Get ready to write with Interactive Rhetorical Situation animations!

For each chapter in Part 2 of the text, Rhetorical Situations for Composing, **English CourseMate** includes an animated tool that helps you establish the writer, audience, and message for the rhetorical situation you are considering.

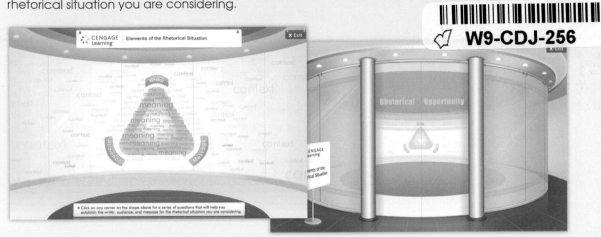

Each screen presents a series of questions to help you map out your rhetorical situation. For example, you'll be prompted to consider your relationship to your audience, what media are available to you, and the essential features of your message. You can also print out your notes and refer to them as you write.

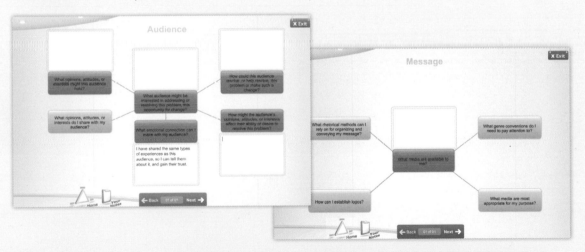

Get started today!

Let **English CourseMate** be your study partner and guide in your composition course. If a printed access card isn't packaged with this text, check your college bookstore or go to **www.cengagebrain.com**, our preferred online store.

The Harbrace Guide to Writing

SECOND EDITION

Cheryl Glenn
The Pennsylvania State University

WADSWORTH
CENGAGE Learning·

Australia • Brazil • Japan • Korea • Mexico • Singapore • Spain • United Kingdom • United States

The Harbrace Guide to Writing, Second Edition
Cheryl Glenn

Senior Publisher: Lyn Uhl

Publisher: Monica Eckman

English Acquisitions Editor: Margaret Leslie

Supervising Development Editor: Leslie Taggart

Development Editor: Stephanie Carpenter

Assistant Editor: Amy Haines

Editorial Assistant: Danielle Warchol

Media Editor: Janine Tangney

Executive Marketing Manager: Stacey Purviance

Marketing Manager: Melissa Holt

Marketing Coordinator: Brittany Blais

Marketing Communications Manager: Linda Yip

Content Project Manager: Rosemary Winfield

Art Director: Jill Ort

Print Buyer: Betsy Donaghey

Rights Acquisition Specialist: Roberta Broyer

Production Service: Lifland et al., Bookmakers

Text Designer: Bill Smith Group

Cover Designer: Bill Smith Group

Cover Image: David Prentice, *Night Light/* Bridgeman Art

Compositor: PreMediaGlobal

For product information and technology assistance, contact us at **Cengage Learning Customer & Sales Support, 1-800-354-9706**

For permission to use material from this text or product, submit all requests online at **www.cengage.com/permissions**. Further permissions questions can be e-mailed to **permissionrequest@cengage.com**.

Library of Congress Control Number: 2011942712

Student Edition:

ISBN-13: 978-1-111-34909-7

ISBN-10: 1-111-34909-6

Wadsworth
20 Channel Center Street
Boston, MA 02210
USA

Cengage Learning is a leading provider of customized learning solutions with office locations around the globe, including Singapore, the United Kingdom, Australia, Mexico, Brazil, and Japan. Locate your local office at: **international.cengage.com/region**.

Cengage Learning products are represented in Canada by Nelson Education, Ltd.

For your course and learning solutions, visit **www.cengage.com**.

Purchase any of our products at your local college store or at our preferred online store **www.cengagebrain.com**.

Instructors: Please visit **login.cengage.com** and log in to access instructor-specific resources.

Printed in China
2 3 4 5 6 7 15 14 13 12

BRIEF CONTENTS

CONTENTS

© Steven Lunetta Photography, 2007

© Martin Jenkinson/Alamy

© Cindy Charles / Photo Edit

© iStockphoto.com/Andres Peiro Palmer

Jacob Silberberg for The New York Times

AP Photo/Mark Humphrey

Waihona Ho'ololi M

Mea Hou ⌘N
Wehe… ⌘O
Pani ⌘W
Mālama ⌘S

Ho'ouka… ⌘T
Ho'oili…

Holoi ⌘D
Ki'i 'Ike ⌘I
Huli… ⌘F
Huli Hou A'e ⌘G

Ho'okuene 'Ao'ao…
Pa'i… ⌘P

Ha'alele ⌘Q

University of Hawai'i ar Hilo

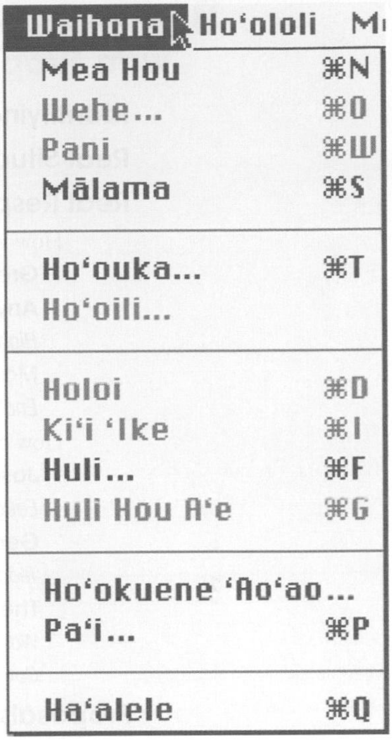

AP Photo/Wisconsin State Journal, John Maniaci

AP Photo/Paul Sakuma

AP Photo/Ben Curtis

Courtesy of Next New Networks

Large Still Life Frieze, Joseph Ablow. Copyright © Joseph Ablow. Reprinted by permission of Pucker Gallery.

fredgoldstein/Big Stock Photo

21 Sentence Structure and Rhetorical Effects 550

© Daniel Koebe/Corbis

PREFACE

We live in a world in which many things are other than they should be: public schools are deeply segregated by race and income; professional athletes pull down bigger salaries than medical researchers; human-caused ecological disasters occur on a regular basis with devastating consequences; Palestine and Israel continue to bomb each other, while our own country continues to bomb Iraq and Afghanistan.

Fortunately, we also live in a world of resolution and possibility, often contingent on the appropriate words being delivered to the appropriate person. Thus, more than ever before, we need to learn how to use language ethically, effectively, and appropriately to address and ultimately resolve conflict—so we can move ahead together and make our world a better place. We need to learn how to use rhetoric purposefully.

The Harbrace Guide to Writing, Second Edition, helps students do just that: It helps them use rhetoric to move forward by addressing and resolving problems, whether those problems are social, academic, or work-related. A comprehensive and richly flexible guide for first-year writers—and their teachers—*The Harbrace Guide to Writing* includes a rhetoric, a reader, a research manual, and a rhetorical handbook. *The Harbrace Guide to Writing* distinguishes itself from other writing guides on the market by its sustained focus on the rhetorical situation and on the specific rhetorical techniques that allow writers to shape their ideas into language that is best suited for their audience and most appropriate for their situation. This writing guide is theoretically sophisticated yet practical: Students will see writing and speaking—using language purposefully—as integral parts of daily life, in and out of school.

In each of its five parts, *The Harbrace Guide to Writing,* Second Edition, translates rhetorical theory into easy-to-follow (and easy-to-teach) techniques that help sharpen the ability to decide which words, assertions, or opinions might work best with a particular audience in a specific situation. In this edition, you'll find many innovations (large and small) that help students understand how to evaluate a rhetorical situation, to identify and respond to an opportunity, and to address a problem. With a sustained focus on authentic issues and opportunities within students' local communities—issues that merit response—this edition offers guidance that supports student writers as they create fitting responses using all of the means of delivery available to them.

How Does the Book Work?

First, the three chapters in Part 1, **Elements of the Rhetorical Situation**, introduce students to the rhetorical principles that underlie all writing situations and provide them with a basic method for using those principles:

▶ To recognize when writing in any of its forms is the best response

▶ To consider strategically their audience and their purpose

▶ To identify language that fits the context and delivers the intended message

▶ To pay close attention to their writing process, from recognizing an opportunity for change to revising, editing, and proofreading

▶ To use the rhetorical methods to develop their paragraphs and essays

Second, the eight chapters in Part 2, **Rhetorical Situations for Composing**, offer writing projects that engage students in responding to real situations:

▶ Assignment options at the start of each chapter prompt students to consider the visual, audio, digital, and print options for responding to the rhetorical situation.

▶ A selection of readings and photos illustrate how others have responded to the same subjects.

▶ An example of writing within a familiar genre (such as a memoir, an investigative report, or a proposal) demonstrates how the genre frames an appropriate response to many similar situations.

▶ Writing in Three Media features refer students to multimodal examples of the genre on the book's English CourseMate website.

▶ A step-by-step guide to writing helps students bring it all together to establish the elements of their rhetorical situation and work within a genre to create a fitting response.

Part 3, **Multimedia Compositions**, offers strategies for approaching the writing process for multimedia. The Part 3 chapters help students learn

▶ to recognize when multimedia is part of a fitting response and when print is most appropriate;

▶ to identify and analyze the rhetorical elements of the multimedia compositions they encounter daily; and

▶ to use rhetorically effective processes for communicating via websites, blogs, wikis, podcasts, Facebook, and even YouTube.

The research manual in Part 4, **A Guide to Research**, draws students into research as a rhetorical activity. Students learn to see a research assignment, not as a set of rules and requirements, but as an effective way of responding to certain rhetorical opportunities. The chapters in Part 4 offer

▶ help in finding print and electronic sources in the library, online, and through databases;

- a comprehensive introduction to field research, with examples of observation, interviews, and questionnaires; and
- information on reading, evaluating, documenting, and responding to sources and help with creating summaries and working bibliographies.

The chapters in Part 5, **A Rhetorical Guide to Grammar and Sentence Style**, reflect an awareness that writers always make grammatical choices in response to their rhetorical situation:

- Each chapter presents grammar rules as statements about how language is commonly used in particular rhetorical situations.
- The chapters include exercises on connected discourse that help put grammar in a broader rhetorical context.

Key Features

- **Brings the rhetorical situation to life**. *The Harbrace Guide to Writing*, Second Edition, introduces students to the rhetorical principles that underlie all writing situations, providing them with a basic method for using those principles. This introduction to rhetoric is adaptable to any composition classroom, and the principles it teaches are transferable to students' other writing tasks.

- **Guides students easily through the writing process**. Step-by-step writing guides help students through the process outlined in Part 1. Students identify an opportunity for change and create a fitting response that takes advantage of all of their available means. In this way, manageable tasks build toward a larger writing project in direct, incremental ways.

- **Offers activities to help students think rhetorically and act locally**. Activities in **Identifying an Opportunity** and **Community Connections** help students consider openings for composing in various media within their communities. **Analyzing the Rhetorical Situation** activities help students understand the elements of a response to a rhetorical situation, and **Your Writing Experiences** and **Write for Five** connect everyday writing with more extensive writing projects.

- **Presents research as a rhetorical response**. Rather than offering a series of lock-step procedures for students to follow as they approach a research project, the research manual in Part 4 draws students into research as a rhetorical activity. Because different research questions require different research methods, the research manual includes information on library, online, and field research.

- **Explains grammar in context**. The chapters on grammar and style in Part 5 teach students that their grammatical and stylistic choices are always made in response to their rhetorical situation.

NEW to This Edition

▶ **Rhetorical concepts updated for the twenty-first century.** *The Harbrace Guide to Writing*, Second Edition, uses student-friendly language to help students apply rhetorical principles to all of their writing situations and bring the rhetorical situation to life.

▶ **New chapters on composing with multimedia.** Because rhetorical opportunities may call for response through more than one medium, *The Harbrace Guide to Writing*, Second Edition, features two new chapters on multimedia composition. **Analyzing Multimedia** (Chapter 12) explores scenarios calling for multimedia responses; **Responding with Multimedia** (Chapter 13) addresses the composition process for websites, blogs, wikis, podcasts, and postings on Facebook and YouTube.

▶ **New focus on multimodal options for writing.** New assignment options at the start of each chapter in Part 2 prompt students to consider the visual, audio, digital, and print options for responding to a rhetorical situation. Students will understand immediately that the elements of the rhetorical situation must guide all considerations related to creating a fitting response.

▶ **New themes for two writing projects.** Providing a context for responding with investigative reports, **Examining the Millennial Generation** (Chapter 6) encourages students to investigate the characteristics of a generation such as the Millennials, Generation X, or the Baby Boomers. **The College of the Future** (Chapter 8) presents opportunities for responding with proposals, asking students to consider what college will be like in the future and how it can be made affordable.

▶ **Engaging new readings.** New readings show students the rhetorical considerations at the heart of such responses as presidential speeches, Steve Jobs's multimedia presentations, and even canvas tote bags.

▶ **More emphasis on student research.** New student-written **Tricks of the Trade** features offer valuable tips for research—such as when to paraphrase or summarize rather than quote and how the bibliography of a good source can yield additional relevant sources. Chapter 16, **Field Research**, includes a transcript of a new student-conducted interview, and an audio recording of the full interview is available at the book's companion website. Chapter 19, **Acknowledging Sources**, features a new student paper written in MLA style about the political satire of Jon Stewart.

 ▶ **New English CourseMate website.** The guide's new English CourseMate website features multimodal examples of student and professional writing for each Part 2 writing project. Interactive guides prompt students to consider and map out each element of their rhetorical situation—characteristics of their audience, the message, and themselves as writers. Access the English CourseMate via cengagebrain.com.

▶ **Clear support of the Council of Writing Program Administrators' (WPA) objectives and outcomes.** To help instructors and students consider shared goals, this edition incorporates the WPA objectives and outcomes. A complete description follows.

How Does *The Harbrace Guide to Writing,* Second Edition, Help Students Achieve the WPA Outcomes?

On the following pages, each of the five primary outcomes of the ***WPA Outcomes Statement for First-Year Composition*** is followed by an explanation and illustration of how—and where—*The Harbrace Guide to Writing,* Second Edition, supports that outcome.

Rhetorical Knowledge

By the end of first year composition, students should

- ▶ Focus on a purpose
- ▶ Respond to the needs of different audiences
- ▶ Respond appropriately to different kinds of rhetorical situations
- ▶ Use conventions of format and structure appropriate to the rhetorical situation
- ▶ Adopt appropriate voice, tone, and level of formality
- ▶ Understand how genres shape reading and writing
- ▶ Write in several genres

From the WPA Outcomes Statement

The Harbrace Guide to Writing, Second Edition, begins with a full introduction to the elements of the rhetorical situation. Examples and activities help students consider the opportunity for change, the writer, the audience, the purpose, the message, and the context, making the book's first two chapters a user-friendly mini-guide to the rhetorical situation.

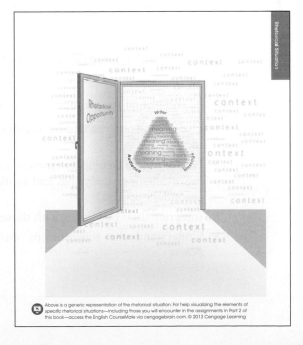

Above is a generic representation of the rhetorical situation. For help visualizing the elements of *specific* rhetorical situations—including those you will encounter in the assignments in Part 2 of this book—access the English CourseMate via cengagebrain.com. © 2013 Cengage Learning

The writing projects in Part 2 guide students in making decisions about the genres and methods of delivery that are most appropriate to their audience and purpose.

Critical Thinking, Reading, and Writing

By the end of first year composition, students should

▶ Use writing and reading for inquiry, learning, thinking, and communicating

▶ Understand a writing assignment as a series of tasks, including finding, evaluating, analyzing, and synthesizing appropriate primary and secondary sources

▶ Integrate their own ideas with those of others

▶ Understand the relationships among language, knowledge, and power

From the WPA Outcomes Statement

Each chapter of *The Harbrace Guide to Writing*, Second Edition, offers activities to help students think rhetorically and yet act locally. Activities in **Identifying an Opportunity** and **Community Connections** help students consider openings for composing within their communities—for addressing or even resolving a problem through the use of language. **Analyzing the Rhetorical Situation** activities help students understand the elements of a fitting response to a rhetorical situation, and **Your Writing Experiences** and **Write for Five** connect everyday writing with more extensive writing projects.

> **> ANALYZING THE RHETORICAL SITUATION**
>
> 1. Compare the excerpts from the writings of Juan F. Perea and Richard Rodriguez. How does each writer explain the invisibility of some people in the United States? What claim does each writer make about this invisibility?
> 2. What reasons does each writer give for the invisibility? What evidence does each author provide to support his claim?
> 3. What do the two writers say about resisting or embracing assimilation into the melting pot? How does each writer evaluate the importance of public language?
> 4. Identify the opportunity, audience, purpose, and context of Perea's and Rodriguez's rhetorical situations. What are the resources and constraints of their contexts? Be prepared to share your answers with the class.

To help students integrate their ideas with those of others, the chapters in **A Guide to Research** (Part 4) guide students in finding, reading, evaluating, and responding to sources at the library, online, and in the field. These six chapters provide many opportunities for students to approach researched writing incrementally by creating a research log, partial and full summaries, and working and annotated bibliographies.

Partial summaries

Jacob Thomas summarized an entire article. Depending on his purpose and the expectations of his audience, he might have chosen to write a partial summary instead. Partial summaries of varying size are frequently found in research papers. A one-sentence summary may be appropriate when a researcher wants to focus on a specific piece of information. If Jacob had been interested in noting what various writers have said about abuses of language, he could have represented William Lutz's ideas as follows:

In "Doubts about Doublespeak," William Lutz describes abuses of language and explains why they are harmful.

Partial summaries of the same source may vary depending on the researcher's purpose. The following partial summary of Lutz's article focuses on its reference to George Orwell's work, rather than on the uses of doublespeak.

SAMPLE PARTIAL SUMMARY

Authors frequently cite the work of George Orwell when discussing the abuses of language. In "Doubts about Doublespeak," William Lutz describes different types of doublespeak—language used to deceive—and explains why they are harmful. He quotes a passage from Orwell's "Politics and the English Language" in order to emphasize his own belief that the doublespeak surrounding the topic of death is the worst form of language abuse: "defenseless villages are bombarded from the air, the inhabitants driven out into the countryside, the cattle machine-gunned, the huts set on fire with incendiary bullets. This is called pacification. Millions of peasants are robbed of their farms and sent trudging along the roads with no more than they can carry. This is called transfer of population or rectification of frontiers" (qtd. in Lutz 24).

Processes

By the end of first year composition, students should

▶ Be aware that it usually takes multiple drafts to create and complete a successful text

▶ Develop flexible strategies for generating, revising, editing, and proofreading

▶ Understand writing as an open process that permits writers to use later invention and re-thinking to revise their work

▶ Understand the collaborative and social aspects of writing processes

▶ Learn to critique their own and others' works

▶ Learn to balance the advantages of relying on others with the responsibility of doing their part

▶ Use a variety of technologies to address a range of audiences

From the WPA Outcomes Statement

Writing Processes and Strategies (Chapter 3) guides students in recognizing an opportunity for change, exploring possible responses, drafting, peer reviewing, revising, and editing. Additionally, the chapter provides examples for employing the rhetorical methods of development.

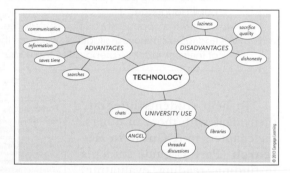

Part 3, **Multimedia Compositions**, offers support for approaching multimodal writing processes.

This website for Texas A&M's VizaGoGo show reached a large and diverse audience.

are the features of the most effective flyer on the bulletin board? Who is the audience for the flyer? What is its purpose? What is the context of the message? What is appealing or unappealing about that flyer? How will you respond to it?

Of course, students are called on to observe and implement these strategies no matter which part of the book they happen to be working within, whether they are reflecting on their writing experiences in Part 1 (**Your Writing Experiences** activities), working through the **Guides to Responding** in Part 2, trying out processes that may involve unfamiliar media in Part 3, generating multiple responses to sources in Part 4, or editing for style in Part 5.

Knowledge of Conventions

By the end of first year composition, students should

▶ Learn common formats for different kinds of texts

▶ Develop knowledge of genre conventions ranging from structure and paragraphing to tone and mechanics

▶ Practice appropriate means of documenting their work

▶ Control such surface features as syntax, grammar, punctuation, and spelling

From the WPA Outcomes Statement

The Myth of Multitasking

@ 2008. Reprinted by permission
Christine Rosen

In one of the many letters he wrote to his son in the 1740s, Lord Chesterfield offered the following advice: "There is time enough for everything in the course of the day, if you do but one thing at once, but there is not time enough in the year, if you will do two things at a time." To Chesterfield, singular focus was not merely a practical way to structure one's time; it was a mark of intelligence. "This steady and undissipated attention to one object, is a sure mark of a superior genius; as hurry, bustle, and agitation, are the never-failing symptoms of a weak and frivolous mind."

In modern times, hurry, bustle, and agitation have become a regular way of life for many people—so much so that we have embraced a word to describe our efforts to respond to the many pressing demands on our time. *multitasking.* Used for decades to describe the parallel processing abilities of computers, multitasking is now shorthand for the human attempt to do simultaneously as many things as possible, as quickly as possible, preferably marshalling the power of as many technologies as possible.

In the late 1990s and early 2000s, one sensed a kind of exuberance about the possibilities of multitasking. Advertisements for new electronic gadgets—particularly the first generation of handheld digital devices—celebrated the notion of using technology to accomplish several things at once. The word *multitasking* began appearing in the "skills" sections of résumés, as office workers restyled themselves as high-tech, high-performing team players. "We have always multitasked—inability to walk and chew gum is a time-honored cause for derision—but never so intensely or self-consciously as now," James Gleick wrote in his 1999 book *Faster.* "We are multitasking connoisseurs—experts in crowding, pressing, packing, and overlapping distinct activities in our all-too-finite moments." An article in the *New York Times Magazine* in 2001 asked, "Who can remember life before multitasking? These days we all do it." The article offered advice on "How to Multitask" with suggestions about giving your brain's "multitasking hot spot" an appropriate workout.

Rosen begins with age-old advice about the wisdom of doing one thing one at a time. She has identified a rhetorical opportunity for addressing a modern-day problem.

Rosen defines her topic in precise terms: multitasking has become a way of life, or at least an expectation.

Rosen provides historical background on multitasking, including differing perspectives on this behavior. She starts with a positive perspective.

Annotated examples of each featured genre in Part 2 identify and describe the conventions common to that genre. Additionally, each **Guide to Responding** begins with a list that identifies features typically found in the genre under discussion; as students work to shape their writing project, a helpful illustration reminds them of how a piece of writing in that genre is commonly shaped or organized.

Introduction
- ▶ Shows readers that the subject is someone they need to know more about
- ▶ Highlights some key feature of the subject's personality, character, or values

Body
- ▶ Presents a fuller description of the subject and his or her life's work
- ▶ Includes details that help readers to visualize the subject's actions and hear the subject's words
- ▶ Provides logical appeals in the form of examples that show how the individual's work affects the lives of people like the readers themselves

Conclusion
- ▶ Often contains one final quote or anecdote that nicely captures the essence of the individual
- ▶ May bring readers into the present day, if the profile has had a historical scope

In Part 4, Chapter 19, **Acknowledging Sources**, discusses MLA and APA style to help students identify the conventions specific to the academic essay genre—and to understand why those conventions exist.

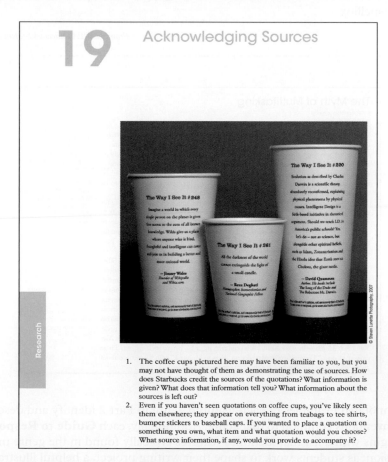

1. The coffee cups pictured here may have been familiar to you, but you may not have thought of them as demonstrating the use of sources. How does Starbucks credit the sources of the quotations? What information is given? What does that information tell you? What information about the sources is left out?
2. Even if you haven't seen quotations on coffee cups, you've likely seen them elsewhere; they appear on everything from teabags to tee shirts, bumper stickers to baseball caps. If you wanted to place a quotation on something you own, what item and what quotation would you choose? What source information, if any, would you provide to accompany it?

Part 5, **A Rhetorical Guide to Grammar and Sentence Style**, presents grammar rules as statements about how language is commonly used in particular rhetorical situations. Whether reviewing word classes, presenting effective style choices, or examining the conventional—and unconventional—uses of punctuation and grammar, the chapters in this part of the book prompt students to consider the rhetorical effect of every grammatical or stylistic choice they make.

Composing in Electronic Environments

Writing in the twenty-first century involves the use of digital technologies for several purposes, from drafting to peer reviewing to editing. Therefore, although the *kinds* of composing processes and texts expected from students vary across programs and institutions, there are nonetheless common expectations.

By the end of first-year composition, students should

▶ Use electronic environments for drafting, reviewing, revising, editing, and sharing texts

▶ Locate, evaluate, organize, and use research material collected from electronic sources, including scholarly library databases; other official databases (e.g., federal government databases); and informal electronic networks and internet sources

▶ Understand and exploit the differences in the rhetorical strategies and in the affordances available for both print and electronic composing processes and texts

From the WPA Outcomes Statement

 The Harbrace Guide to Writing, Second Edition, emphasizes rhetorical situations that students are likely to encounter every day, from writing a text message to a friend to participating in a course wiki. Because many of these rhetorical situations have digital contexts, *The Harbrace Guide to Writing* features examples of those contexts in its chapters and provides an interactive digital environment for viewing multimodal examples and mapping out elements of students' rhetorical situations. The English CourseMate website can be accessed via cengagebrain.com.

Guide to Identifying the Elements of Any Rhetorical Situation

© Steven Lunetta Photography, 2007

As a responsible writer and speaker, you need to understand the elements of any rhetorical situation you decide to enter. Chapters 1 and 2 will help you identify those elements using the following steps.

▶ Identify the opportunity for change that encourages you to enter the situation. Ask yourself: What is it that tugs at me? Why do I feel the need to speak, write, take a photo, share an image? What attitude, action, or opinion do I want to change?

▶ Connect the opportunity to make change with your purpose. Ask yourself: What can I accomplish with rhetoric? How can words or visuals allow me to respond to this opportunity?

▶ Knowing that your purpose is tethered to the nature and character of the audience, carefully consider the composition of that audience: Who are its members? What are they like? What opinions do they hold? What are their feelings about this opportunity to resolve a problem, to make change? How will they react to the message? Different audiences have different needs and expectations, which the responsible writer or speaker tries to meet.

▶ Take into account whatever else has already been said on the subject: Who has been speaking or writing, and what do they say?

▶ Whatever the form of its delivery (spoken, written, or electronic), you'll want your response to be fitting (or appropriate). By calibrating the tone of your response, you can control the attitude you project to your intended audience. When shaping a fitting response, you need to be fully aware that you can come only as close to persuasion as the rhetorical situation allows. A responsible speaker or writer cannot do or expect more.

Assignment options at the start of each Part 2 chapter prompt students to consider the visual, audio, digital, and print options for responding to the rhetorical situation. When students begin writing, they can access examples in each medium online.

IDENTIFYING AN OPPORTUNITY

Throughout this chapter, you'll work to identify an opportunity to profile a person who is successful with words. This person might be someone you're related to, work with, know, or admire from afar: a grandparent, minister, counselor, group leader, politician, public figure, artist, author, or celebrity. As you work to determine the person who most interests you, consider the most fitting means of delivery for your profile:

Print Profile	**Audio Profile**	**Online Profile**
written for a community or campus newspaper or local zine	recorded for a local radio station	composed as a blog entry or multimedia presentation using an online presentation-sharing service (such as SlideShare).

To begin, freewrite for five minutes in response to each of the following questions (or use any of the invention techniques presented on pages 58–61):

1. When have you listened to, read the writing of, or watched a performance by someone whom you consider successful with words?

2. Did reading, hearing, or watching the delivery of this person's words make you think or act differently in response? If so, how did your thinking or behavior change?

3. What qualities or characteristics did this person possess that made him or her an effective speaker or writer? What made his or her words effective?

Analyzing Multimedia (Chapter 12) highlights rhetorical situations that call for multimedia responses and walks students through the process of identifying the key elements of those situations. **Responding with Multimedia** (Chapter 13) addresses the composing process for websites, blogs, wikis, podcasts, and postings on Facebook and YouTube.

Visitors to the site can preview the artists' work in the Gallery.

site. The website could feature "teaser" clips of animations, image galleries of sketches and video stills, and even a history page documenting the development of the show. By giving individual artists and other interested students something to link to (via Twitter, Facebook, or an e-mail message), the website could involve more people in targeting a rhetorical audience for the show. In fact, once the organizers opened the website, it began to reach a wide audience, in part because program alumni who had moved on to careers at ILM, Dreamworks, Disney, and Microsoft shared the site with their coworkers. As the audience expanded, the rhetorical purpose of the website began to change as well.

> ANALYZING THE RHETORICAL SITUATION

Identify one multimedia composition (for instance, a website, podcast, or video) that you have recently been impressed by. Describe the various parts of the rhetorical situation to which the composer of that work is responding; What is the rhetorical opportunity? Who makes up the audience? What is the purpose? What is the context?

Using Multimedia with a Rhetorical Purpose

As you already know, purpose and audience cannot be separated. When the designers of the VizaGoGo website realized that their purpose had broadened, from simply publicizing the art show to interested parties to also promoting themselves to potential employers, they decided that they needed to address this more complicated (dual) rhetorical purpose. The expanded rhetorical purpose

The Harbrace Guide to Writing, Second Edition, also helps students take advantage of technology for research, whether they are locating materials through library databases and the Internet, evaluating and citing those materials, or using a word-processing program to keep track of different sources.

Supplements

Instructor's Manual for Glenn's *The Harbrace Guide to Writing*, Second Edition

The comprehensive Instructor's Manual includes detailed syllabi, sample syllabi, and chapter-by-chapter suggestions for using the guide in your classroom. The detailed syllabi comprise three annotated course plans that can be followed or consulted when teaching with this text in programs that focus on academic writing, writing in the disciplines, or service learning. Activities, exercises, and journal-writing prompts are provided for each class meeting, along with suggested goals and materials for instructors to review. If your course is organized around genres, themes, or rhetorical methods, you'll find each of these approaches addressed by sample syllabi and journal-writing prompt—all created for *The Harbrace Guide to Writing*.

Enhanced InSite™ for Glenn's *The Harbrace Guide to Writing*, Second Edition

You can easily create, assign, and grade writing assignments with Enhanced InSite™ for Glenn's *The Harbrace Guide to Writing*, Second Edition. From a single, easy-to-navigate site, you and your students can manage the flow of papers online, check for originality, and conduct peer reviews. Students can access a multimedia eBook that offers a text-specific workbook, private tutoring options, and resources for writers, including anti-plagiarism tutorials and downloadable grammar podcasts. Enhanced InSite provides the tools and resources you and your students need, plus the training and support you want. Learn more at www.cengage.com/insite.

CourseMate for Glenn's *The Harbrace Guide to Writing*, Second Edition

Printed Access Card
ISBN-10: 1133114121; ISBN-13: 9781133114123
Instant Access Code
ISBN-10: 1133114113; ISBN-13: 9781133114116
Cengage Learning's English CourseMate brings course concepts to life with interactive learning, study, and exam preparation tools that support the printed textbook. Students' comprehension will soar as your class works with the printed textbook and the textbook-specific website. English CourseMate goes beyond the book to deliver what you need! Learn more at cengage.com/coursemate.

Multimedia eBook for Glenn's *The Harbrace Guide to Writing*, Second Edition

Students can do all of their reading online or use the eBook as a handy reference while they're completing coursework. The eBook includes the full text of the print version with interactive exercises; an integrated text-specific workbook; user-friendly navigation, search, and highlight tools; and links to videos that enhance the text content.

Acknowledgments

All books demand time, talent, and plenty of hard work. For that reason, I could not have produced this textbook without the help and support of a number of colleagues and friends. I found myself calling on their expertise at various times throughout the creation of this book. Sarah Summers, Rosalyn Collings Eves, John Belk, and Heather Adams gave generously of their time and wisdom as teachers, scholars, and writers, working with me to create assignments and exercises to which students will want to respond. They helped me conduct research into multimedia sources and locate new readings as well as contributors for various parts of the book. Cristian Nuñez, Alyse Murphy Leininger, and Keith Evans created Tricks of the Trade features. Undergraduate interns Denise Bartolome, Avery James, Daniel Leayman, Jenny Park, Isaac Sharpless Perry, Brooke Senior, Sierra Stovall, Emilie Sunndergrun, and Monique Williams helped with various research and proofreading duties, all demonstrating a professionalism beyond their years. I remain grateful to them all.

At Cengage, Leslie Taggart oversaw the development of the project, relying (as we all have) on the good sense and keen insights of publisher Lyn Uhl, vice-president P. J. Boardman, and, of course, acquisitions editor Margaret Leslie. New to our team in this edition, Jason Sakos has already demonstrated his marketing prowess. Editorial assistants Elizabeth Ramsey and Danielle Warchol and English Sales Specialist Sherry Robertson helped launch the substantive improvements to this edition. For their painstaking production of this book, I thank Rosemary Winfield, Cengage production editor; Jane Hoover and Quica Ostrander, copyeditors and production coordinators at Lifland et al., Bookmakers; Sarah Bonner, image permissions editor; Martha Hall, text permissions editor; and Lillie Caporlingua, the book's designer. My especial thanks go to Stephanie Pelkowski Carpenter, my constant intellectual companion and out-of-this-world development editor.

Finally, I have learned from a phenomenal group of reviewers, including the following instructors who offered their guidance on this second edition:

Jared Abraham, *Weatherford College*
Jeff Andelora, *Mesa Community College*
Amy Azul, *Chaffey College*
Andrea Bewick, *Napa Valley College*
Lee Brewer-Jones, *Georgia Perimeter College*

Sue Briggs, *Salt Lake Community College*
Mark Browning, *Johnson County Community College*
Mary Burkhart, *University of Scranton*
Mary Carden, *Edinboro University of Pennsylvania*
Jo Cavins, *North Dakota State University*
Ron Christiansen, *Salt Lake Community College*
Stephanie Dowdle, *Salt Lake Community College*
Rosalyn Eves, *Brigham Young University*
Eugene Flinn, *New Jersey City University*
Patricia Flinn, *New Jersey City University*
Rebecca Fournier, *Triton College*
Powell Franklin, *Jackson State Community College*
Kevin Griffith, *Capital University*
James Green, *Northern Kentucky University*
Anna Harrington, *Jackson State Community College*
Martha Holder, *Wytheville Community College*
Dawn Hubbell-Staeble, *Bowling Green State University*
James Mayo, *Jackson State Community College*
Kate Mohler, *Mesa Community College*
Sheryl Mylan, *College of DuPage*
Randy Nelson, *Davidson College*
Dana Nkana, *Illinois Central College*
Eden Pearson, *Des Moines Area Community College*
Jason Pickavance, *Salt Lake Community College*
Jeff Pruchnic, *Wayne State University*
Amy Ratto-Parks, *University of Montana*
Marsha Rutter, *Southwestern College*
Adrianne Schott, *Weatherford College*
Wendy Sharer, *East Carolina University*
Noel Sloboda, *Pennsylvania State University-York*
David Swain, *Southern New Hampshire University*
Sharon Tash, *Saddleback College*
Michael Trovato, *Ohio State University–Newark*
Cynthia VanSickle, *McHenry County College*

Cheryl Glenn
October 2011

Elements of the Rhetorical Situation

Too often, the word *rhetoric* refers to empty words, implying manipulation, deception, or persuasion at any cost. But as you'll learn in this book, rhetoric and rhetorical situations are not negative and not manipulative. They are everywhere—as pervasive as the air we breathe—and play an essential role in our daily lives as we work to get things done efficiently and ethically. The following three chapters define rhetoric and the rhetorical situation, show how the rhetorical situation shapes the writing process, and introduce the stages and strategies of that process. You'll begin to develop your rhetorical skills as you work through these chapters, but you'll continue to sharpen them all through your college career and into the workplace. The important point to remember is this: you're probably already pretty good at using rhetoric. So let's build on what you know—and go from there.

Guide to Identifying the Elements of Any Rhetorical Situation

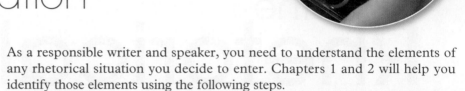

As a responsible writer and speaker, you need to understand the elements of any rhetorical situation you decide to enter. Chapters 1 and 2 will help you identify those elements using the following steps.

▶ Identify the opportunity for change that encourages you to enter the situation. Ask yourself: What is it that tugs at me? Why do I feel the need to speak, write, take a photo, share an image? What attitude, action, or opinion do I want to change?

▶ Connect the opportunity to make change with your purpose. Ask yourself: What can I accomplish with rhetoric? How can words or visuals allow me to respond to this opportunity?

▶ Knowing that your purpose is tethered to the nature and character of the audience, carefully consider the composition of that audience: Who are its members? What are they like? What opinions do they hold? What are their feelings about this opportunity to resolve a problem, to make change? How will they react to the message? Different audiences have different needs and expectations, which the responsible writer or speaker tries to meet.

▶ Take into account whatever else has already been said on the subject: Who has been speaking or writing, and what do they say?

▶ Whatever the form of its delivery (spoken, written, or electronic), you'll want your response to be fitting (or appropriate). By calibrating the tone of your response, you can control the attitude you project to your intended audience. When shaping a fitting response, you need to be fully aware that you can come only as close to persuasion as the rhetorical situation allows. A responsible speaker or writer cannot do or expect more.

Understanding the Rhetorical Situation

1

Rhetoric Surrounds Us

Every day, you use rhetoric. You use it as you read course syllabi and assignments, the directions for hooking up your stereo system, and your mail, as well as e-mails, social network postings, and instant messages. You also use it as you write: when you submit written assignments, answer quiz questions in class, leave notes for your roommate, and send text messages to your friends. Every day, you are surrounded by rhetoric and rhetorical opportunities. In fact, you've been participating in rhetorical situations for most of your life.

> WRITE FOR FIVE

1. Take a few minutes to list the kinds of writing you do every day. Include all instances when you write down information (whether on paper, whiteboard, chalkboard, or computer screen). Beside each entry, jot down the reason for that type of writing. Be prepared to share your answers with the rest of the class.
2. Consider five of the types of writing you identified in the first activity. Who is your audience for these different kinds of writing? In other words, to whom or for whom are you writing? What is your purpose for each kind of writing? What do you hope to achieve?

Rhetoric: The Purposeful Use of Language and Images

Rhetoric is the purposeful use of language and images. That definition covers a great deal of territory—practically every word and visual element you encounter every day. But it's the word *purposeful* that will guide you through the maze of words and images that saturate your life. When you use words or images to achieve a specific purpose—such as explaining to your supervisor why you need next weekend off—you are speaking, writing, or conveying images rhetorically.

The Greek philosopher Aristotle coined an authoritative definition of *rhetoric* over 2,500 years ago: "Rhetoric is the art of observing in any given situation the available means of persuasion." Let's take this definition apart and examine its constituent elements.

The art of observing in any given situation

"Rhetoric is the art [or mental ability] of observing . . . ." Notice that Aristotle does not call for you to overpower your **audience** (your readers or listeners) with words or images, nor does he push you to win an argument. Instead, he encourages you (as a *rhetor*, or user of rhetoric, such as a **writer** or speaker) to observe, as the first step in discovering what you might say or write. For Aristotle, and all of the rhetorical thinkers who have followed, observing before speaking or writing is primary. You need to observe, to take the time to figure out what kind of rhetorical situation you're entering. Whom are you speaking or writing to? What is your relationship to that person or group of people? What is the occasion? Who else is listening? What do you want your language to accomplish (that is, what is your **purpose**)? By answering these questions, you are establishing the elements of the "given situation."

The available means of persuasion

When you consider "the available means," you evaluate the possible methods of communication you might use. You want to choose the one that will best make **meaning** that helps you achieve your purpose. In other words, should you deliver your **message** orally (face to face or over the telephone), in writing (using a letter or note, an e-mail or instant message, or a web page), or via film, video, still images, or other visuals? Where might you most successfully deliver that message: in class, at church, at the coffee shop, at a town meeting?

The spoken word is sometimes most appropriate. If you and a good friend have had an argument, you might not want to put your feelings into writing. It might be better if you simply pick up the telephone and say, "I'm sorry." If you're attending a funeral, you'll want to offer your spoken condolences directly to the bereaved, even if you've already sent a card or flowers. However, if your professor expects you to submit a three-page essay recounting your experiences with technology (a technology autobiography, so to speak) you cannot announce that you'd rather tell her your story over coffee in the student union. The only means available in this situation is the written word. Or is it? Your professor might be impressed if you prepared an electronic presentation to accompany your written essay, complete with video or audio clips. Your available means of communicating are seemingly endless.

The last phrase in Aristotle's definition of *rhetoric* is "of persuasion." Persuasion is not a zero-sum game, with the winner taking all. Think of persuasion as a coming together, a meeting of the minds. Ideally, persuasion results in you and your audience being changed by the experience of understanding one another. When both parties are changed (if only by expanding their understanding of an issue), the rhetorical interaction isn't one-sided: both sides are heard, and both the sender and the receiver(s) benefit.

Aristotle tells us that rhetoric's function is not solely successful persuasion; rather, it is to "discover the means of coming as near such success as the circumstances of each particular case allow." If your only persuasive purpose is to get your own way, you may sometimes succeed; more often, truth be told, you'll find yourself disappointed. But if you think about persuasion in terms of understanding, invitation, and adjustment, you can marshal your rhetorical know-how to achieve success in a broader sense.

Persuasive writers (and speakers) rely on observation in order to get a sense of the **rhetorical situation**, the context in which they are communicating. They know that no two situations are ever exactly the same. Every **context** includes distinctive **resources** (positive influences) and **constraints** (obstacles) that shape the rhetorical transaction:

▶ what has already been said on the subject (by whom and to whom);

▶ when, where, and how the rhetorical exchange takes place;

▶ the writer's credibility; and

▶ the appropriateness of the message in terms of both content and delivery.

Thus, every rhetorical situation calls for you to take note of the available means of persuasion as well as the contextual resources and constraints that will affect your persuasive success.

> ANALYZING THE RHETORICAL SITUATION

Choose two of the following situations and note their similarities and differences in terms of speaker or writer, purpose, audience, and available means (including any resources and constraints). Be prepared to share your observations with the rest of the class.

1. It's time for you to talk with your parents about how you'll spend the coming summer.
2. For the first time, your rent check will be late. You need to explain the reason to your landlord in such a way that the usual late fee will be waived.
3. Your boss has asked you to compose a sign for the store entrance, one that politely asks customers to turn off their cell phones.
4. Your professor has assigned a three-page technology autobiography for Monday.
5. You and your fiancé(e) need to show proof of citizenship or student visas to receive a marriage license.

Analyzing the Rhetorical Situation

You encounter rhetoric—and rhetorical situations—every day, all through the day, from the minute you turn on the morning news to the moment you close your textbook, turn off the light, and go to sleep. In order to develop your skills of persuasion, you need to be able to recognize the elements of rhetorical situations and gauge your own rhetoric accordingly.

As noted above, a rhetorical situation is the context for communicating, the context a writer (or speaker) enters into in order to shape a message that can address a problem and reach an intended audience to change an attitude, action, or opinion. The writer identifies that problem as an **opportunity** to make change through the use of language, whether visual, written, or spoken.

(Such a problem or opportunity is also known as an *exigence*.) For instance, by asking a question, your instructor creates an opportunity for change in the classroom (usually a change in everyone's understanding). The question just hangs there—until someone provides an appropriate response, a **fitting response** in terms of timing, medium of delivery, tone, and content. Similarly, if the company you work for loses online business because its website is outdated, that problem can be resolved only through appropriate use of text and visuals. Once the fitting response comes into being, the opportunity for making a change ("I need an answer" or "We need to update our website") is either partially removed or disappears altogether; then you have responded to the invitation for change.

Sample analysis of a rhetorical situation

If the idea of a rhetorical situation still seems unfamiliar, consider a wedding invitation. Each invitation is rhetorical, embodying every element of a rhetorical situation: opportunity for change, a writer, an audience, a purpose, the message itself, and a context. The need (or desire, in this case) to invite family and friends to their wedding—the problem—provides the happy couple with a rhetorical opportunity. Whether sent to the audience of potential wedding guests through the mail or electronically, the invitation is a response, a way to resolve the specific problem. The meaning of a wedding invitation resonates within a specific context: it announces a joyous celebration for specific people.

TOGETHER WITH THEIR FAMILIES

Reese Jimenez

AND

Krissi Jimroglou

REQUEST THE PLEASURE OF YOUR COMPANY

AT A CEREMONY CELEBRATING THEIR

COMMITMENT AND LOVE

ON SATURDAY, THE SEVENTEENTH OF NOVEMBER

AT FOUR O'CLOCK IN THE AFTERNOON

UNIVERSALIST NATIONAL MEMORIAL CHURCH

1810 SIXTEENTH STREET, NW

WASHINGTON, DC

Courtesy of K. Jimroglou and Matt Batchelder

Every invitation, such as this one for a commitment ceremony, is rhetorical.

Often, one fitting response sparks another opportunity. Imagine that you have received a wedding invitation. The invitation provides you with an opportunity to resolve a specific problem through language: in this case, to respond by informing the couple whether you will attend the wedding. Your response could be as simple as checking a box on a card included with the invitation, indicating that you will attend. If you are close to the couple and have decided you cannot attend the wedding, you might give them a phone call, in addition to checking the "must decline with regret" box on the reply card. The appropriateness of your response depends on your relationship to the couple (your *audience*, in this rhetorical situation) and your purpose in responding.

> ANALYZING THE RHETORICAL SITUATION

For each of the rhetorical situations below, try to identify the opportunity, writer, audience, message, purpose, and context.

1. A guy you met last summer has invited you to be his Facebook friend.
2. You are applying for a scholarship and need three letters of recommendation.

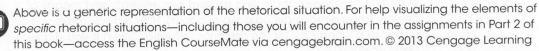

Above is a generic representation of the rhetorical situation. For help visualizing the elements of *specific* rhetorical situations—including those you will encounter in the assignments in Part 2 of this book—access the English CourseMate via cengagebrain.com. © 2013 Cengage Learning

3. As a member of a wedding party, you are expected to make a toast at the reception.
4. You need to request permission to enroll in a class that is already full but is required for your field of study.

The decision to engage

Rhetorical situations may call for your attention, as when you receive a wedding invitation, or they may arise from your interpretation of some event. For instance, if you're in the market for a new car, you might be tantalized by an advertised price for a car that interests you, only to arrive at the dealership and discover that the marked price is higher than the advertised price. If the price discrepancy catches your attention—enough that you want to enter the rhetorical situation—then that's your opportunity.

You'll next have to decide if you want to attempt to change the situation through the use of rhetoric. If you choose to say something about the discrepancy, you'll have to decide on your purpose, what message you want to send, how to send it, and to whom. You'll also need to take into consideration the constraints on your message: perhaps the advertised car had higher mileage than the one on the dealer's lot, or perhaps the advertised price had a time limit. Therefore, if you decide to enter the rhetorical situation, you'll need to shape it in a way that allows you to send a message. If you're annoyed by the price discrepancy but walk away because you don't want to discuss it, let alone negotiate with the car dealership, then you've chosen not to act rhetorically.

On a daily basis, you'll encounter dozens of opportunities to enter rhetorical situations. Some situations you'll decide to enter, and some you'll decide to pass by. If you witness a car accident, for example, you are an observer; you may decide to volunteer to testify about it and thus become a speaker. If you identify an old friend from a newspaper photograph (observer), you may decide to e-mail him (writer). You might hear a song (observer) and decide to perform it and post a video of your performance on YouTube (speaker). Or you might decide to begin introducing yourself to people in an online video game (observer, audience, and writer). Whatever the situations are and however they are delivered (whether spoken, printed, online, or in some other way), you can decide how or whether you want to act on them.

> YOUR WRITING EXPERIENCES

1. To whom have you written today? Why did you write to that person? Take five minutes to describe that rhetorical situation and transaction, identifying the elements of the rhetorical situation (opportunity, writer, audience, purpose, message, constraints, and resources), the means of communication (handwriting or word processing), and means of delivery (mail, e-mail, note on a slip of paper). How did you make your response a fitting one for the rhetorical situation, even if you did so unconsciously?

2. Think of a time when you identified an opportunity to address a problem but didn't respond. Write for five minutes, describing that opportunity for change and explaining why you didn't write or speak in response to it. If you could do it over, how might you respond? How would you take into consideration each element of the rhetorical situation, in order to come as close to persuasion as conditions allowed?

3. What have you learned from reading this section that you didn't know when you started? How might the information about the rhetorical situation help you? Is there a rhetorical situation that is tugging at you now? If you decide to enter that rhetorical situation, how will you do so? How will you take into consideration each element of the rhetorical situation?

Shaping Reasons to Write

Now that you have begun to identify the constituent elements of a rhetorical situation, take a closer look at each of these elements, along with examples from diverse contexts.

What is a rhetorical opportunity?

A rhetorical opportunity (sometimes called an *exigence*) is an opening you identify to address or resolve a problem through spoken or written language. In the example on the next page, student Collin Allan has identified a rhetorical opportunity in his need for a letter of recommendation. His response to that need is in the form of an e-mail (written language) sent to his instructor.

In writing to Dr. Eves, Collin has created a response to his own need (the need for a letter of recommendation). He's also doing his best to present a rhetorical opportunity to which his instructor will respond. After all, he clearly wants his instructor to consider writing him a positive letter of recommendation. Thus, he has set out to resolve his problem using words. Although he has composed an e-mail, he could have written Dr. Eves a letter or spoken to her over the phone or during an office visit. Whether he used spoken or written words, he would not lose sight of the fact that his audience is his instructor and his purpose is to obtain a letter that gives him a good recommendation.

The medium of delivery—spoken or written (with or without visual elements other than text)—is always up to the sender of a message, who must decide which medium of delivery is most appropriate and timely. Suppose you're applying for a scholarship and need some help from your academic advisor. If the semester isn't yet under way, your best option may be to send an e-mail message to your advisor. If you see your advisor almost daily and have taken several classes from him, it might make sense to begin with a spoken request. You could then mail him a set of written documents that include official materials he must fill out and your own materials (illustrating your interests and strengths) that pertain to the application. The materials you supply and the medium you use to communicate with your advisor depend on the elements of the specific rhetorical situation.

From: Collin Allan <csallan2111@hotmail.com>
Date: August 13, 2009 1:19 PM
Subject: Letter of recommendation
To: Rosalyn Eves <rosalyn.eves@gmail.com>

Dear Dr. Eves,

I will be applying to law school this coming semester. Having worked with you both as a student and as a Writing Fellow, I thought that you might be willing to provide a letter of recommendation for me. Most schools require two letters of recommendation from an academic source. If you feel you could write a positive letter of recommendation for me, I would be honored and would deeply appreciate it. I will be out of town until school starts, but, if you are willing, I will get you the necessary information upon my return. I hope that I have contacted you far enough in advance to give you an opportunity to consider writing the letter before the grind of the semester really starts.

Thank you,

Collin Allan

E-mail Courtesy of Collin Allan.

Collin Allan chose e-mail as the most appropriate medium for delivering his request for a letter of recommendation.

Another important characteristic of a rhetorical opportunity for change is that the writer or speaker believes that change can be brought about through language that is spoken or written (or some combination of the two, perhaps combined with visual elements). The woman who picks up the phone to tell her friend she's sorry, the couple who would like to have guests at their wedding, the student who composes an e-mail asking his instructor for a letter of recommendation—all believe that their problems can be resolved through language. If any of these problems were *certain* to be resolved, however, there would be no need to craft a response to them. If a problem could never be resolved, there would also be no point in responding to it.

> ANALYZING THE RHETORICAL SITUATION

Decide whether each problem listed below is also a rhetorical opportunity. Be prepared to share the reasoning behind your responses with the rest of the class.

1. The Internal Revenue Service is charging you $2,000 in back taxes, asserting that you neglected to declare the income from your summer job.

2. Your college library has just sent you an e-mail informing you that you're being fined for several overdue books, all of which you returned a month ago.

3. After Thanksgiving dinner is served, your brothers and mother resume their ongoing argument about U.S. politics: health care, the wars, and the economy.

4. In the student section at the football stadium, some fans throw empty soda cans, toss beach balls, boo the opposing team, and stand during most of the game. You're quickly losing interest in attending the games.

5. If the university's child care center raises its rates again this year, you will have to look elsewhere for affordable child care.

> YOUR WRITING EXPERIENCES

1. Write for five minutes about a specific school-related assignment that created a rhetorical opportunity for you. In other words, try to remember an assignment that posed a problem to which you *wanted* to respond and *felt a need* to respond with spoken or written words or visuals. Be prepared to share your memory of this assignment with the rest of the class.

2. Consider a school-related assignment that you've been given in recent weeks. In your own words, write out the assignment, paying careful attention to the problem you think the assignment is asking you to resolve with language. Does this assignment establish an opportunity that calls for your response? Do you *want* to respond? If so, explain why. If not, explain how the assignment could be rewritten in such a way that you would feel an authentic reason to write. Be prepared to share your ideas with the rest of the class.

Reading a text for rhetorical opportunity

The following essay, "Why I Want a Wife," by Judy Brady, was first published forty years ago, in the inaugural issue of *Ms.* magazine. It remains one of the most widely anthologized essays in the United States. As you read this short essay, try to imagine American domestic life forty years ago. What specific details does the author provide to feed your imagination? Try to determine Brady's reason for writing this essay. What might have been the rhetorical opportunity that called for her written response?

> Why I Want a Wife

Judy Brady

I belong to that classification of people known as wives. I am a Wife. And, not altogether incidentally, I am a mother.

Not too long ago a male friend of mine appeared on the scene from the Midwest fresh from a recent divorce. He had one child, who is, of course, with his ex-wife. He is obviously looking for another wife. As I thought about him while I was ironing one evening, it suddenly occurred to me that I, too, would like to have a wife. Why do I want a wife?

continued

Why I Want a Wife *(continued)*

I would like to go back to school, so that I can become economically independent, support myself, and, if need be, support those dependent upon me. I want a wife who will work and send me to school. And while I am going to school I want a wife to take care of my children. I want a wife to keep track of the children's doctor and dentist appointments. And to keep track of mine, too. I want a wife to make sure my children eat properly and are kept clean. I want a wife who will wash the children's clothes and keep them mended. I want a wife who is a good nurturant attendant to my children, arranges for their schooling, makes sure that they have an adequate social life with their peers, takes them to the park, the zoo, etc. I want a wife who takes care of the children when they are sick, a wife who arranges to be around when the children need special care, because, of course, I cannot miss classes at school. My wife must arrange to lose time at work and not lose the job. It may mean a small cut in my wife's income from time to time, but I guess I can tolerate that. Needless to say, my wife will arrange and pay for the care of the children while my wife is working.

I want a wife who will take care of my physical needs. I want a wife who will keep my house clean. A wife who will pick up after my children, a wife who will pick up after me. I want a wife who will keep my clothes clean, ironed, mended, replaced when need be, and who will see to it that my personal things are kept in their proper place so that I can find what I need the minute I need it. I want a wife who cooks the meals, a wife who is a good cook. I want a wife who will plan the menus, do the necessary grocery shopping, prepare the meals, serve them pleasantly, and then do the cleaning up while I do my studying. I want a wife who will care for me when I am sick and sympathize with my pain and loss of time from school. I want a wife to go along when our family takes a vacation so that someone can continue to care for me and my children when I need a rest and a change of scene.

I want a wife who will take care of details of my social life. When my wife and I are invited out by my friends, I want a wife who will take care of the babysitting arrangements. When I meet people at school that I like and want to entertain, I want a wife who will have the house clean, will prepare a special meal, serve it to me and my friends, and not interrupt when I talk about the things that interest me and my friends. I want a wife who will have arranged that the children are fed and ready for bed before my guests arrive so that the children do not bother us. I want a wife who takes care of the needs of my guests so that they feel comfortable, who makes sure that they have an ashtray, that they are passed the hors d'oeuvres, that they are offered a second helping of the food, that their wine glasses are replenished when necessary, that their coffee is served to them as they like it. And I want a wife who knows that sometimes I need a night out by myself.

I want a wife who is sensitive to my sexual needs, a wife who makes love passionately and eagerly when I feel like it, a wife who makes sure that I am satisfied. And, of course, I want a wife who will not demand sexual attention when I am not in the mood for it. I want a wife who assumes the complete responsibility for birth control, because I do not want more children. I want a wife who will remain sexually faithful to me so that I do not have to clutter up my intellectual life with jealousies. And I want a wife who understands that my sexual needs may entail more than strict adherence to monogamy. I must, after all, be able to relate to people as fully as possible.

If, by chance, I find another person more suitable as a wife than the wife I already have, I want the liberty to replace my present wife with another one. Naturally, I will expect a fresh, new life; my wife will take the children and be solely responsible for them so that I am left free.

When I am through with school and have acquired a job, I want my wife to quit working and remain at home so that my wife can more fully and completely take care of a wife's duties.

My God, why wouldn't I want a wife?

After reading Brady's essay, you may want to spend some class time discussing the merits of her argument, for both the 1970s and today. You may also want to consider her pervasive use of irony (her tongue-in-cheek attitude toward her subject), the extent to which she's being serious, and the potential sexism of the essay. Few readers of this essay can resist registering their agreement or disagreement with its author; you may want to register yours as well.

Whether or not you agree with Brady, it's important for you to be able to analyze her rhetorical situation, starting with the reason she may have written this essay in the first place. Why would she keep repeating "I want a wife . . ."? Why would she write from the husband's point of view? Why would she describe a wife who does all the "heavy lifting" in a marriage? What kind of husband does she evoke? What effects do her rhetorical choices have on you as a reader?

Write your responses to the following questions. In doing so, you are practicing what's known as *rhetorical analysis*.

1. *What does this essay say?* Compile the details of a wife's daily life and describe the writer's feelings about a husband's expectations; then write one sentence that conveys Brady's main argument.
2. *Why does the essay say that?* Drawing on your previous answer, write three or four assertions that support Brady's argument.
3. *Who composed this message?* What information does the writer supply about her identity?
4. *What rhetorical opportunity called for the writing of this essay?* State that opportunity in one sentence.
5. *How does the essay respond to that opportunity?* What change in attitude, opinion, or action does the author wish to influence?

Reading an image for rhetorical opportunity

Responses to rhetorical opportunities are not always verbal. Visual responses to rhetorical opportunities constantly bombard us—from advertisements and promotions to cards from friends and political messages. If you think the Callout Card here addresses the problem of electronic harassment, then you view it as a fitting response to a rhetorical opportunity for change. Obviously, the sender of "David, wrapped in a towel" does not want to receive visuals that are "naughty," maybe even

YOU'LL BE HAPPY TO KNOW THAT THE UNWANTED NAUGHTY PHOTO YOU SENT MADE ME GAG.

THATSNOTCOOL.COM

Sponsored and co-created by the Family Violence Prevention Fund, the Office on Violence Against Women, and the Ad COUNCIL.

This Callout Card, available at Thatsnotcool.com, is a visual response to a rhetorical opportunity.

pornographic. When you consider this image and text in terms of a rhetorical response, you are analyzing it rhetorically, "reading" it more thoroughly than you might have otherwise.

Reading for rhetorical opportunity helps you develop your skills as an active, informed reader and as a rhetorical analyst. Respond to the same questions you answered about "Why I Want a Wife," but this time focus on the Callout Card:

1. *What does the visual "say"—and how?* Describe the visual in one sentence, paying attention to both the statue and the brightly colored text that accompanies it.

2. *Why does the visual say that?* Consider the contexts in which you might usually see a statue such as Michelangelo's *David*. Compare those contexts with this one.

3. *Who composed this message?* Consider what you know or can find out about the groups responsible for the message: the Family Violence Prevention Fund, the Office on Violence Against Women, and the Ad Council for the website Thatsnotcool.com.

4. *What is the rhetorical opportunity that called for the creation of this visual?* Using the information you've compiled in response to questions 1, 2, and 3, identify the opportunity that calls for this visual response.

5. *How does the visual respond to the opportunity?* What message does this visual send to viewers? How might this visual work to address the problem you described in the previous answer? It might help to keep in mind that Callout Cards can be shared through e-mail, Facebook, and MySpace.

Whether you're reading an essay, listening to a speech, or looking at a visual, you'll understand the message better if you begin by determining the rhetorical opportunity that calls for specific words or visuals. Very often, the responses you're reading or viewing call for even further responses. For instance, you may feel a strong urge to respond to "Why I Want a Wife" or to the Callout Card, which are responses in themselves. Whether your response is spoken, written, or composed visually, its power lies in your understanding of the rhetorical opportunity.

Creating or Finding a Rhetorical Opportunity

Unless you perceive something as an opportunity, you cannot respond to it. In other words, *something* needs to stimulate or provoke your interest and call for your response. When you take an essay examination for an American history midterm, you might be given the choice of answering one of three questions:

1. The great increase in size and power of the federal government since the Civil War has long been a dominant theme of American history. Trace the growth of the federal government since 1865, paying particular attention to its evolving involvement in world affairs and the domestic economy. Be sure to support your analysis with relevant historical details.

2. Compare and contrast the attempts to create and safeguard African American civil rights in two historical periods: the first era of reconstruction (post–Civil War years to the early twentieth century) and the second era of reconstruction (1950s to 1970s). Consider government policies, African American strategies, and the responses of white people to those strategies.

3. "When the United States enters a war, it does so in the defense of vital national interests." Assess the accuracy of this statement with reference to any three of the following: the Spanish-American War, World War I, World War II, the Cold War, and the Vietnam War. Be sure to define "national interests" and to support your argument with relevant historical details.

If you're lucky, one of the above questions will call for your response, given your interests and knowledge. You can ignore the other two questions and turn your energies to the one you've chosen. Think of every college writing situation as a rhetorical opportunity for you to use language in order to resolve or address a problem.

Online opportunities

In addition to the spoken and written rhetorical opportunities we encounter, on-line opportunities greet us nearly every time we turn on our computers. If you're familiar with the website Facebook.com, for instance, you know that it presents numerous opportunities for response.

If "Become a Fan" or "What's on Your Mind" doesn't tantalize you, other opportunities will, such as "Status Updates." In other words, different people respond to different online rhetorical opportunities—and those opportunities exist nearly everywhere you browse online.

The family of missing college student Cindy Song, for instance, has resorted to online opportunities in the hope of receiving information about Song, who disappeared on Halloween 2001. Despite an extended, intensive search, an ongoing FBI investigation, and a feature on the TV series *Unsolved Mysteries*, Song's family has

Social networking sites offer many rhetorical opportunities.

Hyun Jong Song
MPCCN Case File: 1529F00

Above Images: Song, circa 2001

Vital Statistics at Time of Disappearance
- **Missing Since:** November 1, 2001 from State College, Pennsylvania
- **Classification:** Endangered Missing
- **Date Of Birth:** February 25, 1980
- **Age:** 21 years old
- **Height and Weight:** 5'1–5'3, 110–130 pounds
- **Distinguishing Characteristics:** Black hair, brown eyes. Song is of Korean descent. Her ears and navel are pierced. Song's nickname is Cindy. Her middle name may be spelled "Jung." Song's first name may be spelled "Hyunjong" or "Hyunjung."

Details of Disappearance
Song was raised in Seoul, South Korea. She moved to the United States in 1995 to live with relatives in Springfield, Virginia near Alexandria. Song graduated from high school and enrolled in Pennsylvania State University, where she majored in integrated arts. She was scheduled to graduate during the spring of 2002.

Song attended a Halloween party during the early morning hours of November 1, 2001 at the *Player's Nite Club* in the 110 block of West College Avenue. She departed from the party at 2:00 a.m., then stopped by a friend's home for two hours. Another friend dropped Song off outside of her residence in *State College Park Apartments* in the 340 block of West Clinton Avenue at approximately 4:00 a.m. She had been drinking that evening and was mildly intoxicated when taken to her apartment. She was last seen wearing her costume, which consisted of a pink sleeveless shirt with a rabbit design imprinted on the front, rabbit ears, a white tennis skirt with a cotton bunny tail attached to the back, brown suede leather knee-

Websites such as this one for missing adults try to create an opportunity to which viewers want to respond.

no leads. So they have set up a web page (above), which asks anyone who might remember any detail about the night Song went missing to contact the local police. Each of the news stories, in addition to the appeal on the web, creates an opportunity for people to respond with language. Every time you come across a story like Song's, you may wish you could respond—but you probably cannot. You have no information about the missing person. Therefore, despite the opportunity, you don't respond (even though you wish you could).

> YOUR WRITING EXPERIENCES

1. When was the last time you identified a rhetorical opportunity to which you felt compelled to respond? Write for five minutes or so, describing the opportunity in terms of the rhetorical situation and how you addressed it. Share your response with the rest of the class.
2. Consider a time when you identified a rhetorical opportunity to which you did not or could not respond. Describe this opportunity and explain what prevented you from responding.

Everyday rhetorical opportunities

Cindy Song's disappearance serves as one of many daily chances you will have to respond to rhetorical opportunities, some joyous, others heartbreaking. If your good friend applies for and gets the job of her dreams, the situation calls for a response. How will she know that you're happy for her unless you send her a congratulatory card, give her a phone call, invite her to a celebratory lunch—or all three? The death of your neighbor creates an opportunity to respond with a letter to the family or a bouquet of flowers and an accompanying condolence note. A friend's illness, an argument with a roommate, a tuition hike, an essay exam, a sales presentation, a job interview, a sorority rush, or children's misbehavior—these are all situations that provide opportunities for response through spoken or written words or through visuals.

Whether you choose to recognize—let alone speak to—a rhetorical opportunity is usually up to you, as are whether you create an elaborate or a simple response and how you deliver your message—whether you choose to write a letter to the editor of the campus newspaper, make a phone call to your state representative's office, prepare a PowerPoint presentation, create a fact sheet, or interrupt someone else and speak. You often have a choice, but not always. Sometimes you're forced to respond and to do so in a specific way.

> ANALYZING THE RHETORICAL SITUATION

1. What is one rhetorical opportunity you are currently considering? Write for a few minutes, describing the overall situation, the problem that can be addressed with language, and the specific call for language.

2. From whom would you like a response? Why is that person (or group) the best source of a response? Write for a few minutes, connecting your answer with that for question 1.

3. What content and medium of response would you prefer? How will people know your preference? Expand on what you wrote for questions 1 and 2 and explain why your preferred content and medium form the best response to this rhetorical opportunity.

4. How might language be a way to respond to the opportunity for making change? In other words, what exactly might language do to relieve or resolve the problem in your life? Add your answer to this question to what you've already written. Be prepared to share your overall analysis with the rest of the class.

5. In class, listen carefully to your classmates' analyses, and take notes. Be prepared to provide suggestions for improving their concepts of rhetorical opportunity, response, and resolution.

Selecting a Rhetorical Audience and Purpose

No doubt many of you have received mailings targeted to you based on your interests and purchases. The message on the following page was sent via e-mail by Barnes & Noble in anticipation of the publication of the last novel in the Harry Potter series. The message was sent to many people—but not to just anyone—for one purpose: to persuade them to come to a celebration at a Barnes & Noble store, and to buy their copy of *Harry Potter and the Deathly Hallows* there, too.

Messages such as this one from Barnes & Noble are created with a *rhetorical audience* in mind.

Of course, not everyone is interested in Harry Potter, let alone in attending a late night party in costume, just to be among the first to get a copy of the newest book in the series. So Barnes & Noble sent this e-mail message to people who had purchased other Harry Potter books or calendars, notebooks, and so on, anticipating that they would be familiar with the tradition of arriving at a store hours ahead of the book's release ("Join us . . . as you count down the final moments to Harry's arrival!"). Additionally, because Barnes & Noble is reaching these people through the medium of e-mail, the message includes information about ordering the book online—just a click away for those already reading e-mail. Thus, the specific audience for the e-mail (people who had purchased Harry Potter items in the past) was closely related to its purpose (enticing these people to purchase Harry Potter items in the near future).

Audience versus rhetorical audience

Audience is a key component of any rhetorical situation. After all, you'll direct your writing, speaking, or visual display to a specific audience in an attempt to change some opinion, attitude, or action. But even as you tailor your verbal or visual language to a specific audience, you must keep in mind that that person or group may not be a rhetorical audience. A **rhetorical audience** consists of *only* those persons who are capable of being influenced by verbal or visual discourse and of bringing about change, either by acting themselves or by influencing others who can create change. The following examples will help clarify the concept of rhetorical audience.

Not every person who received the invitation to come to the Harry Potter party was persuaded to attend, let alone buy the new book. No matter how enticing the e-mail might have been, some people did not even read it: they were not open to being influenced by the message. Others may have looked it over quickly, considered the offer, and *then* deleted it. Still others probably waited to discuss the invitation with their friends before deciding whether to attend. Those who did accept the invitation were capable of bringing about the change that made them guests at the party and consumers of the product.

Now consider the Saab advertisement. Clearly, the purpose of all advertising is to sell a product, so every advertiser must keep a buying audience in mind. The Saab ad tantalizes readers with visual and verbal details, including the $39,995 price tag. The audience for this ad consists of people who appreciate Saabs and perhaps admire Saab owners. Some of them might yearn for a Saab themselves but feel they cannot afford one. The rhetorical audience for this ad, however, consists of those people who can either buy a Saab or influence someone else to buy one. These people can use words to negotiate specific features (color, engine, wheel design, model, and so on) and price if they decide to purchase a Saab. Or they can use words to influence someone else to purchase a Saab. Either way, their actions have been influenced by the ad. But, not every reader of the ad will be influenced by it.

Not every person who listens to a presidential hopeful's speech, watches a Super Bowl ad, or reads about impending tuition hikes is part of a rhetorical audience. After all, not every person is open to being influenced by the discourse and bringing about change or influencing those who can make a change. But some people *are* open to influence. The delegates at the Republican National Convention are a rhetorical audience: they listen to speeches and cast their votes. When the delegates choose the presidential and vice presidential candidates, they eliminate all the other Republican candidates, thereby influencing the voting options of millions of Americans.

Magazine advertisements such as this one seek to persuade those who can buy the product advertised or those who can influence someone else to buy it.

Similarly, many more people are upset—and affected—by tuition hikes than are willing to try to do something about them. Those in the rhetorical audience write or telephone their state representatives, their university's board of trustees, and the university administration to protest tuition hikes. They feel empowered as agents of change and believe that their words can change the minds of the people who determine tuition rates.

The message—whether verbal or visual—can influence a rhetorical audience. You apply this knowledge every time you stand in front of a large display of greeting cards and spend what seems like more time choosing "just the right card" than you spent choosing the gift. You evaluate each card's visual elements and greeting, considering and rejecting cards in rapid succession as you match up the features of the card with the interests of the recipient. After all, you want your influence to be positive, to make the recipient feel appreciated. Whether you choose a card with a Bible verse for your religious friend, a picture of a black lab catching a Frisbee for your dog-loving roommate, or a romantic greeting for your sweetheart, your choice reflects the message you want to send to your audience, the person who is capable of being influenced by the words and pictures that you chose.

Consider the pile of holiday cards you receive each winter. Some may be celebrating Christmas, Hanukkah, or Kwanzaa; some may be reminders of lesser-known holidays—Winter Solstice, Yule, or Ásatrú. Others may just be wishing you "Happy Holidays" or hoping for "Peace on Earth." Whatever the greeting and visual, you are the audience for all the cards you receive. You are capable of being influenced by any of them. But, in actuality, you'll be influenced by only a few: those that give you special pleasure, motivate you to call the sender, surprise you because you don't celebrate *that* particular holiday, or make you feel sentimental about the holiday at hand or friends who are not.

As a member of a rhetorical audience, you're not only capable of being influenced (or changed) by the situation, but also capable of bringing about change as a result of the situation. You can bring about change on your own, or you can influence the people who can make the change.

You are bringing about change, for example, when you pick up the phone to apologize for a long-standing misunderstanding after you read a former friend's moving handwritten message at the bottom of a "Peace on Earth" card. After receiving a "Happy Holidays" card from your brother announcing that he'll be home from Iraq for the holidays, you might recruit all his old buddies for a surprise welcome. Both decisions render you part of the rhetorical audience. When your English instructor writes comments on your drafts, you can become part of her rhetorical audience by following her instructions and writing better essays.

© Steven Lunetta Photography, 2007

Even when choosing a birthday card, you're considering a rhetorical audience.

Considering purpose in terms of rhetorical audience

Many writers equate purpose with their reason for writing: they're fulfilling an assignment or meeting a deadline; they want a good grade or want to see their essay in print; they want to make money or win a contest. When you're writing with a **rhetorical purpose**, however, you move beyond such goals to one of influencing your rhetorical audience. In order to achieve this influence, you'll need to keep in mind the nature of your audience (their control, power, and status) and their character (sympathetic or unsympathetic to, opposed to or in favor of your message).

You already know that rhetorical audience and purpose cannot be separated. You always try to send your message to someone who can be influenced to change an attitude, action, or opinion or resolve a problem of some kind. For example, when you enter a department store to return defective merchandise, you know that you need to speak to a department supervisor or maybe go to the service desk. You don't want to waste your time talking with people who cannot help you.

Once you reach your rhetorical audience, you try to shape your message in terms of content, tone, examples, and timeliness in order to enhance its chances of influencing that audience. Whether you're talking to your instructor, one of your parents, or your physician, you try to keep in mind the kind of information you should deliver—as well as how and when to deliver it. Balancing audience and purpose is a skill you can work to improve.

Reading a cartoon for rhetorical audience and purpose

In June 2009, the reelection of President Mahmoud Ahmadinejad prompted many Iranians to cry foul. Although the government quickly blocked oppositional websites and text messaging services, many Iranians found another available means for getting the word out about the protests that developed in response to the apparently rigged elections: Twitter posts (tweets). Thanks to 140-character Twitter reports and YouTube videos from Iranians, the rest of the world became aware of what they could not see on traditional media outlets.

This cartoon responds to a political opportunity for change.

© RJ Matsor, the *St. Louis Post-Dispatch*, and PoliticalCartoons.com

The cartoon on the preceding page represents an Iranian Lady Liberty, who, like the Statue of Liberty, wears a stola (a robe worn over her dress) and a radiating crown. Instead of a lit torch, she lifts up her cell phone (displaying a photo of a lit torch), a primary tool in the Iranian people's fight to be heard. Like the Statue of Liberty, she also carries a tablet in her left hand. But instead of being engraved with the date of the U.S. Declaration of Independence, it is inscribed with the word *VOTE* and the date of the elections that launched the protests, June 12.

> ANALYZING THE RHETORICAL SITUATION

1. Reread the cartoon, and then write for five minutes about it. List all the information you can possibly glean from its visual and verbal details.

2. Compare your answers to question 1 with those of one or two classmates and write a joint account of the visual and verbal details of the cartoon and its overall impact.

3. What rhetorical opportunity does the cartoon offer? To what rhetorical opportunity does it respond?

4. Who is the intended audience for the cartoon? In what ways does that audience fulfill the definition of a rhetorical audience?

5. Account for your response to the cartoon. Are you a member of the rhetorical audience? If so, list the ways you fulfill the role of a rhetorical audience. Be prepared to share your answer with the rest of the class.

6. What specific visual or verbal details reveal something about the character of the cartoonist? Appeal to your emotions (positively or negatively)? Shape an argument, even if it's one you don't agree with?

Reading a book introduction for rhetorical audience and purpose

English professor Michael Bérubé writes widely about academic matters: curriculum, teaching loads, classroom management, tenure, and cultural studies. But with the birth of his second son, James (Jamie), Bérubé ventured into another kind of writing, writing aimed at a wider audience. The following excerpt is from the introduction to *Life as We Know It: A Father, a Family, and an Exceptional Child*, a chronicle of his family's experiences with Jamie, who has Down syndrome.

Excerpt from

> Life as We Know It

© 1996. Reprinted by permission.

Michael Bérubé

My little Jamie loves lists: foods, colors, animals, numbers, letters, states, classmates, parts of the body, days of the week, modes of transportation, characters who live on Sesame Street, and the names of the people who love him. Early last summer, I hoped his love of lists—and his ability to catalogue things *into* lists—would stand him in good stead during what would undoubtedly be a difficult "vacation" for anyone, let alone a three-year-old child with Down syndrome: a

© Steve Tressler, 2006

three-hour drive to Chicago, a rush-hour flight to LaGuardia, a cab to Grand Central, a train to Connecticut—and *then* smaller trips to New York, Boston, and Old Orchard Beach, Maine. Even accomplishing the first of these mission objectives—arriving safely at O'Hare—required a precision and teamwork I do not always associate with my family. I dropped off Janet and nine-year-old Nick at the terminal with the baggage, then took Jamie to long-term parking with me while they checked in, and then entertained Jamie all the way back to the terminal, via bus and shuttle train. We sang about the driver on the bus, and we counted all the escalator steps and train stops, and when we finally got to our plane, I told Jamie, *Look, there's Mommy and Nick at the gate! They're yelling that we're going to lose our seats! They want to know why it took us forty-five minutes to park the car!*

All went well from that point on, though, and in the end, I suppose you could say Jamie got as much out of his vacation as might any toddler being whisked up and down New England. He's a seasoned traveler, and he thrives on shorelines, family gatherings, and New Haven pizza. And he's good with faces and names.

Then again, as we learned toward the end of our brief stay in Maine, he doesn't care much for amusement parks. Not that Nick did either, at three. But apparently one of the attractions of Old Orchard Beach, for my wife and her siblings, was the small beachfront arcade and amusement park in town, which they associated with their own childhoods. It was an endearing strip, with a roller coaster just the right size for Nick—exciting, mildly scary, but with no loop-the-loops, rings of fire, or oppressive G forces. We strolled among bumper cars, cotton candy, games of chance and skill, and a striking number of French-Canadian tourists: perhaps the first time our two little boys had ever seen more than one Bérubé family in one place. James, however, wanted nothing to do with any of the rides, and though he loves to pretend-drive and has been on bumper cars before, he squalled so industriously before the ride began as to induce the bumper cars operator to let him out of the car and refund his two tickets.

Jamie finally settled in next to a train ride designed for children five and under or thereabouts, which, for two tickets, took its passengers around an oval layout and over a bridge four times. I found out quickly enough that Jamie didn't want to *ride* the ride; he merely wanted to stand at its perimeter, grasping the partition with both hands and counting the cars—one, two, three, four, five, six—as they went by. Sometimes, when the train traversed the bridge, James would punctuate it with tiny jumps, saying, "Up! Up! Up!" But for the most part, he was content to hang onto the metal bars of the partition, grinning and counting—and, when the train came to a stop, pulling my sleeve and saying, "More, again."

This went on for about half an hour, well past the point at which I could convincingly share Jamie's enthusiasm for tracking the train's progress. As it went on my spirits began to sink in a way I do not recall having felt before. Occasionally it will occur to Janet or to me that Jamie will always be "disabled," that his adult and adolescent years will undoubtedly be more difficult emotionally—for him and for us—than his early childhood, that we will never *not* worry about his future, his

continued

Life as We Know It *(continued)*

quality of life, whether we're doing enough for him. But usually these moments occur in the relative comfort of abstraction, when Janet and I are lying in bed at night and wondering what will become of us all. When I'm *with* Jamie, by contrast, I'm almost always fully occupied by taking care of his present needs rather than by worrying about his future. When he asks to hear the Beatles because he loves their cover of Little Richard's "Long Tall Sally," I just play the song, sing along, and watch him dance with delight; I do not concern myself with extraneous questions such as whether he'll ever distinguish early Beatles from late Beatles, Paul's songs from John's, originals from covers. These questions are now central to Nick's enjoyment of the Beatles, but that's Nick for you. Jamie is entirely *sui generis*, and as long as I'm with him I can't think of him as anything but Jamie.

I have tried. Almost as a form of emotional exercise, I have tried, on occasion, to step back and see him as others might see him, as an instance of a category, one item on the long list of human subgroups. *This is a child with Down syndrome,* I say to myself. *This is a child with a developmental disability.* It never works: Jamie remains Jamie to me. I have even tried to imagine him as he would have been seen in other eras, other places: *This is a retarded child.* And even: *This is a Mongoloid child.* This makes for unbearable cognitive dissonance. I can imagine that people might think such things, but I cannot imagine how they might think them in a way that prevents them from seeing Jamie *as* Jamie. I try to recall how I saw such children when I was a child, but here I guiltily draw a blank: I don't remember seeing them at all, which very likely means that I never quite saw them *as* children. Instead I remember a famous passage from Ludwig Wittgenstein's *Philosophical Investigations:* " 'Seeing-as' is not part of perception. And for this reason it is *like* seeing, and then again *not* like." Reading Wittgenstein, I often think, is something like listening to a brilliant and cantankerous uncle with an annoying fondness for koans. But on this one, I know exactly what he means.

> ANALYZING THE RHETORICAL SITUATION

1. To what rhetorical opportunity might Bérubé be responding?
2. Who is the intended audience for Bérubé's book? In what ways does that audience fulfill the definition of a rhetorical audience? How do you know?
3. What rhetorical opportunity does Bérubé offer his audience? Are there specific ways in which his rhetorical audience could be open to effecting change or influencing others who could make change?
4. If you were writing an essay about a remarkable person, whom would you choose to write about? Who would make up your audience? What rhetorical opportunity might you create or perceive in order to shape a fitting response? What would be your purpose? Freewrite for ten minutes and be prepared to share your thoughts with the rest of the class.

COMMUNITY CONNECTIONS

1. Bring a copy of your local or campus newspaper to class. Spend time with a classmate looking over the cartoons, columns, and letters on the editorial page. Choose one of the editorials or cartoons and determine the rhetorical opportunity for change that it presents. Who is the rhetorical audience for the editorial or cartoon? In what specific ways might that audience be influenced to change? What is the overall purpose of the cartoon or editorial? What does the artist or writer want the rhetorical audience to do with the information? Be prepared to share your answers with the rest of the class.

2. Work with one or two classmates to consider someone with influence in your school or community (whether in politics, education, sports, medicine, or the arts) and a rhetorical opportunity for change to which he or she has responded. Describe that opportunity and the person's response. What group of people comprise the rhetorical audience for the response? What would the person have his or her rhetorical audience do? Be prepared to share your answers with the rest of the class.

3. What problem do you face today that can be addressed or resolved through language? What is a possible fitting response to your problem? Who is the rhetorical audience for the response? How would you like that person or those people to be influenced or changed? Write for a few minutes, describing the elements of this rhetorical situation.

4. Consider yourself as a rhetorical audience. For whom do you function as such? In what ways are you considered capable of being influenced by the language of someone else? Capable of implementing change? Capable of influencing those who can make change? Write for five minutes, describing yourself as a rhetorical audience. Prepare to discuss your answer with the rest of the class.

2 Identifying a Fitting Response

The beautiful and extinct Carolina parakeet.

Jean-Pierre Sylvestre/Photo Library

Confronted with the problem of bird extinction, amateur birdwatcher and professor of English Christopher Cokinos began writing *Hope Is the Thing with Feathers*. Cokinos considered his new book to be a fitting response to the rhetorical opportunity for change that called to him. After all, most people knew nothing about important North American birds, particularly those birds that had become extinct, and his book could educate them. He knew he couldn't restore the Carolina parakeet or any of the other five bird species that had been hastened into extinction by logging, the millinery trade, unregulated hunting, and bird collecting. But Cokinos could "restory" these lost beings to human consciousness at the same time as he energized conservation efforts for other endangered nonhuman species.

On an afternoon in late September, in a brisk prairie wind, I watched a bird I'd never seen before, a bird that had strayed far from its usual skies a continent away. Nearly epic in memory, that day began my journey, though I didn't know it then. The journey would take years and retrieve many things: first among them the name of the bird I had watched and didn't know—an escaped parrot that didn't "belong" in Kansas.

Seeing this bird led me to learn of—and revere—America's forgotten Carolina Parakeet, which once colored the sky "like an atmosphere of gems," as one pioneer wrote. The more I learned of the Carolina Parakeet's life, its extinction and its erasure from our memory, the more I wondered: How could we have lost and then forgotten so beautiful a bird? This book is, in part, an attempt to answer those questions and an effort to make certain that we never again forget this species nor the others of which I write. —Christopher Cokinos, from *Hope Is the Thing with Feathers*

> WRITE FOR FIVE

In writing answers to the following questions, think back to a time when you responded to a rhetorical opportunity through some form of writing.

1. In what ways did your response reach and satisfy your intended audience?
2. In what ways was it an appropriate response to the problem you identified?
3. What other appropriate responses would have been possible?

What Is a Fitting Response?

Chapter 1 stressed the importance of identifying the elements of a rhetorical situation (opportunity, purpose, writer, message, audience, and context). Now that you can identify these elements, you can evaluate the wide range of possible responses you can offer. The goal of every person who responds rhetorically to a situation is to shape a **fitting response**, a visual or verbal (written or spoken) response that

▶ addresses the opportunity for change;

▶ is appropriate in content, tone, and timing;

▶ is delivered in an appropriate medium; and thus

▶ reaches, satisfies, and maybe even changes the actions, opinions, or attitudes of the intended audience.

Was Christopher Cokinos's book on the extinction of bird species a fitting response? Yes.

Was his the *only* possible fitting response? No.

Had Cokinos been a different sort of person, having different resources and interests and imagining different rhetorical audiences, he might have made a feature film about these birds, one starring Robert Pattinson and Reese Witherspoon as either hunters or conservationists. He might have put together a public television special, underwritten by the U.S. Department of the Interior. Or maybe he could have induced Pixar Animation Studios to make a children's movie about these birds, with voice-overs by Angelina Jolie, Will Ferrell, and Forest Whitaker. Depending on the problem, responses in different media may reach and satisfy the rhetorical audience.

A fitting response suits the problem

As you know by now, the prime characteristic of a rhetorical situation is that it presents an opportunity for change. Another key feature of a rhetorical situation is that it invites a fitting response. The fitting response is dictated by the situation: by the specific opportunity for response, the writer's relationship with the audience, the constitution of the audience, what that audience might do, the available means of delivering a message, and other constraints and resources of the rhetorical situation. For instance, if you were bothered by your friend's weekend alcohol consumption, you'd want to find a good time and place to talk with her about it, focusing on the dangers to her own well-being or discussing the pros and cons of drinking by college students. This situation invites such a response. On the other hand, the situation does not invite a subpoena, lawsuit, or visit from a physician—at least not yet.

Fraternity parties, post-game celebrations, and spring break have long been part of the college experience. Some have said that these events serve as rites of passage for students as they move from high school into adulthood. But the alcohol consumption that so often accompanies these rites presents a major public health issue. Underage and binge drinking often lead to drunk driving, alcohol dependence, risky sexual behavior, physical injuries, and even death.

According to the Center on Alcohol Marketing and Youth (CAMY), American teenagers are particularly vulnerable to the effects of alcohol. A fact sheet published by the organization indicates that nine U.S. teens are killed each day from alcohol-related causes (including drunk driving). Drinking before the age of twenty-one is believed to impair critical stages of adolescent brain development. Twenty-three percent of sexually active teens and young adults (aged 15–24) blamed having had unprotected sex on drinking (or drug use). Finally, CAMY reports that "alcohol use plays a substantial role in all three leading causes of death among youth—unintentional injuries (including motor vehicle fatalities and drownings), suicides and homicides." Those are just the physical consequences. As you might imagine, the social consequences of underage and binge drinking are innumerable.

One response to the rhetorical situation presented by irresponsible drinking has been a reexamination of drinking practices. The U.S. medical community, for example, has summarized a list of prevention strategies, with the full realization that those strategies can be instituted only within supporting social, political, and economic infrastructure. To that end, the minimum drinking-age laws must be enforced; alcohol tax must be increased; young people must be excluded as targets of alcohol advertising; and educational programs must be instituted. And that's just a start.

Across the United States, college and university administrators have come together in the hope of sparking a national conversation on drinking. They want to work together to discuss the effects of a minimum drinking age and reopen the public debate on what that age should be. These efforts have given rise to what has come to be called the Amethyst Initiative (from the ancient Greek *a methustos*, or "not intoxicated").

Part of the conversation proposed by the Amethyst Initiative is reconsideration of current laws and policies and the creation of a plan for instilling in young people responsible decision making about alcohol use. Toward these ends, college administrators framed an invitational statement expressing their views, a statement that, rather than prescribing specific actions or changes, serves as an invitation for their colleagues across the nation to discuss the possibilities for positive change in the actions, attitudes, and opinions of young people. The statement invites supporters to join the cause—and the conversation. Consider the ways in which the statement constitutes a fitting response to the problem of irresponsible drinking.

Amethyst Initiative's founder John McCardell.

AP Photo/Toby Talbot

> It's Time To Rethink the Drinking Age

www.Chooseresponsibility.org. Used by permission.

The Amethyst Initiative

In 1984 Congress passed the National Minimum Drinking Age Act, which imposed a penalty of 10% of a state's federal highway appropriation on any state setting its drinking age lower than 21.

Twenty-four years later, our experience as college and university presidents convinces us that . . .

Twenty-one is not working

A culture of dangerous, clandestine "binge-drinking"—often conducted off-campus—has developed.

Alcohol education that mandates abstinence as the only legal option has not resulted in significant constructive behavioral change among our students.

Adults under 21 are deemed capable of voting, signing contracts, serving on juries and enlisting in the military, but are told they are not mature enough to have a beer.

By choosing to use fake IDs, students make ethical compromises that erode respect for the law.

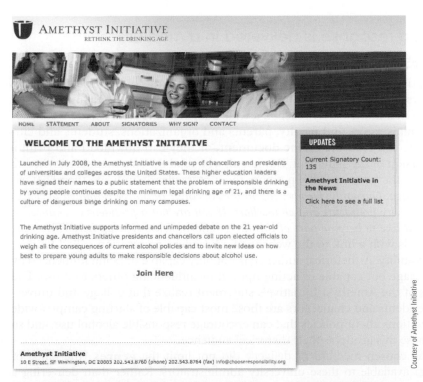

One means available to the Amethyst Initiative for creating a fitting response is this website.

continued

It's Time To Rethink the Drinking Age *(continued)*

How many times must we relearn the lessons of Prohibition?

We call upon our elected officials:

> To support an informed and dispassionate public debate over the effects of the 21 year-old drinking age.
>
> To consider whether the 10% highway fund "incentive" encourages or inhibits that debate.
>
> To invite new ideas about the best ways to prepare young adults to make responsible decisions about alcohol.

We pledge ourselves and our institutions to playing a vigorous, constructive role as these critical discussions unfold.

Please add my signature to this statement:

Name _____

Signature _____

Institution _____

A fitting response is delivered in a medium and genre that reach the audience

In addition to comprising a suitable response to the problem at hand, the Amethyst Initiative's statement was delivered through an easily accessed medium that immediately reached a wide audience: the World Wide Web. College administrators and faculty, parents and organizations, students and citizens alike can read the online document, or they can download and print a PDF version of the statement. But not all who read the statement are invited to sign it. At the bottom of the petition, the writers clearly indicate their rhetorical audience: *Currently, membership in the Amethyst Initiative is limited to college and university presidents and chancellors. If you are not a president or chancellor, but would like to become part of this larger effort, please sign up here.* The sentence ends with a link to the website of a broader organization called Choose Responsibility. A rhetorical audience is not only capable of being influenced by the message but capable of acting upon it or influencing others to do so. The writers of the Amethyst Initiative's statement realize that college and university presidents and chancellors are those most capable of starting campus-wide conversations about policies that can encourage responsible alcohol use, and so they chose this group as their rhetorical audience.

The chosen medium of delivery did not limit the **genres** (the kinds of writing) available to these university administrators. Rather than delivering a statement, the World Wide Web could have delivered anything from a blog entry to a streaming video. But the rhetorical opportunity for change (the need to work toward a national strategy for establishing responsible alcohol use) and other elements of the rhetorical situation (including all the strong arguments surrounding the current drinking age itself) called for a kind of writing that promoted concern, research, and participation, rather than judgment.

By calling on the rhetorical audience to sign the statement, the Amethyst Initiative's writers made use of a genre with a long history—the petition. Consider petitions that you have seen or read, many of which are connected with social activism, all of which involve inviting others to join in the movement for halting or supporting legislation; boycotting or supporting manufacturers, products, or companies; or applauding or protesting decisions. Key characteristics of petitions are

- an explicit statement of the problem,
- essential background information,
- a statement of what should be done to resolve the problem,
- a named audience who can initiate change (that is, a rhetorical audience),
- a request for signatures or support, and
- strategic delivery of the message, often accompanied by some kind of publicity.

Every petition is a response to a rhetorical opportunity for change that calls for spreading the effort more widely. Those who read and sign the petition will likely understand the public nature of the petition because they have encountered that genre before. In other words, the genre has created expectations in readers.

A fitting response satisfies the intended audience

The Amethyst Initiative's petition—fitting response that it is—works on several levels to satisfy the intended audience:

- On a basic level, the petition identifies some of the irresponsible drinking behaviors that constitute health and safety problems—well-known behaviors that worry parents, teachers, and health care professionals, as well as school administrators.
- On a second level, the petition implies that these problems are sufficient cause to reconsider the current drinking age of twenty-one.
- Finally, the authors of the petition don't judge drinkers or drinking behaviors. Rather, they use calm and everyday language, and they call on elected officials to support "informed and unimpeded debate" for the purpose of inviting "new ideas about the best ways to prepare young adults to make responsible decisions about alcohol."

All of these features—identifying a problem, offering an engaged response, and inviting audience participation—are key features of the petition genre that often make such a document a fitting response.

For each of the following problems, decide whether you could shape a response that fulfills the three requirements for being fitting: language that suits the problem, is delivered in an appropriate medium, and satisfies the intended audience. Be prepared to share your answers with the rest of the class.

1. Your university's football coach, whom you have long admired, is receiving a great deal of negative press because the football team is losing.

2. When you and your friends get together, they always try to persuade you to join their church.

3. Your history instructor has assigned a research paper that is due on the same day as your biology midterm.

4. After taking your LSATs, you receive mailings from more than twenty law schools.

5. In order to obtain a green card (indicating U.S. permanent resident status), your Romanian friend wants to arrange a fraudulent American marriage.

Recognizing a Fitting Response

The Amethyst Initiative triggered "push back" from several groups: Mothers Against Drunk Driving (MADD), the Center for Science in the Public Interest (CSPI), the National Institute on Alcohol Abuse and Alcoholism (NIAAA), and the Community Anti-Drug Coalitions of America (CADCA), among others. These national organizations support the current minimum drinking age of twenty-one. Although the Amethyst Initiative suggests that lowering the minimum drinking age will allow multiple educational interventions focusing on responsible drinking, the opposed organizations argue that an overwhelming amount of research has already indicated positive health and safety effects of making twenty-one the minimum drinking age.

The Center for Science in the Public Interest, for instance, posted an online response in the form of a statement given at a press conference by George A. Hacker, Director of CSPI's Alcohol Policies Project. As you read the statement, consider what makes it a fitting response.

Statement by George A. Hacker on Minimum Drinking Age Law

Used by permission of Center for Science in the Public Interest.

One reason CSPI gives for keeping the current drinking age addresses the Amethyst Initiative's call for response.

Since its adoption throughout the United States in the late 1980s, we have learned enough about the benefits of the 21 minimum legal drinking age to know that it would be a disastrous mistake to lower it. Doing so would merely doom many more thousands of young people to premature death and other severe alcohol-related problems. Despite wishful thinking on the part of some, there is no evidence that a lower drinking age would result in fewer alcohol-related problems among young people, and quite a bit of evidence that refutes that view. Since passage of the National Minimum Purchase Age Act in 1983, the percent of high school seniors who report any alcohol use in the past year has dropped nearly 20% (from 88% in 1983 to 73% in 2006) and the proportion who report binge drinking has declined nearly 40% (from 41% in 1983 to 25% in 2006).

Simply having age-21 laws on the books, however, is no panacea. Confronting deeply ingrained alcohol problems requires a real commitment to an effective, comprehensive national prevention strategy. The National Academies of Science Institute of Medicine outlined that evidence-based strategy in a 2003 report to Congress. Among other elements, that groundbreaking report highlighted the need for:

- a well-financed, visible, adult-focused national media campaign to discourage underage drinking;

- higher taxes on alcoholic beverages, especially on beer, to deter youthful drinking and provide funding for prevention and treatment programs; and

- stronger coordination among federal agencies that manage programs addressing underage drinking issues.

The Congress took an important first step toward implementing some of that report's recommendations when it passed the modest Sober Truth on Preventing (STOP) Underage Drinking Act in December, 2006. Much more needs to be done.

The director articulates what CSPI considers the larger issue.

The NASIM is a source the audience of college administrators and others will likely respect.

Rather than inviting "informed and unimpeded public debate," as the Amethyst Initiative did, NASIM (and CSPI) offers specific actions.

For CSPI, the time for debate is past. It's now time to take action.

CSPI spokesperson George A. Hacker delivered a fitting response to the rhetorical opportunity but not the only possible one. Whether or not this response can be considered the best one depends on the context, the audience, the purpose, and so on. Even if the response was not the best one, it was nevertheless a well-researched and well-executed response, one that invited a cascade of responses from other interested parent, professional, and university groups.

All through your life, you have been faced with rhetorical opportunities for change that call for a fitting response of some kind. Right now, as a college student, you are regularly asked to shape fitting responses to opportunities, many of which come in the form of assignments, social dilemmas, and political or religious challenges. In your first-year writing class, your instructor will direct you to a number of opportunities for change that you'll need to analyze and then address in writing. It's doubtful that only one person in the class will shape the perfect resolution for any rhetorical opportunity; more than likely, a number of students will shape fitting responses to each assignment, succeeding even though their responses vary.

The following list of questions can help you evaluate responses to determine whether or not they are fitting.

What makes a response fitting?

When any of the following conditions are not met, your problem may not be a rhetorical opportunity for change or your response may not be a fitting one.

- Is the problem one that can be addressed through language (spoken or written) or visual images?
- Is the response verbal or visual?
- Does the situation invite this response?

▶ Is this response delivered in an appropriate medium that reaches its intended audience?

▶ Is the intended audience also a rhetorical audience? (See Chapter 1.)

▶ Does this response successfully satisfy the intended audience?

> YOUR WRITING EXPERIENCES

1. Think back to one of the most fitting rhetorical responses you've encountered. What, exactly, made that response memorable? Fitting? List its characteristics.

2. When you submit a piece of writing to your instructor, what kind of response do you like most to receive (other than praise, of course)? Answer the following questions to formulate a description of a fitting response to your academic writing:

   a. In what medium (or media) do you like to receive responses to your writing? Verbally? In a conference? In an e-mail message or online course discussion forum? Handwritten in ink on your printed page?

   b. Do you like comments throughout your text or just at the end? Do you like your instructor to correct mechanical errors for you, point them out, or allude to them in a final comment?

   c. What do you want to learn from your instructor's comments and markings?

3. Think of a time when you gave a fitting response to someone else's writing. How exactly did your response address the rhetorical opportunity for change that the writing offered? Describe how your response fit the problem, why the medium you used was appropriate, and how the response successfully satisfied the intended audience.

Reading a resolution as a fitting response

As you already know, people shape different responses to the same rhetorical opportunity for change. Some responses may seem to you more fitting than others, but it can be hard to pinpoint where one falls short and others succeed. To help you become more comfortable evaluating fitting responses, this section presents three different responses to the verdict in the 1992 trial of the white Los Angeles police officers charged with use of excessive force in the arrest of Rodney King, a black man.

On March 3, 1991, after a high-speed chase, two California Highway Patrol (CHP) officers pulled King over for speeding and prepared to arrest him, guns drawn. Four Los Angeles Police Department (LAPD) officers intervened, and three of those officers struck King more than fifty times with their metal batons before handcuffing him and putting him in an ambulance. From a nearby apartment, George Holliday videotaped the entire episode, providing a local television station with nearly nine-and-a-half minutes of footage, including the first ninety seconds when the beatings took place. After much public controversy, involving charges of racism and incompetence against the LAPD, the nearly three-month-long trial began, resulting in the acquittal of all four LAPD officers. (In a federal trial one year later, two of the officers who had struck King were found guilty and were sentenced to serve time in prison.)

The verdict of the trial astounded many Americans. Commentators, news analysts, and race-relations experts rushed to the airwaves, the printed page, and cyberspace to provide what they thought were fitting responses to the verdict. The Academic Senate at San Francisco State University (SFSU), for example, posted a public resolution, questioning "whether the American system of justice treats people equitably under the law." As you read this resolution, which follows, consider how fitting a response it is.

> Resolution Regarding the Rodney King Verdict

Academic Senate of San Francisco State University

At its meeting of May 5, 1992, the Academic Senate approved the following resolution regarding the Rodney King verdict:

WHEREAS The April 29, 1992, verdict in the case of the officers charged with beating Rodney King has raised questions about whether the American system of justice treats people equitably under the law; and

WHEREAS The powerlessness born of having an unequal voice and inadequate representation begets frustration sometimes leading to violence; and

WHEREAS San Francisco State University, through the efforts of its Commission on Human Relations, Working Committee on Multicultural Perspectives in the Curriculum, and other projects has placed a high priority on implementing the principles embodied in its recently adopted statement, "Principles for a Multicultural University"; and

WHEREAS The hostile climate generated by the verdict in this case imperils the foundations of reason, common sense, morality, and compassion which underlie the academic enterprise as well as the larger society which this enterprise serves and is inimical to the equity and diversity goals of this campus; therefore be it

RESOLVED That the San Francisco State University Academic Senate decry the verdict in the case of the officers charged with beating Rodney King; and be it further

RESOLVED That the San Francisco State University Academic Senate reaffirm its commitment to a governance process which actively encourages the participation of all members of the academic community; and be it further

RESOLVED That the San Francisco State University Academic Senate reaffirm its commitment, and redouble its efforts, to provide an academic environment which promotes the empowerment, embraces the diverse viewpoints, and celebrates the contributions of all members of the community which the University serves; and be it further

RESOLVED That this resolution be distributed to the SFSU Campus community, the Chair of the Academic Senate, CSU and to the Chairs of the CSU Campus Senates.

Reading the Los Angeles riots as a fitting response

Although dramatic by academic standards, the SFSU Academic Senate resolution pales in comparison to the most powerful response of all: the three-day riots that began in Los Angeles within two hours after the initial verdict was announced. Arson, looting, and fighting spread throughout South Central Los Angeles, and riots also broke out in several other cities, as far away as Atlanta, Georgia. By the end of the rioting more than fifty people had been killed, over four thousand injured, and over twelve thousand arrested in Los Angeles alone. Many participants in the riots, as well as some onlookers, felt that the riots were, indeed, a fitting response to the opportunity for change offered by the verdict. What do you think?

> ANALYZING THE RHETORICAL SITUATION

1. Use the questions listed under "What Makes a Response Fitting?" (on pages 33–34) to determine whether the Los Angeles riots and the SFSU Academic Senate resolution were fitting responses to the Rodney King verdict. Be sure to respond to all questions for each of the responses.
2. Which response(s) do you consider fitting? If both are fitting, why do you think such different responses can both be fitting? If only one response is fitting, what makes it more fitting than the other?

An immediate response to the Rodney King verdict.

Reading political commentary as a fitting response

If you argue that the Los Angeles riots were, in and of themselves, a kind of visual rhetoric, you might believe them to be the most fitting of all the various responses to the Rodney King verdict. Columnist and activist Barbara Smith certainly believed that the riots were the most fitting response to a terrible verdict. In fact, as the riots waned, Smith commented on their political potential: "the insurrection in Los Angeles will galvanize unprecedented organizing." She also wrote about her own simmering fury. Recounting King's beating and a catalogue of brutalities that preceded it, Smith forged her fury into a verbal response that she felt fit the occasion.

Excerpt from

> The Truth That Never Hurts

Barbara Smith

What I felt at the King verdict and its aftermath was all too familiar. I felt the same gnawing in the pit of my stomach and in my chest when sixteen-year-old Yusuk Hawkins was gunned down on the streets of Bensonhurst, Brooklyn, in 1989. I felt the same impotent rage when the police murdered sixty-seven-year-old Eleanor Bumpurs with a shotgun in the process of evicting her from her Bronx apartment in 1984. I choked back the same bitter tears when I heard the verdict in the 1991 rape case involving a Black woman student and several white male students at St. John's University on Long Island. I was just as terrified when they murdered four Black school girls (my age peers) by bombing a church in Birmingham, Alabama, in 1963. And even though I was too young to understand its meaning, I learned Emmett Till's name in 1955 because of witnessing my family's anguish over his lynching in Mississippi.

So what do we do with all this fury besides burn down our own communities and hurt or kill anyone, white, Black, brown, or yellow who gets in our way? Figuring out what to do next is the incredibly difficult challenge that lies before us.

Above all, the events in Los Angeles have made it perfectly obvious why we need a revolution in this country. Nothing short of a revolution will work. Gross inequalities are built into the current system and Band-Aids, even big ones, won't cure capitalism's fundamental injustice and exploitation.

We need, however, to build analysis, practice, and movements that accurately address the specific ways that racism, capitalism, and all the major systems of oppression interconnect in the United States. It's not a coincidence that the most dramatic political changes have so often been catalyzed by race. In the United States, racism has shaped the nature of capitalism and race relations.

It is our responsibility as Black activists, radicals, and socialists to create vibrant new leadership that offers a real alternative to the tired civil rights

continued

The Truth That Never Hurts *(continued)*

establishment and to the bankrupt "two-party" system. It is our responsibility as we build autonomous Black organizations to make the connections between all of the oppressions and to work in coalition with the movements that have arisen to challenge them.

Recognizing the leadership of radical women of color, feminists, and lesbians is absolutely critical from this moment forward. Women of color are already building a movement that makes the connections between race, class, gender, and sexual identity, a movement that has the potential to win liberation for all of us.

It is past the time to talk. I really want to know how the white left, the white feminist, and the white lesbian and gay movements are going to change now that Los Angeles is burned. It's not enough to say what a shame all of this is or to have a perfect intellectual understanding of what has occurred. It's time for all the white people who say they're committed to freedom to figure out what useful antiracist organizing is and to put it into practice.

Smith says, "Figuring out what to do next is the incredibly difficult challenge that lies before us." You might think of "figuring out what to do next" as the challenge of shaping a fitting response to the opportunity for change within any rhetorical situation. Smith, a socialist, explores a number of options, all of which are "fitting" and some of which are more revolutionary than others.

Look again at Smith's final sentence: "It's time for all the white people who say they're committed to freedom to figure out what useful antiracist organizing is and to put it into practice." That sentence, the last one in her fitting response, opens up another rhetorical opportunity that invites yet another response. In fact, like the Amethyst Initiative's petition regarding the legal drinking age (see pages 29–30), Smith's writing actually prescribes a response, going so far as to dictate the form that response should take.

> ANALYZING THE RHETORICAL SITUATION

1. How is the problem Smith is responding to a rhetorical opportunity for change?
2. Is the response verbal or visual?
3. Does the problem invite this response?
4. Is this response delivered in a medium that reaches its intended audience?
5. Does this response successfully satisfy the intended audience?

Compare your answers with those of your classmates, and then decide, as a class, if Smith's response was fitting for the rhetorical situation. You may also want to consider what result Smith hoped to achieve through her writing.

COMMUNITY CONNECTIONS

1. Your campus or town undoubtedly has unrest or upheaval of some kind, strong dissatisfaction related to economics, employment, politics, justice, race, athletics, or gender. Look through your local newspaper and identify one such incident of unrest. What rhetorical opportunity for change does this incident present? What is one possible fitting response to that opportunity? Be prepared to share your answer with the rest of the class.

2. Celebrations—birthdays, engagements, weddings, commitment ceremonies, graduations, family reunions, athletic victories, and holiday gatherings—invite responses. Fitting responses take the form of letters, cards, songs, speeches, and toasts. Draft a fitting response for an event that you're going to attend soon.

3. Think about the fitting response you drafted for question 2. Choose a different kind of event and explain how you would need to alter your response in order to make it a fitting one for that event. Would you need to change the medium in which you plan to deliver your response? Its length? The specific kind of language used?

Using the Available Means of Persuasion

In Chapter 1, you learned that Aristotle defined *rhetoric* as "the art [mental ability] of observing in any given situation the available means of persuasion." When you consider the available means, you think about the possible methods of communication you might use, whether those are oral (speaking face to face or over the telephone), written (using paper, e-mail, instant messaging, or a web page), visual (using film, video, or still images), digital, or some combination of oral, written, and visual.

You've already had years of experience identifying available means of persuasion and selecting the most appropriate means, whatever the rhetorical situation and whoever the audience. Humans were doing just that long before Aristotle wrote his *Rhetoric*. In fact, one of the earliest examples of humans tapping an available means of persuasion can be found in cave paintings, such as the ones in Lascaux, France, which depict stories of hunting expeditions that took place from 15,000 to 10,000 BCE. Using sharpened tools, iron and manganese oxides, and charcoal, Paleolithic humans recorded

Cave painting in Lascaux, France.

Early stone carvings from the American Southwest.

incidents from their daily lives for the edification of others. From 400 BCE to 1300 CE, people living in what is now the southwestern part of the United States also recorded the stories, events, beliefs, fears, and characters of their daily lives by carving their representations on stone surfaces of various kinds. Using the available means at their disposal (sharpened tools and stones), these First Americans composed stories that continue to speak to and intrigue us.

The contemporary rhetorical scene also offers many varieties of available means—from digital and printed to visual and spoken—for delivering as well as shaping potentially effective information for a specific audience. Let's review some of those means so that you can optimize your choices in order to succeed as a writer or speaker.

What are the available means?

When you successfully use language to address a problem, you've no doubt delivered a fitting response using the available means of persuasion. **Available means** can be defined as the physical material used for delivering the information, the place from which the writer creates and sends the information, and the elements of the presentation itself (elements that include persuasive strategies known as *rhetorical appeals*, the use of evidence or authority, the conventions of style, and the rhetorical methods of development).

We choose intuitively from among all of the means available. With experience and knowledge, each of us can make more conscious, strategic selections, based on the context, the audience, the **constraints** (obstacles) and **resources** (positive influences) of the rhetorical situation (see page 5), and the consequences of our choices. Rhetorical consciousness (and success) comes with recognizing the vast array of options at our disposal, including those already in existence and those we can create as we attempt to negotiate the constraints of our rhetorical situation and reach our intended audience.

The available means deliver information

In the weeks following the September 11, 2001 attacks on the World Trade Center, many Americans responded to the rhetorical opportunity by extending their condolences, whether or not they knew any of the dead and missing personally. The range of fitting responses to the opportunity varied widely: for instance, those whose loved ones were missing contributed to memory walls, filling them with bouquets of flowers and photographs. Others wrote essays and newspaper columns, decrying the terrorists, mourning the victims, and extolling the rescue efforts. Some people presented television and radio programs focusing on what happened on that day and

A visitor at a September 11 memory wall.

how the United States was responding. Still others created online memorial boards and chat rooms. And one inventive author went so far as to hire a sky-writer, posting a message that spoke for and to millions of Americans: "We miss you." Each of these writers chose different physical means of delivering a message.

These writers worked within the constraints and resources of their individual rhetorical situations, whether those constraints and resources were physical ("What passerby or hospital worker may have seen my missing loved one?"), geographical ("How can I reach the survivors in New York City?"), or financial ("I'm going to spend money broadcasting my message in skywriting"). The means of delivery each writer used depended on the writer's expertise, intended audience, and contextual constraints and resources.

The available means are anchored to the writer's place

Every time a writer sends a message, he or she does so from a particular place. Whether that person is writing at a desk, talking on a telephone, preaching from a pulpit, speaking from a podium, or typing on a laptop, both the message itself and its means of delivery are influenced by the constraints and resources of that specific place.

Utah Valley University graduate Urangoo Baatarkhuyag was preparing to move to California to further her education when she learned she had cancer. The Mongolian native was stunned and scared. Hospital personnel told her that she would need a bone marrow transplant to survive, a procedure that costs $350,000. With no health insurance, no family nearby, and relatively poor international students for friends, Baatarkhuyag was not sure what to do, especially given her constraints. How could language possibly help her resolve her problem? She was living away from her home and her family, needing lots of money—and fast.

Fortunately, her friends identified an opportunity for change that could be resolved through language. Because their place (a university community in the United States) offered them easy access to electronic media, they could tap the resources of digital communication to reach a wide audience, rapidly and cheaply. They set up a website to solicit contributions to help their friend in the belief that an Internet request could travel faster than acute myeloid leukemia could progress. Together, the friends' digital know-how (they knew how blogs work as well as how to take advantage of online social networking sites) and the Internet became contextual resources. Providing background information, photos of a healthy Baatarkhuyag, and an easy-to-use PayPal account for donations,

Friends of Urangoo Baatarkhuyag set up this website to help with fundraising for her leukemia treatments.

the website brought in nearly $40,000 within the first month—not enough for chemotherapy, let alone a transplant, but a terrific start, nonetheless. Plus, as the website itself gained momentum, it sparked other kinds of donations: the Latter Day Saints Hospital in Salt Lake City donated a month's worth of chemotherapy and launched an international search for a hospital that could treat her for less money; friends and supporters held silent auctions, fundraisers featuring live entertainment, concerts, and garage sales. They also arranged for Baatarkhuyag's story to be featured on various televised news programs and in local newspapers.

As her friends worked to strengthen the resources of Baatarkhuyag's situation, they surveyed the various means available to them in terms of efficiency and appropriateness. For example, Artan Ismaili, a Brigham Young University student from Kosovo who had never met Baatarkhuyag, worked on her behalf because, like him and his wife, she was an international student with no insurance. Ismaili first learned about Baatarkhuyag's medical crisis when another student alerted members of a class Ismaili was taking, asking them to go to the website to donate whatever amount they could. After Ismaili and his wife donated, they wanted to do even more. He announced the situation and the website to the students in his other classes, arranged with a Mongolian restaurant to hold a fundraiser there, and posted information on Baatarkhuyag's status and how to donate to help her on all his social networking sites. And, since he and his wife planned to move to Boston, they pledged to sell everything they had and donate the money to Baatarkhuyag's medical fund.

Like the best of speakers and writers, then, Ismaili analyzed the resources and constraints of the rhetorical situation and took advantage of as many digital and oral available means as he could think of. Not only did he tap these resources and available means; he also used the appropriate rhetorical methods of development to fulfill his purpose: narration (the story of the uninsured international student and her dire illness), cause-and-effect analysis (what would happen if she did or did not receive the transplant), and process analysis (how to use PayPal, the U.S. postal service, or an electronic bank transfer to donate money to the fund) in order to reach his intended audience (people who could help by donating money). Ismaili's choices were practical ones, influenced by the various resources and constraints. (Sadly, despite the efforts of so many on her behalf, Baatarkhuyag died in 2010.)

Rhetorical choices are often also political ones, for in the United States today, every person (whether international visitor or U.S. citizen) has a right to speak and to speak publicly. However, many speakers and writers in the United States have not enjoyed the right to speak, let alone been able to make use of the available means of persuasion. Many groups of people throughout American history have been denied the right to education, the right to speak publicly, and the right to civic participation on grounds of their gender, race, ethnicity, physical ability, or lack of property. For example, if you think of voting as an available means of persuasion—as a means of sending a message to a specific audience—you understand how punitive the lack of voting rights would be. In 1776, only white Protestant men who owned land had the right to vote. By 1847, all white men could vote, including Catholics and non-Christians. In 1870, black males were awarded the right to vote—but only under certain conditions, including the requirements that they furnish proof of their literacy and that they pay a poll tax. Women were not granted voting rights until 1920, and American Indians not until 1924. Thus, the means of persuasion available to all these groups were fewer than those available to white male landowners.

The available means include the rhetorical elements of the message itself

When a writer or speaker considers the available means for sending a purposeful message to a specific audience, he or she considers the rhetorical elements of the message. Because human beings are not persuaded to believe or act in a certain way based only on facts or only on what can be proved, writers and speakers use **rhetorical appeals**. These three persuasive strategies are **ethos**, the ethical appeal of the writer's credibility; **logos**, the logical appeal of a reasonable, well-supported argument; and **pathos**, the emotional appeal of language and examples that stir the audience's feelings (within a reasonable limit). The use of these appeals is balanced in most successful messages, for to exaggerate any one of the three is to risk losing the audience and thereby failing to achieve the rhetorical purpose.

Many successful messages emphasize each of these appeals separately, but doing so is not the same as exaggerating any one of them. Consider the following excerpts from a speech given at the 1851 Women's Rights Convention in Akron, Ohio. During a time when white women were rarely permitted to speak in public, especially to a "promiscuous assembly" of men and women, former slave Sojourner Truth (born Isabella Baumfree, 1787–1883) faced an audience of educated white Northerners, mostly women, to speak about the importance of women's rights for black women as well as white women. Truth negotiated the constraints and resources of her rhetorical situation to reach her audience.

According to tradition, Truth, the only black person in attendance, had been listening carefully to the speeches, many of which denounced the rights of women. Truth was constrained by being illiterate, black, a Southerner, and a woman, and her spoken ideas (recorded and later published in many versions by white people) would be met with resistance if not outright objection. Some of her constraints, however, proved to be her richest resources. The minute she ascended the platform to address the audience, Truth transgressed all the social norms of the educated Northern white "lady."

In her opening paragraphs, Truth set out the circumference of the struggle for women's rights as she

Library of Congress

Sojourner Truth, whose 1851 speech survives as an example of the available means of persuasion skillfully used.

saw it, establishing her ethos. Notice how her first paragraph establishes common ground with the white women in her audience: both speaker and audience subscribe to the idea that both Northern and Southern women, white and black, share a concern over women's rights. Truth continues to burnish her ethos by demonstrating her goodwill toward her audience, her good sense and knowledge of the subject at hand, and her good character:

> Well, children, where there is so much racket there must be something out of kilter. I think that 'twixt the Negroes of the South and the women of the North, all talking about rights, the white men will be in a fix pretty soon. But what's all this here talking about?
>
> That man over there says that women need to be helped into carriages and lifted over ditches, and to have the best place everywhere. Nobody ever helps me into carriages, or over mud puddles, or gives me any best place! And ain't I a woman? Look at me! Look at my arm! I could have ploughed and planted, and gathered into barns, and no man could head me! And ain't I a woman? I could work as much and eat as much as a man—when I could get it—and bear the lash as well! And ain't I a woman? I have borne thirteen children, and seen them most all sold off to slavery, and when I cried out with my mother's grief, none but Jesus heard me! And ain't I a woman?

A speaker in Truth's position had to devote most of her words to establishing her ethos; after all, she needed to be heard and believed as the black woman she was. But like many successful speakers, Truth spent the body of her speech emphasizing logos, the shape of her reasoning, particularly her response to arguments against women's rights:

> Then they talk about this thing in the head; what's this they call it? ["Intellect," somebody whispers.] That's it, honey. What's that got to do with women's rights or Negros' rights? If my cup won't hold but a pint, and yours holds a quart, wouldn't you be mean not to let me have my little half measure-full?
>
> Then that little man in black back there, he says women can't have as much rights as men, 'cause Christ wasn't a woman! Where did your Christ come from? Where did your Christ come from? From God and a woman! Man had nothing to do with Him.
>
> If the first woman God ever made was strong enough to turn the world upside down all alone, these women together ought to be able to turn it back, and get it right side up again! And now they is asking to do it, the men better let them.

The closing of her speech emphasizes pathos in the form of her gratitude for being allowed to speak.

> Obliged to you for hearing me, and now old Sojourner ain't got nothing more to say.

Ethos, logos, and pathos are often distributed among three sections of any piece of powerful writing in both separate and overlapping forms. Once you start looking for them, you'll discover that these rhetorical appeals appear in much of the reading and writing you do.

Within the message itself, the available means also include the writer's or speaker's use of evidence or authority. You can see for yourself how Truth used the example of her own hardworking life as evidence that women were just as suited for voting rights as men. In fact, her evidence might have been stronger than that offered by any of the well-educated white women who shared the speaker's platform with her. And for authority, Truth wisely went straight to the Bible, the ultimate authority for all her listeners, whether they were Northern or Southern, black or white, male or female, educated or uneducated.

In addition to the rhetorical appeals and the use of evidence and authority, conventions of style constitute yet another feature of the available means. Truth's 1851 speech circulated in at least four versions, all of them recorded by white people, all of them resorting to some version of dialect. The most prominent instance of dialect is the use of the word *ain't*, but it's not the only one. Even allegedly cleaned-up versions of the speech include the expressions *out o' kilter*, *a-talking*, *be in a fix*, and *Aren't I a woman?* No version of her speech has appeared in **Standardized English**, the style of writing and speaking expected in most academic and business settings, which would dictate *Am I not a woman?* as the refrain. The use of dialect authenticates Truth as an uneducated former slave.

Finally, speakers and writers choose the most appropriate of the **rhetorical methods of development** (description, narration, exemplification, classification and division, comparison and contrast, process analysis, cause-and-effect analysis, and definition). In her speech, Truth used definition and narration in the second paragraph: she defined herself as a woman, just not the kind of woman that opponents of women's rights had in mind, and she narrated several incidents from her life that supported her self-definition. In the body of her speech, she used cause-and-effect analysis to bring home her point that women had already set a powerful precedent, one supported by scripture. (Chapter 3 discusses each of the rhetorical methods of development.)

Regardless of the version you examine, Truth's speech provides a useful textual context for examining the available means of persuasion.

> ANALYZING THE RHETORICAL SITUATION

For two or three of the following situations, identify available means of persuasion that take into consideration (1) the physical means of delivering the information, (2) the place from which the author creates and sends the information, and (3) the rhetorical elements (including the rhetorical appeals) of the message itself. Be prepared to share your answers with the rest of the class.

1. You want to support your favorite recording artist, who is under scrutiny for criticizing the current government of the United States.
2. Your family wants to help some neighbors, who have lost all of their worldly possessions in a house fire.
3. You want to change majors, from communications to international business, but your grade-point average is slightly below the necessary minimum for acceptance to the School of Business.
4. Your spouse wants to relocate in order to further his or her career, but you're making good progress on your undergraduate degree at the nearby college.
5. Your economics professor has assigned you a research project: you are to evaluate the kinds of jobs that are appropriate for high school students.

Recognizing Available Means

When Boston University's School of Public Health created Join Together to provide information to individuals and communities interested in fighting and preventing underage drinking and substance abuse, it needed to tap the available means for distributing that information. One of the available means chosen was a website. Under "About Us," the group mentions specific means: coalitions, leadership training for community-based efforts, public education and media, and public policy initiatives—all of which can be realized through print, oral, visual, and electronic means of delivery.

In addition, Join Together's website contains links to many other available means. As you analyze Join Together's website, you'll see that it uses the rhetorical appeals, evidence and authority, a specific style, and various rhetorical methods of development. In fact, the site argues for the importance of its existence not only by recounting specific evidence and making use of the rhetorical appeals of pathos and logos, but also by sending the reader to relevant links to find out how to take further action.

This website is an available means of communication for the organization Join Together.

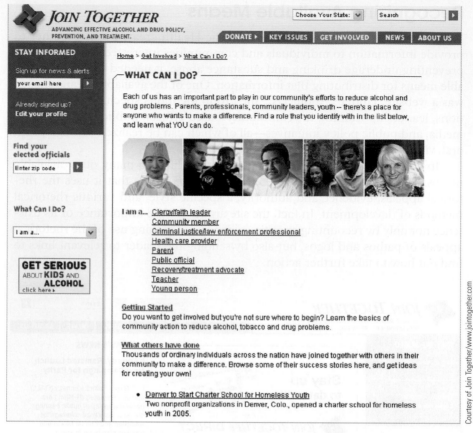

This web page has links to additional available means of response.

No matter what document, website, or television program you're reading or viewing (and analyzing rhetorically), you need to keep in mind that the creators of those communications have tried to choose the best from among all means of communication available to them. As you read and view, then, you'll want to remain alert to the specific choices writers have made and to consider whether those choices are the most fruitful ones.

Rarely will two writers make identical choices in response to a rhetorical opportunity. Each writer's place of composing and status in terms of the situation often complicate those choices. Each writer must negotiate a unique set of rhetorical constraints and resources in order to determine the best available means.

> YOUR WRITING EXPERIENCES

1. Chances are you do not know very many people, if any, in your writing class. Your instructor may not know anyone either. Describe the available means you could use to remedy this situation. How exactly would you do so, and what would be the substance of your message?

2. What means are available to you for letting your writing instructor know what kind of person, student, and writer you are? Write for ten minutes, describing the available means in terms of three constituent parts: (a) the physical means of delivering the information, (b) the place from which you would create and send the information, and (c) the rhetorical elements of the message itself. How might you use the rhetorical appeals (ethos, pathos, and logos) to convey an impression of yourself to your instructor?

3. After you receive a marked and graded piece of writing from your instructor, what are the means available to you for responding? In terms of the three constituents of available means, describe how you usually respond. How might you more profitably respond? Write for five minutes and be prepared to share your answer with the rest of the class.

4. Reconsider the answers you wrote for questions 1, 2, and 3. Carefully translate your three answers into one that takes advantage of the available means of persuasion. Consider your rhetorical constraints and resources (including the rhetorical appeals) as you introduce yourself as a college writer to the rest of your class, including your instructor. Be prepared to share your fitting response with the rest of the class.

Reading an essay for available means

Acclaimed author Susan Orlean has established her career by writing about the ordinary things in life. In an interview at the University of Oregon, Orlean said that she's drawn to the extraordinary in the ordinary: "There's no question in my mind that being a writer is a moral occupation and one that requires an awareness all the time of what that means morally and philosophically." As you read the following excerpt from one of her essays, note the extraordinary features of this ten-year-old's daily existence that Orlean identifies.

Excerpt from

> The American Man, Age Ten

Susan Orlean

If Colin Duffy and I were to get married, we would have matching superhero notebooks. We would wear shorts, big sneakers, and long, baggy T-shirts depicting famous athletes every single day, even in the winter. We would sleep in our clothes. We would both be good at Nintendo Street Fighter II, but Colin would be better than me. We would have some homework, but it would never be too hard and we would always have just finished it. We would eat pizza and candy for all of our meals. We wouldn't have sex, but we would have crushes on each other and, magically, babies would appear in our home. We would win the lottery and then buy land in Wyoming, where we would

Vince Bucci / Getty Images

continued

The American Man, Age Ten (continued)

have one of every kind of cute animal. All the while, Colin would be working in law enforcement—probably the FBI. Our favorite movie star, Morgan Freeman, would visit us occasionally. We would listen to the same Eurythmics song ("Here Comes the Rain Again") over and over again and watch two hours of television every Friday night. We would both be good at football, have best friends, and know how to drive; we would cure AIDS and the garbage problem and everything that hurts animals. We would hang out a lot with Colin's dad. For fun, we would load a slingshot with dog food and shoot it at my butt. We would have a very good life. . . .

Here are the particulars about Colin Duffy: He is ten years old, on the nose. He is four feet eight inches high, weighs seventy-five pounds, and appears to be mostly leg and shoulder blade. He is a handsome kid. He has a broad forehead, dark eyes with dense lashes, and a sharp, dimply smile. I have rarely seen him without a baseball cap. He owns several, but favors a University of Michigan Wolverines model, on account of its pleasing colors. The hat styles his hair into wild disarray. If you ever managed to get the hat off his head, you would see a boy with a nimbus of golden-brown hair, dented in the back, where the hat hits him.

Colin lives with his mother, Elaine; his father, Jim; his older sister, Megan; and his little brother, Chris, in a pretty pale blue Victorian house on a bosky street in Glen Ridge, New Jersey. Glen Ridge is a serene and civilized old town twenty miles west of New York City. It does not have much of a commercial district, but it is a town of amazing lawns. Most of the houses were built around the turn of the century and are set back a gracious, green distance from the street. The rest of the town seems to consist of parks and playing fields and sidewalks and backyards—in other words, it is a far cry from South-Central Los Angeles and from Bedford-Stuyvesant and other, grimmer parts of the country where a very different ten-year-old American man is growing up today.

There is a fine school system in Glen Ridge, but Elaine and Jim, who are both schoolteachers, choose to send their children to a parents' cooperative elementary school in Montclair, a neighboring suburb. Currently Colin is in fifth grade. He is a good student. He plans to go to college, to a place he says is called Oklahoma City State College University. OCSCU satisfies his desire to live out west, to attend a small college, and to study law enforcement, which OCSCU apparently offers as a major. After four years at Oklahoma City State College University, he plans to work for the FBI. He says that getting to be a police officer involves tons of hard work, but working for the FBI will be a cinch, because all you have to do is fill out one form, which he has already gotten from the head FBI office. Colin is quiet in class but loud on the playground. He has a great throwing arm, significant foot speed, and a lot of physical confidence. He is also brave. Huge wild cats with rabies and gross stuff dripping from their teeth, which he says run rampant throughout his neighborhood, do not scare him. Otherwise, he is slightly bashful. This combination of athletic grace and valor and personal reserve accounts for considerable popularity. He has a fluid relationship to many social groups, including the superbright nerds, the ultrajocks, the flashy kids who will someday become extremely popular and socially successful juvenile delinquents, and the kids who will be elected president of the student body. In his opinion, the most popular boy in his class is Christian, who happens to be black, and Colin's favorite television character is Steve Urkel on *Family Matters*, who is black, too, but otherwise he seems uninterested in or oblivious to race. Until this year, he was a Boy Scout. Now he is planning to begin karate lessons. His favorite schoolyard game is football, followed closely by prison dodgeball, blob tag, and bombardo. He's crazy about athletes, although sometimes it isn't clear if he is absolutely sure of the difference between human athletes and Marvel Comics action figures. His current best friend is named Japeth. He used to have another best friend named Ozzie. According to Colin, Ozzie was found on a doorstep, then changed his name to Michael and moved to Massachusetts, and then Colin never saw him or heard from him again.

He has had other losses in his life. He is old enough to know people who have died and to know things about the world that are worrisome. When he dreams, he dreams about moving to Wyoming, which he has visited with his family. His plan is to buy land there and have some sort of ranch that would definitely include horses. Sometimes when he talks about this, it sounds as ordinary and hard-boiled as a real estate appraisal; other times it can sound fantastical and wifty and achingly naïve, informed by the last inklings of childhood—the musings of a balmy real estate appraiser assaying a wonderful and magical landscape that erodes from memory a little bit every day. The collision in his mind of what he understands, what he hears, what he figures out, what popular culture pours into him, what he knows, what he pretends to know, and what he imagines makes an interesting mess. The mess often has the form of what he will probably think like when he is a grown man, but the content of what he is like as a little boy.

He is old enough to begin imagining that he will someday get married, but at ten he is still convinced that the best thing about being married will be that he will be allowed to sleep in his clothes.

The physical means Orlean uses to deliver her information is print, for the most part, despite the fact that one of her books and one of her essays have been made into films (*The Orchid Thief* and *Blue Crush*) and that she's a regular on the lecture circuit. The place in which she composes and from which she sends her message is transitory: she travels to do research and conduct interviews; then she writes about what she learns and observes. All of her writing, however, tends to be tethered to other people, the ones she observes and interviews. The distinctive features of her prose are her clear style and her use of rhetorical appeals, evidence and authority, and rhetorical methods of development.

> ANALYZING THE RHETORICAL SITUATION

Based on the excerpt from Susan Orlean's essay, answer the following questions.

1. If Orlean's purpose is to find the extraordinary in the ordinary, what is her rhetorical opportunity?
2. How does she work to respond to that opportunity through her language? How does her language fit the problem?

3. What are the available means she taps to form her response? Where and how does she use the rhetorical appeals of ethos, pathos, and logos?

4. Who or what does she use as evidence or authority?

5. What stylistic choices does Orlean make that enhance her response as a fitting one?

6. Which of the rhetorical methods of development (see page 46) does she use to shape her response? Which passages in the excerpt are built on those identifiable rhetorical methods?

7. Who might be Orlean's audience? How does her choice of available means suit her intended audience?

COMMUNITY CONNECTIONS

1. Some feature of college life is no doubt a source of dissatisfaction to you: living conditions, roommates, the commute, lack of family time, cost, instructors, course offerings. Choose one feature that is problematic and identify the means available to you for resolving that problem. Make sure that the available means account for each of three features: (a) the physical means of delivering the information, (b) the place from which the information is created and sent, and (c) the rhetorical elements (including the rhetorical appeals) of the message itself. Be prepared to share your response with the rest of the class.

2. Consider a trial being held locally (a case involving irresponsible drinking, murder, embezzlement, theft, assault, or arson, for example). As you keep up with local news (in print or any other medium, even in the form of gossip), try to determine the available means of persuasion being used by the prosecution as well as by the defense. Also identify the means of persuasion that remain either unavailable to or untapped by either the defense or the prosecution. List possible reasons why those specific means are not being used. Be prepared to share your findings with the rest of the class.

Assignment: Writing a Rhetorical Analysis

Now that you are familiar with the features of the rhetorical situation and the ways those features can be employed to shape a fitting response, you can use your knowledge to analyze someone else's rhetoric.

Your task is to select and then analyze a written or visual text, one that appears to be a fitting response. You can choose from the texts in this or the previous chapter or find a text online or in print. You are looking for a piece of writing or a visual produced by a person or a group with a vested interest in the effect of the words or the image. The following two questions will help you determine if the selection you've chosen is appropriate for a rhetorical analysis:

1. Is the text responding to an opportunity to make a change through verbal (spoken or written) or visual language?
2. Is the response verbal or visual?

After you have selected a text, read it carefully, keeping in mind that *the ultimate goal of a rhetorical analysis is twofold: (1) to analyze how well the rhetorical elements work together to create a fitting response and (2) to assess the overall effectiveness of that response.* Then, write answers to the following questions, using textual or visual evidence to support each answer:

1. Who created the text? What credentials or expertise does that person or group have? What opinions or biases did the person or group bring to the text?
2. What is the rhetorical opportunity for change? How is it identified? Why is the creator of the text engaged with this opportunity? Is this an opportunity that can be modified through language?
3. Who is the audience for the message? What opinions or biases might the audience hold? How does the audience feel about this rhetorical opportunity? What relationship is the creator of the text trying to establish with the audience? And, most important, can this audience modify or help bring about a modification of the rhetorical opportunity? How?
4. Identify the rhetorical elements of the message itself. In other words, where and how does the person or group employ the rhetorical appeals of ethos, pathos, and logos? How are credentials, goodwill, or good sense evoked to establish ethos? How is evidence (examples, statistics, data, and so forth) used to establish logos? And how is an emotional connection created to establish pathos? Keep in mind that the rhetorical appeals can sometimes overlap.
5. What kind of language does the creator of the text use? Is it plain or specialized, slang or formal? How does the choice of language reveal how the person or group views the intended audience?
6. What is the place (physical, social, academic, economic, and so on) from which the creator of the text forms and sends the response? What are the resources of that place? What are its constraints (or limitations)?
7. What medium does the creator of the text use to send the response to the audience? How private or public, accessible or inaccessible is the medium? What are the resources and the constraints of that medium?

The next part of your job is to consider whether the response is a fitting and successful one. To achieve that goal, respond in writing to these questions:

1. Is the intended audience for the text a rhetorical audience? Draw on evidence from the text to support your answer.
2. If the audience is a rhetorical one, what can it do to resolve the problem?
3. Does the response address and fit the rhetorical opportunity? How exactly? If not, how might the response be reshaped so that it does fit?

4. Is the response delivered in an appropriate medium that reaches its intended audience? If so, describe why the medium is appropriate. If not, explain how it could be adjusted so that it would be appropriate.

5. Can you think of other responses to similar rhetorical situations? What genre is commonly used to respond to such situations? Does the creator of this text use that genre? If not, what is the effect of going against an audience's expectations?

Now that you have carefully read the text and answered all of the questions, you are ready to write your rhetorical analysis. As you begin, search your answers for an idea that can serve as the basis for your thesis statement. For example, you might focus on the declared goal—if there is one—of the creator of the text and whether it has been achieved. You might assess how successfully that person or group has identified the rhetorical audience, shaped a fitting response, or employed the best available means. Or you might focus on the use of the rhetorical appeals and the overall success of their use. Whether or not you agree with the text is beside the point. Your job is to analyze, in an essay built on a clear thesis statement, how and how well its creator has accomplished the purpose.

Writing Processes and Strategies: From Tentative Idea to Finished Product

3

In this chapter, you'll move through the three general steps of the writing process: planning, drafting, and revising. These steps are the same whether you're working online or off. As you read about each of these steps, you'll learn when to consider the components of the rhetorical situation (components that include a problem or opportunity for change, writer, purpose, message, audience, and context) and when to set those components aside and just write. You'll also learn about the rhetorical methods that are used for developing writing: definition, classification and division, exemplification, description, comparison and contrast, cause-and-effect analysis, process analysis, narration, and argument.

© Cindy Charles / Photo Edit

> WRITE FOR FIVE

Write for five minutes in response to each of the following questions. Be prepared to share your answers with the rest of the class.

1. What is your first reaction to receiving a writing assignment? What kinds of information do you look for in that assignment? Why? When do you actually start the assignment (however you define "start")?
2. Make a list of the kinds of writing you do regularly. Categorize the list according to whether the writing is work-related, school-related, or personal. Which of the available means of delivery do you use most often to deliver that writing?
3. Compare your responses to questions 1 and 2 with those of two classmates. What surprised you about their responses? Pick two things a classmate wrote that made you rethink your answers; then rewrite those answers.

Finding Pleasure in Writing

You've been writing almost all your life. When you were a small child, you grabbed crayons, felt-tip markers, or chalk and wrote on whatever surfaces you could find: paper, coloring books, sidewalks, chalk boards, table tops, walls, lampshades. You might not yet have been talking fluently or reading well, but you were already "writing" as well as your fine-motor skills and linguistic expertise would allow. Like the human animal you are, you were marking your territory—leaving messages for the people who entered your world. When you learned to write cursive or to use a keyboard, you may have felt the same kind of satisfaction that you felt when you scribbled on the sidewalk. You were moving forward into the adult world of writing, a world that feeds our primitive human need to communicate with others.

As you think back on your earliest memories of writing, keep in mind the process of writing that you practiced then. You gathered up your materials and set to work. The entire process—from start to finish—was simple, often fun. Many of you have been writing—and enjoying it—for years. Award-winning author Joyce Carol Oates cannot recall a time when she wasn't writing:

> Before I could write what might be called human words in the English language, I eagerly emulated grown-ups' handwriting in pencil scribbles. My first "novels" . . . were tablets of inspired scribbles illustrated by line drawings of chickens, horses and upright cats.
>
> —**Joyce Carol Oates**, "To Invigorate Literary Mind, Start Moving Literary Feet"

What do you remember about early writing experiences?

Like the writing you did as a child, college writing can also be satisfying, but that is not to say that it will *always* be fun, let alone easy. The process might at times seem demanding, but the results are often exhilarating, something you're proud of. If that weren't the case, you wouldn't worry about writing well or care what your teacher thought of your writing.

Perhaps the best way to make writing a pleasurable activity is to build on what you already do well and enjoy as you write. If you're a person who likes to explore a topic, you may already have a collection of special notebooks in which you jot down notes and observations, write freely about interesting topics, copy delicious phrases or sentences you've heard or read, and make rough outlines.

You may be a writer who especially likes composing the first draft—by hand or keyboard. Maybe you enjoy the tactile sensation of writing with a gel pen on a yellow legal pad or the friction of moving a felt-tipped pen across pulpy paper. Maybe you draft at your computer, entertaining yourself by connecting particular fonts with particular ideas in your draft. Quickly moving between word processing and online audio and video applications, you might share and get feedback on bits of your freewriting or get inspired to use digital media in your composition. At your keyboard, you can rewrite phrase after phrase, sentence after sentence, tinkering that may be especially comforting and pleasurable for you.

Or maybe you're one of those writers who are relieved when they finish a draft so that they can use their energy to work with and against that draft. You may like to print out your piece, sit back in a comfortable chair, and read it line by line, penciling in new sentences, crossing out entire sections, fiddling with your word choice, and drawing arrows to reorganize your paragraphs. You might keep a thesaurus, dictionary, and handbook in a stack nearby, resources for checking your words and punctuation; you might also keep one of your special notebooks nearby so you can weave into your writing some of your favorite phrases or thoughts. Writers who enjoy this final part of the writing process feel that the hardest part is over. These writers especially enjoy polishing their writing until they're proud to submit it. As internationally known writer Susan Sontag put it:

> You write in order to read what you've written and see if it's OK and, since of course it never is, to rewrite it—once, twice, as many times as it takes to get it to be something you can bear to reread.
> —**Susan Sontag**, "Directions: Write, Read, Rewrite. Repeat Steps 2 and 3 as Needed."

For writers like Sontag, the enjoyment they get from rereading their revised work is the best part, whether or not they send it on to someone else to read.

Regardless of which parts of the process they enjoy most, all good writers move through a general, three-step writing process: planning, drafting, and revising. Each of these general steps has smaller steps within it, which is probably why no two writers move through these three basic stages in exactly the same way. Still, most experienced writers use some variation of the general writing process that we'll review in the rest of this chapter. Before we begin, take a few minutes to jot down answers to the following questions, which will reveal what parts of the writing process you already do well and already enjoy.

> YOUR WRITING EXPERIENCES

1. Of the many kinds of writing you do, which one gives you the most pleasure? Is it instant messages; planned, drafted, and revised essays; or some other writing? Why do you do this kind of writing?
2. Which of the means available to you for writing gives you the most pleasure (for example, do you prefer pen and paper, a keyboard, or a touch screen)? Which one makes you feel most confident?
3. How would you describe the process you go through to accomplish this pleasurable writing?
4. What part(s) of your writing process do you most enjoy? Find most difficult? Spend the most time on? Spend the least time on? Can you imagine any ways to make the difficult part(s) easier or more enjoyable?

Recognizing an Opportunity for Change

As you learned in Chapter 1, composing most often begins with an opportunity for change or a problem: a specific reason to use words in order to address an issue. You may think of a due date for a written assignment as a problem that can be addressed only through words—and it is. But even in this case, any authentic essay will be a direct response to a broader problem (for instance, "What characterizes an effective PowerPoint presentation?" or "How do credit card companies make money?"). Often, the opportunity for change is more subtle: a problem that tugs at you for attention. After attending a school board meeting and listening to a discussion of budget cuts, you may feel the need to write a letter to the editor of your local newspaper about the importance of music classes for schoolchildren. At the movie theater, you might find yourself wanting to speak to the manager when you see the sorry state of the restrooms. Or you may be bothered by a controversy—such as the one that arose over President Obama's birth certificate—and feel the need to post your opinion online. The problem you've identified establishes your starting point; it is the opportunity for change that prompts you to enter the conversation.

Planning a Response

Planning to write usually involves three steps: exploration, organization, and consideration of development methods. Experienced writers employ a variety of methods for exploring a topic or inventing things to say about it.

Exploration

The most commonly used methods of exploration (also known as *invention strategies*) are listing, keeping a journal, freewriting, and questioning. But experienced writers also regularly use conversation, meditation, reading, and listening as ways to discover good ideas. They realize that good ideas come to them in all sorts of ways, so they keep a pen and a notebook with them all the time, even at night, because ideas often come just as they're falling asleep. They grab the notebook, scribble down their idea, and sleep soundly, no longer worried that they'll forget the idea.

As you plan your college writing assignments, you'll probably continue to rely on the methods that have worked for you in the past. When you're stuck, however, you may want to try out a new method, if only as a way to jump-start your writing.

Listing As soon as you have some idea of what you're expected to write about, start a list of possibilities—and keep adding to it. Look over some of the lists you made in response to the questions on page 55. These are the kinds of lists that can spark your thinking and writing.

On the first day of the semester, when her professor reviewed the syllabus for the course Writing and Technology, Stacy Simkanin learned about the requirements for her first essay. So, during the first week of classes, she jotted down some tentative ideas, knowing that, as time went by, she'd keep adding possibilities for her formal essay. You can follow Stacy's example and keep your list going for a few days. Or you can jot down all your ideas at one sitting, a kind of listing often referred to as **brainstorming**. What follows is the list Stacy made and kept adding to:

computers	web searches	social networking
chat rooms	Statistical Universe	downloadable essays
visual culture class	plagiarism	forum discussions
photo essays	convenience	electronic requests
quality	online databases	Internet
constantly developing	online course notes	time saver
full-length journal articles	classroom computers	Google

Keeping a journal Some writing instructors expect you to keep a weekly journal, either in print or online. When you're writing in your journal, you don't need to be concerned with punctuation, grammar, spelling, and other mechanical features. If you write three pages a week for a journal or as part of your online class discussion, you may not be able to lift a ready-to-submit essay directly from your work, but you will have accumulated a pool of ideas from which to draw. Even more important, you will have been practicing getting thoughts into words.

In addition to using journal entries as a way to explore your topic, you might also use your journal to write out your understandings of and reactions to your reading and writing assignments and class discussions and lectures. As Stacy considered her own upcoming assignment, she wrote in her ongoing electronic journal:

I think I tend to take modern advances for granted, but when I look at how much more I use technology as a college student than I did, say, eight years ago as a junior high student, it's amazing to think of how much my studies have become dependent on it. I need computer access for almost everything anymore, from writing papers to updating my Facebook status, to doing research on the web. Not only that, but some of my favorite classes have been those that incorporated some form of technology into the course format. I think this is one of technology's major advantages—turning learning into something new and interactive, which gets students involved. I've had courses that used technology in basic ways, like my Biological Science class, in which the class

(continued)

lectures were recorded and saved online for students to listen to later. Some of my other courses, though, have used it in lots of interesting ways. In one of my English classes, for instance, we took a day to hold class in a chat room, and we all logged into the room from our computers at home. It was great as part of our discussions about literacy, because experimenting with computer literacy allowed us all to see how people communicate differently when they're not face to face. Of course, some people would argue that kids my age spend way too much time "chatting" and texting and that instant messenging is one of a student's biggest distracters. I guess, like any good thing, technology also carries with it some disadvantages.

Freewriting Freewriting means just what it says: it's the writing you do that costs you nothing. You don't have to worry about spelling or grammar; you don't even have to worry about writing complete sentences, because no one is going to grade it. In fact, no one (except you) may ever even read it. It's the kind of writing you do to loosen up your thinking and your fingers; it's the kind of no-pressure writing that can yield an explosion of ideas.

When Stacy's teacher asked everyone in class to write for five minutes about the connection between technology and their college success, Stacy wrote the following:

Spanish 3: used chat room discussion.

English 202: used chat room discussion to analyze Internet communication as it relates to literacy.

English 202 and Phil 197: used ANGEL's online forums.

Being an English major, I tend to see the biggest advantages of modern technology as those that have most helped my writing. My courses require hours of writing from me each week, and I know that, without access to all the online resources that have been available to me, the amount of time I have to spend working on a paper would probably double. For instance, technology helps me write a research paper before I've even typed the first word, because I can research my topic so much faster by first consulting the online catalogues, instead of going to the library and getting lost in the stacks. If there is material I need that this library doesn't have, I simply have it sent to me through interlibrary loan. Then, when I actually start writing, the process is made easier through referencing certain websites that I can't live without. And once I'm finished writing my paper, I can choose from plenty of web pages designed to show the proper way to cite any resources I've used. Of course, there are also some things that students get from the Internet that they'd be better to stay away from, such as downloadable essays and book notes that help you skip out of actually reading a text. With technology being so accessible, so fast, so convenient, so easy to use, so full of information, etc., it can be hard to make

(continued)

> sure you don't rely on it *too much*. For instance, I don't think it's a good idea to always use information from the Internet as a replacement for going to the library, because sometimes I've found that the perfect resource for a paper I'm writing is sitting on a shelf in the university library. I think the best way for students to make use of modern advances is to draw on them to help build their own ideas and abilities, and not use them as a means of avoiding any real work.

Notice how Stacy starts with a list of some courses that used technology. She doesn't seem to be heading in any one direction. Then suddenly she's off and running about how the use of technology affects her life as an English major.

After trying several methods of exploration (listing, keeping a journal, and freewriting) and tapping several rhetorical methods of development (process analysis, cause-and-effect analysis, narration, and exemplification), Stacy found that she was starting to repeat herself. She didn't yet have a point she wanted to make, let alone a **thesis**, a controlling idea for her essay. She needed to try a new tack.

Questioning Sometimes when you're in a conversation, someone will ask you a question that takes you by surprise—and forces you to rethink your position or think about the topic in a new way. By using structured questioning, you can push yourself to explore your topic more deeply.

You're probably already familiar with the **journalists' questions**, which can readily serve your purpose: *Who? What? Where? When? Why? How?* As Stacy answered these questions, she began to form an opinion about her topic.

> *Who* is using technology? Teachers, students, librarians–everyone on campus, it seems. But I'm going to talk about how it affects me.
>
> *What* technology is being used, and what is it being used for? All kinds of technology, from e-mail and web searches to PowerPoint presentations and voice mail, is being used, for instruction, homework, student-to-student communication, student-and-teacher communication, and research. I'm going to concentrate on my use of computer technology, mostly access to the Internet.
>
> *Where* is technology being used? At the library, in the classroom, but most often in my bedroom, where my computer is.
>
> *When* is technology being used? Usually at night, after I come home from classes and am doing my homework.
>
> *Why* do students use or not use technology? I use it because it's more convenient than walking over to the library and searching. Not all students have Internet access in their apartments; others may not know all the online research techniques that I know.
>
> *How* are students using it? Some students are using it to advance their education; others are using it to subvert it (like downloading essays and cheating schemes).

Considering genre

Stacy didn't need to think much about the genre in which she would write: her instructor had already determined that fitting responses would take the form of an academic essay, rather than another genre, such as memoir, profile, report, argument, or proposal. But situations will arise when you need to determine which genre is most appropriate. The genre you choose should fulfill your purpose and be deliverable through a medium that will reach your intended audience. In other words, picking the most effective genre is key to making the best use of your available means.

Here are some tips for determining which genre is appropriate to your rhetorical situation:

▶ Consider who else has been faced with a similar rhetorical situation and what genre(s) they used in response.

▶ Locate one or more examples to identify common characteristics of a genre, such as the kind of language used (formal or informal, for example), where and how the rhetorical appeals of ethos, logos, and pathos appear (see page 44), and what kind of evidence (facts, statistics, personal experience, scientific research) is employed.

▶ Ask yourself whether it is most appropriate to use a genre that has been used in similar situations or whether a variation on the expected characteristics of that genre might have a stronger effect.

▶ Finally, consider your available means. To what physical means of delivery do you have access—word processing, PowerPoint, podcast, printed document? What rhetorical methods would make good strategies—definition, classification and division, exemplification, description, comparison, cause-and-effect analysis, process analysis, narration, argument? And what physical and rhetorical means is your audience expecting from you? How do these factors influence your choice of genre and means of delivery?

Organization

Once you've explored your topic as thoroughly as you can, it's time to begin organizing your essay. Two simple methods can help you get started: clustering and outlining.

Clustering Clustering is a visual method for connecting ideas that go together. You might start with words and phrases from a list you compiled or brainstormed and link them with arrows, circles, or lines, the way Stacy did. Notice how Stacy used different sizes of type to accentuate the connections she wanted to make between technology and learning. (You might want to use color as well to help you make connections.) Interestingly, Stacy hasn't yet put herself into her essay's plan.

Outlining An outline establishes the limits of your topic at the same time as it lists the main parts. Outlining is a good way to plan, but only if you think of the result as a rough—not formal or final—outline. You'll want to allow yourself to

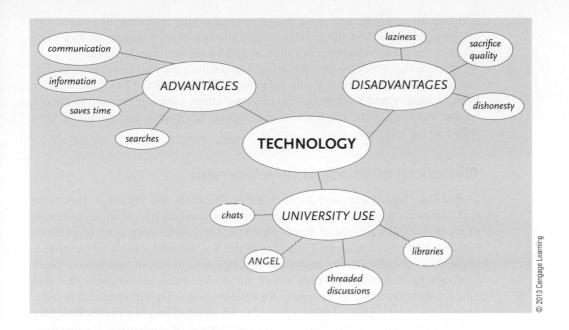

© 2013 Cengage Learning

Technology and Learning

I. Advantages
   - Information
     - fast and convenient
     - online catalogues
     - eBay's First Edition or Rare Books page
     - Google Books
     - online concordances
     - databases
   - Communication
     - ANGEL
     - online forums
     - new forms of interaction
     - chat rooms

II. Disadvantages
   - Academic laziness
     - ignore traditional forms of research
     - quality vs. convenience
     - lose the value of a trip to the library
   - Dishonesty
     - free online book notes
     - downloadable essays
     - plagiarism

add and delete points and move things around so that outlining, like clustering, helps you visualize how things relate to one another. Stacy's outline shows a close relationship to her clustering, but she's added details and a general title.

Notice that Stacy started out using Roman numerals for her main sections, but she switched to simply listing subpoints, thereby making her outline easier to put together and work with. As she was putting together her outline, Stacy began thinking about methods of developing her paper that would be best suited to her purpose.

Rhetorical methods of development

Definition, classification and division, exemplification, description, comparison and contrast, cause-and-effect analysis, process analysis, narration, argument—these rhetorical methods of development are strategies employed to explore, expand, and organize ideas. They're also the way we make sense of the world. Regardless of culture, nationality, gender, age, and ability, we all turn to these methods to find what we want to say and to situate it in a context. We also employ these methods as templates for interpreting what someone else is communicating to us. Each of these methods can stand alone, but more often they complement one another. When we use the method of *comparison*, for instance, we often need to *define* what exactly we are comparing.

Definition If you were to define the animal in the photograph, you might classify it as a "mammal" and then distinguish this mammal from others similar to it, describing its features and perhaps coming up with a definitive name for it. Thus, definition makes use of other strategies such as classification and division, exemplification, and description.

Whenever we're introduced to something new—a new word, academic subject, sport, activity, or language—we need to develop a new vocabulary. Whether we're learning the vocabulary of cooking (*chop, slice, mince, stir, fold, whip, fry*), golf (*ace, birdie, bogey, chip, drive, duff*), or human evolution (*prosimians, hominoids, paleoanthropology, australopithecines, isotopes*), we're expanding our world with new concepts and ideas. Definition is essential to our learning and our understanding.

© Noel Rowe, 2007

No matter what we're learning or learning about, we use definition. And whether or not we're conscious of it, we always employ the three steps of definition:

1. We name the specific concept, action, person, or thing; in other words, we provide a term for it.
2. Then, we classify that term, or place it in a more general category. (See page 66.)
3. Finally, we differentiate the specific term from all the other concepts, actions, persons, or things in that general category, often using examples. (See pages 66–67.)

For instance, if you're studying human evolution, you'll no doubt need to learn what distinguishes primates from other mammals.

Term	Class	Differentiation
Primates are	mammals	that have "a lack of strong specialization in structure; prehensile hands and feet, usually with opposable thumbs and great toes; flattened nails instead of claws on the digits; acute vision with some degree of binocular vision; relatively large brain exhibiting a degree of cortical folding; and prolonged postnatal dependency. No primate exhibits all these features, and indeed the diversity of primate forms has produced disagreement as to their proper classification" (*Encyclopedia Britannica*).

The preceding is a **formal** (or **sentence**) **definition**, the kind you'll find in a reference book. But it's not the only kind of definition. An **extended definition**, such as this one from primate.org, provides additional differentiating information:

> Primates are the mammals that are humankind's closest biological relatives. We share 98.4% of [our] DNA with chimpanzees. Apes, monkeys, and prosimians such as lorises, bush babies, and lemurs make up the 234 species of the family tree. About 90% of the primates live in tropical forests. They play an integral role in the ecology of their habitat. They help the forest by being pollinators, seed predators, and seed dispersers.

A **historical definition**, like this one from chimpanzoo.org/history_of _primates, provides a longitudinal overview of what the term has described over time, offering additional concepts and terms:

> **65 mya** [million years ago]: Paleocene epoch begins. . . . The earliest primates evolve. These primates were small insectivores who were most likely terrestrial. During this epoch, primates began to include food items such as seeds, fruits, nuts and leaves in their diet.
>
> **53.5 mya:** Eocene epoch begins. Primates diversify and some become arboreal. Primates have developed prehensile hands and feet with opposable thumbs and toes and their claws have evolved into nails. Arboreal primates evolve relatively longer lower limbs for vertical clinging and leaping. Their eye sockets are oriented more frontally resulting in stereoscopic vision. Primates of this epoch belong to the prosimian family.

One of the best things about learning a new subject is that the initial vocabulary introduces more vocabulary, so the learning never ends.

Sometimes, you'll need to write a **negative definition** to clarify for your readers not only what a term means but also what it does not mean. In conversation, you might say, "When I talk about success, I'm not talking about making money." For you, success might instead involve having personal integrity, experiencing fulfillment in interpersonal relationships, and taking on exciting professional challenges. Even primates can be defined negatively, as W. E. Le Gros Clark wrote in *The Antecedents of Man*: "The Primates as a whole have preserved rather a generalized anatomy and . . . are to be mainly distinguished . . . by a negative feature—their lack of specialization."

Finally, you may come across or come up with a **stipulative definition**, which limits—or stipulates—the range of a term's meaning or application, thereby announcing to the reader exactly how the writer is using the term in the specific rhetorical situation. For instance, if you find yourself writing about *success*, you might define your meaning for your readers like this: "In this paper, *success* will be defined in terms of how quickly college graduates obtain employment in their chosen fields." Or if you're writing about *primates*, you might stipulate that you're concentrating on a twenty-first century conception of them. As you can see, definition provides the foundation for learning, understanding, and communicating. As you'll see in the following pages, classification and division, exemplification, and description all work in service of definition.

Classification and division Like definition, **classification and division** first places something in a general category and then distinguishes it from other things within that category. Department stores, hospitals, telephone books, libraries, grocery stores, and bookstores are all classified and divided in order to enhance accessibility to their information or contents. When you go into a hospital, for instance, you look at the directory by the entrance to find out how the areas in the building are classified (reception area, visitor information, emergency room, outpatient clinic, waiting room, obstetrics, patient rooms, gift shop, and cafeteria). Then, when you make your way to one of those areas (patient rooms, for instance), you look to see how that general area has been divided up (into floors and individual rooms on those floors). In important ways, the classification of hospital areas and the further division and distinction of those same areas define those locations. The hospital room you want to find is defined by belonging to the category of *patient rooms* and then differentiated from (or divided from) other patient rooms by being on the fifth floor, at the end of the hallway, to the left. Just as with definition, then, when you use classification and division, you provide a term and then place that term in its general category of origin.

Exemplification The rhetorical strategy of **exemplification** involves making a generalization and using an example or series of examples in support of that generalization. If you want to clarify why Veronica is the best salesclerk in your favorite sporting goods store, you can provide a series of examples that define *best salesclerk:* Veronica is herself a competitive athlete; she has positive energy and is knowledgeable about all the equipment, from running shoes and jackets to cycles and kayaks. She lets you know when items will be going on sale, and, best of all, she never pushes a sale. She realizes by now that if you really want it, you'll come back for it when you have the money. Or if you want to add interest to a generalization about your terrific Santa Fe vacation, you might talk about the clear blue skies, warm days, and cool nights; you could include anecdotes about the bargain rate you found online for your hotel room, running into Jessica Simpson at the Folk Art Museum, attending the Santa Domingo Pueblo feast day, and joining a Friday night art gallery walk and meeting artists; you could describe shopping on the plaza, where you found turquoise jewelry,

Acoma Pueblo pottery, and Hopi-made Christmas presents. You could also include tantalizing, sensory descriptions of the delicious regional food—Frito pie, chocolate-covered chile creams, *carne adovada*, and *natillas*. All these examples not only add interest to the generalization that you had a "terrific vacation" but also help define exactly what you mean by that phrase.

© Vulpix/Big Stock Photo

In the passage that follows, Pulitzer Prize–winner William Styron defines *suicidal* through his examples of suicidal thoughts.

> He asked me if I was suicidal, and I reluctantly told him yes. I did not particularize—since there seemed no need to—did not tell him that in truth many of the artifacts of my house had become potential devices for my own destruction: the attic rafters (and an outside maple or two) a means to hang myself, the garage a place to inhale carbon monoxide, the bathtub a vessel to receive the flow from my opened arteries. The kitchen knives in their drawers had but one purpose for me. Death by heart attack seemed particularly inviting, absolving me as it would of active responsibility, and I had toyed with the idea of self-induced pneumonia—a long, frigid, shirt-sleeved hike through the rainy woods. Nor had I overlooked an ostensible accident . . . by walking in front of a truck on the highway nearby. These thoughts may seem outlandishly macabre—a strained joked—but they are genuine. —**William Styron**, *Darkness Visible*

Styron admits to his physician that he is, indeed, depressed to the point of being suicidal, but he reserves the persuasive examples of his mental state for readers of his memoir.

Description Specific details converge in **description**, a verbal accounting of what we have experienced physically and mentally. Thus, our descriptions always carry with them **sensory details** having to do with our physical sensations (what we see, hear, smell, touch, or taste) or **sensibility details** having to do with our intellectual, emotional, or physical states (alertness, gullibility, grief, fear, loathing, exuberance, clumsiness, relaxation, agitation, and so on).

José Antonio Burciaga's description (and extended definition) of *tortilla* relies heavily on sensory details:

> For Mexicans over the centuries, the *tortilla* has served as the spoon and fork, the plate and the napkin. . . . When I was growing up in El Paso, . . . I used to visit a *tortilla* factory in an ancient adobe building near the open *mercado* in Ciudad Juárez. As I approached, I could hear the rhythmic slapping of the *masa* as the skilled vendors outside the factory formed it into balls and patted them into perfectly round corn cakes between the palms of their hands. The wonderful aroma and the speed with which the women counted so many dozens of *tortillas* out of warm wicker baskets still linger in my mind. Watching them at work convinced me that the most handsome and *deliciosas tortillas* are handmade. Although machines are faster, they can never adequately replace generation-to-generation experience. There's no place in the factory assembly line for the tender slaps that give each

tortilla character. The best thing that can be said about mass-producing *tortillas* is that it makes it possible for many people to enjoy them. **—José Antonio Burciaga, "I Remember Masa"**

The sensory details that infuse Burciaga's description of *tortilla* make it entertaining and memorable. Because description relies on details, it defines what is being described in specific ways.

Comparison and contrast We use **comparison and contrast**, a two-part method of rhetorical development, from the moment we wake up (often comparing the advantages of getting up without enough rest with those of staying in bed) until we go to bed at night (comparing the option of getting rest with that of staying up and working). We use **comparison** to consider how two or more things are alike, and we use **contrast** to show how related things are different. This rhetorical strategy, which helps us clarify issues, can be used to explain, make a decision, shape an argument, open a discussion, or craft an entertaining narrative.

When you do decide to get up, you might want to choose a cereal to have for breakfast, knowing that you have Lucky Charms and Cheerios on your shelf. Because both of these share the characteristics of cold breakfast cereals, you have a **basis for comparison**. In order to decide which you want to eat, you'll intuitively set up **points of comparison** to clarify the ways in which the two are the same (both are cereals, served cold, eaten for breakfast) as well as the ways in which they are different (in terms of taste, nutrition, ingredients). You may already know the answers to the questions of which cereal tastes better, which one is better for you, and which one will sustain you until lunch. But you may not be familiar with the information that supports those answers, information that appears on the cereal boxes themselves.

© Steven Lunetta Photography, 2007

The nutritional information panels on the boxes indicate that both cold cereals have been approved by the American Heart Association because both are low in saturated fats and cholesterol, with 0 grams of saturated fat and 0 milligrams of cholesterol. Both are also pretty low in sodium (200 milligrams and 210 milligrams), carbohydrates (25 grams and 22 grams), and protein (2 grams and 3 grams). But neither of the cereals comes close to fulfilling recommended daily allowances (RDAs) of carbohydrates and protein, as the charts on the boxes show. What about the recommended daily requirements (RDRs) for vitamins and minerals? The nutrition charts show that these cereals provide the same amounts of vitamins A, C, D, B_6, and B_{12}. In terms of other nutrients—calcium, thiamin, riboflavin, niacin, folic acid, and zinc—they are also the same. Cheerios, however, offers more iron (nearly half the RDR), phosphorus, magnesium, and copper. But will those differences affect your choice?

What distinctive contrast will be the deciding factor? The amount of sugar? Lucky Charms has 13 grams, whereas Cheerios has only 1 gram. The extra sugar might make Lucky Charms taste better, which may tip the scale. If you want enough energy to sustain you until lunch, however, you might choose Cheerios, so that you don't start your day with a sugar high and then crash midmorning.

The information you can glean from the side of a cereal box helps you understand the ingredients of the cereal and make an informed choice. If you wanted to discuss the choice of cereal with children and argue for the "right" choice, you could use much of that information. Whether you could ultimately persuade them to choose Cheerios over Lucky Charms is, of course, another story. You would, however, be informing them through the method of comparison and contrast.

Cause-and-effect analysis Whenever you find yourself concentrating on either causes or effects, explaining why certain events have occurred or predicting that particular events or situations will lead to specific effects, you're conducting a **cause-and-effect analysis** (sometimes referred to as a *cause-and-consequence analysis*). The opportunity for change in these situations comes with your ability to use words to address your questions, to explore why some things happen, or to predict the effects of an event or situation. Cause-and-effect analysis can be used to explain (your opinion on why Ohio State is going to the Rose Bowl), to entertain (your description of what happens when the family gathers for Thanksgiving), to speculate (your thoughts on the causes of autism), or to argue a point (your stance on the effects of pollution).

We spend a good deal of time considering the causes of situations. For instance, when one of your bookshelves collapses, you check to see if the shelf braces are screwed into studs, if the books are too heavy, or if you need additional supporting braces. If you have a fender bender on the way to school, you think about what led to the accident. Some of the reasons may be outside your control: low visibility, an icy road, a poorly marked road, missing taillights on the car in front of you. Other causes may reside in you: your tailgating, speeding, or inattention (due to eating, putting a CD in, talking or texting on your cell phone).

Image courtesy of NOAA

We spend just as much time—maybe even more—evaluating the effects of situations and events. You're enrolled in college and already considering the effects of having a college degree, most of them positive (you'll have to pay for your coursework and work hard, but you're likely to be well employed when you're finished). If you're considering marriage, you're analyzing the positive and not-so-positive effects of that decision (you'll live with the love of your life, but you'll have to relocate to Sacramento, where you may not be able to transfer all your credits). If you follow current events, you know that the effects of the controversial wars in Iraq and Afghanistan include the deaths of nearly six thousand Americans, over one hundred thousand Iraqis, approximately twenty thousand Afghanis (estimates vary), and a good deal of public discontent.

Before-and-after photographs, such as the dramatic ones above and on the facing page, often lead us to wonder what happened and what was the cause. The first of this pair of photographs shows a beautiful old church surrounded by big trees. It's Trinity Episcopal Church in Pass Christian, Mississippi, which was built in 1849. Set among live oaks and lush lawns, Trinity served as a landmark for over a century. In the second photo, some—but not all—of the big trees are still standing, but there's no church, just the stairs and pathway leading up to the church. This second photograph was taken on August 18, 1969, the day after Hurricane Camille smashed into the Mississippi Gulf Coast, with wind speeds in excess of two hundred miles per hour and water levels twenty-four feet above normal high tide, making it the strongest storm in U.S. history. The effects of Camille, by the time it had dissipated on August 22, included 256 deaths and $1.4 billion in damages, the equivalent of $8.4 billion in 2010. Even though chances are slim that anyone in your class will have heard of, let alone remember, Hurricane Camille, you understand its effects. Developing your ability to examine situations or events for their causes or effects, teasing out a relevant analysis, will help you better understand your world.

Process analysis Whenever you develop your ideas in order to explain how something is done, you're engaging in **process analysis**. Process analysis involves dividing up an entire process into a series of ordered steps so that your audience can understand the relationship among those steps and maybe even replicate them. To that end, process analysis always includes a series of separate, chronological steps that provide details about a process and often reads like a narration. Many process analyses take the form of a list, with distinct and often numbered steps, as in recipes, instruction manuals (for tasks from using a small appliance to assembling a toy), and installation guides (for everything from showerheads and garbage disposals to computer software). Whether the purpose of the process analysis is to inform (how volcanoes erupt, how leukemia is treated), entertain (how to gain weight on vacation, how a ten-year-old boy makes hot chocolate), or argue a point (the best way to quit a job, learn to write, develop as a reader), the analysis itself responds to a problem: someone needs to know how to do something or wants to learn how something is done.

Television programs and DVDs present processes we can duplicate or appreciate: we can watch the Food Network to learn about Paula Deen's plan for an easy-to-prepare Thanksgiving dinner (one that includes deep-fried turkey and double-chocolate gooey cake) or be entertained by *Say Yes to the Dress*, a not-always-flattering analysis of the process brides-to-be move through in their search for the perfect wedding dress. We can view DVDs to learn how to compose an iron-clad will or *How to Draw Comics the Marvel Way*, although these analyses might not provide enough training for us to duplicate the processes they describe. Whether processes are conveyed orally, in writing, or visually, whether we're taking directions from our mom, reading a car-repair manual, or watching *30 Minute Meals*, we're using process analysis.

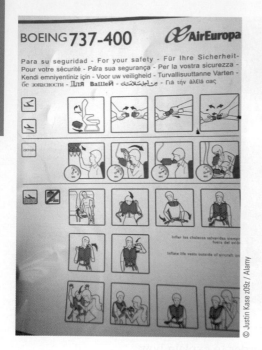

BOEING **737-400**   *AirEuropa*

Para su seguridad - For your safety - Für Ihre Sicherheit-
Pour votre sécurité - Pára sua segurança - Per la vostra sicurezza -
Kendi emniyentiniz için - Voor uw veiligheid - Turvallisuuttanne Varten -
бе зопасности - Для Вашей - ... - Γιά τήν άλεΐά οας

© Justin Kase z09z / Alamy

Process analyses come in two basic forms. **Directive process analysis** is used to teach the audience how to do something, how to duplicate the process. **Informative process analysis**, on the other hand, is used to explain a process so that the audience can understand, enjoy, or be persuaded. Either kind of process analysis can constitute an entire message or be one part of a larger message (within a novel, proposal, report, or essay, for example).

If you've ever taken an airplane trip, you're familiar with directive process analyses. Both the passenger safety card in the pocket of the seat in front of you (as shown to the left) and the oral instructions from the flight attendant serve as perfect examples. As you follow along with the card, the attendant recites and enacts the step-by-step directions for various safety procedures during takeoffs, landings, and emergencies: how to buckle and unbuckle your seat belt, how to put an oxygen mask on yourself and help a child do so, how to locate and inflate the life preserver, and so on. Many passengers can understand the language in which the flight attendant is giving the instructions, but, for those who cannot, the visuals on the card provide the details necessary for full understanding. Whether the passengers take in the information aurally, visually, or both aurally and visually, the directive process analysis allows them to duplicate the steps described.

The following example of the second type of process analysis, informative process analysis, comes from a suspense novel. The author uses process analysis to address the problem emerging in the opening paragraph.

> Detective Matt Chacon knew that unlike the TV cop shows—where actors sit in front of a computer monitor and instantaneously pull up a digital fingerprint record that matches a perp or a victim—trying to ID someone using prints in the real world can be mind-numbing work. There are thousands of prints that have never been entered into the computer data banks, and thousands more on file that, because of poor quality, are virtually unusable for comparison purposes. On top of that, figure in the small cop shops who haven't got the money, manpower, and equipment to transfer print records to computers, and the unknown number of print records that were left in closed felony cases and sit forgotten in basement archives at police departments all over the country, and you've got a data-bank system that is woefully inadequate and incomplete. Finally, while each fingerprint is unique, the difference between prints can be so slight that a very careful analysis must be made to confirm a perfect match. Even then, different experts can debate the results endlessly, since it isn't an exact science.
>
> Chacon had started his career in law enforcement as a crime scene technician with a specialty in fingerprint and tool-mark identification, so of course Lieutenant Molina had sent him off to the state police headquarters to work the state and federal data banks to see if he could get a match.

He'd been at it all night long and his coffee was starting to taste like sludge, his eyes were itchy, and his butt was numb. Using an automated identification system, Chacon had digitally stored the victim's prints in the computer and then started scanning for a match against those already on file.

The computer system could identify possible matches quickly, but then it became a process of carefully analyzing each one and scoring them according to a detailed classification system. So far, Chacon had examined six dozen sets of prints that looked like possible equivalents and had struck out. But there was another baker's dozen to review.

He clicked on the next record, adjusted the monitor to enhance the resolution of the smudged prints, and began scoring them in sequence. Whoever had printed the subject had done a piss-poor job. He glanced at the agency identifier. It was a Department of Corrections submission.

Chacon finished the sequence and used a split screen to compare his scoring to the victim's print. It showed a match. He rechecked the scoring and verified his findings.

—**Michael McGarrity,** *Everyone Dies*

As it informs and entertains, this process analysis argues a point—that fingerprint matching is a complicated and often time-consuming procedure, not the quick fix depicted by popular media. Process analysis provides the overall structure of the passage—a thesis statement, chronological organization, and purposeful point of view. In addition, the passage uses several other rhetorical strategies for development: comparison and contrast, narration, description, exemplification, and cause-and-effect analysis.

In our culture, directions are no longer given and received only through print or face-to-face interaction. Instead of reading a cookbook, we might turn on the Food Network; instead of hiring a plumber, we might visit homedepot.com. So whether you decide to convey a process analysis in English or another language, over the telephone or by e-mail, in laborious detail or in shorthand, with or without an accompanying visual depends on your audience's native language, access to various means of communication, and understanding of the subject matter. With process analysis, as with other rhetorical methods, it's important to consider the physical means of delivering and receiving information.

Narration One of the rhetorical methods for development that you already know well is **narration**, which tells a story that has **characters** (people in the story), **dialogue** (direct speech by the characters), a **setting** (the time and place), **description** (selected sensory and sensibility details about the characters, dialogue, and setting), and **plot** (the sequence of events). Narrations help us make sense of the world for ourselves and for others—whether we're retelling a fairy tale or family legend or recounting the final minutes of the Super Bowl or our canyon-bottom tour of Canyon de Chelly (pictured on next page).

Narration can frame an entire story ("Robin Hood" or the first Thanksgiving), or it can provide an example (why you can depend on your brother) and support an argument (those final plays proved the Steelers to be the better team). Usually narrations are verbal—we want to tell "what happened."

Courtesy of the author

Verbal narration, which appears in newspapers, in movies, and in reports on television and radio, tells us, for example, about University of California students protesting tuition hikes, the latest child-abduction tragedy, the president's travels to the Middle East, a murder mystery or police procedural, a girl who's been sneezing for two weeks, obituaries, and the local school board meeting. Such verbal narrations might consist of one particular sequence of events or include a series of separate incidents that shape an overall narrative.

Were you to compose a narration about the photograph of the jeep and flood water at Canyon de Chelly, what might it be? Would your narration account for your entire vacation, beginning when you left home, or might you concentrate only on the canyon-bottom tour? In addition to tapping all the elements of a narration (characters, dialogue, setting, description, and plot), would you also use an **anecdote** (a brief, illustrative story that propels the narrative)? From what **point of view** would you tell the story? Your own, that of the Navajo guide, your parents', or your sibling's? And what might be the **climax** of your narration, the turning point toward a resolution? Would you recount your narration in chronological order, or might you use **flashback** to account for past events or **flashforward** to account for future events? Purposefully interruptive, these techniques add interest to a story, providing glimpses of other times, which illuminate the present as it is being recounted in an otherwise straightforward, chronological organization.

Whether used to supply information, explain, provide an example, set a mood, or argue a point, narration easily reaches most audiences and often serves as a fitting response to opportunities for change. Given its versatility, narration can serve as the basis for a good deal of your academic, personal, and work-related writing.

Argument The words *argument* and *persuasion* are often used interchangeably, despite the technical distinctions between the two terms. **Argument** refers to the verbal or visual delivery of a point of view and the use of logical reasoning to help an audience understand that point of view as true or valid. **Persuasion**, on the other hand, refers to the use of emotions as well as logical reasoning to move the audience a step or two beyond the understanding that accompanies successful argument. The goal of persuasion is to change the mind, point of view, or actions of the audience. Because any visual or verbal argument can easily include emotional appeals as well as logical reasoning and because any argument holds the potential for changing the collective mind or actions of an audience, the broader term *argument* will be used throughout this chapter and book.

We employ and respond to arguments all day long, as we work to understand and explain to others the world around or within us. Sometimes, our arguments focus on defending our opinions or questioning the opinions of others—opinions about whether Charlie Sheen should have returned to *Two and a Half Men*, where to get the best pizza, which music venue offers the best nightlife, or whether a vegan diet is truly healthful. Sometimes, argument involves exploring and clarifying our own opinions, so we weigh all sides of an issue and various possible consequences of our final opinion. Often, we employ that kind of analytical argument when we're considering some of life's big issues: surgery, divorce, marriage, a new job, racism, sexism, and so on.

Other times, argument is invitational, in that it invites the audience to understand your position (even if they're not convinced to change their minds or action) and to explain their position to you (even if you're not convinced to change your mind or action). Invitational argument works especially well when the speaker and the audience need to work together to solve a problem (what to do about school violence, the spread of the AIDS virus, or unemployment), construct a position that represents diverse interests (for or against universal health coverage, the professionalization of college athletics, or affirmative action), or implement a policy that requires broad support (on establishing a draft system or allowing gay marriage).

When we analyze an argument—our own or one someone else is presenting to us—we can consider several elements: an identifiable issue, a claim, common ground, and rhetorical appeals.

An **identifiable issue** is the topic under discussion, one that we choose from a multitude of issues we confront daily, from limited service at the university health center to poverty, homelessness, poor-quality schooling, and so on. We don't always take the time to address any one of those problems in any productive way, perhaps because we cannot pinpoint the specific issue within that problem that we want to argue for or against. In other words, we cannot identify an opportunity for change that can be addressed with words.

But suppose you were experiencing both bad service and bad food at a restaurant. That experience might not be a very big deal unless you became violently ill and you thought it was from the salmon, which didn't taste quite right. Now you have identified a specific issue you can argue as you express your opinion that either the storage of the fresh seafood or the sanitary conditions of that restaurant are in need of improvement. Or suppose you've identified one specific issue that contributes to the poor test scores of your neighborhood school: most children don't eat breakfast before they come to school.

Once you've identified an issue (that hungry schoolchildren test poorly), you can make a **claim** about it, an arguable position you take regarding that issue. Your claim could be that the school should launch a free breakfast program for students. The need for free school breakfasts would be the position you'd take in your argument to parents, teachers, administrators, and the school board. As you think through the various claims that could be made about the issue (parents should feed their children themselves; parents should provide better after-school support; children need to work harder; teachers need to concentrate on the basics, and so on), you'll want to make sure that your claim is one that can be argued and responded to. Citing research can be one of the most persuasive kinds of support, as the U.S. Department of Agriculture demonstrates in a flyer it produced:

Courtesy of the author

There are many benefits of breakfast for children. Breakfast provides children with the energy and essential nutrients they need to concentrate on school work and learn. Studies show that breakfast provides as much as 25 percent of the recommended daily allowance for key nutrients, such as calcium, protein, vitamins A and B6, magnesium, iron and zinc.

Research shows that children who eat breakfast have higher achievement scores, lower rates of absence and tardiness, and increased concentration in the classroom. . . .

Another important benefit of breakfast for children is that establishing the healthy habit of eating breakfast early in life could stave off many adulthood health problems associated with poor diet, such as diabetes and obesity.

Among all the possible views of school breakfast programs, yours—that school breakfast programs contribute to academic performance—will ground your thesis statement.

In addition to supplying support for your claim, you'll also need to establish **common ground**: the goal, belief, value, or assumption that you share with your audience. In this case, you might say that "academic performance needs to improve," and you could be reasonably certain that your audience would agree. Once you've established common ground, you've assured your audience that, despite any misunderstandings or disagreements, you both actually share a good deal, which provides a starting point for you to speak or write.

You'll also employ the rhetorical appeals of ethos, logos, and pathos to make connections with your audience (see pages 44–45). By establishing common ground and speaking to a nationwide problem involving children and their school performance, you've emphasized ethos. By citing research to support your assertion that eating breakfast improves students' health, behavior, and academic performance, you're employing logos. And by listing ten reasons children should eat breakfast, starting with the obvious one that no child should go hungry, you're employing pathos.

Argument is a common part of everyday life, whether we're negotiating to change an airline ticket, discussing why Ohio State fired football coach Jim Tressel, or explaining why we don't want our roommate borrowing our clothes. In some ways, then, everything's an argument. Every time you transfer meaning or understanding from yourself to another person, you've made a successful argument. And every time you've understood what someone else is saying to you, you've responded to a successful argument. No matter what kind they are—visual or verbal, angry or informative, personal or bureaucratic—arguments work to fulfill one of three rhetorical purposes: to express or defend a position, to question or argue against an established belief or course of action, or to invite or persuade an audience to change an opinion or action.

You can find additional help with writing arguments in Chapter 2, which discusses the rhetorical appeals of ethos, logos, and pathos; Chapter 7, which discusses and gives examples of position arguments and rhetorical fallacies; and Chapter 8, which discusses and gives examples of proposals.

> WRITE FOR FIVE

Write for five minutes in response to each of the following questions. Be prepared to share your answers with the rest of the class.

1. What was the last opportunity for change you responded to in writing? Why did you choose to respond to it? What did you think your words could do?
2. How did you go about exploring possible responses? Which of the invention strategies did you employ?
3. How did you begin organizing your response? What organizational methods did you explore? How was your response organized in its final form?
4. What means did you use to deliver your response—words, visuals, paper, electronic files? Why did you choose that specific means of delivery?
5. Compare your answers with those of two classmates. What surprised you about their answers? List two things a classmate wrote that made you rethink your own answers. Then rewrite those answers.

Drafting a Response

Reconsidering audience, resources, and constraints

After you've explored your topic, loosely organized your paper, and considered which of the rhetorical methods of development are best suited to your purpose, you'll begin drafting. While some writers find the first draft the toughest part of the process, many others derive great pleasure from the two-step drafting process: drafting and evaluating. The joy of putting words together is exhilarating for many writers; they enjoy the freedom of combining an outline with a freewrite as they work to attend to all the elements of the rhetorical situation (see Chapter 1). A first draft is just that—words you'll revisit again and again as you adjust your message to take into account all the elements in your rhetorical situation.

When you're drafting, you'll be considering your intended audience as well, particularly in terms of what you're hoping your audience can do to address (or help you address) the opportunity for change that sparked your writing in the first place. The following list may help you as you reconsider audience:

▶ Who can resolve the opportunity for change (or the problem) that you've identified?

▶ What exactly might that audience do to address, resolve, or help resolve it?

▶ What opportunities (if any) are there for you to receive feedback from that audience?

Answers to these questions will help you tie your purpose to your particular audience.

By thinking of her assignment as a rhetorical situation, Stacy Simkanin developed a better idea of how to approach her draft. When an instructor doesn't write out an assignment, you should feel free to ask him or her to explain it in terms of the rhetorical situation—that is, ask your instructor specific questions about purpose, audience (or receiver), context, and constraints.

Here is Stacy's first draft.

Technology for teaching and learning is especially strong here at State. It provides many advantages for students and teachers alike, but it also brings with it some disadvantages. In this essay, I'm going to talk about my experiences with technology, the advantages I've experienced and the disadvantages I feel. I'll draw upon my experiences in Spanish 3, English 202, Philosophy 197, Biological Sciences, Art History, and my internship.

Technology is rapidly becoming increasingly advanced, and much of it is used to enhance learning and writing. Not only does it increase the amount of information available, but it allows for stronger writing. I can search libraries around the world, use eBay to find rare manuscripts, use interlibrary loan, and file electronic requests for needed items.

Technology also makes the writing process faster, more convenient. I often access online concordances, view library books on my PC, e-mail librarians, and read full-text journal articles online. This technology is also allowing for more ways to develop ideas and new forms of written communication. For instance, I'm now experienced with chat room communication, forum discussions, and photo essays.

(continued)

But at the same time that technology brings these advantages, it also inhibits learning and writing. I know that when I'm conducting online research I may be missing out on information or lowering the quality of information because I'm limiting my searching to electronic sources. Nowadays, students don't really have to learn to use the library, where often more information can be found than what appears in an online search. I fear that students are placing convenience over quality. I know I do sometimes. The information online isn't always reliable, either. Students don't often take the time to investigate sources.

For these reasons, campus technology may be promoting academic laziness in some students, and dishonesty as well. So much information is available that you can practically write a book report without ever reading the book. And online papers make plagiarism easy. In conclusion . . .

Stacy's first draft has begun to address the components of the rhetorical situation: she understands that she needs to talk about her own experiences with technology and describe the technology that she uses. In getting her thoughts down, she's beginning to sketch out an organizational structure that starts with the advantages of this technology and ends with the disadvantages. She has made certain to add that some students take advantage of technology only in a way that cheapens their learning experience. Notice that she hasn't begun to shape a strong thesis yet, let alone a conclusion. Still, she's ready to begin revising.

> ## WRITE FOR FIVE

1. What methods do you use to launch your first draft?
2. What's the easiest part of drafting for you? The most difficult? Why?
3. How does having a specific sense of audience help or hinder you?
4. Many writers concentrate on the big picture when drafting; others find themselves slowing down and filling in some details as well. How would you describe your process of producing a first draft? Be prepared to share your answers with the rest of the class.
5. How does your means of delivery (print, electronic file, visual, oral presentation) affect your process? In other words, which means of delivery help or hinder you?

Revising a Response

Revision means evaluating and rethinking your writing in terms of the rhetorical situation. Writers use several techniques during revision. Some put the draft aside for twenty-four hours or more in order to return to it with fresh ideas and a more objective viewpoint. Others like to print out the draft and actually cut it into different sections so that they can experiment with organization. One of the most popular—and most effective—revision techniques is peer evaluation.

Peer evaluation is a form of collaboration that provides productive advice and response from a fellow student writer. If the thought of letting a peer (a classmate or friend) read your first draft makes you uncomfortable, if you've tried peer evaluation before and it didn't work, or if you're worried that you won't receive good advice, please reconsider. All effective writing is the result of some measure of collaboration, whether between colleagues, editors and writers, publishers and writers, actors and writers, students and teachers, or friends. Just consider for a moment all the writing you read, hear, and see every day—newspapers, magazines, online chat, billboards, commercials, sitcoms, newscasts. A great majority of the words that you experience daily come to you as a result of collaboration and peer evaluation. Every day, experienced writers are showing their first drafts to someone else in order to get another point of view, advice, and evaluation.

Peer evaluation is a valuable step in the writing process that you, too, will want to experience. No matter how good a writer you are, you'll benefit from hearing what one or more real readers have to say about your message. They may ask you questions that prompt you to clarify points you want to make, nudge you to provide more examples so that your prose comes alive, or point out attention-getting passages. When you respond to a peer's first draft, you are not only helping that writer but also strengthening your own skills as a reader and writer. As you discover strengths and weaknesses in someone else's writing, you also improve your ability to find them in your own. Most important, the successful writing of a peer will energize your own writing in ways that the successful writing of a professional might not. A peer can show you how attainable good writing can be.

Although it is sometimes helpful to get pointers on things like grammar and word choice, you'll usually want a peer reviewer to focus first on how well your draft responds to your rhetorical situation. The following set of ten questions can help guide a peer reviewer:

PEER EVALUATION QUESTIONS

1. What opportunity for change (or problem) sparked this essay?
2. What is the topic of this essay? What is the main idea the writer wants to convey about this topic?
3. What can you tell about the writer of this essay? What is his or her relationship to this topic?
4. Who is the audience? What information in the essay reveals the audience to you? What do you imagine are the needs and concerns of this audience? What might this audience do to address, resolve, or help resolve this problem?
5. What seems to be the relationship between the writer and the audience? How is the writer meeting the needs and concerns of this audience? What specific passages demonstrate the writer's use of the rhetorical appeals (ethos, pathos, and logos)?

6. What is the purpose of the writer's message? What is the relationship among the writer, the audience, and the writer's purpose? Do you have any other comments about the purpose?
7. What means is the writer using to deliver this message? How is this means appropriate to the situation?
8. What constraints are on the writer and this message?
9. What idea or passage in the essay is handled most successfully? Least successfully?
10. What are two questions you have for this writer?

These questions can be answered fairly quickly. Although you might be tempted to have your peer reviewer go through them quickly and orally, you'll be better served if you ask the peer reviewer to write his or her answers either on a separate piece of paper or directly on your draft. When it's your turn to evaluate a peer's draft, you may well come away from the experience surprised at how much you learned about your own writing. There's no better way to improve your own understanding than to explain something to someone else.

The peer reviewer of Stacy's paper offered her a good deal of advice, most of which had to do with large-scale revising, as you can see from his responses to questions 6 and 9:

6. I cannot tell for sure what your purpose is in writing this essay. You describe technology, but I'm not sure why. Do you want to explain the opportunities, or do you want to show how bad it can be for students? And I cannot tell who you're writing to—maybe just any reader? Still, I think you have a good start on a strong essay because you know so much neat stuff about all the technology here at school. I didn't know half this stuff.

9. The beginning of your essay is the least successful part; I can't tell by reading it where you're headed with your topic, so I think you're going to want to revise with a stronger purpose in mind. But as I said earlier, the strongest part of your essay is all the specific information you already know about using technology. No wonder you get such good grades. You don't have any conclusion yet. I think if you get a better start on your introduction that you can pull together your overall argument in your conclusion. Maybe talk about how technology is always thought of as being better, an improvement, but that it's not always, not really.

The peer reviewer confirmed what Stacy already thought: the introduction of the essay, especially the thesis statement, merited more of her attention. Earlier in this chapter, a **thesis** was defined as a controlling idea. More specifically, a **thesis statement** is a central idea stated in the form of an assertion, or claim, which indicates what you believe to be true, interesting, or valuable about your topic. A thesis statement also gives readers a clear idea of your purpose in writing, and it sometimes outlines the approach you'll take. Although it is often phrased as a single sentence, it doesn't need to be. Here is Stacy's first attempt at a thesis statement:

> Technology provides many advantages for students and teachers alike, but it also brings with it some disadvantages. In this essay, I'm going to talk about my experiences with technology, the advantages I've experienced and the disadvantages I feel.

Stacy identified her topic—use of technology by students and teachers—and forecast that she would be talking about both advantages and disadvantages. Her peer reviewer, though, was unclear about what Stacy's purpose was. So Stacy must concentrate on the connection between her purpose and audience as she creates a thesis statement that narrows her topic and makes a comment on that topic.

Editing and Proofreading a Response

Although the peer reviewer focused on Stacy's approach to the rhetorical situation, other evaluative responses had to do with smaller issues related to editing: improving word choice, adding specific details, and structuring sentences more effectively. Some writers revise, edit, and proofread simultaneously, while others focus their efforts on resolving the big issues (thesis statement, organization, and supporting information) before tackling editing and proofreading.

After the peer reviewer finished responding to Stacy's essay (and she to his), Stacy took his advice, wrote two more drafts, and edited and proofread her way to her final draft. Like most writers, Stacy stopped revising because she'd run out of time—not because she thought her essay was perfect in every way.

> WRITE FOR FIVE

1. How do you define *revision*?
2. When do you revise? Can you name the last piece of writing that you revised? Why did you choose to revise that particular piece?
3. What are your strengths as a reviser? Your weaknesses?
4. What features of revision do you like to have help with?
5. What features of proofreading and editing are you good at? Which could you use help with? Be prepared to share your answers with the rest of the class.

A Final Draft

Stacy's final draft appears on the following pages. She formatted her paper according to Modern Language Association (MLA) guidelines (see Chapter 19).

Simkanin 1

Anastasia Simkanin

Professor Glenn

Writing and Technology, English 270

22 October 2010

Technology and the Learning Process: One Student's View

Could today's college student survive without a microwave to heat
Easy Mac in her dorm room, a smartphone to check in on *Facebook* friends,
and a laptop streaming movies or music to escape the tedium of another
evening spent doing coursework? The answer is debatable. What's *not*
debatable, however, is that even though technology of various forms has
brought a certain ease to the lives of today's college students, it has also
allowed them to embark on serious academic pursuits that would not be
possible without technological innovation. •

> The thesis statement presents Stacy's position on the topic.

The Internet, for instance, offers students a wealth of advanced search
engines and online library databases. Many students find that such tools
open up a world of information, allowing more expedient research and, in
turn, stronger essays. But some people argue that the ease of computer
searching and the availability of almost anything over the Internet expose
students to the dangers of academic laziness and dishonesty. Which side is
right? The incorporation of technology into the learning process is a complex
matter and, like any powerful innovation, brings potential pitfalls as well as
advantages. Perhaps the best way to approach both sides of the issue is to
draw a clear picture of the pros and the cons, thereby assessing the different
ways that technology has revolutionized learning in today's universities. •

> Stacy forecasts her approach, which involves looking at both pros and cons of the use of technology, and also clarifies her purpose: to assess technology's effect on learning.

One major way that technological advances have facilitated the
learning process is by supplying students with a wealth of information that
could not be obtained without Internet resources. Online catalogues such

as *WorldCat*, for instance, allow users to search libraries anywhere in the world for books, articles, and more in a single step. *Borrow Direct* allows students to simultaneously search all Ivy League university libraries, and the University Library (sponsored by the Committee on Institutional Cooperation)

This is one of the places where Stacy responds to the peer reviewer's suggestion by including specific details about using resources.

allows the same type of search within Big Ten schools. Alternatively, students can opt to go to a specific library website, such as the online catalogue of Oxford University libraries, and begin their search there. With such a vast array of resources available, only very rarely is a student unable to find pertinent information. Having located a needed item, a student can file an electronic request through interlibrary loan and have the item delivered to a convenient location or even made available as a PDF download. A student in the United States who needs a rare manuscript held at the University of Cambridge in England can view important pages online. Whereas once students' research was limited to the resources in their own neighborhood, technology now allows them access to information in libraries across the Atlantic.

Not only does the Internet allow users to find information that is hard to obtain because it is held in distant locations, but it also allows them

This transition sentence links this paragraph to the preceding one.

access to information that is hard to obtain for a variety of other reasons. On those rare occasions when students are unable to find a needed item by searching library catalogues, they can look on sites such as eBay's *First Edition* and *Rare Books* and possibly locate a volume that is to be found only in someone's living room.

Besides searching *for* books, searching *through* them has been aided by technology as well. Writing a paper on *Great Expectations* and want to find the exact passage where Pip admits that Biddy is "immeasurably better than Estella"? Web resources such as the *Concordance of Great Books* allow users to type in a word or phrase and instantly see all the occurrences of those words in a book, along with the surrounding text and chapter numbers. *Google Book Search* and *Hathi Trust Digital Library* let users search for keywords and phrases within millions of books without any more effort than it takes to Google their topic. The above quotation, by the way, is found in chapter 17 of the Penguin edition.

Even with all the time it can save a student, the average dot-com site is not necessarily the top rung of the ladder of searching expediency. Today's students can easily write stronger, more persuasive papers by taking advantage of the information that online databases place at their fingertips. Compare, for instance, the effectiveness of saying "State University conferred many doctoral degrees in 2009" with the effectiveness of saying "State University conferred 513 doctoral degrees in 2009." Including statistics in their papers can make students' points sharper and more vivid, and databases such as *Historical Statistics of the United States* allow students to achieve this result. Other databases, such as *JSTOR* and *MUSE*, let students sort through full-length journal articles simply by moving their mouse. With libraries containing thousands of volumes of journals and periodicals, the amount of time saved through computer searches is immense. And, of course, consulting a database is a lot faster than surveying the 6,165 graduate students who were enrolled at State University in 2009.

> Stacy includes another specific detail that makes the essay more persuasive.

Not only is technology improving traditional methods of research and writing, it is also providing students with new ways to communicate and develop ideas. State University's *ANGEL* site is designed to give professors and students online space for managing their courses. By accessing *ANGEL*, students can click on the link for a course and view daily reminders, weekly assignments, selected lecture notes, and more. A favorite feature of *ANGEL* is its threaded discussion board. Online forums and live (online) office hours allow students and instructors to carry on the one-on-one discussion that is precluded by large class sizes and limited lecture time. In another step toward moving course discussion beyond the classroom setting, some instructors at State University—especially those who teach language classes—have experimented with "holding class" in a chat room. Online chats allow students to carry on multiple conversations at once, which gives them more opportunities to share and develop ideas. The fact that most students enjoy chat room discussion is an added bonus, as the appeal of something new and fun can go a long way in keeping students interested and eager to learn.

Given all the ways that technology is changing life for students, it is not surprising that some of the effects are less welcome than others. One possible pitfall of relying on technology is that, ironically, ignoring more traditional ways of research can sometimes reduce information—or at least information quality. Searching a library's database from home while a stereo plays in the background is more appealing to most students than taking a trip to the stacks, but what many students do not realize is that, though online catalogues are a great place to start, they are often not enough by themselves. Finding the approximate spot where a needed item is located and then looking through items on adjacent shelves or discussing resources with a reference librarian will almost always turn up more results than does an online catalogue search alone. When it comes to finding that approximate location, however, the catalogues are indeed the place to begin. The danger lies in placing convenience over quality. What many students find to be most convenient is conducting a simple online search using an engine like *Google*, but this method has its own set of problems. Anyone can create a page on the Internet: for example, my fourteen-year-old brother could post his middle school paper on how Jane Eyre's inheritance reveals Charlotte Brontë's secret obsession with the power of money. Would such a paper help a college student write a sophomore-level essay? Probably not. Being lured by the convenience of Web searches, students can sometimes forget to investigate the reliability of sources, thus compromising the quality of their work.

Perhaps the most serious dangers of depending too much on technology are the possibilities of academic laziness and dishonesty. There is *so* much information available online that a student can practically write a paper on a book without even opening it. Sites like *SparkNotes* are great when a student is running late for class and needs to quickly find out what happens in a particular chapter of a text or needs to refresh his or her memory of something read earlier, but a student will never get as much out of summary notes as out of reading the book. With free online literature notes replacing $5.99-a-copy *Cliffs Notes*, however, the temptation to skip out on one's assignments is becoming all the more pervasive.

More serious than simply consulting summary notes is another danger: plagiarism. Not only are notes on books available online, but so are entire essays on them. Whole sites are devoted to selling papers to students who are looking to avoid writing an essay themselves, and papers are sometimes available for free. Every college student knows the feeling of sitting at a computer screen late at night, trying to write a paper but having little success because of fatigue. Times like these are when the temptation to abuse technology arises, and a student might simply download someone else's essay, hand it in as her or his own, and get some sleep. While having an abundance of information available is usually a wonderful thing, today's college students need to be wary of letting technology do their work *for* them, rather than just helping them with it.

Because technology affects the learning process in so many ways, it cannot be judged as wholly positive or wholly negative. Perhaps it would not be fair to say either but to agree, instead, that though the value of Web content depends on how one uses it, the dramatic changes that have been brought on by recent advances are amazing. Technology is changing the way students learn and the way they write. Visual Culture, a 400-level English course at State University, encourages students to "write" essays in new ways, using images instead of words. Many students choose to obtain their images off the Internet or to present their visual essay in the form of a PowerPoint presentation or YouTube video. With "writing an essay" no longer requiring actual *writing*, there's little—if any—room to doubt that education today is being constantly shaped and molded as technology continues to progress. It will be interesting to see what the future brings.

Closing the essay with a focus on a course at her school demonstrates Stacy's awareness of her audience—her instructor.

> YOUR WRITING EXPERIENCES

1. Where does your best writing appear? What qualities of this writing lead you to judge it to be your best?
2. What writing do you feel most proud of? Why does this writing make you feel proud?
3. What opportunities for change (or problems) spur your best writing? Who is your audience? What is your purpose? What is the context? What is your medium for writing?
4. After reading this chapter and studying Stacy's writing process, describe two specific ways in which you could improve your own writing process. Be prepared to share your answer with the rest of the class.

Sharing the Experience
or Taste: Responding
th Memoirs

Rhetorical Situations for Composing

2

You already know how to engage in rhetorical situations; after all, for most of your life, you've been observing the elements of such situations (opportunity, audience, message, purpose, and context) in order to shape your messages purposefully into the most fitting responses. The following eight chapters will help you become more familiar with types of writing you've likely already practiced, even if you don't know them by the names used here. You'll come to understand how memoirs, profiles, investigative reports, position arguments, proposals, evaluations, and critical and literary analyses can serve as appropriate responses to rhetorical situations. As you work through the chapters, you'll recognize the everyday nature of rhetorical theory and practice. In addition, you'll understand how well you're already using rhetorical techniques, how you resort to these kinds of writing as your response, and how you can quickly become even more skilled in their use.

4 Sharing the Experience of Taste: Responding with Memoirs

Many college students—and former students—have had highly animated conversations about the cafeteria food at their schools. Legends have been passed down through the generations about the quality of the food and the havoc it could wreak on unsuspecting students. *Boston Globe* reporter Taryn Plumb interviewed University of New Hampshire students who "expressed unease about the long-standing rumor—common to many college campuses—that servers mix laxatives into recipes to safeguard against food poisoning or botulism." In his January 2000 article on the website epinions .com, "Fond Memories of a Congenital Glutton," Jonathan Kibera offered a different rumor, which circulated among the students at Harvard University: "We used to joke that there was one chicken dish at Harvard, the leftovers of which were reheated under different names throughout the week. General Wong's chicken on Monday had morphed into some greasy Kung Pao derivative by Wednesday, and could well have been the Soup du Jour by Friday."

© iStockphoto.com/Chris Schmidt

Chances are that more than once during your times in the college cafeteria you've longed for a home-cooked meal. Some alumni, on the other hand, have fond memories of the food they enjoyed while relaxing with their friends after a long day of classes. Readers of the food-related website Chowhound .com were asked to post stories about their college dining experiences in order to determine which college has the best food. Many contributors to the online discussion expressed longing for their school's unique delicacies. "Lidi B" of Penn State University opined, "Oh, to have a grilled sticky from the Ye Olde College Diner à la mode with Penn State Creamery ice cream . . . that would just about be heaven . . . ," and "Quick" from Cornell University admitted, "I still remember the great reuben and chicken salad sandwiches from Cascadeli, the Dijon burger and roast chicken from Ivy room, and the awesome breakfasts from Hughes." For each of these contributors, the thoughts of college food brought back pleasant memories—not only of the food itself but also of fun and relaxation with friends.

Memoirs are a kind of writing used to narrate and analyze significant experiences in our lives, including those concerning certain foods. Food-related memoirs, which are appearing in greater numbers on bookshelves around the world, present past experiences with food that resonate with a larger historical, psychological, or social meaning. For example, Diana Abu-Jaber's memoir of her childhood in upstate New York and Jordan, *The Language of Baklava*, centers on food but is also a reflection on living between two cultures. In other words, a good food-related memoir, like any memoir, is a kind of history that captures distinctive moments in the life of the writer and the larger society. Food memories are primarily sensory, starting with an aroma, a texture, or a visual delight but then encompassing an event, an occasion, or an interaction.

IDENTIFYING AN OPPORTUNITY

Throughout this chapter, you'll work to identify an opportunity for writing a memoir of an experience with food. You might focus on the food itself (how it's produced or prepared), or you might describe the sensory experience of eating it. Your memoir might capture a compelling food-related moment from your childhood or one from the more recent past. As you determine what you want to share, consider the most fitting means of delivery for your memoir:

Print Memoir

written for a community or campus newspaper or a local zine

Audio Memoir

recorded for a local radio station

Online Memoir

written as a blog entry or a contribution to a website

To begin, freewrite for five minutes in response to each of the following questions (or use any of the invention techniques presented on pages 58–61):

1. What kinds of food best represent your childhood? In other words, what foods did you eat at home and with your family? Of those foods, which ones were your personal favorites? If you are now living away from home at college, what kind of memories and emotions do thoughts of this food bring to mind?

2. What locations and foods make up the culture of food on your campus or in your community? Think about the restaurants, dining halls, convenience stores, snacks, take-out meals, and cafeteria offerings that make your school's or community's culture of food unique.

3. Select the location or food from the preceding questions that you find most significant, most memorable, or most satisfying. Write about the experiences you've had in this location or with this food or the memories that it brings to mind for you. Be as specific as possible when describing your experiences or memories.

Real Situations

Many food memories, like the ones the alumni posted online at Chowhound .com, are positive. On a discussion forum for Roadfood's website, "Mosca" reminisced similarly about a food truck just off Cornell's campus: "After 30 years I can still taste the (great) heartburn from the Ithaca hot truck, which was the source of my personal 'freshman 15.'" That hot truck is just one of numerous food trucks serving college campuses today or in the past, such as the Chinese Kitchen at Harvard, the grease trucks at Rutgers, Chuck's at the University of Miami, and the enchilada trucks at the University of Arizona.

This food truck at UCLA will no doubt become part of many students' memories.

Chocolate, perhaps more than any other food, provides delightful memories for people of all ages. Clotilde Dusoulier, the author of the blog *Chocolate & Zucchini*, prefers to enjoy high-quality chocolate with fresh coffee—for her, that combination simply makes for happiness.

On a Sunday afternoon, after a copious lunch, wait for your next-door neighbor Patricia to knock on your window with a wooden spoon. Agree to come over to their place for coffee. From the special chocolate cabinet in your kitchen (surely you must have one) grab what's left of the excellent dark chocolate with fragments of roasted cocoa beans that your friend Marie-Laure brought you last time she came for dinner. Walk next door in your socks. Leave Maxence and Stéphan to chat about Mac OS-X and guitar tuners in the living room, while you watch Patricia brew coffee on their espresso machine. When asked, opt for the designer coffee cups. Bring the four cups to the table on a metal tray. Take a cup, break a square of the chocolate, sit down, relax. Have a bite of chocolate, then a sip of coffee. —**Clotilde Dusoulier, "Happiness (A Recipe)"**

Some food memories are negative—yet still entertaining—as shown by the following excerpt from Ruth Reichl's food memoir:

This is a true story.

Imagine a New York City apartment at six in the morning. It is a modest apartment in Greenwich Village. Coffee is bubbling in an electric percolator. On the table is a basket of rye bread, an entire coffee cake, a few cheeses, a platter of cold cuts. My mother has been making breakfast—a major meal in our house, one where we sit down to fresh orange juice every morning, clink our glasses as if they held wine, and toast each other with "Cheerio. Have a nice day."

Right now she is the only one awake, but she is getting impatient for the day to begin and she cranks WQXR up a little louder on the radio, hoping that the noise will rouse everyone else. But Dad and I are good sleepers, and when the sounds of martial music have no effect she barges into the bedroom and shakes my father awake.

"Darling," she says, "I need you. Get up and come into the kitchen."

My father, a sweet and accommodating person, shuffles sleepily down the hall. He is wearing loose pajamas, and the strand of hair he combs over his bald spot stands straight up. He leans against the sink, holding on to it a little, and obediently opens his mouth when my mother says, "Try this."

Later, when he told the story, he attempted to convey the awfulness of what she had given him. The first time he said that it tasted like cat toes and rotted barley, but over the years the description got better. Two years later it had turned into pigs' snouts and mud and five years later he had refined the flavor into a mixture of antique anchovies and moldy chocolate.

AP Photo/Jeff Geissler

Ruth Reichl, formerly editor-in-chief of *Gourmet* magazine.

© Photos 12/Alamy

Food, Inc. has reached international markets with its hard look at the American food industry.

Whatever it tasted like, he said it was the worst thing he had ever had in his mouth, so terrible that it was impossible to swallow, so terrible that he leaned over and spit it into the sink and then grabbed the coffeepot, put the spout into his mouth, and tried to eradicate the flavor.

My mother stood there watching all this. When my father finally put the coffeepot down she smiled and said, "Just as I thought. Spoiled."

And then she threw the mess into the garbage can and sat down to drink her orange juice.

—**Ruth Reichl, "The Queen of Mold"**

As Reichl makes clear elsewhere in her memoir, Americans are not known for their appreciation of fine food. In fact, internationally, Americans are better known for their love of junk food and fast food. Eric Schlosser captures the fast food experience in the following excerpt:

Pull open the glass door, feel the rush of cool air, walk in, get in line, study the backlit color photographs above the counter, place your order, hand over a few dollars. Watch teenagers in uniforms pushing various buttons, and moments later take hold of a plastic tray full of food wrapped in colored paper and cardboard. The whole experience of buying fast food has become so routine, so thoroughly unexceptional and mundane, that it is now taken for granted, like brushing your teeth or stopping for a red light. It has become a social custom as American as a small, rectangular, hand-held, frozen and reheated apple pie.

—**Eric Schlosser,** *Fast Food Nation*

In recent years, the American culture of food has been the focus of a good deal of criticism. You've no doubt seen articles about the obesity epidemic in the United States, an epidemic linked directly to overconsumption of fast food. With 65.4 percent of Americans either overweight or obese, the detrimental effects of fast food consumption have been well publicized in books; in movies such as *Fast Food Nation, Super Size Me,* and *Food, Inc*; in public debates; and even in lawsuits.

In industrialized, developed nations like the United States, the culture of food is increasingly characterized by an overabundance of choices—from dozens of ethnic cuisines and hundreds of snack and frozen food products to fresh fruits, vegetables, and fish imported from around the globe and available twelve months a year. The once strong connection between eating and ritual, represented by Dusoulier's chocolate-and-espresso routine, is weakening in the United States. On-the-go eating habits and reliance on fast food don't necessarily lend themselves to meaningful experiences with nourishment, but many people still have vivid and personally significant memories of their experiences with food.

DESCRIBING THE CULTURE OF FOOD

1. Identify a key moment when you were first introduced to an unfamiliar kind of food. How did that event affect you?

2. Our food experiences are often shaped just as much by our visual sense as by smell or taste. We might think a food looks disgusting and thus resist tasting it, or we might favor a particular restaurant as much for its hip décor as for its food. Choose one of the images in this chapter and write for five minutes about what it suggests to you.

3. Working with a classmate, make a list of ways in which the eating habits of current college students either differ from those of past generations of students or differ from how those students ate when they lived with their parents. Explain how, when, and where you learned about these differences.

4. Call up a memory about awaiting a particular food—something that had not yet come into season, something only available at your family's vacation spot, something you would seek out upon your return to your hometown, or something always served at a holiday meal. Now write a description of that food and the anticipation of it.

5. Recall a negative stereotype about food on your college campus or in a nearby neighborhood, the ill effects of a particular food, or the students who eat that specific food. Write for several minutes about how that stereotype is perpetuated—or how you came to hear of it.

Real Responses to Real Situations

Telling the stories of their kitchens

With the proliferation of cable television channels such as the Food Network and Fine Living, specialty magazines such as *Cooking Light* and *Everyday Food,* and smartphone apps such as Epicurious, Yelp, and Urban Spoon, food lovers now have more ways than ever to satisfy their appetite for new recipe ideas, reviews of local restaurants and bars, descriptions of how their favorite foods are made, and stories about food industry personalities.

One particularly noteworthy contribution of the cooking and dining community to the entertainment industry has been the food memoir. Many good family recipes have interesting stories behind them, from Grandma and Grandpa's ill-fated experimentation with prune-filled pierogies on Christmas Eve in 1953 to a father's tale of picking onions in the blazing hot Texas summers, the same kind of onions his children are now piling high on top of their chili. The food memoir brings those narratives from the realm of family folklore and the margins of cookbooks to the *New York Times* bestseller list. Steve Inskeep, host of National Public Radio's *Morning Edition*, interviewed food memoirist Ruth Reichl, who helped him and his listeners understand this popular genre.

> Interview with Ruth Reichl: Favorite Food Memoirs

Steve Inskeep

STEVE INSKEEP: Okay. Some people love to eat, some people love to write about what they eat, and apparently many people love to read other people's writing about what they eat. Walk into a big bookstore and you may find an entire shelf devoted to food memoirs. So, this morning, we'll pull some books off that shelf to review them.

Our reviewer is Ruth Reichl, the editor of *Gourmet* magazine. She has written two food memoirs of her own, so she is the perfect person to answer this question. Would you explain what a food memoir is for somebody who's never read one?

RUTH REICHL: It's a sort of new genre where people are writing about their lives and food. I mean, they are actually looking at the world food-first. . . .

INSKEEP: You begin with the meal that you prepare and go on from there. There's actually a quote from George Orwell in one of these books. . . . This book by Bill Buford, called *Heat*, included a quote from George Orwell, which begins, "A human being is primarily a bag for putting food into."

REICHL: Many of the other authors that we will meet today don't quite agree with that.

INSKEEP: They think that there's meaning in food itself, and they try to draw out that meaning and try to draw larger meanings, don't they?

REICHL: Exactly.

INSKEEP: Let's talk about one of these books that you have selected here, *Animal, Vegetable, Miracle* by Barbara Kingsolver. Maybe that's an example of someone drawing a larger meaning out of what they eat.

REICHL: Well, Barbara Kingsolver . . . is by anybody's measure just an extraordinary writer. I just sort of opened the book at random and picked out one sentence. This is just her description of cactuses. It says, "The tall, dehydrated saguaros stood around all teetery and sucked in like very prickly super models." So here's this extraordinary writer who decides that for a year she and her family are going to try and raise all their food or get it from neighbors.

INSKEEP: What do they have to do without, if anything?

REICHL: Citrus, because . . .

INSKEEP: [It's from Florida and] they're in Virginia.

REICHL: Exactly. They had to do without almost all processed foods. They each got to choose one thing that would be outside of this law. So her husband chose coffee because, of course, there would be no coffee if you were totally feeding yourself.

INSKEEP: Did you find yourself thinking about what would be the one thing that you would insist on not doing without if you were doing this?

REICHL: Oh, there were so many things. And there are actually moments where you find them cheating a little. They do a party for her fiftieth birthday and suddenly they're doing these Vietnamese rice rolls. And I'm thinking, wait a minute, these rice paper wrappers, I don't believe that they were grown in Virginia.

INSKEEP: Now, how is a year of eating depicted differently, if at all, when we move to a book called *The Kitchen Diaries: A Year in the Kitchen with Nigel Slater*?

REICHL: I cannot tell you how much I love this book. Nigel Slater is an English writer and chef, and I don't think anybody has ever made food sound more delicious. When he describes a beet, for instance, it comes alive for you on the page and you suddenly want to run out and eat as many beets as you possibly can. . . . This is from late May. He says, "There were beets at the farmers market today. I buy six, each the size of a plum and the color of damson jam. The stalks are young and translucent, a vivid magenta purple, yet the beets have the coarse, curly whiskers of an old man. They need no washing, just a rub with a wet thumb and a while in a very hot oven. I cut off the stalks, leaving a short tuft behind, then put the beets in a roasting tin with a splash of water and cover the tin with foil. An hour in the oven and they are done. Their skin slides off effortlessly to reveal sweet, ruby flesh." And everything he talks about is like that, and I mean there's no "shoulds" in this. It's just sheer pleasure and sensuousness in food.

INSKEEP: How long has this sort of food memoir been around?

REICHL: I think that M. F. K. Fisher really, at least for us in the United States, is the person who first wrote a food memoir. And hers was written in the forties. She wrote a book called *The Gastronomical Me*. She says that when she's writing about food, what she's really writing about are larger things, about love and our need for it. And she has a wonderful quote when she says she believes that we would all be better people if we paid attention to our appetites.

INSKEEP: May I read a sentence or two from that very book? This is from—she's remembering something that happened in 1912. She says: "The first thing I remember tasting and then wanting to taste again is the grayish-pink fuzz my grandmother skimmed from a spitting kettle of strawberry jam. I suppose I was about four." That doesn't actually sound very delectable, but it's clearly about the relationship there, isn't it?

REICHL: It is about the relationship, and it's about the memory. And actually, Barbara Kingsolver has a wonderful quote where she talks about when she's cooking, all the people who taught her to cook are standing in the kitchen with her and that there's a sort of communion of the stove and that they're all there, you know, every time she cooks. And it's that same idea, that the act of cooking is sort of going down through the ages and it's, you know, passed on from mother to daughter, from grandmother to child, and that there's a kind of sacred place in the kitchen where your relatives come to join you when you cook.

Julie Powell, author of *Julie & Julia* and *The Julie/Julia Project*.

Even though every bookstore offers at least a shelf's worth of food memoirs, and cable television features round-the-clock cooking shows, our appetite for food-related media has not yet been satisfied. The increasing popularity of cooking shows such as the Food Network's *Iron Chef America* and Bravo's *Top Chef* and of cookbooks such as Jamie Oliver's *Jamie's Food Revolution* and Renee Behnke and Cynthia Nims's *Memorable Recipes to Share with Family and Friends* is proof.

But books and television shows are not the only indications that we Americans have an insatiable hunger for food-related media. Food-focused blogs have become a cottage industry, with literally thousands appearing online daily. Some of these blogs are compelling, well-written, and photographically stunning; they focus on bacon, chocolate, finding the best tamale, cooking professionally or at home, and an array of other topics. One of the most successful of such blogs was *The Julie/Julia Project*, which attracted forty, fifty, sometimes even eighty comments a day from readers interested in Julie Powell's culinary and personal journey. In the blog, as in Powell's spin-off food memoir (*Julie & Julia: 365 Days, 524 Recipes, 1 Tiny Apartment Kitchen*) and the movie based on it (*Julie & Julia*), Powell narrates her year-long effort to pull herself out of a rut of living in a run-down New York apartment, working in dead-end secretarial jobs, and approaching her thirtieth birthday without a clear direction in her life. Her recovery came in the form of her mother's battered copy of Julia Child's classic cookbook, *Mastering the Art of French Cooking*. Powell cooked every recipe in Child's influential cookbook—from Filets de Poisson Bercy aux Champignons and Poulet Rôti to Carottes à la Concierge and Crème Brûlée—and recorded her reflections on these cooking ventures on her blog. In Powell's blog and memoir (as well as in the movie), Julia Child becomes a model, not just for aspiring cooks, but for anyone who wants to keep learning while growing older.

Excerpt from

> The Julie/Julia Project

Julie Powell

Working with the book, one comes to know Julia as a teacher—a brilliant one, with a spark of humor, a passion for her subject, and an unfailing intuition for how to create a feeling of comfort in the midst of chaotic striving. But in her shows, and particularly her later ones, "Cooking with Master Chefs," . . . Julia proves an exemplary, and inspirational, student. She is endlessly curious—every time she sticks her big, curled paws into a pot of boiling water, or right under the flying knife of a chef forty years her junior, to pick up some bit of something to taste, the tiny bit of my soul that still harbors a belief in a higher power squeezes its eyes shut and crosses its fingers and prays as hard as it can that when I am her age, I'll be just like Julia. She asks endless questions—in the episode PBS is so obsessed with that they show it about once a week, it's the anti-flatulence properties of epazote that holds her attention, to a rather unseemly degree—and always seems glad to learn from the people she brings on to the show, often wet-eared young whippersnappers who treat her like she's some dotty old biddy until I want to grab them by the shoulders and shake them— "Show some respect, kid, this is *Julia,* and you wouldn't be here if it wasn't for her!!!" But she never seems to feel slighted or disrespected—really, in the end, how could she? She is Julia—always changing, but always, utterly, herself. As a student, on these shows, she's teaching us all how to learn.

She has a wonderful aside in [the] endlessly repeated episode about lard—when she gets off the epazote for a minute. "We should talk about this," she warbles, as Rick dumps a nice big scoop of lard into a frying pan, "because everyone's so *afraid* of lard." They discuss the pros and cons of the stuff—less cholesterol than butter, but more saturated fats, the authenticity lard lends to Latin American dishes, etc. . . . , and Julia says, "The point is, if you don't want to make something right, *don't make it.* Choose something else. Like making tamales with olive oil, it's *TERRIBLE!"* And her voice swoops briefly up into the stratosphere, and you feel this passion in her, and yes, she's probably had a glass or two of wine, which God love her she deserves, but to me the wonderful thing is the hint that there's yet another Julia, another face. I've learned from the teacher and I've learned again from the student, but when she talks of lard, Julia hints that there is another, wilder, Julia beneath it all, a rebellious, passionate, dare I say *dangerous* individual. Was it this Julia who joined [the] OSS and created shark repellent? Or maybe just this Julia who walked into a cooking school in France—no longer a spring chicken herself, but with an unquenchable fire in her that she herself didn't quite understand. That's the Julia I'm striving toward, the Julia that I hope someday to be like.

> ANALYZING THE RHETORICAL SITUATION

The texts in this section suggest that food memoirs have great appeal for many people in the United States. The following questions ask you to consider this kind of writing in terms of the elements of the rhetorical situation. You'll want to reread the excerpts in this section carefully before answering.

1. Who might be the intended audience of Julie Powell's food blog *The Julie/Julia Project*? What textual evidence can you provide for your answer? Be prepared to share your answers with the rest of the class.

2. To what rhetorical opportunity is Steve Inskeep responding? How does his interview address that opportunity?

3. Who might be the intended audience for Inskeep's interview with Ruth Reichl on food memoirs? How does Inskeep's audience differ from Powell's? What textual evidence supports your conclusions?

4. Is the purpose of each excerpt in this section evident? If so, what is the purpose of each one? What are the differences among the excerpts in terms of purpose? And how does each purpose relate to the writer's or speaker's intended audience? Again, be prepared to share your answers with the rest of the class.

5. The publication or recording of each of the pieces in this section occurred in the past. Keeping that in mind, suggest a rhetorical opportunity for change to which each piece might be a response. How does the piece work to resolve or address that opportunity?

6. How does each writer and speaker demonstrate his or her use of the rhetorical appeals of ethos, logos, and pathos to fulfill the purpose? Cite passages from the texts to support your answer.

The changing significance of food

Some food memoirists share their experience of tasting the fresh winter-into-spring salad or their first failed attempt at flipping omelets; others have focused their attention on better understanding people's relationship to food and the consequences of that relationship. Indeed, the growing popularity of food writing and programming within the entertainment industry suggests that

Americans connect food more with pleasure and fun than with nourishment and sustenance. Newspaper headlines over the past few years have begun to warn readers about scientific findings that link growing health epidemics to problematic obsessions with food. However, this evolving relationship with food has been a topic that some anthropologists and sociologists have been writing and speaking about for decades.

Margaret Mead (1901–1978) was the most influential and the most persistent explorer of the American culture of food. A graduate of Barnard College with a degree in psychology, Mead went on to earn a PhD in anthropology at Columbia University. After graduate school, believing that understanding human behavior held great promise for the future, Mead conducted research among adolescents in Samoa, which culminated in the 1928 publication of the now classic *Coming of Age in Samoa*. In another of her studies, Mead argued that the biological differences between men and women should not preclude women's full participation in the world. All of Mead's anthropological work—whether

AP Photo

Margaret Mead holds a baby on Admiralty Island, Papua New Guinea, in 1954.

on indigenous cultures, social roles, or family structure—advanced the idea that human traits are primarily social, not biological.

Mead's observations on the social influences on human traits were continued in her sociological studies of Americans' eating habits. During World War II (1939–1945), for instance, she focused her research on the culture of food in the United States. At that time, she was one of the scientists and social scientists recruited by the U.S. government to conduct various "national character" studies and then to give public policy advice. As an anthropologist already versed in the interconnectedness of all aspects of human life, Mead understood the connections among the elements of national character, including ritual, belief, and identity—and the ways those elements linked up with the culture of food.

Mead remained interested in food and nutrition throughout the tremendous social and cultural changes of the 1960s in the United States. As a skilled writer and observer of human behavior and social structures, she continued to study both domestic and international changes in the availability of food and the consequences of the increased efficiency, automation, and industrialization of the food industry. She had good reason to be concerned with such issues: famine struck India and Pakistan in the late 1960s. And despite the great progress of U.S. agriculture during that same time, hunger was a major American problem as well, as Marion Nestle, author of *Food Politics,* points out. Even today, despite agricultural advances, hunger affects 50 million Americans, or one-sixth of the nation's population, with children and the elderly at the greatest risk, according to the organization Food First.

When President Lyndon Baines Johnson took office in 1963, poverty and hunger affected one-fifth of all Americans. He declared a war on poverty and established food assistance programs, some of which still remain. Around that same time, Margaret Mead dedicated herself to updating the World War II–era findings of the National Research Council's Committee for the Study of Food Habits, believing that social and technological developments had significantly altered the way people ate in the United States. In a section of her update, Mead observes the following:

> In the United States, within the lifetime of one generation, there has been a dramatic shift from malnutrition as a significant nutritional state on a national scale, to over-nutrition as one of the principal dangers to the nation's health. Over-nutrition, in the United States, may be attributed to food habits carried over from a situation of relative scarcity to one of plenty and to the development of food vending methods which continually expose people to an extreme amount and variety of foods. . . . Today we may distinguish an increasing number of affluent industrialized countries in which it is essential to develop an educational system within which children can learn self-regulation in the face of tremendous variety. Conditions in these countries contrast sharply with those which prevail—and may be expected to continue to prevail—in the underdeveloped areas of the world, where children must still be taught a rather rigid adherence to a diet that is only just sufficient for survival.
>
> —**Margaret Mead,** *Food Habits Research: Problems of the 1960s*

Prepackaged and highly processed foods are often consumed along with entertainment today.

Mead's observations about Americans' eating habits led her to consider the changing significance of food in people's lives. No longer was food being used to commemorate special events or traditions; instead, it was used for easy consumption or quick entertainment, with little thought for its nutritional value. In her update, Mead also noted dramatic alterations in the way food was produced (mass production), prepared (breaded and fried), and distributed (frozen and canned). Given the current debates over American diets, eating habits, and agricultural practices—as well as the presence of widespread hunger—Mead's writing now seems prophetic. She brought national attention to the split between food as nourishment and food as a commercial commodity as well as to the profound postwar changes in the foods produced by industrialized nations and their distribution (or lack thereof).

In 1970, Mead published what would become one of her most famous essays, "The Changing Significance of Food," which appeared in the magazine *American Scientist.* Mead argued that despite all the national attention, the United States remained dangerously ignorant of its food-related challenges and capabilities. "Today, for the first time in the history of mankind," she asserts, "we have the productive capacity to feed everyone in the world." But the United States was not feeding every American, let alone everyone else in the world. World hunger and food scarcity simply had not yet been properly addressed. Mead used this essay, then, to single out conditions that had contributed to this refusal or inability to recognize the severity of the situation. In the following passage, Mead describes one such condition—the increase in the "diseases of affluence."

Excerpt from

> # The Changing Significance of Food

Margaret Mead

In a country pronounced only twenty years before to be one-third ill-fed, we suddenly began to have pronouncements from nutritional specialists that the major nutritional disease of the American people was over-nutrition. If this had simply meant overeating, the old puritan ethics might have been more easily invoked, but it was over-nutrition that was at stake. And this in a country where our ideas of nutrition had been dominated by a dichotomy which distinguished food that was "good for you, but not good" from food that was "good, but not good for you." This split in man's needs, into our cultural conception of the need for nourishment and the search for pleasure, originally symbolized [by] the rewards for eating spinach or finishing what was on one's plate if one wanted to have dessert, lay back of the movement to produce, commercially, nonnourishing foods. Beverages and snacks came in particularly for this demand, as it was the addition of between-meal eating to the three square, nutritionally adequate meals a day that was responsible for much of the trouble.

We began manufacturing, on a terrifying scale, foods and beverages that were guaranteed not to nourish. The resources and the ingenuity of industry were diverted from the preparation of foods necessary for life and growth to foods non-expensive to prepare, expensive to buy. And every label reassuring the buyer that the product was not nourishing increased our sense that the trouble with Americans was that they were too well nourished. The diseases of affluence, represented by new forms of death in middle-age, had appeared before we had . . . conquered the diseases of poverty—the ill-fed pregnant women and lactating women, sometimes resulting in irreversible damage to the ill-weaned children, the school children so poorly fed that they could not learn. . . .

It was hard for the average American to believe that while he struggled, and paid, so as not to be overnourished, other people, several millions, right in this country, were hungry and near starvation. The contradiction was too great. . . . How can the country be overnourished and undernourished at the same time?

For Mead, the increased availability of highly processed snack foods and drinks and American businesses' focus on these products were proof that the United States had a problem with over-nutrition and food abundance. The boom in consumer goods and prepared foods—from TV dinners to baby formula—rendered nearly invisible the millions of Americans who were not

AP Photo/Columbus Dispatch, Eric Albrecht

In a cafeteria at Kenyon University in Ohio, the word *Local* on the salad bar sneeze guard tells diners that the food came from a nearby family farm.

benefiting from food surpluses. Mead warned that once food became an international commodity, a product separated entirely from its cultural and nutritional significance, its production, distribution, and consumption would become a huge international problem.

Margaret Mead warned about the trend toward easy-to-make, prepackaged foods that were believed to be a solution to the world's nutrition problems because they seemed easier to distribute and consume. You likely have experienced the end results of this trend in the school cafeterias where you went to grade school, high school, and college. These facilities have long struggled to balance the need to provide students with nourishing foods with the constraint of a limited budget, while keeping students happy that they're eating something that tastes good. If you're like many college students, you may be more than a little skeptical about or resistant to some of the culinary offerings in your college cafeteria, and you may even buy into the rumors about what the cooks may be stirring into your dinner.

Many college dining facilities are seeking to change students' negative impressions and to assume nutritional responsibility for their students and ecological responsibility for their communities at the same time. And while they're at it, these new-and-improved cafeterias are having an influence on the college recruiting process. The following excerpt from an article in the *Atlantic Monthly* describes efforts by Yale University to provide students with delicious foods while also teaching them the value of producing foods in locally sustainable ways.

> Good-bye Cryovac

Corby Kummer

I recently washed up after a supper consisting of four kinds of vegetables from the farmers' market—all four of them vegetables I usually buy at the local right-minded supermarket. As I considered the vivid, distinctive flavor of every bite, I thought, What is that stuff I've been eating the rest of the year?

One of the twelve residential colleges at Yale University is trying to give students that kind of summertime epiphany at every meal, by serving dishes made from produce raised as close to New Haven as possible. In just two years the Yale Sustainable Food Project has launched two ambitious initiatives to bridge the distance from farm to table: the complete revamping of menus in Berkeley College's dining hall to respect seasonality and simplicity, and the conversion of an overgrown lot near campus to an Edenic organic garden. The garden does not supply the dining hall—it couldn't. Rather, it serves as a kind of Greenwich Mean Time, suggesting what is best to serve, and when, by illustrating what grows in the southern New England climate in any given week. The goal of the project is to sell students on the superior flavor of food raised locally in environmentally responsible (but not always organic) ways, so that they will seek it the rest of their lives.

A few dishes I tasted last summer during a pre-term recipe-testing marathon in Berkeley's kitchen convinced me that this goal is within reach for any college meals program willing to make an initial outlay for staff training and an ongoing investment in fewer but better ingredients. I would be happy to eat pasta with parsnips once a week, for example, the candy-sweet roots sharpened by fresh parsley and Parmesan. In fact, I demanded the recipe. Any restaurant would be pleased to serve fresh asparagus roasted with a subtle seasoning of balsamic vinegar and olive oil alongside, say, filet of beef. Even the chicken breasts, coated with black pepper, grilled, and served with a shallot, garlic, and white-wine sauce, tasted like chicken.

Not long ago a college would never have thought to mention food in a brochure or on a school tour—except, perhaps, in a deprecating aside. Now food is a competitive marketing tool, and by the second or third stop on the college circuit parents and students practically expect to be shown the organic salad bar and told about the vegan options and the menus resulting directly from student surveys. Yale has gone these colleges what I consider to be a giant step further, showing students what they should want and making them want it.

As caring about food has become interwoven with caring about the environment, enjoying good food has lost some of the elitist, hedonistic taint that long barred gourmets from the ranks of the politically correct. The challenge, as with any political movement, is to bring about practical institutional change that incorporates ideals.

It's a very big challenge with college food, almost all of which is provided by enormous catering companies like Sodexho, Chartwells, and Aramark, the company that has run Yale's dining services since 1998. These companies have long offered vegetarian, organic, and vegan choices. But none of those options—not

continued

even, sadly, going organic—necessarily supports local farmers and local econo-mies, or shows students how much better food tastes when it's made from scratch with what's fresh. Vegetarian, organic, and vegan foods can all be processed, over-seasoned, and generally gunked up, and in the hands of institutional food-service providers they usually are. . . .

Whatever the argument for spending more money on food . . . , the practi-cal successes at Yale should encourage other schools to consider similar changes. [Associate Director of the Yale Sustainable Food Project Josh] Viertel gives the example of granola, a simple seduction tool. At the beginning of this year the Food Project's formula of organic oats, almonds, and raisins, a local honey, and New England maple syrup was so popular that Commons had to take over mak-ing it for every college. And the project's recipe is actually cheaper than buying pre-made granola in bulk. Viertel recently began a composting program; the first step is asking students to scrape their own plates, which shows close up the waste involved when they take, say, just one bite of cheese lasagne. Other schools ought to take that same step, even if they stop there. . . .

Kummer's description of this food project at Yale University illustrates the kinds of efforts going on at some colleges to combat the disturbing trend to-ward "over-nutrition" that Mead saw four decades ago. While Mead emphasized the social and, elsewhere in her writings, the environmental benefits that would follow from producing more locally based diets, Kummer adds the element of economic gain that colleges and universities would achieve by enticing more stu-dents to their schools. Indeed, we can all imagine that such locally oriented dining experiences might someday leave all of us longing for the days in college cafete-rias, not only because we experienced such great times relaxing and telling stories with friends, but also because we were eating such delicious, inventive foods.

> ANALYZING THE RHETORICAL SITUATION

1. What is "over-nutrition," and how does Mead argue that it came to be a problem?
2. What evidence does Mead provide to demonstrate that diseases of affluence result not just from biological traits but also from social traits? Who is the audience for this argument? What is her purpose?
3. What problems (or rhetorical opportunities) does Mead address? What arguments does she make about the roots of these problems? What evidence does she provide to support these claims about the sources of the problems?
4. What is Mead's purpose, given her audience? Provide textual evidence for your answer.
5. What are Mead's proposals for solving the problems she identifies? Referring to your answer to question 4, suggest how her intended audience might help her resolve or address the problem she's investigating.

6. How does Mead use the rhetorical appeals to build the arguments in her two pieces? Provide textual evidence to support your answer. Which of the rhetorical appeals does she rely on most? Be prepared to share your answer with the rest of the class.

7. What rhetorical opportunities prompted Kummer's piece on the Sustainable Food Project at Yale University? How would you characterize the relationship between his work and Mead's theories? In what ways is he helping to develop the conversation about the culture of food in the United States?

COMMUNITY CONNECTIONS

1. How do Julie Powell's reflections and descriptions coincide with or diverge from your experiences with cooking and with food? Take about ten minutes to write your response.

2. Now do the same for the pieces by Mead and Kummer: how do their analyses coincide with or diverge from your experiences or observations about the culture of food in the United States?

3. Do you agree with Mead's argument that "ideas of nutrition [in the United States have] been dominated by a dichotomy which distinguished food that was 'good for you, but not good' from food that was 'good, but not good for you'"? Draw on your experiences in childhood or in college to support your answer.

4. Now that you have considered various arguments made about humans and their relationships with food, how would you describe the culture of food on your campus or in your community? What food options or eating habits seem most significant to you? What economic, political, social, cultural, or biological forces have shaped the culture of food?

Memoirs: A Fitting Response

A memoir on food and culture

Food triggers vivid memories for all of us—some joyous or satisfying, others painful or awkward. Food can also serve to define our relationships with family, friends, and even complete strangers. Many writers have discussed their experiences with food in their memoirs precisely to trigger reflections on defining moments in their lives or to crystallize their own perceptions of people and cultures. Pooja Makhijani provides one such reflective memoir in her essay "School Lunch." As you read, notice the rich details that Makhijani provides to help readers visualize, smell, taste, and even feel the food that her mother packed for her each day before she left for school. As you take pleasure in these descriptions, though, see how Makhijani uses her descriptions of food to illustrate a larger point about her relationship with her mother and with the American culture in which she wants to immerse herself.

School Lunch

© 2003. Reprinted by permission.

Pooja Makhijani

Mom says she is being "sensible" about what I eat and she likes to pack "sensible" lunches. Plastic sandwich bags filled with blood-red pomegranate seeds. Fresh raisin bread wrapped in foil. Homemade vegetable biryani made with brown rice and lima beans. Yellow pressed rice with potatoes and onions. A silver thermos full of warm tamarind-infused lentil soup. Blue and white Tupperware containers that can be reused. Lunch sacks that have to be brought home every day. Silverware.

I don't want her lunches. I want to touch a cold, red Coca-Cola can that will hiss when I open it. I want to pull out a yellow Lunchables box so I can assemble bite-size sandwiches with Ritz crackers and smoked turkey. I want to smell tuna salad with mayonnaise and pickles. I want bologna on white bread, Capri Sun Fruit Punch, and Cool Ranch Doritos in a brown paper bag. I want plastic forks that I can throw away when I am done eating. But I am too scared to ask her. I know she will say, "No."

"Why don't you invite Chrissy over this Friday after school?" Mom ladles a spoonful of sweetened, homemade yogurt into a white ceramic bowl. "You've already been to her house twice." I hoist myself onto one of the high chairs at my kitchen table and pull my breakfast toward me. I tear the hot masala roti into eight irregular pieces and dip the largest one into the cold yogurt.

"I will, I will." I rub my fingers on the paper towel in my lap. The last time I went to Chrissy's house, Mrs. Pizarro gave us mini–hot dogs wrapped in pastry topped with a squirt of mustard, and tall glasses of Hawaiian Punch as an after-school snack. I can't imagine Chrissy coming to our house and munching on cauliflower and broccoli florets while gulping down chilled milk. I don't want to think about all the questions she will ask. When she sees the bronze Ganesh idol on the wooden stool near the sofa, she will inquire, *What is that elephant-headed statue in your living room?* When she sniffs the odor of spices that permeates the bedrooms, she will question, *What's the smell?* And when she accidentally touches my mother's henna colored sari, she will query, *What's your mom wearing?*

"I will," I say between bites so Mom won't ask me again. "Just not this week."

She glances at the clock on the oven. "Hurry up with your food, beti. Nishaat Aunty will be here any second." She grabs the rest of the roti, dunks it into the yogurt, and shovels it into my mouth. Thick globs of yogurt slide in rivulets down her palms and she licks it off once I am done eating. She wipes her hands on her red gingham apron and hands me a bulging brown paper bag. "Your lunch," she says.

"What did you pack today?" I ask as I shove the bag into my purple canvas backpack alongside my spelling and math textbooks.

"Aloo tikkis. Left over from last night."

"Oh." I part the curtains of the kitchen window and look for Nishaat Aunty's midnight-blue station wagon. "Chrissy brought Coke with her to school yesterday." I look into her eyes, hoping she will understand.

The writer provides examples with details to help readers visualize the contents of the lunches she totes to school. She also introduces the main characters of her memoir, including herself as the narrator.

With the short first sentence of the second paragraph, the writer creates tension between her and her mother, tension that will give momentum to the rest of the memoir.

The writer also introduces dialogue, which reveals the first-person point of view. The essay moves from scene to scene during a pivotal period of the author's life.

The writer uses description to help readers visualize the cultural differences she believes are keeping her distanced from friends at school.

As she uses flashforward to describe what will happen in the future, the writer concentrates on, detailed descriptions, characters, setting, and a sequence of events.

"Coca-Cola! During school?" she says. "Of course, that's what those American parents do. That's why their children are so hyper and don't concentrate on their studies." I am not allowed to drink soda, except on Saturdays when Mom makes fried fish. Recently, I've been drinking lots of apple juice because she is worried that there is too much acidity in orange juice.

"Okay, class, time for lunch." Miss Brown, my fifth-grade teacher, puts down the piece of chalk and rubs her hands on her chocolate-brown pleated pants, leaving behind ghostly prints. She grabs her cardigan off her chair and heads to the teachers' lounge near the gym.

Our lunch aide, Ms. Bauer, walks into the classroom. Her long silver hair cascades over her shoulders and down her back, hiding her ears.

Describing the aide calling out the rows one by one provides transitions for the movement in this scene.

"Row One, you can go to the closets and get your money or your food," Ms. Bauer's raspy voice instructs the five students in the front of the room. I wait for her to call "Row Four" so I can run to the back of the classroom and yank my sack off the top shelf of the closet. Every day, I take my food out of my sack and slide it into my desk. I leave it there until the end of the day so I can throw it away in the large garbage bin next to Principal Ward's office before I head home.

"Row Two." I look out the window. I see the rusty swing set in the front of Washington School. Before Christmas, there were three wooden planks attached to the bar. This spring, only one remains and it sways, lonely, in an early April breeze.

"Row Three." By now, several of my classmates have lined up near the globes in front of the room. They will wait there until everyone whose parents gave them a dollar and two quarters this morning have lined up. Ms. Bauer will walk them down the hall to the temporary lunch stations and they will bring back compartmentalized Styrofoam trays loaded with food.

The writer builds the readers' sense of anticipation: what's she going to do once Ms. Bauer calls "Row Four"? Building a sense of anticipation also builds toward the climax, or turning point, of the narrative.

"Row Four." I bolt. As I reach for my sack, I feel someone tug on my pink turtleneck. I turn around to see who tapped me on the shoulder.

"Aisha." She reintroduces herself.

It's the new girl. Mr. Ward brought her to our classroom on Monday, right after we had finished the Pledge of Allegiance. "Aisha's family just came from Pakistan two days ago," he said. "Please make her feel welcome."

Miss Brown rearranged our desks a bit, and put Aisha in the center of the room. Then she pulled down the world map and gave everyone a quick geography lesson. "Now, who can find Pakistan?" she asked. Even though I knew, I didn't raise my hand. Months before, we'd studied India and Pakistan and Bangladesh in our South Asia unit in social studies. As we took turns reading aloud paragraphs, Miss Brown asked me to read the longest section on topography of the subcontinent. "And in the northeast, Nepal is separated from Tibet by the mighty Himalayan Mountains," I concluded as I heard snickers behind me.

Finding Pakistan on the map serves an important purpose in the story: it deepens the readers' sense of the writer's awkwardness as she tries to blend into her American surroundings.

"Hima-aa-layan," Eddie whispered to no one in particular.

"It's Him-a-lay-an." Miss Brown corrected me at the same time. An accent of the first syllable. Short 'a' sounds. Four quick strokes and not the drawn-out vowels that had rolled off my tongue.

I wasn't going to pronounce "Pakistan" the way I knew how to—with a hissing "st" sound not heard in the English language.

"Will you have lunch at my desk today?" she asks. Today, just like yesterday, she wears her fanciest salwaar khameez to school. Yesterday, she wore a blue kurta over a satin

The inclusion of undefined cultural terms demonstrates the writer's fluency with the terms and enhances her sense of not fitting in.

white churidaar, and today she wears a shimmery lavender top decorated with clusters of pearls along the edges. She slings her dupatta over her left shoulder. It is longer in the front than in the back and the end gets caught in the heel of her white chappal.

I look down at my cuffed jeans and wonder if she wants to wear sneakers. Will everyone ask Aisha questions about what she is wearing, why she has an accent, or where she comes from? I have always said "No, thank you" when Chrissy or Heather have asked me to eat with them because I don't want to explain anything that makes me different from them. Will I have to explain things about Aisha too? I don't know whether to say yes and be nice, or say no, and read a book while waiting for recess.

"Sure, I'll eat with you," I say finally. I know she has asked me to sit at her desk because I am the only person in the classroom who looks somewhat like her.

She looks relieved. "I have to go buy some food." She rummages through her fleece-lined jacket and takes out $1.50. "Pull your chair up to my desk. I will be back in ten minutes." I watch her get into the lunch line that Ms. Bauer directs out the door.

I drag my chair over to the front of the room. I haven't had a chance to stuff my lunch into my desk, so I peer inside my bag.

I see Mom's aloo tikkis. She's stuffed the leftover potato patties inside a hard roll from La Bonbonniere bakery. The deep-fried flattened ball of potato is spiked with garam masala and shoved into a bun slathered with fresh coriander chutney, which Mom makes with coarsely ground almonds that crunch in my mouth when I least expect it. Below the sandwich are a bunch of grapes in a Ziplock bag. No dripping-wet can of Sprite. No Little Debbie apple pie. No Hostess chocolate cupcakes filled with vanilla cream. No strawberry Pop-Tarts.

I zip up my bag again and wait for Aisha to return. She brings back her tray and places it on her desk. Today's lunch is six chicken nuggets, a spoonful of corn, sticky peach halves floating in sugar syrup, and a tough dinner roll.

"I thought you would have started eating by now." Aisha pierces her chocolate milk carton with a straw.

"I am not that hungry." My stomach growls. I am used to ignoring the sounds. I can usually get through the day on the normal, easily-explainable-if-anyone-sees food. Carrot sticks, apple slices, or Saltines.

"But you brought your lunch. I saw you take something out of the bag. What is it?" she insists.

I reach inside my bag and feel the crusty bread. I draw it out, pressing it between my fingers and thumb, flattening it into a tiny Frisbee, mashing the roll into the soft potatoes.

"See, it is just bread." The disk is so flat that you can't see the tikki inside.

"No, there's something inside it." Aisha peers at the sandwich. "Is that an aloo tikki in a bun? I wish my mother would pack them in my lunch for me. Yesterday, I bought peanut-butter-and-jelly sandwiches. I've never had peanut butter before. It's such a funny food. It stuck to the back of my teeth and I could taste it for the rest of the day."

I look at the flattened mess in my hands and think about licking peanut butter from the crevices in my mouth. I gaze at Aisha's chicken nuggets.

"Wanna trade?" I ask.

"Are you sure? If I were you, I'd keep my food." She cocks her head and her eyes dart between the multicolored array in front of her and the earth-tone concoction just a few inches away from her.

The writer doesn't stop at describing the food that is in her lunch bag; she also describes the food that is not there. In this way, she sets up a comparison and contrast that leads into the following scene comparing Pooja's and Aisha's comfort levels with American culture.

"If you want it, you can have it." My fingers inch over to her side of the desk.

"You can have everything except the corn. I like that." She passes her plate to me and I hand my lunch to her.

"How long have you been here?" I devour all the chicken nuggets before Aisha changes her mind.

"We just got here last weekend. We are living in Edison Village, right near the train station." She nibbles her way around the entire circumference of the bun. "You've probably been here longer than that. You sound American."

I realize she is commenting on the way I pronounce words. Her accent sounds like my mother's. "I was born in New York. I've lived in Edison as long as I can remember."

"Then why don't you eat the school lunch?" Aisha spoons the corn into her mouth.

I don't have an answer for Aisha. I know it's not because it's too expensive or that Styrofoam trays are environmentally unsound. It's because Mom thinks her deep-fried aloo tikkis and freshly ground masalas are what good Indian parents give their daughters. She doesn't understand that good Indian daughters just want to become American. •

It's too complicated an issue to explain. Like my mother, Aisha won't understand it.

"Time for recess." Ms. Bauer claps her hands three times. I throw the tray and the plastic utensils in the garbage can in the front of the room, and Aisha walks with me back to the closets to put my lunch sack back on the shelf. I race back towards the front of the line that is heading out the door, a few steps behind Chrissy and Heather, following them to the asphalt playground. The boys bolt off to play kickball, their four bases taking up most of the space on the grounds. The girls congregate near the fence around Ms. Bauer as she pulls multicolored jump ropes out of her tote bags.

"Cookies, candies in a dish. How many pieces do you wish?" Chrissy and Heather both jump into the twirling rope. "One, two, three, four," twenty-five girls chant. "Twelve, thirteen. . . ." The rope gets caught under Heather's sneaker.

"Aisha, would you like to try?" Ms. Bauer turns to Aisha and me, who both watch intently.

"Okay." She kicks off her chappals and ties her dupatta round her waist. "But I don't know any of the songs."

"Don't worry. I will pick one for you." Aisha stands between the two lunch ladies, the rope swaying in the wind against her bare feet. I collapse down onto the ground and sit, legs crossed, as I usually do, singing along, but never joining in. "Cinderella, dressed in yella. Went upstairs to see her fella. How many kisses did she get?" Aisha is jumping furiously in time with the music. "Twenty-eight, twenty-nine, thirty, thirty …" Aisha missteps and stumbles.

"That was fun." She sits down next to me.

I smile. "You are very good."

"There is a new girl in our class," I tell Mom after school as I peel the tangerine she's given me. "She's from Pakistan." I pull the segments apart and arrange them in a circle on the napkin.

"When did they come?"

"Last weekend." I tell her all the stories Aisha told me at lunch—about her all-girls school in Islamabad, her two younger brothers, and how busy her parents are trying to find a job in New Jersey. I pick up a single slice of the tangerine and glide it between my teeth. "She even wore Indian—I mean, Pakistani—clothes to school every day this week."

"You should do that too." She sweeps the discarded peel with her hands.

All good memoir writers pause in their narration of events to reflect on the significance of those events to their personal development and worldview.

Memoirs

I sink my incisors into the fruit. A burst of juice fills my mouth. "She just came from there. That's why she does it," I rationalize to her. "She doesn't have American clothes. And she eats the school lunch." I hope that she picks up on my second subtle hint of the day.

"I am sure once they are all settled in, Aisha's mother will be giving her biryani as well." She wipes the tangerine juice that's dribbled out of my mouth onto my chin, and I lower myself from the chair. "They'll want to hold onto that in this country. Don't you want your banana today?"

"No, I am not hungry. I ate lunch."

Aisha and I continue to exchange meals for the rest of the school year. I give her more of my mom's aloo tikkis, and she hands over her pizza bagels. I demolish her macaroni and cheese, and she inhales my masala rice. Aisha starts to wear jeans by June. She always takes off her sneakers and socks before jumping rope, though; she says it's easier that way.

Every day, at 3:15, as I jump into our ice-blue Dodge Caravan, Mom asks me, "Did you finish the lunch I packed you for today?"

"Yes, Mom," I lie. I am not about to spoil my arrangement.

Understanding the Rhetorical Situation

When you want to narrate and analyze a significant experience in your life, consider composing a memoir. Memoirs share the following characteristics:

- Memoirs focus on a particularly significant experience or series of experiences in the writer's life. Rather than narrating from birth to adulthood, the way an autobiography does, a memoir focuses on those experiences or events that carry the most significance for shaping who the writer is and his or her perspective on the world.
- Memoirs contain ample sensory details to help readers visualize, hear, smell, taste, or feel key events, characters, experiences, and objects.
- Memoirs include dialogue or quoted speech that reveals something unique about or central to a character or the character's relationship with other people, events, or objects in the story.
- Memoirs include clear transitional phrases to show how events relate to one another in time and how the action of the narrative unfolds.
- Memoirs provide reflection on or analysis of the key narrative events to help readers understand their significance for the writer's development and his or her perspective on everyday life.

The following sections will help you compose a memoir about an experience with food. To work with an online guide to the elements of the rhetorical situation, access your English CourseMate through cengagebrain.com.

Identifying an opportunity

Consider the foods, the recipes, and the dining spots that you find most familiar and most comforting—or, conversely, most alien and most unpleasant—so that you can begin the process of thinking about how the culture of food has shaped who you are. You might, for example, think back to a time when a parent or other relative calmed your anxieties about a bad result on an exam or your distress following a devastating break-up with a comforting meal. Or you might remember the specific details of a meal at your favorite diner or coffee shop in your hometown, the one where you and your friends still congregate when you are all home for semester break. What you are searching for is an experience or event or relationship within which food has played a vital role—and helped you to understand something about life that you want other people to know.

1. Make a list of the foods that are most pleasurable, most memorable, or most meaningful to you, including those you might have written about in response to the questions on page 92. Describe at least one experience involving each food. Explain why the experiences were positive or negative, providing as

Memoirs

many details as possible. If anything could have made the bad experiences better, explain what and how. For each experience, include as many contributing factors as you can: the people you were with when you were eating the food, the place where you were eating the food, the occasion, the events that led up to the moment or that followed immediately after it, and so forth.

2. Choosing one or two foods, make sketches or take photos of the food or the location where you enjoyed it from different vantage points, paying particular attention to the details and features that you find most intriguing about the experience of eating the food.

3. Choose the food you want to write about and compose four or five descriptions of the significance that food has for you. Vary your descriptions by emphasizing different features of the situation in which you have eaten or most often eat the food. For example, one description might emphasize your pleasant or unpleasant memories of the first time you ate the food. Another description might emphasize a particular person the food reminds you of, and yet another might deal with the sense of belonging or alienation that eating this food has created in you.

Locating an audience

The following questions will help you locate your rhetorical audience as well as identify their relationship to the food-related experience you've decided to write about. Having identified your audience, you'll be able to choose the most descriptive details to include and the best way to deliver the message you want that audience to receive, whether that message is informative, entertaining, argumentative, analytical, or explanatory.

1. List the names of the persons or groups who might be most interested in hearing about your experiences with this particular food or who might be most resistant to your story but need to hear about it anyway.

2. Next to the name of each potential audience, write reasons that audience could have for acknowledging the significance of your experience. In other words, what would convince these audiences that you have a unique and interesting story to tell—a story they need to hear more about in order to think more deeply about the food experiences in their own lives?

3. What kinds of responses to your writing could you reasonably expect from each of these audiences? In other words, what would you like your audience to do with the information you're providing? Think here about similar experiences that the audience might have had, as well as the audience's openness to new perspectives or desire for familiar experiences.

4. With your audience's interests, experiences, and perspectives in mind, look again at the descriptions and visual illustrations of food experiences and their significance that you composed in the preceding section on identifying an opportunity. Decide which descriptions will most likely engage your audience and help your audience connect your food-related experience with their own. At this point, it is probably necessary to revise your best descriptions to tailor them to your audience.

Identifying a fitting response

Because different purposes and different audiences require different kinds of texts—different media—you'll want to consider all of the options available to you. For example, the desire to recount your inability to resist the temptations of the college cafeteria's dessert table might prompt you to write a humorous column for the school's alumni magazine. Your narrative describing how your grandfather taught you to cook his delicious stir-fry recipe might find a place in your family's scrapbook or be preserved in an audio recording as part of your family's oral history. The point is that once you identify your opportunity, audience, and purpose, you need to determine what kind of format will best respond to the rhetorical situation.

Use the following questions to help you narrow your purpose and shape your response:

1. What specific message do you want to convey about your food-related experience? What is the purpose of your message?
2. What kind of reaction do you want from your audience? Are you asking the audience to be more thoughtful about the experiences that have shaped their own lives? Are you asking the audience to reconsider foods that they tend to think of as "different" or "bad"? Or are you asking the audience to perform a particular action?
3. What is the best way to connect with your audience? That is, what kind of text is this audience most likely to have access to and most likely to respond to? (Chapter 13 can help you explore options for media and design.)

Writing a Memoir: Working with Your Available Means

Shaping your memoir

As you have probably figured out by now, a memoir is a genre arranged much like a fictional work such as a novel or a short story. The **introduction** hooks readers by dropping them right in the middle of an interesting situation or by presenting them with an especially vivid description (see Chapter 3). This introduction announces the focal point of your memoir, whether that is a specific food, a significant culinary experience, or a particular aspect of your present personality that was shaped by an earlier experience with a food or eating. Pooja Makhijani, for example, opens her memoir with descriptions of what her mother packs in her lunch bag and what she yearns for instead—what would be on her classmates' lunch trays that day. In so doing, she introduces the tension between herself and her mother, which manifests itself in their different ideas about what is appropriate or desirable food, at the same time that she establishes her ethos. But Makhijani also begins to build a conflict for the rest of her memoir by leaving this tension unspoken. Rather than being open about her desire to eat bologna on white bread and Cool Ranch Doritos like her classmates, she says nothing. In short, Makhijani, like all good memoir writers, creates effective

pages 67–68

pathos through the introduction of her piece—she describes the characters and their actions in such a way as to get readers emotionally invested in her topic.

The **body** of a memoir presents the narrative, the plot or the major sequence of events. As you've learned in this chapter, a memoir focuses on a specific event or series of events that is significant, rather than narrating each and every event in a person's life. The events or experiences that you choose to include should be those that have proven to be most meaningful for you, that best illustrate the point you want to make, or that best convey the message you want to send. As you describe the specific events, choose concrete, precise verbs that reveal the actions taken by the different characters and use transitional phrases such as *by that time* and *later in the day* to show the sequence of events and help readers see how the events relate to one another in time.

In addition, the body of a memoir provides specific sensory details. You'll want to describe the food you ate, the place where you ate it, and the people you were with (the characters in your memoir). Makhijani helps readers to understand the care with which her mother made those school lunches by describing pages 68–69 each piece of food in mouth-watering detail; she contrasts these homemade lunches with the bland, mass-produced foods on her classmates' lunch trays. Such sensory details are important for helping readers to imagine the events, the foods, and the characters at the heart of your memoir; they also help you to deliver the specific message you want to convey to readers. Vivid descriptions invite readers to connect emotionally with and invest themselves in the lives and activities of the major characters. In Makhijani's memoir, her vivid details help readers feel just how strong her desire to assimilate is, so strong that she would rather eat peaches from a can than her mother's deep-fried potato patties "spiked with garam masala" and "slathered with fresh coriander chutney."

The body of a memoir also develops the various characters. You'll certainly want to use sensory details to help readers visualize the key features and actions of each character. Equally important, you'll want to create dialogue between the characters to reveal important aspects about their personalities and relationship to one another. For example, Makhijani never directly asks her mother if she can buy school lunches. Instead, because she fears what her mother will say, she speaks indirectly about what her classmates do and eat ("Chrissy brought Coke with her to school yesterday") in the hope that her mother will get her point. It's important to use dialogue or quoted speech purposefully, to give readers deeper insight into the thoughts and emotions of your characters.

One more element to incorporate into the body of your memoir is reflec-pages 73–74 tion on or analysis of the events that you're narrating. Reflection and analysis encourage readers to notice particular details or help them understand the significance of a particular experience for a character's self-development. Drawing on the methods of critical analysis allows you to craft compelling rhetorical appeals. In the case of logos, you may try to convince readers that your analysis is the best way to interpret the significance of certain events in the memoir. In terms of ethos, you may present an analysis that seems to consider the perspectives of all characters involved in order to cast yourself as an open-minded, well-reasoned observer of events. For example, look again at the paragraph that comes immediately after Aisha asks, "Then why don't you eat the school

Introduction
▶ Announces focal point
▶ Establishes ethos

Body
▶ Presents the main narrative
▶ Provides specific sensory details
▶ Develops characters
▶ Reflects and analyzes

Conclusion
▶ Reinforces message
▶ Leaves readers with an understanding of events' significance for writer and reader

© 2013 Cengage Learning

lunch?" Makhijani's reflection not only gives dramatic pause but also reveals her perception of herself: "I know it's not because it's too expensive or that Styrofoam trays are environmentally unsound. It's because Mom thinks her deep-fried aloo tikkis and freshly ground masalas are what good Indian parents give their daughters. She doesn't understand that good Indian daughters just want to become American." This allows readers to see how Makhijani's relationship to her mother's food was directly connected to her desire to identify herself as an "American." As you narrate the events in your memoir, look for places where you can help readers understand the significance of specific details or events by stopping the action and providing a few sentences of reflection or analysis.

The **conclusion** of a memoir reinforces the message, or the point of the story. The important consideration here is to be sure the events you've narrated, the details you've provided, and the reflection or analysis you've composed all work together to deliver a clear, coherent message. You might, as Makhijani does, conclude your memoir with a scene that captures precisely the mood you want readers to experience or the image you want them to remember. Or you might decide to conclude your memoir with a more traditional paragraph that, like your reflective components, speaks fairly explicitly about the point of the events that you've described. Either way, your readers will respond favorably to your conclusion if it helps them to see how the events have significance both for you as the writer and for them as your readers.

Revision and peer review

After you've drafted your memoir, ask one of your classmates to read it. You'll want your classmate to respond to your work in a way that helps you revise it into the strongest memoir it can be, one that addresses your intended audience, helps you fulfill your purpose, and is delivered in the most appropriate means available to you.

Questions for a peer reviewer
1. To what opportunity for change is the writer responding?
2. Who might be the writer's intended audience?
3. What might be the writer's purpose? How does purpose connect with audience?

4. What information did you receive from the introduction? What suggestions do you have for the writer for enhancing the effectiveness of the introduction?

5. Note the key narrative events in the memoir. Are transitions used in a way that helps the reader keep track of the narrative? If not, identify places that could use transitional words or phrases.

6. Note passages in which the writer reflects on or analyzes the key narrative events. What seems to be the significance of these events for the writer?

7. How does the writer establish ethos? How can the writer strengthen this appeal?

8. What material does the writer use to establish logos? How might the writer strengthen this appeal?

9. How does the writer make use of pathos? Does the writer rely on pathos too much or too little? How might the writer strike a balance?

10. What did you learn from the conclusion that you didn't already know after reading the introduction and the body? What information does the writer want you to take away from the memoir? Does the writer attempt to change your attitude, action, or opinion?

11. What section of the memoir did you most enjoy? Why?

MEMOIRS IN THREE MEDIA

Audio Memoir

This audio memoir about an Italian American family restaurant was recorded for StoryCorps. To listen, find *Writing in Three Media* in your English CourseMate, accessed through cengagebrain.com.

Courtesy of StoryCorps, a national nonprofit dedicated to recording and collecting stories of everyday people: www.storycorps.org

Online Memoir

This blog entry by Ree Drummond, also known as "Pioneer Woman," presents an illustrated memoir about her first encounter with Nova salmon. To read the blog, find *Writing in Three Media* in your English Course-Mate, accessed through cengagebrain.com.

barbaradudzinska/Shutterstock.com

Print Memoir

In the following memoir, student writer Anna Seitz remembers her first experience "processing" a chicken.

Anton Novik/Shutterstock.com

pages 75-77

Anna's lesson in chicken killing could have been relayed in any of several genres or media. If her purpose had been to inform other novices, she could have posted a how-to guide on YouTube. If she wanted her somewhat gory descriptions to make a direct argument against eating meat, she could have written a position argument. A letter tucked inside a birthday card to her cousin would have conveyed a funny anecdote about the perils of animal husbandry. Instead, Anna wanted her readers to feel the conflict she experienced, and she knew that to replicate those feelings, she would need to appeal to her readers' physical senses and to pay particular attention to the ethos she was creating for herself. She also knew that her experience was about more than just chickens—and that she could describe it in a way that made clear its larger significance. Thus, Anna knew a memoir was appropriate for her rhetorical situation. She chose the print format because it fit the requirements of her class assignment.

Memoirs

Anna Seitz

English 260

Professor Lundin

22 April 2010

Herb's Chicken

Last year, my husband Bill and I, fueled by farmers' market fantasies, decided we wanted to keep some backyard chickens. Since we had to wait until spring to order birds, we spent the winter getting our coop, and ourselves, ready. We read stacks of books and magazines on raising chickens, and we decided to ask our friend Herb to teach us to "process" them.

When we pulled into Herb's driveway on the big day, he was already hanging out the back door, gesturing to the cane at the bottom of the steps. He's 87 years old and has been a poultry farmer since he got back from the war. He shuffles slowly, hunched over. He can't hear much of what we say. When he can hear, he usually just rolls his eyes. Bill handed him the cane, and Herb led us to the last of his coops that still has chickens. His farm of 6,000 birds is down to 75. "Well, how many you want?" Herb asks.

"I don't know," said my husband. "Got one that's not layin'?"

"Get that one there," said Herb. He pointed his finger in the direction of a group of three birds, and my husband, appearing to know which one Herb meant, took a couple of steps toward them. They immediately dispersed.

Herb grabbed a long handle with a hook at the end, resembling the sort of wand I've used to roast weenies over a campfire, and handed it to Bill. He pointed again. "There," he said. Bill grabbed the tool and managed to at least tangle up the bird's feet. Herb snapped up the bird with the efficient movement of someone who has snapped up tens of thousands of birds, and handed the bird, upside-down, to me.

Margin annotations:

Anna's memoir uses the narrative form, which includes a setting, characters, dialogue, and a sequence of events.

The significant experience related in this memoir arose from Anna's "farmers' market fantasy" of raising chickens.

Anna includes many sensory details to help her readers visualize the setting and Herb's character.

The dialogue reveals the characters' relationships to one another as well as to the raising of chickens.

I held it carefully by the ankles and got a little shiver. It flapped its wings a few times, but it didn't really try to fight me. It actually looked pretty pitiful hanging there. Herb was already walking back to the house.

"Pull up that bird feeder, Billy," barked Herb, in his thin voice.

My husband had worked digging graves with Herb since he was fifteen, and he was used to taking orders. "Yup," he said. He walked up to a bird feeder on a stake and pulled it up from the ground.

Herb unhooked a metal cone which he'd been using on the stake as a squirrel deterrent and slid it off the bottom. "For the chicken," he told me as I caught up to them. "I'll open the cellar."

This paragraph works as a transition between the present series of events and the past relationship of the characters.

Bill and I waited outside the bulkhead for Herb. He opened it up, still holding the metal cone in his hand. "Come on," he instructed. We made our way down into the dark. The chicken tried to arch its head up, to peck me. I handed it over to Bill.

In the cellar, Herb hooked the cone to a beam. "Give me that," he said to me, gesturing at a dusty bucket on the floor next to me. I pushed it with my foot until it was under the cone.

"All right!" said my husband brightly. I stiffened. He pushed the chicken head-first into the cone, until her head poked through the opening at the bottom and her feet stuck out the top. The chicken got one wing free, but my husband put a rubber band around her feet and hooked it on the nail that held the cone. She was stuck.

Herb fished through his pocket for his knife, and my eyelids started to wrinkle. I held my lips tightly closed. "You just need to go through the roof of the mouth and get them right in the brain," said Herb. "It's better than chopping the head off because they don't tense up. Makes it easier to get the feathers off."

This series of five short paragraphs includes graphic details and purposeful dialogue.

"Won't it bite you?" I asked.

"So what if it does?" answered Herb. "Last thing it'll ever do." Herb easily pried the mouth open with his left hand, and with his right, he pushed the knife into its brain and turned it. It was over. I furrowed my brow.

"Then you gotta bleed it," he said. Herb pulled the knife down, and in one quick motion, cut the chicken's throat from the inside. Blood spilled from its open beak into the bucket. My husband watched with interest, offering the same occasional "Yup" or "Uh-huh" that he uses when listening to any good story. I watched with my eyes squinted and my face half turned away.

Herb rinsed the knife in the washbasin and announced, "Gotta get the water. Anna, it's on the stove. Hot but not boiling." I went up to the kitchen and fiddled with the temperature under a big soup pot. It looked about right, I guessed.

By the time I got the water down to the cellar, Herb and Bill had already pulled the chicken out of the cone and tossed the head into the bloody bucket. It looked more like food when I couldn't see the eyes. Herb told my husband to dip the bird in the hot water a few times, and he did, holding it by the rubber-banded legs. When he pulled it out, some of the feathers on its chest started to drop off.

This is a strong transitional sentence.

From under the stairs, Herb pulled out a large plastic drum, the sides dotted with rubber fingers. He put the chicken inside and switched it on. After a few minutes, he pulled out a mostly featherless chicken. The feathers stuck to the sides of the drum. "Get that," he said to Bill. While Bill pulled feathers out of the plucker, Herb held the chicken by the feet and pulled off the remaining feathers—mostly large wing and tail feathers, and a few small pin feathers. By now there really wasn't any blood left, and the chicken looked pretty close to what you might get in the store, except skinnier.

Bill brought the chicken and the bucket up to the kitchen, and Herb and I followed. Herb took the bird and dropped it down into the sink with a smack. "Now, you cut out the crop," Herb said. He pointed to something I couldn't see, then cut into the throat and showed us a little sack full of stones and grain. "It's how they chew, I guess," he added. He tugged on it, and it brought with it a large section of the windpipe. "To get the rest of the guts out, you gotta cut in the back."

Herb made an incision and stuck in his hand, making a squishy sound. He pulled out a handful of guts and dropped most of it into the bucket. He cut off one section and held it toward Bill. "You got the wrong bird," he said. The slimy tube was sort of transparent, and through it we could see a string of about eight little eggs of increasing size, beginning with a tiny yolk, and ending with an almost full-sized egg.

"Can you eat 'em?" I asked.

"Guess you could," said Herb, throwing the whole mess into the bucket, "but I got eggs." He turned the chicken, lopped off the feet, and tossed them into the bucket. They landed toes up, like a grotesque garnish. "Well, want a plastic bag?"

I accepted the grocery bag and some plastic wrap and wrapped the carcass up while Herb and Bill took the bucket outside. They talked for a while, and then Herb directed Bill up onto a ladder to check a gutter. I stood with my back to the carcass, examining Herb's wife's display of whimsical salt and pepper shakers.

When my husband and I got back in the car, I put the carcass at my feet. "That was great!" said my husband. "Think we can do it on our own?"

I thought through the steps in my mind. "I think I can," I chirped. I thought of the bucket and the toe garnish. "But I'm not eating it."

Anna reflects on the narrative events, helping her readers understand their significance to her changing perspective.

Alternatives to the Memoir

Fitting responses come in many forms, not just memoirs. Your instructor might call upon you to consider one of the following opportunities for writing.

1. Have you recently had a satisfying experience dining out that you want your friends and classmates to enjoy as well? Or have you suffered through a restaurant meal that you would not wish on your worst enemy? What aspects of your experience made it satisfying and enjoyable or unfulfilling and unpleasant? Write a critical review of that dining experience. Be sure to specify the criteria on which you're basing your evaluation and to provide specific examples that show how the food, the service, and the atmosphere contributed to the overall dining experience.

2. In *Fast Food Nation,* Eric Schlosser notes a disturbing trend in the culture of food in industrialized nations, and he investigates this trend (particularly in terms of its consequences). In an investigative report, analyze a positive or negative feature of food culture on your campus or in your community. Be sure to provide concrete evidence and details to support your analysis.

3. Margaret Mead identified a particular problem in the American culture of food and offered a difficult solution for that problem. Identify a problem concerning the culture of food on your campus or in your community and write a proposal in which you outline a plan for solving that problem. Be sure to identify the rhetorical audience for your proposal (that is, some person or group in a position to act on it) and to describe the problem in a way that emphasizes the importance of addressing the problem right away. Present your solution in specific detail and include analysis that shows its appropriateness and feasibility.

Portraying Successful Speakers and Writers: Responding with Profiles

5

Profiles

What thoughts come to your mind when you see the famous image of the Reverend Dr. Martin Luther King, Jr., speaking at the March on Washington for Jobs and Freedom, on August 28, 1963? Perhaps you think about the values in which King believed and the civil rights for which he fought. Perhaps you think of his nonviolent resistance to the oppression faced by African Americans in the 1950s and 1960s. Perhaps you remember other images from the civil rights movement—marchers beaten back by powerful streams of water or sit-ins at segregated lunch counters. Chances are, though, that this image brings to your mind the famous words spoken on that day in 1963 on the steps of the Lincoln Memorial:

AP Photo

> So even though we face the difficulties of today and tomorrow, I still have a dream. I have a dream that one day this nation will rise up and live out the true meaning of its creed . . . that all men are created equal. I have a dream that one day even the state of Mississippi, a state sweltering with the heat of oppression, will be transformed into an oasis of freedom and justice. I have a dream that my four little children will one day live in a nation where they will not be judged by the color of their skin but by the content of their character. I have a dream today. And if America is to be a great nation, this must become true.
>
> —**Martin Luther King, Jr.,** **"I Have a Dream"**
> © 1963. Reprinted by permission.

King's legacy in U.S. history centers on his great victories in the civil rights movement. This legacy was shaped, in part, by his enviable ability to put his message into words. He could create moving narratives, vivid images, and logical arguments. He employed a host of rhetorical tools to persuade Americans of the need to act to ensure universal civil rights.

There have been times in all of our lives when we have been moved to tears or to action or have been angered by the words of a public figure. What makes language move us in this way? How does the speaker or the writer craft language that can move us? As curious human beings, we often want to learn about what motivates a person to say or write the things that he or she does or to learn when, where, and how the person learned to use language as effectively and as powerfully as he or she does. In pursuing answers to these questions, we often learn that how a person comes to craft a speech or a piece of writing is just as interesting as what any particular passage might say.

Every bit as important as how a person crafts the message is how those words are delivered. Given our highly digital world, you may already have a great deal of experience—maybe even expertise—in delivering your ideas electronically, whether you're using words, visuals, video, audio, or some combination of these. You are also likely an experienced and good speaker when the situation calls for it, even if you don't feel like an expert when giving a formal oral presentation. If you're not already, you can become a confident writer and speaker.

Successful speakers and writers know the importance of gauging the relationship between the content of their message and the expectations of their intended audience. Therefore, they spend a good deal of time preparing their message to fit the context. They adjust their assertions, examples, choice of words, and the delivery of those words at the same time that they weigh the decision whether to deliver their message orally, in writing, or in images—or to combine these forms. Most of the successful speakers and writers profiled in this chapter, like Martin Luther King, Jr., say good things—and say those good things very well.

Writers have used profiles—biographical sketches—to help others better understand how the most eloquent writers and speakers have honed their skills and how they have deployed them to effective ends. As readers of a **profile**, we gain glimpses into a person's private life and see how personal experiences affect the often very visible work that the person does. A profile of Dr. Martin Luther King, Jr., for example, might help us to better understand how his daily life experiences as a black man and as a father affected his ideas about the value of words in public life. A profile might also help us to better understand how King viewed his public speaking in relation to his actions, whether boycotting, marching, or conducting acts of civil disobedience such as those that landed him in the Birmingham jail.

Writers create profiles to help readers gain a deeper understanding of a public figure—or of a person their readers might not otherwise have heard of. Often, writers create profiles to analyze the individuals who have shaped history. In profiles, writers paint portraits with words, to describe a person in detail and to show how the pieces fit together to form the whole person.

IDENTIFYING AN OPPORTUNITY

Throughout this chapter, you'll work to identify an opportunity to profile a person who is successful with words. This person might be someone you're related to, work with, know, or admire from afar: a grandparent, minister, counselor, group leader, politician, public figure, artist, author, or celebrity. As you work to determine the person who most interests you, consider the most fitting means of delivery for your profile:

Print Profile

written for a community or campus newspaper or local zine

Audio Profile

recorded for a local radio station

Online Profile

composed as a blog entry or multimedia presentation using an online presentation-sharing service (such as SlideShare).

To begin, freewrite for five minutes in response to each of the following questions (or use any of the invention techniques presented on pages 58–61):

1. When have you listened to, read the writing of, or watched a performance by someone whom you consider successful with words?

2. Did reading, hearing, or watching the delivery of this person's words make you think or act differently in response? If so, how did your thinking or behavior change?

3. What qualities or characteristics did this person possess that made him or her an effective speaker or writer? What made his or her words effective?

Real Situations

Your college or university may require you to take a public speaking course. Such a requirement, like the requirement that all students take at least one writing course, is grounded in the belief that professionals need to possess more than the technical knowledge at the heart of their field or discipline—they need to be able to communicate this knowledge to others, as well. Moreover, your experiences in your public speaking course are meant to instill in you the ability to appreciate and engage in informed discussions in your other courses and in your community. Many colleges and universities also give their students extracurricular opportunities to improve their abilities in public speaking through participation in debate teams. Students on these teams learn to generate arguments in response to challenging ethical, legal, and political questions and to present their positions in a logically reasoned and stylistically polished way. Many students use their experiences on college debate teams as preparation for future careers in the law, business, or politics.

Public speaking is such an important skill in professional life that many organizations hire coaches to help their executives improve. Carmine Gallo is one such speaking coach, one who draws his advice directly from what he has noticed about the presentations of Apple CEO Steve Jobs. Here are the five elements every Jobs presentation includes (Gallo's observations are reprinted in full on pages 140–141):

1. **A headline.** Steve Jobs positions every product with a headline that fits well within a 140-character Twitter post. . . .

2. **A villain.** In every classic story, the hero fights the villain. . . . This idea of conquering a shared enemy is a powerful motivator and turns customers into evangelists.

3. **A simple slide.** Apple products are easy to use because of the elimination of clutter. The same approach applies to the slides in a Steve Jobs presentation. . . .

4. **A demo.** Neuroscientists have discovered that the brain gets bored easily. Steve Jobs doesn't give you time to lose interest. [In most of his presentations] he's . . . demonstrating a new product or feature and having fun doing it. . . .

5. **A holy smokes moment.** Every Steve Jobs presentation has one moment that neuroscientists call an "emotionally charged event." The emotionally charged event is the equivalent of a mental post-it note that tells the brain, Remember this! . . . (© 2009. Reprinted by permission.)

College public speaking courses and the work of professional coaches like Gallo are premised on the belief that anyone can become a more effective wielder of words by learning to apply some basic skills and keeping in mind

A student speaks at the YMCA Youth and Government mock trial competition.

some valuable advice. Most people, however, are somewhat awed by public figures who, like King, possess a powerful ability to move people through words. Where did they gain this ability? Were they born with it? Did they learn it? What motivates their work, and how do they approach their tasks?

In this chapter, you'll gain insight into some successful and effective speakers and writers. Just as important, you'll learn about the profile, a kind of writing that can give readers a fuller understanding of how public figures have come to their lives' work, how they have learned to use words effectively, and what motivates them to wield this power in their professional lives.

DESCRIBING SUCCESSFUL SPEAKERS

1. What do you know about Dr. Martin Luther King, Jr.'s abilities with words? What skills did he use most effectively or most often? Where did he acquire those skills? What motivated him to use words in the ways that he did? After freewriting in response to these questions for several minutes, conduct online research to learn what others have said about King's ability to achieve things with words.

2. Conduct online research on the topic of effective public speaking. What do your searches reveal about common beliefs and attitudes concerning the importance of wielding the spoken word effectively?

3. What do the images in this chapter suggest to you about successful speakers and writers?

Real Responses to Real Situations

Persuasion from the presidential podium

When President Barack Obama ran for president in 2008, he had a modest political résumé: eight years in the Illinois state senate and only three as a U.S. senator. To get himself elected, he had to marshal all the means of persuasion available to him, both verbal and visual. Even if you don't remember the words he used, you may remember his widely circulated campaign poster (designed by Shepard Fairey), which presented in visual form his biracial, forward-looking character, his red-white-and-blue patriotism, and his campaign theme of "hope."

The campaign poster was just one of the available means of persuasion that Obama and his team employed to rally supporters and publicize his plans and policies. Obama's campaign was distinguished by its integrated use of technology, employing both digital and analog means and profiting from the efficiency of the Internet in bringing about real time distribution of his messages. As many of you know, Obama's team targeted the under-thirty age group by employing online forums and social networking websites (such as MySpace, Facebook, and Neighbor-to-Neighbor) to engage this specific group in discussing the issues most important to them. In addition, the YouTube videos that "mashed up" Obama's speeches into songs (will.i.am's "Yes We Can," Ruwanga Samth and Maxwell D's "Make It to the Sun," JFC's "Barack Obama," and Misa/Misa's "Unite the Nation") generated support for Obama among the young (and young in spirit). And the YouTube versions of "They Said This Day Would Never Come" functioned as oral profiles of Obama the candidate and Obama the man.

By circulating his policies, ideas, and speeches digitally (through e-mail, text messages, and online), Obama set himself apart from the other candidates, especially from his toughest political foes, the ones with more political experience (Hillary Clinton and John McCain, for instance). His use of technology to engage in continual dialogue with his supporters transformed this conventional liberal Democratic senator into a "techno-cool" presidential candidate.

Obama's use of communication technology was a boon to his campaign, to be sure, but his messages ("Change We Can Believe In" and "Yes, We Can") were every bit as crucial to his ultimate success. He had plenty of ideas about health care, social security, immigration, and banking—some of them controversial—so he needed to avail himself of the best staff possible, people who could assist him in successfully transforming his ideas of "hope,"

Shepard Fairey standing in front of the campaign poster he designed.

"change," and "progress" into actual votes. This first African American man to be a strong contender for president needed to be more than an inspirational, charismatic speaker. Because his opponents were using his eloquence against him, he had to demonstrate both style and substance, not either alone. The man who was promising change and unity needed to win. And he needed help to do so.

Obama turned to speechwriting genius Jon Favreau. Only twenty-six years old, Favreau was nonetheless an experienced speechwriter who could help Obama craft the words to express his substantial and concrete ideas in ethical, and ultimately persuasive, language. Ashley Parker's January 2008 profile of Favreau in the *New York Times* introduces readers to someone they likely don't know, giving information about his background and outlining his impressive accomplishments in specific ways.

> What Would Obama Say?

Ashley Parker

At the Radisson Hotel in Nashua, N.H., Jon Favreau sipped Diet Coke and munched on carrot sticks and crackers to pass the time. His boss, Senator Barack Obama, wandered in and out of the room.

Finally, results from the New Hampshire Democratic primary started coming in, surprising everyone. Hillary Clinton was pulling past Senator Obama, who had won the Iowa caucuses only five days earlier.

Mr. Favreau, the campaign's 26-year-old head speechwriter, found himself in the hotel lounge with less than three hours to revise what was to have been a victory speech. What made it particularly strange was that his words were being challenged. Mrs. Clinton had helped turn her campaign around by discounting Mr. Obama's elegant oratory, saying, "You campaign in poetry, but you govern in prose."

"To be honest," Mr. Favreau said, "the first time I really stopped to think about how it felt was when he started giving the speech. I looked around at the senior staff, and they were all smiling. And I looked around the room and thought, 'This is going to be O.K.' "

Mr. Favreau, or Favs, as everyone calls him, looks every bit his age, with a baby face and closely shorn stubble. And he leads a team of two other young speechwriters: 26-year-old Adam Frankel, who worked with John Kennedy's adviser and speechwriter Theodore C. Sorensen on his memoirs, and Ben Rhodes, who, at 30, calls himself the "elder statesman" of the group and who helped write the Iraq Study Group report as an assistant to Lee H. Hamilton.

Together they are working for a politician who not only is known for his speaking ability but also wrote two best-selling books and gave the much-lauded keynote speech at the 2004 Democratic National Convention.

"You're like Ted Williams's batting coach," Mr. Favreau said.

But even Ted Williams needed a little help with his swing.

"Barack trusts him," said David Axelrod, Mr. Obama's chief campaign strategist. "And Barack doesn't trust too many folks with that—the notion of surrendering that much authority over his own words."

When he first met Mr. Obama, Mr. Favreau was 23, a recent graduate of the College of the Holy Cross in Worcester, Mass., near where he grew up. Mr. Obama was rehearsing his 2004 convention speech backstage, when Mr. Favreau, then a member of John Kerry's staff, interrupted him: the senator needed to rewrite a line from his speech to avoid an overlap.

"He kind of looked at me, kind of confused—like, 'Who is this kid?' " Mr. Favreau recalled.

Mr. Obama became his boss the following year. Mr. Favreau had risen to a job as a speechwriter on the Kerry campaign, but by then was unemployed. He was, he said, "broke, taking advantage of all the happy-hour specials I could find in Washington."

Robert Gibbs, Mr. Obama's communications director, had known Mr. Favreau during the Kerry campaign, and recommended him as a writer.

Life was relatively quiet then, and Mr. Obama and Mr. Favreau had some time to hang out. When Mr. Obama's White Sox swept Mr. Favreau's beloved Red Sox three games to none in their American League 2005 division series, the senator walked over to his speechwriter's desk with a little broom and started sweeping it off.

Speechwriter Jon Favreau on the Obama campaign trail.

Mr. Favreau also used this time to master Mr. Obama's voice. He took down almost everything the senator said and absorbed it. Now, he said, when he sits down to write, he just channels Mr. Obama—his ideas, his sentences, his phrases.

"The trick of speechwriting, if you will, is making the client say your brilliant words while somehow managing to make it sound as though they issued straight from their own soul," said the writer Christopher Buckley, who was a speechwriter for the first President Bush. "Imagine putting the words 'Ask not what your country can do for you' into the mouth of Ron Paul, and you can see the problem."

Many Democratic candidates have attempted to evoke both John and Robert Kennedy, but Senator Obama seems to have had more success than most. It helps that Mr. Obama seems to have the élan that John Kennedy had, not to mention a photogenic family.

For his inspiration, Mr. Favreau said, "I actually read a lot of Bobby" Kennedy.

"I see shades of J.F.K., R.F.K.," he said, and then added, "King."

continued

Not everyone is so enamored. Mr. Obama excels at inspirational speeches read from a teleprompter before television cameras, critics have noted, but many of his other speeches on the campaign trail have failed to electrify.

Ted Widmer, a historian at Brown University, said that Mr. Obama's speeches "were perfect for getting to where he was early in the race, but I think now that we're in a serious campaign, it would be helpful to hear more concrete proposals."

"There's more to governing, there's more to being president, than speechwriting," he added.

Mr. Favreau said that when he is writing, he stays up until 3 A.M. and gets up as early as 5. He hasn't slept for more than six hours in as long as he can remember, he said.

Coffee helped him through the Iowa caucuses. Two days before the victory there, he walked across the street from the campaign's Des Moines headquarters and cloistered himself inside a local cafe.

He and Mr. Obama had talked about the post-caucus speech for about 30 minutes, settling on a theme of unity and an opening line: "They said this day would never come."

"I knew that it would have multiple meanings to multiple people," Mr. Favreau said. "Barack and I talked about it, and it was one that worked for the campaign. There were many months during the campaign when they said he'd never win. And of course there was the day that would never come, when an African-American would be winning the first primary in a white state."

In discussions about the speech, the issue of race never came up, Mr. Favreau said. But, he added, "I know I thought about it."

As Senator Obama's star has risen, so has Mr. Favreau's. In New Hampshire, Mr. Favreau stood in the back of a gym watching his boss campaign when Michael Gerson, a former speechwriter to the current President Bush, introduced himself. He complimented him on the Iowa victory speech.

The campaign staff has started teasing Mr. Favreau about his newfound celebrity. Not that it's any great pickup line. Mr. Favreau, who said he doesn't have a girlfriend, observed somewhat dryly that "the rigors of this campaign have prevented any sort of serious relationship."

"There's been a few times when people have said, 'I don't believe you, that you're Barack Obama's speechwriter,' " he went on. "To which I reply, 'If I really wanted to hit on you, don't you think I'd make up something more outlandish?' "

He does have other things to worry about. "Can you get through this process and keep the core of yourself?" Mr. Favreau asked. "You know, we're finding out. I'm confident he can. And I think I can, too."

This profile gives you a sense of the speechwriter-candidate relationship, the ways Obama and Favreau collaborated and took advantage of one another's strengths all through the presidential campaign, and some of the reasons that Obama eventually won the Iowa caucuses and then the presidency itself. The profile also mentioned Obama's idea for opening a post-caucus speech: "They said this day would never come." That speech follows.

> Caucus Speech

Barack Obama

You know, they said this day would never come.

They said our sights were set too high. They said this country was too divided, too disillusioned to ever come together around a common purpose.

But on this January night, at this defining moment in history, you have done what the cynics said we couldn't do. You have done what the state of New Hampshire can do in five days. You have done what America can do in this new year, 2008. In lines that stretched around schools and churches, in small towns and in big cities, you came together as Democrats, Republicans and independents, to stand up and say that we are one nation. We are one people. And our time for change has come.

You said the time has come to move beyond the bitterness and pettiness and anger that's consumed Washington. To end the political strategy that's been all about division, and instead make it about addition. To build a coalition for change that stretches through red states and blue states.

Because that's how we'll win in November, and that's how we'll finally meet the challenges that we face as a nation.

We are choosing hope over fear. We're choosing unity over division, and sending a powerful message that change is coming to America.

You said the time has come to tell the lobbyists who think their money and their influence speak louder than our voices that they don't own this government—we do. And we are here to take it back. The time has come for a president who will be honest about the choices and the challenges we face, who will listen to you and learn from you, even when we disagree, who won't just tell you what you want to hear, but what you need to know.

And in New Hampshire, if you give me the same chance that Iowa did tonight, I will be that president for America. I'll be a president who finally makes health care affordable and available to every single American, the same way I expanded health care in Illinois, by bringing Democrats and Republicans together to get the job done. I'll be a president who ends the tax breaks for companies that ship our jobs overseas and put a middle-class tax cut into the pockets of working Americans who deserve it. I'll be a president who harnesses the ingenuity of farmers and scientists and entrepreneurs to free this nation from the tyranny of oil once and for all. And I'll be a president who ends this war in Iraq and finally brings our troops home, who restores our moral standing, who understands that 9/11 is not a way to scare up votes but a challenge that should unite America and the world against the common threats of the 21st century. Common threats of terrorism and nuclear weapons, climate change and poverty, genocide and disease.

Tonight, we are one step closer to that vision of America because of what you did here in Iowa.

And so I'd especially like to thank the organizers and the precinct captains, the volunteers and the staff who made this all possible. And while I'm at it on thank yous, I think it makes sense for me to thank the love of my life, the rock of the Obama family, the closer on the campaign trail. Give it up for Michelle Obama.

continued

I know you didn't do this for me. You did this—you did this because you believed so deeply in the most American of ideas—that in the face of impossible odds, people who love this country can change it.

I know this. I know this because while I may be standing here tonight, I'll never forget that my journey began on the streets of Chicago doing what so many of you have done for this campaign and all the campaigns here in Iowa, organizing and working and fighting to make people's lives just a little bit better.

I know how hard it is. It comes with little sleep, little pay and a lot of sacrifice. There are days of disappointment. But sometimes, just sometimes, there are nights like this; a night that, years from now, when we've made the changes we believe in, when more families can afford to see a doctor, when our children—when Malia and Sasha and your children inherit a planet that's a little cleaner and safer, when the world sees America differently, and America sees itself as a nation less divided and more united, you'll be able to look back with pride and say that this was the moment when it all began. This was the moment when the improbable beat what Washington always said was inevitable. This was the moment when we tore down barriers that have divided us for too long; when we rallied people of all parties and ages to a common cause; when we finally gave Americans who have never participated in politics a reason to stand up and to do so. This was the moment when we finally beat back the [politics] of fear and doubts and cynicism, the politics where we tear each other down instead of lifting this country up. This was the moment.

Years from now, you'll look back and you'll say that this was the moment, this was the place where America remembered what it means to hope. For many months, we've been teased, even derided for talking about hope. But we always knew that hope is not blind optimism. It's not ignoring the enormity of the tasks ahead or the roadblocks that stand in our path. It's not sitting on the sidelines or shirking from a fight. Hope is that thing inside us that insists, despite all the evidence to the contrary, that something better awaits us if we have the courage to reach for it and to work for it and to fight for it.

Hope is what I saw in the eyes of the young woman in Cedar Rapids who works the night shift after a full day of college and still can't afford health care for a sister who's ill. A young woman who still believes that this country will give her the chance to live out her dreams.

Hope is what I heard in the voice of the New Hampshire woman who told me that she hasn't been able to breathe since her nephew left for Iraq. Who still goes to bed each night praying for his safe return.

Hope is what led a band of colonists to rise up against an empire. What led the greatest of generations to free a continent and heal a nation. What led young women and young men to sit at lunch counters and brave fire hoses and march through Selma and Montgomery for freedom's cause.

Hope—hope is what led me here today. With a father from Kenya, a mother from Kansas and a story that could only happen in the United States of America.

Hope is the bedrock of this nation. The belief that our destiny will not be written for us, but by us, by all those men and women who are not content to settle for the world as it is, who have the courage to remake the world as it should be.

Profiles

That is what we started here in Iowa and that is the message we can now carry to New Hampshire and beyond. The same message we had when we were up and when we were down; the one that can save this country, brick by brick, block by block, callused hand by callused hand, that together, ordinary people can do extraordinary things.

Because we are not a collection of red states and blue states. We are the United States of America. And in this moment, in this election, we are ready to believe again.

Peggy Noonan worked as a speechwriter for Presidents Ronald Reagan and George H. W. Bush. She also authored *What I Saw at the Revolution: A Political Life in the Reagan Era*. In the following excerpt from that book, Noonan gives readers a glimpse into the process of crafting presidential rhetoric and helps them to evaluate how it works and achieves—or fails to achieve—its desired ends. Her reflections on her own writing process also help readers understand the ways all good communicators envision their audiences so they can connect with them through the spoken or written word.

Excerpt from

> What I Saw at the Revolution: A Political Life in the Reagan Era

© 1989. Reprinted by permission.

Peggy Noonan

All speechwriters have things they think of when they write. I think of being a child in my family at the dinner table, with seven kids and hubbub and parents distracted by worries and responsibilities. Before I would say anything at the table, before I would approach my parents, I would plan what I would say. I would map out the narrative, sharpen the details, add color, plan momentum. This way I could hold their attention. This way I became a writer.

The American people too are distracted by worries and responsibilities and the demands of daily life, and you have to know that and respect it—and plan the narrative, sharpen the details, add color and momentum.

Peggy Noonan with President Ronald Reagan.

I work with an image: the child in the mall. When candidates for president are on the campaign trail they always go by a mall and walk through followed by a pack of minicams and reporters. They go by Colonel Sanders and have their picture taken eating a piece of chicken, they josh around with the lady in the mall information booth, they shake hands with the shoppers. But watch: Always there is a child, a ten-year-old girl, perhaps, in an inexpensive, tired-looking jacket.

continued

Perhaps she is by herself, perhaps with a friend. But she stands back, afraid of the lights, and as the candidate comes she runs away. She is afraid of his fame, afraid of the way the lights make his wire-rim glasses shine, afraid of dramatic moments, dense moments. When you are a speechwriter you should think of her when you write, and of her parents. They are Americans. They are good people for whom life has not been easy. Show them respect and be honest and logical in your approach and they will understand every word you say and hear—and know that you thought of them.

The irony of modern speeches is that as our ability to disseminate them has exploded (an American president can speak live not only to America but to Europe, to most of the world), their quality has declined.

Why? Lots of reasons, including that we as a nation no longer learn the rhythms of public utterance from Shakespeare and the Bible. When young Lincoln was sprawled in front of the fireplace reading *Julius Caesar*—"Th' abuse of greatness is, when it disjoins remorse from power"—he was, unconsciously, learning to be a poet. You say, "That was Lincoln, not the common man." But the common man was flocking to the docks to get the latest installment of Dickens off the ship from England.

The modern egalitarian impulse has made politicians leery of flaunting high rhetoric; attempts to reach, to find the right if sometimes esoteric quote or allusion seem pretentious. They don't really know what "the common man" knows anymore; they forget that we've all had at least some education and a number of us read on our own and read certain classics in junior high and high school. The guy at the gas station read *Call of the Wild* when he was fourteen, and sometimes thinks about it. Moreover, he has imagination. Politicians forget. They go in for the lowest common denominator—like a newscaster.

People say the problem is soundbites. But no it isn't. . . .

Soundbites in themselves are not bad. "We have nothing to fear. . ." is a soundbite. "Ask not. . ." is a soundbite. So are "You shall not crucify mankind upon a cross of gold," and "With malice toward none; with charity for all. . . ."

Great speeches have always had great soundbites. The problem is that the young technicians who put together speeches are paying attention only to the soundbite, not to the text as a whole, not realizing that all great soundbites happen by accident, which is to say, all great soundbites are yielded up inevitably, as part of the natural expression of the text. They are part of the tapestry, they aren't a little flower somebody sewed on.

They sum up a point, or make a point in language that is pithy or profound. They are what the politician is saying! They are not separate and discrete little one-liners that a bright young speechwriter just promoted out of the press office and two years out of business school slaps on.

But that is what they've become. Young speechwriters forget the speech and write the soundbite, plop down a hunk of porridge and stick on what they think is a raisin. (In the Dukakis campaign they underlined them in the text.)

The problem is not the soundbitization of rhetoric, it's the Where's-the-beefization. The good news: Everyone in America is catching on to the game, and it's beginning not to work anymore. A modest hope: Politicians will stop hiring communications majors to write their speeches and go to history majors, literature majors, writers—people who can translate the candidate's impulses into literature that is alive, and true.

> ANALYZING THE RHETORICAL SITUATION

1. Who do you think might be the intended audience of Peggy Noonan's book? In what ways might Noonan's book-reading audience differ from Ashley Parker's newspaper-reading audience? What textual evidence have you analyzed that leads you to these conclusions? Be prepared to share your answers with the rest of the class.

2. Given their intended audiences, what purpose do Noonan and Parker each want to fulfill with their writing? What opinions does each writer want readers to leave with? What are the specific differences in the purposes of these two pieces? How does the purpose of each intersect with the writer's intended audience? Again, be prepared to share your answers with the rest of the class.

3. To what opportunity for writing might Noonan and Parker be responding? How does each piece of writing work to address that opportunity?

4. How do Noonan and Parker mobilize the rhetorical appeals of ethos, logos, and pathos to support an opinion on presidential rhetoric? Draw on passages from the texts to support your answer.

5. Parker's profile reveals that Favreau and then–presidential candidate Obama understood the import of opening the post-caucus speech with "They said this day would never come." Such an opening "would have multiple meanings to multiple people." Which people (audiences) were Favreau and Obama trying to reach? How might those audiences interpret that opening?

6. In their original forms, the three pieces of writing were delivered through three different means: a printed book (Noonan), a newspaper article (Parker), and a speech (Obama). Choose one of these pieces and examine how the choice of delivery was fitting for the particular rhetorical situation.

Rhetorical success in a digital world

Writer Virginia Heffernan writes a weekly article for the *New York Times Magazine*. "The Medium" focuses on the convergence of television and the Internet, analyzing the wide variety of online images and stories (from political rants to celebrity exposés) and the ever-expanding online means of visual and oral delivery (including, as Heffernan reports in her description of the column, "Web video, viral video, user-driven video, custom interactive video, embedded video ads, Web-based VOD [video on demand], broadband television, diavlogs [video blogs involving at least two people], vcasts, vlogs, video podcasts, mobisodes, Webisodes, mashups, and more"). In the following column, Heffernan analyzes the TED talks to which she's so addicted. As she informs her readers about the TED world, TEDsters, and their various personalities and agendas, she entertains her readers with her TED experience.

> Confessions of a TED Addict

Virginia Heffernan

Help. Here I go. My pulse is racing. I'm completely manic.

Oh why oh why have I been bingeing on TED talks again? I promised myself I would quit watching the ecstatic series of head-rush disquisitions, available online, from violinists, political prisoners, brain scientists, novelists and Bill Clinton. But I can't. Each hortatory TED talk starts with a bang and keeps banging till it explodes in fireworks. How can I shut it off? The speakers seem fevered, possessed, Pentecostal. No wonder I am, too, now.

A TED talk begins as an auditorium speech given at the multidisciplinary, invitation-only annual TED conference. . . . TED then creates videos of the speeches and puts them online so they can find a broader audience—and usurp my life. There are around 370 speeches and counting on Ted.com. A new one is added every weekday.

TED (which stands for "Technology, Entertainment, Design") was founded in 1984 by the architect Richard Saul Wurman and his partners. Their first conference included one of the first demonstrations of the Macintosh computer. In 2001, TED was acquired and is now run by Chris Anderson, the new-media entrepreneur who started Business 2.0, among other magazines and websites. Giving a TED talk has become an opportunity for name-in-lights speakers to throw down, set forth "ideas worth spreading" and prove their intellectual heroism.

According to June Cohen, the executive producer of TED Media, the speeches were once filmed and cut for a TV pilot. ("The idea of a 'lecture series' wasn't exactly greeted with enthusiasm by the networks," she says.) But she had another idea when she brought on Jason Wishnow, an online-video virtuoso. Together, they made the TED talks streamable on the Web in 2006. In less than three years, the talks have become a huge hit, attracting sponsorship from BMW and others. Karen Armstrong, Jeff Bezos, Jared Diamond, Helen Fisher, Peter Gabriel, Jane Goodall, Stephen Hawking, Maira Kalman, Nellie McKay, Isaac Mizrahi, Jimmy Wales and Rick Warren have all given TED talks. As of this month, the talks have been viewed more than 90 million times.

I have seen about 40. Let me say straight up that one of my favorites is "Simplicity Patterns," by the designer John Maeda. His talk made clear to me the uncanny resemblance between a block of tofu (the kind Maeda grew up making in his family's business in Seattle) and the I. M. Pei building that houses the M.I.T. Media Lab (where Maeda, who is now the president of the Rhode Island School of Design, used to work). Almost haphazardly associative, Maeda's talk expresses respect for the mandate of the talks—to change the world—without becoming sententious. You get rapid, straight-to-the-bloodstream access to his mental life.

Richard Termine/The New York Times

Singer-songwriter Nellie McKay is one of those who have presented TED talks.

Profiles

The other talk that does this poetically is Jill Bolte Taylor's "My Stroke of Insight." A brain scientist who studied the way she lost her own faculties during and after she suffered a stroke, Taylor urges the audience to pay attention to the sybaritic, present-tense right brain. Repeatedly, she recalls the pleasurable aspects of her stroke with such sensory precision that she seems to enter a rapturous trance. Not only do I buy her case for unfettered right-brain experience, but I began scheming to unfetter my right brain then and there.

While looking for your perfect TED talk, don't make the mistake I first did. I started with the 10 most popular. If you do that, you could form the impression that TED talkers are nutcase bullies like the self-help entrepreneur Tony Robbins, who gave a menacing, abrasive performance in "Why We Do What We Do, and How We Can Do It Better." Boasting about his renegade ways, he gunned through a series of piggish sophistries, only to fault fellow TEDster Al Gore—who was sitting in the front row, no less—for not making an emotional connection with the American electorate. (This was 2006.)

Once you start watching TED talks, ordinary life falls away. The corridor from Silicon Alley to Valley seems to crackle, and a new in-crowd emerges: the one that loves Linux, organic produce, behavioral economics, transhistorical theories and "An Inconvenient Truth." Even though there are certain TED poses that I don't warm to—the dour atheist, the environmental scold—the crowd as a whole glows with charisma. I love their greed for hope, their confidence in ingenuity, their organized but goofy ways of talking and thinking.

TED supplies its speakers with strict guidelines. "Start strong" is the most obvious one, and there is virtually no throat clearing or contrived thanking. Instead, speakers blaze onto the stage like stand-up comics, hellbent on room domination. Some consult notes and stay close by their audiovisual equipment—PowerPoint is used for emphasis, but it never directs the talks—while others pace, spread their arms wide and take up space. No one apologizes for himself. No one fails to make jokes. The appreciative room roars at humor, when they're not literally oohing and aahing at insight.

It's not easy to admit, then, that no single idea put forth in the TED talks seized me with its specifics. The necessary fiction at TED is that matters of substance— policy, practice, code—will emerge from the talks. But it's unlikely that a plan to disarm Iran or treat autism will surface; there's too much razzle-dazzle for brass tacks. What's really on display is much more right brain, and that's what I've come to be addicted to: the exposure to vigorous minds whirring as they work hard.

Right now I'm holed up on TED.com, sampling the talks. The TEDsters bellow their ideas at me, and I try to brook more stimulation. These are the people of the brain, after all, the understanders. They have only to chant some nostrums and cast rhetorical spells and I'm suddenly thinking some combination of *It's all going to be all right* and *The heck it is—but only I can stop it!* Thanks, TED. I'm clearly inspired out of my mind.

As mentioned earlier in this chapter, communications coach Carmine Gallo helps businesses do business better. Whether he's training executives in crisis management or meeting skills or talking with sales professionals about commitment to customers or persuasive presentations, he talks about motivation and engagement.

An Emmy award–winning television anchor (he has worked for CNN, CNET, and CBS) and media consultant for many major companies (such as Intel, Toshiba, SanDisk, and Clorox), Gallo has written a number of motivational books for business leaders. He also contributes a weekly column to Businessweek.com. "Uncovering Steve Jobs' Presentation Secrets" is one such column.

> Uncovering Steve Jobs' Presentation Secrets

Carmine Gallo

The Apple music event of Sept. 9, 2009, marked the return of the world's greatest corporate storyteller. For more than three decades, Apple co-founder and CEO Steve Jobs has raised product launches to an art form. In my new book, *The Presentation Secrets of Steve Jobs: How to Be Insanely Great in Front of Any Audience*, I reveal the techniques that Jobs uses to create and deliver mind-blowing keynote presentations.

Steve Jobs does not sell computers; he sells an experience. The same holds true for his presentations that are meant to inform, educate, and entertain. An Apple presentation has all the elements of a great theatrical production—a great script, heroes and villains, stage props, breathtaking visuals, and one moment that makes the price of admission well worth it. Here are the five elements of every Steve Jobs presentation. Incorporate these elements into your own presentations to sell your product or ideas the Steve Jobs way.

1. **A headline.** Steve Jobs positions every product with a headline that fits well within a 140-character Twitter post. For example, Jobs described the MacBook Air as "the world's thinnest notebook." That phrase appeared on his presentation slides, the Apple website, and Apple's press releases at the same time. What is the one thing you want people to know about your product? This headline must be consistent in all of your marketing and presentation material.

2. **A villain.** In every classic story, the hero fights the villain. In 1984, the villain, according to Apple, was IBM. Before Jobs introduced the famous 1984 television ad to the Apple sales team for the first time, he told a story of how IBM was bent on dominating the computer industry. "IBM wants it all and is aiming its guns on its last obstacle to industry control: Apple." Today, the "villain" in Apple's narrative is played by Microsoft. One can argue that the popular "I'm a Mac" television ads are hero/villain vignettes. This idea of conquering a shared enemy is a powerful motivator and turns customers into evangelists.

3. **A simple slide.** Apple products are easy to use because of the elimination of clutter. The same approach applies to the slides in a Steve Jobs presentation. They are strikingly simple, visual, and yes, devoid of bullet points. Pictures are dominant. When Jobs introduced the MacBook Air,

no words could replace a photo of a hand pulling the notebook computer out of an interoffice manila envelope. Think about it this way—the average PowerPoint slide has 40 words. In some presentations, Steve Jobs has a total of seven words in 10 slides. And why are you cluttering up your slides with too many words?

4. **A demo.** Neuroscientists have discovered that the brain gets bored easily. Steve Jobs doesn't give you time to lose interest. Ten minutes into a presentation he's often demonstrating a new product or feature and having fun doing it. When he introduced the iPhone at Macworld 2007, Jobs demonstrated how Google Maps worked on the device. He pulled up a list of Starbucks stores in the local area and said, "Let's call one." When someone answered, Jobs said: "I'd like to order 4,000 lattes to go, please. No, just kidding."

5. **A holy smokes moment.** Every Steve Jobs presentation has one moment that neuroscientists call an "emotionally charged event." The emotionally charged event is the equivalent of a mental post-it note that tells the brain, Remember this! For example, at Macworld 2007, Jobs could have opened the presentation by telling the audience that Apple was unveiling a new mobile phone that also played music, games, and video. Instead he built up the drama. "Today, we are introducing three revolutionary products. The first one is a widescreen iPod with touch controls. The second is a revolutionary mobile phone. And the third is a breakthrough Internet communications device . . . an iPod, a phone, an Internet communicator . . . an iPod, a phone, are you getting it? These are not three devices. This is one device!" The audience erupted in cheers because it was so unexpected, and very entertaining. By the way, the holy smokes moment on Sept. 9 had nothing to do with a product. It was Steve Jobs himself appearing onstage for the first time after undergoing a liver transplant.

One more thing . . . sell dreams. Charismatic speakers like Steve Jobs are driven by a nearly messianic zeal to create new experiences. When he launched the iPod in 2001, Jobs said, "In our own small way we're going to make the world a better place." Where most people saw the iPod as a music player, Jobs recognized its potential as a tool to enrich people's lives. Cultivate a sense of mission. Passion, emotion, and enthusiasm are grossly underestimated ingredients in professional business communications, and yet, passion and emotion will motivate others. Steve Jobs once said that his goal was not to die the richest man in the cemetery. It was to go to bed at night thinking that he and his team had done something wonderful. Do something wonderful. Make your brand stand for something meaningful.

AP Photo/Paul Sakuma

> ANALYZING THE RHETORICAL SITUATION

1. What opportunity might Heffernan be responding to by writing a weekly column on new media? How does her column respond to that opportunity for change? What are the constraints and resources of her rhetorical situation?

2. Who might be Heffernan's intended audience? What might be the audience's concerns, values, or knowledge?

3. Who is Gallo's intended audience? How does Gallo use the rhetorical appeals to connect with that audience? What is his rhetorical purpose?

4. How does Gallo deliver his message? What media and genre does he choose?

5. How does the arrangement of Gallo's text match what is being said? What effect does the form have? How does he use style and tone purposefully?

COMMUNITY CONNECTIONS

1. Spend several minutes freewriting about your response to President Obama's speech. Why was this speech important? Next, spend several minutes freewriting about whether Peggy Noonan's description of speechwriting made you think differently about the effectiveness, purpose, or value of Obama's speech. Why or why not? Refer to specific passages from the text as you compose your response.

2. What reasons does Noonan offer for the importance of political speeches? What is your opinion of each of these reasons? In what ways have technological innovations since 1990, when Noonan presented her ideas, affected political speeches?

3. Ashley Parker writes "[Hillary] Clinton had helped turn her campaign around by discounting Mr. Obama's elegant oratory, saying, 'You campaign in poetry, but you govern in prose.'" What did Clinton mean by such a statement? How might her ranking in the polls have influenced her statement?

4. Think of a time when you believed that someone's actions did not or could not live up to his or her words. What was the rhetorical situation? What was the outcome? What features of the rhetorical situation led to the outcome that proved you right—or maybe even wrong?

5. Perhaps you hadn't considered that public figures (political candidates, university presidents and administrators, CEOs, and so on) often rely on

professional speechwriters. As you reconsider the Favreau piece, can you imagine any people you know or listen to who might be using speechwriters? What makes you think so? What are the results of using—or not using—a trustworthy speechwriter?

6. Identify two or three speeches or presentations—formal or informal—that you've heard in the past year. Of these, choose one that you consider a success, and explain what made it successful.

Profiles: A Fitting Response

A profile of a professional who shapes his world with words

We seem to be fascinated by people who have demonstrated unique abilities to establish a character, connect with our emotions, and move others to action through words. Profiles serve as a means through which readers can understand what motivates these writers and speakers and what experiences have helped them develop their abilities with words.

In the following profile, Marisa Lagos examines Tommie Lindsey's efforts to help students at Logan High School in California improve their abilities in public speaking and debate.

Successes Speak Well for Debate Coach

Marisa Lagos

Logan High School forensics coach Tommie Lindsey's classroom says a thing or two about his success: It's crowded with banners, trophies and kids. On this morning, Lindsey is just minutes from loading 38 high school students into buses and heading to Long Beach, where they will compete in the Jack Howe Invitational. More than 60 schools from across the nation would participate in the three-day forensics challenge, competing in public speaking, presentation and debate. The Logan High team would take the grand sweepstakes award as well as six individual first-place awards.

Lindsey, a 15-year teacher at the Bay Area school, was recently named one of 23 recipients of the MacArthur Foundation's annual $500,000 award—a so-called "genius grant" the foundation disburses over a five-year period with no strings attached. Meant to underscore "the importance of a creative individual in society," according to the foundation, "fellows are selected for their originality, creativity, and the potential to do more in the future."

Recipients of the grants are nominated anonymously, but Lindsey's qualifications are obvious. Logan High, a public school in a middle- to low-income area, has claimed four

The writer shows that she not only interviewed her subject but spent time with him engaged in the activity that has made him newsworthy.

The writer explains why the subject is interesting and important—he's a prestigious award winner (a "genius," no less).

state forensics titles and many other awards in a type of academic competition usually more suited for prep schools than public schools. Typically, the 16 forensic categories include speech, interpretation and acting.

This paragraph gives details about how the subject is making a difference in his community.

Lindsey, 53, a Mississippi transplant, is known for his dedication. He usually works seven days and up to 150 hours a week. If he's not practicing with the 300-plus-member team—most schools have about 40 members and as many as eight coaches—he's attending weekend tournaments from 6 A.M. to 11 P.M. "I think every teacher does a lot," said Alphonso Thompson, Lindsey's substitute teacher and former student, "but what Lindsey does goes above and beyond the call of duty a million times over. I don't know where I would be if it wasn't for Mr. Lindsey." He has had numerous offers, mostly from private schools, to bring his expertise, and his assistant coach, Tim Campbell, elsewhere, and says he has entertained some of those offers seriously, especially since learning that the program's funding for next year is threatened. For now, Lindsey is still at Logan, where he has taught public speaking and debate to about 3,000 students, many of them from poor and/or single-parent homes.

This paragraph gives readers a sense of the specific types of work that the subject does as well as the attitude with which the subject approaches his job.

When Lindsey started at Logan in 1989 there were many skeptics. "Even the principal didn't think we would be able to do forensics at Logan," he said. So Lindsey began recruiting athletes, whom he believed would take to competition. "I went out and started getting athletes and putting them to the challenge. I would say, 'I don't think you can do this.' . . . Finally, they would come out and find that they love it."

It's that mix of tough love, confidence and intuition that makes Lindsey both a friend and a foe. But most of all, it's what sparks his students. Varun Mitra, a senior at Logan, started on the team as a freshman. "Mr. Lindsey sacrifices a lot," Mitra said. "He never gives up on you if you say no to him. . . . He'll keep going after you to the point where you realize he was right, until he molds you into a better life." Before forensics, Mitra had planned to go to a University of California campus because his parents encouraged it. Now, he has even grander plans: after a bachelor's degree, law school. "Four years ago when I came in, I wasn't able to speak in front of anyone. . . . This program made me want to pursue a career in public speaking—as a lawyer, in politics," he said. "This program has helped me decide what I want to do in life."

The writer doesn't simply tell readers that Lindsey "sparks his students"; she lets one student's experiences serve as an example to show how Lindsey motivates students.

Not all of Logan's students fit the typical mold for a forensics team, however. Many have been diagnosed with learning disabilities; others have never made academics their focus. And half the team members are female, still somewhat unusual in forensics.

But what really sets Lindsey's program apart is that its popularity has made being smart cool, mainly because the students see each other getting good grades. "When you join the program it creates expectations that you're going to further your education in college," said Mike Joshi, a senior. He plans to apply to several Ivy League colleges this year. "There are kids in honors classes that need the intellectual outlet," Lindsey said, "but many of the kids may not fit into standard academics. Some have been labeled special ed, and they come in and we find a place for them. . . . It's a matter of believing in a kid and finding a special something the kid does."

The writer has consulted more than one source in putting together this profile: the subject himself and several students.

It's also about pushing students to do what they never thought possible: More than 90% of them go on to attend college. "I presently have a kid living in a two-bedroom apartment with five people. He sleeps on the couch. . . . But he wants to be able to do forensics, because it's an outlet," Lindsey said. "Once you're involved in this group, you start thinking about four-year colleges. Not if, but when." Lindsey moved to west Oakland as a child and graduated from Castelmont High School. He received a bachelor of arts degree from the University of San Francisco—where he was the school's first African American valedictorian—and went on to get a bachelor of science degree and secondary teaching certificate there. Lindsey then went to law school for a year and simultaneously began teaching to "pay the bills." He was hooked, and after five years teaching at Alameda County's Juvenile Hall, Lindsey landed a full-time teaching job at El Rancho Verde High School, where he stayed until moving to Logan.

He is the father of two Logan students—Terrence, a junior at the school, and Erica, 21, now a student at UCLA. It was his children he thought of first when he was awarded the grant last month, he said. "With this money, we're finally going to get some relief here. Most important is my daughter and son's educations." That help is well-deserved, say Lindsey's colleagues and students, who are pleased that the money is for him alone.

Lindsey said he was surprised and happy when he got the call. "It's great, not just because I was honored, but because teachers are not respected as they should be. Teaching changes lives and builds kids up. . . . They should be given more recognition than they receive," he said. "I was so happy the MacArthur Foundation is now looking at public school teachers, because it's very different. You have to be loyal to work in a public setting. I was shocked, and very appreciative."

Lindsey said he ended up in forensics because he was always fascinated by oration—including listening as a child to sermons at the Baptist churches he attended and to civil rights speeches by the Rev. Martin Luther King, Jr. While in high school, Lindsey decided he wanted to speak at the graduation ceremony. Though his teacher doubted him, she said he could try, then handed him his topic: "Investing in Learning to Cultivate the Intellect." After his initial frustration melted away, Lindsey sat down with a neighbor and hashed out a speech—one that got him a standing ovation at the ceremony. "I took that negative energy and propelled it," he said, adding that he still looks after that neighbor, who is now 102. The students at Logan are not the only ones to gain something, however. Logan journalism teacher Patrick Hannigan said: "At the end of my career, what I will remember is that I worked with Tommie Lindsey."

The profile turns to Lindsey's past to show how his experiences have informed his present-day efforts to motivate students to attend college.

The writer shows readers how the concerns Lindsey has for his family also shape his encouraging of his students.

The writer helps readers see what motivates the subject.

The anecdote reveals how the subject's own experiences showed him the power and possibilities of effective public speaking; it also helps to bring the subject to life.

■ GUIDE TO RESPONDING TO THE RHETORICAL SITUATION

Understanding the Rhetorical Situation

When you want to share your understanding of somebody with an audience, consider composing a profile. Profiles commonly have the following features:

- Profiles have as their subject someone readers will find compelling or interesting.
- Profiles provide descriptive details to help readers imagine how the subject looks, sounds, or acts.
- Profiles include several direct quotations from the subject or others that help readers understand the person's opinions and perspectives.
- Profiles draw on evidence and insights from a variety of sources, such as personal observations, interviews, and research.
- Profiles present several anecdotes about the subject that show readers the background and experiences that have shaped the subject.
- Profiles lead readers to a particular emotional response or logical conclusion about the subject.

 The following sections will help you compose a profile about someone who is successful with words. To work with an online guide to the elements of the rhetorical situation, access your English CourseMate through cengagebrain.com.

Identifying an opportunity

Consider the people who work or study in the community around you. You might listen to those individuals on campus whose voices have shaped the dialogue about pressing concerns. Or you might listen to others whose voices influence the people in your community, such as the preachers who craft their messages with deft rhetorical style or the teachers and debate coaches who create learning opportunities for students to develop writing and speaking skills they can put to use as active civic participants.

1. Make a list of the interesting writers you've read or the inspiring speakers you've heard over the past few weeks or months, including the one you wrote about in response to the questions on page 127. Have any of your fellow students inspired others to action through their words? Do you know of any teachers who have inspired students to develop their own voices in their writing and add these voices to the important conversations on campus? Are there any poets, rappers, or writers pushing the boundaries of how words are used in our everyday lives? For each one, write a few sentences describing your initial impressions of the speaker or writer. To help explain your impressions, write down as many details about the writer's presentation or the speaker's performance as you can.

2. For one or two of the writers or speakers whom you wrote about in response to question 1, locate images—or, if the opportunity presents itself, take photos—that capture some aspects of the individual's personality. Then spend several minutes writing about what the visuals convey about the person's ability to inject life and energy into his or her words.

3. Choose the writer or speaker you would like to profile and compose four or five sentences that describe the ways in which that person has succeeded. Then spend several minutes freewriting about the contexts in which this person's words have had influence and the specific ways in which they move people: What is the purpose of the person's writing or speeches? When and where do this person's words have the most influence, and who has been the audience for these words? Describe what you know about the person's background and analyze how this background might be influencing the person's public success with words. If your profile will feature a particular text or speech, describe how you interpreted it when you initially encountered it and after you thought about it.

pages 67–68

Locating an audience

The following questions will help you identify your rhetorical audience for your profile. Your answers will also help you describe and analyze your subject's effective way with words.

1. List the names of the persons or groups (students, faculty, administrators, community members, or alumni) likely to be engaged—positively or negatively—by your subject's words.

2. Next to the name of each potential audience, write reasons that audience could have for appreciating the subject's rhetorical prowess. In other words, what would persuade these audiences that they need to learn about this person's experiences, perspectives, and motivations in greater detail?

3. How could each of these audiences be influenced by a profile of this individual? In other words, what emotional responses or logical conclusions could you expect your profile of this successful speaker to lead to? Consider the implications of these emotional responses or logical conclusions for each audience and the motivations each audience might have for learning more about the personal experiences, values, and worldview that have affected your subject.

4. With these different audiences' interests and motivations in mind, return to the descriptions of the subject's speaking or writing that you composed in the preceding section. Add descriptive details, images, and compelling quotes or audio snippets (you may need to conduct some interviews or do other kinds of research) that will enable your readers to feel invested in exploring the life of this person who has shaped the campus or the local or broader community with his or her words. A good description will help your audience more clearly visualize the person at work, hear how he or she has moved people to action through speeches or writing, and understand how this individual has affected the school or the local or broader community. Tailor your best description to connect closely to your audience's needs and interests.

Identifying a fitting response

As you've been learning throughout this book, different purposes and different audiences require different kinds of texts—delivered through different media. For example, if you're writing about a student leader on campus, you might want to compose a feature article to appear in the student newspaper, the alumni magazine, or on the website of the Office of Student Life. If you're writing about a community activist, your profile could take the form of a creative piece for a local zine. Your profile of a community business or political leader could be the PowerPoint centerpiece of a program for an awards banquet honoring that person. You could record an audio profile of an inspiring professor for your campus radio station or for a podcast, encouraging other students to take this professor's course next semester. The point is that once you identify your opportunity, locate your audience, and find your purpose, you will want to determine what kind of text will best respond to the rhetorical situation.

Use the following questions to help you narrow your purpose and shape your response:

1. What kinds of facts and details do you need to provide in order to create a vivid picture of your subject and his or her success?
2. What past experiences or current activities and actions make your subject compelling to your audience?
3. What do your readers need to know in order to understand what motivates this speaker or writer and to appreciate the significance of this person's words for the school or community?
4. Are you asking the audience to adopt a new perspective on this individual? Or do you want to prompt the audience to take a specific action in response to your message?
5. What is the best way to reach this audience? That is, to what kind of text will this audience most likely respond? (Chapter 13 can help you explore options for media and design.)

Writing a Profile: Working with Your Available Means

Shaping your profile

One major reason writers create profiles is to let others know more about the people who are important to them or who shape the world in which we live. A writer using this genre often uses the rhetorical appeal of pathos in the introduction to connect the subject to the readers' emotions and values. In short, the introduction to a profile needs to show readers that the subject is someone they need to know more about—right now. Marisa Lagos, for example, immediately offers evidence of Tommie Lindsey's success: banners and trophies won by his students and his own "genius grant." Writers also use the introduction of a profile to highlight some key feature of the subject's personality, character, or values; by noting that genius grants are given to original and creative individuals, Lagos draws attention to these characteristics of Lindsey.

Introduction	Body	Conclusion
▶ Shows readers that the subject is someone they need to know more about ▶ Highlights some key feature of the subject's personality, character, or values	▶ Presents a fuller description of the subject and his or her life's work ▶ Includes details that help readers to visualize the subject's actions and hear the subject's words ▶ Provides logical appeals in the form of examples that show how the individual's work affects the lives of people like the readers themselves	▶ Often contains one final quote or anecdote that nicely captures the essence of the individual ▶ May bring readers into the present day, if the profile has had a historical scope

© 2013 Cengage Learning

After capturing readers' attention with a brief image of the subject, the writer may begin the body of the profile by presenting a fuller description of the subject and his or her life's work. Lagos, for example, lets readers know that Lindsey possesses "obvious" credentials for the MacArthur Foundation's grant because of his work in helping students from a middle- to low-income area win several state titles "in a type of academic competition usually more suited for prep schools than public schools." Lagos uses the rhetorical appeal of pathos as she describes Lindsey as a "genius." This appeal to the emotions of the readers—who's not fascinated by geniuses and interested in learning how they see the world?—helps convince them that Lindsey is worth learning more about.

The body of a profile also includes descriptive details that help readers visualize the subject's actions and hear the subject's words. Readers of Lagos's profile, for example, learn that Lindsey "usually works seven days and up to 150 hours a week. If he's not practicing with the 300-plus-member team . . . he's attending weekend tournaments from 6 A.M. to 11 P.M." Lagos incorporates these and other details into her profile in order to draw readers closer to the subject and to let them feel they're learning about aspects of Lindsey's personality that make him unique and influence the ways in which he works with words.

Writers also use the body of a profile to provide logical appeals in the form of numerous examples that show that the subject is indeed making a difference in the community. The crux of the logical appeal, in fact, is the explanation of how the individual's work affects the lives of people like the readers themselves. Lagos, for example, presents the story of Varun Mitra, a senior at Logan High School whose participation on Lindsey's forensics team has inspired him to work toward a law degree. Readers see from exemplification pages 66–67 that Lindsey has indeed helped to inspire many students to continue their education. Through details supporting Lindsey's success in improving the lives of students often ignored and marginalized in public education, Lagos connects his achievements with a value her readers no doubt hold: the importance of all students having equal access to quality education and equal opportunities to succeed in life.

Lagos strengthens this logical appeal by providing quotations from Varun Mitra and Lindsey's colleague Patrick Hannigan. These quotations lend support to Lagos's assertions about Lindsey's significance to his community. The strength of Lagos's logical appeal ultimately rests on the assumption that her readers value people who expend the energy and effort necessary to make contributions to their communities. The quotations from Lindsey's students and colleague, as well as quotations from Lindsey himself, also help Lagos create an ethical appeal. That Lagos talked directly with several people before composing the profile strengthens the credibility of her claims about Lindsey's abilities to motivate his students as well as to inspire his fellow teachers. If Lagos had created an audio profile, the quotations could have been incorporated as audio snippets from her interviews, thereby literally bringing new voices into the profile.

Finally, the conclusion of a profile often contains one final quote or anecdote that nicely captures the essence of the individual. Lagos, for example, leaves readers with a quotation conveying high praise from one of Lindsey's colleagues: "At the end of my career, what I will remember is that I worked with Tommie Lindsey."

Revision and peer review

After you've drafted a strong version of your profile, ask one of your classmates to read through or look over it. You'll want your classmate to respond to your work in a way that helps you revise it into the strongest profile it can be, one that addresses your intended audience, helps you fulfill your purpose, and is delivered in the most appropriate means available to you.

Questions for a peer reviewer

1. To what opportunity for change is the writer responding?
2. Who might be the writer's intended audience?
3. What might be the writer's purpose?
4. What information did you receive from the introduction? How effective is the introduction in terms of establishing an emotional connection between the subject and the audience? What suggestions do you have for the writer regarding the introduction?
5. Note the facts and details the writer provides in order to create a vivid picture of the subject and his or her success.
6. What past experiences or current activities and actions does the writer point out to make the subject compelling to you? How could the writer help you better understand what motivates his or her subject?
7. How does the writer establish ethos? How could the writer strengthen this appeal?
8. What material does the writer use to establish logos? How might the writer strengthen this appeal (see questions 5 and 6)?
9. Other than in the introduction, how does the writer make use of pathos?
10. What did you learn from the conclusion that you didn't already know after reading the introduction and body? What information does the writer want you to take away from the profile? Does the writer attempt to change your attitude, action, or opinion?
11. What section of the profile did you most enjoy? Why?

PROFILES IN THREE MEDIA

Audio Profile

The audio profile of Bill McKibben was written and recorded by Alena Martin and produced at WBYX at the University of Oregon. To listen, find *Writing in Three Media* in your English CourseMate, accessed through cengagebrain .com.

AP Photo/Toby Talbot

Online Profile

The online profile of Beverly Wright of the Deep South Center for Environmental Justice was composed by Faiza Elmasry. To read it, find *Writing in Three Media* in your English Course-Mate, accessed through cengagebrain.com.

Lori Waselchuk/The New York Times/Redux

Print Profile

In the following profile, student writer Matthew Glasgow addresses the rhetorical opportunity of capturing a classroom experience. ....

Photo by Richie Wireman, Courtesy of the University of Kentucky.

pages 75–77

Matthew could have worked in various genres or media to present his professor's skills. If his purpose had been to persuade his fellow education majors of the power of particular teaching practices, he could have written a position argument for their newsletter. If he had wanted to nominate his professor for a teaching award, he could have drafted a formal letter to the nominating committee. Or, if he had wanted to share his musings on why some people are so good with words, he could have composed a blog entry. Matthew knew that his subject was someone that his audience—his college classmates—didn't know well but would find compelling. He also knew that he had several anecdotes based on experiences in and out of the classroom that he could combine with observations and direct quotations to provide a well-rounded picture of his subject—in a word, a profile. He chose the printed form because the piece was turned in as a class assignment.

Profiles

Matthew Glasgow

Professor Goldthwaite

English 215

20 November 2009

The Liberating Mind

Colloquially speaking, he's rad. He entered the lecture hall donning his

Matthew's first sentence aims to establish a connection between the subject and college-age readers.

sleek black-rimmed glasses, in one hand a notebook and a text, our first

reading, Plato's *Five Dialogues*. Bookmarks jutted out on all sides, drawing

attention to the annotated pages within, which he had no doubt read

upwards of twenty times throughout his relatively young lifetime. In the other

hand he carried a cup of coffee, envied by most students, particularly

myself, at 8:30 a.m. on that first Tuesday of the fall semester at Saint Joseph's

University. After placing each item on the table, Dr. Arnold Farr began to

read off the names listed on his roster, thus launching his course The Human

Person, which, for many of us, served as our first experience in the realm of

philosophy.

Not only is the professor "rad," but he's teaching a course that college-age students would be interested in. Thus, a connection is made.

Though quickly impressed with the subtleties of Dr. Farr's professional

mien, I soon came to increasingly respect the process behind his work and

the way he successfully communicated with his students and colleagues.

Throughout the course he was able to identify with his students by

relating the texts to topics that a college student might be more prone to

understand. The first of these many connections occurred during our studies

Matthew identifies a key feature of the subject's ability to successfully communicate: relating texts to topics a college student would likely understand.

of Sigmund Freud and Herbert Marcuse.

When discussing Marcuse's interpretation of the Freudian Performance

Principle, Dr. Farr informed us that he does not carry a cell phone. The

principle refers to how socially and historically created structures serve as

guidelines for what societies should desire. Marcuse believed that such a standard of behavior functioned as a subtle form of oppression, isolating those who differed from the societal norm.

"If you don't have a cell phone, people look at you funny," Farr explained, yet he found his life simplified by using only his office and home phones when necessary. This example shows not only how he explains philosophy in more readily understood terms, but also the way in which he himself manifests his philosophical beliefs in his own life.

The cell phone example shows how Farr successfully communicates with his students.

Another clarifying example came from the music industry. During our study of Marcuse's "Dialectic of Civilization," we considered culture's influence on communities. Marcuse identified Eros as a pleasure-seeking and creative principle, which finds itself in conflict with the death instinct. This death instinct also seeks pleasure; however, its qualities are more destructive and produce aggression. To help us understand the relationship between Eros and the death instinct, Dr. Farr explained that the history of music and the music industry have a similar relationship. Originally musicians wrote songs and melodies as a means of personal, social, and cultural expression, but as record labels emerged as major corporations seeking greater profits, artists' music became increasingly formulaic. By repressing musicians' freedom of expression, the music industry destroyed what the art of music was meant to achieve.

Again, Farr taps the contemporary scene to explain a complex philosophical idea, thereby successfully communicating to his students.

Farr's explanations in his course lectures provided guidance for his students; however, in several functions on campus, Dr. Farr also identified with people of various walks of life. "In a way I am still the same kid from years ago, while a part of me has also matured as well," Farr said of this ability to speak several forms of English, which proved vital when he lectured to students, fellow professors, and members of the local community simultaneously.

Matthew develops the body of his profile essay with fuller descriptions of how the professor works toward successful communication.

Fig. 1. Dr. Arnold Farr in his office (Photo by Richie Wireman, Courtesy of the University of Kentucky)

As part of the celebration of black history in February, he organized multiple events, including an African-American Read-In and a campus visit by actress Ruby Dee Davis. Farr spoke at both events, sharing a passage by Dr. Cornel West at the read-in and providing an introduction for Davis, to audiences of students, professors, and many residents of the Philadelphia area. With such a range of people, most of whom spoke to Farr prior to or following the festivities, it was not hard to notice the appreciation and respect he had earned over the years through his cordial nature and stimulating intellectual activities.

In yet another significant contribution to the community, Dr. Farr organized the Alain Locke Conference, an event celebrating and discussing the work of the praised African-American philosopher. Through Farr's efforts, several of the top Lockeian experts from across the country joined together to present their own essays interpreting and expanding upon Locke's philosophies. In addition to hosting and organizing the conference, Dr. Farr presented his essay entitled "Beyond Repressive Tolerance: Alain Locke's Hermeneutics of Democracy as a Response to Herbert Marcuse's Deconstruction of the Same."

Though the extensive title of his work appeared to be slightly intimidating, Dr. Farr provided a clear lecture to ensure clarity for all persons present. He examined the extent to which tolerance serves as a democratic value, specifically questioning the tolerance of harmful views and ideas. When misunderstood by a colleague, Farr clarified his thesis by explaining the need for a struggle and potential for change. Interpreting values as contingent rather than dogmatic, Farr stated that one's ability to change or legitimate one's views over time allowed for a greater chance for true tolerance.

After Dr. Farr's thoughts on "the problem of tolerance as a democratic value" were clarified, the man replied, "if that is what you are saying, then I understand and I agree with you." Once again, Farr's communication through his essay and his words following its presentation revealed the ease with which he can educate both young and old, scholar and student.

As the semester progressed, we reached one of the more sensitive subjects—race and its prevalence in the philosophical realm. Race, in itself, arose as an intriguing medium through which to consider the philosophies of liberation, criminalization, and dialectics of past and present human relations.

For this subject we turned to the writings of Angela Davis, who had made a much publicized visit to the campus the previous year, tainted by unfair assaults on her character. Prior to her visit, flyers produced by a select group of students and faculty were posted labeling Davis as a "lesbian, communist, and black panther" among other things. As a friend of Davis and the administrator who had invited her to speak, Dr. Farr quickly came to her defense and even e-mailed a colleague who had been involved with the flyers and negative articles in the newspapers. He simply asked his coworker if he had ever taken the time to read any of Davis's work, which his colleague had not.

A student later posted on a website created to rate professors that Dr. Farr's class was aimed at making white people feel bad about slavery and the oppression of African Americans. Upon discovering this accusation, Farr decided to incorporate a question on his final exam asking his students to agree with or deny this statement based upon the readings and class focus. The responses overwhelmingly disproved the allegation, primarily discussing the calls by Davis for change and liberation in the future, rather than sympathy for slavery.

What keeps this profile believable (thereby enhancing the ethos of the writer) is that Farr is portrayed authentically. Many students admire him, but at least one does not. Being a human being (with feelings), Farr not only checks out his ratings but tries to resolve the criticism he finds on the ratings website.

Strangely enough, the attacks were manifestations of many of the philosophies in Davis's texts and discussed by Farr during course lectures. Due to the events surrounding his friend's visit and the need for greater understanding of the role of race in philosophy, Dr. Farr committed himself to teaching Davis's texts in every semester of The Human Person. His professional and humorous responses to these unfortunate claims emphasize his clever use of language to resolve conflict and succeed at his position as teacher, philosopher, and friend.

"I have always advocated the ability to think critically," Farr has said, careful to differentiate between critique and criticism. Farr referred to social critique in philosophy as a means of improving injustices and liberating individuals in the future, while criticism offers only negative responses without any means of progress.

"I also take into account the historical context which gave birth to all these ideas. It is important to understand how language has come to be in itself," Farr said of his appreciation of the history of both the philosophical ideologies and the language by which they are communicated.

At the conclusion of the semester, I interviewed Dr. Farr concerning a documentary I had been crafting entitled *War and Peace*. Hundreds of texts lined the walls of his office, all surely consolidated in the man before me who spoke of Immanuel Kant's "Perpetual Peace" and mankind's current inability to reconcile differences without violence.

"We have to be careful to not always assume we are the 'good guy'," he told me. "You cannot force democracy on people, and we have not yet completed our democratic experiment here." These words were not spoken with spite, like many in the political realm, but rather were grounded in reason and conscientious thought.

These words were a product of his extensive studies at Carson-Newman College and the University of Kentucky, where he received his master's and doctoral degrees. He remembers those years at the University of Kentucky as ones that changed and matured his way of thinking, providing a constant value for education.

And now, as the educator, Dr. Arnold Farr recognizes himself as one person attempting to inspire many young people, but realizes his students have the same opportunities he once did. "Teaching is difficult when students have no interest," he says, "but I hope that by the end of the semester some lights go on." And though those lights may be sparse in a world where philosophy seems to be fading, each new gleam sheds hope on the future. •

Matthew closes with a moving quotation by Farr that captures the essence of the professor's key characteristic.

The final sentence brings readers to the present and leads them into a hopeful future.

Profiles

Alternatives to the Profile

Fitting responses come in many forms, not just profiles. Your instructor might call on you to consider one of the following opportunities for writing.

pages 66–67

1. What have you accomplished through the persuasive or inventive use of language? What specific events exemplify your ability to get things done or to move people to action through words? What life experiences propelled you to this success? Write a memoir that describes how you succeeded with spoken or written words. Be sure to include details and quotations to help your readers imagine what that experience must have been like, as well as a concise analysis of the insights you gained through that experience.

pages 69–70

2. How effective are eloquent, rhetorically powerful speeches? What political, cultural, or social consequences have followed from them? In an analytical essay, trace the effects of one public address that many people claim is historically significant or even timeless. As you conduct this analysis, consider the extent to which this speech contributed to actions that followed it.

3. Write a critical review of a speech or a public document that addressed an issue of particular importance to your campus or your community. Identify the criteria that you will use to evaluate the effectiveness of the speech or text and then evaluate the extent to which it does or does not meet those criteria. Be sure to provide specific evidence and details from the speech or public document in order to support your conclusion.

Examining the Millennial Generation: Responding with Investigative Reports

College students who will graduate in 2014 and were born in or around 1992 are members of the Millennial Generation, also known as Generation Y. This generation shares many of the characteristics, viewpoints, and experiences that appear on the Beloit College Mindset List (www.beloit.edu/mindset). Ten of the seventy-five items of the list for the class of 2014 are shown on page 160, and just a glance at those items will tell you if you are a Millennial. If you are a first-year student who was born earlier than 1992 (like the great and growing number of those entering college as older adults) or later (like a number of advanced young people), you may not feel as though you share this mindset with your classmates.

At the start of each fall semester since 1998, Beloit College has released the Mindset List for the incoming college class, noting touchstones that have shaped the lives of that class. Created by Beloit's Keefer Professor of the Humanities Tom McBride and former Public Affairs Director Ron Nief, the Mindset List reminds faculty members of their dated references and of the experiences and values of their incoming students. For college faculty, the assassinations of Mohandas Gandhi, John F. Kennedy, Malcolm X, Robert F. Kennedy, Dr. Martin Luther King, Jr., and John Lennon may have marked critical moments in their younger lives; for incoming college students, those assassinations are ancient history, comparable to the assassinations of Abraham Lincoln or Julius Caesar.

AP Photo/Mark Humphrey

The Beloit College Mindset List for the Class of 2014

Most students entering college for the first time this fall—the Class of 2014—were born in 1992. For these students, Benny Hill, Sam Kinison, Sam Walton, Bert Parks and Tony Perkins have always been dead.

1. Few in the class know how to write in cursive.
2. E-mail is just too slow, and they seldom if ever use snail mail.
3. "Go West, Young College Grad" has always implied "and don't stop until you get to Asia . . . and learn Chinese along the way."
4. Al Gore has always been animated.
5. Los Angelenos have always been trying to get along.
6. Buffy has always been meeting her obligations to hunt down Lothos and the other blood-suckers at Hemery High.
7. "Caramel macchiato" and "venti half-caf vanilla latte" have always been street corner lingo.
8. With increasing numbers of ramps, Braille signs, and handicapped parking spaces, the world has always been trying harder to accommodate people with disabilities.
9. Had it remained operational, the villainous computer HAL could be their college classmate this fall, but they have a better chance of running into Miley Cyrus's folks on Parents' Weekend.
10. Entering college this fall in a country where a quarter of young people under 18 have at least one immigrant parent, they aren't afraid of immigration . . . unless it involves "real" aliens from another planet.

According to the Mindset List, "e-mail is just too slow" for the Millennials. Little wonder, then, that for this generation, doing just one thing at a time can seem outdated. The numerous distractions in the working and learning environments of Millennials and others close to their age provided a rhetorical opportunity for Christine Rosen, who published an investigative report titled "The Myth of Multitasking" (see pages 181–184). **Investigative reports** like Rosen's are commonly used to present the results of research. In her report, Rosen takes the opportunity to explain to readers the common perceptions—and misperceptions—about multitasking. At a time when far too many people celebrate their ability to multitask (and when employers may expect them to do it), Rosen analyzes the consequences of this behavior.

IDENTIFYING AN OPPORTUNITY

Throughout this chapter, you'll work to identify an opportunity to investigate a specific characteristic of the Millennials or of another generation. As you know, pundits are called on to hypothesize about up-and-coming generations for the mass media. As an investigative researcher, you will be doing more than hypothesizing: you will be making observations, conducting interviews, developing surveys, drawing from your personal experience, or doing library, online, or archival research and then presenting your findings to your audience. Whether or not you consider yourself a member of the Millennials, you can offer important insights or observations about a cultural touchstone, behavior, or value of a specific generation. As you work to determine what you want to investigate, consider the most fitting means of delivery for your report:

Print Report

written for a community or campus newspaper or local zine

Video Report

filmed for a campus television station or filmed and uploaded to YouTube

Online Report

for your online campus newspaper

To begin, freewrite for five minutes in response to each of the following questions (or use any of the invention techniques presented on pages 58–61):

1. Which physical spaces on your campus (or in your town) attract the Millennials—coffee shops, gyms, computer labs, multimedia labs, libraries? Do any of those spaces attract people of other generations as well? What physical spaces attract mostly students who are older or younger than the Millennials—study rooms, eating facilities, game rooms, sports areas? Describe a specific physical space and its inhabitants in as much detail as possible.

2. Consider the expectations of the Millennials (or students from an older or younger generation) on your campus. What particular services have been customized to meet those expectations? Think about career services, services for international students, academic services, and student life services as well as the offerings of the dining services and libraries. What specific evidence can you supply for your observation? Who might be interested in or disagree with your observation?

3. What would you like to know about the effects of the presence on your campus or in your community of the Millennial generation (or another older or younger generation)? Where might you begin researching for information to answer your question? Who, besides you, might be interested in what you find out?

4. What groups, both on campus and off, might be interested in or have a stake in the findings of an investigative report on the relationship between a specific generation and your school or your town? Make a list of the potential findings of an investigative report about Millennials (or another specific generation), based on what you've observed and experienced so far.

Real Situations

Though it may seem odd to label any generation, especially your own, consider the generational labels that have become common. The United States population contains a number of named generations: the Lost Generation, people who fought in or lived through World War I; the Greatest Generation, those who fought in World War II; the Silent Generation, those born between 1928 and 1945; the Baby Boomers, who were born after World War II, between 1946 and 1964; and Generation X, people born from 1965 through 1980. The very numerous

What's in a Name?

Generational names are the handiwork of popular culture. Some are drawn from a historic event; others from rapid social or demographic change; others from a big turn in the calendar.

The Millennial Generation falls into the third category. The label refers those born after 1980 – the first generation to come of age in the new millennium.

Generation X covers people born from 1965 through 1980. The label long ago overtook the first name affixed to this generation: the Baby Bust. Xers are often depicted as savvy, entrepreneurial loners.

The Baby Boomer label is drawn from the great spike in fertility that began in 1946, right after the end of World War II, and ended almost as abruptly in 1964, around the time the birth control pill went on the market. It's a classic example of a demography-driven name.

The Silent Generation describes adults born from 1928 through 1945. Children of the Great Depression and World War II, their "Silent" label refers to their conformist and civic instincts. It also makes for a nice contrast with the noisy ways of the anti-establishment Boomers.

The Greatest Generation (those born before 1928) "saved the world" when it was young, in the memorable phrase of Ronald Reagan. It's the generation that fought and won World War II.

Generational names are works in progress. The zeitgeist changes, and labels that once seemed spot-on fall out of fashion. It's not clear if the Millennial tag will endure, although a calendar change that comes along only once in a thousand years seems like a pretty secure anchor.

In 2010, the Pew Research Center published a report on the Millennials that included this list of generational names.

Boomers created a cultural and economic phenomenon with their purchasing power and their rejection of traditional values. The Gen Xers have been considered to be without a clear identity, as their defining experiences have been instability (including the series of economic calamities since their birth and the high rate of divorce among their parents). Gen Xers were the first generation to take personal electronic devices for granted; home computers, cell phones, video games, and the Internet all became commonplace during their youth. The Millennial Generation, or Generation Y, characterized by the Beloit College Mindset List at the beginning of this chapter, consists of those born between about 1981 and the turn of the century. Following the Millennial Generation is Generation Z, or the Internet Generation, those who have never known a world without online capabilities.

The effects of such labels can spark strong reactions—for example, frustration in the Baby Boomers, whose name reminds people of the burden their large number will be for the Social Security system, and pride in the Greatest Generation, many of whom feel they deserve their tag, given their sacrifices during a world war and an economic depression. If you're a member of the Millennial Generation, you might resist the labels that pundits have applied to you and your cohort. You've been called "digital natives," which rings true only if the digital world is the only place you feel at home. Those among the Millennials who are the most digitally connected have been called "socially inept," because their obsession with online communication and entertainment often seems to have diminished their person-to-person, real-life social skills. If you're bristling at these labels, you might envy the positive attributes ascribed to members of earlier generations, especially since the Millennials have also been described as narcissistic and characterized as neither hard-working nor selfless. In contrast, the Millennials are also considered to be civic-minded (think about all the recent college graduates who have joined Teach for America) and better connected socially (with peers and older folks alike) than any other generation.

DESCRIBING THE MILLENNIAL GENERATION

1. How would you define the generation born between 1981 and 2001? Make a list of the distinguishing characteristics and cultural touchstones that you think define this generation.

2. How have you heard others define the generation born between 1981 and 2001? Work with a classmate or two to make a list of all the things you've heard about this generation. Be prepared to share your list with the rest of the class.

3. In what ways do the definitions from questions 1 and 2 overlap? Where do they diverge?

4. What do the images in this chapter suggest to you about the Millennials? What kind of visual is missing?

Real Responses to Real Situations

A number of writers have employed their available means to respond to rhetorical opportunities concerning the Millennial Generation. As you explore the responses presented here, ask yourself how what these writers have to say relates to your understanding of this generation. For example, if your parents are Baby Boomers, they know the feeling of having music, clothing, television, movies, education, and social policies fashioned to reflect and cater to their interests, estimated longevity, and spending capacity. Despite the raised eyebrows of their elders, their spending power, social freedoms, and seemingly unlimited educational and professional opportunities have allowed the Boomers to move optimistically forward with their lives. The same might be said of the Millennials.

Ted Horowitz

Millennials tend to get along well with their parents and others in older generations.

Defining a generation

Labeling generations has long been the norm, not surprisingly, since members of the same generation represent a demographic that can be both analyzed and exploited. Some generations have been named only after they have aged; the Greatest Generation is a case in point. But the Millennials were named early on and have been described in sometimes conflicting terms ever since. Even the span of their birth years (between 1981 and 2001, give or take a couple of years on either end) has been debated. In "The Millennial Muddle," award-winning writer Eric Hoover tells us that "figuring out young people has always been a chore, [and] today it's also an industry." He goes on to say that "colleges and corporations pay experts big bucks to help them understand the fresh-faced hordes that pack the nation's dorms and office buildings" and that "everyone in higher education has pondered 'The Millennials.'" Given the widespread and seemingly nonstop discussion of this generation, it is no surprise that a variety of opinions about it are in circulation. According to Hoover, depending on the so-called expert, "this generation either will save the planet, one soup kitchen at a time, or crash-land on a lonely moon where nobody ever reads." The Pew Research Center's report on the Millennials, whose overview is excerpted here, represents one of the positive depictions of this generation.

Excerpt from

> The Millennials: Confident. Connected. Open to Change.

Pew Research Center

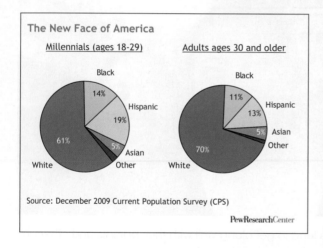

The New Face of America

Millennials (ages 18-29) — Black 14%, Hispanic 19%, White 61%, Asian 5%, Other

Adults ages 30 and older — Black 11%, Hispanic 13%, Asian 5%, Other, White 70%

Source: December 2009 Current Population Survey (CPS)

PewResearchCenter

Generations, like people, have personalities, and Millennials—the American teens and twenty-somethings who are making the passage into adulthood at the start of a new millennium—have begun to forge theirs: confident, self-expressive, liberal, upbeat and open to change.

They are more ethnically and racially diverse than older adults. They're less religious, less likely to have served in the military, and are on track to become the most educated generation in American history.

Their entry into careers and first jobs has been badly set back by the Great Recession, but they are more upbeat than their elders about their own economic futures as well as about the overall state of the nation.

They are history's first "always connected" generation. Steeped in digital technology and social media, they treat their multi-tasking hand-held gadgets almost like a body part—for better and worse. More than eight-in-ten say they sleep with a cell phone glowing by the bed, poised to disgorge texts, phone calls, e-mails, songs, news, videos, games and wake-up jingles. But sometimes convenience yields to temptation. Nearly two-thirds admit to texting while driving.

They embrace multiple modes of self-expression. Three-quarters have created a profile on a social networking site. One-in-five have posted a video of themselves online. Nearly four-in-ten have a tattoo (and for most who do, one is not enough: about half of those with tattoos have two to five and 18% have six or more). Nearly one-in-four have a piercing in some place other than an earlobe—about six times the share of older adults who've done this. But their look-at-me tendencies are not without limits. Most Millennials have placed privacy boundaries on their social media profiles. And 70% say their tattoos are hidden beneath clothing.

Despite struggling (and often failing) to find jobs in the teeth of a recession, about nine-in-ten either say that they currently have enough money or that they will eventually meet their long-term financial goals. But [in early 2010], fully 37% of 18-to-29-year-olds are unemployed or out of the workforce, the highest share among this age group in more than three decades.

Whether as a by-product of protective parents, the age of terrorism or a media culture that focuses on dangers, they cast a wary eye on human nature. Two-thirds say "you can't be too careful" when dealing with people. Yet they are less skeptical than their elders of government. More so than other generations, they believe government should do more to solve problems.

They are the least overtly religious American generation in modern times. One-in-four are unaffiliated with any religion, far more than the share of older adults when they were ages 18 to 29. Yet not belonging does not necessarily mean not believing. Millennials pray about as often as their elders did in their own youth.

Only about six-in-ten were raised by both parents—a smaller share than was the case with older generations. In weighing their own life priorities, Millennials (like older adults) place parenthood and marriage far above career and financial success. But they aren't rushing to the altar. Just one-in-five Millennials (21%) are married now, half the share of their parents' generation at the same stage of life. About a third (34%) are parents.

Millennials are on course to become the most educated generation in American history, a trend driven largely by the demands of a modern knowledge-based economy, but most likely accelerated in recent years by the millions of 20-somethings enrolling in graduate schools, colleges or community colleges in part because they can't find a job. Among 18 to 24 year olds a record share—39.6%—was enrolled in college as of 2008, according to census data.

They get along well with their parents. Looking back at their teenage years, Millennials report having had fewer spats with mom or dad than older adults say they had with their own parents when they were growing up. And now, hard times have kept a significant share of adult Millennials and their parents under the same roof. About one-in-ten older Millennials (ages 22 and older) say they've "boomeranged" back to a parent's home because of the recession.

They respect their elders. A majority say that the older generation is superior to the younger generation when it comes to moral values and work ethic. Also, more than six-in-ten say that families have a responsibility to have an elderly parent come live with them if that parent wants to. By contrast, fewer than four-in-ten adults ages 60 and older agree that this is a family responsibility.

continued

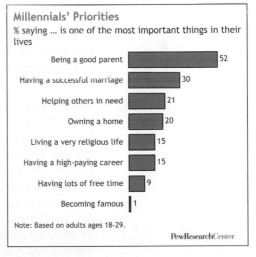

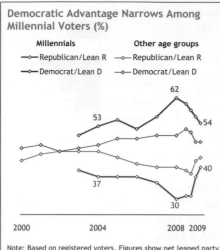

Democratic Advantage Narrows Among Millennial Voters (%)

Note: Based on registered voters. Figures show net leaned party identification as yearly totals from 2000 through 2008 and quarterly for 2009.
Source: Pew Reseach Center surveys

PewResearchCenter

Despite coming of age at a time when the United States has been waging two wars, relatively few Millennials—just 2% of males—are military veterans. At a comparable stage of their life cycle, 6% of Gen Xer men, 13% of Baby Boomer men and 24% of Silent men were veterans.

Politically, Millennials were among Barack Obama's strongest supporters in 2008, backing him for president by more than a two-to-one ratio (66% to 32%) while older adults were giving just 50% of their votes to the Democratic nominee. This was the largest disparity between younger and older voters recorded in four decades of modern election day exit polling. Moreover, after decades of low voter participation by the young, the turnout gap in 2008 between voters under and over the age of 30 was the smallest it had been since 18- to 20-year-olds were given the right to vote in 1972.

But the political enthusiasms of Millennials have since cooled—for Obama and his message of change, for the Democratic Party and, quite possibly, for politics itself. About half of Millennials say the president has failed to change the way Washington works, which had been the central promise of his candidacy. Of those who say this, three-in-ten blame Obama himself, while more than half blame his political opponents and special interests.

To be sure, Millennials remain the most likely of any generation to self-identify as liberals; they are less supportive than their elders of an assertive national security policy and more supportive of a progressive domestic social agenda. They are still more likely than any other age group to identify as Democrats. Yet by early 2010, their support for Obama and the Democrats had receded, as evidenced both by survey data and by their low level of participation in recent off-year and special elections.

The Millennial Identity

Most Millennials (61%) in our January, 2010 survey say their generation has a unique and distinctive identity. That doesn't make them unusual, however. Roughly two-thirds of Silents, nearly six-in-ten Boomers and about half of Xers feel the same way about their generation.

But Millennials have a distinctive reason for feeling distinctive. In response to an open-ended follow-up question, 24% say it's because of their use of technology. Gen Xers also cite technology as their generation's biggest source of distinctiveness, but far fewer—just 12%—say this. Boomers' feelings of distinctiveness coalesce mainly around work ethic, which 17% cite as their most prominent identity badge. For Silents, it's the shared experience of the Depression and World War II, which 14% cite as the biggest reason their generation stands apart.

Millennials' technological exceptionalism is chronicled throughout the survey. It's not just their gadgets—it's the way they've fused their social lives into them. For example, three-quarters of Millennials have created a profile on a social networking site, compared with half of Xers, 30% of Boomers and 6% of Silents. There are big

Investigative Reports

What Makes Your Generation Unique?

Millennial	Gen X	Boomer	Silent
1. Technology use (24%)	Technology use (12%)	Work ethic (17%)	WW II, Depression (14%)
2. Music/Pop culture (11%)	Work ethic (11%)	Respectful (14%)	Smarter (13%)
3. Liberal/tolerant (7%)	Conservative/Trad'l (7%)	Values/Morals (8%)	Honest (12%)
4. Smarter (6%)	Smarter (6%)	"Baby Boomers" (6%)	Work ethic (10%)
5. Clothes (5%)	Respectful (5%)	Smarter (5%)	Values/Morals (10%)

Note: Based on respondents who said their generation was unique/distinct. Items represent individual, open-ended responses. Top five responses are shown for each age group. Sample sizes for sub-groups are as follows: Millennials, n=527; Gen X, n=173; Boomers, n=283; Silent, n=205.

generation gaps, as well, in using wireless technology, playing video games and posting self-created videos online. Millennials are also more likely than older adults to say technology makes life easier and brings family and friends closer together (though the generation gaps on these questions are relatively narrow).

Work Ethic, Moral Values, Race Relations

Of the four generations, Millennials are the only one that doesn't cite "work ethic" as one of their principal claims to distinctiveness. A nationwide Pew Research Center survey taken in 2009 may help explain why. This one focused on differences between young and old rather than between specific age groups. Nonetheless, its findings are instructive.

Nearly six-in-ten respondents cited work ethic as one of the big sources of differences between young and old. Asked who has the better work ethic, about three-fourths of respondents said that older people do. By similar margins, survey respondents also found older adults have the upper hand when it comes to moral values and their respect for others.

It might be tempting to dismiss these findings as a typical older adult gripe about "kids today." But when it comes to each of these traits—work ethic, moral values, respect for others—young adults *agree* that older adults have the better of it. In short, Millennials may be a self-confident generation, but they display little appetite for claims of moral superiority.

That 2009 survey also found that the public—young and old alike—thinks the younger generation is more racially tolerant than their elders. More than two decades of Pew Research surveys confirm that assessment. In their views about interracial dating, for example, Millennials are the most open to change of any generation, followed closely by Gen Xers, then Boomers, then Silents.

Likewise, Millennials are more receptive to immigrants than are their elders. Nearly six-in-ten (58%) say immigrants strengthen the country, according to a 2009 Pew Research survey; just 43% of adults ages 30 and older agree.

The same pattern holds on a range of attitudes about nontraditional family arrangements, from mothers of young children working outside the home, to adults living together without being married, to more people of different races marrying each other. Millennials are more accepting than older generations of these more modern family arrangements, followed closely by Gen Xers. To be sure, acceptance does not in all cases translate into outright approval. But it does mean Millennials disapprove less.

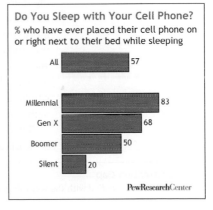

Do You Sleep with Your Cell Phone?
% who have ever placed their cell phone on or right next to their bed while sleeping

All	57
Millennial	83
Gen X	68
Boomer	50
Silent	20

PewResearchCenter

continued

The Millennials: Confident. Connected. Open to Change. *(continued)*

Weighing Trends in Marriage and Parenthood, by Generation % saying this is a bad thing for society				
	Millennial	Gen X	Boomer	Silent
More single women deciding to have children	59	54	65	72
More gay couples raising children	32	36	48	55
More mothers of young children working outside the home	23	29	39	38
More people living together w/o getting married	22	31	44	58
More people of different races marrying each other	5	10	14	26

Note: "Good thing", "Doesn't make much difference", and "Don't know" responses not shown.

A Gentler Generation Gap

A 1969 survey, taken near the height of the social and political upheavals of that turbulent decade, found that 74% of the public believed there was a "generation gap" in American society. Surprisingly, when that same question was asked in a Pew Research Center survey [in 2009]—in an era marked by hard economic times but little if any overt age-based social tension—the share of the public saying there was a generation gap had risen slightly to 79%.

But as the 2009 results also make clear, this modern generation gap is a much more benign affair than the one that cast a shadow over the 1960s. The public says this one is mostly about the different ways that old and young use technology—and relatively few people see that gap as a source of conflict. Indeed, only about a quarter of the respondents in the 2009 survey said they see big conflicts between young and old in America. Many more see conflicts between immigrants and the native born, between rich and poor, and between blacks and whites.

There is one generation gap that *has* widened notably in recent years. It has to do with satisfaction over the state of the nation. In recent decades the young have always tended to be a bit more upbeat than their elders on this key measure, but the gap is wider now than it has been in at least twenty years. Some 41% of Millennials say they are satisfied with the way things are going in the country, compared with just 26% of those ages 30 and older. Whatever toll a recession, a housing crisis, a financial meltdown and a pair of wars may have taken on the national psyche in the past few years, it appears to have hit the old harder than the young.

But this speaks to a difference in outlook and attitude; it's not a source of conflict or tension. As they make their way into adulthood, Millennials have already distinguished themselves as a generation that gets along well with others, especially their elders. For a nation whose population is rapidly going gray, that could prove to be a most welcome character trait.

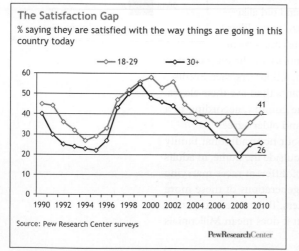

The Satisfaction Gap
% saying they are satisfied with the way things are going in this country today

— 18-29   — 30+

Source: Pew Research Center surveys

PewResearchCenter

Author Derek Thompson, himself a member of the Millennial Generation, has written at length in an effort to define his generation, focusing on its members' personalities, outlooks, identities, maturation, employment problems and possibilities, education, and social practices and values. Thompson begins by summarizing the article to which he is responding, which provided his rhetorical opportunity.

> What's Really the Matter with 20-Somethings

Derek Thompson

What is the deal with 20-somethings, these days? That's the question burning up the Internet and family room tables across the country since Robin Marantz Henig posed it in a mammoth *New York Times* Magazine article. In the last 30 years, Generation Y (or the Millennials) have pushed back each of the five milestones of adulthood: completing school, leaving home, becoming financially independent, marrying and having a child. We're not children, not yet adults, but rather in some Britney Spearsesque middle world of psychological development.

There are three levels to what author Henig calls "emerging adulthood." The first level is science and psychology: it's the idea that 20-somethings' brains and bodies might not be as grown up as we thought. The second level is today's culture: it's why Millennials, as opposed to all of history's young adults, are more likely to take time to "grow up." The third and final level is economic. The unemployment rate is 15.7 percent for workers aged 20 to 24. For 20-something African Americans and Hispanics without college degrees, that number is in the mid-20s. You can't become financially independent on food stamps.

The article mentions the bad economy only twice, both times by dismissing its impact ("it's a development that predates the current economic doldrums") to focus on developmental psychology. It's fine for the author Robin Marantz Henig to be more interested in science than economics.* But it's not fine for the *Times* Magazine to publish a front-page story called "What Is It About 20-Somethings?" when "it" is still the economy, stupid.

First, where Henig is correct: the bad economy has *accentuated* certain trends in the workforce rather than created a new generational identity overnight. Some of us were already delaying marrying and moving back with our parents before the recession. But some of these trends have nothing to do with our brains and everything to do with how we've chosen to use them.

Women and College

In 1970, women accounted for 36 percent of college graduates. Today they account for the majority. College educated women marry later, have fewer children, and are less likely to view marriage as "financial security," according to a

continued

---

*By the same token, since I am more interested and versed in economic trends than developmental psychology, this analysis might make too much of the recession and too little of brain development.

2010 Wharton study . . . . You can't explain delayed marriages and older mothers without talking about college.

Student Debt

Student debt recently eclipsed total credit card [debt] in this country at $860 billion. Before the recession, in 2006, the average public college student owed $17,250 from loans, according to the American Association of State Colleges and Universities. That number incredibly *doubled* from $8,000 in 1996. So put yourself in the shoes of a 22-year old from a relatively affluent family. You've graduated with $15,000 in debt, you can't find a job that pays more than $23,000 without benefits, and you don't hate your parents. Why *wouldn't* you live at home for a year?

Recession

Unemployment is 50 percent higher for 20-somethings than the general population. As *National Journal*'s Ron Brownstein has said, a functioning economy works like an escalator. You step on at high school, ascend through college, and step off into a decent paying job. But today, the escalator is jammed at the top. Senior workers won't leave their jobs because the recession devastated their 401(k) plans. Middle workers can't get promotions. And graduating seniors get stuck. Large employers hired 42 percent fewer graduating students in 2009, according to a Michigan State University study.

Something deeper is happening: it's the rise of a shadow job market without benefits or proper accounting. It's the emerging Freelancer Economy. Between 1995 and 2005, the number of self-employed independent contractors grew by 27 percent to almost 9 million workers. This phenomenon is especially prevalent in New York City, where self-employment accounted for two thirds of the job growth between 1975 and 2007, according to the Chicago Fed. Part-time jobs might be good for productivity and company output. But they come without health care or wage protection or the guarantee that they'll exist in a month. If we're moving slower toward adulthood, the economy is providing one hell of a headwind.

Half a century ago, it might have been normal to graduate from college (or not), marry in your lower 20s, have a kid, settle down at a nice firm, put in your 40 years and clock out with a good-looking pension. But that's not the world we live in. Horizontal mobility, part-time projects, rapidly changing jobs: this is the new normal. Maybe it's because we've been hopelessly coddled and our brains, with their flaccid synapses, have been massaged into thinking we could land our dream job at 23. Or! Maybe it's because the world changed, and it doesn't make sense to start a family at 24 in the shadow of $15,000 in debt with a thimbleful of jobs that don't provide health care or the promise of stability.

Henig's lengthy piece is impressive in its scope of developmental psychology and in its sensitivity to the question of whether 20-somethings need more help than we thought. Her concern is noted, and appreciated. But there are cultural and economic reasons why 20-somethings aren't growing up that have nothing to do with the pruning of our synapses. When people ask what's the matter with my generation, part of me wants to say: Have you seen the economy you created? *What's the matter with yours?*

But that's churlish. So instead, let's make a deal. Boomers, fix what you did to the country. And I promise you, the kids will be alright.

Currently director of the University Center for Innovation in Teaching and Education at Case Western Reserve University, theoretical physicist and social commentator Mano Singham regularly contributes to the *Chronicle of Higher Education*, where the following article originally appeared. A prolific writer (whose works include *God vs. Darwin: The War Between Evolution and Creationism in the Classroom*, *The Achievement Gap in US Education: Canaries in the Mine*, and *Quest for Truth: Scientific Progress and Religious Beliefs*), Singham posts his thoughts on subjects ranging from science, religion, and politics to the media, education, books, and film on his blog (http://blog.case.edu/singham).

> More than Millennials: Teachers Must Look Beyond Generational Stereotypes

Mano Singham

Until the 1990s, generations were thought by most people to span about 20 years, and labeling a generation with a catchy name usually meant that the cohort represented some major demographic trend. The births of the baby boomers, for example, had serious implications for social policy because of the need to project future needs in education, social services, and retirement. Giving that cohort an easily identifiable label made sense.

Now, however, it seems that a new generation is named every decade or less, driven by sweeping generalizations from the mass media and supported by little more than alleged changes in character traits as described by pop sociologists. One could dismiss all the generational splitting as the harmless fun of people in the news business, who need filler for their arts-and-style and pop-culture sections—except for the fact that it has seeped into academic conversations and may actually be influencing how we interact with college students, and not in a good way.

The first of the new breed of compressed generations was the so-called Generation X, consisting of those born after 1965, who are supposedly characterized by qualities of independence, resilience, and adaptability.

Tragically, before that generation could even reach its teenage years, it was killed off and replaced by Generation Y, consisting of those born after 1977. But it seems that Generation Y was unhappy with the label, and one can understand why. The letter X carries with it an aura of mystery, while Y is merely the letter after X, always playing second fiddle. Even in graphs, X is the independent variable, adventurously staking out new ground, while Y is the plodding dependent variable, following along in X's wake. Who wants to be part of that crowd? So Generation Y was rechristened as the Millennials, a catchy title for those coming of age at the turn of the century, and it has stuck.

And what do we know about these Millennials? A lot, it seems. Here's one description, from "Generation X and the Millennials: What You Need to Know

continued

About Mentoring the New Generations," by Diane Thielfoldt and Devon Scheef:

> The 75 million members of this generation are being raised at the most child-centric time in our history. Perhaps it's because of the showers of attention and high expectations from parents that they display a great deal of self-confidence. . . . Millennials are typically team-oriented, banding together to date and socialize. . . . They work well in groups, preferring this to individual endeavors. They're good multitaskers, having juggled sports, school, and social interests as children, so expect them to work hard. Millennials seem to expect structure in the workplace. They acknowledge and respect positions and titles, and want a relationship with their boss. . . . They are definitely in need of mentoring. . . . and they'll respond well to the personal attention. Because they appreciate structure and stability, mentoring Millennials should be more formal, with set meetings and a more authoritative attitude on the mentor's part.

Really? We seem to have those 75 million people pegged, don't we?

The Millennial label was so successful that we were loath to let it go, so that generation was allowed to grow into adulthood until 1998, when the news media decided that it was time for a new one. Generation Z was thus born, comprising those born from the mid- to late-1990s through the 2000s. Their arrival is now indelibly linked with the events of September 11, 2001, and Generation Z's worldview is supposedly shaped by that one event.

But that's not all. With the source of generation labels shifting from demographics to character traits and the influence of significant contemporaneous events, we have now gone back in time and cut earlier generations into more finely grained slices that encompass smaller age cohorts. Generation Next consists of people born between 1982 and 1989 who, according to the Pew Research Center, "have grown up with personal computers, cell phones, and the Internet and are now taking their place in a world where the only constant is rapid change." The MTV Generation consists of those who occupy the space between Generation X and Generation Y. Even the venerable baby boomers have succumbed to this generational Balkanization, with those born between 1954 and 1965 being peeled off and given their own enigmatic label of Generation Jones. Why? Because late boomers are presumed to have been too young to be deeply affected by the Vietnam War and Woodstock—supposedly the cultural touchstones that shaped the worldview of early boomers.

I suspect that student-life and admissions administrators are the first to be influenced by such generational bandwagons. They have to deal with parents and with students' nonacademic lives, and thus must keep their antennae tuned to what is going [on] in popular culture. From them these terms diffuse into general university conversation.

I attended a conference on college teaching recently and was amazed at how often generational stereotypes were brought up and used as a valid basis for dealing with students. All it took was one person dropping the word "Millennial" into the discussion, and the anecdotes started pouring out: The students who demand instant gratification, those who send repeated e-mail messages to their professors in the middle of the night and are annoyed when they don't get an immediate reply, those who expect professors to give them a wake-up call on field trips because that is what their parents did, those whose parents cling to them and intercede on their behalf, those who cling to their parents, those who confide intimate details about their lives that professors need not (and would rather not) know, those who demand to be told exactly what they need to do on assignments, and so on. Such stories seem to spring from an inexhaustible well. And the picture of the Millennials that emerges is that of a whiny, needy, instant-gratification-seeking, grade-oriented bunch of students.

It should be borne in mind that those stories were not told by bitter, curmudgeonly, "you kids get off my lawn!"-type professors who hate being in the company of students and think that universities would be much better places if no pesky undergraduates were around to interrupt the day. The puzzle is that the people who attend such teaching conferences and make such comments are often some of the best and most caring teachers—the ones who are constantly trying to find ways to improve their teaching and reach more students.

The willingness of such professors to accept generational stereotypes stands in stark contrast to their sensitivity when it comes to gender and ethnic stereotypes. During one session on identifying and dealing with classroom incivilities, a couple of professors ventured the suggestion that what students considered incivil may depend on their culture: that Korean students may unwittingly commit plagiarism because they believe that citing sources is an insult to their professor; that Saudi Arabian students like to negotiate grades with their professors because they come from a bargaining culture; that Latin American students think that something is cheating only if you get caught. There was immediate pushback from other professors that such generalizations are not valid—and are in fact harmful, because they prevent us from seeing the individuality in students. Generalizations about the Millennials, however, went unchallenged.

Why are we in academe so accepting of media-driven constructs like the ever-multiplying generation labels? Paradoxically, it may be because we want to help students. Thoughtful academics are problem solvers, and when dealing with disengaged students, giving the problem a label gives one the sense that one understands it and can set about dealing with it.

But generational stereotypes are of no value for professors—and not because they are entirely false. After all, stereotypes are usually based on some reality. But even if different populations exhibit, on average, their own distinct traits, large populations like nations and generations include so many deviations from the norm that stereotypes are of little use in predicting the traits that any given person is likely to display.

It would be silly to argue that student behavior hasn't changed over time. But what we are observing may not be a result of new traits emerging, but rather old traits manifesting themselves in novel forms because of changes in external conditions. Maybe parents have not become more clingy or students more psychologically dependent on them. Perhaps the truth is simply that college has become vastly more complicated and difficult to navigate, with its explosion of majors, minors, and other programs—not to mention the byzantine rules for financial aid—so perhaps some parents have felt obliged to step in more than they might have in earlier generations to act on their children's behalf.

Similarly, we have always had students who were uninhibited, socially awkward, or needed instant gratification. But now e-mail and Facebook enable them to

continued

display those qualities in ways they couldn't before—such as by expecting immediate responses to midnight queries or revealing personal information online they should keep to themselves.

Students are diverse and have always been diverse. I've taught for over three decades and have my own cache of funny or poignant stories about needy, annoying, or self-absorbed students. We teachers love stories about students, and treasure and accumulate them like anglers or golfers do about their pastimes. While my own stories can fit those spread around about the Millennials, many of them are about students from long ago, before it became fashionable to label students according to their birth years.

Bertrand Russell said that "no man can be a good teacher unless he has feelings of warm affection toward his pupils and a genuine desire to impart to them what he himself believes to be of value." The trouble with generational stereotyping is that it sucks the individuality out of our students, the very thing that generates those feelings of warm affection. It makes them into generic types, whose personalities and motivations we think we can discern without having to go to all the bother of actually getting to know them.

> ANALYZING THE RHETORICAL SITUATION

1. To what rhetorical opportunity is each of the three pieces of writing in this section responding?
2. What characteristic of the Millennial Generation does each piece of writing investigate?
3. Who is the specific audience for each of the three pieces? For what purpose was each written? How do the purpose and audience of each piece connect?
4. What facts and evidence does each piece of writing present to help readers better understand the Millennials? What kinds of research do you think were needed to find those facts and that evidence?
5. How do each of these pieces draw on the rhetorical appeals of ethos, logos, and pathos to support opinions about the Millennials? Work with another classmate or two to find passages from each of the texts to support your answers. Be prepared to share your answers with the rest of the class.

Investigating what it means to grow up in a digital world

Most college students are fluent digital communicators, whether they use handheld devices, touch-screen devices, or personal computers. As one of those students, your expertise has likely been forged by long use of electronic devices, perhaps starting with a desktop computer. Although some experts argue that people who rely on electronic communication do so at the expense of their person-to-person social skills, you might not agree. In fact, your own life may prove that just the opposite is true. You might be one of those people who mails out personalized, handwritten holiday cards every winter. Between envelope-addressing sessions, you might check your e-mail and Facebook accounts to see who has accepted an invitation to the annual holiday party—at your home, at your place of worship, or at one of your social clubs, where you see and talk with your friends and associates face to face. Just because you're digitally savvy doesn't necessarily mean you're socially inept; the two qualities are not mutually exclusive.

The following articles explore the complicated cause-and-consequence relationships between the use of digital methods of communication and the users' social and educational lives. David Fallarme, the author of the first article, is a digital marketing professional, consultant to businesses, and author of the blog *The Marketing Student.*

> A Look at How Gen Y Communicates

Used by permission.
David Fallarme

Boomers had it pretty simple back in their youth. Want to connect with your friends? Write them a letter, give them a call or go and see them.

Gen X-ers had a little more fun. They could've e-mailed each other over 28.8 [phone-line dial-up for the Internet] or used their pagers to send 1-sentence messages back and forth.

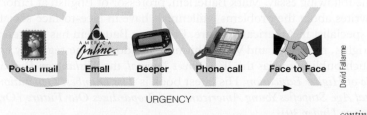

continued

Here's what **Generation Y** uses to stay in touch.

To an outsider, it can be confusing to understand how Gen Y uses those channels just to talk to each other. After all, Boomers just had three channels and they made friends just fine. To put things in context, here's what my communication habits are like and how I use the above.

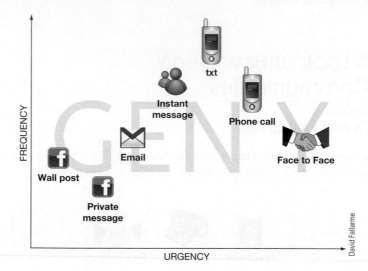

Looking at that chart makes me envy my father's generation. They didn't have to worry about drunk texts. Or having personal information all over the internet.

In the following essay, Mark Bauerlein, professor of English at Emory University, writes about the problems Millennials have in face-to-face social situations. A specialist in American culture, Professor Bauerlein has written widely on civil rights, race riots, and Walt Whitman. In addition, he regularly contributes to such publications as the *Wall Street Journal*, the *Washington Post*, and the *Chronicle of Higher Education*. His latest book is *The Dumbest Generation: How the Digital Age Stupefies Young Americans and Jeopardizes Our Future (Or, Don't Trust Anyone Under 30)*.

> Why Gen-Y Johnny Can't Read Non-Verbal Cues

Mark Bauerlein

In September 2008, when Nielsen Mobile announced that teenagers with cellphones each sent and received, on average, 1,742 text messages a month, the number sounded high, but just a few months later Nielsen raised the tally to 2,272. A year earlier, the National School Boards Association estimated that middle- and high-school students devoted an average of nine hours to social networking each week. Add e-mail, blogging, IM, tweets and other digital customs and you realize what kind of hurried, 24/7 communications system young people experience today.

Unfortunately, nearly all of their communication tools involve the exchange of written words alone. At least phones, cellular and otherwise, allow the transmission of tone of voice, pauses and the like. But even these clues are absent in the text-dependent world. Users insert smiley-faces into e-mails, but they don't see each others' actual faces. They read comments on Facebook, but they don't "read" each others' posture, hand gestures, eye movements, shifts in personal space and other nonverbal—and expressive—behaviors.

Back in 1959, anthropologist Edward T. Hall labeled these expressive human attributes "the Silent Language." Hall passed away last month in Santa Fe at age 95, but his writings on nonverbal communication deserve continued attention. He argued that body language, facial expressions and stock mannerisms function "in juxtaposition to words," imparting feelings, attitudes, reactions and judgments in a different register.

This is why, Hall explained, U.S. diplomats could enter a foreign country fully competent in the native language and yet still flounder from one miscommunication to another, having failed to decode the manners, gestures and subtle protocols that go along with words. And how could they, for the "silent language" is acquired through acculturation, not schooling. Not only is it unspoken; it is largely unconscious. The meanings that pass through it remain implicit, more felt than understood.

They are, however, operative. Much of our social and workplace lives runs on them. For Hall, breakdowns in nonverbal communication took place most damagingly in cross-cultural circumstances—for instance, federal workers dealing with Navajo Indians and misconstruing their basic conceptions of time. Within cultures, Hall assumed, people more or less "spoke" the same silent language.

They may no longer, thanks to the avalanche of all-verbal communication. In Silicon Valley itself, as the Los Angeles Times reported last year, some companies have installed the "topless" meeting—in which not only laptops but iPhones and other tools are banned—to combat a new problem: "continuous partial attention." With a device close by, attendees at workplace meetings simply cannot keep their focus on the speaker. It's too easy to check e-mail, stock quotes and Facebook. While a quick log-on may seem, to the user, a harmless break, others in the room receive it as a silent dismissal. It announces: "I'm not interested." So the tools must now remain at the door.

continued

Older employees might well accept such a ban, but younger ones might not understand it. Reading a text message in the middle of a conversation isn't a lapse to them—it's what you do. It has, they assume, no nonverbal meaning to anyone else.

It does, of course, but how would they know it? We live in a culture where young people—outfitted with iPhone and laptop and devoting hours every evening from age 10 onward to messaging of one kind and another—are ever less likely to develop the "silent fluency" that comes from face-to-face interaction. It is a skill that we all must learn, in actual social settings, from people (often older) who are adept in the idiom. As text-centered messaging increases, such occasions diminish. The digital natives improve their adroitness at the keyboard, but when it comes to their capacity to "read" the behavior of others, they are all thumbs.

Nobody knows the extent of the problem. It is too early to assess the effect of digital habits, and the tools change so quickly that research can't keep up with them. By the time investigators design a study, secure funding, collect results and publish them, the technology has changed and the study is outdated.

Still, we might reasonably pose questions about silent-language acquisition in a digital environment. Lots of folks grumble about the diffidence, self-absorption and general uncommunicativeness of Generation Y. The next time they face a twenty-something who doesn't look them in the eye, who slouches and sighs for no apparent reason, who seems distracted and unaware of the rising frustration of the other people in the room, and who turns aside to answer a text message with glee and facility, they shouldn't think, "What a rude kid." Instead, they should show a little compassion and, perhaps, seize on a teachable moment. "Ah," they might think instead, "another texter who doesn't realize that he is communicating, right now, with every glance and movement—and that we're reading him all too well."

Prolific writer and artist Laurie Fendrich is professor at Hofstra University, where she teaches courses in drawing, painting, humanities, and art appreciation. Her own artwork (paintings, drawings, and installations) has appeared in galleries all over North America. Her productive professional life also includes writing, which she does regularly for the *Chronicle of Higher Education.* Her view of the Millennial Generation seems more respectful and sympathetic than the views of some of her contemporaries.

> Bad Student Writing? Not So Fast!

Reprinted by permission.

Laurie Fendrich

It would be good for the blood pressure of everyone involved in criticizing education—state legislators, education policy professionals, professors, school administrators, parents—to take a deep breath. Put aside the statistics, the studies, the anecdotes, and take a look at the big picture.

Here's what Edith Hamilton had to say about education, in *The Echo of Greece* (1957), one of her many trenchant books on the subject of the ancient Greeks:

> If people feel that things are going from bad to worse and look at the new generation to see if they can be trusted to take charge among such dangers, they invariably conclude that they cannot and that these irresponsible young people have not been trained properly. Then the cry goes up, "What is wrong with our education?" and many answers are always forthcoming.

Note the droll and ironic, "and many answers are always forthcoming." Perhaps studying people who lived so long ago—people who invented the very idea of education as a route to genuine freedom, and understood freedom to be worthwhile only when coupled with self-control—gave Hamilton one of those calm, stoical uber-minds that comprehends competing pronouncements about education never to be more than opinion.

While the rest of us thrash about interpreting the parade of studies and tests demonstrating that students can no longer think, read, write, do math, know the dates of the Civil War or the fall of Byzantium, or identify a water molecule when it's softly floating on a glass slide, Hamilton calmly sees 'twas ever thus. In an interesting aside, she also observes that there's an increase in "educational fervor" whenever there's a lack of confidence in the state.

I'd go further. The problem of "control freaks" applies to generations as well as to individuals. Older generations never voluntarily let go. They embrace new ideas only grudgingly, and often won't even try to understand the younger generation they themselves spawned. One of the many tragedies of existence is that the only species that's equipped by nature to have back-and-forth conversations between generations resists such conversations with all its might.

Clive Thompson's article on the "new literacy" (*Wired Magazine*, 24 August [2011]) urges those of us who are fretting about the decline in writing, in particular, to buck up. Unlike Hamilton, who points to the eternal past for comfort, Thompson points to the present and the future. He reports on a large, ongoing study at Stanford—the Stanford Study of Writing—directed by Andrea Lunsford, a professor of writing and rhetoric at Stanford University. Her conclusion? "I think we're in the midst of a literacy revolution the likes of which we haven't seen since Greek civilization."

Thompson writes, "Technology isn't killing our ability to write. It's reviving it—and pushing our literacy in bold new directions." The Stanford study, although incomplete, already shows that young people today write far, far more than any previous generation, and a lot of it they do outside the classroom (!).

While the older generation worries endlessly (frequently employing pretentious prose in the process) over the quality of the writing on Facebook, blogs and Twitter, the younger generation enthusiastically probes new ways to express themselves clearly and concisely (texting and Twitter), to exchange open opinions about every matter under the sun (Twitter and Facebook), and to do all these things in clever, inventive ways. Lunsford sees a link between the modern world of online writing—feisty, conversational, out in public, and concise—and the ancient Greek tradition of argument.

What if the younger generation ends up better writers than their parents—and their professors? Perish the thought!

> ANALYZING THE RHETORICAL SITUATION

1. To what rhetorical opportunity are David Fallarme, Mark Bauerlein, and Laurie Fendrich each responding?
2. What specific argument does each writer appear to be making?
3. Fendrich urges readers to "Put aside the statistics, the studies, the anecdotes, and take a look at the big picture." What point do you think she is making about those kinds of evidence? What kinds of details and evidence does she use to support her argument? Work with another classmate or two to compose your answers and be prepared to share them with the rest of the class.

COMMUNITY CONNECTIONS

1. Write for ten minutes in response to one of the pieces you've just read about the effects of the use of technology. How do the descriptions or examples offered by the writer coincide with or diverge from your own experiences?

2. Chart your use of communication technologies in the way that David Fallarme does (in terms of frequency and urgency). How often are you prompted to interpret nonverbal communication when using technology? How often do you rely solely on writing when using communication technology?

3. Write for ten minutes about the causes or the consequences of using one type of communication technology. Work with another classmate or two to determine which communication technology you'll focus on. Be prepared to share your list of causes or consequences with the rest of the class.

Investigative Reports: A Fitting Response

As many of the pieces of writing in this chapter demonstrate, an investigative report can sometimes be the most fitting response to a rhetorical opportunity. Each of the pieces is a response to the question of what characterizes the Millennial Generation. Because there is vigorous disagreement about the definition of that generation, each of the authors conducted research (library, experiential, observational, or online) to support his or her findings. Thus, their pieces *define* the nature of the Millennial Generation, *clarify* how this generation can be distinguished from other generations, and *illustrate* a conception of the Millennials with examples.

A report investigating the causes and consequences of multitasking

In her investigative report, which appeared in *The New Atlantis: A Journal of Technology & Society*, Christine Rosen explores what is really happening in our brains when we try to pay attention to many things at once. She uses cause-and-consequence analysis to organize her piece.

The Myth of Multitasking

Christine Rosen

In one of the many letters he wrote to his son in the 1740s, Lord Chesterfield offered the following advice: "There is time enough for everything in the course of the day, if you do but one thing at once, but there is not time enough in the year, if you will do two things at a time." To Chesterfield, singular focus was not merely a practical way to structure one's time; it was a mark of intelligence. "This steady and undissipated attention to one object, is a sure mark of a superior genius; as hurry, bustle, and agitation, are the never-failing symptoms of a weak and frivolous mind."

In modern times, hurry, bustle, and agitation have become a regular way of life for many people—so much so that we have embraced a word to describe our efforts to respond to the many pressing demands on our time: *multitasking*. Used for decades to describe the parallel processing abilities of computers, multitasking is now shorthand for the human attempt to do simultaneously as many things as possible, as quickly as possible, preferably marshalling the power of as many technologies as possible.

In the late 1990s and early 2000s, one sensed a kind of exuberance about the possibilities of multitasking. Advertisements for new electronic gadgets—particularly the first generation of handheld digital devices—celebrated the notion of using technology to accomplish several things at once. The word *multitasking* began appearing in the "skills" sections of résumés, as office workers restyled themselves as high-tech, high-performing team players. "We have always multitasked—inability to walk and chew gum is a time-honored cause for derision—but never so intensely or self-consciously as now," James Gleick wrote in his 1999 book *Faster*. "We are multitasking connoisseurs—experts in crowding, pressing, packing, and overlapping distinct activities in our all-too-finite moments." An article in the *New York Times Magazine* in 2001 asked, "Who can remember life before multitasking? These days we all do it." The article offered advice on "How to Multitask" with suggestions about giving your brain's "multitasking hot spot" an appropriate workout.

But more recently, challenges to the ethos of multitasking have begun to emerge. Numerous studies have shown the sometimes-fatal danger of using cell phones and other electronic devices while driving, for example, and several states have now made that particular form of multitasking illegal. In the business world, where concerns about time-management are perennial, warnings about workplace distractions spawned by a multitasking culture are on the rise. In 2005, the BBC reported on a research study, funded by Hewlett-Packard and conducted by the Institute of Psychiatry at the University of London, that found, "Workers distracted by e-mail and phone calls suffer a fall in IQ more than twice

Evidence from careful research helps Rosen establish her ethos and enhances the logos of her overall argument.

that found in marijuana smokers." The psychologist who led the study called this new "infomania" a serious threat to workplace productivity. One of the *Harvard Business Review*'s "Breakthrough Ideas" for 2007 was Linda Stone's notion of "continuous partial attention," which might be understood as a subspecies of multitasking: using mobile computing power and the Internet, we are "constantly scanning for opportunities and staying on top of contacts, events, and activities in an effort to miss nothing."

Dr. Edward Hallowell, a Massachusetts-based psychiatrist who specializes in the treatment of attention deficit/hyperactivity disorder and has written a book with the self-explanatory title *CrazyBusy*, has been offering therapies to combat extreme multitasking for years; in his book he calls multitasking a "mythical activity in which people believe they can perform two or more tasks simultaneously." In a 2005 article, he described a new condition, "Attention Deficit Trait," which he claims is rampant in the business world. ADT is "purely a response to the hyperkinetic environment in which we live," writes Hallowell, and its hallmark symptoms mimic those of ADD. "Never in history has the human brain been asked to track so many data points," Hallowell argues, and this challenge "can be controlled only by creatively engineering one's environment and one's emotional and physical health." Limiting multitasking is essential. Best-selling business advice author Timothy Ferriss also extols the virtues of "single-tasking" in his book, *The 4-Hour Workweek*.

Multitasking might also be taking a toll on the economy. One study by researchers at the University of California at Irvine monitored interruptions among office workers; they found that workers took an average of twenty-five minutes to recover from interruptions such as phone calls or answering e-mail and return to their original task. Discussing multitasking with the *New York Times* in 2007, Jonathan B. Spira, an analyst at the business research firm Basex, estimated that extreme multitasking—information overload—costs the U.S. economy $650 billion a year in lost productivity.

Changing Our Brains

To better understand the multitasking phenomenon, neurologists and psychologists have studied the workings of the brain. In 1999, Jordan Grafman, chief of cognitive neuroscience at the National Institute of Neurological Disorders and Stroke (part of the National Institutes of Health), used functional magnetic resonance imaging (fMRI) scans to determine that when people engage in "task-switching"—that is, multitasking behavior—the flow of blood increases to a region of the frontal cortex called Brodmann area 10. (The flow of blood to particular regions of the brain is taken as a proxy indication of activity in those regions.) "This is presumably the last part of the brain to evolve, the most mysterious and exciting part," Grafman told the *New York Times* in 2001—adding, with a touch of hyperbole, "It's what makes us most human."

Citing a wide range of credited sources helps Rosen convey to readers that she has conducted a fair, balanced investigation.

It is also what makes multitasking a poor long-term strategy for learning. Other studies, such as those performed by psychologist René Marois of Vanderbilt University, have used fMRI to demonstrate the brain's response to handling multiple tasks. Marois found evidence of a "response selection bottleneck" that occurs when the brain is forced to respond to several stimuli at once. As a result, task-switching leads to time lost as the brain determines which task to perform. Psychologist David Meyer at the University of Michigan believes that rather than a bottleneck in the brain, a process of "adaptive executive control" takes place, which "schedules task processes appropriately to obey instructions about their relative priorities and serial order," as he described to the *New Scientist*. Unlike many other researchers who study multitasking, Meyer is optimistic that, with training, the brain can learn to task-switch more effectively, and there is some evidence that certain simple tasks are amenable to such practice. But his research has also found that multitasking contributes to the release of stress hormones and adrenaline, which can cause long-term health problems if not controlled, and contributes to the loss of short-term memory.

In one recent study, Russell Poldrack, a psychology professor at the University of California, Los Angeles, found that "multitasking adversely affects how you learn. Even if you learn while multitasking, that learning is less flexible and more specialized, so you cannot retrieve the information as easily." His research demonstrates that people use different areas of the brain for learning and storing new information when they are distracted: brain scans of people who are distracted or multitasking show activity in the striatum, a region of the brain involved in learning new skills; brain scans of people who are not distracted show activity in the hippocampus, a region involved in storing and recalling information. Discussing his research on National Public Radio recently, Poldrack warned, "We have to be aware that there is a cost to the way that our society is changing, that humans are not built to work this way. We're really built to focus. And when we sort of force ourselves to multitask, we're driving ourselves to perhaps be less efficient in the long run even though it sometimes feels like we're being more efficient."

If, as Poldrack concluded, "multitasking changes the way people learn," what might this mean for today's children and teens, raised with an excess of new entertainment and educational technology, and avidly multitasking at a young age? Poldrack calls this the "million-dollar question." Media multitasking—that is, the simultaneous use of several different media, such as television, the Internet, video games, text messages, telephones, and e-mail—is clearly on the rise, as a 2006 report from the Kaiser Family Foundation showed: in 1999, only 16 percent of the time people spent using any of those media was spent on multiple media at once; by 2005, 26 percent of media time was spent multitasking. "I multitask every single second I am online," confessed one study participant. "At this very moment I am watching TV, checking my e-mail every two minutes, reading a newsgroup about who shot JFK, burning some music to a CD, and writing this message."

The Kaiser report noted several factors that increase the likelihood of media multitasking, including "having a computer and being able to see a television from it." Also, "sensation-seeking" personality types are more likely to multitask, as are those living in "a highly TV-oriented household." The picture that emerges of these pubescent multitasking mavens is of a generation of great technical facility and intelligence but of extreme impatience, unsatisfied with slowness and uncomfortable with silence: "I get bored if it's not all going at once, because everything has gaps—waiting for a website to come up, commercials on TV, etc." one participant said. The report concludes on a very peculiar note, perhaps intended to be optimistic: "In this media-heavy world, it is likely that brains that are more adept at media multitasking will be passed along and these changes will be naturally selected," the report states. "After all, information is power, and if one can process more information all at once, perhaps one can be more powerful." This is techno-social Darwinism, nature red in pixel and claw.

Other experts aren't so sure. As neurologist Jordan Grafman told *Time* magazine: "Kids that are instant messaging while doing homework, playing games online and watching TV, I predict, aren't going to do well in the long run." "I think this generation of kids is guinea pigs," educational psychologist Jane Healy told the *San Francisco Chronicle*; she worries that they might become adults who engage in "very quick but very shallow thinking." Or, as the novelist Walter Kirn suggests in a deft essay in *The Atlantic*, we might be headed for an "Attention-Deficit Recession."

Noting potential negative effects on children is a good way for Rosen to establish pathos, to make a strong emotional connection with her readers.

Paying Attention

When we talk about multitasking, we are really talking about attention: the art of paying attention, the ability to shift our attention, and, more broadly, to exercise judgment about what objects are worthy of our attention. People who have achieved great things often credit for their success a finely honed skill for paying attention. When asked about his particular genius, Isaac Newton responded that if he had made any discoveries, it was "owing more to patient attention than to any other talent."

William James, the great psychologist, wrote at length about the varieties of human attention. In *The Principles of Psychology* (1890), he outlined the differences among "sensorial attention," "intellectual attention," "passive attention," and the like, and noted the "gray chaotic indiscriminateness" of the minds of people who were incapable of paying attention. James compared our stream of thought to a river, and his observations presaged the cognitive "bottlenecks" described later by neurologists: "On the whole easy simple flowing predominates in it, the drift of things is with the pull of gravity, and effortless attention is the rule," he wrote. "But at intervals an obstruction, a set-back, a log-jam occurs, stops the current, creates an eddy, and makes things temporarily move the other way."

To James, steady attention was thus the default condition of a mature mind, an ordinary state undone only by perturbation. To readers a century later, that placid portrayal may seem alien—as though depicting a bygone world. Instead, today's multitasking adult may find something more familiar in James's description of the youthful mind: an "extreme mobility of the attention" that "makes the child seem to belong less to himself than to every object which happens to catch his notice." For some people, James noted, this challenge is never overcome; such people only get their work done "in the interstices of their mind-wandering." Like Chesterfield, James believed that the transition from youthful distraction to mature attention was in large part the result of personal mastery and discipline—and so was illustrative of character. "The faculty of voluntarily bringing back a wandering attention, over and over again," he wrote, "is the very root of judgment, character, and will."

Today, our collective will to pay attention seems fairly weak. We require advice books to teach us how to avoid distraction. In the not-too-distant future we may even employ new devices to help us overcome the unintended attention deficits created by today's gadgets. As one *New York Times* article recently suggested, "Further research could help create clever technology, like sensors or smart software that workers could instruct with their preferences and priorities to serve as a high tech 'time nanny' to ease the modern multitasker's plight." Perhaps we will all accept as a matter of course a computer governor—like the devices placed on engines so that people can't drive cars beyond a certain speed. Our technological governors might prompt us with reminders to set mental limits when we try to do too much, too quickly, all at once.

Then again, perhaps we will simply adjust and come to accept what James called "acquired inattention." E-mails pouring in, cell phones ringing, televisions blaring, podcasts streaming—all this may become background noise, like the "din of a foundry or factory" that James observed workers could scarcely avoid at first, but which eventually became just another part of their daily routine. For the younger generation of multitaskers, the great electronic din is an expected part of everyday life. And given what neuroscience and anecdotal evidence have shown us, this state of constant intentional self-distraction could well be of profound detriment to individual and cultural well-being. When people do their work only in the "interstices of their mind-wandering," with crumbs of attention rationed out among many competing tasks, their culture may gain in information, but it will surely weaken in wisdom.

Rosen moves toward a conclusion by quoting Newton and James, historical figures whose contributions to culture have been monumental. Each of them, like Lord Chesterfield, recommends paying attention to one thing at a time.

Rosen reaches the conclusion that "our collective will to pay attention seems fairly weak," and she has provided a good deal of evidence to support that conclusion.

Rosen admits that perhaps it's too late to turn back the clock on multitasking and that modern society may need to resign itself to a tradeoff between information and wisdom.

■ GUIDE TO RESPONDING TO THE RHETORICAL SITUATION

Understanding the Rhetorical Situation

When you want to present the results of research you have done, consider composing an investigative report. Such a report commonly has the following features:

- An investigative report defines an issue or phenomenon in precise terms.
- An investigative report makes clear why the issue or phenomenon is one that needs to be investigated.
- An investigative report provides convincing facts and details to help readers understand how the issue or phenomenon affects different groups that have some stake in the situation.
- An investigative report uses direct quotations to vividly convey the perspectives of various groups with a stake in the issue or phenomenon.
- An investigative report clearly identifies the conclusion readers should reach.

The following sections will help you compose an investigative report about the Millennial Generation or another generation that interests you. To work with an online guide to the elements of the rhetorical situation, access your English CourseMate through cengagebrain.com.

Identifying an opportunity

Until you read this chapter, you may not have given much thought to generational labels. Now that you have been considering what it means to be part of a generation, you may be wondering just how accurate and appropriate such labels are. Are they fair ("the greatest") or unfair ("narcissistic")? Are any of them mutually exclusive or overlapping?

As you consider a specific generation, what do you want to know more about? Do you want to investigate the existing label for that generation or find out more about some of its members, their values, accomplishments, and hopes? Maybe you're interested in investigating how generational labels relate to the activities or functions of on-campus offices: the Office of Student Affairs, the Office of Career Services, the Admissions Office, or the Alumni Office. Have you noticed that you are treated differently at any of those offices than a student from another generation? Have older or younger students reported different treatment and expectations from any of those offices? Perhaps you have noticed behaviors, cultural touchstones, or values that are common to a generation but that others have overlooked? Whatever details you have noticed or experiences you have had, you should tap them as you launch your own investigation of generational identity.

1. Make a list of values, behaviors, cultural touchstones, or other characteristics associated with a particular generation. (You might be able to draw

on the writing you've done in response to questions presented earlier in this chapter.) Who do you know who embodies the label of a specific generation? What evidence from that person's life or behavior can you provide that helps support your assertion?

2. Where and when do the various generations of students (or instructors) on campus display their differing characteristics? Which characteristics are immediately identifiable or familiar? Which characteristics are less obvious or unfamiliar? How do you know that someone has those less obvious qualities? Write for a few minutes about these considerations. Be prepared to share your response with the rest of the class.

3. Choose a single characteristic of any generation you would like to explore further, in order to determine its causes and consequences. Write four or five sentences that describe that characteristic and explain how it affects the generation itself or other generations. Be prepared to share your sentences with the rest of the class.

Locating an audience

The following questions will help you identify the rhetorical audience for your investigative report on some characteristic of (or label for) a specific generation. Once you identify an audience who will be interested in or affected by your analysis, you'll be able to choose the best way to deliver your report.

1. List the names of the persons or groups who are affected by or have an interest in the particular generational characteristic (or label) you're going to explore. (This step may require some research.)

2. Next to the name of each potential audience, write reasons that audience could have for acknowledging the significance of this generational characteristic (or label). In other words, what information might convince that audience that an investigation of this particular characteristic (or label) could be important to them?

3. What motivation might each potential audience have for learning more about the generational characteristic (or label)? What emotional response might each audience be expected to have to your investigative report? What logical conclusions might the potential audiences reach about generational labels or mislabels? In what ways might each audience help you confirm or disprove the accuracy of such labels? What actions could these audiences reasonably be expected to take in response to your report?

4. With your audience's interests and motivation in mind, look again at the descriptions of generational characteristics that you composed in the preceding section. Decide which description will enable your audience to feel invested in exploring this particular characteristic (or label) in greater detail in order to understand why and how it affects them. At this point, it will probably be necessary to revise your best description to tailor it to the audiences.

Identifying a fitting response

As you know by now, different purposes and different audiences call for different kinds of texts delivered through different media. For example, realizing that the preferences of an older generation are being overlooked by your school's food services might prompt you to write a flyer and circulate it in the student union, in order to raise awareness of the predominance of fast food on campus and its implications for students' health and satisfaction. Or perhaps discovering that your generation lacks experience in public speaking might lead you to compose and deliver a multimedia presentation to your first-year writing classmates, with the purpose of explaining the curricular opportunities that can help them address this shortcoming. The point is that once you identify your rhetorical opportunity, audience, and purpose, you need to determine what kind of text will best respond to the rhetorical situation.

Use the following questions to help you narrow your purpose and shape your response:

1. What facts and details do you need to provide in order to get your audience to recognize the validity or significance of the specific generational feature (characteristic or label) you are investigating?
2. What are the various (perhaps conflicting) perspectives on this generation that you must acknowledge?
3. Are you asking the audience to adopt a new perspective, or do you want the audience to perform a particular action in response to your writing?
4. What is the best way to reach this audience? That is, to what kind of text is this audience most likely to respond? (Chapter 13 can help you explore options for media and design.)

Writing an Investigative Report: Working with Your Available Means

Shaping your investigative report

Like many other genres, investigative reports take advantage of the power of the rhetorical appeals. While establishing the writer's ethos, the introduction of an investigative report provides readers with a specific description or definition of the issue or phenomenon to be explored as well as the writer's stance concerning that issue. Mark Bauerlein, for example, opens his investigative report with statistics—2,272 texts a month, nine hours of social networking a week—about young people's communication methods. After these descriptive numbers, he identifies the topic of his report: that visible nonverbal behaviors are missing from these communication methods. pages 64–65, 67–68

The body of an investigative report provides facts, details, and direct quotations that further clarify the issue or phenomenon being examined while shaping the logic (and thus the persuasiveness) of the writer's argument. A successful investigative report is one in which the writer displays good sense in the presentation and analysis of evidence. The writer uses attributive tags to show where each piece of pages 75–77 evidence came from and to indicate that each source is credible and knowledgable about the topic, thereby enhancing the writer's ethos as well as the report's logos. For example, Bauerlein refers to the research of influential anthropologist Edward Hall, who wrote about the "silent language" as early as 1959. In describing Hall's research on how communication breaks down across cultures, Bauerlein clarifies his purpose: he is applying Hall's cross-cultural communication research findings to instances of miscommunication within a single culture. In particular, Bauerlein is investigating miscommunication that occurs because some participants are less adept at reading nonverbal signals than others. Bauerlein's citations and quotations support his thesis and help build the logos of his argument. If Bauerlein had used video to deliver his report (in the form of a short documentary, for example, or a segment on a news show), he could have shown clips from archived interviews with Hall and presented graphics to illustrate the quantitative research from which he is drawing. Such visual information would further support his credibility.

The body of an investigative report also traces the effects of the issue or phenomenon on various groups. Every use of examples, facts, statistics, and other data builds the ethos of the writer at the same time as it establishes the appeal of logos.

In addition, the body of an investigative report characterizes fairly the positions and motivations of the various groups interested in or affected by the issue or phenomenon, thereby strengthening the writer's ethos and logos. As you can see, all the rhetorical appeals must continually overlap, even if one appeal is emphasized over others at certain points. In a successful investigative report, the writer presents different perspectives in a fair, even-handed way, balancing the ethical appeal of good sense with the logical appeal of supporting information. The writer attends carefully to the connotations of words used to describe the different perspectives of the various groups and gives voice to members of these different groups by quoting them directly.

Finally, the conclusion of an investigative report brings together the various perspectives on the issue or phenomenon and sometimes makes a final appeal

Introduction
- ► Establishes ethos
- ► Describes or defines the issue
- ► States the thesis

Body
- ► Establishes logos
- ► Provides facts, details, and direct quotations
- ► Traces the effects of the issue on various groups

Conclusion
- ► Brings together various perspectives, making an emotional connection
- ► Makes a final attempt to connect with the audience, establishing pathos
- ► Includes a (reasonable) appeal to the audience to adopt a particular attitude or undertake a specific action

© 2013 Cengage Learning

for readers to adopt a specific attitude or opinion or take a specific action, using the emotional appeal (of pathos) by connecting the writer's cause with the interests of the readers.

Revision and peer review

After you've drafted a strong version of your investigative report, ask one of your classmates to read it. You'll want your classmate to respond to your work in a way that helps you revise it so that it is the strongest investigative report it can be, one that identifies a rhetorical opportunity, addresses your intended audience, helps you fulfill your purpose, and is delivered in the most appropriate means available to you and your audience.

Questions for a peer reviewer
1. To what opportunity for change is the writer responding?
2. Who might be the writer's intended audience? What might be the writer's purpose? How do audience and purpose come together?
3. What information did you receive from the introduction? Does the writer define the issue or phenomenon in terms that will make sense to the audience? What suggestions do you have for the writer regarding the introduction?
4. Note the writer's thesis statement. If you cannot locate a thesis statement, what thesis statement might work for this report?
5. Note the assertions the writer makes to support the report's thesis. Are the assertions presented in chronological or emphatic order? How does that order enhance the report's overall effectiveness? Which of the assertions might you reorder? Why?
6. If you cannot locate a series of assertions, what assertions could be made to support the thesis? In what order?
7. Mark the supporting ideas (presented using narration, cause-and-consequence analysis, description, exemplification, process analysis, or definition) that the writer offers to support the assertions.
8. What reasons are given for investigating the issue or phenomenon?
9. What facts and details are provided to explain how the issue or phenomenon affects different groups that might have an interest in or connection to it?
10. Whom does the writer quote? What evidence does the writer provide for the credibility of the sources quoted? Whose perspectives are represented in direct quotations? Whose perspectives are not represented through the use of quotations? Can you ascertain why the writer made those decisions?
11. How does the writer establish ethos? How could the writer strengthen this appeal?
12. How does the writer make use of pathos? How exactly does the writer connect his or her cause with the interests of the rhetorical audience?
13. What specific conclusion do you reach about the issue or phenomenon as a result of reading the report?
14. What section of the report did you most enjoy? Least enjoy? Why?

INVESTIGATIVE REPORTS IN THREE MEDIA

Online Report

Ryan Healy's investigation responds to the question "Why Isn't Mainstream Gen Y Buying into the New Web?" in his blog post for *Employee Evolution*. To read it, find *Writing in Three Media* in your English Course-Mate, accessed through cengagebrain.com.

Courtesy Ryan Healy

Video Report

PBS NewsHour filmed a report on the Pew Research Center's study of the Millennials. To view it, find *Writing in Three Media* in your English Course-Mate, accessed through cengagebrain.com.

Courtesy of PBS

Print Report

In the following report, Columbia University student Jenn Mayer investigates what music videos and MTV programming mean to her generation.

Helga Esteb/Shutterstock.com

Jenn could easily have explored her generation's relationship to the music video using any of a variety of genres and media. If her main purpose had been to reflect on the ways in which *Total Request Live* had a formative effect on her, she might have written a memoir to post on her blog. If she had wanted to convince others that the music video is truly the "lasting art form" that she labels it, she could have gathered her evidence into a position argument. But Jenn realized that her extensive research, including interviews with Columbia College classmates, lent itself to an investigative report. And, as a writer for *The Eye*, the weekly magazine affiliated with the *Columbia Daily Spectator* (an undergraduate newspaper), she was able to use that publication to deliver her report to a large audience likely to be interested in the same topic: her college peers who also grew up with *TRL*, *Pop-Up Video*, Britney Spears, and the Backstreet Boys.

The Last of the Music Videos

a dying art form finds a new home

by Jenn Mayer

Video killed the radio star, but who killed the video?

MTV's *Total Request Live* was canceled late last year after a decade-long run. In a sense, *TRL* defined a generation—ours. In the late '90s and early '00s, scores of tweens would rush home from middle school to see the hottest Britney Spears and Backstreet Boys videos. On the show, pop stars showcased synchronized dance moves and flawless bodies that made teenage girls shriek and cry. While *TRL* was culturally crucial in our younger years, the show's former popularity also indicates how important music videos once were for MTV. The end of the *TRL* era also seemed to symbolize the end of the era of music videos.

The demise of music videos seems clear now that MTV has all but done away with them. In the past, MTV played videos around the clock, providing an additional, visual outlet for artists to expose themselves and for viewers to hear new music. The golden age of the music video began with Michael Jackson's "Thriller" in 1983. When MTV began to credit the directors of music videos in 1992, videos started to take on a cinematic, short-film quality. Video directors like Spike Jonze, F. Gary Gray, and Michel Gondry later went on to direct full-length films.

To help fuel this nascent art form, MTV developed programs like *Making the Video*, which gave viewers a behind-the-scenes look into the creation of a different hit video every episode. VH1, MTV's corporate cousin, had a similar show in *Pop-Up Video*. Videos were almost ubiquitous, the source of iconic images for our generation—who doesn't remember Sisqó's silver hair in the "Thong Song" video or the members of *NSYNC posing as puppets in "Bye Bye Bye"?

Jenn makes clear that the audience for her report is the generation of readers who were middle schoolers from about 1998 to 2003, and she appeals to pathos by identifying herself as part of that generation.

Jenn defines the topic of her investigative report in clear terms: the decline of the music video, a favorite form of media for some Millennials.

Jenn presents details about specific music videos that establish her ethos and support her appeal to pathos.

Just as the quasi-innocent image of Britney Spears in her ". . . Baby One More Time" schoolgirl outfit has been replaced in our minds with the image of a shaved head and umbrella, MTV has replaced music videos with reality programming, a field it pioneered with *The Real World*. Now that reality shows dominate prime time, MTV has expanded its offerings to include a slew of dating shows, competitions, and forays into celebrity lifestyles. To remain relevant, it seems as though MTV has been forced to alter its original design to match other major networks.

She presents evidence that the growing popularity of reality shows was the main cause for the decline of music videos.

In addition to MTV's reality programming, YouTube has also contributed to putting the nail in the video coffin. On the site, music videos with A-list directors and multi-million dollar budgets mingle equally with fan-made videos. As Henry Jones, SEAS [School of Engineering and Applied Science] '12, says, "If there's a song I really like, I'll search to see if there's a video. But I don't go on YouTube exclusively to watch multiple videos. It just doesn't seem logical anymore to sit down and actively watch a music video."

This shift away from music videos is also a signal of major change for the music industry. Illegal file-sharing and waning CD sales have crippled the industry, forcing it to adapt in order to stay afloat. But while stories like the lawsuits against college students who download illegally and the closing of the Virgin Megastore have consistently made headlines, it seems as though music videos have more or less disappeared silently from the airwaves.

Jenn identifies the significance of the decline in music video programming.

But, as Jones suggests, while many people don't search deliberately for music videos, they are directed to them by links or friends' suggestions. This type of viral marketing represents how popular culture continues to embrace music videos, despite their ousting from television. Videos for songs such as MGMT's "Electric Feel" gained popularity through word of mouth, and everyone had seen Beyoncé's "Single Ladies" video even before it was parodied on *Saturday Night Live.*[*]

Jenn's references to specific artists and songs further supports her appeal to pathos.

Furthermore, the original concept of the music video as an additional link to the artist continues to attract viewers. Emma Gillespie, CC [Columbia College] '09, tunes into videos both online and through MTV sister channels that have continued to show videos, like MTV Jams and MTV Hits. "Videos put a story with the music, and it's fun to see what the artist's interpretation of the song is," she says.

Although MTV has abandoned music videos on its main channel, it does make over 16,000 videos available for online streaming. Britney Spears' "Circus" video, which marked her highly publicized comeback, boasts over 2 million MTV views. One of the many YouTube versions of the same video reports almost 25 million.

Though the music video is not fully dead, it has begun to take on the qualities of a has-been pop star. While today's tweens may not have the same relationship to music videos as teens in the '80s or the TRL generation did, the simple fact is that people continue to invest time in watching them. Rather than lamenting the days when music videos ruled the airwaves, we can rejoice in the medium's status as a lasting art form. Music videos will continue to garner attention and inspire parody for years to come.

Alternatives to the Investigative Report

Fitting responses come in many forms, not just reports. Your instructor might call upon you to consider one of the following opportunities for writing.

1. As you read in the introduction to this chapter, generational labels are generalizations about specific groups with which some people may not agree. Compose an essay that defines your generation in a fresh way. What name would you give your generation? What characterizes your generation? What differentiates it from and connects it to other generations?

pages 64–66

2. Compose a narrative about a day in the life of a fellow student from a generation other than your own. Describe in vivid detail how and where your campus accommodates—or does not accommodate—someone from that generation. You will probably need to do library or online research and/or conduct interviews to fulfill this assignment.

3. Identify a particular problem on your campus that results from lack of attention to a specific generational characteristic (of your generation or another). Write a proposal that describes the problem and argues for a particular practical solution. As you write, make sure to consider your audience (whose members should be in a position to help implement your solution) and the feasibility of your proposal (its cost and how it might affect the institution's research, teaching, and service missions).

Persuading in a Multilingual Context: Responding with Position Arguments

7

According to the latest census figures, over 55 million people in the United States speak a language other than English in their homes. Of the more than 230 million other inhabitants who do speak English in their homes, very few claim knowledge of the rules and conventions that govern what they might call "correct" English. This is another term for **Standardized English**, the English used in schools, businesses, government, textbooks, standardized tests, entrance examinations, and other kinds of official places and documents.

WORD COURT

BY BARBARA WALLRAFF

CAROLYN SIMON, of Tucson, Ariz., writes: "I am seeking evidence to present to the activities committee here at my retirement center. Each evening on our closed-circuit TV channel a feature film is broadcast. In the past we've had variety. Now we have a new activities director. I suggested *Babel*, and one of our members said, 'No, it has the F word!' I said that the F word is part of today's accepted vernacular and often simply means 'Omigosh!' or 'Oops!' or 'Look what I did!' Our activities director has been swayed by the puritan wing of our committee. What do you think?"

I think saying the F word, like doing the F thing, is appropriate behavior for consenting adults in private. Newspapers and many magazines are concerned mainly with the public sphere, so they (we) tend to shy away from the word unless it's part of a quotation that was uttered in public. Saying the word in public demonstrates recklessness, crassness, or both. But movies almost inevitably portray private life. Here the word, like the deed, tends to come up. Anyone who is truly shocked when he

word *dubious* where I'm certain the writer means *doubtful*. I see this error in newspapers and in books by respected writers. It upsets me every time I see it. Is *dubious* now synonymous with *doubtful*?"

Even worse: *Dubious* has been synonymous with *doubtful* for centuries. The two main definitions for *dubious* in the *Oxford English Dictionary* begin "objectively *doubtful*; fraught with doubt or uncertainty" (the supporting citations include this one, from 1548: "To abide the fortune of battayle,

f word

indifferent musical performance, *sure* of a *sure* thing. Granted, this imprecision could give rise to misunderstandings. But it hardly ever does: Does the chair feel *comfortable* or does it make us feel that way? You say that when you read *dubious*, sometimes you're "certain the writer means *doubtful*." That's about as much clarity as you can reasonably expect.

HAROLD SIMON, of Camarillo, Calif., writes: "An article in *Time* magazine, a very positive one about a popular TV personality, called her 'antisnob and utterly *nonaspirational*.' My medical background complained. *Aspiration*, medically, is the oral ingestion of a substance into the trachea instead of the esophagus, and it may have serious consequences. Am I being picky or reasonable?"

Aspiration in medical lingo is one thing; in common parlance it's something else. Though the word comes from the Latin for *breathe*, its meaning is often more nearly "desire." As for *aspirational*, time was it tended to have to do with lofty spiritual desires. In recent

In "Word Court," a feature in the *Atlantic Monthly*, Barbara Wallraff regularly settles disputes for people who concern themselves with the rules and conventions of English grammar and usage. For instance, Frederick G. Rodgers wrote asking Wallraff about the trend of "people using the word *do* as an alternative to a more fitting verb": "When I hear statements such [as] 'I often *do* French bread twice a week' and 'The mayor is not planning to *do* an investigation yet,' I automatically wonder why *bake* in the first statement and *order* in the second were not used." After pointing her finger at Nike for its successful "Just do it" campaign, Wallraff maintains that beyond the world of advertising, this overuse of *do* "sabotages communication," allowing us to "express ourselves in ways that can mean anything listeners want." For many American readers, "Word Court" would feed anxieties about their use of spoken and written English, about their inability to use English "right"—either in English class or outside of it. Even those of us who speak English fluently freeze up the minute we have to speak or write something that other people will be judging for correctness. Paradoxically, these are the kinds of experiences that lead so many Americans to believe in the importance of Standardized English for maintaining civility and precise communication in U.S. public life.

A **position argument**—the delivery of a point of view and the use of logical, emotional, and ethical appeals to help an audience understand that point of view—is one means of asserting how and why Americans ought to use English. Given the increasing linguistic and cultural diversity of the United States, however, questions about "correctness" are complicated to address. Whether the overuse of *do* signals the decline of the English language or any similar issue is overshadowed by the larger concern of whether English is the national (i.e., official) language of the United States, especially given the public presence of Spanish, Mandarin Chinese, and Tagalog. Position arguments can serve as individuals' and groups' means for participating in debates concerning speaking and writing in this increasingly multilingual context.

IDENTIFYING AN OPPORTUNITY

Throughout this chapter, you'll work to identify an opportunity to compose a position argument. You might want to consider your home dialect or language, particularly if you're comfortable with it and it contrasts with Standardized American English. You might want to explore an issue of discrimination—or advantage—based on language. Or perhaps you'll want to reflect on how some particular feature of your language has changed as you've become more educated. As you work to determine the language issue you want to argue, consider the most fitting means of delivery:

Print Argument
written in essay form (with or without visuals for illustration) for a community or academic publication

Visual Argument
composed as a cartoon or an advertisement for a print or online publication

Online Argument
written as a blog entry or a contribution to a website

To begin, freewrite for five minutes in response to each of the following questions (or use any of the invention techniques presented on pages 58–61):

1. Look at the images in this chapter. What specific argument does each visual make about the relationship between language and diversity in the United States? What details in the image lead you to your conclusions?

2. Select the particular image that resonates most strongly for you as you think about the language differences in the United States. What seems most familiar—or disorienting—in this image? What interests you the most about it?

3. In what ways does this particular image seem to support or oppose a viewpoint you have about language differences?

Real Situations

The last page of the *Atlantic Monthly* provides a space for people to police the boundaries of "correct" English, but one hundred years ago, the magazine featured a series of articles critiquing an educational policy aimed at eradicating the languages and cultural ways of Native American tribes. In three successive issues, autobiographical essays by Zitkala-Ša argued for the end of that educational policy. Zitkala-Ša, born in 1876 on the Yankton Reservation in South Dakota and later a student and teacher at the off-reservation

Courtesy of Cumberland County Historical Society.

Cover of the 1895 catalogue for the federal Indian School in Carlisle, Pennsylvania, one of many off-reservation boarding schools.

Indian School in Carlisle, Pennsylvania, published "Impressions of an Indian Childhood," "The School Days of an Indian Girl," and "An Indian Teacher among Indians" in 1900. She criticized the school's policy of forbidding students to use their tribal languages to communicate with teachers or to converse with fellow students. While directors at the school claimed to be freeing the students from their "savage ways" by teaching them English, Zitkala-Ša declared in "Impressions of an Indian Childhood" that, as she lost her native language, "I no longer felt free to be myself, or to voice my own feelings." She argued, in effect, that rather than dictating students' language choices and deciding what constitutes "correct" and "proper" language use, U.S. schools should give students opportunities to learn English while also maintaining the language of their cultural heritage.

Zitkala-Ša's arguments speak to the difficulties faced by thousands of Native American students at off-reservation boarding schools at the turn of the twentieth century. But those difficulties remain for many students in the twenty-first century. As you will read later in this chapter, students from language minority groups continue to experience cultural tensions in their formal schooling, often being forced to leave behind the language of their friends, families, and relatives. Other groups of non-English speakers in the United States, however, live in tightly knit communities where they can thrive without using English at all, conducting their domestic life and daily business in the language with which they feel most comfortable. In still other settings, speakers of several

In parts of the United States where Spanish speakers are numerous, advertisers often use that language to appeal to consumers.

languages encounter situations that require them to mix their languages. Such mixing sometimes helps a person express exactly something a single language could not convey; it can also, however, make a person feel uncertain about issues of identity. Puerto Rican poet Sandra Mariá Esteves uses Spanglish in her poem "Not Neither," in which she identifies herself as both "Puertor-riqueña" and "Americana" but shows that she does not feel a full member of either community: "Pero ni portorra, pero sí portorra too / Pero ni que what am I?" The billboard on the facing page attests to one business's "strategic" mixing of Spanish and English to tap into patrons' linguistic preferences—and to make profits.

During the past forty years, arguments echoing those by Zitkala-Ša and others have helped to make the use of languages other than English more evident in American political, educational, journalistic, and legal arenas. According to the Voting Rights Act of 1965, when 5 percent of the voting-age citizens in any state or political subdivision are members of a single language minority group, local election boards must print ballots and other relevant materials in that language. The Federal Bilingual Education Act of 1968 allowed languages other than English to be used in schools across the nation. (That practice has since been at the center of public debate on educational policies, most notably concerning California's Proposition 227, whose adoption meant that all public school instruction in California had to be conducted in English only.) In 2010, there were nearly twenty Spanish-language television networks in the United States, with Univision reaching 95 percent of Hispanic households with televisions and Telemundo reaching 86 percent. Annually, nearly 200,000 federal court proceedings require the work of qualified translators and interpreters. Close to 95 percent of these cases involve Spanish, with the remainder involving over 100 other languages. The prevalence of Spanish and other languages in the U.S. political, educational, journalistic, and legal arenas gives added layers of meaning to the question Robert Mac-Neil and William Cran pose in the title of their book, *Do You Speak American?*

As the linguistic and ethnic demographics of the U.S. population continue to change, local, state, and federal agencies have explored ways of making public services and public communications more accessible to language minority groups. For example, the city government of Minneapolis, Minnesota, posted a sign printed in four languages: English, Hmong, Spanish, and Somali. Medical service providers similarly have sought to make printed and online materials available in multiple languages in order to communicate essential health information to all the language groups in a

Courtesy of The National Institutes of Health

Public notices and government publications are increasingly multilingual or bilingual.

Joey Vento with his controversial "Speak English" sign.

community. The National Institutes of Health, for example, published a booklet on cholesterol levels in a side-by-side, English-Spanish format.

Some people in the United States, however, consider the visible presence of non-English languages as a threat to the English language's prominence in the nation's public affairs. These people want to halt the use of languages other than English in the public sphere. Joey Vento, a third-generation Italian American and owner of Geno's Steaks in Philadelphia, Pennsylvania, went so far as to post a sign at the counter where restaurant patrons place their orders instructing them to do so in English. This sign sparked an intense month-long debate in the local newspapers and on radio and television talk shows. The Philadelphia Commission on Human Relations even filed a discrimination complaint, arguing that the sign violates the city's Fair Practices Ordinance, which prohibits discrimination in public accommodation. In several interviews, including one con-

Members of the Dominican vocal group Voz a Voz get ready to sing in an ensemble performance of "Nuestro Himno" at Ellis Island in New York.

ducted by Neil Cavuto of Fox News, Vento responded that he simply wants all Americans to learn English the way his ancestors did when they arrived in the United States.

A similar debate centers on a Spanish-language version of the U.S. national anthem. British music producer Adam Kidron created the song in 2006 as a response to the immigration debate in the United States. The recording, entitled "Nuestro Himno" ("Our Anthem"), features Puerto Rican singers Carlos Ponce and Olga Tanon and hip-hop artists including Wyclef Jean and Pitbull singing Spanish lyrics based on those of "The Star-Spangled Banner." At certain points, however, the song switches to English and directs sharp criticism at U.S. immigration policy; for example:

> These kids have no parents
> 'cause all of these mean laws . . .
> let's not start a war with all these hard workers
> they can't help where they were born.
>
> Used by permission.

NEW YORK'S BEST (AND NICEST) BOUNTY HUNTER / THE REAL BILLIE HOLIDAY

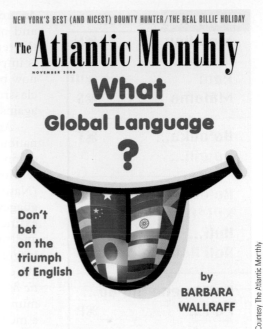

The Atlantic Monthly

NOVEMBER 2000

What Global Language ?

Don't bet on the triumph of English

by **BARBARA WALLRAFF**

Position Arguments

Cover of the *Atlantic Monthly,* questioning the status of English as the global language.

Pitbull suggested that "the American dream is in that record: struggle, freedom, opportunity, everything they are trying to shut down on us."

Despite such appeals to Americans' democratic values, countless numbers of critics have expressed outrage that the U.S. national anthem might be sung in anything but English. U.S. Senator Lamar Alexander, a Republican from Tennessee, went so far as to propose a resolution:

> . . . giving senators an opportunity to remind the country why we sing our National Anthem in English . . . . We Americans are a unique nation of immigrants united by a common language and a belief in principles expressed in our Declaration of Independence and our Constitution, not by our race, ancestry or country of origin. We are proud of the countries we have come from, but we are prouder to be Americans.

In expressing his pride in the common culture and political ideals of the United States, Alexander argues for a specific view of how citizens can and should reaffirm the nation's democratic principles.

Ironically, as calls for using only English to reaffirm the nation's political and cultural values have multiplied, the U.S. Defense Department has argued that language education plays a key role in strengthening U.S. security capabilities. The Defense Department came to see language education as a national security concern shortly after September 11, 2001, when it realized that it did not have enough linguists and translators to read the covert

Waihona Ho'ololi M	
Mea Hou	⌘N
Wehe...	⌘O
Pani	⌘W
Mālama	⌘S
Ho'ouka...	⌘T
Ho'oili...	
Holoi	⌘D
Ki'i 'Ike	⌘I
Huli...	⌘F
Huli Hou A'e	⌘G
Ho'okuene 'Ao'ao...	
Pa'i...	⌘P
Ha'alele	⌘Q

A pull-down menu translated into Hawaiian increases the perception of that language as a living one.

Savage Chickens   by Doug Savage

PIRATE TEXT MESSAGING

www.savagechickens.com

How does text messaging affect language use?

documents (written in Arabic, Chinese, Korean, Russian, and other less frequently taught languages) warning of the terrorists' attack. Concluding that language education is important to the military, Defense Department officials now believe that schools—and, in particular, language arts classrooms—are valuable resources for securing the nation against terrorist threats.

And while the U.S. government is striving to build the nation's expertise in certain foreign languages, scholars and community activists have launched campaigns to draw attention to and revitalize the nation's heritage languages (Native American, Alaska Native, and Native Hawaiian languages), many of which have died out or are threatened with extinction as a result of monolingual educational policies and the use of English in the mass media. In effect, these language revitalization projects are attempting to reverse the effects of the educational legacy Zitkala-Ša warned *Atlantic Monthly* readers about in 1900. The projects bring communities together physically or virtually in order to create a meaningful context for learning and using their heritage languages. Scholars and community leaders in Hawaii, for instance, have successfully adapted Apple software to meet the needs of their language revitalization project by translating computer commands into the Hawaiian language. Most recently, Hawaiian language scholars have worked with Google to make its search page available in Hawaiian. This adaptation of literacy tools helps students to see Hawaiian as a living language they can use to communicate with others across the Hawaiian island chain.

While revitalization advocates try to breathe life into languages that have declined because educational, political, and technological trends have established English's prominence in the world, others have turned their attention to what English might be like in the United States in the years to come, given immigration, the growth of the Spanish-speaking population, and technological advances that abridge the language. One thing is certain: within the next fifty years in the United States, native speakers of English will be outnumbered by nonnative speakers of English, and all Americans will use English in a multilingual context. Consequently, while some readers of the *Atlantic Monthly* hold fast to the seemingly fixed rules of Standardized English and bring cases before the "Word Court," the notion of plural "Englishes" may prove to be a more useful way of characterizing the language usage of the future.

DESCRIBING LANGUAGE USE IN THE UNITED STATES

1. Write for five to ten minutes about your experiences using, listening to, or reading languages other than English in the United States. Is your reaction to the use of these languages in public spaces positive, negative, or neutral?

2. Write for five minutes about the experiences your parents (or children) have had with languages other than English in the United States. Are their experiences like yours or different? What is their level of frustration or acceptance?

3. Finally, take five minutes to consider your viewpoint on language diversity in the United States by composing a claim (or assertion). What reason can you provide for your claim? What evidence supports that reason?

4. Does your viewpoint match that of your family members, or is it different from theirs? How do you account for the similarity or difference?

Real Responses to Real Situations

Should we make English the official language of the United States?

There would be no United States were it not for immigration. In fact, the history of this country is directly linked to a sequence of immigrants. The dominant image for the assimilation of the various national and ethnic groups has long been the melting pot. Although many people see the melting pot as a symbol of Americans' openness to immigrants, each new wave of immigrants—Irish, Italians, Eastern Europeans, Asians, or Mexicans—became an object of scorn for those who were already citizens. Throughout U.S. history, immigrants have come to this country to escape danger, poverty, or persecution and to improve their lives. Those who had the easiest time assimilating had Northern European backgrounds, which made it easier for them to blend into the mainstream.

When huge numbers of Latin Americans and Asians arrived in the United States between 1970 and 1990, many joined ever-growing linguistic communities of Chinese, Korean, Japanese, and Spanish speakers who live out their entire lives without learning, let alone using, English. Perceiving these non–English-speaking communities as a threat to English as the dominant U.S. language, some citizens began rallying to make English the official language of the United States. Supporters of this position argue that Americans—regardless of native language—should all speak the same language in order to work toward common national goals and participate fully in public life.

S. I. Hayakawa (1906–1992) served California as a Republican Senator from 1977 to 1983. In 1981, he introduced the first English language amendment to the Constitution. After serving his state and nation, Hayakawa, the son of immigrants and a speaker of English as a second language, helped to found the organization U.S. English, whose dual missions are generating public support for an English language amendment to the Constitution and lobbying congressional representatives to enact such legislation. Subcommittees of the Senate Judiciary Committee, in 1984, and the House Judiciary Committee, in 1988, conducted public hearings on Hayakawa's proposed amendment. Although the U.S. Congress has taken no action to add an English language amendment to the Constitution, about thirty states have adopted English as the official state language, through an amendment to the state constitution or a legislative statute. Hayakawa outlined the vision guiding English-only supporters in his 1985 policy paper "One Nation . . . Indivisible? The English Language Amendment." According to Hayakawa, an English language amendment to the U.S. Constitution would reinforce the nation's political and cultural values.

Excerpt from

> # One Nation . . . Indivisible? The English Language Amendment

Reprinted by permission.

S. I. Hayakawa

What is it that has made a society out of the hodgepodge of nationalities, races, and colors represented in the immigrant hordes that people our nation? It is language, of course, that has made communication among all these elements possible. It is with a common language that we have dissolved distrust and fear. It is with language that we have drawn up the understandings and agreements and social contracts that make a society possible. . . .

One need not speak faultless American English to become an American. Indeed, one may continue to speak English with an appalling foreign accent. This is true of some of my friends, but they are seen as fully American because of the warmth and enthusiasm with which they enter into the life of the communities in which they live. . . .

In the past several years, strong resistance to the "melting pot" idea has arisen, especially for those who claim to speak for the Hispanic peoples. Instead of a melting pot, they say, the national ideal should be a "salad bowl," in which different elements are thrown together but not "melted," so that the original ingredients retain their distinctive character. . . .

I welcome the Hispanic—and as a Californian, I especially welcome the Mexican—influence on our culture. My wife was wise enough to insist that both our son and daughter learn Spanish as children and to keep reading Spanish as they were growing up. Consequently, my son, a newspaperman, was able to work for six months as an exchange writer for a newspaper in Costa Rica, while a Costa Rican reporter took my son's place in Oregon. My daughter, a graduate of the University of California at Santa Cruz, speaks Spanish, French, and after a year in Monterey Language School, Japanese.

The ethnic chauvinism of the present Hispanic leadership is an unhealthy trend in present-day America. It threatens a division perhaps more ominous in the long run than the division between blacks and whites. Blacks and whites have problems enough with each other, to be sure, but they quarrel with each other in one language. Even Malcolm X, in his fiery denunciation of the racial situation in America, wrote excellent and eloquent English. But the present politically ambitious "Hispanic Caucus" looks forward to a destiny for Spanish-speaking Americans separate from that of Anglo-, Italian-, Polish-, Greek-, Lebanese-, Chinese-, and Afro-Americans, and all the rest of us who rejoice in our ethnic diversity, which gives us our richness as a culture, and the English language, which keeps us in communication with each other to create a unique and vibrant culture.

© Bettmann/CORBIS

The advocates of Spanish language and Hispanic culture are not at all unhappy about the fact that "bilingual education," originally instituted as the best way to teach English, often results in no English being taught at all. Nor does Hispanic leadership seem to be alarmed that large populations of Mexican Americans, Cubans, and Puerto Ricans do not speak English and have no intention of learning. Hispanic spokesmen rejoice when still another concession is made to the Spanish-speaking public, such as the Spanish-language Yellow Pages telephone directory now available in Los Angeles.

"Let's face it. We're not going to be a totally English-speaking country any more," says Aurora Helton of the governor of Oklahoma's Hispanic Advisory Committee. "Spanish should be included in commercials shown throughout America. Every American child ought to be taught both English and Spanish," says Mario Obledo, president of the League of United Latin American Citizens, which was founded more than a half-century ago to help Hispanics learn English and enter the American mainstream. "Citizenship is what makes us all American. Nowhere does the Constitution say that English is our language," says Maurice Ferré, mayor of Miami, Florida.

"Nowhere does the Constitution say that English is our language." It was to correct this omission that I introduced in April 1981 a constitutional amendment which read as follows: "The English language shall be the official language of the United States." Although there were ten cosponsors to this resolution, and some speeches were given on the Senate floor, it died without being acted upon in the 97th Congress.

But the movement to make English the official language of the nation is clearly gaining momentum. It is likely to suffer an occasional setback in state legislatures because of the doctrinaire liberals' assumption that every demand made by an ethnic minority must be yielded to. But whenever the question of English as the official language has been submitted to a popular referendum or ballot initiative, it has won by a majority of 70 percent or better.

It is not without significance that pressure against English language legislation does not come from any immigrant group other than the Hispanic: not from the Chinese or Koreans or Filipinos or Vietnamese; nor from immigrant Iranians, Turks, Greeks, East Indians, Ghanians, Ethiopians, Italians, or Swedes. The only people who have any quarrel with the English language are the Hispanics—at least the Hispanic politicians and

continued

"bilingual" teachers and lobbying organizations. One wonders about the Hispanic rank and file. Are they all in agreement with their leadership? And what does it profit the Hispanic leadership if it gains power and fame, while 50 percent of the boys and girls of their communities, speaking little or no English, cannot make it through high school?

While the U.S. Congress has yet to ratify an English language amendment to the Constitution, English-only legislation is periodically introduced in both houses. On May 6, 2009, for example, Oklahoma Republican Senator James Inhofe introduced a bill to declare English the "national language of the Government of the United States" in order "to promote the patriotic integration of prospective U.S. citizens," further declaring that "no person has a right, entitlement, or claim to have the Government of the United States or any of its officials or representatives act, communicate, perform or provide services, or provide materials in any language other than English" (U.S. Senate, Bill 992).

From the first time an English language amendment was introduced in the U.S. Congress in 1981, the idea has met significant opposition from people who argue that negative legal, social, and cultural consequences would follow passage of such a constitutional amendment. In 1988, a diverse collection of groups (American Civil Liberties Union, American Jewish Congress, Chinese for Affirmative Action, Haitian Refugee Center, Mexican American Legal Defense and Educational Fund, Organization of Chinese Americans, and Teachers of English to Speakers of Other Languages) rallied to counter the English-only movement by forming the English Plus Information Clearinghouse (EPIC). EPIC called on the federal government to expand access to comprehensive English-language instruction and social services in order "to ensure all persons the ability to exercise the rights and responsibilities of full participation in society," a policy EPIC referred to as "English Plus." In addition, EPIC encouraged the federal government to foster multilingualism for all people in order to advance the national interest economically and politically as well as to strengthen the nation's commitment to democratic and cultural pluralism.

The various ethnic groups represented in EPIC reflect a broad-based concern over official English legislation. Some critics (including Juan F. Perea, who is featured later in this chapter) have labeled the ideas of Hayakawa, U.S. English, and the entire English-only movement as anti-immigrant, even nativist; others have questioned the assumptions about language, culture, and politics on which the English-only movement builds its case.

Linguist Geoffrey Nunberg, a researcher at Stanford University's Center for the Study of Language and Information, has attempted to understand the motivations of official English proponents, who continue to push for an English language amendment to the U.S. Constitution. His findings indicate that Hayakawa, U.S. English, and other English-only advocates concern themselves far more with the symbolic importance of the English language—that is, what an individual's competency in English seems to signal about his or her commitment to American ideals and values—than with the practical matters affecting bilingual education and social services.

The Official English Movement: Reimagining America

Geoffrey Nunberg

[L]inguistic diversity is more conspicuous than it was a century ago. To be aware of the large numbers of non-English speakers in 1900, it was necessary to live in or near one of their communities, whereas today it is only necessary to flip through a cable television dial, drive past a Spanish-language billboard, or (in many states) apply for a driver's license. As a best guess, there are fewer speakers of foreign languages in America now than there were then, in both absolute and relative numbers. But what matter

Courtesy of Geoffrey Nunberg

symbolically [are] the widespread impressions of linguistic diversity, particularly among people who have no actual contact with speakers of languages other than English. . . .

[T]he debate is no longer concerned with the content or effect of particular programs, but the symbolic importance that people have come to attach to these matters. Official English advocates admit as much when they emphasize that their real goal is to "send a message" about the role of English in American life. From this point of view, it is immaterial whether the provision of interpreters for workers' compensation hearings or of foreign-language nutrition information actually constitute a "disincentive" to learning English, or whether their discontinuation would work a hardship on recent immigrants. Programs like these merely happen to be high-visibility examples of government's apparent willingness to allow the public use of languages other than English for any purpose whatsoever. In fact, one suspects that most Official English advocates are not especially concerned about specific programs per se, since they will be able to achieve their symbolic goals even if bilingual services are protected by judicial intervention or legislative inaction (as has generally been the case where Official English measures have passed). The real objective of the campaign is the "message" that it intends to send.

What actually is the message? . . . Proponents of Official English claim that they seek merely to recognize a state of affairs that has existed since the founding of the nation. After two hundred years of common-law cohabitation with English, we have simply decided to make an honest woman of her, for the sake of the children. To make the English language "official," however, is not merely to acknowledge it as the language commonly used in commerce, mass communications, and public affairs. Rather, it is to invest English with a symbolic role in national life and to endorse a cultural conception of American identity as the basis for political unity.

Nunberg sees the official English movement granting a symbolic power to language that previous generations of Americans did not. He explains that the nation's founders believed "the free institutions of the new nation would naturally lead to the formation of a new and independent culture," symbolized by an American variety of English increasingly distinct from the British variety, but today's advocates for official English legislation consider a common language to be a guarantee of the cultural sameness they believe is necessary for political unity.

Every ten years, the U.S. Census Bureau collects, distributes, and analyzes information concerning the demographics of the population, including data on race, age, sex, ancestry, income, and household types. Beginning in 1890, one hundred years after the first census, the Census Bureau started inquiring about language use. The following excerpt discusses some of the bureau's findings on the daily language practices of the U.S. public.

Excerpt from

> Language Use and English-Speaking Ability: Census 2000 Brief

Hyon B. Shin with Rosalind Bruno

The ability to communicate with government and private service providers, schools, businesses, emergency personnel, and many other people in the United States depends on the ability to speak English. In Census 2000, as in the two previous censuses, the U.S. Census Bureau asked people aged 5 and over if they spoke a language other than English at home. Among the 262.4 million people aged 5 and over, 47.0 million (18 percent) spoke a language other than English at home. . . .

These figures were up from 14 percent (31.8 million) in 1990 and 11 percent (23.1 million) in 1980. The number of people who spoke a language other than English at home grew by 38 percent in the 1980s and by 47 percent in the 1990s. While the population aged 5 and over grew by one-fourth from 1980 to 2000, the number who spoke a language other than English at home more than doubled.

In 2000, more people who spoke a language other than English at home reported they spoke English "Very well" (55 percent, or 25.6 million people). When they are combined with those who spoke only English at home, 92 percent of the population aged 5 and over had no difficulty speaking English. The proportion of the population aged 5 and over who spoke English less than "Very well" grew from 4.8 percent in 1980, to 6.1 percent in 1990, and to 8.1 percent in 2000.

. . . Spanish was the largest of the four major language groups (Spanish, Other Indo-European language, Asian and Pacific Island languages, and All other languages), and just over half of the 28.1 million Spanish speakers spoke English "Very well."

Other Indo-European language speakers composed the second largest group, with 10.0 million speakers, almost two-thirds of whom spoke English "Very well." Slightly less than half of the 7.0 million Asian and Pacific Island language speakers spoke English "Very well" (3.4 million). Of the 1.9 million people who composed the All other languages category, 1.3 million spoke English "Very well."

After English and Spanish, Chinese was the most commonly spoken at home (2.0 million speakers), followed by French (1.6 million speakers) and German (1.4 million speakers . . .). Reflecting historical patterns of immigration, the numbers of Italian, Polish, and German speakers fell between 1990 and 2000, while the number of speakers of many other languages increased.

Spanish speakers grew by about 60 percent and Spanish continued to be the non-English language most frequently spoken at home in the United States. The Chinese language, however, jumped from the fifth to the second most widely spoken non-English language, as the number of Chinese speakers rose from 1.2 million to 2.0 million people. . . . The number of Vietnamese speakers doubled over the decade, from about 507,000 speakers to just over 1 million speakers.

Of the 20 non-English languages most frequently spoken at home . . . , the largest proportional increase was for Russian speakers, who nearly tripled from 242,000 to 706,000. The second largest increase was for French Creole speakers (the language group that includes Haitian Creoles), whose numbers more than doubled from 188,000 to 453,000. . . .

In the United States, the ability to speak English plays a large role in how well people can perform daily activities. How well a person speaks English may indicate how well he or she communicates with public officials, medical personnel, and other service providers. It could also affect other activities outside the home, such as grocery shopping or banking. People who do not have a strong command of English and who do not have someone in their household to help them on a regular basis are at even more of a disadvantage. They are defined here as "linguistically isolated."

In 2000, 4.4 million households encompassing 11.9 million people were linguistically isolated. These numbers were significantly higher than in 1990, when 2.9 million households and 7.7 million people lived in [linguistically isolated] households.

> ANALYZING THE RHETORICAL SITUATION

The texts you have just read demonstrate that the issue of making English the official U.S. language is a complex one, not easily settled on the basis of a few examples or statistics. The following questions ask you to consider the writings of S. I. Hayakawa and Geoffrey Nunberg in terms of the elements of their respective rhetorical situations. Be sure to reread each excerpt carefully before answering.

1. Who might be the intended audience of each of the two excerpts? How do the audiences for the two excerpts differ? What textual evidence can you provide for your answers?

2. Is the purpose of each excerpt evident? If so, what is it? What are the differences between the excerpts in terms of purpose? How does each purpose relate to the intended audience?

3. To what rhetorical opportunity might each writer be responding? How does each piece of writing work to resolve the problem? Who holds the power to resolve or affect the resolution of the problem?
4. How does each writer deploy the rhetorical appeals of ethos, pathos, and logos to support an opinion of the official English movement? Use passages from each excerpt to support your answer.

© Steven Lunetta Photography, 2007

Evidence of linguistic diversity in the United States is on display at newsstands in any major U.S. city.

Living on the margins of English-speaking America

The official English movement has been opposed by a number of professional and public advocacy groups in addition to EPIC. Bilingual educators have argued about the cultural perspective and the sense of cultural identity that nonnative English speakers gain from having their native languages valued in school. And legal scholars have criticized the legal viability of English-only laws, arguing that they constitute national-origin discrimination, which was made illegal by the Civil Rights Act of 1964.

Legal scholar Juan F. Perea, best known for his analyses of the social consequences of English language amendments, has long worked to confront anti-immigration laws and attitudes, as well as national-origin discrimination, in the United States. In the following excerpt, Perea writes of the social and legal situations that prevent ethnic and linguistic minorities from participating fully in U.S. society. For Perea, English language amendments give nonnative English speakers no incentive to learn English or to enter the melting pot. Perea's argument encourages his readers to think more carefully about how the language of Spanish-speaking U.S. citizens affects their public identity.

Excerpt from

> Los Olvidados: On the Making of Invisible People

© 1995. Reprinted by permission.

Juan F. Perea

In his recent book, *Latinos*, Earl Shorris poignantly describes Bienvenida Pation, a Jewish Latino immigrant, who clings to her language and culture "as if they were life itself." When Bienvenida dies, it is "not of illness, but of English." Bienvenida dies of English when she is confined to a nursing home where no one speaks Spanish, an environment in which she cannot communicate and in which no one cares about her language and culture.

"Death by English" is a death of the spirit, the slow death that occurs when one's own identity is replaced, reconfigured, overwhelmed, or rejected by a more powerful, dominant identity. For Latinos, illness by English of varying degree, even death by English, is a common affliction, without known cure. It may be identified, however, by some of its symptoms.

The mere sound of Spanish offends and frightens many English-only speakers, who sense in the language a loss of control over what they regard as "their" country. Spanish also frightens many Latinos, for it proclaims their identity as Latinos, for all to hear. The Latino's fear is rational. Spanish may subject Latinos to the harsh price of difference in the United States: the loss of a job, instant scapegoating, and identification as an outsider. Giving in to this fear and denying one's own identity as a Latino is, perhaps, to begin to die of English.

Latino invisibility is the principal cause of illness by English. When I write of Latino invisibility, I mean a relative lack of positive public identity and legitimacy. Invisibility in this sense is created in several ways. Sometimes we are rendered invisible through the absence of public recognition and portrayal. Sometimes we are silenced through prohibitions on the use of Spanish. Sometimes we are rendered politically invisible, or nearly so, through the attribution of foreignness, what I shall call "symbolic deportation." I do not maintain that Latinos are the only people rendered invisible in America. In many respects the processes of invisibility have more general application. . . . however, I shall discuss only the invisibility I know best: How American culture, history, and laws make "invisible people" out of American Latinos who arrived before the English. . . .

According to its English conquerors, America was always meant to belong to white Englishmen. In 1788, John Jay, writing in the *Federalist* Number 2, declared, "Providence has been pleased to give this one connected country to one united people—a people descended from the same ancestors, speaking the same language, professing the same religion, attached to the same principles of government, very similar in their manner and customs." Although Jay's statement was wrong—early American society was remarkably diverse—his wish that America be a homogeneous, white, English-speaking Anglo society was widely shared by the Framers of the Constitution and other prominent leaders. . . .

The Framers' white America also had to be a predominantly English-speaking America in the words of John Jay and later echoes by Thomas Jefferson. Benjamin Franklin's dislike of the German language was palpable. I will use two examples to illustrate the perceived need for a white and English-speaking America.

In 1807, Jefferson proposed the resettlement, at government expense, of thirty thousand presumably English-speaking Americans in Louisiana in order to "make the majority American, [and] make it an American instead of French State." The first governor of Louisiana, William Claiborne, unsuccessfully attempted to require that all the laws of Louisiana be published in English.

The saga of New Mexico's admission to statehood also illustrates the perceived need for a white and English-speaking America. Despite repeated attempts beginning in 1850, New Mexico did not become a state until 1912, when a majority of its population was English-speaking for the first time. Statehood was withheld from New Mexico for over sixty years because of Congress's unwillingness

continued

to grant statehood to a predominantly Spanish-speaking territory populated by Mexican people.

A tremendous disparity, of course, separated the country the Framers desired and the one they came to possess. The country was composed of many groups, of different hues and speaking different languages. Several examples of governmental recognition of American multilingualism illustrate my point. The Continental Congress, hoping to communicate with and win the allegiance of American peoples whose language was different from English, published many significant documents in German and French. After the Revolutionary War, the Articles of Confederation were published in official English, German, and French editions.

Particularly during much of the nineteenth century, several states had rich legal histories of official bilingualism, by which I mean statutory or constitutional recognitions of languages other than English: Pennsylvania was officially bilingual in German and English; California and New Mexico were officially bilingual in Spanish and English; and Louisiana was officially bilingual in French and English. The implementation of official bilingualism in these several states shared common features. All of the laws of those states were required to be published in more than one language. Although this state-sponsored bilingualism mostly died out during the nineteenth century, New Mexico's official bilingualism was remarkably long-lived. New Mexico was officially bilingual between 1846 and early 1953, over one hundred years.

Most people are not aware of the existence and the extent of American multilingualism and its official, state-sponsored character. I am not aware of any United States history texts that include this material. Nor will you find it in any legal history text. . . .

Latinos are made invisible and foreign . . . despite our longtime presence, substance, and citizenship. Latinos must be recognized as full and equal members of our community. This equality I describe is an equality of respect and of dignity for the full identity and personhood of Latino people. It is an equality and respect for the similarities we share with our fellow Americans. It is also an equality and respect for the differences we contribute to American identity. In 1883, Walt Whitman complained that the states "showed too much of the British and German influence." . . . "To that composite American identity of the future," Whitman wrote, "Spanish character will supply some of the most needed parts." Our Mexican and Latino character continues to supply some of our most needed parts.

In *Hunger of Memory,* Richard Rodriguez reflects on his educational experiences, particularly how his Spanish-language identity at home conflicted with the English-speaking identity he felt that he needed to succeed in public school. For him, learning the English of the classroom offered the public identity necessary for participating in American civic life. In the following excerpt from his book, Rodriguez describes how he came to believe that English should be his "public language" and Spanish his home language. He argues from his own experience that immigrants to the United States remain invisible until they learn the public language of English.

Excerpt from

> Hunger of Memory

Richard Rodriguez

Supporters of bilingual education today imply that students like me miss a great deal by not being taught in their family's language. What they seem not to recognize is that, as a socially disadvantaged child, I considered Spanish to be a private language. What I needed to learn in school was that I had the right—and the obligation—to speak the public language of los gringos. The odd truth is that my first-grade classmates could have become bilingual, in the conventional sense of that word, more easily than I. Had they been taught (as upper-middle-class children are often taught early) a second language like Spanish or French, they could have regarded it simply as that: another public language. In my case such bilingualism could not have been so quickly achieved. What I did not believe was that I could speak a single public language.

Without question, it would have pleased me to hear my teachers address me in Spanish when I entered the classroom. I would have felt much less afraid. I would have trusted them and responded with ease. But I would have delayed—for how long postponed?—having to learn the language of public society. I would have evaded—and for how long could I have afforded to delay?—learning the great lesson of school, that I had a public identity.

Fortunately, my teachers were unsentimental about their responsibility. What they understood was that I needed to speak a public language. So their voices would search me out, asking me questions. Each time I'd hear them, I'd look up in surprise to see a nun's face frowning at me. I'd mumble, not really meaning to answer. The nun would persist, "Richard, stand up. Don't look at the floor. Speak up. Speak to the entire class, not just to me!" But I couldn't believe that the English language was mine to use. (In part, I did not want to believe it.) I continued to mumble. I resisted the teacher's demands. (Did I somehow suspect that once I learned public language my pleasing family life would be changed?) Silent, waiting for the bell to sound, I remained dazed, diffident, afraid. . . .

Today I hear bilingual educators say that children lose a degree of "individuality" by becoming assimilated into public society. (Bilingual schooling was popularized in the seventies, that decade when middle-class ethnics began to resist the process of assimilation—the American melting pot.) But the bilingualists simplistically scorn the value and necessity of assimilation. They do not seem to realize that there are two ways a person is individualized. So they do not realize that while one suffers a diminished sense of private individuality by becoming assimilated into public society, such assimilation makes possible the achievement of public individuality.

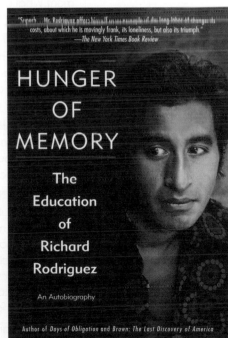

"Superb . . . Mr. Rodriguez offers himself as an example of the long labor of change: its costs, about which he is movingly frank, its loneliness, but also its triumph."
—The New York Times Book Review

HUNGER
OF
MEMORY

The
Education
of
Richard
Rodriguez

An Autobiography

Author of Days of Obligation and Brown: The Last Discovery of America

Jacket cover: copyright © 1983 by Bantam Books, a division of Random House, Inc., from HUNGER OF MEMORY by Richard Rodriguez. Used by permission of Bantam Books, a division of Random House, Inc.

> ANALYZING THE RHETORICAL SITUATION

1. Compare the excerpts from the writings of Juan F. Perea and Richard Rodriguez. How does each writer explain the invisibility of some people in the United States? What claim does each writer make about this invisibility?

2. What reasons does each writer give for the invisibility? What evidence does each author provide to support his claim?

3. What do the two writers say about resisting or embracing assimilation into the melting pot? How does each writer evaluate the importance of public language?

4. Identify the opportunity, audience, purpose, and context of Perea's and Rodriguez's rhetorical situations. What are the resources and constraints of their contexts? Be prepared to share your answers with the class.

COMMUNITY CONNECTIONS

1. Write for ten minutes about your own perspective on the English-only movement. What do you think about Hayakawa's aim of adding an English language amendment to the U.S. Constitution or about the arguments of U.S. English? What statement, or claim, can you make to summarize your position?

2. Write for five minutes about the vision of public life that Hayakawa believes an English language amendment will reflect. What positive consequences does he see arising from making English the official language of the United States? What claim might you make about such positive effects?

3. Write for another five minutes about the negative consequences that might follow from making English the official language of the United States. What claim can you make? What reasons can you provide to back up your claim? What evidence can you provide?

4. Perea writes, "Most people are not aware of the existence and the extent of American multilingualism and its official, state-sponsored character." Were you aware of the multilingual history of the United States? If so, where and when did you learn about it? If not, why do you suppose you never heard of it? Write for ten minutes about your response to Perea's historical overview, including how you knew—or why you didn't know—about the history of American multilingualism. At the end of the ten minutes, write one sentence that captures your opinion on multilingualism. If possible, make a claim about multilingualism.

5. Both Perea and Rodriguez talk about how language shapes both public and private identities. How would you characterize the language-based

differences between these two identities? What are the roots of these differences? Using your own experiences or those of someone you know well, write for five to ten minutes on how a person can use language to distinguish his or her public and private selves.

6. Rodriguez argues that Latinos who push for public bilingualism think they can "have it both ways"—that is, can participate in public life while retaining their cultural and ethnic identities. Drawing on your observations of life in the United States and within your community, do you think it is possible for people to "have it both ways"? On what evidence do you base your conclusion?

7. Perea and Rodriguez have different views of the emphasis the mainstream culture in the United States should place on the cultural and linguistic heritages of minority communities. After writing a sentence that captures the view of each of these writers, write for ten minutes about whether each view has crucial implications for education, focusing on your own campus community or hometown. Provide specific evidence from both excerpts to support your claim.

Position Arguments: A Fitting Response

An argument about language diversity in the United States

As you have learned in this chapter, many people—from politicians and scholars to activist groups and individuals—have made arguments about the political, economic, social, and cultural consequences of the use of non-English languages in the United States. Some of these arguments (Hayakawa's and Perea's, for instance) attempt to present objective analyses of how particular laws or policies will or will not bring about certain ends. Equally compelling are the narratives of writers such as Rodriguez who argue for or against official recognition of language diversity in the United States by describing personal experiences.

Let's consider another example of an argument from personal experience. In an editorial, Gabriela Kuntz, a retired elementary-school teacher living in Cape Girardeau, Missouri, tells why her own painful experiences of ethnic and linguistic discrimination have led her to decide not to teach her children Spanish.

My Spanish Standoff

Gabriela Kuntz

Once again my 17-year-old daughter comes home from a foreign-language fair at her high school and accusingly tells me about the pluses of being able to speak two languages. Speaker after speaker has extolled the virtues of becoming fluent in another language. My daughter is frustrated by the fact that I'm bilingual and have purposely declined to teach her to speak Spanish, my native tongue. She is not the only one who

Kuntz indirectly presents her position in the introduction. She alludes to the counterarguments, too.

This final sentence creates the impression that the writer has thought hard about her decision and has strong reasons to support her argument.

has wondered why my children don't speak Spanish. Over the years friends, acquaintances and family have asked me the same question. Teachers have asked my children. My family, of course, has been more judgmental.

I was born in Lima, Peru, and came to the United States for the first time in the early '50s, when I was 6 years old. At the parochial school my sister and I attended in Hollywood, Calif., there were only three Hispanic families at the time. I don't know when or how I learned English. I guess it was a matter of survival. My teacher spoke no Spanish. Neither did my classmates. All I can say is that at some point I no longer needed to translate. When I spoke in English I thought in English, and when I spoke in Spanish I thought in Spanish. I also learned about peanut-butter-and-jelly sandwiches, Halloween and Girl Scouts.

By saying that she "also learned about peanut-butter-and-jelly sandwiches, Halloween and Girl Scouts," Kuntz implicitly argues that learning English marks an important part of the process of becoming "American."

We went to a high school in Burbank. Again, there were few Hispanic students at the time. My sister and I spoke English without an "accent." This pleased my father to no end. He would beam with pleasure when teachers, meeting him and my mother for the first time and hearing their labored English, would comment that they had no idea English was not our native tongue.

My brother was born in Los Angeles in 1959, and we would speak both English and Spanish to him. When he began to talk, he would point to an object and say its name in both languages. He was, in effect, a walking, talking English-Spanish dictionary. I have often wondered how his English would have turned out, but circumstances beyond our control prevented it. Because of political changes in Peru in the early '60s (my father being a diplomat), we had to return to Peru. Although we had no formal schooling in Spanish, we were able to communicate in the language. I was thankful my parents had insisted that we speak Spanish at home. At first our relatives said that we spoke Spanish with a slight accent. But over time the accent disappeared, and we became immersed in the culture, our culture. My brother began his schooling in Peru, and even though he attended a school in which English was taught, he speaks the language with an accent. I find that ironic because he was the one born in the United States, and my sister and I are the naturalized citizens.

Kuntz juxtaposes the uncontrollable circumstances that influenced her brother's language development and those surrounding her daughter, which Kuntz has controlled as much as possible.

In 1972 I fell in love and married an American who had been living in Peru for a number of years. Our first son was born there, but when he was 6 months old, we came back to the States. My husband was going to get his doctorate at a university in Texas.

Kuntz concedes a point to those who disagree with her position. She has yet to reveal her reasons for not teaching her child Spanish.

It was in Texas that, for the first time, I lived in a community with many Hispanics in the United States. I encountered them at the grocery store, the laundry, the mall, church. I also began to see how the Anglos in the community treated them. Of course, I don't mean all, but enough to make me feel uncomfortable. Because I'm dark and have dark eyes and hair, I personally experienced that look, that unspoken and spoken word expressing prejudice. If I entered a department store, one of two things was likely to happen. Either I was ignored, or I was followed closely by the salesperson. The garments I took into the changing room were carefully counted. My check at the grocery store took more scrutiny than an Anglo's. My children were complimented on how "clean" they were instead of how cute. Somehow, all Hispanics seemed to be lumped into the category of illegal immigrants, notwithstanding that many Hispanic families have lived for generations in Texas and other Southwestern states.

The writer signals that she is shifting to the reasons supporting her argument. Yet this paragraph does not mention the Spanish language.

To be fair, I also noticed that the Latinos lived in their own enclaves, attended their own churches, and many of them spoke English with an accent. And with their roots firmly established in the United States, their Spanish was not perfect either.

Kuntz uses the phrase "to be fair" to anticipate readers' objections.

It was the fact that they spoke neither language well and the prejudice I experienced that prompted my husband and me to decide that English, and English only, would be spoken in our house. By this time my second dark-haired, dark-eyed son had been born, and we did not want to take a chance that if I spoke Spanish to them, somehow their English would be compromised. In other words, they would have an accent. I had learned to speak English without one, but I wasn't sure they would.

When our eldest daughter was born in 1980, we were living in southeast Missouri. Again, we decided on an English-only policy. If our children were going to live in the United States, then their English should be beyond reproach. Of course, by eliminating Spanish we have also eliminated part of their heritage. Am I sorry? About the culture, yes; about the language, no. In the Missouri Legislature, there are bills pending for some sort of English-only law. I recently read an article in a national magazine about the Ozarks where some of the townspeople are concerned about the numbers of Hispanics who have come to work in poultry plants there. It seemed to me that their "concerns" were actually prejudice. There is a definite creeping in of anti-Hispanic sentiment in this country. Even my daughter, yes, the one who is upset over not being bilingual, admits to hearing "Hispanic jokes" said in front of her at school. You see, many don't realize, despite her looks, that she's a minority. I want to believe that her flawless English is a contributing factor.

Last summer I took my 10-year-old daughter to visit my brother, who is working in Mexico City. She picked up a few phrases and words with the facility that only the very young can. I just might teach her Spanish. You see, she is fair with light brown hair and blue eyes.

Position Arguments

Kuntz presents the major reasons supporting her argument that she's doing her daughter a service by not teaching her Spanish.

Kuntz anticipates readers' counterarguments with this question and then answers them in the next sentences.

Kuntz begins to situate her personal decision within the context of larger public events.

Kuntz ties together earlier strands of her argument in which she juxtaposed racial discrimination and linguistic discrimination.

Understanding the Rhetorical Situation

When you want to help an audience understand your point of view—and you're prepared to use logical, emotional, and ethical appeals to deliver that point— you want to consider composing a position argument. Arguments commonly have the following features:

- Arguments vividly describe a problem or issue.
- Arguments are directed toward an audience with a clear connection to or investment in the problem being addressed.
- Arguments include a concise statement of the writer's point of view.
- Arguments provide reasons in support of the writer's position, and each supporting reason takes into account the audience's beliefs, attitudes, and values.
- Arguments contain specific evidence—details, examples, and direct quotations—to back each supporting reason.
- Arguments describe the benefits that will be achieved by responding to the writer's position in the intended way or the negative situation that will result from ignoring it.

 The following sections will help you compose a position argument about language diversity. To work with an online guide to the elements of the rhetorical situation, access your English CourseMate through cengagebrain.com.

Identifying an opportunity

Consider the communities you are part of—academic, activist, artistic, athletic, professional, civic, ethnic, national, political, or religious. What language practices or attitudes toward language have shaped your experiences within each group? You might, for example, think about how your soccer team developed a shared vocabulary for cheering each other on, one not shared by family members or friends on the sidelines. Or perhaps you've noticed that your ability to communicate in more than one language has been seen as a positive thing in many of your communities but not, strangely, in others. Maybe you're a member of an online community in which certain rules have been established about language use. The point is to reflect on the unique role that language plays within a particular group so that you can identify a rhetorical opportunity.

1. Make a list of the communities with which you identify most strongly. For each group, list several significant or unique language experiences that have marked your participation in that group. If the experiences were positive, explain why, providing as many details as possible. If the experiences were negative, describe the factors that made them difficult or unpleasant. Also,

write down any rules—whether written or unwritten—that influence the ways in which you or other group members use language to participate in the community.

2. Choosing one or two of your communities, take photos or sketch pictures of group members speaking, writing, texting, posting updates to Facebook or Twitter, or engaging in some other use of language. Or download a screenshot illustrating a relevant example of the group's online communication. Whatever visual you choose should illustrate details or features that make the community's language use compelling to examine.

3. Choose the community whose language practices or rules you want to write about and compose four or five descriptions of a problem related to language use in that community. Vary the ways you describe the problem. For example, one description might emphasize how some people are marginalized by an online community member's language practice, and another might emphasize the ways in which others in the community respond to or ignore this language practice. Another description might focus on the process by which rules for language use are communicated to new group members, and yet another might describe what ideal seems to guide the online community's language use.

Locating an audience

The following questions can help you locate your rhetorical audience as well as identify the audience's relationship to the problem you're addressing. Then, you'll be able to choose the best way to describe that problem.

1. List the names of the persons or groups who are affected directly or indirectly by the problem you're addressing.

2. Next to the name of each potential audience, write reasons that audience could have for acknowledging the existence of your problem. In other words, what would persuade these audiences that something needs to change or that they need to view the situation in a new way?

3. What actions could these audiences reasonably be persuaded to perform? What new perspectives could they be expected to adopt? In other words, consider what each audience would be able to do to resolve this problem.

4. With your audience's interests and capabilities in mind, look again at the descriptions of the problem that you composed in the preceding section. Decide which description will best help your audience feel connected to the situation as you've described it. Be open to revising your best description in order to tailor it to the audience's attitudes, beliefs, experiences, and values.

Identifying a fitting response

Different purposes and different audiences require different kinds of texts. For example, a lack of local resources for people who speak languages other than English might prompt you to create a newsletter that draws attention to the daily challenges these people face and argues for a greater public commitment to addressing this problem. Community debate over an English-only policy or a bilingual education program might lead you to write a letter to the county commissioners or the school board to highlight an important aspect of the issue they may be overlooking. As these two examples suggest, once you identify your problem, audience, and purpose, you need to determine what kind of text will best respond to the rhetorical situation.

Use the following questions to help you narrow your purpose and shape your response:

1. What reasons support the argument you want to make? What evidence or examples can you provide to persuade readers that each supporting reason is valid?
2. Which supporting reasons are most likely to resonate with your audience? What are the audience's beliefs, attitudes, or experiences that lead you to this conclusion?
3. What specific response are you hoping to draw from your audience? Do you want the audience to feel more confident in its current position? Do you want the audience to listen to and consider an overlooked position? Or do you want the audience to take some specific action to address the problem you're trying to resolve?
4. What is the best way to present your argument to your audience? That is, what kind of text is this audience most likely to respond to? (Chapter 13 can help you explore options for media and design.)

Writing a Position Argument: Working with Your Available Means

Shaping your position argument

You are likely familiar with the form and arrangement of position arguments because you come across examples of this genre in your daily life. The introduc-

pages 67–68

tion of an argumentative essay grabs an audience's attention as it describes the problem in a way that helps readers see how it concerns them as well as why the situation needs their attention right now. The introduction also states the thesis, which presents the writer's argument in a single sentence or short string of sentences; supporting reasons might also be presented in the introduction in a cluster of concise sentences following the thesis statement.

The body of an argumentative essay provides the major reasons supporting the argument. Here the writer not only presents the supporting reasons but also explains how each reason strengthens his or her larger argument. And, as you have already learned, the stronger supporting reasons are those that connect to readers' beliefs, values, and attitudes. For example, Gabriela Kuntz grounds much of her argument in support of English-only education on two interrelated supporting reasons: learning to speak and write only in English improves one's ability to speak the language "without an accent"; speaking "without an accent" improves one's ability to live in the United States without facing discrimination

Introduction
- ▶ Establishes ethos
- ▶ Describes the problem
- ▶ Makes clear how the problem concerns the audience
- ▶ Emphasizes why the time to address the problem is now
- ▶ States the thesis

Body
- ▶ Outlines the major reasons supporting the argument
- ▶ Connects the reasons to the thesis
- ▶ Presents evidence and examples in the form of facts and figures, direct quotations, brief narratives
- ▶ In other words, establishes logos

Conclusion
- ▶ Reinforces the benefits for an audience of responding to the writer's argument in the intended way
- ▶ May illustrate the negative situation that will result if the writer's argument is ignored

© 2013 Cengage Learning

and to fully assimilate into mainstream culture. The first of Kuntz's supporting reasons projects a logical appeal, as it reinforces readers' commonsense understanding of how language learning works (although many bilingual educators would refute this claim). Kuntz's second supporting reason creates an emotional appeal, as it connects with readers' belief that all people should have an equal opportunity to succeed in life. Ultimately, the success of most arguments depends on how well the writer has identified the audience's core beliefs and values and how successfully the writer has supported her or his argument with reasons that speak to those beliefs and values.

In addition, writers use the body of an argumentative essay to present evidence and examples that create stronger logos and ethos appeals. Writers present facts and figures, direct quotations, and brief narratives to persuade readers that each supporting reason does strengthen the larger argument. Any of these supports may be presented through words (written or spoken) or images. For example, Juan F. Perea uses historical evidence to show that the belief that the United States should have English as its official language is long-standing. By quoting John Jay and Thomas Jefferson, Perea supports his analysis of the ways in which Latinos have been made to seem invisible in the language of government documents. Perea presents historical evidence to advance both a logical and an ethical appeal, demonstrating that he has the good sense to draw on a documented, shared history to support his argument. pages 66–67

The body of an argumentative essay also acknowledges and responds to counterarguments and opposing viewpoints. This rhetorical move helps writers not only to create stronger logical appeals, as they address possible gaps in their arguments, but also to project more convincing ethical appeals, as they show readers that they are open to considering alternative perspectives on the issue. Kuntz, for example, acknowledges that "by eliminating Spanish" from her children's education, she and her husband "have also eliminated part of their heritage." She presents herself as being open to the views of English-only opponents who lament the loss of people's culture and who perceive "a definite creeping in of anti-Hispanic sentiment in this country." At the same time, though, Kuntz asserts that she's not sorry her daughter has lost the language of her heritage because, Kuntz explains, her daughter's "flawless English" has helped her to assimilate into mainstream U.S. culture. Ultimately, Kuntz shows readers she has weighed her argument against compelling counterarguments.

Finally, the conclusion of an argumentative essay reinforces the benefits that will be realized if the audience responds to the writer's argument in the intended way. Or, conversely, the conclusion may illustrate the negative situation that will result if the writer's argument is ignored.

Avoiding rhetorical fallacies

As you develop information that advances your thesis and supports specific points in your argument, you'll want to take care that your reasoning is logical, that you're enhancing the overall effectiveness of your argument as well as your own ethos. Constructing your argument logically requires avoiding **rhetorical fallacies**, which are errors in reasoning or logic.

Sloppy reasoning, snap judgments, quickly drawn conclusions, missing data, one-sided opinions—all of these signal that a writer's or speaker's thinking is not trustworthy and that the argument is not well reasoned. When we encounter problems in someone else's argument, we respond with "That's simply not so," "That's an unfair tactic," "Just because X happened doesn't mean Y will," or "What does that have to do with anything?" Because it's often easier to detect the flaws in someone else's argument than in our own, even the most experienced writers inadvertently make these errors in arguments.

Non sequitur The phrase *non sequitur* is Latin for "it does not follow." The non sequitur rhetorical fallacy serves as the basis for many other fallacies, for it is an error in cause-and-effect analysis, a faulty conclusion about consequences. "Helen loves the stars; she'll major in astronomy." "My client is not guilty of speeding because he did not see the posted speed limit." "I need a raise because of my child support payments." "The war in Vietnam was a disaster for the United States; therefore, U.S. troops should not be in Iraq." Each of these statements is based on the faulty claim that there's a logical connection between the parts of the statement.

pages 69–70

Ad hominem The Latin phrase *ad hominem* translates as "toward the man himself." The ad hominem fallacy is an attack on a person, which draws attention away from the actual issue under consideration. So, for example, rather than discussing the problem of fidelity in your relationship, you criticize your partner's weight. You attack the person rather than the opinion that person holds: "I don't want golfing tips from my neighbor, even if she is a professional golfer—that woman believes in X." Whether the belief relates to a woman's right to abortion, the value of plastic surgery, the importance of a war in Iraq, gay marriage, a comprehensive health plan, or lower taxes, the speaker is refusing the golf tips for the wrong reason.

Appeal to tradition Many people resist change—it unsettles their routines and makes them uncomfortable. Such people often invoke an appeal to tradition; in other words, "That's how we've always done it, so you should, too" or, to put it another way, "That's how it's always been done, so it should continue." This appeal is often used in political campaigns ("Four more years"), by social groups ("We've never invited X or Y to Thanksgiving; why would we start?"), and in many other situations ("My family always fills the gas tank before getting on the highway, so you should fill up now"; "My mother always uses Crisco in her pie crust, so I should, too").

Bandwagon The bandwagon argument is "Everyone's doing or thinking it, so you should, too." Highway patrol officers often hear "Everyone else was speeding, so I was merely keeping up with the traffic." Parents hear from their children that everyone else is getting to go to that concert, everyone else has a certain kind of cell phone, and everyone else text-messages during the night.

Begging the question Often referred to as a "circular argument" and similar to equivocation, begging the question involves simply restating the initial arguable claim as though it were a conclusion or a good reason. In other words, that arguable claim has not been supported in any way. "O. J. Simpson did not kill his wife because he is a world-class football player, not a murderer." "I can talk to my parents any way I choose because of freedom of speech." "We must test students more in order to improve their test scores." In each of these examples, the initial claim needs to be established and argued, whether it's Simpson's innocence, your right to speak to your parents as you choose, or that low test scores can be blamed on too little testing.

False analogy Effective writers and speakers often use analogies to equate two unlike things, explaining one in terms of the other—for example, comparing a generous grandma with an ATM machine or a diamond ring with eternal love. False analogies, however, stretch beyond the valid resemblance to create an invalid comparison. "Vietnam War veterans were greeted by the animosity of an antiwar U.S. populace; Iraqi war veterans will surely return to the same antipathy." "Like the beautiful and talented Elizabeth Taylor, Jennifer Lopez will also be married at least eight times."

False authority One of the most prevalent rhetorical fallacies, false authority assumes that an expert in one field is credible in another field. Just think of all the professional athletes and celebrities who argue that a particular brand of car, coffee, undershorts, or soft drink or a particular vacation, charge card, or political candidate is the best one, and you'll understand immediately how false authority works—and why it's often undetected. When celebrity Jenny McCarthy discovered that her son presented the symptoms of autism, she set to work, investigating the biomedical reasons for his symptoms and drastically changing his diet and her family's cleaning, eating, and living habits. She also helped launch Generation Rescue, a coalition of doctors, parents, and children who believe that autism and related neurological disorders "are environmental illnesses caused by an overload of heavy metals, live viruses, and bacteria. Proper treatment . . . is leading to recovery for thousands."

AP Photo/Jose Luis Magana

In her role as spokeswoman for the organization, McCarthy writes, "I want to offer you the same hope that Generation Rescue offered me. Many children can and do recover from autism. Recovery is real!" McCarthy's words have encouraged many families to follow her lead. But where does her authority lie? She's an actress, an activist, and a mom, but not a physician.

False cause Also referred to by the Latin phrase *post hoc, ergo propter hoc*, the fallacy of false cause is the assumption that because A occurs before B, A is therefore the *cause* of B. We all know that events that follow each other do not necessarily have a causal relationship—although I sneezed right before the lights went out, my sneeze did not cause the electrical outage. The false-cause fallacy, however, occurs when there might actually be some relationship between the two events but not a direct one: "Jim got fired from his job, and his wife divorced him; therefore, his job loss caused his divorce." Jim's job loss might have been the last of several job losses he suffered in the past three years, and his wife, tired of depending on him to hold a job, filed for divorce.

False dilemma Also referred to as the "either/or fallacy," the false-dilemma fallacy sets up only two choices in a complex situation, when in fact there are more than two choices. In addition, the false dilemma offers the writer's or speaker's choice as the only good choice, presenting the only other choice as unthinkable. "If we don't spank our children, they will run wild." "If you don't get straight A's, you won't be able to get a job." These examples offer only one right choice and no analysis of a complex situation.

Guilt by association An unfair attempt to make someone responsible for the beliefs or actions of others, guilt by association is one of the reasons so many Arabs living in the United States were brutally beaten and persecuted in other ways after the September 11th attacks. Many innocent Arabs suffered for the deeds of the Arab terrorists. Social tensions in the United States often stem from this fallacy and are passed on for the same reason: "those people" are bad—whether they are members of a racial, ethnic, or religious group, a particular profession, or a certain family.

Hasty generalization A conclusion based on too little evidence or on exceptional or biased evidence, the hasty generalization results in statements such as "Fred will never get into law school when he didn't even pass his poli sci exam" or "Mexican food is fattening." The otherwise very intelligent Fred may have a good reason for failing one exam, and although beef and cheese burritos may well be high in calories, many Mexican dishes rely on the healthy staples of black beans and rice.

Oversimplification Closely related to hasty generalization, oversimplification occurs when a speaker or writer jumps to conclusions by omitting relevant considerations. "Just say 'No'" was the antidrug battle cry of the 1980s, but avoiding drug use can be much more complicated than just saying no. The "virginity pledge" is an oversimplified solution to the problem of unwanted teenage pregnancy, as it ignores the fact that many teenagers need to become educated about human sexuality, safe sex practices, sexually transmitted disease, and aspects of teen social and sexual behavior.

Red herring A false clue or an assertion intended to divert attention from the real issue under consideration, the red herring is intended to mislead, whether it appears in a mystery novel or in an argument. "Why go to the doctor for a mammogram when I haven't been able to stop smoking, and smoking is known to cause cancer?" "We cannot defeat the piracy in Somalia when we're involved in the Israeli-Palestinian conflict." The real issues in the preceding statements (the importance of getting a mammogram and defeating piracy) are blurred by other issues that, while important, are not the primary ones under consideration.

"Decoy ducks on the lake, scapegoats in the paddock, and red herrings on the fishing line. If this is a cover-up, it's big..."

Slippery slope In order to show that an initial claim is unacceptable, the slippery slope fallacy presents a sequence of increasingly unacceptable events that are said to be sure to follow from that initial claim: "Confidential letters of recommendation allow for damning comments." "If I accept your late paper, I'll have to let anyone else who asks turn in late papers." "Marijuana is the gateway drug to crack cocaine and then heroin." "A national health plan will lead to 'death panels.'" We hear these kinds of slippery slope arguments every day, in contexts from weight loss ("You're losing too much weight; you'll end up anorexic") to taste in music ("Once you start listening to gansta rap, you'll become violent").

Revision and peer review

After you've drafted your argument, ask one of your classmates to read it. You'll want your classmate to respond to your work in a way that helps you revise it into the strongest argument it can be, one that addresses your intended audience, helps you fulfill your purpose, and is delivered in the most appropriate means available to you.

Questions for a peer reviewer

1. To what opportunity for change is the writer responding?
2. Who might be the writer's intended audience?
3. What might be the writer's purpose?
4. What information did you receive from the introduction? How effective is the introduction? What suggestions do you have for the writer for improving the introduction?
5. Note the writer's thesis statement. If you cannot locate a thesis statement, what thesis statement might work for this argument?
6. Note the assertions the writer makes to support the thesis. Are they presented in chronological or emphatic order? Does the writer use the order that seems most effective? Would you re-order some of the assertions?

7. If you cannot locate a series of assertions, what assertions could be made to support the thesis statement?

8. Note the supporting ideas (presented through narration, cause-and-effect analysis, description, exemplification, process analysis, or definition) that the writer uses to support his or her assertions.

9. How does the writer establish ethos? How could the writer strengthen this appeal?

10. What material does the writer use to establish logos? How might the writer strengthen this appeal (see questions 6–8)?

11. How does the writer make use of pathos?

12. What did you learn from the conclusion that you didn't already know after reading the introduction and the body? What information does the writer want you to take away from the argument? Does the writer attempt to change your attitude, action, or opinion?

13. What section of the argument did you most enjoy? Why?

ARGUMENTS IN THREE MEDIA

Visual Argument

This visual argument is in the form of an editorial cartoon by John Darkow. To view the cartoon, find *Writing in Three Media* in your English CourseMate, accessed through cengagebrain.com.

John Darkow, Columbia Daily Tribune, Missouri/Cagle Cartoons

Online Argument

Anand Giridharadas of the *New York Times* has written an argument about language in the digital age. To read the article, find *Writing in Three Media* in your English CourseMate, accessed through cengagebrain.com.

Photo by Priya Parker

Print Argument

In the following essay, student Alicia Williams develops her position on American Sign Language (ASL), which she believes is an authentic, live, and vibrant language with a rich history and vital present.

Courtesy of the author of the student paper.

Alicia Williams has strong opinions about the status of ASL as a language and became interested in how the English-only movement might affect it. Alicia knew that she could have written a personal narrative such as a memoir or autobiography that would shed light on her experiences and beliefs as a deaf person. She could also have joined forces with others concerned about English-only education and started a letter-writing campaign to influence the local school board. But Alicia decided that a good first step would be to further understand how ASL, like Spanish, Tagalog, or Mandarin Chinese, is a language affected by English-only policies. She could then use a position argument to help her develop and present her thoughts for others to consider. Notice that she includes photographs that she has taken herself to support her argument and aid readers who do not know ASL.

Alicia Williams

Professor Glenn

English 275

20 November 2009

The Ethos of American Sign Language

The termination of the Bilingual Education Act was followed by the No Child Left Behind Act (2001), thus removing a bilingual approach from the education tracks of non-English native speakers.•The loss of bilingual education has caused the political group English First to lobby hard for an English-only education that purports to produce truly American citizens. This, in turn, produces more momentum for the group's side project: making English the official language of the United States of America. Not only does this negate the melting pot of languages in America, but it diminishes the impact of a truly unique language— American Sign Language (ASL). The drive for English-only education treats the manifestations of language through a purely verbal platform, thereby perpetuating long-held prejudices and the common mistaken assumption that ASL is not, in fact, a language.

•Only fifty years ago did ASL receive its long overdue recognition as a distinct language, rather than being perceived as a "hindrance to English," a "bastardization of English," or even a "communication disorder." By the end of the nineteenth century, during the rise of formal educational instruction in ASL for the Deaf, an oppositional camp known as Oralists had fervently portrayed signing by the Deaf community as a pathological version of spoken language.[1] A few even preposterously correlated deafness with low intelligence. Ironically, the husband of a Deaf woman, Alexander Graham Bell, who was the inventor of the telephone and hearing aids, was a

Alicia identifies a problem and establishes herself as an informed, engaged, and reasonable writer (ethos). At the end of this paragraph, she directs her readers to her thesis, a concise statement of her point of view regarding the problem.

Alicia provides a historical overview of the problem as well as reasons for her point of view. She includes specific details and a direct quotation (logos).

supporter of the Oralists' philosophy. He endorsed "genetic counseling for the deaf, outlawing intermarriages between deaf persons, suppression of sign language, elimination of residential schools for the deaf, and the prohibition of deaf teachers of the deaf " (Stewart and Akamatsu 242).

Oralism faced counteractions by the numerous, though less famous, people who were working for the needs of the Deaf community as its educators. They understood that ASL is requisite for a deaf person's social, cultural, and lingual needs. The Deaf community managed to keep its educational programs intact without losing ASL, though not without struggle. It was not until a half-century later, in the 1960s, that William Stokoe's linguistic analysis of ASL produced the much-needed equilibrium between the Deaf and hearing communities concerning the legitimacy of ASL. Even so, when most people talk about language, their thinking assumes communication through speaking: most classify as unconventional forms of language outside of a verbal modality. Native signers such as myself understand that our minority language must coexist with a dominant majority language, but the practice of reducing ASL to a type of communication disorder or, worse, obliterating it for the spoken English-only movement, ignores the historical presence of Deaf culture in America, as well as the key characteristics ASL shares with the evolution of languages.

Alicia makes an assertion related to her thesis, which is followed by specific narrative details, arranged in chronological order (logos). She ends this paragraph with an emotional connection with her audience (pathos).

ASL was derived from French Sign Language (FSL) in the early nineteenth century. Harlan Lane and François Grosjean, prominent ASL linguists, found supporting evidence for this date from "the establishment of the first American school for the deaf in 1817 at Hartford, Connecticut. . . . Its founders, Thomas Gallaudet and Laurent Clerc, were both educated in the use of FSL prior to 1817" (Stewart and Akamatsu 237). Historically speaking, David Stewart and C. Tane Akamatsu have determined that "approximately

Alicia continues to shape her argument with additional specific details and facts (logos).

60% of the signs in present-day ASL had their origin in FSL" (237). The modification of a parent language, such as FSL for the birth of ASL, is part of the process spoken language has undergone in its evolution throughout history, producing our contemporary languages. For instance, the English spoken in England during Shakespeare's lifetime is not the same English spoken in America today; nonetheless, they are both of English tradition.

Alicia opens this paragraph with another assertion that supports her thesis (logos), using process analysis with information arranged chronologically for support.

Another characteristic that ASL has in common with other languages is that it changes from one generation to another. Undoubtedly, spoken languages continue to change. For instance, slang words used now may not be the same when the toddlers of today are in college. ASL also experiences these changes, which is contrary to a common misconception that the signs in ASL are concrete in nature, meaning there are no changes. For example, an obsolete sign for "will/future" is conveyed by holding your right arm bent in a ninety-degree angle with your fingertips parallel to the ground. Then you move your entire forearm upward to a forty-five-degree angle in one swift movement. The modern sign starts with an open palm touching the right jawline, underneath the ear; then the forearm moves forward until the arm is in a ninety-degree position, equivalent to the starting position of the arm in the old form. The evolution of signs is comparable to the changing connotations of various words found in the history of languages.

Another assertion is supported with a detailed comparison-and-contrast analysis and direct quotations (logos).

In the process of its shift to physical hand gestures and appropriate facial expressions, ASL does not discard the traditional syntax of language, maintaining its legitimacy as a distinct language. The rich complexity of ASL's syntax conveys itself through designated facial expressions and specific sign constructions, demonstrating that "ASL is governed by the same organizational principles as spoken languages . . . [despite] essential differences based on the fact that ASL is produced in three-dimensional space" (Neidle et al. 30). As every language has a syntactical structure, so does ASL.

Despite its similarities to languages such as English, it is a mistake to think of ASL as pathology of spoken English. Perpetuating this myth is the misconception that ASL signs are direct translations of English. ASL has rules of its own, which are not identical to those of English syntax. In English, for instance, one says, "Who hates Smitty?" but in ASL, it is signed "Hate Smitty who?" The photos in Fig. 1 show another example of how signs in ASL are not a direct translation of English, but also show how differing hand placements denote different pronouns used with the verb *give*.

An assertion is supported with specific examples, including the use of visuals (logos).

Stokoe's work establishing the legitimacy of ASL spurred a movement for a bilingual approach in educating the deaf. The teaching of ASL was a top priority because of the hardship of expecting the Deaf community to acquire English as our native language, which carries a disadvantage by working on a modality inaccessible to us—hearing. In the bilingual approach, after the deaf child has attained a solid working background in ASL, some parents elect to have oral English taught as a second language. The success of

More historical background leads into Alicia's personal experience as a deaf person, thereby establishing logos, ethos, and pathos.

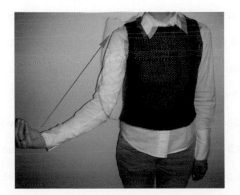

Fig. 1. The photograph on the left shows the signing of "Me give to him or her," and the photograph on the right shows that of "Me give to you." (Photographs by the author.)

English as a second language is largely subject to the individual's capabilities, which are dependent on numerous factors. My parents chose the bilingual approach in my education track at Rufus Putnam Elementary School (for the Deaf). While I maintained my fluency in ASL, I developed an efficacy at speech reading (informally known as lip reading). For instance, when I speak, I am able to convince hearing persons that I am not deaf. In my Deaf community, I always resort to my first language—ASL. All this would not be possible if Oralism or English First were successful in a push for *spoken* English only.

My bilingual background has been met with fierce opposition from hearing people who believe ASL is a crutch language and that it is an antiquated solution for the Deaf community. In other words, they believe the advances of medical technology will enable researchers to develop revolutionary digital hearing aids, while aggressively diagnosing deaf children at younger ages should cause a decreasing need for ASL, which they assume is a diminished form of English. But if ASL meets all other criteria of what linguists consider a language—with the exception of the use of a vocal apparatus—how can it be called a "crutch language"? And hearing aids only amplify whatever remaining hearing a deaf person has, if any at all; they do not compensate for hearing loss. Even if a doctor diagnoses a deaf child at birth, the child's sensorineural hearing loss may be so severe that spoken language will be impractical to acquire, whereas ASL will be a better approach for the child.[2] In rare cases, adults who become deaf later in their lives find comfort in ASL, rather than English. The naturalization associated with the visual-spatial lingual framework of ASL is uniquely characteristic of the Deaf community because it operates to their advantage, bypassing the confines of oral-aural languages. The use of a verbal apparatus in spoken languages is a natural reaction from the body possessing a functional audio-physiological system. Often this is not the case

Alicia addresses the opposing point of view and refutes it with specific support for her stance, reasonable questions, and good examples. In this paragraph, she augments her ethos, logos, and pathos.

within the Deaf community; hence that is why ASL is deeply embedded in its culture and will remain the staple of its community, regardless of technology's novelty or the hearing community's desire to push for English-only education.

•The most primeval function of language is to create a medium for people's desire to outwardly express themselves to others. Whatever form language may take—visual or verbal—it lays the foundation for humanity's collective identity as great storytellers. Through language we have been able to pass on stories of past heroes and enemies, warn future generations of failed philosophies, create new ideals for better living, share our aspirations and fears, even express our wonder at all that remains unknown to us. Language binds us as humans, and its diverse forms are reflected in the embodiments of its heterogeneous natives. ASL is but another paintbrush of language, and yet proof of humanity's palette of mutability.

The final paragraph establishes a strong emotional connection with the audience (pathos).

Notes

[1] I realize the use of the term *Deaf* might seem archaic, but for the purpose of this paper, it is representative of all members who psychologically or linguistically identify themselves as members of the Deaf community through ASL as their common language, regardless of their physiological hearing capacity.

[2] There are three basic types of hearing loss: conductive hearing loss, sensorineural hearing loss, and mixed hearing loss, which is any combination of the first two. All three types can make speech hard to acquire.

Works Cited

Neidle, Carol, et al. *The Syntax of American Sign Language: Functional Categories and Hierarchical Structures.* Cambridge: MIT P, 2000. Print.

Stewart, David A., and C. Tane Akamatsu. "The Coming of Age of American Sign Language." *Anthropology & Educational Quarterly* 19.3 (Sept. 1988): 235–52. Web. 7 Nov. 2009.

Fitting responses come in many forms, not just position arguments. Your instructor might call upon you to consider one of the following opportunities for writing.

Alternatives to the Position Argument

1. Compose a three- to four-page critical essay analyzing the consequences of legislation making English the official language. To fully understand the political, social, and cultural context in which the legislation was passed, conduct research to find print materials (newspaper articles, editorials and letters to the editor, transcripts of legislative hearings and testimony) from the time when the legislation was being considered. Use these materials to try to discern the stated and unstated goals of the advocates of the English language legislation. You also will want to conduct interviews with community leaders and local citizens, as well as other primary research, to determine what effects, if any, such legislation has had at the local level, such as restrictions on access to social services or implicit or explicit policies and practices in local workplaces.

2. Many supporters of English-only legislation draw attention to the costs of providing public services in languages other than English. Several opponents of English-only legislation suggest that these costs are not as significant as activists such as S. I. Hayakawa argue; others emphasize the costs of failing to provide such services. Respond to this debate by composing a four-page, double-spaced investigative report that explores the specific costs associated with multilingualism in your community. Conduct research on local, state, and federal government resources in order to create strong logical and ethical appeals in your report; you might also consider interviewing local policymakers as part of your research process.

3. How do English-as-a-second-language speakers experience life on your campus or in your community? What atmosphere of linguistic diversity or homogeneity do they perceive in their daily lives, and how does this atmosphere manifest itself in their academic, professional, and extracurricular activities? Interview a student or community member who speaks English as his or her second language, and write a profile of that person that helps readers better understand how multilingual people move between languages in their daily lives and what motivates them either to maintain their abilities in their first language or to let these abilities erode.

The College of the Future: Responding with Proposals

Wherever you are attending college—even if it's a parent's or grandparent's alma mater—your college experience is not like that of previous generations. The college of the twenty-first century is different from that of the twentieth in all sorts of ways: the gender, racial, and ethnic-cultural diversity of its students, faculty, and course offerings; its high-tech computer labs and state-of-the-art exercise and classroom facilities; its co-ed dorms and sports programs; the wide range of eateries, both on and off campus; and the seemingly countless campus-community collaborations, going-green initiatives, pre-professional internship opportunities, and student activities.

Even though these changes might surprise those who attended college as recently as a decade ago, the college of the twenty-first century feels familiar to you. You may be a product of dual-enrollment and AP programs, someone who can easily handle expectations for online interactions related to course enrollment, library research, and coursework; you may also be juggling family or work obligations along with your academic ones. Your college experience might be more convenient for you than it was for your forebears in terms of attending classes online from home or from your dorm room. But college today is not easier or less expensive than in the past. Today's students collaborate with community-service agencies or businesses to fulfill their research or writing assignments, rent their textbooks or e-books, conduct scholarly collaborative projects via social networking sites, and spend their summers as interns, earning professional experience rather than money for next semester's expenses.

The classroom experience of today is quite different from that of just twenty years ago.

Despite the ever-increasing complications of undergraduate life, students are being pressured to move through college more quickly, to take heavier course loads in order to graduate sooner—and at the same time to take out hefty student loans and work part-time during the academic year in order to pay for their schooling. If it's difficult to create a one-size-fits-all depiction of contemporary college life, it's nearly impossible to predict what the college of the future might be like. The only way to imagine the college of the future is to anchor the vision in current practices and trends—and to reconsider perennial questions concerning college. The most enduring question about a college education has not asked how courses should be taught, how much college should cost, or who should attend. Rather, it concerns the basic purpose of a college education. Should college prepare people to make a good living or to live a good life? Or both?

Recently, Alain de Botton, whose proposal for changing the way we look at the humanities appears on page 260, identified a problem with higher education. According to de Botton, college is charged with teaching "both how to make a living and how to live," but it falls far short of the second goal. To address this rhetorical opportunity, de Botton and his colleagues proposed and eventually opened the School of Life, whose subjects include "marriage, child-rearing, choosing a career, changing the world, and death." **Proposals** like de Botton's are a common response to this question: How can something be improved? But that simple question leads to a number of other questions: Why is something a problem in the first place? What are viable solutions to the problem? Why is one solution better than others? What will it take to enact the best solution? Who will be affected by this solution? This chapter will challenge you to respond to these questions rhetorically as you identify an opportunity to propose a solution to some problem with higher education.

IDENTIFYING AN OPPORTUNITY

Throughout this chapter, you will work to identify an opportunity to propose a solution about higher education. What should the college of the future look like? What should its priorities be? What needs to be addressed today so that a college education can be made more affordable and more accessible tomorrow? As you think about the various elements of a college education (cost, accessibility, expectations for teaching and learning, use of electronic media, student-instructor relationships, preprofessional training, and so on), consider which element stimulates your sensibilities and opinions or suggests a problem that you might like to address, maybe even resolve. And as you consider that element, also consider the most fitting means of delivery for your proposal:

Print Proposal

written for a community or campus newspaper or sent directly to the rhetorical audience

Online Proposal

featuring images illustrating the problem and/or solution and posted to an appropriate site

Oral Proposal or Short Film

recorded as a short film or video podcast

To begin, freewrite for five minutes in response to each of the following questions (or use any of the invention techniques presented on pages 58–61):

1. List the reasons you came to college and the goals you are working toward at college. If you can, link some of the reasons to some of the goals.

2. Next to each goal, list the resources you are drawing on to work toward that goal. Consider people (instructors, advisors, mentors, fellow students, and family members), programs of study (your biology minor, for instance, or your Spanish courses), extracurricular programs (such as a lecture series, sports, or social organizations), and material resources (like a computer lab equipped with film-editing software or a 24-hour study lounge). Which of these resources are most essential to your goals?

3. If you could change just one thing about the resources available to you, what would it be? How could any of the resources better accommodate your needs and desires? (Consider, too, how other students, current and future, would be accommodated.) Be as specific as you can about your proposal for improvement as well as the potential beneficiaries of the improvement.

Real Situations

You don't have to be in college long to realize that college life has its frustrations and limitations. Perhaps you have access to lectures from some of the greatest researchers in the nation, but you cannot ask them any questions; all your questions must be posed online to their hard-working (but not as experienced) teaching assistants. Or, you may have planned to work part-time all year long in order to pay for your courses, only to discover that your major requires you to spend a summer interning with no pay. Textbook prices seem to be soaring, and you always buy all the books—so you're annoyed when an instructor neglects to assign anything from one of them. Yet, as hard as you work and as

Marvi Lacar/Getty Images

Aurelia Ventura/La Opinion/Newscom

Like online courses, coursework in nontraditional fields takes the college experience beyond the campus.

motivated as you are, you still tend to believe that college students in Europe and Asia are getting better college educations. Their college education is often free; they're reading the classics; and they're working long and hard on math, science, and accounting. To your mind, their college education comes with a real payoff: a promising future. As you consider your education and that of your international peers, what do you think is the most important outcome of obtaining a college degree?

DESCRIBING THE COLLEGE OF THE FUTURE

1. Working with a classmate or two, identify two features of higher education that you think will change significantly in the coming years. You might consider academics, the social scene, the application or registration process, the student population, teaching, learning, or other features of the college experience.

2. How can you describe the current status of those two features of higher education? Focusing on your campus, make a list of specific descriptive details. Be prepared to share your answers with the rest of the class.

3. Which details in your list describe resources? Which ones describe limitations?

4. Translate one or more of the limitations into a one-sentence problem.

5. What solution can you imagine for the problem you stated? What specific action could be taken to resolve the problem? What money, time, or cooperative effort is necessary for the success of such an action?

Some observers believe that, like many other traditional features of college life, printed books will eventually become obsolete.

Real Responses to Real Situations

How will a higher education be delivered?

Making reasonable predictions about higher education (or anything else, for that matter) starts with careful observation of a present trend (its distinctive features and effects), followed by reasonable projections about what that trend might lead to if it continues along the same trajectory. One easily observable trend in today's colleges is the increasing use of technology for coursework and research. In the following essay, cultural commentator Gregory M. Lamb predicts the ways in which the Internet will continue to affect a college education and experience.

>The Future of College May Be Virtual

Gregory M. Lamb

In many ways, education hasn't changed much since students sat at the feet of Socrates more than two millenniums ago. Learners still gather each autumn at colleges to listen to and be questioned by professors.

But the Internet has caused sudden shifts in other industries, from the way people read news to the way they buy music or plan travel. Might higher education be nearing such a jolt?

Aside from the massive dent put in their endowments by Wall Street's woes, colleges and universities mostly have been conducting business as usual. Costs have soared compared with general inflation, but students still flock to classes.

Many have theorized that the Internet could give education a rude shock. Recently, an opinion piece by Zephyr Teachout, a law professor at Fordham University in New York who once served as an Internet organizer for presidential candidate Howard Dean, put the possibility in dramatic terms.

"Students starting school this year may be part of the last generation for which 'going to college' means packing up, getting a dorm room, and listening to tenured professors," she wrote in *The Washington Post*. "Undergraduate education is on the verge of a radical reordering. Colleges, like newspapers, will be torn apart by new ways of sharing information enabled by the Internet."

She's not the first to see newspapers moving from print to online and wonder whether something similar could happen to colleges. Online newspaper readers tend to seek out individual stories, not what papers as a whole have to say. Might finding the right class online become more important than which institution was offering it? What happens if colleges or even specialized online-only education companies provide essentially the same Economics 101 course? Does geography cease to matter and do low-cost providers win out?

Some think it could happen, perhaps sooner than expected. "Three years ago nobody thought the newspaper industry was going to collapse," says Kevin Carey, policy director of Education Sector, an independent education think tank in Washington, D.C.

Today, a college education is more than twice as expensive as it was in the early 1990s, even after adjusting for inflation.

"It's getting worse all the time. There's no end in sight," Mr. Carey says.

Colleges "have set the bar pretty low for competitors" through a lack of competition, he says. At the same time, many potential students are being underserved. "We need more institutions that are good at serving working students, immigrant students, low-income students, students who are basically going to college because they want to get a credential and have a career," he says.

Carey points to the fledgling company Straighterline.com, which offers college courses in subjects from algebra to business statistics, English composition, and accounting. Students can take as many courses as they want for $99 per month, the company's website says. The price includes 10 hours each month of one-on-one live

continued

support and a course adviser. Passing courses results in "real college credit" from one of several colleges affiliated with the program.

About 30 percent of the undergraduate credits given each year at US colleges and universities derive from only 20 or 30 introductory classes. It seems logical, then, that these could be turned into "commodities" sold at the lowest price online.

"Econ 101 for $99 is online, today. 201 and 301 will come," Carey writes in an essay, "College for $99 a Month," in *Washington Monthly*. "The Internet doesn't treat middlemen kindly." He describes an unemployed woman in Chicago who was able to complete four college courses for less than $200 on Straighterline. com. The same courses would have cost $2,700 at a local university.

Of course, colleges and universities have discovered online learning themselves. They already offer thousands of online courses to their registered students. According to one recent survey, nearly 4 million college students, more than 20 percent of all students, have taken at least one online course.

But colleges don't generally offer a lower price for online courses. The reason is that the courses actually take more work to prepare and teach than similar classroom courses, says Janet Poley, president of the American Distance Education Consortium in Lincoln, Neb. Members of the consortium, made up of public universities and community colleges, find that they often must provide extra resources to faculty who are preparing to teach online for the first time, such as help from a graduate assistant or a lighter teaching load, she says.

Online learning at these institutions "has been growing very fast," Dr. Poley says. Students appreciate the flexibility to be able to take courses whenever they want, allowing them to keep their jobs or avoid paying baby sitters or commuting to campus as often.

What's holding back more online courses, she says, is the lack of good broadband Internet options in some places, especially rural areas.

What may be evolving, Poley says, is a "home institution model," in which students take introductory courses online but come on campus for work in their major field and for graduate study.

"I don't really care whether there are students on campus or not," she says. But "I think there will still be folks who like to be in a community with others while they are learning." Some students enjoy athletics and other on-campus activities, she says. "I don't think people are ready to give that up."

Online courses, the latest form of distance learning, have had a reputation for being of lower quality than on-campus work, Carey says—something advertised in the back pages of a magazine. But that may be out of date.

Online education is continually improving, he says. "It's better now than it was 10 years ago."

A study of 12 years of online teaching by SRI International on behalf of the US Department of Education concluded earlier this year that "On average, students in online learning conditions performed better than those receiving face-to-face instruction."

What's more, this wasn't true only of lower-level courses. "Online learning appeared to be an effective option for both undergraduates . . . and for graduate students and professionals . . . in a wide range of academic and professional studies," the study said.

The Obama administration has talked in general terms about online education as part of a grand plan to give the US the highest proportion of college-educated citizens in the world by 2020. The plan … could include funds to develop more online course materials and make them freely available.

If other online education start-ups like Straighterline.com do appear, they won't be looking for "18-year-olds from suburban high schools who want to go to Harvard," Carey says. Elite schools will always offer other reasons to attend, such as making social connections. "Exclusivity never goes out of style," he says.

Professor Teachout is reminded of the 19th century, when wealthy Americans sent their children off to Europe to absorb its cultural treasures on a so-called Grand Tour. "I can imagine the off-line, brick-and-mortar, elegant, beautiful MIT experience becoming the Grand Tour" of tomorrow, she says in an interview.

Reaction to her article has been strong and varied. Some, including her father, also a law professor, have said, "This is horrible. This is the end of the world," she says. Those she calls "techno-Utopians" have said, "This is fantastic!"

An online learning experience for the self-motivated, organized person could be "extraordinary," she says. And we've only scratched the surface. "The totally free online university that is stitched together from MIT-quality professors is going to happen very soon."

Others remain skeptical.

"I do question whether things are really as dire as she says, and whether we're moving toward a model where the online [courses] will almost completely displace the classroom," says Dan Colman, associate dean and director of continuing studies at Stanford University in California. He also has founded openculture .com, a website that points visitors to free educational courses online.

"I think there could be a day when a lot . . . could be done online, but I don't think it's in 20 years. I think it's further out."

As you know well, computer-assisted learning and teaching (through online courses, web content, podcasts, video links, course-management systems, PowerPoint presentations, and other kinds of electronic aids) are here to stay. In fact, you may be so familiar with the uses of computers that their assistance seems almost "invisible" to you. Taking an online course may seem more natural, even preferable, to you than sitting in a traditional classroom, listening to an instructor who speaks from notes and writes on the board.

Not everyone, though, is convinced that computer-assisted learning and teaching will continue, let alone thrive, in college-based settings. Some futuristic (they might prefer to be called "practical") academics argue that the entire notion of what makes a "university" needs to be redefined. Arguing that a traditional college education leaves most students in debt and without the skills and knowledge that they want and need, these academics want to transform the ways in which a college education is delivered, accredited, and assessed. These academics, the "edupunks" journalist Anya Kamenetz writes about in the following article, believe that they can use open-source course materials from the most prestigious of universities to provide students the best education. All that's necessary is the technology to convene communities of scholars from around the world. Kamenetz regularly writes about issues affecting higher education, including for-profit universities, student debt, nonpaying internships, and online influences.

> How Web-Savvy Edupunks Are Transforming American Higher Education

Anya Kamenetz

Is a college education really like a string quartet? Back in 1966, that was the assertion of economists William Bowen, later president of Princeton, and William Baumol. In a seminal study, Bowen and Baumol used the analogy to show why universities can't easily improve efficiency.

If you want to perform a proper string quartet, they noted, you can't cut out the cellist nor can you squeeze in more performances by playing the music faster. But that was then—before MP3s and iPods proved just how freely music could flow. Before Google scanned and digitized 7 million books and Wikipedia users created the world's largest encyclopedia. Before YouTube Edu and iTunes U made video and audio lectures by the best professors in the country available for free, and before college students built Facebook into the world's largest social network, changing the way we all share information. Suddenly, it is possible to imagine a new model of education using online resources to serve more students, more cheaply than ever before.

"The Internet disrupts any industry whose core product can be reduced to ones and zeros," says Jose Ferreira, founder and CEO of education startup Knewton. Education, he says, "is the biggest virgin forest out there." Ferreira is among a loose-knit band of education 2.0 architects sharpening their saws for that forest. Their first foray was at MIT in 2001, when the school agreed to put coursework online for free. Today, you can find the full syllabi, lecture notes, class exercises, tests, and some video and audio for every course MIT offers, from physics to art history. This trove has been accessed by 56 million current and prospective students, alumni, professors, and armchair enthusiasts around the world. "The advent of the Web brings the ability to disseminate high-quality materials at almost no cost, leveling the playing field," says Cathy Casserly, a senior partner at the Carnegie Foundation for the Advancement of Teaching, who in her former role at the Hewlett Foundation provided seed funding for MIT's project. "We're changing the culture of how we think about knowledge and how it should be shared and who are the owners of knowledge."

But higher education remains, on the whole, a string quartet. MIT's courseware may be free, yet an MIT degree still costs upward of $189,000. College tuition has gone up more than any other good or service since 1990, and our nation's students and graduates hold a staggering $714 billion in outstanding student-loan debt. Once the world's most educated country, the United States today ranks 10th globally in the percentage of young people with postsecondary degrees. "Colleges have become outrageously expensive, yet there remains

MIT offers materials for all of its courses online, for free, through its OpenCourseWare site.

a general refusal to acknowledge the implications of new technologies," says Jim Groom, an "instructional technologist" at Virginia's University of Mary Washington and a prominent voice in the blogosphere for blowing up college as we know it. Groom, a chain-smoker with an ever-present five days' growth of beard, coined the term "edupunk" to describe the growing movement toward high-tech do-it-yourself education. "Edupunk," he tells me in the opening notes of his first email, "is about the utter irresponsibility and lethargy of educational institutions and the means by which they are financially cannibalizing their own mission."

The edupunks are on the march. From VC-funded [venture capital–funded] startups to the ivied walls of Harvard, new experiments and business models are springing up from entrepreneurs, professors, and students alike. Want a class that's structured like a role-playing game? An accredited bachelor's degree for a few thousand dollars? A free, peer-to-peer Wiki university? These all exist today, the overture to a complete educational remix.

The architects of education 2.0 predict that traditional universities that cling to the string-quartet model will find themselves on the wrong side of history, along-side newspaper chains and record stores. "If universities can't find the will to in-novate and adapt to changes in the world around them," professor David Wiley of Brigham Young University has written, "universities will be irrelevant by 2020."

continued

Wiley doesn't come off immediately as a bomb thrower. He is a 37-year-old member of the Church of Jesus Christ of Latter-day Saints with five kids. He has close-cropped gray hair, glasses, and speaks softly in a West Virginia accent. But he employs his niceness strategically, as a general in the intellectual vanguard of the transformation of higher education. The challenge is not to bring technology into the classroom, he points out. The millennials, with their Facebook and their cell phones, have done that. The challenge is to capture the potential of technology to lower costs and improve learning for all.

Wiley has been experimenting with open educational content and tools since the early days of the Internet. As a college junior, he was hired as the first Webmaster of his small, resource-starved alma mater, Marshall University, in West Virginia. "I was working on developing a JavaScript calculator for a Web page when it occurred to me that this calculator, unlike a real one in our elementary schools, can be used by 100,000 people all at the same time," he says. "When you put materials online, they're different in that particular way; you can pay to produce them once and they can be used by an infinite number of people. That seemed to be somewhere between terribly fascinating and the kind of realization that it makes sense to spend the rest of your life working on." In 1998, when Wiley arrived at Brigham Young to do a PhD in instructional psychology and technology, he learned about open-source software programs and operating systems like Linux that are produced collaboratively and shared freely. "I said, 'Hey, that's exactly what we need to do with educational materials. Let's call it open content.'"

Today, "open content" is the biggest front of innovation in higher education. The movement that started at MIT has spread to more than 200 institutions in 32 countries that have posted courses online at the OpenCourseWare Consortium. But, as Wiley points out, there's still a big gap between viewing such resources as a homework aid and building a recognized, accredited degree out of a bunch of podcasts and YouTube videos. "Why is it that my kid can't take robotics at Carnegie Mellon, linear algebra at MIT, law at Stanford? And why can't we put 130 of those together and make it a degree?" Wiley asks. "There are all these kinds of innovations waiting to happen. A sufficient infrastructure of freely available content is step one in a much longer endgame that transforms everything we know about higher education."

Wiley is pursuing several different strategies toward this endgame. He has cofounded a free, not-for-profit, online public charter high school that draws on open courseware, letting Utah students complete their degree from home. He is "chief openness officer" at a for-profit startup, Flat World Knowledge, that commissions professors to write open-source textbooks that are free online, $19.95 for a download, or $29.95 for a print-on-demand copy. (Flat World closed $8 million in VC funding earlier this spring.) He has also offered five of his courses to anyone on the Web for free; he donates his own time to review nonenrolled students' work, awarding a signed certificate in lieu of course credit. Wiley's most recent open course was formatted as an online role-playing game, with students divided into "guilds" completing "quests"—a learning community inspired by the world of online gamers. "If you didn't need human interaction and someone to answer your questions, then the library would never have evolved into the university," Wiley says. "We all realize that content is just the first step."

"Open courseware is hard for the self-learner," agrees Neeru Paharia, a PhD student at Harvard Business School. Building a social network to make it easier is the goal of her newest project, Peer2Peer University. The daughter of two Indian-born Silicon Valley engineers, Paharia is a former McKinsey consultant and an early employee of Creative Commons, a not-for-profit set up to create the intellectual and legal framework to share and remix content without the expense and red tape of commercial copyright. In 2005, she started AcaWiki, a crowdsourced compilation of free summaries of academic papers. Now, she says, she wants to address "all the other things that a university does for you: It provides you a clear path from A to B, provides social infrastructure of teachers and other students, and accreditation so you actually get credit for what you do. So the question becomes, Is there a way of hacking something like this together?"

At a conference in Croatia last year, Paharia met Jan Philipp Schmidt, a German computer scientist working on open courseware in South Africa; together with a Canadian and an Australian, they started Peer2Peer University, which has become one of the most buzzed-about initiatives in open education. Would-be students can use the Web site to convene and schedule classes, meet online, and tutor one another; a volunteer facilitator for each course helps the process along. Peer2Peer got a $70,000 seed grant from the Hewlett Foundation to launch its first 10 pilot courses, in topics from behavioral economics to Wikipedia visualization—content areas that already have online audiences of self-motivated learners.

Paharia's idea of "hacking" education—putting something together on the fly—is important. All of these projects are still very much works in progress. Not even the most starry-eyed geeks are claiming that an LCD monitor can and should replace the richest, most fully textured college experience out there (at least not yet). But it could certainly represent an upgrade in opportunity for those who can't afford college, or for the half of American college students who attend community colleges, or even the 80% who attend nonselective universities.

Ultimately what interests Paharia is proving the model, demonstrating that there's a way to provide education cheaply or even for free to all who are qualified. "I ride the Boston T around and I see these ads for schools, and it bothers me that so much hope is rested on having an education, and yet at the end of the day you end up with $100,000 in debt. What are you paying for? And is this the best way of setting up the system?"

Peer2Peer is not the only attempt to bridge the gap between free material and cheap education. The online University of the People, founded by Shai Reshef, who made his fortune in for-profit education, signed up its first class this fall—300 students from nearly 100 countries. While it has yet to get accreditation, the not-for-profit plans to offer bachelor's degrees in business and computer science using open courseware and volunteer faculty; fees would add up to about $4,000 for a full four-year degree.

Richard Ludlow, a 23-year-old Yale graduate, has his own ideas about a workable business model for open educational resources. His for-profit startup, Academic

continued

Earth, is a Web site that brings together video lectures and other academic content from various sources. As an undergrad looking for help grokking a tough concept in his linear algebra class, he stumbled onto MIT's OpenCourseWare. He realized that there were some really cool educational resources out there and that most of his classmates didn't know about them. "My idea was to first, aggregate this huge critical mass of content disconnected over various sites; second, apply best practices in user interface design and Web standards to do for educational content what Hulu has done [for TV]; and third, build an educational ecosystem around the content," Ludlow explains. "Showing the videos is one thing, but building the right interactive tools and the right commenting system will really create something of value."

The Hulu comparison is a striking one. When you look at the cultural industries that have fallen under the spell of the Internet, the transformation has happened unevenly: newspapers before television, music before books. Hulu.com, launched just 18 months ago, is widely considered to be the first Web site to prove that mass broadcast-television viewing as we know it can and will shift online. Hulu did that by being attractive, well-designed, and easy to use, and by having a viable business model with actual paying advertisers—and soon, subscribers.

"We're talking about revenue sharing with a lot of universities," says Ludlow. "Most of this content is licensed noncommercial, but with endowments dropping, universities have to be selective about what they're funding. We're trying to find a way to make this sustainable by generating revenue and making sure it's in sync with the university's brand."

If open courseware is about applying technology to sharing knowledge, and Peer2Peer is about social networking for teaching and learning, Bob Mendenhall, president of the online Western Governors University, is proudest of his college's innovation in the third, hardest-to-crack dimension of education: accreditation and assessment. WGU was formed in the late 1990s, when the governors of 19 western states decided to take advantage of the newfangled Internet and create an online university to expand access to students in rural communities across their region. Today, it's an all-online university with 12,000 students in all 50 states. It's a private not-for-profit, like Harvard; the only state money was an initial $100,000 stake from each founding state. WGU runs entirely on tuition: $2,890 for a six-month term.

"We said, 'Let's create a university that actually measures learning,'" Mendenhall says. "We do not have credit hours, we do not have grades. We simply have a series of assessments that measure competencies, and on that basis, award the degree."

WGU began by convening a national advisory board of employers, including Google and Tenet Healthcare. "We asked them, 'What is it the graduates you're hiring can't do that you wish they could?' We've never had a silence after that question." Then assessments were created to measure each competency area. Mendenhall recalls one student who had been self-employed in IT for 15 years but never earned a degree; he passed all the required assessments in six months and took home his bachelor's without taking a course.

Most students, though, do the full coursework, working at their own pace through online course modules, playlists of prerecorded lectures, readings, projects, and quizzes. For every 80 students, a PhD faculty member, certified in the discipline, serves as a full-time mentor. "Our faculty are there to guide, direct, counsel, coach, encourage, motivate, keep on track, and that's their whole job," Mendenhall says. Multiple-choice tests are scored by computer, while essays and in-person evaluations are judged by a separate cadre of graders. What WGU is doing is using the Internet to disaggregate the various functions of teaching: the "sage on the stage" conveyor of information, the cheerleader and helpmate, and the evaluator. WGU constantly surveys both graduates and their employers to find out if they are lacking in any competencies so they can continue to fine-tune their programs.

Mendenhall is impatient with those who argue that what he's doing with education and technology is unworkable. "Technology has changed the productivity equation of every industry except education," he says. "We're simply trying to demonstrate that it can do it in education—if you change the way you do education as opposed to just adding technology on top."

So far, the open-education movement has been supported, to an astonishing extent, by a single donor: The Hewlett Foundation has made $68 million worth of grants to initiatives at Berkeley, Carnegie Mellon, MIT, Rice, Stanford, and Tufts. Today, such foundation money is slowing, but new sources of financing are emerging. President Barack Obama has directed $100 billion in stimulus money to education at all levels, and he recently appointed a prominent advocate of open education to be undersecretary of education (Martha Kanter, who helped launch the 100-member Community College Consortium for Open Educational Resources and the Community College Open Textbook Project) Meanwhile, outfits such as Flat World and Knewton are attracting venture funding .... The Carnegie Foundation's Casserly is helping existing open-courseware projects generate metrics that demonstrate their value to universities. "We need to figure out the models for this stuff," she says. "If it were easy, it wouldn't be such a fun challenge."

The transformation of education may happen faster than we realize. However futuristic it may seem, what we're living through is an echo of the university's earliest history. Universitas doesn't mean campus, or class, or a particular body of knowledge; it means the guild, the group of people united in scholarship. The university as we know it was born around AD 1100, when communities formed in Bologna, Italy; Oxford, England; and Paris around a scarce, precious information technology: the handwritten book. Illuminated manuscripts of the period show a professor at a podium lecturing from a revered volume while rows of students sit with paper and quill—the same basic format that most classes take 1,000 years later.

Today, we've gone from scarcity of knowledge to unimaginable abundance. It's only natural that these new, rapidly evolving information technologies would convene new communities of scholars, both inside and outside existing institutions. The string-quartet model of education is no longer sustainable. The university of the future can't be far away.

While some experts argue for the value of face-to-face teaching and learning and others propose an entirely new kind of university, still others remind us of the need to keep in mind the purpose of higher education: to educate all the students who come to college. In the following essay, Mark David Milliron, who serves as the Deputy Director for Postsecondary Improvement, US Programs, for the Bill and Melinda Gates Foundation, identifies some of the most serious roadblocks to student achievement and graduation. (The percentage of students who leave college without a degree is referred to as the *attrition rate.*) The reasons college students drop out include not being helped by remedial programs, lacking a social support network, and having a lower socioeconomic background or being a first in one's family to attend college (referred to as a *first-generation student*). Milliron points out that redesigning courses, increasing academic momentum, and creating an online student support system are all ways that higher education can be improved so that more students graduate from college.

> Online Education vs. Traditional Learning: Time to End the Family Feud

Reprinted by permission.

Mark David Milliron

Online learning tools and techniques—including fully online courses, blended learning, mobile learning, game-based learning, and social networking—are some of the newest and rowdiest children in the family of higher-education resources. They hold the promise of expanding, improving, and deepening learning for our students. A quick exploration of Carnegie Mellon's Open Learning Initiative, or the Monterey Institute for Technology and Education's National Repository of Online Courses, or Florida Virtual School's Conspiracy Code (a history course in a game) gives you a sense of what's possible and what's coming.

However, too many innovators brag at length about the bells and whistles of their tech-savvy children. They wax poetic about their exciting features and ever-growing functions that may or may not have anything to do with student achievement. Moreover, in the quest to increase credibility, some advocates for online learning argue that technology-enabled learning is vastly superior to traditional chalk-and-talk methods. Some of the more vocal zealots regularly lambast all lectures and mock any required face time as anachronistic. In their minds, these are vestiges of a failed system. In response, traditionalists scold the newcomers, reject their innovations, and pine for a simpler time.

So the family feud continues, each side shrieking that the other is sucking resources and has little proof of quality. The irony is that, in some ways, both are right. And with the financial challenges at hand, coming demographic changes, and education aspirations of the day, both are necessary, but neither is sufficient.

It's time we move beyond these dichotomous diatribes to a more nuanced exploration of how we can apply the entire family of tools, techniques, and resources at our disposal to help our students learn deeply, become active citizens, and complete their educational journeys with a credential in hand. It's time to put online-learning conversations in a larger context of learning resources and, more importantly, help them stay on purpose.

Let me offer a few of the most powerful possible purposes. Only about half the students who begin higher education finish. The number is less than one-fourth when you look at low-income students, and slips far lower if you include first-generation students. Our country has dropped from first in educational attainment to 12th, and we're on target to turn out a generation that is less educated than the one that proceeded it. Even more challenging is that the types of students who are least likely to succeed—low-income, minority, part-time, and adult learners—represent the fastest-growing segment of higher education. The headline: traditional methods aimed at traditional students won't work.

Given these challenges, we should be innovating with all our might and using any resource at our disposal to help all students succeed. Online-learning resources should be a powerful part of this work, especially in the following areas:

Plugging the Loss Points

Take a hard look at the data on student pathways through higher education, and you can't help but notice the key loss points—places where huge numbers of students stumble and fall off the path to a certificate or degree. While rushed or sloppy application of online learning to these loss points could actually make the situation worse, the thoughtful use of online tools holds the potential to be a major difference maker.

Remedial education, for example, is the Bermuda Triangle of higher education. Students who are shuffled off into a sequence of such courses are most likely never to be seen again. However, with more nuanced assessments that better discern remediation needs, these students can catch up more quickly using an interactive blend of online-learning tools (often used in on-campus labs) and on-ground tutoring support. El Paso Community College has had success with its early pilots of this model—based on Virginia Tech's Math Emporium, which leverages self-paced digital courseware in a lab environment staffed with tutors and support staff—and is expanding it to all of its campuses.

Technology can be applied with purpose beyond developmental education. Ask any community-college or university leaders where students fall off the path, and they will point you to the same set of core courses that wipe out huge numbers of students each year. The failure rates of these gatekeeper courses used to be a badge of honor for some, but now these data are viewed as lost opportunities, wasted dollars, and deferred dreams, all the result of a Darwinian attempt to assure quality.

Course-redesign efforts such as those led by the National Center for Academic Transformation have helped colleges and universities re-engineer these courses with significant success. The redesigns, which make strategic use of online resources, most often in a blended format, lead to significantly improved student achievement and reduced costs. In an attempt to outfit other colleges with improved resources to respond to this same challenge, the first wave of a $20-million national grant program called the Next Generation Learning Challenges was just released by Educause. This program is asking colleges and consortia to innovate with online courseware and blended learning models specifically for these gatekeeper courses.

continued

Finally, "life happens" is still the most often reported challenge for working, part-time, and returning students. Kids get sick, parents fall ill, work schedules change, jobs get lost, cars break down—and learning takes a back seat. Leaders at Corporate Voices for Working Families, a nonprofit group that is doing significant work catalyzing the conversation between education and employers about supporting working students, find that simply adding an online section or even a blended component to a course can significantly increase the likelihood that a working student or parent will not only attend but succeed.

Increasing Academic Momentum

In addition to plugging loss, we should focus on increasing academic momentum. Purdue University's Signals project shows the power of analyzing data gathered from student use of Purdue's online-learning-management system to keep students working in gatekeeper courses like chemistry. Simply giving up-to-the-minute, predictive-model-based feedback in the form of traffic lights—red, yellow, and green—lets students know how they're doing along the way and helps them succeed at significantly higher rates. In an age where students are used to getting immediate feedback on performance through video games, it's not surprising that this kind of resource works.

In a related but broader effort, Valencia Community College created an online student-service support system called Atlas that builds momentum for the student from first contact through completion. Students fill out a full profile and degree plan in a first-semester course devoted to student success, which helps them develop their "Life Map" through to a degree. From that point on, Atlas/ Life Map is their virtual connection to the college and pathway to their academic goal. A part of a larger group of reforms, this type of strategy has contributed to Valencia's graduation rate being almost triple that of its peer institutions.

Western Governors University uses this type of holistic pathway support with its faculty-mentor strategy. The university's faculty members—who are mostly full time and online—focus almost exclusively on guiding students through to success. The university champions a competency-based learning model that allows students to leverage online-learning resources and work at their own pace— completing degrees that often take 55 months in 30.

Reducing Costs and Increasing Quality

With tools like OER Commons, Connexions, Curriki, iTunes U, Academic Earth, and MIT OpenCourseWare, we have more free education resources at our fingertips than ever before—much to the delight of cash-strapped students buying ridiculously expensive textbooks they seldom use. However, the quality development and curation of these resources is a challenge—as is their thoughtful integration into instructional practice. We're moving from traditional text- and textbook-based curricular resource strategies to more robust "play lists" of digital resources aimed at helping students master better-defined learning goals.

As these conversations continue, I'm intrigued by the faculty who are looking to displace as much as possible online—including lectures—to ensure that precious

Proposals

time with students is increasingly used for questioning, mentoring, interacting, and other deeper learning activities. Moreover, others are basing their instructional design on heavily researched learning-science models, not on simple online replicas of current teaching. They are asking hard questions about what works, what doesn't, and with which students; and harder questions about pacing, timing, and presentation strategies that maximize learning. It's compelling work, and there is much to be learned about the effective mix of online and on-ground strategies.

We need to end the family feud over learning strategies. Particularly for low-income students, the journey to and through our institutions is the pathway to possibility. We owe it to them to steer our conversations about online learning away from the tired "use it versus don't use it" arguments. Like the examples cited here, we need to get online learning explorations and efforts on purpose, and begin the process of envisioning a new generation of learning that leverages all the resources at hand to help all students make the most of their time with us.

> ANALYZING THE RHETORICAL SITUATION

As the articles in this section demonstrate, one major way in which higher education is changing is in how courses are being delivered, with online delivery perhaps having the greatest impact. The following questions ask you to consider these changes (and the effects of these changes) in terms of the elements of the rhetorical situation. You'll want to reread the essays carefully before answering.

1. Who might be the intended audience for each article? How do the audiences for the articles differ? What characteristics do these audiences share? What textual evidence can you provide to support your answers? Be prepared to share your answers with the rest of the class.

2. Is the purpose of each article evident? If so, what is it? How do the articles differ in terms of purpose? And how does each purpose correspond to the intended audience? Again, be prepared to share your answers with the rest of the class.

3. To what rhetorical opportunity might each writer be responding? How does each piece of writing work to resolve the problem? Who has the capability to resolve or affect the resolution of that problem?

4. How does each writer draw on the rhetorical appeals of ethos, logos, and pathos? Cite passages from the texts to support your answer.

How can college be made affordable?

Given the rising costs of higher education, one important question in any conversation about the college of the future concerns ways to make it affordable for all who want to attend. The writers of the texts in the preceding section suggest that online courses are perceived to lower costs. However, online courses require hiring a significant number of personnel who will assist teachers and students alike and to work in computer labs. Computers themselves are, of course, expensive, as are the software, computer-lab space, Ethernet wiring, wireless installations, and all the other components needed to translate "chalk-and-talk" education into online and computer-assisted teaching and learning. Still, the most expensive part of a higher education is typically tuition and books, rather than computer-related expenses. The following articles address the question of affordability, describing the efforts of various schools to lower the costs of tuition and detailing the sometimes overlooked economic benefits of attending a two-year college.

The authors of the following proposal examine some of the economic forces that are currently working to make higher education unaffordable for many. Joseph Marr Cronin and Howard E. Horton bring their professional expertise to the question of what it will take to make college more affordable for more students, particularly in terms of lowering or freezing tuition. Cronin writes from his perspective as President of the Massachusetts Higher Education Assistance Corporation and Chairman of the Board of the New England Education Loan Marketing Corporation; Horton writes as President of the New England College of Business and Finance. According to these writers, what's at stake is the ultimate value of a college education. In other words, is a college education a good financial investment or not?

> Will Higher Education Be the Next Bubble to Burst?

Joseph Marr Cronin and Howard E. Horton

The public has become all too aware of the term "bubble" to describe an asset that is irrationally and artificially overvalued and cannot be sustained. The dot-com bubble burst by 2000. More recently the overextended housing market collapsed, helping to trigger a credit meltdown. The stock market has declined more than 30 percent in the past year, as companies once considered flagship investments have withered in value.

Is it possible that higher education might be the next bubble to burst? Some early warnings suggest that it could be.

With tuitions, fees, and room and board at dozens of colleges now reaching $50,000 a year, the ability to sustain private higher education for all but the very well-heeled is questionable. According to the National Center for Public Policy and Higher Education, over the past 25 years, average college tuition and fees have risen by 440 percent—more than four times the rate of inflation and almost twice the rate of medical care. Patrick M. Callan, the center's president, has warned that low-income students will find college unaffordable.

Meanwhile, the middle class, which has paid for higher education in the past mainly by taking out loans, may now be precluded from doing so as the private student-loan market has all but dried up. In addition, endowment cushions that allowed colleges to engage in steep tuition discounting are gone. Declines in housing valuations are making it difficult for families to rely on home-equity loans for college financing. Even when the equity is there, parents are reluctant to further leverage themselves into a future where job security is uncertain.

Consumers who have questioned whether it is worth spending $1,000 a square foot for a home are now asking whether it is worth spending $1,000 a week to send their kids to college. There is a growing sense among the public that higher education might be overpriced and under-delivering.

In such a climate, it is not surprising that applications to some community colleges and other public institutions have risen by as much as 40 percent. Those institutions, particularly community colleges, will become a more-attractive option for a larger swath of the collegebound. Taking the first two years of college while living at home has been an attractive option since the 1920s, but it is now poised to grow significantly.

With a drift toward higher enrollments in public institutions, all but the most competitive highly endowed private colleges are beginning to wonder if their enrollments may start to evaporate. In an effort to secure students, some institutions, like Merrimack College near Boston, are freezing their tuition for the first time in decades.

Could it get worse for colleges in the coming years? The numbers of college-aged students in the "baby-boom echo," which crested with [2009's] high-school senior class, will decline over the next decade. Certain Great Plains and North-eastern states may lose 10 percent of the 12th-graders eligible for college. Vermont is expected to lose 20 percent by 2020.

In the meantime, online, nontraditional institutions are becoming increasingly successful at challenging high-priced private colleges and those public universities that charge $25,000 or more per year. The best known is the for-profit University of Phoenix, which now teaches courses to more than 300,000 students a year—including traditional-age college students—half of them online. But other competitors are emerging. In collaboration with an organization called Higher Ed Holdings—which is affiliated with Whitney International University, owner of New England College of Business and Finance, where one of us is president and the other a trustee—some state universities have begun taking back market share by attracting thousands of students to online programs at reduced tuition rates. One such institution is Lamar University, in Texas, which has seen its enrollment mushroom since working with Higher Ed Holdings to increase access to some of its programs.

Moreover, increases in federal financial aid and state scholarships have been unable to keep up with the incessant annual increases in tuition at traditional four-year colleges. For example, Congress has raised the Pell Grant limits from $4,731 to $5,350 a year by scrubbing the federal loan programs of bank subsidies thought to be excessive. But $5,350 pays for only about four to six weeks at a high-priced private college.

A few prominent universities, including Harvard and Princeton, have made commitments to reduce or eliminate loans for those students from families earning less than $75,000 or even $100,000 a year. But the hundreds of less-endowed colleges cannot reduce the price of education in that fashion. It is those colleges that are most at risk.

continued

What can they do to keep the bubble from bursting? They can look for more efficiency and other sources of tuition.

Two former college presidents, Charles Karelis of Colgate University and Stephen J. Trachtenberg of George Washington University, recently argued for the year-round university, noting that the two-semester format now in vogue places students in classrooms barely 60 percent of the year, or 30 weeks out of 52. They propose a 15-percent increase in productivity without adding buildings if students agree to study one summer and spend one semester abroad or in another site, like Washington or New York. Such a model may command attention if more education is offered without more tuition.

Brigham Young University–Idaho charges only $3,000 in tuition a year, and $6,000 for room and board. Classes are held for three semesters, each 14 weeks, for 42 weeks a year. Faculty members teach three full semesters, which has helped to increase capacity from 25,000 students over two semesters to close to 38,000 over three, with everyone taking one month (August) off. The president, Kim B. Clark, is a former dean of the Harvard Business School and an authority on using technology to achieve efficiencies. By 2012 the university also plans to increase its online offerings to 20 percent of all courses, with 120 online courses that students can take to enrich or accelerate degree completion.

Colleges can also make productivity gains by using technology and re-engineering courses. For the past 10 years, the National Center for Academic Transformation, supported by the Pew Charitable Trusts, has helped major universities use technology to cut instructional costs by an average of 40 percent while reducing the number of large course sections, graduate teaching assistants, and faculty time on correcting quizzes. Grades have increased, and fewer students have dropped out. Meanwhile, students have a choice of learning styles and ways to get help online from either fellow students or faculty members. That "transformation" requires a commitment to break away from the medieval guild tradition of one faculty member controlling all forms of communication, and to give serious attention to helping students think and solve problems in new formats.

The economist Richard Vedder of Ohio University, a member of the federal Spellings Commission, offers more radical solutions. He urges that university presidents' salaries include incentives to contain and reduce costs, to make "affordability" a goal. In addition, he proposes that state policy makers conduct cost-benefit studies to see what the universities that receive state support are actually accomplishing.

Fortunately, some other forces are at work that might help save higher education. The federal government recently raised significantly the amount of money that returning veterans might claim to pursue higher-education degrees, so it reaches at least the level of tuition and fees at many public universities.

In addition, the rest of the world respects American higher education, and whether studying at a college here or an American-based one abroad, the families of international students usually pay in full. The number of international students could rise from 600,000 to a million a year if visa reviews are expedited; the crisis of September 11, 2001, temporarily reduced the upward trajectory of overseas enrollments in American colleges. Accrediting agencies could also develop standards to expedite the exporting of American education into the international market.

But colleges cannot, and should not, rely on those trends. Although questions about the mounting prices of colleges have been raised for more than 30 years and just a few private colleges have closed, the stakes and volume of the warnings are mounting. Only during a critical moment in economic history can one warn of bubbles and suggest that the day of reckoning for higher education is, in fact, drawing near.

George D. Kuh is Chancellor's Professor Emeritus of Higher Education at Indiana University Bloomington and current director of the National Institute for Learning Outcomes Assessment at Indiana University and the University of Illinois. In addressing the controversy surrounding the cost of attending college and the pressures of balancing school work and employment, Kuh argues for combining both kinds of work. What if a student's job responsibilities and courses were mutually beneficial? What if there were employment possibilities that enriched academics—and vice versa? Teachers, students, and their employers might all benefit from such an arrangement.

> Maybe Experience Really Can Be the Best Teacher

© 2010. Reprinted by permission.

George D. Kuh

College students work for different reasons. Many take jobs to pay tuition and related educational expenses. Others work to afford electronic gadgets (often ones that we, their professors, don't yet know exist). Regardless of the reasons, many professors and administrators consider students' working during college to be an unfortunate distraction from what should be their primary focus: their academic studies.

Mark Shaver

Nonetheless, next to going to class, work is by far the most common activity in which undergraduates take part. At least two-thirds of students at four-year colleges and four-fifths of their counterparts at two-year colleges work at some point during college, either on or off campus. And, contrary to long-held beliefs, findings from the 2008 National Survey of Student Engagement show that working is positively related to several dimensions of student engagement, especially for full-time students.

Given that policy makers and institutional leaders are looking for low- or no-cost ways to improve student success—especially for part-time and older students and [students] from historically underrepresented groups—it's high time we look for ways to use the work experience to enrich rather than detract from learning and college completion.

Substantial research suggests that working during college is related to acquiring such employer-preferred skills as [the ability to work in a team] and time

continued

management. Employment also has the potential to deepen and enrich learning, as is the case when students participate in such "high impact" activities as learning communities, student-faculty research, study abroad, capstone seminars, and internships both paid and unpaid. When done well, those and other high-impact activities require students to connect, reflect on, and integrate what they are learning from their classes with other life experiences. Doing so helps students see firsthand the practical value of their classroom learning by applying it in real-life settings—which, additionally, often helps to clarify their career aspirations.

For more than a century, integrating learning and work along with service has been the mission of the seven federally recognized work colleges in the United States: the College of the Ozarks and Alice Lloyd, Berea, Blackburn, Ecclesia, Sterling, and Warren Wilson Colleges. These institutions meet the eligibility criteria for funds from the Work-Colleges Program administered by the U.S. Department of Education, including featuring work, learning, and service in their educational philosophy; requiring that all students work at least five hours a week (though most students at work colleges average between 10 [and] 15 hours); and making student performance on the job as well as the classroom part of the student record. The goal is to help students learn to balance study, service to others, and the demands of their jobs.

Other institutions are pursuing similar ends. The University of Maine at Farmington has created more on-campus jobs to help students see the connections between curriculum and work. Boston's Northeastern University and the University of Waterloo, in Ontario, offer large numbers of high-quality off-campus internships.

As part of a two-day visit to the University of Iowa in 2009, I encouraged staff members in the division of student services to teach their student employees to connect and apply what they were learning in class to their jobs, and vice versa. They subsequently started a small pilot program with students working in different kinds of jobs—clerking at the campus bookstore, assisting at the health center, and answering questions at the residence-hall information desk, to name just a few.

Supervisors met with their student employees twice during the semester. To focus those conversations, they provided students with a list of questions in advance:

▶ How is this job fitting in with your academics?

▶ What are you learning here at work that is helping you in class?

▶ What are you learning in class that you can apply here at work?

▶ Can you give a couple of examples of what you are learning here at work that you will use in your chosen profession?

Although only about half of the 33 students who had the structured meetings with their supervisors responded, the results of the survey comparing them with 373 co-workers who did not have such meetings were striking. On virtually every measure, the pilot-program group was much more positive. For example, about 70 percent of the students in the pilot program agreed that they had made connections between their work experience and their major-field course work, compared with only 29 percent of their co-workers. Sixty-nine percent of the pilot-program workers reported that their work had helped improve their written communication skills, compared with 17 percent of their peers. Seventy-seven percent of the pilot-program workers said their jobs had helped them use critical-thinking skills to solve problems, compared with 56 percent of the others.

Iowa is expanding the program this year, making an effort to include more students working in areas such as food service, where integrating academic learning with the work experience may be more challenging. Any college can adapt this generic, low-cost, potentially high-payoff approach.

For students in off-campus jobs, a classroom-based model can achieve similar ends. Professors can create assignments that encourage such students to make connections between course materials and their jobs, and can lead discussions that ask students to reflect on and integrate their learning. For example, in an upper-division writing course, a professor could ask students to analyze, in a genre appropriate for the field, the relevance of key concepts presented in class readings to one's workplace, or to dealing effectively with a low-performing co-worker.

Getting students to talk, in the company of their peers, about how they are applying their learning can be a significant challenge. One way to jump-start meaningful exchanges is to include in the class an upper-division student who is articulate in such matters. After a few sessions, students will very likely begin making and discussing connections themselves.

Not every course needs to be so structured for students to derive benefits from connecting learning and work. If working students have just one or two such courses in the first year, and again a few more times in [their] major, they would begin to develop an enhanced, practiced capacity for reflection and integration that they can use in other classes and settings.

So how can colleges build on those successes? One way is for a consortium of colleges and universities to seek funds to develop course modules focused on connecting learning and employment. The challenges and rewards of using work to educational advantage could then be documented and adapted by colleges with large numbers of working students.

There are many good ideas for enhancing college achievement and helping more undergraduates succeed. Few promise to deliver as much bang for the buck as making work more relevant to learning, and vice versa.

Some colleges and universities are offering reduced tuition to students whose families earn less than $75,000 to $100,000 a year; others are offering reduced rates to all veterans. Few colleges and universities have instituted tuition reductions for all students, however. In response to the continuing high cost of a college education, the Center for College Affordability and Productivity compiled twenty-five ways for students to reduce that cost, the first being to attend a community college, which may be one of the best bargains in higher education. Other cost-reducing actions suggested by the center include enrolling in dual-enrollment programs, taking online courses, and moving more quickly through college by taking heavier course loads.

Excerpt from

> 25 Ways to Reduce the Cost of College, #1: Encourage More Students to Attend Community Colleges

The Center for College Affordability and Productivity

The average cost of educating a person at a community college is markedly lower than that of four-year institutions. Tuition levels for students are seldom much more than one-half of what they are at four-year schools, and governmental subsidies per student tend to be lower as well. A very significant savings in overall college costs could occur simply by increasing the proportion of Americans attending lower cost schools, including for-profit proprietary institutions.

A large portion of students attending both two- and four-year schools drop out, often because of academic difficulties. Too many students whose high school grades and test scores indicate they would have difficulty with four-year schools enroll anyhow. These students not only accrue large personal debts but also impose a burden on society in the form of federal financial assistance and unwarranted subsidies to state schools. Four-year schools should be discouraged—perhaps even actively prohibited—from accepting many of these students. Students instead should be encouraged to enroll in two-year colleges; those who succeed academically can then move on to four-year schools.

One difficulty with the scenario above is that it is often difficult for students to transfer to four-year schools without a significant loss of credit—meaning the total college experience extends beyond four years and therefore becomes more costly. State higher education coordinating boards, state boards of education, state governments and, above all, school officials should work to make credit transfer relatively seamless and cost efficient. This means there should be more communication and coordination between the two types of higher educational institutions. Perhaps financial incentives need to be offered to the four-year schools [that] demonstrate that they are accepting more and more community college transfers—students who are actually ready for their third year of college.

How much can be saved by increasing the proportion of students in two-year community colleges? A lot. Let us compare two otherwise identical states [that] both educate two- and four- year students, respectively, at a cost to society of $10,000 and $25,000 each annually. Suppose the first state has 75 percent of its undergraduates in four-year schools and 25 percent in two-year ones, while the second state has equal numbers in each type of institution. Total per student costs for the first state would be $21,250, while for the second state they would be $17,500, or 17.6 percent less.

> ANALYZING THE RHETORICAL SITUATION

1. What problem does each proposal in this section address? Who can resolve or help bring about a resolution to that problem?
2. How do the writers propose resolving the problem? What actions do they want their audiences to take?
3. Who might be the intended audience for each proposal? What textual evidence can you provide for your response?
4. What seems to be the purpose of each proposal? How do the proposals differ in purpose?
5. How do the writers use ethos, pathos, and logos to reinforce their arguments? Provide textual evidence to support your answer. On which of the rhetorical appeals do they rely most heavily? Be prepared to share your answer with the rest of the class.
6. How do the writers evaluate the feasibility of their proposals in terms of the necessary time, money, and people? Provide textual evidence to support your answer.

COMMUNITY CONNECTIONS

1. Write for ten minutes in response to Joseph Marr Cronin and Howard E. Horton's proposal to keep the higher education "bubble" from bursting. How does their information coincide with or diverge from your experiences in college?

2. Write for ten minutes in response to George D. Kuh's proposal to combine work and learning. How does his analysis coincide with or diverge from your experiences juggling college and work?

3. In your own experience, what is your biggest educational expense? What are the positive and negative effects of incurring that expense?

4. Although cost may be the biggest challenge facing higher education, there are other challenges as well. Write for five minutes describing another challenge to higher education—such as the undue attention to athletics, the devaluation of a college degree, the lure of parties and bars, or the unpreparedness of first-year students.

5. Write for ten minutes about the causes or the consequences of the challenge you identified in question 4. How do you think this phenomenon becomes a problem? What are its immediate and long-term effects? Be prepared to share your response with the rest of the class.

6. Given your college experiences so far, what is your definition of a good college education? What elements constitute (or should constitute) a good education? Write for ten minutes and be prepared to share your responses.

Proposals: A Fitting Response

As the readings in this chapter illustrate, higher education is of concern to more than just college and university administrators. What is studied, how it's studied, how campuses are designed, and who they're ultimately designed for— these issues and others create a need for conversation. To set forth their own visions for resolving such issues, many writers offer proposals, which can be distributed to the intended audience in a variety of ways.

A proposal for reframing the humanities

The potential for computers and technology to enhance (or detract from) education continues to receive vast amounts of attention. Still, some scholars are concerned with the substance of college courses rather than the ways in which course content is delivered. Author Alain de Botton is a philosopher of the everyday. He founded and helps run the School of Life, in London, which is dedicated to a new vision of education. In the following proposal, de Botton focuses on the enduring value of great books and works—the benefits that works of art, religion, history, philosophy, and literature bring to life, work, and family. At his School of Life, de Botton offers a curriculum featuring courses on wisdom, the challenges of marriage, and anger, using such works to illuminate authentic issues in students' lives. Although it may seem to some to be an antiquated view, de Botton believes that the humanities should "help us to live" and to "face our most pressing personal and professional issues." His assessment of the value of a college education harkens back to centuries past, during which influential writers extolled the capacity of a good education to help inspire "capable and cultivated human beings."

Can Tolstoy Save Your Marriage?

Alain de Botton

De Botton uses his opening paragraph to identify the rhetorical opportunity to which he is responding.

Hard-working, pragmatic types, who abound in the United States, have always been suspicious of university education in the humanities. What good does it do to study the works of Milton or Rousseau, let alone the enigmatic pronouncements of Buddha or the Zen poet Basho? The unemployment rate hovers near 10%, and the Chinese are feeding their undergraduates a strict diet of engineering and accountancy. How can we pampered, decadent sorts possibly still be indulging our youth with lectures on Roman poetry and Renaissance painting?

De Botton addresses an audience of people who are interested in education, specifically in the value of a college education.

Unfortunately, university professors in the humanities tend to get unproductively upset when asked to explain the importance of what they do. They know that their opposite numbers in the technical and scientific departments can justify their work in utilitarian terms to impatient government officials and donors. But fearing that they cannot compete effectively, the denizens of the humanities prefer to take refuge in ambiguity and silence, having carefully calculated that they retain just enough prestige to get away with leaving the reasons for their existence somewhat murky.

My own answer to what the humanities are for is simple: They should help us to live.
We should look to culture as a storehouse of useful ideas about how to face our most
pressing personal and professional issues. Novels and historical narratives can impart
moral instruction and edification. Great paintings can suggest the requirements for happiness. Philosophy can probe our anxieties and offer consolation. It should be the job of
a university education to tease out the therapeutic and illuminative aspects of culture,
so that we emerge from a period of study as slightly less disturbed, selfish and blink-
ered human beings. Such a transformation benefits not only the economy but also our
friends, children and spouses.

After a rich Intro-
duction, de Botton
presents his thesis
statement.

I'm hardly the first to express these hopes of education. In mid-19th-century Victorian Britain, we find men like John Stuart Mill saying that "the object of universities is not to make skillful lawyers, physicians or engineers" but "to make capable and
cultivated human beings." His contemporary Matthew Arnold sounded similar notes,
arguing that liberal education should help to inspire in us "a love of our neighbour, a
desire for clearing human confusion and for diminishing human misery." At its most
ambitious, it should even engender the "noble aspiration to leave the world better and
happier than we found it."

The writer quotes
other intellectuals
who agree with his
thesis. Then, he pro-
vides some historical
background for his
argument.

These well-meaning mid-Victorians wanted universities to become our new churches,
places that would teach us how to live, but without dogma or superstition. Given the
dramatic decline in religious belief in the 19th century in Europe, anguished questions
were raised about how, in the absence of a Christian framework, people would manage
to find meaning, understand themselves, behave in a moral fashion, forgive their fellow
humans and confront their own mortality. It was hoped that cultural works might hence-
forth be consulted in place of the biblical texts.

The claim that culture can stand in for scripture—that "Middlemarch" or the essays
of Schopenhauer can take up the responsibilities previously handled by the Psalms—still
has a way of sounding eccentric or insane. But the ambition is not misplaced: Culture
can and should change and save our lives. The problem is the way that culture is taught
at our universities, which have a knack for killing its higher possibilities.

In a variation of his
thesis statement, de
Botton emphasizes
his point.

The modern university has achieved unparalleled expertise in imparting factual information about culture, but it remains wholly uninterested in training students to use
culture as a repertoire of wisdom—that is, a kind of knowledge concerned with things
that are not only true but also inwardly beneficial, providing comfort in the face of life's
infinite challenges, from a tyrannical employer to a fatal diagnosis. Our universities have
never offered what churches invariably focus on: guidance.

The writer provides a
definition of the mod-
ern university, what
it offers and what it
does not.

It is a basic tenet of contemporary scholarship that no academic should connect
works of culture to individual sorrows. It remains shocking to ask what "Tess of the
d'Urbervilles" might usefully teach us about love or to read the novels of Henry James
as if they might contain instructive parables. When confronted by those who demand
that a university education should be relevant and useful, that it should offer advice on
how to choose a career or survive the end of a marriage, how to contain sexual impulses
or cope with the news of a medical death sentence, the guardians of culture become
disdainful. They prefer students who are mature, independent, temperamentally able to
live with questions rather than answers, and ready to put aside their own needs for the
sake of years of disinterested study.

Whatever the rhetoric of promotional prospectuses and graduation ceremonies, the
modern university has precious little interest in teaching us any emotional or ethical

Proposals

life skills: how to love our neighbors, clear human confusion, diminish human misery and "leave the world better and happier than we found it." To judge by what they do rather than what they airily declaim, universities are in the business of turning out tightly focused professionals and a minority of culturally well-informed but ethically confused arts graduates, who have limited prospects for employment. We have charged our higher-education system with a dual and possibly contradictory mission: to teach us both how to make a living and how to live. But we have left the second of these aims recklessly vague and unattended.

Because this situation cries out for a remedy, a few years ago I joined with a group of similarly disaffected academics, artists and writers and helped to start a new kind of university. We call it, plainly, the School of Life, and it operates from a modest space in central London. On the menu of our school, you won't find subjects like philosophy, French and history. You'll find courses in marriage, child-rearing, choosing a career, changing the world and death. Along the way, our students encounter many of the books and ideas that traditional universities serve up, but they seldom get bored—and often come away with a different take on the world.

The School of Life draws upon the same rich catalog of culture treated by its traditional counterparts; we study novels, histories, plays and paintings. But we teach this material with a view to illuminating students' lives rather than merely prodding them toward academic goals. "Anna Karenina" and "Madame Bovary" are assigned in a course on understanding the tensions of marriage instead of in one focused on narrative trends in 19th-century fiction. Epicurus and Plato appear in the syllabus for a course about wisdom rather than in a survey of Hellenistic philosophy.

We are currently teaching a class on anger using the works of Seneca, the Stoic philosopher who proposed that anger results not from an uncontrollable eruption of the passions but from a basic (and correctible) error of reasoning. In his view, what makes us angry is having dangerously optimistic ideas about what the world and other people are like. How badly we react to frustration is critically determined by what we consider to be normal. We may be frustrated by a rain storm, but we are unlikely to respond to one with anger. So Seneca's answer to anger is to disappoint ourselves fully before life has a chance to do it for us. Students who thought they had enrolled merely to read some old books have come away with tools to live in a better way. There's a waiting list for almost every course we run.

A university might follow this model by identifying the problematic areas in people's lives and designing courses that address them head on. There should be classes devoted to, among other things: being alone, reconsidering work, improving relationships with children, reconnecting with nature and facing illness. A university alive to its true responsibilities in a secular age would establish a Department for Relationships, an Institute of Dying and a Center for Self-Knowledge. This is less a matter of finding new books to teach than of asking the right questions of the ones we already have.

Our most celebrated intellectual institutions rarely consent to ask, let alone to answer, the most serious questions of the soul. Oprah Winfrey may not provide the deepest possible analysis of the human condition, but her questions are often more probing and meaningful than those posed by Ivy League professors in the humanities. It is time for humanistic education to outgrow its fears of irrelevance and to engage directly with our most pressing personal and spiritual needs.

What the contemporary university does not teach—skills relevant to actual life and living—is exactly what the writer wants it to teach. He gives specific examples of those skills.

The writer enhances his ethos by noting his role in establishing the School of Life. The mention of a "modest space" also supports this ethos.

The writer gives examples of the works the school uses and elucidates the positive effects of such an education.

These two paragraphs explain just how the School of Life operates and thus establish the writer's logos.

De Botton ends his essay with a call for action in line with his thesis.

■ GUIDE TO RESPONDING TO THE RHETORICAL SITUATION

Understanding the Rhetorical Situation

When you want to argue for the best way to improve upon a situation, consider composing a proposal. Proposals commonly have the following features:

- There is a clear, identifiable problem that the proposal seeks to resolve.
- This problem is of concern to a significant number of people.
- The proposed solution will resolve the problem in a way these people will find acceptable.
- The proposal contains specific details about the costs and benefits of the solution.
- The proposal is directed to an appropriate audience and demonstrates a good understanding of that audience's needs and interests.
- The proposal clearly explains the steps or processes required to enact the solution.

The following sections will help you compose a proposal about a feature of higher education you would like to change. To work with an online guide to the elements of the rhetorical situation, access your English CourseMate through cengagebrain.com.

Identifying an opportunity

Consider the resources that have enriched your college life so far, whether in the classroom, the library, the student center, the gym, or with particular persons or groups. You might also consider your experiences with your school before you enrolled as a student. Which resources, if any, are a focus of contention? Perhaps you have sensed tension over your school's relationship with members of the surrounding community, whether businesses or individuals. Maybe your experience with the admissions process or with the kinds of classes offered in your major have been disappointing in some way. Or maybe you have had a wonderful experience, and you want to point out how others can best use the resources. The following activities can help you identify an opportunity.

1. Make a list of resources associated with your college experience, including those you wrote about in response to the questions on page 237.
2. If your experiences with these resources have been positive, explain why, providing as many details as possible. If anything could have made the experiences better, explain how. If any of the experiences have been negative, describe the factors that made them difficult or unpleasant. Identify as many contributing factors as you can: the rules or guidelines for using a resource, the quality or accessibility of the resource, the effects of the resource on you or on others, and so forth.

3. Choose the feature of higher education you would like to write about and compose four or five sentences describing some problem with it. Vary your description of the problem. For example, one sentence might emphasize one group of people who are affected by the problem, and another might emphasize a different group.

Locating an audience

The following questions can help you locate your rhetorical audience as well as identify its relationship to the problem you've identified. Then, you'll be able to choose the best way to describe that problem.

1. List the names of the persons or groups who are in the best position to help with your problem. This step may require some research and some legwork.
2. Next to the name of each potential audience, write reasons that audience could have for acknowledging the existence of your problem. In other words, what would persuade these audiences that something needs to change?
3. What actions could these audiences reasonably be persuaded to perform? In other words, consider what each audience would be able to do to address the problem.
4. With your audience's interests and capabilities in mind, look again at the descriptions of the problem that you composed in the preceding section. Decide which description will best help your audience feel connected to the features of higher education in question and invested in improving them. At this point, it may be necessary to revise your best description to tailor it to your audience. Remember to consider whether the most fitting description will include images, video, or audio.

Identifying a fitting response

Identifying a problem and getting others to recognize it as a problem are only the first steps in responding to a rhetorical situation. You also need to identify and support a suitable solution to the problem. Your solution should consider the information you gathered about your audience, such as their interests and capabilities. It should also be feasible, in the sense of being an efficient and cost-effective way to go about making a positive change.

As you know, different purposes and different audiences require different kinds of texts—delivered through different media. For example, if your school could better serve its growing population of single parents by extending the hours of its on-campus daycare facility, better serve its health-conscious students by expanding the food options on campus, or better serve its entire student body by increasing the number of computer labs, you might draft a petition to circulate among your classmates. None of these situations necessarily calls for an extended, formal proposal. The point is that once you have identified your problem, audience, and purpose, you need to determine what kind of text will best respond to your rhetorical situation.

Use the following questions to help you narrow your purpose and shape your response:

1. How would you efficiently and effectively solve the problem you've identified?
2. What would this solution require of your audience?
3. Are you asking your audience simply to support your solution or to perform a particular action?
4. What is the best way to reach this audience? That is, what kind of presentation is this audience most likely to respond to? (Chapter 13 can help you explore options for media and design.)

Considering your proposal's acceptability and feasibility

The next step has to do with two concepts that are particularly important to proposals: acceptability and feasibility. Audiences are more likely to be persuaded by solutions that make responsible use of resources and that benefit some group rather than just a few individuals. Once you have identified and defined the problem for a particular audience, one that can affect the resolution of the problem by showing support or giving permission or working on the solution, you can begin to consider the acceptability and feasibility of your proposal.

1. What resources—time, money, and human effort—are needed to accomplish the solution you're proposing? Write about each of these needs separately.
2. What positive consequences will follow from your proposed solution? List them.
3. What examples can you provide of other instances in which your proposed solution (or a similar one) has had positive results?
4. What logistical challenges does your solution face? List them.
5. What can be done to address each of these challenges?

Writing a Proposal: Working with Your Available Means

Shaping your proposal

As you have probably figured out, a proposal is arranged much like an argument. The introduction provides enough background information to describe and define the problem (perhaps in terms of its causes or consequences) and states a reasonable thesis, which conveys the essence of the proposed sensible solution, all of which helps establish ethos.

The body of a proposal provides supporting evidence for the suggested solution, particularly in terms of its consequences or results. The shape and content of the overall argument help establish logos. In addition, the body accounts for the feasibility of the proposed solution in terms of time, money, and human effort. In other words, what resources are necessary for implementing the

pages 67–68
pages 64–66

pages 75–77

Introduction
▶ Defines and describes the problem by offering necessary background
▶ Establishes common ground (ethos)
▶ States thesis (the writer's sensible solution)

Body
▶ Supports the proposed solution with evidence (logos)
▶ Discusses feasibility of the solution: the time, money, and effort required
▶ Addresses possible objections

Conclusion
▶ Predicts positive outcomes of the solution
▶ Makes an emotional connection with the audience, linking the solution to their interests (pathos)

© 2013 Cengage Learning

solution? What needs to be done first, second, and next? How much time will it take? How much will it cost? Who needs to do what? And when?

The body of a proposal also acknowledges possible objections and criticisms (whether they have to do with the disadvantages of the solution, the superiority of another alternative, or the costs) by including a point-by-point defense of the solution. Successful proposals often discuss trade-offs in this section.

Finally, the conclusion of a proposal predicts the positive consequences or improvements that will result from the proposed solution. Also, the conclusion should make an emotional connection with the audience, using the rhetorical appeal of pathos. The goal is to identify the solution with the interests of the audience.

Revision and peer review

After you've drafted your proposal, ask one of your classmates to read it. You'll want your classmate to respond to your work in a way that helps you revise it into the strongest proposal it can be, one that addresses your intended audience, helps you fulfill your purpose, and is delivered in the most appropriate means available to you.

Questions for a peer reviewer

1. To what rhetorical opportunity is the writer responding? How does the writer define the problem to which he or she is responding?
2. Who might be the writer's intended audience?
3. Where does the writer indicate how the problem will affect the audience?
4. Identify the writer's thesis statement, in which the writer clearly states the solution he or she proposes. If you cannot locate a thesis statement, what thesis statement might work for this document?
5. Identify the evidence the writer provides in support of the proposed solution. Where does the writer address potential objections to the solution?
6. Identify the supporting ideas (presented through narration, cause-and-effect analysis, description, exemplification, process analysis, or definition) that the writer uses to support his or her assertions.

7. How feasible does the solution seem? What additional evidence could the writer provide to better support the solution's feasibility?
8. What does the solution ask of the audience? Is the requested action explicit or merely implied?
9. How does the writer make use of images? Is there any place where a graph or chart could be included, to display costs or otherwise provide readers with a sense of what will be expected of them or the community?
10. How does the writer establish pathos?
11. What did you learn from the conclusion that you didn't already know after reading the introduction and the body? What information does the writer want the reader to take away from the proposal? Does the writer attempt to change readers' attitudes, actions, or opinions?
12. What section of the proposal did you most enjoy? Why?

Online Proposal

The slide show *Universities in the "Free" Era,* by Peg Faimon and Glenn Platt, was delivered at the South by Southwest (SXSW) Interactive Conference and recorded so that it could be uploaded to Slideshare .net and viewed by more than just the original audience. To experience the slide show, find *Writing in Three Media* in your English Course-Mate, accessed through cengagebrain.com.

Courtesy of Glenn Platt, Armstrong Institute for Interactive Media Studies

Oral Proposal or Short Film

A short presentation by creativity expert Sir Ken Robinson, titled "Changing Education Paradigms," proposes a radical change in the conceptualization of public education and college. To view the video, find *Writing in Three Media* in your English CourseMate, accessed through cengagebrain .com.

Courtesy of the Royal Society for the Encouragement of Arts, Manufactures and Commerce (RSA)

Print Proposal

In the following proposal, student Ryan T. Normandin argues for continued funding for MIT's Open-CourseWare project, a program described in the article by Anya Kamenetz that begins on page 242 of this chapter.

Courtesy Ryan Normandin

Instead of writing a proposal, Ryan might have decided to write to an appropriate governing body at his school, such as a board of trustees, asking them to retain the OpenCourseWare program. Given the importance of the program to a national audience, he might also have created a Facebook page called "Save Funding for OpenCourseWare" and asked his Facebook friends to "Like" it and spread the word through their own extensive networks. But Ryan knew he needed to appeal to the community most affected by the MIT budget: MIT students, faculty, and staff. As a staff columnist for the student newspaper, he knew he could reach that audience through an editorial published in the print and online versions of that paper.

Proposals

OpenCourseWare and the Future of Education

by Ryan T. Normandin

As we are all aware, MIT has and will continue to make relatively large cuts to its budget in light of the recent financial meltdown. The administration established the Institute-Wide Planning Task Force to evaluate ways to make these cuts with minimal impact to the MIT community. One proposal is to cut funding to OpenCourseWare (OCW) or continue funding only until the grant funding that has paid for 72 percent of OCW since its creation runs out.

For those not familiar with OCW, it is a brilliant piece of intellectual philanthropy that MIT opened to the public in September of 2002. Essentially, anyone in the world can access the same knowledge and information that MIT students are inundated with by classes. Not just a few classes here and there in the most common disciplines—as of May 2006 there were 1400 courses online. This is an unbelievable resource that has been utilized by about 60 million people, both on and off the campus. Twenty years ago, the thought that one could log onto a computer and access nearly the entire curriculum at MIT would be unthinkable. But now it can be done.

The author demonstrates a clear understanding of OCW as he lists its benefits and costs.

Yet what of the costs? OCW is more than simply recording lectures and posting problem sets and exams. A dedicated staff is necessary to deal with publishing the various formats of media and keeping OCW updated and relevant. This sums to $4.1 million per year, although OCW has managed to cut about $500,000 from its budget in FY 2009. Since its creation, 22 percent of OCW's expenditures have been covered by the Institute, 72 percent has been paid for through grants from the William and Flora Hewlett Foundation and the Andrew Mellon Foundation, and 6 percent has been covered by donations, revenue, and other sources. Unfortunately,

In layman's terms, he explains how OCW works as well as the steps for implementing it.

grant funding runs out in two years. With that in mind, while many are asking how OCW can be sustained, others are wondering if it should be at all.

Answering this question necessitates a broader view on education. In the United States, the federal government provides free public education, grades K–12, to every citizen of the country. We take this for granted, but I cannot stress enough how utterly remarkable this actually is. Eighteen-year-olds leave high school with more knowledge than a citizen of the 18th century could even dream of. Knowledge of math that took the Greeks generations to uncover is imparted in a few weeks in a free high school math course to every American student. This model of education is absolutely revolutionary, and most take it for granted. The model clearly is not perfect, but it is certainly an excellent foundation upon which we can build.

However, once a student graduates from high school, a guaranteed free public education ends. From that point on, families must find a way to pay for a college education should a student decide to continue [his or her] studies. And, quite frankly, without a college degree, their horizons are extremely limited. Is this the right model? Sure, families can get loans, students can earn scholarships through hard work and dedication, and state colleges can attempt to increase accessibility by keeping costs low. Yet some students spend the rest of their lives paying off debt from college loans and others cannot even hope to afford it in the first place.

OCW is a way to remedy this inequity. With its immense power anyone, from the student who could not get accepted to any college to the senior citizen who is curious about quantum mechanics, can access information that historically has been restricted to those within the walls of a university. Thus, completely free, public education can continue beyond high school. Of course, no degree can be earned through the completion of an online

Ryan identifies a problem that affects many students.

He also demonstrates his understanding of the interests and needs of his audience.

The author offers a solution to the problem.

Proposals

OCW course, but the very fact that the dissemination of knowledge is no longer restricted to those who can afford it is valuable. We have unlocked the secrets of the human genome; we understand the motion of both the planets and subatomic particles; we comprehend things that people long ago could not even imagine. Why should that information be restricted to a select number of people?

Some argue against making this information accessible to everyone. Suppose MIT continues to make OCW accessible, even continuing to expand it. The average student at MIT can then simply go online to OCW and watch the lectures, do the problem sets, show up for the final, pass, and get a degree. This leads to empty lecture halls and vacant recitations. There is no longer a need for professors or TAs. But, detractors of universal knowledge claim, if all of the professors and TAs are let go, how can OCW continue to be updated?

A related argument states that if anyone can simply go online and access an MIT education, then what's the point of paying to attend the school? There goes MIT's source of income. Finally, some claim that the program is far too socialistic. These people feel that education must be earned. If you work hard through high school, get good grades, develop a good character, and manage to stand out, they claim that you will get into a school, earning the opportunities that will follow.

While respectable, none of these arguments hold enough sway to cut funding to OCW. The first argument will never actually come to fruition; videos for many classes' lectures, including 3.091 and 7.012 (Introduction to Solid-State Chemistry and Introductory Biology, respectively), are already posted online following the lecture. While some students take advantage of this, the lecture halls have yet to become empty. And if, hypothetically, such

The author understands the limitations of his proposed solution, as well as how this solution would affect his audience.

The author demonstrates his understanding of opposing views.

Proposals

a thing did happen as a result of an OCW-like program, all MIT would have to do is institute a mandatory attendance policy.

The author carefully addresses the short-comings of the opposing views.

• The answer to the second argument is quite simple: yes, anyone can essentially get an MIT education online, but you don't get the degree unless you attend the school. Without a degree in a certain course from an accredited institution, employers will not take you seriously. Claiming that you're qualified to operate a nuclear reactor because you "watched MIT lectures on it online" is not likely to convince an employer to hire you.

The final argument is more ideological. Once again, the age-old capitalism-versus-socialism debate. Opponents to OCW programs argue that not everyone has "a right" to this knowledge. People have spent lots of money, lots of time, and lots of ingenuity to develop the knowledge that we have today, and this should not simply be given away. Unless you're willing to earn it, it should not be made available to you.

Such a philosophy would also mean that opponents of OCW would also oppose the current public education system. In the end, what it comes down to is that the rich can get this knowledge while the poor are left out. Yes, a poor student who excels will get scholarships and admittance to universities and rich students who fail will not. However, an average poor student may get accepted but earn no scholarships. An average rich student may also get accepted and likewise earn no scholarships. But the only thing that differentiates these students is the wealth of their parents, the rich student will be able to afford a college education while the poor student will not. Any system that favors wealth over ability, character, and dedication is wrong.

MIT should continue to support OCW because it is the first step to promoting free public education at a higher level than grade 12. The

Proposals

academic climate in the United States is changing. Due to the tough economy, state colleges, which are the government's attempt to provide an affordable higher education, are becoming more competitive than ever before. The country is also undergoing an "inflation" of college degrees. While a bachelor's degree would get you nearly any job in the past, a bachelor's is now expected and it is a master's that provides better chances of getting a job today. Therefore, people who get rejected from a college or are unable to afford a higher education have far fewer opportunities than those who attain a bachelor's and master's degree.

Some might argue that if just anyone is let into college, then the country will be flooded with unqualified individuals. This is not true—as long as standards are kept high, individuals who are unqualified will flunk out and be unable to earn their degree. It is wrong to deny an individual the right to an education and, as a result, a good job with a livable wage, on the basis that their parents cannot afford it. For logical and moral reasons, free higher level education is a necessity. OpenCourseWare is a harbinger of the future of education, and MIT would do well to continue to ensure its continued availability. ●

Finally, the author asserts again why his proposal is a good one: it's the "future of education."

Alternatives to the Proposal

Fitting responses come in many forms, not just proposals. Your instructor might call on you to consider one of the following opportunities for writing.

1. Not everyone thinks that higher education needs to be improved. In an essay of three to four pages, discuss your positive college experiences. Be specific about these experiences and employ details and descriptions to support your assertions. Various rhetorical methods of development—process analysis, comparison and contrast, cause-and-consequence analysis, exemplification, and classification and division—may help you conceptualize and then arrange your essay.
2. Colleges and universities are often considered to be successful examples of planned public spaces. Identify a familiar public space on your campus

and, in an essay of three to four pages, evaluate it according to specific criteria (function, identity or character, arrangement, access and circulation, seating and refreshments, and so on). As you write, consider your audience (who may or may not share your ideas about criteria), your purpose (which should align with your audience), and the constraints and resources of your rhetorical situation.

3. Since you've started college, you've no doubt had to make adjustments to your daily life related to scheduling classes, studying, socializing, being with friends and family, and reaching your professional goals. Draft an essay of three to four pages in which you analyze the process of becoming a successful college student. Be sure to identify habits and practices that enhance and detract from student life and to consider your rhetorical opportunity, audience, purpose, constraints and resources, and available means.

Reviewing Visual Culture: Responding with Evaluations

It's more than likely that your first introduction to the college or university where you're now studying came through a brochure, a booklet, or a website describing the school's programs, its student body, and campus life. At the University of Kansas, prospective students can download the official KU app to their iPhones. Like the school's website, the iPhone app offers news, sports scores, campus photographs and maps, and a schedule of events, all awash in Jayhawk red and blue.

Students considering Lewis & Clark College in Portland, Oregon, can scroll through a host of photos and student blogs that depict "Real Life at Lewis & Clark College." Seeing images of real students and reading their accounts of

Courtesy of the University of Kansas

Real Life

A Journal By:

CAMPUS JOURNAL   CAMPUS JOURNAL   CAMPUS JOURNAL   CAMPUS JOURNAL   CAMPUS JOURNAL   CAMPUS JOURNAL

The Latest Posts

Maisha Foster-O'Neal: test run cooking

Springtime in Portland is always such a messy affair. In the past two weeks I've experienced shorts and mild sunburns, a series of deluges, cold winds, and a hail storm. Spring break itself tripped all over itself in the weather department. My brother came home from San Luis Obispo for spring break, and we spent our week just chilling out. We hiked to the top of **Multnomah Falls**, hill-walked Portland, threw sticks for our fetch-obsessed cocker spaniel Moki on **Sauvie Island** beach, and drank a lot of tea. I finally got around to seeing Avatar, but the 3-D glasses gave me a killer headache, because they didn't fit over my regular glasses very well. I also spent a good portion of break reading and researching for class.

A lot of the research I did over break was for my Gender in Relational Communication final project. I read academic articles

What is Real Life?

Real life is an online journal where students tell you their everyday — what it's like to live, breathe and study in Portland Oregon at Lewis & Clark. The Admissions Office has sponsored this journal since 2003. If you'd like, you can read some of the past five years of posts.

Topics

THE TOP THIRTY

dscn0151.JPG

See More

2009-10

April 2010

March 2010

February 2010

Courtesy of Lewis & Clark College

college life may persuade viewers that Lewis & Clark College is the place for them to pursue their undergraduate careers.

Web pages and phone apps—in addition to the countless brochures and pamphlets published in order to stimulate recruitment—are two means by which colleges and universities craft a recruitment message to send to prospective students and their parents. Each school wants potential students to appreciate all the available opportunities of that particular school and to imagine themselves as successful there. When you were a prospective student, it was up to you to decide how you were going to evaluate these highly visual messages.

Evaluations—spoken or written texts that argue whether something meets a particular set of criteria—are particularly useful for understanding how well individuals and groups portray themselves visually and what kinds of decisions readers or viewers make in response to those portrayals. Evaluations consider such questions as the following: What is the immediate overall effect of the visual? What are the specific parts of the visual? How are these parts pieced together? What is the overall effectiveness of the visual? These are the types of questions you will be asking and responding to in this chapter, questions that lead not only to detailed evaluations of images but also to thoughtful analyses of how the visual culture in which we are increasingly immersed is shaping our society.

Evaluations

IDENTIFYING AN OPPORTUNITY

Throughout this chapter, you will work to identify an opportunity to evaluate a visual element of our culture. As you determine the specific interest or appeal of this element (whether it's your school's or company's website, a product logo, an advertisement, the architecture of a familiar building, or a movie or video game), consider also the most fitting means of delivery for your evaluation:

Print Evaluation

written for a community or campus newspaper or local zine

Online Evaluation

posted on a film review site, a video game review site, or other website

Oral Evaluation

using video, a digital slide show, or presentation software and presented live to your rhetorical audience

To begin, freewrite for five minutes in response to each of the following questions (or use any of the invention techniques presented on pages 58–61):

1. Look at the images on the next few pages of this chapter. Which of them represent a designed space or object that is familiar to you? Which ones represent something unfamiliar? How do you ordinarily interact with the familiar scenes or objects? How might you interact with the unfamiliar ones?

2. What kinds of images or designed spaces do you encounter in your everyday life? What details of these images or designs do you find most memorable? How do you interact with or respond to these images or designs?

3. Which of the images in this section do you find especially interesting? Which ones would stimulate you to look twice or think more deeply were you to pass them on your way across campus?

4. What kinds of words would you use to describe the especially stimulating images? What specific details prompt you to think about these images in this particular way?

Real Situations

Once on campus, you are immersed in a sea of images, some that are portrayed in the official brochures and some that are not. On your walk to class, you may step over chalk drawings urging you to attend an upcoming lecture or pass by flyers urging you to participate in an upcoming Critical Mass bike ride. When eating lunch at the student union, you may glance at posters encouraging you to sell your chemistry textbook back to the bookstore during finals week. You may read advertisements in the student newspaper persuading you to spend your hard-earned money on dinner-and-drink specials at restaurants in town.

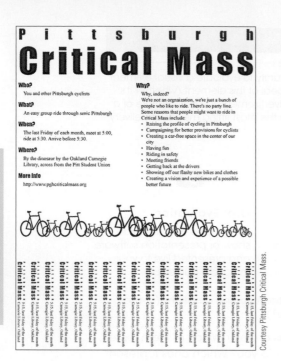

Courtesy Pittsburgh Critical Mass.

Flyers like this one are among the many visuals competing for attention on college campuses.

And while visiting your friend's dorm room, you may spend a few moments looking at the posters of abstract art or the hundreds of photos of her family and friends that she has scattered over every available inch of wall space. All of these kinds of visual texts use images as a means of capturing a particular mood, delivering a specific message, or provoking a specific action.

As you know well, personal computers, smartphones, and tablet computers are playing an increasingly central role in our leisure time, and as a result we are becoming ever more enmeshed in a world of images and multimedia, from the personal to the academic. Many students (maybe including you) present themselves through a careful construction of photos, videos, and text on a personal blog or on sites such as Facebook and Twitter. More students than ever before read about and watch the news on visually rich online magazines and newspapers, such as Salon.com, msnbc.com, FoxNews.com, and Yahoo! News. All of these sites offer visually intense environments, with photos and text situated alongside colorful banner ads, animated graphics, and links to sponsors' websites. And, in addition to tapping the resources of social and political sites, students are also taking advantage of the possibilities of academic-related multimedia sites by participating in online courses, viewing online slide shows for Art Appreciation 101, or creating, contributing to, and editing a course wiki.

The ways in which you and your fellow students experience visual culture do not end with the more obvious forms of photographs, posters, advertisements, web pages, and movies. The visual design of the buildings, green spaces, and monuments on your college or university campus creates a particular atmosphere. For example, the prominent Bonfire Memorial at Texas A&M University seeks to reinforce a deep respect for that school's unique traditions. The visual design of the classrooms and labs on your campus creates particular types of learning environments. The digital writing classrooms at Stanford University have been redesigned to foster collaboration and innovation, with computers clustered in groups of three to enable students to work on writing projects in teams. And the visual design of the chairs, tables, lights, and bookshelves in the Humanities Reading Room in Penn State University's Pattee Library creates a comfortable space in

Many dorm rooms are visual presentations of students' interests and self-image.

The Bonfire Memorial at Texas A&M University.

which students and faculty members are invited to focus their energy on their individual reading and writing projects.

If you look around your own campus, you'll see an environment rich in visuals. Whether or not you have thought much about it, living within this visual culture shapes the ways you seek and communicate information every day. Charles A. Hill, a professor of rhetoric and writing at the University of Wisconsin, Oshkosh, describes the effects in this way:

> [T]he students now entering our classrooms have grown up with one hundred channels of television, and the World Wide Web is no longer a novelty, but part of their social, academic, and working lives. If we include nonelectronic sources of visual communication such as billboards, print advertisements, and the ubiquitous packaging that has taken such an important place in our consumer culture, then we have to conclude that most of the information our students are exposed to is in a visual form.

For Hill, this high level of immersion in an increasingly visual culture calls for both teachers and students to know how to read what images communicate.

Courtesy of Alyssa O'Brien, Stanford University

A redesigned digital writing classroom at Stanford University allows for effective collaboration.

Courtesy of Public Relations and Marketing, Penn State University Libraries.

The Humanities Reading Room in Penn State University's Pattee Library.

DESCRIBING IMAGES ON CAMPUS

1. Choose two of the photographs in this section of the chapter and list the specific details you notice about the images—for example, the way objects and people are arranged, the lighting, or a contrast in color or sizes. Be prepared to share your answers with the rest of the class.

2. Who do you imagine designed the spaces or arranged the objects? Who produced the actual images?

3. What might be the rhetorical audience for and purpose of each image?

4. What adjectives come to mind when you consider these images? Which of the details that you used to answer question 1 illustrate each of those adjectives?

5. Translate the purposes, adjectives, and details into a single statement about each of the images. Then compose a list of criteria by which you might best evaluate each image. Be prepared to share your statement and list with the rest of the class.

Real Responses to Real Situations

One good way to explore visual culture in this country is to consider one of its most common forms: movies. In 2004, the average American watched more than two thousand hours of filmed entertainment, and the evaluation of movies in the United States is a mini-industry itself. We rely on the professional assessments of Roger Ebert and Gene Shalit, on publications such as *Entertainment Weekly* and websites such as rottentomatoes.com, and on the regular columns in our local and school newspapers. Every day, we have easy access to evaluations of this part of our visual culture—even though we don't always think in these terms when we search online for movie reviews or read an opinion piece about the latest crop of action films.

A reasonable and insightful movie evaluation includes judgments about overall quality, strengths and weaknesses, cast, setting, and technical features. In addition, a good evaluation might include a consideration of the cultural referents of the film, such as costumes or historical references in the movie's plot line. Whatever the reviewer argues, it is paramount that he or she supply specific evidence to support that claim (for example, that a movie is groundbreaking or derivative, suspenseful or confusing).

Evaluating the visual spectacle of a Hollywood film: *The Matrix*

One film that has generated an enormous amount of critical evaluation from a variety of perspectives is *The Matrix*, written and directed by Andy and Larry Wachowski. *The Matrix* was released in 1999 and was an instant box-office hit, generating $27.8 million in its opening weekend—the biggest opening weekend of that year. Not only was *The Matrix* widely reviewed, but it soon became the subject of articles, classroom discussions, and books. *The Matrix* proved to be one of those unusual films enjoyed by both casual moviegoers of a wide variety of ages, ethnicities, and regions and devoted fans who gave it cult status.

When *The Matrix* was first released, most people had never seen anything like it. The film combined cinematic techniques from popular Hong Kong action movies, kung fu films, and Japanese anime with sophisticated digital technology. One technique, which the directors call "bullet-time photography," gives key action sequences in the film a slow-motion, 360-degree view in which the characters appear to be able to halt or slow down time. This technique was combined with digital special effects and "wire" fighting scenes adapted from Asian martial arts movies to create a movie that was new and startling. As one reviewer for the *Village Voice* observed, "It's that rare sci-fi film that actually looked like it was from the future."

According to critic Joshua Clover, *The Matrix*'s story is based on two popular premises in many science fiction stories: "the war between man and machine, and the possibility that reality is a hoax." The movie is set in what may be the twenty-second century, when intelligent machines have taken over the world, conquered humanity, and turned people into living "battery packs" farmed by the machines for energy. The plot centers around a small band of free rebels (played by Keanu Reeves, Laurence Fishburne, Carrie-Anne Moss,

WARNER BROS. / THE KOBAL COLLECTION

The cast of *The Matrix*, a film that continues to inspire critical evaluation.

WARNER BROS. / THE KOBAL COLLECTION

and Joe Pantoliano) who are searching for "The One" to help them conquer the ruling machines and end the virtual reality called "The Matrix" that the machines have created to fool humanity.

The Matrix won four Academy Awards: Best Visual Effects, Best Film Editing, Best Sound, and Best Sound Effects Editing. It inspired two sequel films, *The Matrix Reloaded* (2003) and *The Matrix Revolutions* (2003), which most viewers judged to be disappointing in comparison with the original. Nonetheless, more than a dozen popular books on the film's cinematography, philosophy, religion, and artwork (just to name a few of the most common themes)—as well as countless reviews, fan sites, a comic book series, animated movies, and an online computer game—have since been published about *The Matrix*. The evaluative conversation about the meaning and merits of this movie is an active one.

In an early review of the film, professional film critic Kenneth Turan gave *The Matrix* a positive evaluation. Like many of the first reviewers, Turan praises the film primarily for its visual look and feel, its energy, and its action sequences. He clearly lays out all the criteria he uses to evaluate a film, and he provides vivid descriptions of scenes and characters to explain how he sees the film stacking up on these criteria. He acknowledges where *The Matrix* falls short, but he leaves readers with a strong sense that, overall, the movie's combination of interesting story line and innovative visual techniques makes it worth seeing.

> An Apocalypse of Kinetic Joy

Kenneth Turan

"Imagine you're feeling a little like Alice, tumbling down the rabbit hole," someone says in the dazzling and disorienting "The Matrix," and who has the strength to argue?

A wildly cinematic futuristic thriller that is determined to overpower the imagination, "The Matrix" combines traditional science-fiction premises with spanking new visual technology in a way that almost defies description. Like it or not, this is one movie that words don't come close to approximating.

Written and directed by the Wachowski brothers, Larry and Andy, "The Matrix" is the unlikely spiritual love child of dark futurist Philip K. Dick and the snap and dazzle of Hong Kong filmmaking, with digital technology serving as the helpful midwife.

Yet because this tale has been on the Wachowskis' minds for so long—it was written before their 1996 debut film, "Bound"—"The Matrix" never feels patched together. And its story, constructed though it is from familiar elements and pseudo-mystical musings, is nevertheless strong enough to support the film's rip-roaring visuals.

Thomas Anderson (Keanu Reeves), a software programmer in a world very much like our own who goes by his nighttime hacker moniker of Neo, has heard the Matrix whispered about his whole life, but no one knows what it is. All the beautiful Trinity (Carrie-Anne Moss of TV's "Dark Justice") can tell him is that "it's looking for you," which is certainly scary but not a great deal of help.

For that Neo has to turn to Trinity's partner, the legendary Morpheus (Laurence Fishburne), considered the most dangerous man alive by the authorities. What he says is more than frightening: What Neo thinks is the real world is no more than a computer-generated dreamscape, a virtual reality created by the artificial intelligence that really controls things to distract our human minds while our bodies are systematically plundered as an energy source to keep those nefarious machines up and running.

Sometimes those machines take human form as agents, robotic parodies of FBI men, like the chilling Agent Smith (Hugo Weaving of "Proof" and "The Adventures of Priscilla, Queen of the Desert"), who wear security earpieces, sunglasses and white shirts with ties and are terrifyingly close to indestructible.

These Matrix men have a special interest in Neo. There's a feeling in the air, one that Morpheus and his ragtag colleagues (including "Bound" veteran Joe Pantoliano) are tempted to share, that Neo might be the One, the foretold liberator who has the power to destroy the Matrix and free the human race. But only the Oracle (a fine cameo by Gloria Foster) knows for sure, and everything she says is, well, oracular.

Obviously, there's a great deal that's familiar about "The Matrix," starting with its sturdy themes of alternate realities, the deadly rivalry between men and machines, the resilient power of the human mind and the creeping dangers of conformity. And the film's fake-Zen dialogue, lines like "Don't think you are; know you are" and "There's a difference between knowing the path and walking the path," isn't going to win any ovations for originality.

On the other hand, the somber quality of the dialogue suits the apocalyptic quality of "The Matrix" story, and the gravity of the actors, especially the always magisterial Fishburne and the magnetically phlegmatic Reeves, makes the words more bemusing than bothersome.

Helping most of all are the riveting visuals shot by Bill Pope. The Wachowskis do have a taste for the bizarre (witness an electronic bug that turns into a body-piercing insect) but this tendency pays off in bravura moments like a mesmerizing vista of a body farm without end (inspired by the work of comic-book artist Geof

continued

Darrow) where humans are relentlessly harvested for energy like so many replaceable Eveready batteries.

Just as exciting are "The Matrix"'s two kinds of action sequences. One . . . involves John Woo–type expenditures of massive amounts of ammunition shot in super slow-motion and the other uses both Hong Kong–style stunt work and a technique the press notes refer to as "bullet-time photography" that involved shooting film at the computer-aided equivalent of 12,000 frames per second.

"The Matrix" cast members who were involved in the film's eye-catching kung fu fight sequences also apparently committed to four months of pre-production work with Hong Kong director and stunt coordinator Yuen Wo Ping, someone who specializes in the technique, known as wire fighting, that gives H.K. films like "Drunken Master," "Once Upon a Time in China" and "Fist of Legend" their distinctive high-flying look.

Not everything in "The Matrix" makes even minimal sense, but the Wachowski brothers, said to be major fans of comic books and graphic novels, are sure-handed enough to smoothly pull us over the rough spots. When a film is as successful as this one is at hooking into the kinetic joy of adrenalized movie making, quibbling with it feels beside the point.

Taking a different position from Kenneth Turan's largely positive review, Bob Graham, senior writer for the *San Francisco Chronicle*, argues that *The Matrix*'s technology is all the movie actually is, calling the movie a "pretentious sci-fi thriller" that is "also a special effects spectacle" but not a memorable film. For him, special effects alone do not a movie make. "Technical expertise and visual imagination" should always be put in the service of plot development and character growth.

> Lost in the Matrix

Bob Graham

The Keanu Reeves cyberspace opera, "The Matrix," is a wonderful movie to chew up and spit out.

Larry and Andy Wachowski, the hotshot-brothers writing and directing team, clearly set out to astonish with this one, and they certainly do.

It's astonishing that so much money, talent, technical expertise and visual imagination can be put in the service of something so stupid.

Folly on such a monumental scale is almost exhilarating.

So this is what more than 100 years of cinema history has come to: special effects with no movie.

"The Matrix" is about nothing less than the nature of reality, heaven help us. The Wachowskis have discovered that there is a real world behind the apparent one. This may be a tremendous subject in the hands of somebody like Plato, but when the Wachowskis get their mitts on it, watch out. Somebody ought to adjust their medication.

If anybody ever wanted to see Reeves shaved naked and covered with slime, now is the chance.

He plays a computer hacker who stumbles into a vague awareness—with him, everything is vague—that this world is but the dim reflection of a controlling cyberworld "out there."

"The Matrix" is the film that asks the question, "Ever had that feeling you're not sure if you're awake or still dreaming?"

Frequently.

Characters have names like Neo, Morpheus, Trinity and Cypher that take us into the quagmire of allegory, and the unfortunate actors attached to these names have to deliver speeches accordingly.

"It's like a splinter in your mind driving you mad," someone says. Splinters in your mind will do that.

This movie is so pretentious that it invites speculation in kind. The neo-Wagnerian soundtrack score falsely raises hopes that "The Matrix" has aspirations of becoming the all-encompassing multimedia philosophical artwork that the German genius might have created if only moving pictures hadn't waited so long to be invented. In fact, the Wachowskis seem to be masters of the Wagnerian art of transition. In one stunning shot, the camera closes in on a static TV monitor view of Reeves in an interrogation room. The camera seamlessly merges into the shot on the monitor and then independently moves about the interrogation room. It is breathtaking, and there are other displays of visual virtuosity that almost equal it, including a shot into a fiber-optics cable. To say nothing of the insect-like monsters, among them one that enters Reeves' belly button.

As he moves back and forth between this world and that, Reeves materializes at one point as a kung fu artist. After the audience gets though digesting that one, he flies through the air like a refugee from some Hong Kong fantasy, more empty technical razzmatazz.

Maybe the DVD version will have an option to eliminate the dialogue, but in the meantime we have to put up with oppressive acting here.

We know that Reeves is puzzled about which reality he currently occupies because he squinches up his eyebrows. Laurence Fishburne has the chore, as a mysterious cyberworld overlord, of making absolute nonsense sound like he believes it. He does this by e-nun-ci-a-ting every syllable.

In a throwback to the Wachowskis' "Bound," Carrie-Anne Moss in black leather plays the Gina Gershon ambiguous lesbian character.

Australian actor Hugo Weaving ("The Adventures of Priscilla, Queen of the Desert") is a "Men in Black"-style special agent. His mannered performance is briefly fun until it becomes apparent that's all there is and he intends to go on and on with it.

As one of the overlord's underlings, Joe Pantoliano ("The Fugitive") at first seems to be the actor who will rescue the honor of the profession. He is the only one who has a spark of wit, but even he is eventually swamped by the hopeless muddle that "The Matrix" becomes.

Like Turan, Graham weighs various criteria (plot, visual effects, character development, and acting) in order to evaluate *The Matrix,* and he presents in clear terms how he sees the film meeting or falling short of each one. For him, the plot is "about nothing less than the nature of reality," which merits his scoff, "heaven help us." And the visual look that Turan found so stunning and difficult to put into words seems to Graham to consist of "money, talent, technical expertise, and visual imagination. . . . put in the service of something . . . stupid." Graham calls out the allegorical names of the characters (Neo, Morpheus, Trinity, and Cypher), lamenting that the "unfortunate actors attached to these names have to deliver speeches accordingly." And he criticizes the acting itself, citing Keanu Reeves' movie-long puzzlement, enacted by "squinch[ing] up his eyebrows," and Laurence Fishburne's demonstration of his mysterious character by "e-nun-ci-a-ting every syllable" of his nonsensical dialogue. Thus, even though Graham presents a set of evaluation criteria similar to those of Turan, Graham arrives at a markedly different conclusion, a negative conclusion that he supports with specific evidence and compelling examples. Ultimately, both Turan and Graham are trying to persuade their readers that the criteria they use to evaluate the film (and the examples from the film to which they apply the criteria) are the most important ones to consider.

> ANALYZING THE RHETORICAL SITUATION

1. State Kenneth Turan's main evaluative claim about *The Matrix* in one sentence. What reason(s) does Turan use to support his claim? What specific evidence does he provide to support his reason(s)?

2. State Bob Graham's main evaluative claim in one sentence. What reason(s) does he use to support his claim? What specific evidence does he provide to support his reason(s)? How is some of the same evidence used by Turan used differently in this evaluation?

3. You have read both a positive review of *The Matrix* (Turan's) and a negative one (Graham's). Which one seems more persuasive to you? Why? Be prepared to share your answer with the class.

COMMUNITY CONNECTIONS

1. Write for ten minutes about your response to one of the evaluations of *The Matrix.* How do the various elements of the movie that this evaluation explores coincide with or diverge from the elements that you normally consider when evaluating a movie?

2. Now write for ten minutes about the other evaluation of *The Matrix.* What criteria does the writer use to evaluate the movie, and how are these criteria similar to or different from the criteria that you use to evaluate a film?

3. What visually compelling images on your campus or in your community have grabbed your attention over the past few weeks? Write for ten minutes about your initial impressions of one visually compelling image. Describe, with as much detail as you can, the image and the context in which you first saw it.

4. Now consider the rhetorical situation for the image you've just described: Who created this image? Who was intended to see and respond to the image? What rhetorical opportunity might have prompted this image?

5. What criteria would you use to evaluate the image you've described? On what basis would you evaluate it?

6. What do you understand to be the purpose of evaluating the visual elements in our everyday lives? What particular kinds of rhetorical situations call for evaluation, and what does evaluation allow us to do in response to those situations?

Evaluating visual culture in our everyday lives

We tend to think first of television, movies, magazines, and other media when we consider visual culture. In doing so, we overlook other visual elements we encounter every day: an attractive chair in the student lounge, a sign on a storefront, a new laptop computer, the look of a coffee mug, a canvas tote bag, or a backpack. The designers who created these objects considered not only the object's function and purpose but also how the object's aesthetic dimensions influence the user's experience with it. Just as we can analyze and evaluate movies, we can assess the ways in which the design of everyday objects speaks to our needs for function and aesthetic pleasure.

One of the most everyday of everyday objects is the reusable tote bag. In response to the proliferation of those lightweight plastic bags that have replaced brown paper bags—and begun to clog our waterways, landfills, and roadsides—grocery stores, discount retailers, and high-end boutiques are all pushing their own brands of reusable bags. Often artfully designed with catchy sayings, these tote bags are one way to "go green," now that going green has become fashionable. In the following essay written for the blog *Design Observer*, Dmitri Siegel, Web art director for Urban Outfitters, evaluates the trend in reusable tote bags.

> Paper, Plastic, or Canvas?

Dmitri Siegel

Amidst all the despair in the last few years about the slow extinction of various design-friendly formats—the vinyl LP, the newspaper, the book, etc.—one vehicle for graphic design has vaulted to almost instant ubiquity: the canvas tote. The medium is not new, of course. Public television stations have been giving them

continued

"Whale" tote bag, Hugo Guiness, 2008.

"Jacobs by Marc Jacobs . . ." tote bag, Marc Jacobs, 2008.

away during fund-raisers for decades and L. L. Bean's "Boat and Tote" has been a New England staple even longer. But the timely environmental appeal of these reusable bags and the easy application of graphics catapulted the canvas tote from the health food store to the runway in a few short years. Graphic designers have embraced the form as a venue for their imagery and messages on par with the tee shirt. The ensuing glut of these bags, however, raises questions about the sustainability of any product regardless of the intention behind it, and the role that design plays in consumption.

It's difficult to pinpoint when the recent canvas tote craze really started, but there was a pivotal moment two years ago when Anya Hindmarch released the "I'm Not a Plastic Bag" tote in collaboration with the global social change movement We Are What We Do. The bag was originally sold in limited numbers at Hindmarch boutiques, Colette and Dover Street Market in London, but when it went into wide release at Sainsbury's 80,000 people lined up to get one. When the bag hit stores in Taiwan, there was so much demand that the riot police had to be called in to control a stampede, which sent 30 people to the hospital. Suddenly the formerly crunchy canvas tote had cachet.

Marc Jacobs skewered his own eponymous empire with his "marc by marc for marc" tote. This fascination with cheap bags seemed like part reaction to and part extension of the high-end handbag frenzy that gripped the fashion industry for much of the 00s. It had all the same qualities of exclusivity and brand envy, but also seemed at least in part to be an acknowledgment that things had gone too far. Was Mr. Jacobs' self-mocking tote a *mea culpa* for the astronomical handbag prices he had helped engineer at Louis Vuitton or was it a sly attempt to mainstream the phenomenon?

Simultaneous with the fashion world's affair with the tote, the graphic design community seemed to rediscover this humble sack. The canvas tote is a great medium for graphic design because it is flat and easy to print on. The canvas provides a beautiful off-white ground and the material is as wonderfully suited to silk-screen printing as primed canvas is to oil paint. The recent show at Open Space in Beacon, NY demonstrated the material appeal of the bags and the adaptability of their flat surface. Short-run printing and the quick transfer of graphic files make it remarkably easy to produce a relatively high quality bag. Design blogs have become enthralled by the never-ending stream of canvas totes—each one made unique by a clever and/or beautiful graphic.

But the primary reason that designers in both fields have embraced canvas totes so quickly and nearly universally is their compelling social benefits. Not only is canvas a renewable resource, but the bags are biodegradable and sturdy enough to stand up to years of use. Reusing canvas bags could reduce the number of plastic bags that are used and discarded every year. According to Vincent Cobb, founder of reusablebags.com, somewhere between 500 billion and a trillion plastic bags are consumed worldwide each year. The impact of the super-thin plastic bags given away free with purchase at supermarkets and shops is so severe that governments from Ireland to San Francisco to China have banned their distribution altogether.

With the devastating effects of global warming and pollution becoming a feature of everyday life, designers and consumers alike latched onto [the] reusable canvas tote as a tangible step they could take to help the environment. Canvas totes are often cited as an example of how good design can help the environment because of the promise that they will replace plastic bags.

Ironically, however, [the] plastic bag problem can in large part be traced back to the quality of its design as well. Before the introduction of the ultra thin plastic bags in the 1980s groceries were packed almost exclusively in paper bags. Plastic bags were touted as a way to save trees. Within a few years plastic was dominant and now commands 80% of grocery and supermarket traffic. Comparing a plastic bag to a paper bag, it is easy to see why: the ultra thin plastic bag is a vastly superior design. It consumes 40 percent less energy, generates 80 percent less solid waste, produces 70 percent fewer atmospheric emissions, and releases up to 94 percent fewer water-borne wastes. A plastic bag costs roughly a quarter as much to produce as a paper bag and is substantially lighter so it takes a great [deal] less [. . .] fossil fuel to transport. Plastic bags are among the most highly reused items in the home and are just as recyclable as paper.

The problem is that what is marvelous about an individual plastic bag becomes menacing when multiplied out to accommodate a rapidly growing global economy. The low cost of the bags allowed merchants to give them away, and despite the strength of an individual bag, they are routinely packed with a single item or double-bagged unnecessarily. The bag was so cleverly designed that there is simply no barrier to their indiscriminate distribution. Their incredible durability means it can take up to hundreds of years for them to decompose (a process that releases hazardous toxins). Although plastic bags are recyclable, the evidence suggests that even after ten years, in-store recycling programs have barely managed to achieve a one percent recycle rate. It is simply too easy and efficient to keep making and distributing more plastic bags. Meanwhile consumers mistakenly try to recycle the bags through their curbside recycling programs (perhaps because of the recycle symbols printed on the bags), creating a sorting nightmare at recycling facilities across the country.

Are we headed for the same kind of catch-22 with the adoption of the cleverly designed canvas tote with its renewable materials and infinite potential for customization? I am certainly an outlier in this case but I recently found twenty-three canvas totes in my house. Most of them were given to me as promotional materials for design studios, start-ups, boutique shops; more than one came from an environmental event or organization; one even commemorates a friend's wedding. A local community group recently delivered a reusable shopping bag to every house in my neighborhood to promote local holiday shopping. On the one hand all this interest in reusable bags is inspiring, but just like the story of Anya Hindmarch's "I'm Not a Plastic Bag" it also reveals the fundamental contradiction of the canvas tote phenomenon. Best intentions are almost immediately buried under an avalanche of conspicuous consumption and proliferation of choice. The environmental promise of reusable bags becomes pretty dubious when there are closets and drawers full of them in every home.

This contradiction can largely be traced back to the influence of graphic design. Once this gorgeous flat surface presented itself, it quickly became simply a substrate

ABCDEF GHIJKLM NO PQRSTU VWXYZ

Daniel Eatock/Eatock Ltd.

"Alphabet" tote bag, Daniel Eatock, 2008.

continued

"For Like Ever" tote bag, Village.

Design: Tracy Jenkins of Village / Photo: Rey Banogon

for messaging, branding, promotion, etc. Judging by the cost, producing one tote is roughly equivalent to producing 400 plastic bags. That's fine if you actually use the tote 400 times, but what if you just end up with 40 totes in your closet? Once the emphasis shifts from reusing a bag to having a bag that reflects your status or personality, the environmental goal starts drifting out of sight.

I could not find any data on the subject of how much the use of canvas totes has decreased the number of plastic bags, but at best the totes can only be a catalyst for the act of reusing. Designers are correct in thinking that making a more appealing bag increases the likelihood that it will be reused, but the environmental benefit does not come from people acquiring bags. It comes from people reusing them. Successful attempts to reduce the number of plastic bags have all focused on (not surprisingly) depressing the consumption of plastic bags. For example, in 2001, Ireland consumed 1.2 billion plastic bags, or 316 per person. In 2002 they introduced what they called a PlasTax—15 cents for every plastic bag consumed. The program reduced consumption of plastic bags in that country by 90%! This seems to undercut the whole strategy of selling canvas totes as a way to help the environment. Based on the Irish example, even a 15 cent price-tag might actually inhibit the use of canvas totes by 90%. In terms of actually reducing the number of plastic bags, programs like the one at IKEA, which charges customers 5 cents per plastic bag and donates the proceeds to a conservation group, are probably more likely to have an impact than selling a canvas alternative. The best thing for the environment is reuse and that can be accomplished just as easily by reusing plastic bags.

The canvas tote is a great example of the power and the paradox of design in a consumer society. On the one hand design has allowed for personal expression, and fantastic variation in an otherwise mundane object. Every well-designed tote has the potential to replace some of the estimated 1000 plastic bags that each family brings home every year. The aesthetic power of a single design raised more awareness about the impact of plastic bags on our environment than any government or non-governmental organization. On the other hand, it is unclear that a consumable can counteract the effects of consumption. The designs that make each bag unique contribute to an over-abundance of things that are essentially identical and the constant stream of newness discourages reuse. Just as the remarkable efficiency of the plastic bag ended up making it a menace to the environment, graphic design's ability to generate options and choices may turn a sustainable idea into an environmental calamity.

The following essay, which appeared on the *Art & Design* blog of the British newspaper the *Guardian*, is the twelfth in Jonathan Glancey's series of evaluations of everyday objects. In his series, Glancey asks readers to reappreciate the form and design of the ordinary paper clip, to pause a moment to admire the "smartly uniformed, practical, and long-lived" UPS trucks passing them on the street, and, in the following posting, to share his pleasure in the neon light.

Evaluations

> Classics of Everyday Design No 12

Jonathan Glancey

Stepping out of Copenhagen station a few weeks ago in the winter dark, I felt welcomed by the colourful glow of the rooftops of the otherwise straight-laced office blocks and hotels of the close-by neighbourhood. These are crowned with neon advertisements. Nothing fancy, and yet warm, alive and happily cheerful in the otherwise biting winter gloom.

Here is an example of subtle neon lighting used to make a winter night in a dark and cold winter city shine like some modern, and urban, equivalent of Jacob's coat of many colours. Not exactly Piccadilly Circus, not quite Times Square, but rainbow-like, heart-warming and fun.

The neon sign is indeed one of the great everyday classic designs. It can be subtle. It can be all singing, all dancing, yet never ever dull.

The mastermind, and master eye, behind the cheerful neon sign was Georges Claude (1870–1960), a French chemist, engineer and inventor. Claude discovered that an electric charge applied to a sealed tube of neon gas would produce a joyous coloured light. Red. And, that other of the family of gases to which neon belongs, treated in the same way, would bring alive other colours, too. Blue in the case of mercury. White with CO_2. Helium turned gas and electricity to gold. Phosphor-coated glass tubes could spin any number of colours—some 150 to date.

Neon itself had been identified by the British scientists, William Ramsey and M. W. Travers, in 1898; yet, it was up to Claude to suggest its popular and commercial potential. The gas was certainly special—just one part in 65,000 of the Earth's atmosphere—but once distilled, could enliven shops, arcades, squares and city centres from Los Angeles via London to Rome and Shanghai.

Claude demonstrated the first neon sign in Paris at the World Expo of 1910, although the first commercial application—above the door of a Parisian barber's shop—had to wait another two years. Claude first exported the invention, or concept, to the US in 1923 when ritzy neon lamps showcased a Packard car dealer's showroom in Los Angeles, and the rest was colourfully-lit history.

Neon lighting can, of course, be wholly over-the-top, and absurdly vulgar; yet, at its best, it warms the cockles, and cornices, of any number of otherwise dark buildings and glum streets in winter, and whenever, in fact, the blazing sun, all hydrogen and helium, and only a tiny bit of neon, disappears.

Evaluations

> ANALYZING THE RHETORICAL SITUATION

1. Look again at the photographs of the various canvas tote bags. What do these images convey to you about the bags' surge in popularity?
2. What specific features of a tote bag does Dmitri Siegel evaluate?
3. What criteria does he use to evaluate the simple tote bag? How does he describe the various totes in terms of these criteria?
4. Who is the specific audience for each of the two evaluations in this section? What purpose does each writer hope to achieve? How does that purpose relate to the audience for each evaluation?
5. What kinds of specific details and evidence does each writer provide in order to evaluate the everyday object? What rhetorical method(s) of development does each author use? What kinds of questions do the writers ask about tote bags or neon lights in order to draw out these types of details and evidence?
6. What rhetorical opportunity prompted each of the visual evaluations in this section? How would you characterize each one's contribution to the ongoing professional and public conversation about everyday design?

COMMUNITY CONNECTIONS

1. Write for ten minutes about your response to the evaluation of the tote bag. How do the criteria used by the writer coincide with or diverge from the criteria that you would apply to evaluate a tote bag you use every day? How do those criteria relate to those you consider most important for evaluating some other common object?

2. Write for ten minutes about the evaluation of the neon light. What criteria does the writer use to evaluate neon lights? How do these criteria relate to those you consider most important for evaluating a light or another common object?

3. What object other than a tote bag or a neon light that you encounter every day has a design that affects how you work or play? Who made the design decisions that shaped this object? How and why do you come into contact with this object?

4. Write for ten minutes about the design of the object you chose in question 3. Provide as many specific visual and tactile details as you can in describing it. Then, write for five minutes about the ways in which you use this object. Be sure to specify where and when (places and time of day) you use it. Finally, write for five minutes about how the visual design of this object affects your attitude toward the work or play that you do. Be prepared to share your answers.

Evaluations: A Fitting Response

The readings in this chapter illustrate the use of evaluation to understand how visual elements shape our everyday experiences. Visual effects in movies such as *The Matrix* can lead us, in the words of Morpheus, to "free our minds" and consider the limits of human thought. A nighttime walk down a neon-lit city street can lead us, like Jonathan Glancey, to take pleasure in the efficient functioning of everyday objects. Clearly, evaluating visuals in our culture helps us to better understand the logical and emotional responses they produce in us.

An evaluation of images in contemporary culture

As you have seen throughout this chapter, there are many visual elements in our culture that affect the ways in which we live and work, whether we realize it or not. Critics compose evaluative essays as a means for exploring the ways in which our lives are shaped by images and design. In the following essay, critic Mike D'Angelo evaluates two movies in terms of the technique used in their creation.

Unreally, Really Cool: Stop-Motion Movies May Be Old School, but They Still Eat Other Animation for Breakfast

Reprinted by permission.

Mike D'Angelo

As a filmgoer, I have virtually no allegiances. My goal is basically to avoid things that suck. However brilliant the actor, I have no interest in watching him sort his laundry or demonstrate that even the mentally retarded can be wonderful parents, thereby teaching Michelle Pfeiffer the true meaning of family. You say your movie is about lesbian vampire Catholic schoolgirls on a submarine? It may take zero stars from every critic on the face of the planet to keep me away . . . but if it does get the pan of a lifetime, I can resist. Or at least wait for the DVD.

That said, no amount of negative buzz could keep me away from two of this season's tastiest offerings: Tim Burton's *Corpse Bride* . . . and *Wallace & Gromit: The Curse of the Were-rabbit*. . . . If there's one thing in the vast world of cinema that qualifies as inherently compelling, that thing is stop-motion animation. Almost as old as the medium itself—you can see stop motion at work in Georges Méliès's classic short *A Trip to the Moon* (1902)—the basic process has remained unchanged. The original King Kong, the dueling skeletons in Ray Harryhausen

© Louis Quail/Corbis

The writer provides a succinct definition of the phenomenon he will evaluate.

adventures, the barnyard animals in *Chicken Run*—all involve miniature puppets being painstakingly manipulated one frame at a time. •

Pixar may have the most consistently impressive track record since the glory days of Walt Disney, but a Pixar CG [computer-generated] movie with a mediocre script and generic voice characterizations would be . . . well, it'd be *Madagascar*. Traditional cel animation, too, no matter how beautiful, can be deadly dull. Stop motion is different. There is no such thing as a stop-motion film that isn't fascinating to watch. Obviously, some are better than others—and there's reason to hope that *Corpse Bride*, a typically macabre Burton fable about a man who inadvertently marries a cadaver, and *Were-rabbit*, the long-awaited feature debut of Nick Park's beloved duo, will both be terrific. But all of them share the same singular, outré visual allure.•They're uncanny.

One criterion D'Angelo will use is whether the film is "outré"— unconventional or eccentric.

Consider Gromit.•(I've been waiting years to say that.) If you've seen any of Park's Oscar-winning shorts about the adventures of a cheerful English nincompoop and his faithful, tolerant canine companion, you're familiar with the character's look and temperament: big floppy ears, deep-set goggle eyes, silently unperturbable demeanor. You probably have a favorite Gromit moment, and it probably involves nothing more dynamic than a single styptic blink in response to escalating lunacy. But I submit that Gromit would not be half as funny or as endearing were he hand drawn or computer generated, no matter how expertly the animators replicated his appearance and mannerisms. Whether we're conscious of it or not, his oddball charisma is rooted in a combination of tactility and artificiality that's unique to stop motion.•It's a very different kind of response from the one we have to Dumbo or Buzz Lightyear. We love Gromit because he's at once real and not real.

The word *Consider* signals that the writer is going to begin providing evidence and examples to support his claim.

D'Angelo introduces two more criteria: the objects on the screen should combine tactility and artificiality.

Human beings are drawn to borders, gray areas, the mystery of the in-between. The director's favorite time of day is dusk, also known as the "magic hour": no longer light, not yet dark. Many movie stars have vaguely androgynous features (Julia Roberts looks exactly like Eric Roberts to me), and movies themselves tend to appeal to us the more they resemble our dreams, that world weirdly suspended between waking and sleeping. What makes stop motion so arresting, regardless of whether we're involved in the story or the characters, is that it pushes this dichotomy one step further, straddling the line that separates reality from imagination.•Cel animation and computer animation, no matter how aesthetically pleasing, never offer anything more than a simulacrum of reality; they are clearly make-believe. But when we look at one of the grandiosely morbid sets in Burton's *The Nightmare Before Christmas*, we can plainly see that those ornate tombstones and grinning jack-o'-lanterns and curlicue hills are really there, physically present. (The next time you watch *Nightmare*, notice how many objects have grooves cut into them, or have surfaces that are stippled. That sort of three-dimensional detail works only in stop motion.) And there's something oddly riveting about watching puppets navigate this tactile landscape 1/24 of a second at a time.

One more criterion D'Angelo uses to evaluate animated films is the blurring of the line between reality and imagination.

That's another thing about stop motion: There are no shortcuts. Cel animation is exacting work, but there are numerous ways to economize, as any *Speed Racer* fan knows all too well. Computer animation allows for endless revision. But stop motion is always and only moving everything a fraction of an inch, taking a picture, moving everything a fraction of an inch, taking a picture—day in, day out, for years and years. Screw something up and you have to do it all . . . over . . . again. It's like building a skyscraper using a pair of tweezers. Consequently, the folks who toil in this nearly moribund field tend to be perfectionists— not just when it comes to technical matters but in every aspect of filmmaking.•*Corpse Bride* and *Were-rabbit* don't have to be good. But I bet you they will be.

D'Angelo makes a final assertion to persuade readers— that the people who make stop-motion animated films attend to all the specific details that make an animated film great.

Understanding the Rhetorical Situation

When you want to present your thoughts on a facet of visual culture, you want to consider composing an evaluation. Evaluations commonly have the following features:

- Evaluations describe the particular object or phenomenon in a way that the rhetorical audience will understand.
- Evaluations make clear why a particular object or phenomenon should be evaluated.
- Evaluations identify the precise category into which the object or phenomenon fits.
- The criteria on which the object or phenomenon is to be evaluated are presented clearly.
- Concrete evidence and examples illustrate the ways in which the object or phenomenon does or does not meet each evaluative criterion.
- Evaluations articulate a clear argument about whether or not the object or phenomenon meets the criteria on which it is being evaluated.

The following sections will help you evaluate an element of visual culture. To work with an online guide to the elements of the rhetorical situation, access your English CourseMate through cengagebrain.com.

Identifying an opportunity

Consider your campus. Are there any buildings with unarguably unique architecture? Are there any pages on the school's website that are either visually compelling or aesthetically uninspired? Are there any advertisements in the campus newspaper, in a building stairwell, or on a campus bus that you think have particularly innovative imagery or layout? Is there any public artwork that made you do a double-take when you first walked by it? Are there any computer labs that make you feel mentally and physically exhausted—or all revved up? Are there any couches or chairs in the common area of your dormitory that seem to be particularly inviting—or just the opposite? Are any of your friends' dorm rooms creatively decorated?

1. Make a list of five interesting images or designs that you have noticed over the past week, a list that might include some elements you wrote about in response to the questions on page 277. For each one, write a few sentences describing your initial impressions. Were your impressions positive or negative? Provide as many details as you can to explain why. Also identify the contextual factors that may have shaped your impression of each image or design: where and when (place and time of day) you saw it, what you were doing at that time, the emotion or response evoked.

2. Choose two of the images or designs you listed and take photos of them. Pay particular attention to documenting the physical context in which the image or design appears.

3. Choose the image or design you want to write about and compose four or five sentences that describe its visual features in concrete, specific detail. After composing these descriptions, spend several minutes freewriting about the context of the image or design. Respond to questions such as these: What do you think the purpose of this image or design might be? When and where do you tend to interact with it in your everyday life? If you are writing about the visual design of an everyday object, what are the purposes for which you use the object? If you are writing about an image, how do you view it and in what ways do you interpret it and make sense of it?

Locating an audience

The following questions can help you locate your rhetorical audience as well as identify the relationship they have to the visual element you're writing about. Answering them can help you determine the best way to present your evaluation of that image or design.

1. List the names of the persons or groups—students, faculty, administrators, community members, alumni, parents—most likely to see and be affected by the visual element you've chosen. These are potential audiences for your evaluation.

2. Next to the name of each audience, write reasons that audience might have for thinking in greater depth about this particular image or design. In other words, what would persuade these audiences that the visual element needs to be evaluated?

3. How could each of these audiences reasonably be influenced by an evaluation of this image or design? In other words, what emotional responses could they be expected to have or what logical conclusions could they be expected to arrive at after reading your evaluative essay? Consider what motivations each group might have for analyzing the specific details that make up an object's design or an image's composition.

4. With your audience's interests and motivations in mind, look again at the descriptions of the image or design that you composed in the preceding section. Which description(s) will enable your readers to feel engaged in your evaluation and invested in exploring this image or design in greater depth? The better description not only allows readers to create a vivid mental picture of the visual element but also helps them understand why and how it affects them. At this point, it may be necessary to revise your best description to tailor it to your audience's needs and interests.

Identifying a fitting response

As you know, narrowing your purpose is important, because different purposes require different kinds of texts, delivered through different media. For example, if you are evaluating an image such as a photograph or a painting, you might want to compose an essay that would appear as part of a museum display or in an exhibition catalog. Your evaluation of a visually uninspiring web page could be crafted as a letter to the staff in the admissions or alumni relations office. Your evaluation of the dysfunctional design of a computer lab could take the form of a pamphlet or flyer to be distributed to other students in order to gain their support for change. The point is that once you have identified your opportunity, audience, and purpose, you need to determine what kind of text will best respond to your rhetorical situation.

Use the following questions to help you narrow your purpose and shape your response:

1. What kinds of facts or details about the image or design do you need to provide in order to precisely define the contexts in which it influences or interacts with people's everyday lives on campus?
2. What kinds of facts or details about the visual image or visual design make it particularly compelling?
3. What cultural, social, economic, or political details do you need to know in order to better understand the purpose of this visual design and its significance for the people who created it as well as for the people who interact with it, whether regularly or only once?
4. Are you asking the audience to adopt a new perspective on this particular object or image, or do you want the audience to perform a particular action in response to your writing?
5. What is the best way to reach this audience? That is, what kind of text is this audience most likely to respond to? (Chapter 13 can help you explore options for media and design.)

Writing an Evaluation: Working with Your Available Means

Shaping your evaluation

You are no doubt familiar with evaluations because you have seen many examples of this genre in the form of movie reviews in newspapers and magazines and product reviews in print and online publications such as *Consumer Reports* and *PC Magazine*. What you may not have noticed, however, are the ways in which evaluations use the rhetorical methods of development. For instance, the introduction of an evaluation provides readers with a concise definition of what is to be evaluated, the reasons it merits evaluation, and the particular ways in which it is to be evaluated. By the end of the introduction, then, the writer has begun to establish his or her expertise and good sense, asserting a position as a qualified evaluator and thereby establishing his or her ethos. For example, by the end of his second paragraph, Mike D'Angelo has provided a brief definition of stop-motion animation ("miniature puppets being painstakingly manipulated one frame at a time") and explained how he thinks animated films should be evaluated (by whether

pages 64–66

or not they provide compelling movie-going experiences). Writers of evaluations also use the introduction to show readers why they need to consider the evaluation. D'Angelo is no exception: he tells readers that two stop-motion movies will be released soon. By providing an in-depth explanation, D'Angelo establishes his expertise and knowledge.

pages 75–77

The body of an evaluation generally provides the criteria according to which the particular object or phenomenon will be evaluated. These criteria help make—and shape—the argument at the same time that they establish the logos (the logical appeals) of the evaluation. To accompany each criterion (and further emphasize logos), the writer offers facts and direct quotations to show how the object or phenomenon does or does not meet it. The body of an evaluation also describes the object or phenomenon in as much specific detail as possible, again maintaining the appeal to logos. Photos and audio or video clips can

pages 64–66

help provide details, as can careful verbal description. Readers of D'Angelo's essay, for example, can imagine Gromit's "big floppy ears, deep-set goggle eyes, silently unperturbable demeanor" and see the grooves cut into the tombstones in *The Nightmare Before Christmas*. These details grab and maintain the readers' interest. Just as important, sensory details help the writer to persuade his or her readers that the evaluation is based on a careful, complete analysis of all the elements that make up the object or phenomenon, and they provide the evidence to support the writer's argument and make the readers believe that it is based on sound reasons. Indeed, the reader of D'Angelo's essay is no doubt convinced that stop-motion animators "tend to be perfectionists—not just when it comes to technical matters but in every aspect of filmmaking."

The body of an evaluation often attempts to explain the political, economic, social, or cultural context that gives this object or phenomenon particular significance. D'Angelo, for example, argues that "movies themselves tend to appeal to us the more they resemble our dreams." Thus, stop-motion animation is particularly compelling because this method of composing visual imagery

Introduction	Body	Conclusion
▶ Establishes the author's ethos by ▶ Defining the subject to be evaluated ▶ Explaining why the subject should be evaluated ▶ Identifying the ways in which the subject is to be evaluated ▶ Explaining why readers should pay attention to the evaluation	▶ Provides criteria for evaluating the subject ▶ Describes the subject in detail ▶ Offers specific facts, examples, and direct quotations to show how the subject meets or does not meet those criteria ▶ Explains the political, economic, social, or cultural context that gives the subject particular significance ▶ Establishes logos	▶ Synthesizes criteria and collected evidence ▶ Makes one final appeal for readers to adopt a specific attitude or opinion ▶ Establishes pathos

© 2013 Cengage Learning

in a film "pushes this dichotomy [between waking and sleeping] one step further, straddling the line that separates reality from imagination." This contextual evaluation helps deepen readers' understanding of how the animated films fit into contemporary visual culture and influence their daily lives.

Finally, the conclusion of an evaluation brings together the various criteria and the collected evidence in order to make one final appeal for readers to adopt a specific attitude or opinion. D'Angelo connects with his readers on an emotional level (establishing pathos), urging them to appreciate the technical artistry of stop-motion animated movies and the "folks who toil" to create these films.

Revision and peer review

After you've drafted your evaluation, ask one of your classmates to read it. You'll want your classmate to respond to your work in a way that helps you revise it into the strongest evaluation it can be, one that addresses your intended audience, helps you fulfill your purpose, and is delivered in the most appropriate means available to you.

Questions for a peer reviewer

1. To what opportunity for change is the writer responding?
2. Who might be the writer's intended audience?
3. What might be the writer's purpose? How do audience and purpose come together in this evaluation?
4. What information did you receive from the introduction? How does the writer introduce the particular object or phenomenon he or she is exploring? How does the writer suggest why it needs to be evaluated? What suggestions do you have for the writer regarding the introduction?
5. Note the writer's thesis statement. If you cannot locate a thesis statement, what thesis statement might work for this evaluation?
6. Note the assertions the writer makes to support the thesis. (These may be in the form of criteria the writer establishes.) Are they presented in chronological or emphatic order? Does the writer use the order that seems most effective? How could the writer improve the order of these assertions?
7. If you cannot locate a series of assertions, what assertions could be made to support the thesis statement?
8. Note the concrete evidence and examples that the writer uses to show how the subject meets or does not meet the criteria established.
9. How does the writer establish ethos? How could the writer strengthen this appeal?
10. What material does the writer use to establish logos? How might the writer strengthen this appeal (see questions 6–8)?
11. How does the writer make use of pathos?
12. What did you learn from the conclusion that you didn't already know after reading the introduction and body? What information does the writer want you to take away from the evaluation? Does the writer attempt to change your attitude, action, or opinion?
13. What section of the evaluation did you most enjoy? Why?

EVALUATIONS IN THREE MEDIA

Online Evaluation

Stephanie Zacharek posted her evaluation of *Clash of the Titans* (2010) on the site Salon.com. To read the review, find *Writing in Three Media* in your English Course-Mate, accessed through cengagebrain.com.

Frank Trapper/Corbis

Oral Evaluation

EDU Checkup is a video blog (vlog) that reviews college and university websites. To view the evaluation of Southwest Minnesota State University's website, find *Writing in Three Media* in your English CourseMate, accessed through cengagebrain. com.

© Nick Denardis

Print Evaluation

In the following essay, student Alexis Walker locates a rhetorical opportunity in the changing landscape of her city's downtown.

Courtesy of James Kirkhuff.

If Alexis had wanted to argue against the sale of a downtown shop to Dunkin' Donuts, she could have organized her thoughts into talking points and spoken at a city council meeting. Or, if she had wanted to focus on architectural details that were obscured by the new sign, she might have written a letter to the local preservation association. As a long-time resident witnessing a shift in the aesthetics of the downtown area, Alexis wanted to evaluate the effects of this latest change in order to influence the perceptions of other residents—so that they might use the criteria she establishes in her critical review to evaluate future developments.

Alexis Walker

Professor Davis

English 251

27 September 2009

Donuts at Easton's Center Circle: Slam Dunk or Cycle of Deterioration?

• The way a city looks—its skyline, the buildings, the streets, even the greenery—affects how we feel in that city and the perception of what it has to offer. From the hectic environment of New York to the calming quality of a rural farm, these feelings are informed by what surrounds us. • With that in mind, the center of a city should, ideally, portray the best the city has to offer. Visual clues, such as the type of businesses that thrive in the area, indicate something about the town.

A quick scan around downtown Easton on a winter weekday afternoon, however, makes clear that there is much to be desired in this eastern Pennsylvania town. For instance, the prominence of the Peace Candle, standing proudly in the center of the traffic circle, assumes a grandiosity that fails to actualize itself. No matter which direction one enters the circle from, the peace candle sits straight ahead. The off-white concrete representing the wax looks grungy and neglected. Some melted wax drips down the sides in light blue cascades of color encrusting each corner. The stiff flame of orange and red metal sits atop the structure, too unassuming to project the proper vibrancy. It's all supported by a series of black visible cables emphasizing the candle's behemoth existence as almost menacing. The display of fire intends to signify energy and soul, an attempt to spark downtown into a bustling hub of city commerce full of life rather than old and dull as the mostly rundown space actually is. Instead, darkened windowpanes and boarded up entrances encircle the mammoth centerpiece.

Alexis opens her evaluation by describing the scene she plans to analyze in a way that all her readers can easily understand.

In a two-sentence thesis statement, Alexis asserts why the scene she describes merits evaluation.

Evaluations

Fig. 1. Historic downtown's Dunkin' Donuts (photograph courtesy of James Kirkhuff).

Freshly painted buildings and the presence of patrons constitute the two criteria for an appealing city center or, in this case, center circle.

• The bright white, freshly painted outside of the new Dunkin' Donuts provides a clear contrast to the lifeless grey buildings that surround it. The signature orange and pink lettering adorns both sides of this corner edifice, and its large windows showcase the patrons the establishment actually is attracting. All of these attributes, dissimilar to the dreary display downtown Easton usually offers, might suggest that the area is on the rise. Indeed, the revamped Dunkin' Donuts building and the business it brings are nice.

This and following paragraphs contain details that illuminate how well Easton is meeting each of the two criteria that Alexis is using to evaluate the overall appeal of the center circle.

• There are a few more exceptions to the lifeless environment intermittently placed among the abandoned properties. Pearly Baker's restaurant sits inconspicuously in one corner despite its neon green sign. Easton is also home to Crayola crayons, and across the street, a building complex dominates the scene, advertising all things Crayola (and a McDonald's to boot!); a giant crayon box acts as a sign to identify—if gaudily—the gift shop entrance. It is also a relatively new building with plenty of windows and one of the taller buildings in the circle.

Considering the already successful Crayola complex and built-in McDonald's, it is clear that bigger corporations are not new to downtown.

Now, though, with the addition of a Dunkin' Donuts, the precedent is set for what kind of companies can be successful within the circle: anything with a brand name. Crayola and Dunkin' Donuts both have name recognition, which is a primary reason they are the most prominent attractions to Easton's center. The chance the center circle once had to become a thriving, eclectic neighborhood now seems impossible. Even if small businesses remain for a while, it is the Dunkin' Donuts that will draw the most business from Crayola's downtown existence, and vice versa. The patronage these two businesses will bring to downtown might create some spillover business for the other establishments, but these two primary attractions seem to complement each other the most. And so the problem remains: less patronage for small businesses begets fewer attractions to offer Eastonians. There won't be any compelling postcards of the hustle and bustle of the charming city to sell. An image of a humdrum town with an emerging strip mall for a downtown region, however, is easily imaginable, if less compelling.

There are bright spots within this dismal image, though. During the summertime, provided good weather, Easton's center circle plays host to a farmers' market every week. Consisting of stands selling products from produce to freshly milled soap, it is a time when there is an alternative offering—transient as it may be—to draw a crowd. And that crowd is outside and socializing, delivering a livelier image than the downtown area used to.

Should one take a picture of these two different downtown environments, position them next to each other, and then draw conclusions about what type of place Easton is to live in, the results would obviously be quite different. Whether one picture is more accurate, or whether the real Easton experience is somewhere in between, ultimately is irrelevant. The fact remains that a city projects a certain experience through its surroundings.

In this passage, Alexis explains what kinds of business will succeed in Easton's center circle.

Next, she points out a concrete reason why the circle won't succeed: most businesses don't meet the criteria for success.

In mentioning the farmers' market, Alexis offers one concrete example of how the center circle might meet the second criterion, that of having patrons visit the downtown.

Evaluations

Is it welcoming, impressive, expansive, busy, or a combination? Usually a trip to Easton's center circle would not yield a particularly promising impression of what Easton has to offer. Maybe the recent addition of a Dunkin' Donuts will improve downtown's condition. On the other hand, maybe it will cement its deterioration.

Finally, Alexis articulates a clear argument that Easton is not meeting the criteria required for a thriving center circle.

Alternatives to the Evaluation

Fitting responses come in many forms, not just evaluations. Your instructor might call upon you to consider one of the following opportunities for writing.

1. What happens when a familiar image gets printed in a different medium or a familiar design appears in a different context? How does this new medium or context affect a viewer's or a user's experience of that image or that object? For example, how does the visual effect of a painting by Vincent van Gogh differ when the painting is displayed in a gallery and when it's reprinted on mugs and t-shirts? Or, how does a response to a urinal differ when it appears in a bathroom and when it appears in a museum? Compose an analysis of how the medium or the context affects a response to an image or object.

2. As you learned throughout this chapter, descriptive details are at the heart of any evaluation of visual culture. In a descriptive essay, help readers visualize a particular image or object and try to draw out a particular emotional response to the image or object.

3. Designers such as Marc Jacobs and Anya Hindmarch took up tote bags not only as a way to express their creative vision but also to solve a problem of everyday life—too much plastic waste. Identify a design problem that affects the work or play of people on your campus or in the surrounding community. In an investigative report, describe the problem and help readers better understand how it shapes their lives in negative ways and how their lives might be different if the design were improved.

Exploring the Global Village: Responding with Critical Analyses

10

Cell phones are ubiquitous on college campuses; students and teachers alike punch keys on their way out of the classroom. Text messages, Facebook updates, and phone calls keep students connected to their friends on campus or their families in their hometowns. Now that technologies such as cell phones, satellite television, and the Internet have brought communities around the world into close contact with one another, many people speak of the global village, in which news flows between communities on different continents faster than it spreads among people living in the same town.

You have probably heard the phrase *global village* many times before. It usually suggests the positive potential for people in different parts of the world to form relationships, learn from each other, and participate in cultural exchange. The global village has also become a common metaphor for the Internet's effect of connecting millions of people all over the world. But you may have heard about negative effects of the increasing interconnectedness of the world's cultures. For example, the communications networks that link so many of us create inequalities worldwide because they exclude communities that lack access to the necessary technology. Thus, a digital divide exists between those with access and those without, people in the United States and people elsewhere on the globe. Even though 70 percent of Facebook users live *outside* the United States, discrepancies in access to social networking technology lead to

AP/M. Lakshman

AP Photo/Themba Hadebe

Created by students at the University of Texas for a holiday card, this image shows a positive perspective on the idea of a global village.

the question of how connected (interconnected) various parts of the world really are.

Writers have used **critical analysis** to understand the specific cultural, economic, political, and social forces that have given shape to the global village, as well as to explore the consequences that have occurred or might occur as a result of its existence. This type of analysis, writers hope, can help people become more aware of how and why they use technologies in their daily lives. In some cases, writers hope to change how people use technologies to create the kinds of virtual and physical communities in which they want to live and work.

IDENTIFYING AN OPPORTUNITY

Throughout this chapter, you'll work to identify an opportunity to analyze the causes or consequences of some feature of communication in the global village. If you aren't already aware of how often you participate in the global village, keep a one-day record of your use of media and technology. How does each encounter affect you, particularly in terms of your relationship to a larger community? Which of your encounters leave you feeling connected and optimistic, and which leave you feeling isolated, or puzzled, or maybe even disconnected? If you are alert to these encounters for an entire day, you may be surprised at how plugged into the global village you are. As you work to determine the feature of communication in the global village that interests you, consider the most fitting means of delivering your analysis to your rhetorical audience:

Print Analysis

written for a community or campus newspaper

Online Analysis

posted on a blog

Oral/Multimedia Analysis

presented live to your rhetorical audience

To begin, freewrite for five minutes in response to each of the following questions (or use any of the invention techniques presented on pages 58–61):

1. Consider your experiences using technology such as a cell phone, satellite television, or the Internet to communicate with or learn about people in other parts of the world. What are you curious about, specifically? What kinds of information tend to come to you without your making much effort? What kinds of information must you work harder to discover?

2. Now consider your experiences communicating face to face with people from other parts of the world—either when traveling abroad or through contacts with visitors to this country. What, in particular, have you learned about these people, their cultures, and their worldviews through these types of interactions? What information seems to fit your preconceptions? What information seems surprising or totally unexpected? Be prepared to share your conclusions with the rest of the class.

3. Take five minutes to analyze the differences between your virtual and physical interactions with people from around the world. How and what do you learn through each type of interaction? Be prepared to share your analysis with the rest of the class.

4. Reread your responses to questions 1–3, and then spend five to ten minutes writing about the consequences (for yourself personally, for people in your particular community or country, or for people in the world at large) of living, working, and communicating within the global village.

Real Situations

Students searching the Internet read articles from sites hosted around the world; farmers in rural areas use computers to keep up with international food prices; and an earthquake in Japan prompts an international outpouring of sympathy and monetary support only hours later. These are just a few examples of what it means to live in a world where electronic technology connects many people instantly. You know how to use e-mail, to access movies made in foreign countries, to find web pages in many languages, to read news from reporters based in Afghanistan—in short, how to navigate the information highway. In fact, you may believe that, in many ways, communications technology has shrunk the world to the size of a global village.

With technological developments allowing messages to be sent instantaneously around the

Journalists bring news from around the world to readers while the events are unfolding.

Nicolas Torres/LatinContent/Getty Images

Students in China use the Internet.

world, many more people know about the affairs of communities and countries that may have once seemed distant from them—not only physically but intellectually as well. Being concerned with the news and affairs of others, especially those far away, is at the heart of the concept of the global village. Whereas news once spread from person to person and from home to home, it now spreads via cable and satellite to distant places. People no longer face only their own daily concerns but become vicariously—and directly—invested in what happens in far-flung places.

Along with the technological developments that led to cell phones, satellite television, and the Internet have come developments in the ways in which people create and circulate information. Individuals and organizations now create blogs to draw attention to a range of cultural perspectives and to voices rarely heard in the mainstream media. Twitter extends a microphone to thousands, giving rise to on-the-ground, live reports from individual citizens. Blog and Twitter posts attract the attention of mainstream media outlets such as CNN and Fox News, which regularly stream comments from viewers.

People around the globe can watch television programs from thousands of miles away via satellite.

Despite such evidence of a trend toward media inclusiveness and representation, a significant percentage of the world's population is not part of the global village. Limited access to communications technologies means that only groups with access get to participate in and shape the global village. That is, the images and words that represent communities without access are chosen by those who *do* have access.

Many activist groups, philanthropic organizations, and academic institutions are working to remedy this digital divide. Their shared goal is to provide marginalized populations with Internet access as a platform for speaking for themselves and participating in the global village. Some of these groups and organizations are providing the technology necessary for access; others are teaching the rhetorical skills necessary for producing online content. The hope is that more people will make contributions and help to shape the global village, rather than simply consume information from it. In "Community Computing and Citizen Productivity," Jeffrey T. Grabill claims that computer networks can only be helpful to marginalized communities if they can be used in "village building," not as "information dumps" but as "communicative and productive spaces."

Of course, many individuals and groups are marginalized and voiceless within their own cities or countries, to say nothing of the global village. Sometimes, marginalized people find that the only way they can circulate their messages is to use the communications technologies available to them. Later in this chapter, you'll read about the Zapatistas (officially known as the Ejército Zapatista de Liberación Nacional, or the EZLN), who gained international attention for their subversive use of fax machines, radio, satellite television, and the Internet. Because they have no access to the officially sanctioned Mexican media, the Zapatistas use other means to promote indigenous musicians and storytellers and broadcast political speeches by EZLN leaders directly to the global village.

The concern about access to the global village, then, involves important questions about who participates, what their participation entails, how various communities are represented online and in other global media, and just what (and whose) information and ideas are available throughout this village.

John Davies displays the Classmate PC, a low-cost laptop computer created by Intel for schoolchildren in Brazil.

A member of the Zapatistas, a group whose use of communications technologies has attracted wide attention.

1. Look again at the images in this section. In what ways does each one prompt you to think about what the global village is and why it's important to analyze this phenomenon more thoroughly?

2. Select the two images that resonate most strongly with you. What interests you the most about these particular images?

3. Write for five minutes about what each of the two images you chose makes you think about the causes or the consequences of living, learning, and working within the global village. Be prepared to share your answers with your classmates.

4. Look once more at all the images in this section. Which ones challenge your thinking about the global village and the positive or negative consequences that follow from it? In what specific ways do they present an opposing perspective to your own?

Real Responses to Real Situations

Tracing the causes and consequences of the global village

© Canada Post Corporation (1851). Reproduced with permission.

Marshall McLuhan sought to understand the impact of electronic media.

For a decade, from the mid-1960s to the mid-1970s, Marshall McLuhan was North America's media guru. His provocative theories and public pronouncements about media, technology, and the effects of electronic communication made him a leading pop cultural figure. He was interviewed on national television in Canada and the United States, featured on the cover of *Newsweek,* and parodied in *New Yorker* cartoons; his opinions on the social and cultural effects of media were debated internationally in newspapers, in classrooms, and on television. His best-known books, *Understanding Media: The Extensions of Man* and *The Medium Is the Massage* (not *message,* as most people believe), sold millions of copies around the world.

McLuhan was fascinated by the explosion of mass media that occurred in the post–World War II economic boom, and he was passionately concerned with the direction in which it was taking society. He was worried that not enough people were paying attention to the role media and electronic communication played in their lives. In an interview with journalist Eric Norden, he reiterated this caution:

Today, in the electronic age of instantaneous communication, I believe that our survival, and at the very least our comfort and happiness, is predicated on understanding the nature of our new environment, because unlike previous environmental changes, the electric media constitute a total and near instantaneous transformation of culture, values, and attitudes. This upheaval generates great pain and identity loss, which can be ameliorated only through a consciousness of its dynamics. If we understand the revolutionary transformations caused by new media, we can anticipate and control them; but if we continue in our self-induced subliminal trance, we will be their slaves.

McLuhan was convinced that everyone living in developed nations needed to understand how technology was shaping their social and political life as the world moved from the industrial revolution to the information revolution.

It was McLuhan's 1964 electronic media project (in particular, *Understanding Media: The Extensions of Man*) that would make him a household name as well as a sensation on the lecture and interview circuit. In *Understanding Media,* McLuhan observed that modern society was moving into a new era of "all-at-onceness" defined by a tremendous speedup in daily life, the connection of people and economies around the world regardless of time and space, and "almost overnight cultural change." During an interview on the Canadian television show *Explorations,* McLuhan explained what he meant: "The world is now like a continually sounding tribal drum, where everybody gets the message all the time—a princess gets married in England and boom, boom, boom go the drums. We all hear about it. An earthquake in North Africa, a Hollywood star gets drunk, away go the drums again." The nature of electronic media was making the world smaller and more interconnected—what McLuhan identified as a global village.

In *Understanding Media,* McLuhan highlighted the unifying effects of this technology. We are all interconnected, McLuhan seemed to be arguing, and people should begin to consider the consequences of this new interconnectedness.

Excerpt from

> Understanding Media: The Extensions of Man

Marshall McLuhan

Today, the instantaneous world of electric information media involves us all, all at once. Ours is a brand-new world of all-at-onceness. Time, in a sense, has ceased and space has vanished. Like primitives, we now live in a global village of our own making, a simultaneous happening. The global village is not created by the motor car or even by the airplane. It is created by instant electronic information movement. The global village is at once as wide as the planet and as small as the little town where everybody is maliciously engaged in poking his nose into everybody else's business. The global village is a world in which you don't necessarily have harmony; you have extreme concern with everybody else's business and much involvement in everybody else's life. It's a sort of Ann Landers column written

continued

larger. And it doesn't necessarily mean harmony and peace and quiet, but it does mean huge involvement in everybody else's affairs. And so, the global village is as big as a planet and as small as the village post office. . . .

Tokyo isn't much farther away than the suburbs in point of time. So the patterns of human association vary enormously with the amount of acceleration possible. I think now of the city as the planet itself, the urban village or global village. And, in fact, you could say that with the satellite, the global village has become a global theater, with everybody on the planet simultaneously participating as actors. Students around the globe feel an entire unity among themselves; they feel a homogeneity of interest. They live in an information environment created by electricity. They share the same information or electric environment of information and they share the same outlook around the world. . . .

Electric speed in bringing all social and political functions together in a sudden implosion has heightened human awareness of responsibility to an intense degree. It is this implosive factor that alters the position of the Negro, the teenager, and some other groups. They can no longer be *contained,* in the political sense of limited association. They are now involved in our lives, as we in theirs, thanks to the electric media.

This is the Age of Anxiety for the reason of the electric implosion that compels commitment and participation, quite regardless of any "point of view." . . .

Electric speed . . . has revealed the lines of force . . . from Western technology in the remotest areas of bush, savannah, and desert. One example is the Bedouin with his battery radio on board the camel. Submerging natives with floods of concepts for which nothing has prepared them is the normal action of all of our technology. But with electric media Western man himself experiences exactly the same inundation as the remote native. We are no more prepared to encounter radio and TV in our literate milieu than the native of Ghana is able to cope with the literacy that takes him out of his collective tribal world and beaches him in individual isolation. We are as numb in our new electronic world as the native involved in our literature and mechanical culture. Electric speed mingles the cultures of prehistory with the dregs of industrial marketers, the nonliterate with the semiliterate and the postliterate. Mental breakdown of varying degrees is the very common result of uprooting and inundation with new information and endless new patterns of information.

Though many people enthusiastically embraced McLuhan's argument that electronic media would bring an eventual unification of people and points of view, the concept of the global village was not wholly positive. Electronic media might be making the world smaller but were not necessarily making it a better place. According to McLuhan, the greater unification and interconnectedness of the world would be disturbing to its people. No village, not even the global village, could be without conflict and violence. Writing about the potential power of technology to make the world one small village, McLuhan admonished his readers to think about the negative consequences of that power.

Today, we may see positive and unifying effects from various Internet campaigns, such as the "It Gets Better" YouTube campaign to reassure young people, particularly young gay people and others who encounter bullying, that life does get better. But we also recall the ways in which bullying and the Internet, tragedy and the invasion of privacy are linked. The suicide of Tyler Clementi, a Rutgers student whose encounter with another male student was allegedly filmed by his roommate and posted online, happened only one day after Dan Savage and his partner, Terry Miller, uploaded the first "It Gets Better" video to YouTube. In the wake of this event and others like it that prompted the "It Gets Better" campaign in the first place, we may ask questions about the nature of privacy in the age of social networking or about what bullying looks like online. In the global village of the twenty-first century, we are constantly prompted toward such debates. But well over forty years ago—long before web cams, the Internet, Facebook, or Twitter were in anyone's imagination—McLuhan had already recognized that the race toward electronic technology (whatever that technology might turn out to be) would not lead to unilaterally positive results and might even lead to "mental breakdown."

One writer who continues to analyze the ways in which "everything is connected" is anthropologist Michael Wesch. Wesch has explored how Internet use affects the ways we communicate. He published his research results online, as a YouTube video, entitled "The Machine Is Us/ing Us." In the following interview with blogger John Battelle, Wesch discusses his understanding of the global village as "not a very equitable one," but one in which the availability of digital tools might help all of us connect more usefully.

Excerpt from

> A Brief Interview with Michael Wesch (The Creator of That Wonderful Video . . .)

Reprinted by permission.
John Battelle

Michael Wesch, PhD, is Assistant Professor of Cultural Anthropology at Kansas State University. If you've been reading *Searchblog*, then you know him as the guy behind this amazing video.

After I saw the film, I had to talk to the man who made it. Michael is a very thoughtful fellow, as one might expect, but he comes to "Web 2.0" from an entirely different perspective than your typical Valley entrepreneur (yet he seems to know more than most of us!). For more, read on. . . .

You did your fieldwork in Melanesia, and teach at Kansas State. How did you end up making such a compelling video, one that resonates so deeply with folks like, well, those who read *Searchblog*?

For me, cultural anthropology is a continuous exercise in expanding my mind and my empathy, building primarily from one simple principle: everything is connected. This is true on many levels. First, everything including the environment,

continued

CHOGO/Xinhua/Landov

technology, economy, social structure, politics, religion, art and more are all interconnected. As I tried to illustrate in the video, this means that a change in one area (such as the way we communicate) can have a profound effect on everything else, including family, love, and our sense of being itself. Second, everything is connected throughout all time, and so as anthropologists we take a very broad view of human history, looking thousands or even millions of years into the past and into the future as well. And finally, all people on the planet are connected. This has always been true environmentally because we share the same planet. Today it is even more true with increasing economic and media globalization.

My friends in Papua New Guinea are experts in relationships and grasp the ways that we are all connected in much more profound ways than we do. They go so far as to suggest that their own health is dependent on strong relations with others. When they get sick they carefully examine their relations with others and try to heal those relations in order to heal their bodies. In contrast, we tend to emphasize our independence and individuality, failing to realize just how interconnected we are with each other and the rest of the world, and disregarding the health of our relationships with others. This became clear to me when I saw a small boy in a Papua New Guinea village wearing a torn and tattered University of Nebraska sweatshirt, the only item of clothing he owned. The grim reality for me at that moment was that the same village was producing coffee which eventually found its way onto shelves in my hometown in Nebraska, and this boy may never be able to afford to drink the coffee produced in his own village.

So if there is a global village, it is not a very equitable one, and if there is a tragedy of our times, it may be that we are all interconnected but we fail to see it and take care of our relationships with others. For me, the ultimate promise of digital technology is that it might enable us to truly see one another once again and all the ways we are interconnected. It might help us create a truly global view that can spark the kind of empathy we need to create a better world for all of humankind. I'm not being overly utopian and naively saying that the Web will make this happen. In fact, if we don't understand our digital technology and its effects, it can actually make humans and human needs even more invisible than ever before. But the technology also creates a remarkable opportunity for us to make a profound difference in the world.

So that's some of the more personal and philosophical background behind this video. I wanted to show people how digital technology has evolved and give them a sense of where it might be going and to give some momentum to the all-important conversation about the consequences of that on our global society. I did not know it would reach so many people, but I had hoped that for those it did reach it would spark some reflection on the power of the technology they were using. Because without proper understanding and reflection, "the machine" is using us—all of us—even those that don't have access to the machine at all.

Your video was quite sophisticated about how the web works, and the production quality was quite high as well. Where did you pick up those skills?

I made my first website in 1998 using notepad and HTML while I was a graduate student at the University of Virginia. It was slow-going but I saw a tremendous potential for transforming the way we present our research. Since then I have had a passion for exploring the latest technologies and how they can be used to communicate ideas in more effective ways. I like to learn these technologies on my own through trial and error, because sometimes the errors turn out to be new uses for the tool that I might not have discovered through formal training. I'm always looking for ways to use tools in ways other than for what they were intended. The great thing about our current era is that the tools are not only easier to use (as evidenced by an anthropology professor being able to learn them in his spare time), they are also more flexible than ever, allowing for some creative uses that seem to re-invent the tools all over again.

> ANALYZING THE RHETORICAL SITUATION

1. Who might have been the intended audience for Marshall McLuhan's book *Understanding Media*? What textual evidence can you provide to support your answer?
2. To what rhetorical opportunity might McLuhan have been responding in his book *Understanding Media* (keep in mind that it was published in 1964)?
3. How do Marshall McLuhan and Michael Wesch use the rhetorical appeals of ethos, logos, and pathos? Which of the appeals is most dominant in each selection? Provide textual evidence to support your answer.
4. Why do you think Wesch says "if we don't understand our digital technology and its effects, it can actually make humans and human needs even more invisible than ever before"?
5. What do you think Wesch means when he cautions that "without proper understanding and reflection 'the machine' is using us—all of us"? What is the machine he refers to? Do you agree with him? Why or why not?

Tools for bringing the world together

Since Marshall McLuhan first discussed the global village, the world has been shaped in profound ways by the spread of communications technologies such as cell phones, satellite television, and the Internet. You can stay on top of political events around the globe on cable television news outlets such as CNN, Fox News, and MSNBC. Using Google Earth, you can witness the effects of the genocide in Darfur through interactive mapping technologies enhanced with research from

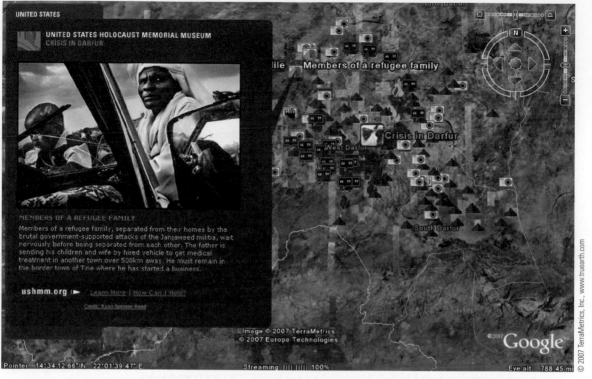

Google Earth's Crisis in Darfur project tracks the devastating effects of genocide in that region.

the United States Holocaust Museum. You can also write blog entries or Twitter posts to narrate your daily experiences, from the incredible to the mundane, or comment on the atmosphere for women on campus or the political leanings of the candidates for president of the student government; you can link readers of your blog to a hilarious video you just saw on YouTube or review the latest CD by your favorite musician. You can create friendships with students at colleges and universities all over the world through online forums such as MySpace and Facebook. All of these activities make use of digital technologies in ways that seem to forge new connections between people around the globe, bringing the news and the opinions of many individuals and groups into public view.

As news analysts and cultural commentators look at digital archives (blogs and podcasts) and online forums (Wikipedia and YouTube), they see a radical reshaping of both the production and the distribution of knowledge throughout the world. As more individuals are gaining access to the Internet (as a way to communicate their ideas and the events of their lives), the global village is quickly becoming more pluralistic and more democratic. In other words, average people are shaping the global village, an idea *Time* magazine celebrated when naming its 2006 Person of the Year: "You." Four years later, *Time*'s editors selected as Person of the Year Facebook founder Mark Zuckerberg, who has also used the Internet to transform the global village.

One of Facebook's overseas offices.

AP Photo/The Canadian Press, Frank Gunn

From the pages of *TIME*:

> Only Connect (Person of the Year, Mark Zuckerberg)

Richard Stengel, December 27, 2010/January 3, 2011

"On or about December 1910, human character changed."
—*Virginia Woolf, 1924*

AP Photo/Paul Sakuma

She was exaggerating—but only a little. Woolf saw a fundamental shift in human relations taking place at the beginning of the 20th century "between masters and servants, husbands and wives, parents and children." Those changes, she predicted, would bring about transformations in every sphere of life, from religion to politics to human behavior. Few would say she got it wrong.

A century later, we are living through another transition. The way we connect with one another and with the institutions in our lives is evolving. There is an erosion of trust in authority, a decentralizing of power and at the same time, perhaps, a greater faith in one another. Our sense of identity is more variable, while our sense of privacy is expanding. What was once considered intimate is now shared among millions with a keystroke.

More than anyone else on the world stage, Facebook's Mark Zuckerberg is at the center of these changes. Born in 1984, the same year the Macintosh computer was launched, he is both a product of his generation and an architect of it. The social-networking platform he invented is closing in on 600 million users. In a single day, about a billion new pieces

continued

of content are posted on Facebook. It is the connective tissue for nearly a tenth of the planet. Facebook is now the third largest country on earth and surely has more information about its citizens than any government does. Zuckerberg, a Harvard dropout, is its T-shirt–wearing head of state.

Evolutionary biologists suggest there is a correlation between the size of the cerebral neocortex and the number of social relationships a primate species can have. Humans have the largest neocortex and the widest social circle—about 150, according to the scientist Robin Dunbar. Dunbar's number—150—also happens to mirror the average number of friends people have on Facebook. Because of airplanes and telephones and now social media, human beings touch the lives of vastly more people than did our ancestors, who might have encountered only 150 people in their lifetime. Now the possibility of connection is accelerating at an extraordinary pace. As the great biologist E. O. Wilson says, "We're in uncharted territory."

All social media involve a mixture of narcissism and voyeurism. Most of us display a combination of the two, which is why social media are flourishing faster and penetrating deeper than any other social development in memory. Social media play into the parts of human character that don't change, even while changing the nature of what once seemed immutable.

Like two of our runners-up this year, Julian Assange and the Tea Party, Mark Zuckerberg doesn't have a whole lot of veneration for traditional authority. In a sense, Zuckerberg and Assange are two sides of the same coin. Both express a desire for openness and transparency. While Assange attacks big institutions and governments through involuntary transparency with the goal of disempowering them, Zuckerberg enables individuals to voluntarily share information with the idea of empowering them. Assange sees the world as filled with real and imagined enemies; Zuckerberg sees the world as filled with potential friends. Both have a certain disdain for privacy: in Assange's case because he feels it allows malevolence to flourish; in Zuckerberg's case because he sees it as a cultural anachronism, an impediment to a more efficient and open connection between people.

At 26, Zuckerberg is a year older than our first Person of the Year, Charles Lindbergh—another young man who used technology to bridge continents. He is the same age as Queen Elizabeth when she was Person of the Year, for 1952. But unlike the Queen, he did not inherit an empire; he created one. (The Queen, by the way, launched a Facebook page this year.) Person of the Year is not and never has been an honor. It is a recognition of the power of individuals to shape our world. For connecting more than half a billion people and mapping the social relations among them (something that has never been done before); for creating a new system of exchanging information that has become both indispensable and sometimes a little scary; and finally, for changing how we all live our lives in ways that are innovative and even optimistic, Mark Elliot Zuckerberg is TIME's 2010 Person of the Year.

As increasing numbers of people communicate about their lives through blogs, Facebook, Twitter, podcasts, and YouTube, their online activities make them seem more influential than people with little or no access to technologies such as computers, Internet connections, and digital and audio production equipment. Commentators argue that getting such technologies into the hands of people living on the economic, political, and cultural margins of society will make the global village a more inclusive, but also potentially more revolutionary, place. In fact, the so-called digital divide between black and white Americans seems to have been successfully bridged (if it ever existed at all), according to the following analysis by journalist and novelist Michael E. Ross. This article appeared on theGrio.com, which reports news of particular interest to African Americans.

> Twitter-verse Draws More Black Followers into Its Orbit

Michael E. Ross

First lady Michelle Obama officially entered the Twitter-verse last Saturday, at the White House Correspondents Dinner. The popular social messaging service deepened its reach into the public when she sent her message, brief enough and consistent with the "what are you doing now?" Twitter ethos: "from flotus: here at dinner this is officially my first Tweet. i am looking forward to some good laughs from the potus and jay," she wrote, in a reference to President Obama and Jay Leno.

Michelle Obama's first, benign message underscores the inroads that Twitter has made in black life and culture. A new report on who's using Twitter bears that out with startling results. The comprehensive report on Twitter usage released April 29 by Edison Research and Arbitron reveals, among other things, that the service "does appear to be disproportionately popular with African-Americans." The study finds that 24 percent of the 17 million Americans "tweeting" at any given time are African-American, "which is approximately double the percentage of African-Americans in the current U.S. population."

"Indeed, many of the 'trending topics' on Twitter on a typical day are reflective of African-American culture, memes [ideas, styles, and so on], and topics," says the report, which elaborates on Twitter's impact on the nation as a whole.

The Twitter report represents responses to a survey of 1,753 Americans age 12 and over, [which] was conducted through landline and mobile phone interviews done in February. It's the culmination of three years of research into Twitter usage trends.

The study finds that, overall, all Americans' awareness of Twitter has "exploded" from 5 percent in 2008 to 87 percent in 2010, a fact that's created an unlikely situation: "With the percentage of Americans who have access to the Internet stalled at roughly 85 percent, more people are *aware* of Twitter than could possibly *use* the service," the report states, blaming that anomaly on the way Twitter has saturated the culture, fueling our everyday conversations at water coolers and in break rooms everywhere.

The Twitter report's data on black users is startling enough on its own; what gives its findings deeper significance is how they conform with those of the Pew Internet report on wireless Internet use, released in July 2009. Together, the surveys past and present reveal dovetailing results that strongly suggest the storied

continued

"digital divide" between black and white America, once taken as a kind of socio-economic truism, is no longer true at all.

The Pew report says that, among users of the Internet on mobile platforms—thought to be the next frontier in Internet access—"African Americans are the most active users of the mobile Internet—and their use of it is also growing the fastest."

The Pew report found that 48 percent of African Americans have at one time used mobile Internet access for information, e-mail or instant messaging, twice the national average of 32 percent. Some 29 percent of African Americans use the Internet on their handheld on an average day, way above the national average of 19 percent.

And Pew found that between 2007 and 2009, mobile Internet access among African Americans soared by 141 percent.

The reasons vary as to why the black American presence on Twitter, and the online experience in general, have gotten so strong. One reason is availability. As communications technology has evolved, devices have gotten smaller, less expensive, and more affordable for households with smaller incomes.

Major companies such as software giant Microsoft have invested heavily in technology centers tasked with enhancing computer literacy, making it easier for black Americans (younger ones in particular) to acquire experience with computers and the Web.

And with advances in wi-fi technology and proliferation of Web-enabled kiosks at airports and so-called Internet cafes, the Web is just more accessible, more in your face, than ever before. With Twitter, the celebrity factor can't be overlooked. Like countless others in America, black people take many of their cultural cues from celebrities and athletes. A wide range of black figures in sports and popular culture, including Questlove of the Roots, *Grey's Anatomy* creator Shonda Rhimes, Tyrese Gibson, Tyra Banks and 50 Cent have embraced the Twitter phenomenon, an extension of both the African American "grapevine" and our national passion for good celebrity dish.

"It's penetrated different pockets of African-American culture," said Tom Webster, author of the Twitter report. "I wouldn't say it's a global phenomenon, but NBA stars tweeting is a real bubble of usage. [Shaquille O'Neal's Twitter address] the_real_shaq has almost three million followers. You have a lot of major African-American celebrities accumulating massive amounts of followers—white, black, Hispanic, they're from everywhere."

And the embrace of Twitter speaks to an age-old survival strategy for African-Americans: In ways more surprising to Internet analysts than to black Americans, Twitter taps into our historical experience of making more out of less: in this case, getting a black perspective across to the world—and doing it 140 characters at a time.

> ANALYZING THE RHETORICAL SITUATION

1. Analyze your own access to and use of communications technology. List the online tools you use regularly and the reasons you use them. What rhetorical opportunities are you addressing? Who exactly comprises your various audiences? What technologies or online tools are new to you? Which do you want to learn more about?

2. What evidence does Michael E. Ross include to support his argument that African Americans are regularly accessing digital technologies? What evidence does Richard Stengel provide to document that we are undergoing a "fundamental shift in human relations"?

3. What rhetorical opportunity sparks Ross's analysis? What problem does he analyze?

4. How does Ross define issues of access to online technologies? What positive consequences follow from such access? What specific evidence does Ross provide to support his analysis?

5. How do Ross and Stengel use ethos, pathos, and logos to build their arguments? (Provide textual evidence to support your answer.) Which of the rhetorical appeals is most evident in their analyses? Be prepared to share your answer with the rest of the class.

COMMUNITY CONNECTIONS

1. Write for ten minutes about your response to the analysis of communications technologies and the global village crafted by Marshall McLuhan or Michael Wesch. How does that analysis align with your own experiences with such technologies?

2. Write for ten minutes responding to the arguments of Michael Wesch and Michael E. Ross. How do their arguments coincide with or diverge from your experiences in working with old or new forms of media?

3. In terms of the views expressed by McLuhan, Wesch, Stengel, and Ross, how does your campus or community relate to the global village? What specific developments (technological, economic, cultural, political, or social) enable students or local citizens to contribute to or consume within the global village? Which of those developments have been planned and unplanned?

4. How would you describe the ideal global village? What practices would shape it? What activities would take place within it? Who would contribute to and participate in these practices?

Critical Analyses: A Fitting Response

A critical analysis of the global village

There can be little doubt that digital media and communications technologies have shaped today's societies in significant ways. Disagreement arises, however, when people begin to debate the causes and the consequences of this technological and social transformation. Some ask whether the characteristics of certain media lead people to feel closer to or more remote from what they see and hear from communities around the globe; some question the extent to which the global village does or does not represent the perspectives of all groups, particularly the poor and the powerless, in various societies. The proliferation of digital media and the integration of communications technologies into so many people's lives—and the lack of integration into the lives of so many others—create a particularly compelling opportunity for critical analysis.

In the following article from *Newsweek*, writer Russell Watson (along with contributors John Barry, Christopher Dickey, and Tim Padgett) examines how a community that traditionally lacked a political voice in its country appropriated communications technologies to announce its presence within and transmit its messages throughout the global village.

When Words Are the Best Weapon

Russell Watson

Watson presents a detailed example in the introductory paragraph as a way of engaging readers' interest and revealing his rhetorical opportunity.

Here's how to wage a revolution in the Information Age: two weeks ago Mexican government troops lunged into the rain forests of Chiapas state in renewed pursuit of the Zapatista rebels. When the federal soldiers reached an insurgent stronghold at Guadalupe Tepeyac, the guerrillas melted into the jungle, leaving behind a few trucks but taking with them their most valuable equipment—fax machines and laptop computers. In retreat, the Zapatistas faxed out a communiqué claiming that the army was "killing children, beating and raping women … and bombing us." Soon the government was taking another public relations beating. It stopped the offensive and allowed reporters into the area. They found no signs of atrocities or bombing. But the government attack had been thwarted, and the rebels were free to fight on, with words as their best weapons.

Watson uses a direct quotation from Subcomandante Marcos to offer readers the revolutionary group's perspective.

The writer makes an assertion here about information technology, and he supports this claim in the sentences that follow.

The Zapatistas' chief spokesman, Subcomandante Marcos (the government says his name is Rafael Guillén), knows that he will never obtain political power from the barrel of a gun. "What governments should really fear," he told a *Newsweek* reporter last summer, "is a communications expert." Information technology has always been seen as a potentially revolutionary weapon. Almost as soon as the printing press was invented, governments and churches tried to control it, and the Ottoman Empire shunned the technology for almost 300 years. The American Revolution was spurred on by Benjamin Franklin, a printer; Thomas Paine, a pamphleteer; and Samuel Adams, a propagandist. In the modern era, vulnerable governments have been challenged by proliferating means of communication. Long-distance telephone service, for example, helped to undermine the Soviet Union, connecting dissidents to each other and to supporters outside the country. Other Communist regimes have been weakened by radio and television signals: West German programs beamed into East Germany, and broadcasts from Hong Kong feeding the appetite for reform in mainland China.

Violent revolutions, especially those that resort to terrorism, often have the most success with relatively low-tech weapons. But like the Zapatistas, many of today's revolutionaries are better talkers than fighters, accomplishing little or nothing on the battlefield. "These new insurgencies, in the end, are aimed more at high-intensity lobbying and low-intensity fighting," says William LeoGrande of the American University in Washington, an expert on leftist movements. Now they have the tools they need. Older communications technology, such as radio and television, is centralized and subject to government control, if only through the assignment of frequencies and the jamming of unauthorized signals. The latest gear, such as satellite television receivers or computers linked to the Internet, is decentralized, diffused and—so far—almost impossible to police or control.

The Internet is the fastest-growing communication tool, with as many as 30 million subscribers in 92 countries. Even Chinese dissidents are beginning to use e-mail. News about the fight against Chinese repression in Tibet is regularly gathered and circulated by the London-based Tibet Information Network, one of dozens of human-rights organizations using the Information Superhighway. In the Soviet Union, the Internet played a small but vital role in defeating the attempted coup by Communist hard-liners in 1991. Soviet computer scientists had hooked up to the Internet only a few months before. When Boris Yeltsin and his reformists holed up in the White House, the Russian republic's Parliament, someone inside the building started sending bulletins, including Yeltsin's edicts, on the Internet. They were picked up by the Voice of America (VOA), which broadcast them back to the Soviet Union by radio, helping to rally public support for Yeltsin.

Since then, the VOA has made a big investment in the Internet. It now offers computer users written news reports in 47 languages and audio bulletins in 16. Access is obtained through two of the Internet's standard communications protocols: Internet Gopher and FTP (File Transfer Protocol). Those aren't the most advanced access gates, but that's precisely why the VOA chose them; more users overseas are likely to have them. The VOA currently logs about 100,000 uses of its Internet service each week. That's minuscule compared with the 92 million weekly VOA radio listeners. But Christopher Kern, the VOA's director of computer services, says the Internet has "wonderful demographics"; users are educated and influential. They also seem to have sensitive political antennae. Recently, when Washington and Beijing got into a nasty dispute over trade, no one in China logged on to the VOA Internet for an entire week. The next week, with the trade issue under negotiation, they came back online.

On a much more modest scale, the Internet also has become a platform for the Zapatistas. One of the services offering information about the movement is run from Mexico City by Barbara Pillsbury, a 24-year-old American who works for a development organization. She transmits bulletins about the Zapatistas and communiqués from Subcomandante Marcos to subscribers around the world. . . . She says interest in the Zapatistas helped introduce many Mexicans to cyberspace. "Beyond their concerns about Chiapas," says Pillsbury, "Mexicans have realized that they need to be part of this technology."

Satellite TV is much easier to use, given the proper dish-shaped antenna and decoding equipment. The technology has become popular in many countries where the native TV menu is limited. There are thought to be more than 150,000 dishes in Saudi Arabia, pulling

Watson underscores his claim about the importance of information technology for present-day revolutionary groups. He further supports his claim with the quotation from an expert that follows.

Watson provides several (recent) historical examples to support his point in the previous paragraph that the latest communications technologies are "almost impossible to police or control."

The two previous sentences make another analytical point: many Internet users have "sensitive political antennae" that make them attentive to, if not necessarily in agreement with, the revolutionary messages being broadcast within the global village.

Watson here makes a clear transition from analyzing use of the Internet to analyzing use of satellite TV.

in programming as varied as CNN, Italian game shows, soft pornography from Turkey, sitcoms from Israel and religious fulminations from Iran, the kingdom's archenemy. China, where dishes are institutionally owned, would seem to be at the opposite end of the scale as a market for satellite TV. But four months ago the VOA began [by aiming] a weekly hour of TV news in Mandarin Chinese from the AsiaSat, which has a good broadcast "footprint" over the mainland. Is anyone watching? The VOA doesn't know yet. "We shot an arrow in the air," says Kern.

Authoritarian governments of all political persuasions would like to shoot down satellite TV. Jamming is much more difficult than with radio, which uses a narrower and more vulnerable bandwidth. A more productive approach is to outlaw the dish antennas. The conservative Saudi government banned them last year, threatening a fine of $180,000 on anyone who continues to use them. Fundamentalist Iran outlawed the dishes last month. The mullahs who rule Iran have been fighting a rear-guard action against communications technology ever since they took power in 1979. Previously they tried—and failed—to suppress videocassettes and camcorders.

The irony is that Ayatollah Ruhollah Khomeini and his followers overthrew the Shah of Iran by using even more primitive communications technology. While Khomeini was still exiled in Paris, his calls to rebel against the shah were disseminated throughout Iran on tape cassettes. Any means of communication can be an instrument of revolution, as long as it's in fairly widespread use. For years, Iraqi dictator Saddam Hussein banned private ownership of typewriters. He remembered the subversive power of the mimeograph machine when he was an ambitious young rebel plotting his own takeover.

The most tightly closed societies, such as North Korea, and the most violently repressive ones, such as Iraq or Libya, may not be susceptible to an Information Age revolution. In North Korea, shortwave radios are unavailable, even to the few who could afford them. Fax machines, privately owned computers and satellite TV are unheard-of. Partly to constrict the flow of information, travel is severely limited, within the country as well as outside it; even bicycles were banned until about three years ago. Iraq and Libya have considerably more open societies, but their regimes remain in power through the most ruthless terror tactics, killing off opponents, real or imagined, and utterly intimidating the rest of the population, which in any case has little access to outside information.

Even in less rigid dictatorships, communications technology cannot make a revolution by itself. The Soviet Union was done in by its own economic failures and a ruinous arms race, not by long-distance phone calls or foreign radio broadcasts. In Iran, the conditions for revolution were created by the shah's brutal repression and his breakneck modernization program, which outraged Muslim tradition. But the flow of information helps to undermine such regimes, and the faster it flows, the more trouble they're in. Few states can afford to opt out of the Information Age; they have to keep up with at least some of the latest scientific, technical and commercial developments. "We have a kind of knowledge market going on which is, in a way, impervious to the efforts of states to control it," says Paul Wilkinson, professor of international relations at the University of St. Andrews in Britain. If dictatorships want to play any part in the modern world, they have to risk exposing themselves to ideas and information that could inspire reform or spark a revolution.

In this paragraph, Watson examines counterexamples that may tend to weaken his claim about the potential revolutionary consequences of information age technologies.

Watson builds his appeals of ethos and logos here as he qualifies his argument about the consequences that follow from revolutionary groups' use of communications technologies.

■ GUIDE TO RESPONDING TO THE RHETORICAL SITUATION

Understanding the Rhetorical Situation

When you want to explore the causes and/or consequences of a situation or phenomenon, consider composing a critical analysis. Whether you are writing or reading, you will notice that critical analyses typically include the following features:

- Description is used to help readers understand why the situation or phenomenon needs to be examined and to help them feel invested in the analysis.
- The causes and/or the consequences seem logically connected to the situation or phenomenon.
- The critical analysis includes sufficient evidence and examples to assure readers that a logical connection exists between the situation or phenomenon and its causes or consequences.
- Alternative perspectives on the situation or phenomenon are acknowledged and responded to.
- The critical analysis informs readers as to how the situation or phenomenon affects their lives.

The following sections will help you compose a critical analysis of some feature of communication in the global village. To work with an online guide to the elements of the rhetorical situation, access your English CourseMate through cengagebrain.com.

Identifying an opportunity

Consider the kinds of communications technologies you use in your everyday life: the Internet, a cell phone or smartphone, radio and broadcast or cable TV, iPad or tablet PC. Or, think about the specific kinds of content you consume through these technologies: virtual tourism sites, Facebook posts, news updates from South America, YouTube videos of political demonstrations in eastern Europe, podcasts from artists in central Africa. How exactly are you participating in the global village—as both consumer and producer of information or entertainment? Can you identify the social interests, economic developments, or political or cultural views that underpin the information you're consuming (or producing)? What interests or perspectives might be missing from the global village? What do you gain personally from participating in the global village?

Consider your understanding of and participation in the global village in terms of the people with whom you communicate, such as students in other countries who share similar academic, cultural, or political interests. Maybe you have increased your understanding of and empathy for the experiences of students in other cultures as you read their tweets or watched videos depicting their experiences, or perhaps you have sensed that you cannot get the whole picture about them in these ways. You may even feel overwhelmed by the sheer volume of information on the Internet or at times want to unplug yourself from it.

1. Make a list of the communications technologies you use regularly to participate in the global village, a list that might include the encounters with technology you identified in response to the questions on page 307. For each technology, list the kinds of content you create or consume. Providing as many details as possible, describe each type of content and explain whether you found your experiences with that type of content to be positive or negative.

2. Make two columns—in which you list the positive and negative features of the types of content you have experienced through communications technology: subject matter, quality of the audio or visual components, language differences, presence or absence of instant communication with other people, and so forth. Provide specific details about each feature.

3. Choosing one or two kinds of content, save a screenshot that best represents some positive or negative feature you discussed in question 2. Or take photos or make sketches of yourself using a form of communications technology, paying particular attention to the physical details that best characterize the nature of your participation within the global village.

4. Choose a type of content and draft four or five brief descriptions of its positive or negative features. Vary the descriptions: for example, one description might focus on a group of people who are obviously affected by the content; another description could focus on a group that is seemingly unaffected (especially if you think they should be affected). Or you could emphasize the sensory details that were evident on the website, video, podcast, or news program where you encountered the content.

Locating an audience

The following questions can help you locate your rhetorical audience as well as identify the relationship they have to the situation or phenomenon you're analyzing. Then, you'll be able to choose the best way to present your analysis.

1. List names of groups who directly contribute to or who are affected by the situation or phenomenon you're analyzing. On another list, write the names of groups who indirectly contribute to or are indirectly affected by the situation or phenomenon. You may need to do some research to compose a list that accounts for all the various groups with a stake in analyzing this situation or phenomenon more fully.

2. Next to the name of each potential audience, write possible reasons that audience could have for wanting a better understanding of the causes

or consequences of the situation or phenomenon. In other words, what would motivate these audiences to analyze how communications activities or technologies influence their lives?

3. What responses could these audiences reasonably be expected to have to your analysis? In other words, what conclusions might they be persuaded to draw, what attitudes might they be likely to adopt, what opinions might they be willing to reconsider? After exploring these possible responses, decide which audience you most want or need to reach with your critical analysis.

4. With your audience's interests and capabilities in mind, look again at the descriptions of the types of content that you composed in the preceding section on identifying a rhetorical opportunity. Decide which description might enable these readers to feel connected to the situation or phenomenon you want to analyze—might help them become invested in understanding its causes or consequences. At this point, you may need to revise, tailoring your best description to your intended audience.

Identifying a fitting response

As you know, different audiences and different purposes require different kinds of texts, delivered through different media. For example, for a critical analysis of the consequences for international understanding that could arise from virtual tourism websites or software such as Google Earth, you might create your own web page or post an extended comment on the message board of such a site. Your analysis of the causes that lead to the emergence of online communities for the world's youth might lead you to create a pamphlet for distribution at local public libraries. As these two examples suggest, once you identify your opportunity, audience, and purpose, you need to determine what kind of text will best respond to your rhetorical situation.

Use the following questions to help you narrow your purpose and shape your response:

1. What specific assertion do you want to make about the causes or the consequences of the situation or phenomenon you're analyzing? What reasons support this particular claim? What evidence or examples can you provide to convince readers that each reason logically supports your analysis?

2. Which supporting reasons are most likely to resonate with or be convincing to your audience? What are the audience's beliefs, attitudes, or experiences that lead you to this conclusion?

3. What specific response are you hoping to draw from your audience? Do you want to affirm readers' existing beliefs about some negative or positive features of the global village? Do you want to draw their attention to overlooked content on the Internet or have them reconsider their views on a particular type of content? Do you want readers to perform different types of activities as they participate in the global village?

4. What might be the best way to present your analysis to your audience? That is, what kind of text is this audience most likely to respond to? (Chapter 13 can help you explore options for media and design.)

Writing a Critical Analysis: Working with Your Available Means

Shaping your critical analysis

pages 67–68

You are probably familiar with the form and arrangement of critical analyses because you read many of them in your daily life: editorials and feature articles, for example, are often in this genre. The introduction of a critical analysis hooks readers' attention, presenting a detailed example or description that helps them recognize the rhetorical opportunity and understand why this situation or phenomenon should be analyzed. The introduction also presents the writer's thesis,

pages 69–70

a claim about the causes or the consequences of the situation or phenomenon, and provides some support for it to establish the writer's ethos.

The body of a critical analysis presents and elaborates on the primary (and, depending on the depth of the analysis, the secondary) causes and/or consequences of the situation or phenomenon being analyzed. Here the writer clearly articulates how each cause contributes to or each consequence follows from the situation or phenomenon. The writer creates a strong appeal to logos as he or she presents reasons supporting the claim about each cause or consequence. Russell Watson, for instance, describes a situation in which the rebel group the Zapatistas use communications technology as "a potentially revolutionary weapon," and he

Introduction
▸ Describes the situation or phenomenon
▸ Establishes the rhetorical opportunity for analysis
▸ States the thesis, a claim about causes or consequences
▸ Builds the writer's ethos by providing support for the claim

Body
▸ Presents and elaborates on causes and/or consequences of the situation or phenomenon
▸ Articulates how each cause contributes to or each consequence follows from the situation
▸ Presents reasons supporting the claim about each cause or consequence
▸ Acknowledges and responds to alternative viewpoints
▸ Creates appeal to logos and enhances the writer's ethos

Conclusion
▸ Reinforces the positive benefits to readers from analyzing the situation or phenomenon or the negative situation that may result if such analysis is ignored
▸ Presents an effective appeal to pathos

points to specific technological and cultural changes that helped to bring about this situation. He continues throughout subsequent body paragraphs to more fully develop his argument that the primary cause of revolutionary groups' political advances is the ability to connect to the global village.

Writers also create strong appeals to logos as they present brief anecdotes, direct quotations, and statistics to strengthen each supporting reason and to help readers see more clearly how each cause or consequence is linked to the situation or phenomenon. For example, Watson details the Zapatistas' use of the Internet as an international platform via the bulletins and communiqués that Barbara Pillsbury transmits "to subscribers around the world." And he explains that the Zapatistas' Internet use has motivated more Mexicans to try to obtain access to cyberspace. Watson reinforces this point with a short, focused quote from Pillsbury: "Beyond their concerns about Chiapas, Mexicans have realized that they need to be part of this technology." Often, direct quotations can help writers establish persuasive appeals to ethos, as they signal to readers that the writers have sought out experts' opinions in order to deepen their knowledge about the topic.

The body paragraphs of a critical analysis also acknowledge and respond to alternative viewpoints about the situation or phenomenon being analyzed. Writers make this rhetorical move to improve both their appeals to logos, as they acknowledge and fill gaps in their arguments, and their appeals to ethos, as they present themselves as thoughtful appraisers of the perspectives of other stakeholders in the issue. Watson, for example, concedes the fact that the "most tightly closed societies, such as North Korea, and the most violently repressive ones, such as Iraq or Libya, may not be susceptible to an Information Age revolution"; he continues through the rest of that paragraph to present concrete examples of specific measures governments in those countries have taken to limit revolutionary groups' ability to use communications technology. And he also explains that "[e]ven in less rigid dictatorships, communications technology cannot make a revolution by itself." Through such statements, Watson acknowledges counterarguments to his claim about the revolutionary possibilities of the Internet and satellite television.

Finally, the conclusion of a critical analysis reinforces the positive benefits that readers can reap from analyzing this situation or phenomenon. Or, depending on the topic, the conclusion can illustrate the negative situation that may result if readers ignore the writer's critical analysis. The writer can also use the conclusion to present effective appeals to pathos.

Revision and peer review

After you've drafted a strong version of your critical analysis, ask one of your classmates to read it. You'll want your classmate to respond to your work in a way that helps you revise it into the strongest analysis it can be, one that addresses your intended audience, helps you fulfill your purpose, and is delivered in the most appropriate means available to you.

Questions for a peer reviewer

1. To what opportunity for change is the writer responding?
2. Does the writer clearly describe the situation or phenomenon? How might he or she help the audience better visualize the situation?
3. How does the writer establish the need to analyze this particular situation or phenomenon?
4. Who might be the writer's intended audience?
5. Where does the writer indicate how the situation or phenomenon concerns the audience?
6. Identify the thesis statement of the analysis, in which the writer clearly states his or her claim about the causes or the consequences of the situation or phenomenon being analyzed. If you cannot locate a thesis statement, what thesis statement might work for this document?
7. Identify the evidence and examples the writer provides in support of the claim.
8. Does the writer address varying perspectives on the causes or consequences of the situation or phenomenon being analyzed?
9. How does the writer establish pathos?
10. What did you learn from the conclusion that wasn't already in the document? What does the writer want you to take away from the document in terms of information, attitude, or action?
11. What section of the document did you most enjoy? Why?

Online Analysis

This online article analyzes the consequences of the YouTube video "Star Wars Kid," which is in the *Guinness Book of World Records* for most video downloads. To read the article, find *Writing in Three Media* in your English CourseMate, accessed through cengagebrain.com.

Oral/Multimedia Analysis

In this interview, a young Malawian man named William Kamkwamba explains the causes that led him to build a windmill to harness electricity at his rural home and traces the amazing consequences. A link is also available to "Moving Windmills," a short film. To watch the videos, find *Writing in Three Media* in your English CourseMate, accessed through cengagebrain .com.

Print Analysis

In the following essay, student writer Anna Seitz analyzes some consequences of getting an online degree.

WILLIAM WLUT/AFP/Getty Images

Bonita R. Cheshier/Shutterstock.com

© Corbis Premium RF/Alamy

Critical Analyses

Anna's experience with online learning could have been the basis for a fascinating memoir, if her purpose had been to look back on the years she spent getting her degree and recreate her experience for others. If she had been primarily interested in giving advice to a nephew who was considering getting a degree online, she might have written up a list of pros and cons in an informal e-mail—or relayed the information in a phone call. But Anna wanted to examine her experience in a way that clarified her conclusions for others. Her critical analysis does just that.

Critical Analyses

Anna Seitz

Professor James

English 275

31 January 2011

The Real-Time Consequences of an Online Degree

I'm a mother of three small children, and I'm much more interested in spending time with my kids than spending time in a classroom. When I decided to pursue an advanced degree, I opted for an online program. I didn't know exactly what it would be like, but I knew what I wanted out of it—flexibility to complete the program on my own schedule. And while I got that, I also found that my decision had other consequences.

The immediate consequence of taking online classes was that I did, in fact, have even more flexibility than I'd imagined. That was good and bad. I had an impressive selection of electives each term, especially because my advisor gave me almost total freedom to select my courses. The more remote consequence of this freedom is that I won't be graduating with the exact same skills and experiences as everyone else in my class—we all have different specialties and will be competing for different jobs. Also, none of my classes had set meeting or chat times, and I was able to do my readings, write my papers, and participate in discussion forums in fits and spurts (and in pajamas!). I read at night and during nap times, in the car, and at the playground. I learned to do most of my research online, and when I had to use local libraries, I simply packed up my gang for the children's story hour. Some of my professors provided the entire term's contents on day one, which helped me plan my work.

The flip side of this particular consequence was that planning my work was a bigger challenge than doing the work. Because my days with

Anna sets up her thesis: that there are both expected and unexpected consequences of working toward a degree online.

She opens with a positive consequence, one familiar to the millions of students getting degrees online.

She provides detailed support for her assertion about the first consequence.

Anna moves on to a second consequence, which isn't as positive. This paragraph is detailed with incidents from her life, a life familiar to many parents who are working toward a degree (online or off).

the children were always unpredictable, I lost a lot of sleep while learning how to pace myself in terms of taking care of my family and keeping up with my school work. There were times when my kids got stuck with a distracted mommy who cut corners on suppers and bedtime stories. I had to keep careful records of tasks and due dates, and I had to create my own deadlines as I learned how to divide big projects into manageable sections. After all, with online courses, the only regular reminders and announcements from the teachers are discussion board reminders (only useful if you log in and read them, of course). I'm nearly finished with the program, and I still haven't settled on an acceptable frequency for checking the class message board. Either I waste time checking constantly and finding nothing, or I go out for a day only to come home and find out that I've missed contributing to some major discussion or development.

Taking responsibility for my own learning at my own pace has always been comfortable for me. I've always been independent, and the idea of doing these classes "all by myself" was very appealing. Unfortunately, a secondary consequence of the online environment caught me by surprise. I was soon forced to admit that as much as I wanted to do things myself, my way, my professors and my classmates profoundly affected my learning, my grades, and my enjoyment of the classes. I had a few professors who spent as much or more time on my online classes as they would have on a face-to-face class, producing online PowerPoint lectures, enrichment activities, and discussion prompts, and making personal contact with each student. In those classes, I got to know my classmates, worked with others on projects, and learned things that I can still remember years later. The efforts of our professors inspired us to put in our own best efforts, and I would count those experiences to be on par with my best face-to-face classroom experiences.

Anna claims that independent learning feels natural and easy to her—but admits that her independent nature doesn't always lend itself to online learning.

I also had a few "teachers" who simply selected textbooks that came with lots of extras, such as a publisher's Web site with quizzes and assignments. In one of those classes, the publisher's Web site actually did the grading for the quizzes and calculated my class grade. I was really offended and kind of disgusted that my "teacher" would be so lazy. I felt that I wasn't getting what I'd paid for, and I felt neglected. Ultimately, I was embarrassed because I felt that it gave merit to all of the criticisms that I'd heard about online education. In one of those classes, I simply sat down with my textbook and did the entire term's quizzes in one night. I didn't learn a thing. I should have acted like a grown-up and made the best of it, but I just jumped through the hoops and collected my credits. I got an A in that class doing work which would have flunked me out of any face-to-face class, and that made me mad, too.

One of the remote consequences is that I began to consider my teacher's performance, and to discuss it with my classmates. When I was in college at 18, I was more focused on what I was putting into my classes than what I was getting out of them. I didn't notice what the teachers were or were not doing. In my current program, however, nearly all of the students are busy adults with careers and families who are paying their own way through school so that they can enhance their careers. My classmates and I are only there to improve our skills and we want to get our money's worth. There are a lot of complaints when we don't. I can think of dozens of examples of students voicing their complaints about the teacher, materials, or assignments as part of the class discussion, and since the communication is public, the teachers nearly always have to make improvements.

Another remote consequence is that there is surprisingly little privacy in an online class when compared to a face-to-face class, and that was very

As she provides logical support for her assertions (establishing logos), Anna also gives readers authentic glimpses into her self, a rhetorical move that emphasizes her positive ethos.

Anna carefully differentiates the immediate from the remote consequences of taking an online degree.

difficult to get used to. I can't just slink in, sit in the back of the class, keep my head down, and hope the teacher never learns my name. The comments I am required to post each week can be read, and in fact *must be read* by the entire class. Everyone knows what I've read, what I think about it, and how well I express myself. Everyone reads my papers, and I read theirs. For an independent person like me, this was tough to swallow. I didn't like comparing my work to others', even when it compared favorably. I dreaded the times when it compared unfavorably, and when I saw a classmate do particularly good work, I wanted to, too. It was a healthy and productive sort of peer pressure, and I did things I'd never tried to do before, and sometimes even did them well.

Anna's obvious connection with her fellow students helps her successfully establish pathos.

Ultimately, the primary consequence is that I am completing my degree, so my goal of getting a degree while managing my family responsibilities will soon be met. I did have a few complaints, but I could get bad teachers anywhere, and it's not just any program that would allow me to stay home with my kids all day while earning a degree. I missed a few of my teachers' e-mails, forgot people's names because I never saw their faces, and gave up hundreds of hours of sleep, but in the end, online education did work for me.

Alternatives to the Critical Analysis

Critical analyses are a fitting response to some, but not all, rhetorical situations. Your instructor might call on you to consider one of the following opportunities for writing.

1. In what ways are other students at your school or other people in your community contributing to or consuming information from the global village? What specific technologies are they using to link to others around the world? What specific kinds of content are they creating and reading, watching, or viewing? What do they learn from the virtual exchanges? What do they seem to be ignoring about their participation in the global village? Conduct primary research to learn more about the spe-

cific activities that classmates or fellow community members undertake in relation to the global village. Then compose a four-page investigative report on these activities, paying particular attention to the political, economic, social, and cultural realities that make such participation in the global village possible.

2. Write a four-page memoir exploring an experience you have had using technology to navigate within the global village. Describe your experience in as much specific detail as possible, using quotations and exemplification to help answer these questions: In what specific ways did the particular experience with technology bring you closer to the concerns and feelings of other people? In what ways did it create distance between you and other people and issues with which you are not directly concerned? What might be different about your academic, civic, or personal life if you did not have access to the online technology? If you had greater access? As you compose your memoir, consider who might be most interested in reading about what you learned through your experience.

pages 66–67

pages 75–77

3. Locate a website, television program, or some other media presentation that seems to represent some part of the global village. Consider all of the various materials (visuals, videos, audio clips, and texts) that the media presentation uses to depict places, cultures, or events from another part of the world, as well as the implicit or explicit argument that it makes about the people and places it presents. Then compose a four-page critical review of the presentation, focusing on the message it seeks to convey as well as the means through which it seeks to do so. Be sure to create a clear set of evaluative criteria to use and to provide evidence and examples to support your evaluation.

Everyday Reading: Responding with Literary Analyses

11

Since 1996, television show host and entrepreneur Oprah Winfrey has sparked significant public discussion about literature. For Oprah's Book Club, she selected over sixty-five books, including classics, contemporary fiction, and memoirs for viewers of *The Oprah Winfrey Show* to read. Special episodes of the show, such as the program featuring Toni Morrison in 1996, were devoted to interviewing the authors of these books and fostering audience discussion. Winfrey also devoted a section of her web page to hosting message boards for discussing the books, giving viewers opportunities to join smaller online reading groups, sponsoring essay writing contests about the books, providing tips to help interested viewers host their own book discussions in their communities, answering questions that readers might have about the books, and presenting "Reader of the Week" to feature one member of Oprah's Book Club. Winfrey's OWN Network is scheduled to continue the book club.

Although it stimulated interest in reading, Oprah's Book Club sometimes generated controversy. Jonathan Franzen, author of the novel Winfrey planned to feature in September 2001, was unsettled by all the attention Winfrey was receiving for his book. Franzen told the *Portland Oregonian* that he was thrilled to learn that his publisher had printed 800,000 copies of *The Corrections*—but

© Reuters/Corbis

every copy had the Oprah's Book Club logo on the front cover. "I see this as my book, my creation, and I didn't want that logo of corporate ownership on it," Franzen said. Shortly after Franzen made this and other comments, Winfrey revoked her invitation to him to appear on her show, creating even more controversy. But, by 2010, they had resolved their conflict: Franzen appeared on Winfrey's show, and his new book, *Freedom*, was named an Oprah's Book Club selection.

Despite occasional controversy, Winfrey's ability to motivate people to read more literature—especially her personal selections—cannot be denied: both contemporary and classic novels achieved bestseller status once they were stamped with the Oprah's Book Club logo. Little wonder then that publishers, such as Knopf Publishing Group chairman Sonny Mehta, have been forthright in acknowledging Winfrey's influence. According to Mehta, the book club has "brought the act of reading home to people in a way that publishers have not always been successful at doing."

The resurgence in widespread public projects aimed at encouraging communities to read, discuss, and write about literature has been spurred on by campaigns similar to Oprah's Book Club. The Seattle-based Washington Center for the Book, for example, initiated One Book, One Community, a series of reading promotion programs. For these programs, which have been run in towns, cities, counties, and regions in all fifty states as well as the District of Columbia, one book is selected for all residents to read. Responses to the book take the form of community discussions, public readings, essay contests, and other activities. In some places, separate One Book, One Community programs have been created for local youth; in Evansville, Indiana, for example, the youth program focused on Margaret McMullan's Civil War novel, *How I Found the Strong*.

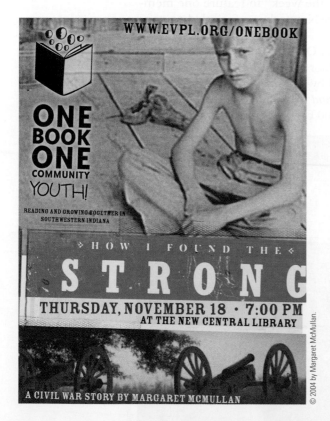

When people come together to discuss a book, they are usually analyzing that text. The purpose of a **literary analysis** is to explain and interpret a work. During the process of such an analysis, readers or writers sharpen their ability to synthesize meaning from the various elements of a text: the plot, setting, characters, point of view, and stylistic techniques of a novel, short story, poem, or play. When you write a literary analysis, you will come to better understand more about each of these individual elements and the ways in which they interact with one another.

IDENTIFYING AN OPPORTUNITY

In this chapter, your goal will be to identify a rhetorical opportunity for analyzing a literary work. Perhaps you have felt the urge to discuss one of Oprah's Book Club selections with an online or other book group. Maybe you've given a favorite novel to a friend with a note saying, "Drop everything and read this book." Or perhaps you've returned from a stage adaptation of a favorite novel complaining that one of the characters was miscast. In each of these situations, you were responding to and analyzing a literary work. Such a situation provides a starting point for determining what most interests you. As you work, then, consider the most fitting means of delivery for your literary analysis:

Print Literary Analysis

written for an undergraduate journal

Oral Literary Analysis

recorded as a podcast

Online Literary Analysis

posted on a website such as GoodReads.com or LibraryThing.com

To begin, freewrite for five minutes in response to each of the following questions (or use any of the invention techniques presented on pages 58-61):

1. Examine the images on the next several pages of this chapter. Which of them seems familiar to you? In other words, have you ever seen or encountered literature in an everyday context like that portrayed in any of the images?

2. Which of the images depicts a situation involving a literary work or a form of literary expression that you'd like to encounter? Why?

3. Which of the images surprised you the most? Why did it surprise you to find this image in a discussion of reading and writing about literature?

4. Which of the images depicts a form of text that you would normally not characterize as literary? What leads you to characterize that text as you do?

5. Select the form of literary expression that you would be most interested in learning more about or analyzing in more detail. What most interests you about this form? What about this kind of text or the context in which it would normally be encountered makes it particularly compelling to you? Be as specific as you can.

Real Situations

Oprah's Book Club and the One Book, One Community programs have sought to encourage people to carve out time and space to enjoy and discuss literature, but other public campaigns have aimed to bring literature to people in the midst of their daily routines. The Poetry Society of America, for example, teamed with Barnes & Noble Booksellers and New York's Metropolitan Transit Authority to create Poetry in Motion. A major part of this campaign was the placement of Poetry in Motion posters in New York City subways and buses.

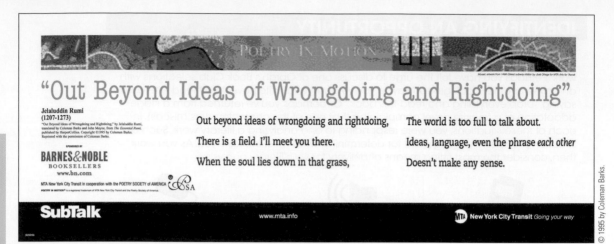

Poetry in Motion poster featuring "Out Beyond Ideas of Wrongdoing and Rightdoing," by Jelaluddin Rumi.

The posters encouraged commuters, local residents, and visitors to take a few minutes' break from their hectic schedules to contemplate some ideas and images that poets have created with language.

All of us have encountered verses on the greeting cards we send at birthdays, anniversaries, graduations, and other special occasions, but some established literary authors have circulated their poems through this form. Former U.S. poet laureate Maya Angelou produced her own collection of greeting cards for Hallmark Cards, Inc. She explained, "My partnership with Hallmark creates a new way for my message to reach millions of women and families, many of whom may not be familiar with my work, but most of whom seek an expanded viewpoint on courage, spirituality, and personal expression." Angelou's comments express a view held by many that everyday encounters with literature can help people gain new perspectives on their professional, communal, and familial lives.

Angelou drew international attention to the uses of poetry when she read her poem "On the Pulse of the Morning" at the first inauguration of U.S. President Clinton on January 20, 1993. Although Angelou was only the second person in history to read a poem at a U.S. presidential inauguration, the trend may be catching on: three of the five ceremonies between 1993 and 2009 featured poets, among them Elizabeth Alexander.

Poets are chosen to read at presidential inaugurations to mark a significant national event, but many other people regularly read their poetry to audiences in clubs, bars, coffeehouses, libraries, student unions, and writing centers

Elizabeth Alexander reads her poem, "Praise Song for the Day" at the inauguration of President Obama.

Beau Sia reads his poetry at the Poetry Slam Face Off at the Nuyorican Poets Café in New York City.

in cities, communities, and colleges across the country. A prominent part of the movement to make poetry and other literary forms public has been the Poetry Slam circuit. A poetry slam involves a spoken performance of poetry in a competitive setting, where randomly selected members of the audience judge the different poets on their lyrical skills as well as their stage presence. Some literary critics have attacked Poetry Slam and warned that the popularity of the movement, in the words of Harold Bloom, signals "the death of art." But who gets to decide what is or is not "art"? The Poetry Slam competitions wrest that decision from academic and literary critics, who have long held sole power over it. These events place this power in the hands of the audience members, who decide what performances and poems do and do not move them.

Given the broad popularity of poetry of all kinds, we're all likely to interact with poetry in public spaces— from hearing it on a daily walk to class

Alexis Ignatovich writes a poem in Union Square Park.

AP Photo/Eddy Palumbo

A passerby rearranges words on the magnetic poetry wall at the University of Pennsylvania.

to seeing it posted on buses or subways. Artists of all types use public spaces to express ideas and images with language.

But people don't need to write in chalk on sidewalks to contribute to public engagement with literary texts. The company Magnetic Poetry, Inc., produces magnetic poetry kits that can inspire people to put their own poems on refrigerators and filing cabinets in their homes and offices. Some groups have made such magnetic poetry available in public spaces. The University of Pennsylvania, for example, set up a magnetic poetry wall project on the College Green as part of a celebration of National Poetry Month in 1998. In addition, former U.S. Poet Laureate Robert Pinsky launched the Favorite Poem Project, whose website invites citizens of all ages to send in a video or podcast of themselves reading aloud their favorite poem. The website also provides online resources and space for people's discussions and analyses of various poems. These sorts of public poetry projects aim to get more people engaged with literature—talking about it and experiencing the excitement of composing their own literary creations.

Twitter posts often sound like haiku, and the combination of poetry and tweet has come to be called the *twaiku*. Poet Matt Morden regularly posts twaiku like the following:

small town swim gala / the tinkle of medals / round the winner's neck #haiku #micropoetry #NaHaiWriMo

Note that Morden reserves the final 31 characters for Twitter hashtags, used to organize feeds.

These are just a few of the ways you might encounter literature in daily life—you can probably think of many more. This chapter will give you an opportunity to sharpen your ability to read, interpret, and formulate ideas about

Favorite Poem Project

Americans Saying Poems They Love

Todd Hellems reading Cullen, "Yet Do I Marvel"

Home
The Project
The Videos
The Books & DVD
For Teachers
Get Involved
Contact
Donate
Summer Institute
for K-12 Teachers

Like   225 likes. Sign Up to see what your friends like.

BOSTON UNIVERSITY   A partnership among Boston University, the Library of Congress and other organizations with major funding from the National Endowment from the Arts and the Carnegie Corporation of New York.

Courtesy of the Favorite Poem Project

The Favorite Poem Project encourages people to engage with literature.

the significance of literary texts. You will use writing throughout this chapter not just to present your polished ideas about a literary work but also to record your thoughts and perceptions before, during, and after you read it. Rereading your own developing thoughts about a text will help you to identify a critical question that you find interesting and that will sustain your writing.

DESCRIBING EVERYDAY ENCOUNTERS WITH LITERATURE

1. Working with a classmate, choose two of the images in this section and list specific details about that public presentation of creative writing. What can you tell about the contexts within which people encounter these texts? When might people see these texts? Where might they see them? How long might they spend reading these texts or talking or writing about them?

2. How do the contexts for the texts influence the ways in which people read and respond to the texts? How might these contexts affect the meaning that people take from these pieces of writing?

3. Who is the audience that the writer of each text wanted to reach? What kind of responses do you think this writer wanted to evoke in this audience? How might the context in which this text was to be read or heard have affected the way the writer created it?

4. If you wanted to respond to one of these pieces of writing, what means (or media) are available to you? In other words, what physical means do you have for developing a response? How many kinds of fitting responses can you imagine?

Real Responses to Real Situations

Writers on reading

We read texts with a variety of purposes in mind. We read instruction sets to follow some process, such as installing a new program on a computer or preparing a package of macaroni and cheese. We read textbooks to learn more about topics in academic fields of study, such as the functions of mitochondria or the probable causes of the Civil War. We read literary works for specific purposes, too. Some of us read science fiction novels to imagine what life on Earth might be like in the distant future. Others read literature about groups whose cultures and lives differ from our own in order to learn about their experiences. Some of us read plays by William Shakespeare to gain greater insight into the depths of human motivations and passions; others read these texts merely to enjoy the poetic language of Elizabethan dramatic verse.

Whatever our motivations might be for reading literary works, the needs or desires that shape *why* we read affect *how* we read. Each of us pays particular attention to certain characters, certain scenes, or certain sentences or phrases that seem most important to us, given the interests and experiences we bring to the text. The following readings illustrate this fact. The first was written by a literary and philosophical scholar; the second and third were written by successful literary writers. The topic of each is the act of reading itself.

Throughout his career, Mortimer Adler committed himself to persuading all Americans, not just those privileged enough to formally pursue higher education, to acquire a liberal education and appreciate the insights to be gained from great writings in philosophy, science, religion, history, and literature. To further these goals, Adler co-founded the Center for the Study of the Great Ideas, the Great Books Foundation, and the University of Chicago's Basic Program of Liberal Education for Adults. Adler also developed and edited the book series Great Books of the Western World and served as editor-in-chief of the journal *Philosophy Is Everybody's Business.* His essay "How to Mark a Book," which first appeared in the *Saturday Review of Literature* in 1940, reflects his pursuit of this lifelong goal of encouraging all adults, no matter their background, to read, analyze, and discuss classical works of literature. Adler believed that a person truly possesses a book only when he or she has written in it, actively engaged with it, and made personal responses to the ideas in its pages.

> How to Mark a Book

Mortimer Adler

You know you have to read "between the lines" to get the most out of anything. I want to persuade you to do something equally important in the course of your reading. I want to persuade you to "write between the lines." Unless you do, you are not likely to do the most efficient kind of reading. I contend, quite bluntly, that marking up a book is not an act of mutilation but of love.

You shouldn't mark up a book which isn't yours. Librarians (or your friends) who lend you books expect you to keep them clean, and you should. If you decide that I am right about the usefulness of marking books, you will have to buy them. Most of the world's great books are available today, in reprint editions, at less than a dollar.

There are two ways in which one can own a book. The first is the property right you establish by paying for it, just as you pay for clothes and furniture. But this act of purchase is only the prelude to possession. Full ownership comes only when you have made it a part of yourself, and the best way to make yourself a part of it is by writing in it. An illustration may make the point clear. You buy a beefsteak and transfer it from the butcher's icebox to your own. But you do not own the beefsteak in the most important sense until you consume it and get it into your bloodstream. I am arguing that books, too, must be absorbed in your bloodstream to do you any good.

Confusion about what it means to *own* a book leads people to a false reverence for paper, binding, and type—a respect for the physical thing—the craft of the printer rather than the genius of the author. They forget that it is possible for a man to acquire the idea, to possess the beauty, which a great book contains, without staking his claim by pasting his bookplate inside the cover. Having a fine library doesn't prove that its owner has a mind enriched by books; it proves nothing more than that he, his father, or his wife, was rich enough to buy them.

There are three kinds of book owners. The first has all the standard sets and best sellers—unread, untouched. (This deluded individual owns woodpulp and ink, not books.) The second has a great many books—a few of them read through, most of them dipped into, but all of them as clean and shiny as the day they were bought. (This person would probably like to make books his own, but is restrained by a false respect for their physical appearance.) The third has a few books or many—every one of them dog-eared and dilapidated, shaken and loosened by continual use, marked and scribbled in from front to back. (This man owns books.)

Is it false respect, you may ask, to preserve intact and unblemished a beautifully printed book, an elegantly bound edition? Of course not. I'd no more scribble all over a first edition of *Paradise Lost* than I'd give my baby a set of crayons and an original Rembrandt. I wouldn't mark up a painting or a statue. Its soul, so to speak, is inseparable from its body. And the beauty of a rare edition or of a richly manufactured volume is like that of a painting or a statue.

But the soul of a book *can* be separate from its body. A book is more like the score of a piece of music than it is like a painting. No great musician confuses a

continued

Literary Analyses

symphony with the printed sheets of music. Arturo Toscanini reveres Brahms, but Toscanini's score of the G Minor Symphony is so thoroughly marked up that no one but the maestro himself can read it. The reason why a great conductor makes notations on his musical scores—marks them up again and again each time he returns to study them—is the reason why you should mark your books. If your respect for magnificent binding or typography gets in the way, buy yourself a cheap edition and pay your respects to the author.

Why is marking up a book indispensable to reading? First, it keeps you awake. (And I don't mean merely conscious; I mean awake.) In the second place, reading, if it is active, is thinking, and thinking tends to express itself in words, spoken or written. The marked book is usually the thought-through book. Finally, writing helps you remember the thoughts you had, or the thoughts the author expressed. Let me develop these three points.

If reading is to accomplish anything more than passing time, it must be active. You can't let your eyes glide across the lines of a book and come up with an understanding of what you have read. Now an ordinary piece of light fiction, like, say, *Gone With the Wind,* doesn't require the most active kind of reading. The books you read for pleasure can be read in a state of relaxation, and nothing is lost. But a great book, rich in ideas and beauty, a book that raises and tries to answer great fundamental questions, demands the most active reading of which you are capable. You don't absorb the ideas of John Dewey the way you absorb the crooning of Mr. Vallee. You have to reach for them. That you cannot do while you're asleep.

If, when you've finished reading a book, the pages are filled with your notes, you know that you read actively. The most famous active reader of great books I know is President Hutchins, of the University of Chicago. He also has the hardest schedule of business activities of any man I know. He invariably reads with a pencil, and sometimes, when he picks up a book and pencil in the evening, he finds himself, instead of making intelligent notes, drawing what he calls "caviar factories" on the margins. When that happens, he puts the book down. He knows he's too tired to read, and he's just wasting time.

But, you may ask, why is writing necessary? Well, the physical act of writing, with your own hand, brings words and sentences more sharply before your mind and preserves them better in your memory. To set down your reaction to important words and sentences you have read, and the questions they have raised in your mind, is to preserve those reactions and sharpen those questions.

Even if you wrote on a scratch pad, and threw the paper away when you had finished writing, your grasp of the book would be surer. But you don't have to throw the paper away. The margins (top and bottom, as well as side), the end-papers, the very space between the lines, are all available. They aren't sacred. And, best of all, your marks and notes become an integral part of the book and stay there forever. You can pick up the book the following week or year, and there are all your points of agreement, disagreement, doubt, and inquiry. It's like resuming an interrupted conversation with the advantage of being able to pick up where you left off.

And that is exactly what reading a book should be: a conversation between you and the author. Presumably he knows more about the subject than you do; naturally, you'll have the proper humility as you approach him. But don't let anybody tell you that a reader is supposed to be solely on the receiving end. Understanding is a two-way operation; learning doesn't consist in being an empty receptacle. The learner has to question himself and question the teacher. He even has to argue with the teacher, once he understands what the teacher is saying. And marking a book is literally an expression of differences, or agreements of opinion, with the author.

There are all kinds of devices for marking a book intelligently and fruitfully. Here's the way I do it:

1. *Underlining (or highlighting):* of major points, of important or forceful statements.

2. *Vertical lines at the margin:* to emphasize a statement already underlined.

3. *Star, asterisk, or other doodad at the margin:* to be used sparingly, to emphasize the ten or twenty most important statements in the book. (You may want to fold the bottom corner of each page on which you use such marks. It won't hurt the sturdy paper on which most modern books are printed, and you will be able take the book off the shelf at any time and, by opening it at the folded-corner page, refresh your recollection of the book.)

4. *Numbers in the margin:* to indicate the sequence of points the author makes in developing a single argument.

5. *Numbers of other pages in the margin:* to indicate where else in the book the author made points relevant to the point marked; to tie up the ideas in a book, which, though they may be separated by many pages, belong together.

6. *Circling or highlighting of key words or phrases.*

7. *Writing in the margin, or at the top or bottom of the page, for the sake of:* recording questions (and perhaps answers) which a passage raised in your mind; reducing a complicated discussion to a simple statement; recording the sequence of major points right through the [books]. I use the endpapers at the back of the book to make a personal index of the author's points in the order of their appearance.

The front end-papers are to me the most important. Some people reserve them for a fancy bookplate. I reserve them for fancy thinking. After I have finished reading the book and making my personal index on the back end-papers, I turn to the front and try to outline the book, not page by page or point by point (I've already done that at the back), but as an integrated structure, with a basic unity and an order of parts. This outline is, to me, the measure of my understanding of the work.

If you're a die-hard anti-book-marker, you may object that the margins, the space between the lines, and the end-papers don't give you room enough. All right. How about using a scratch pad slightly smaller than the page-size of the book—so that the edges of the sheets won't protrude? Make your index, outlines and even your notes on the pad, and then insert these sheets permanently inside the front and back covers of the book.

Or, you may say that this business of marking books is going to slow up your reading. It probably will. That's one of the reasons for doing it. Most of us have

continued

been taken in by the notion that speed of reading is a measure of our intelligence. There is no such thing as the right speed for intelligent reading. Some things should be read quickly and effortlessly and some should be read slowly and even laboriously. The sign of intelligence in reading is the ability to read different things differently according to their worth. In the case of good books, the point is not to see how many of them you can get through, but rather how many can get through you—how many you can make your own. A few friends are better than a thousand acquaintances. If this be your aim, as it should be, you will not be impatient if it takes more time and effort to read a great book than it does a newspaper.

You may have one final objection to marking books. You can't lend them to your friends because nobody else can read them without being distracted by your notes. Furthermore, you won't want to lend them because a marked copy is kind of an intellectual diary, and lending it is almost like giving your mind away.

If your friend wishes to read your *Plutarch's Lives*, *Shakespeare*, or *The Federalist Papers*, tell him gently but firmly, to buy a copy. You will lend him your car or your coat—but your books are as much a part of you as your head or your heart.

Sherman Alexie, a Spokane/Coeur d'Alene from Wellpinit, Washington, wrote the following essay in 1998 for the *Los Angeles Times*' series "The Joy of Reading and Writing." In this essay, Alexie describes his first encounters with the material of literature—bound books and their texts—and explains how his family and community experiences have shaped his experiences of reading and writing. Alexie encourages his readers to reflect on how cultural and economic circumstances shape reading practices and on the value and use of reading and writing. He wants to encourage today's Native American students to see that writing is not "something beyond Indians" and to motivate them to save their cultures through recording, reworking, and reviving their communities' stories, experiences, and worldviews.

> Superman and Me

Sherman Alexie

I learned to read with a Superman comic book. Simple enough, I suppose. I cannot recall which particular Superman comic book I read, nor can I remember which villain he fought in that issue. I cannot remember the plot, nor the means by which I obtained the comic book. What I can remember is this: I was 3 years old, a Spokane Indian boy living with his family on the Spokane Indian Reservation in eastern Washington state. We were poor by most standards, but one of my parents usually managed to find some minimum-wage job or another, which made us middle-class by reservation standards. I had a brother and three sisters. We lived on a combination of irregular paychecks, hope, fear and government surplus food.

AP Photo/Jim Cooper

My father, who is one of the few Indians who went to Catholic school on purpose, was an avid reader of westerns, spy thrillers, murder mysteries, gangster epics, basketball player biographies and anything else he could find. He bought his books by the pound at Dutch's Pawn Shop, Goodwill, Salvation Army and Value Village. When he had extra money, he bought new novels at supermarkets, convenience stores and hospital gift shops. Our house was filled with books. They were stacked in crazy piles in the bathroom, bedrooms and living room. In a fit of unemployment-inspired creative energy, my father built a set of bookshelves and soon filled them with a random assortment of books about the Kennedy assassination, Watergate, the Vietnam War and the entire 23-book series of the Apache westerns. My father loved books, and since I loved my father with an aching devotion, I decided to love books as well.

I can remember picking up my father's books before I could read. The words themselves were mostly foreign, but I still remember the exact moment when I first understood, with a sudden clarity, the purpose of a paragraph. I didn't have the vocabulary to say "paragraph," but I realized that a paragraph was a fence that held words. The words inside a paragraph worked together for a common purpose. They had some specific reason for being inside the same fence. This knowledge delighted me. I began to think of everything in terms of paragraphs. Our reservation was a small paragraph within the United States. My family's house was a paragraph, distinct from the other paragraphs of the LeBrets to the north, the Fords to our south and the Tribal School to the west. Inside our house, each family member existed as a separate paragraph but still had genetics and common experiences to link us. Now, using this logic, I can see my changed family as an essay of seven paragraphs: mother, father, older brother, the deceased sister, my younger twin sisters and our adopted little brother.

At the same time I was seeing the world in paragraphs, I also picked up that Superman comic book. Each panel, complete with picture, dialogue and narrative was a three-dimensional paragraph. In one panel, Superman breaks through a door. His suit is red, blue and yellow. The brown door shatters into many pieces. I look at the narrative above the picture. I cannot read the words, but I assume it tells me that "Superman is breaking down the door." Aloud, I pretend to read the words and say, "Superman is breaking down the door." Words, dialogue, also float out of Superman's mouth. Because he is breaking down the door, I assume he says, "I am breaking down the door." Once again, I pretend to read the words and say aloud, "I am breaking down the door." In this way, I learned to read.

This might be an interesting story all by itself. A little Indian boy teaches himself to read at an early age and advances quickly. He reads "Grapes of Wrath" in kindergarten when other children are struggling through "Dick and Jane." If he'd been anything but an Indian boy living on the reservation, he might have been called a prodigy. But he is an Indian boy living on the reservation and is simply an oddity. He grows into a man who often speaks of his childhood in the third-person, as if it will somehow dull the pain and make him sound more modest about his talents.

A smart Indian is a dangerous person, widely feared and ridiculed by Indians and non-Indians alike. I fought with my classmates on a daily basis. They wanted me to stay quiet when the non-Indian teacher asked for answers, for volunteers, for help. We were Indian children who were expected to be stupid.

continued

Most lived up to those expectations inside the classroom but subverted them on the outside. They struggled with basic reading in school but could remember how to sing a few dozen powwow songs. They were monosyllabic in front of their non-Indian teachers but could tell complicated stories and jokes at the dinner table. They submissively ducked their heads when confronted by a non-Indian adult but would slug it out with the Indian bully who was 10 years older. As Indian children, we were expected to fail in the non-Indian world. Those who failed were ceremonially accepted by other Indians and appropriately pitied by non-Indians.

I refused to fail. I was smart. I was arrogant. I was lucky. I read books late into the night, until I could barely keep my eyes open. I read books at recess, then during lunch, and in the few minutes left after I had finished my classroom assignments. I read books in the car when my family traveled to powwows or basketball games. In shopping malls, I ran to the bookstores and read bits and pieces of as many books as I could. I read the books my father brought home from the pawnshops and secondhand. I read the books I borrowed from the library. I read the backs of cereal boxes. I read the newspaper. I read the bulletins posted on the walls of the school, the clinic, the tribal offices, the post office. I read junk mail. I read auto-repair manuals. I read magazines. I read anything that had words and paragraphs. I read with equal parts joy and desperation. I loved those books, but I also knew that love had only one purpose. I was trying to save my life. Despite all the books I read, I am still surprised I became a writer. I was going to be a pediatrician. These days, I write novels, short stories, and poems. I visit schools and teach creative writing to Indian kids. In all my years in the reservation school system, I was never taught how to write poetry, short stories or novels. I was certainly never taught that Indians wrote poetry, short stories and novels. Writing was something beyond Indians. I cannot recall a single time that a guest teacher visited the reservation. There must have been visiting teachers. Who were they? Where are they now? Do they exist? I visit the schools as often as possible. The Indian kids crowd the classroom. Many are writing their own poems, short stories and novels. They have read my books. They have read many other books. They look at me with bright eyes and arrogant wonder. They are trying to save their lives. Then there are the sullen and already defeated Indian kids who sit in the back rows and ignore me with theatrical precision. The pages of their notebooks are empty. They carry neither pencil nor pen. They stare out the window. They refuse and resist. "Books," I say to them. "Books," I say. I throw my weight against their locked doors. The door holds. I am smart. I am arrogant. I am lucky. I am trying to save our lives.

Marianne Gingher has written four books, including the novel *Bobby Rex's Greatest Hit* and a memoir, *A Girl's Life: Horses, Boys, Weddings & Luck*. She teaches creative writing at the University of North Carolina at Chapel Hill. The following excerpt is from an essay about a book by Eudora Welty. Gingher's experience reading Eudora Welty's novel inspired her toward a career in writing, as she came to realize the miracle that fiction writers perform as they "transform the drudge and drone of prose into language as airborne as birdsong."

> The Most Double-D-Daring Book I Read

Marianne Gingher

It was gentle Eudora Welty's rowdy little romance, *The Robber Bridegroom,* that incited me to throw protocol and every good manner my mother ever taught me out the window and barge my way into a party, uninvited. I blame that book entirely with its spitfire heroine, its rollicking blend of American folklore, European fairy tale, and confection of language so luscious I wanted to eat every page. Best of all, *The Robber Bridegroom* was written in 1943, when political correctness was only a tyrannical gleam in the critic's eye. Just imagine! A writer could write about a bandit who kidnapped a plantation owner's daughter, deflowered her (the maid enjoyed it!), and set her up cooking and cleaning for him and his band of rogues in an isolated hovel. Not only does she not complain, she whistles like a lark while she love-slaves her life away.

Welty's only thematic agenda was to weave a sly and witty entertainment, wicked with hyperbole, that portrays the profound gains and losses inherent in civilizing a behemoth Southern wilderness. This is a madcap bucking bronco of a book filled with galloping diversions that have confounded and irritated literary scholars looking to rein it in. That must be the chief reason it enthralled me.

I came upon it at a time in my education when I relished the refreshment of literature that reminded me of why I had loved reading as a child—for the sensation of wholehearted adventure.

I didn't read Eudora Welty until the early 1970s, when I was in graduate school. Somehow, although I had grown up in the South, I had missed all the Southern writers, except Faulkner. Not all of Welty's fiction is as fanciful as *The Robber Bridegroom,* of course, but the chief appeal to me of all her writing is its Yeats-like lyricism and imagery as concrete and well aimed as a stone expertly skipped across water. I thought of myself in those days as a failed poet. That Welty, a writer of fiction, could transform the drudge and drone of prose into language as airborne as birdsong seemed nothing short of miraculous to me—and an inspiration.

My teacher, Fred Chappel, frequently suggested books I might enjoy, recommending everything from Aristotle to Tolstoy to H. P. Lovecraft. On one occasion we were standing near a bookshelf in his den, and something I had said made him reach for *The Robber Bridegroom.* . . .

I took *The Robber Bridegroom* home and gulped it down in one sitting, admiring its mix of beauty and rambunctiousness. On a second reading I paid close attention to the many liberties Welty takes with the conventions of the tale. Her heroine, Rosamond, is no passive fairy tale princess waiting for some prince to rouse her from her stupor with a kiss. Rosamond is spirited, industrious, and loyal; but she is also habituated to lying and takes a few pratfalls normally reserved for the buffoon. The book's hero, Jamie Lockhart, thief and lover, is no paragon of family values. He is however, a hero "with the power to look both ways and see a thing from all sides." Sometimes his hesitation and thoughtfulness waylay his success. It's the couple's lack of perfection, their rascally virtue that defines Jamie and Rosamond as recognizably modern.

continued

My third reading of the book was a submersion in language. I found myself trying to memorize passages I admired so that when I returned the book—which was then out of print—the afterglow of its imagery would permanently flicker across my brain. I read of one character so festooned with jewelry "that she gave out spangles the way a porcupine gives out quills." A bucket of fresh milk had "the sound of foam in it." Daylight was so tentative "that the green was first there, then not there in the treetops, but green seemed to beat on the air like a pulse." Six ugly girls were "as weighted down with freckles as a fig tree is with figs."

Several months passed before I felt ready to part with the book. To tell the truth, my brain felt feverish from reading it so many times, a little wild and woolly. When Fred opened the door, I'm sure I looked like somebody who needed to have her temperature taken. I apologized for the late return. "How'd you like it?" he asked.

"It's one of the most unruly books I ever read," I declared. Fred laughed. As he took the book, I imagined he could feel its palpitations in sync with my own.

"Romance, murder, sorrow, comedy, violence, charm, and poetry—it has everything. I loved it so much I've been trying to memorize it."

Marianne Moore was one of the leading poets of the modernist movement in the United States, which spanned the first four decades of the twentieth century. She published her poems in the leading literary journals of her time (*Others, Poetry: A Magazine of Verse*, and the *Dial*), and the poems were then reprinted in small books, including *Poems* (1921), *Observations* (1924), *What Are Years?* (1941), and *Nevertheless* (1944). Her *Collected Poems* (1951) won the Pulitzer Prize and the National Book Award in 1952. As she accepted the National Book Award, Moore suggested that critics called her work "poetry" because there simply weren't any other categories to put it in. Moore often spoke of enjoying her biology courses while earning her BA at Bryn Mawr College from 1905 to 1909; literary scholars Elaine Oswald and Robert L. Gale suggest that this enjoyment of scientific study probably resulted in Moore's "love of intricately shaped animals" and her "life respect for precision in description." Moore makes a call for precise writing in the following poem. All types of writing are important, Moore suggests, but poetry, with its precise descriptions of both the physical world and the ideas conjured up by the human imagination, helps us better understand ourselves and the world around us.

© Gordon Converse

While serving as the judge for Mount Holyoke College's 1955 Glascock Poetry Competition, Marianne Moore spoke with student Sylvia Plath.

Literary Analyses

> Poetry

Marianne Moore

I, too, dislike it: there are things that are important beyond all this fiddle.
    Reading it, however, with a perfect contempt for it, one discovers that there is in
    it after all, a place for the genuine.
    Hands that can grasp, eyes
        that can dilate, hair that can rise
            if it must, these things are important not because a
high-sounding interpretation can be put upon them but because they are
    useful. When they become so derivative as to become unintelligible,
    the same thing may be said for all of us, that we
        do not admire what
        we cannot understand: the bat
            holding on upside down or in quest of something to
eat, elephants pushing, a wild horse taking a roll, a tireless wolf under
    a tree, the immovable critic twitching his skin like a horse that feels a flea, the
    base
    ball fan, the statistician—
        nor is it valid
        to discriminate against "business documents and
school-books"; all these phenomena are important. One must make a distinction
    however: when dragged into prominence by half poets, the result is not poetry,
    nor till the poets among us can be
    "literalists of
        "the imagination"—above
            insolence and triviality and can present
for inspection, "imaginary gardens with real toads in them," shall we have
    it. In the meantime, if you demand on the one hand,
    the raw material of poetry in
        all its rawness and
    that which is on the other hand
        genuine, you are interested in poetry.

> ANALYZING THE RHETORICAL SITUATION

1. Spend several minutes describing your own strategies for reading a literary work. Do you read with a pen, pencil, or highlighter in your hand? Do you use any of the marking techniques Mortimer Adler recommends? Or do you read on an e-book reader, using different techniques afforded by the digital medium? How do these reading strategies affect how you respond to a literary work and what you later remember about that text?

2. Why did Sherman Alexie read when he was a student at the reservation school? What evidence for your answer does his essay

provide? For Alexie, what is the purpose of reading for children on the reservation?

3. Given what you have learned about Alexie from his essay, how would you describe his reading process? What textual features would he be most likely to notice and remember? On what features would he be least likely to focus? How might Alexie's personal experiences have shaped his reading preferences and practices?

4. How did Marianne Gingher read *The Robber Bridegroom*? How did her ways of interpreting, analyzing, or appreciating the novel change during subsequent readings?

5. Why might Marianne Moore have begun "Poetry" with the line "I, too, dislike it"? With whom might she be agreeing? What rhetorical opportunity does Moore want to address with her poem?

6. What is poetry, according to Moore? How does Moore use comparison and contrast to clarify her definition? What purpose does she see in writing poetry, and what does she believe people can gain from reading it? Be sure to cite passages from "Poetry" to support your answers.

7. Spend several minutes writing in as much detail as you can about a memorable reading experience you have had. What were you reading, and why were you reading it? To what features of the text were you paying the most attention? What were your initial reactions while reading the text? Describe how your reactions to or thoughts about the text have changed since you initially read it.

COMMUNITY CONNECTIONS

1. Write for ten minutes about your response to one of the four texts in this section. How do the writer's arguments or opinions about reading coincide with or diverge from your own perspective on reading?

2. Write for ten minutes in response to another of the four texts. How do this writer's arguments or opinions about reading coincide with or diverge from your perspective?

3. Write for ten minutes about how any of the four texts in this section either caused you to think differently about literature, reading, and the importance of interpretation or confirmed your own perspective.

Literary Analyses: A Fitting Response

Genres of literature

As you've seen in earlier chapters of this book, genres such as investigative reports, memoirs, and proposals can be identified by their particular features and conventions. Literary genres are no different. Some genres are timeless and culturally universal (drama and poetry, for instance); others have developed within a specific period and culture (detective fiction is a recent Western cultural phenomenon). Just as you can recognize film genres—action, suspense, horror, comedy, animated, Western, and science fiction—you can identify various literary genres: from poetry and drama to essays and narratives. Just as film genres sometimes overlap (for example, when an action film is partially animated), so do literary genres. Some poems are referred to as prose poems, some plays are written in verse. But even when genres overlap, the identifiable features of each genre remain evident.

Some of the most widely studied literary genres are fiction, drama, and poetry, though many forms of nonfiction (including personal essays and memoirs, literacy narratives, and manifestos) are being studied in college courses on literature. All imaginative literature can be characterized as fictional, but the term **fiction** applies specifically to novels and short stories.

Drama differs from all other imaginative literature in one specific way: it is meant to be performed—whether on stage, on film, or on television—with the director and actors imprinting the lines with their own interpretations. In fact, the method of presentation distinguishes drama from fiction, even though the two genres share many of the same elements (setting, character, plot, and dialogue). In a novel, you often find extensive descriptions of characters and setting, as well as passages revealing what characters are thinking. In a play, you learn what a character is thinking when he or she shares thoughts with another character in dialogue or presents a **dramatic soliloquy** (a speech delivered to the audience by an actor alone on the stage). And like fiction, nonfiction, and poetry, drama can be read; in which case, you bring your interpretative abilities to what is on the printed page rather than to a performance of the work.

Poetry shares many of the components of fiction and drama. It, too, may have a narrator with a point of view. Dramatic monologues and narrative poems sometimes have a plot, a setting, and characters. But poetry is primarily characterized by its extensive use of concentrated language, or language that relies on imagery, allusions, figures of speech, symbols, sound and rhythm, and precise word choice, all of which allow poets to make a point in one or two words rather than spelling it out explicitly.

Elements of literary texts

Characters The characters are the humans or humanlike personalities (aliens, creatures, robots, animals, and so on) who carry along the action. The main character is called the **protagonist**, who is in external conflict with another character or an institution or in internal conflict with himself or herself. This conflict usually reveals the theme, or the central idea of the work.

Because writing about literature often requires character analysis, you need to understand the characters in any work you read. You can do so by paying close attention to their appearance, their language, and their actions. You also need to pay attention to what the narrator or other characters are saying about any character in terms of physical, mental, or social attributes. Whether you are writing about characters in a novel, a play, or a poem, you will want to concentrate on what those characters do and say—and why.

Point of view Each literary work is told by a **narrator**, and this speaking voice can be that of a specific character (or those of characters taking turns), can seem to be that of the work's author (referred to as the **persona**, or the **speaker**, and not to be confused with the actual author), or can be that of an all-knowing presence (referred to as an **omniscient narrator**) that transcends both characters and author. Whatever the voice, the narrator's tone reveals his or her attitude toward events and characters and even, in some circumstances, toward readers.

In some literary texts, the narrator tells the story using the first-person pronoun *I*. As a reader, you are able to understand this narrator not only from his or her actions and speech but also from his or her thoughts, which are revealed. First-person narration can reveal a reliable narrator—one who seems to convey the story fairly accurately—but a first-person narrator can also be unreliable, meaning that he or she reveals thoughts that suggest he or she is not telling the reader the whole, unvarnished truth. An unreliable narrator is sometimes a child or mentally distressed person who for one reason or another is incapable of describing events and other characters accurately.

In other texts, the point of view is third person, and all characters are referred to by name or third-person pronoun (*he* or *she*). If the narrator appears to follow one character around and reveal just that character's thoughts, the point of view is **third person**, **limited**. If the narrator knows and tells readers about the thoughts, motivations, and attitudes of all the characters, the point of view is **third person**, **omniscient**.

Once you are able to identify the perspective from which the story is being told, you'll want to consider what this perspective allows you and other readers to know about different characters and events, as well as what this perspective does not allow you to know.

Plot The **plot** is what happens, the sequence of significant events (the narrative)—and more. Narrative answers "What comes next?" and plot answers "Why?" Plot usually begins with a conflict, an unstable situation that sets events in motion. In what is called the **exposition**, the author introduces the characters, setting, and background—the elements that not only constitute the unstable situation but also relate to the events that follow. The subsequent series of events leads to the climax, the most intense **turning point**, and what follows is **falling action** (or **dénouement**) that leads to a resolution of the conflict and a stable situation. Thus, the plot establishes how events are patterned or related in terms of conflict and resolution.

Setting **Setting** involves place—not just the physical setting, but also the social setting (the morals, manners, and customs of the characters). Setting also involves time—not only historical time, but also the length of time covered by the narrative. Setting includes **atmosphere**, or the emotional response to the situation, often shared by the reader with the characters. Elements of the setting can often help you understand the motivations of characters or the reasons for certain events in the plot. Ask yourself this question as you consider how, if at all, the setting may shape a text you are reading: would the story be significantly different if it took place somewhere else?

Figurative language Writers often use metaphors and similes as a means of communicating complex ideas and meanings to readers. **Metaphors** are statements in which the writer says that an object or idea is something else, as when Hisaye Yamamoto compares a character's money to a pair of scissors: "his money was a sharp pair of scissors that snipped rapidly through tangles of red tape." Such a statement encourages readers to see how the first object or idea takes on specific qualities or characteristics of the second. **Similes** are statements in which the writer says that an object, idea, or person is *like* something else, as in Alice Walker's comparison of a man to a piece of china: "He was like a piece of rare and delicate china which was always being saved from breaking and finally fell." Despite the slight difference in language, the purpose of a simile is the same as that of a metaphor—to help readers understand something complicated or unfamiliar by comparing it to something readers might be more familiar with.

Symbol and imagery Frequently used by writers of literature, a **symbol** is an object, usually concrete, that stands for something else, usually abstract. For example, the kitchen table in Joy Harjo's poem "Perhaps the World Ends Here" (which appears later in this chapter) has meaning beyond its simple composition of a flat surface and four legs, meaning that Harjo attempts to convey through her careful, vivid description of the significant and everyday experiences that take place on and around the table.

When you write about a particular symbol, first note where it appears in the literary work. To determine what the symbol might mean, consider why it appears where it does and to what effect. Once you have an idea about the meaning, trace the incidents in the literary work that reinforce your interpretation.

Imagery refers to words and phrases that appeal to readers' senses. Most imagery is visual and helps readers "see" a particular image in their mind's eye (think, for instance, of how Marianne Moore called on poets to help readers visualize "real toads" in "imaginary gardens"). However, writers also use imagery to appeal to readers' senses of hearing, smell, taste, and touch. Vivid imagery involves the use of precise nouns and verbs and concrete descriptive details.

Rhythm and rhyme Most writers give considerable thought to the sound of the language they use in their literary works. Poets, in particular, pay utmost attention to rhythm and rhyme. A poet creates the rhythm of a poem through careful arrangement of syllables, words, and line breaks. Some poems have a regular rhythm, with each line containing a particular pattern of short and long syllables; other poems have a less structured, even patternless (yet no less significant) rhythm of words and syllables. Rhyming of words, either within the same line or between different lines, can also help poets create or stress a particular rhythm. Whether regular or irregular, a poem's rhythm can evoke emotions in readers or emphasize specific words and ideas, either by speeding readers through one or more lines and then slowing them down in subsequent lines or by forcing them to consider an image or idea more carefully.

Theme The **theme** of a literary work is the particular message the text delivers about a character, a relationship, an event, or a place. Depending on how they interpret a work, readers may identify different themes. To test whether the theme you have identified is central to the work in question, check to see if it is supported by the setting, plot, characters, point of view, and symbols. If you can relate these components to the idea you are considering, then that idea can be considered the work's theme. The most prominent literary themes arise out of conflict: person versus person, person versus self, person versus nature or technology, or person versus society.

A literary analysis

People write literary analyses in order to make arguments about how other readers should interpret the elements of a text and make meaning from them. Rhetorical situations compel writers to compose a literary analysis when they sense that readers are ignoring, misreading, or failing to understand significant features of a text. In other instances, writers compose literary analyses in order to discover answers to interesting questions, questions about the text itself or about its potential influence on people and their interactions.

The latter type of rhetorical opportunity motivated Ralph Rees to write the following literary analysis about the poetry of Marianne Moore. As his introduction suggests, Rees wrote this article partly in order to contribute to a conversation about a question that many literary critics have long tried to answer: What do authors of literary works help us to understand about the relationship between reality and imagination? Rees writes about Marianne Moore's work because he thinks that Moore offers a compelling perspective on how imagination and reality interact with one another. In his literary analysis, he presents evidence from her poem "Poetry."

Literary analyses like Rees's can be challenging to read—until you get used to the specialized vocabulary and dense language. If you take the time to work through them, though, they can be very rewarding. As you read the following analysis, take your time, pausing at the end of each sentence to be sure you've understood and looking up unfamiliar words as you go. You might even try out some of Mortimer Adler's techniques for marking a text.

The Reality of Imagination in the Poetry of Marianne Moore

Reprinted by permission.
Ralph Rees

Rees uses a conventional strategy to open his essay. After telling readers the general topic—different perspectives on reality—in his first sentence, he presents several examples of different perspectives. Then he explains which perspective is Marianne Moore's.

Reality means different things to different people. To most, fact and the stimuli of the senses define reality; to some, the products of the intellect may be added to the above; to a few, the offspring of the imagination must also be considered. Marianne Moore belongs to the last group, for she finds imagination as much a part of reality as fact. Many realists ignore the figments of the mind because they do not feel that such things have actuality; they deal only with the apparent, the sensed. Moore finds a more immediate reality in thoughts than in facts and the things that arouse the senses. The imagined, because it is more individual and more personal than the other phenomena, seems to her the very essence of reality. The way a thing *seems* is truth; its definitions and its composition are not realities but stimuli to the imagination, which creates actuality. The experience of the fact and the sensed is reality.

In speaking of poetry, Moore says,

> nor till the poets among us can be
> "literalists of
> the imagination"—above
>   insolence and triviality and can present
> for inspection, "imaginary gardens with real toads in them," shall we have
> it. In the meantime, if you demand on the one hand,
> the raw material of poetry in
>   all its rawness and
>   that which is on the other hand
>   genuine, you are interested in poetry.[1]

It can be seen that she wants poets to accept the products of their imaginations as realities that can be put down in their poems as actualities. She sees no need for the poet to separate his imaginings from that which is sensed or founded in fact. A truer actuality exists in mental experiences than in sensuality. "A single shawl—Imagination's—is wrapped tightly round us since we are poor."[2] Morton Zabel says,

> In her poem on [poetry] Miss Moore improves [William Butler] Yeats' characterization of [William] Blake by insisting that poets must be "literalists of the imagination"; they must see the visible at that focus of intelligence where sight and concept coincide, and where it becomes transformed into the pure and total idealism of ideas. By this realism, the imagination permits ideas to claim energy from what is usually denied them—the vital nature that exists and suffers, and which alone can give poetic validity to the abstract or permit the abstract intelligence to enhance experience.[3]

In finding "the visible at that focus of intelligence where sight and concept coincide" Moore discovers the matter and the method of her poetry. With such an approach a poet can find material in everything; no limits restrict a poetic concept. "The idealism of ideas" accepts everything and rejects nothing in establishing material suitable to poetry. As R. P. Blackmur has said,

> The whole flux of experience and interpretation is appropriate subject matter to an imagination *literal* enough to see poetry in it; an imagination, that is, as intent on the dramatic texture (on what is involved, is tacit, is immanent) of the quotidian, as the imagination of the painter is intent, in Velasquez, on the visual texture of lace.[4]

Imagination, then, must be looked upon as the force which blends the other qualities together; through imagination the experienced, the observed, the studied are brought into a single heightened experience, which enhances the singularity of the idea of a thing while discarding much that has adhered to it through constant usage and casual observance.

. . . This emphasis on imagination gives the cohesive quality to many of her poems. At first, the reader may have difficulty in finding the connections between the various subjects brought into a single poem; the search for traditional logical development deludes him. When he is willing to accept the imaginative connections between the various matters of the poem, he will readily see that the common qualities are brought about by the ideal states of the many things mentioned. For this reason, most ideas can

continued

Although he doesn't signal it explicitly, Rees presents his thesis in the second half of this paragraph. He also begins to build his argument that his interpretation of Moore's ideas is the appropriate way to read her work.

Rees presents a passage from Moore's "Poetry" as evidence to support his argument.

Rees follows the quoted passage with his own analysis because he wants readers to understand it in a specific way. He uses an attributive tag before the direct quotation so that readers know the source.

Rees quotes other literary scholars' interpretations of Moore's work as a means of supporting his own argument.

Just as he did with the passage from "Poetry," Rees follows quotations from other scholars with his own analysis of their arguments.

be compared with objects, with other ideas, with animals, and with man. Within the world of the imagination no barriers limit the poet or the reader to believe that only obvious likes may be compared with each other or that comparisons may be made only between members of a single class.

Moore has said that "the artist biased by imagination is a poet."[5] By this definition many of our so-called poets may be placed in the artist class, which she seems to place below that of poet. The true poet, the person with aesthetic possibilities, permits his imagination to be the guide to his artistic capabilities. Such a person does not draw close distinctions between that which is dreamed of and that which is sensed. He accepts as the world of poetry all things that he can experience, whether physically or mentally. Imagination not only allows the poet to invoke comparisons that are fresh, interesting and constructive but to achieve a level of thought that is all-encompassing. The poet is the artist without bias, barriers, or prejudices of any kind; he permits his imagination to have full control of his creative processes and, by so doing, creates a world which seems new and startling to the unimaginative reader although the poet would say that this is the world that has always had existence, that has always remained the same while the factual was constantly changing through new concepts and ideas.

The power of imagination in its stimulation and growth from the factual and the sensed has the utmost importance to the poet. It demonstrates the mind at its most original and refreshing. The rest of experience is important only as stimuli; experience that does not stimulate the imagination is of little value. It is for this reason that Moore says, "The power of the visible / is the invisible."[6] The "visible" gains importance only as it affects the imagination. In other words, Moore finds that the factual and the sensed, those things which most people accept as the "all" of reality, are important only as the stimuli of the imagination. Such an idea turns the world of the realist upside down; actuality becomes that which is not concrete and which can never be "proved.". . .

It has been shown that Marianne Moore is a realist, by her own definition and by her own actions. The standard conception of realist would exclude her and her poetic creations; but, by showing that only that which she herself has experienced has actuality for her, she has designated herself a realist of the imagination. In his essay "Jubal, Jabal and Moore," M. L. Rosenthal says,

> Miss Moore's vivid emphasis on the details of subhuman organic life—she is the botanist's and the zoologist's poet, as well as the poet's poet—makes her poetry swarm with symbolic observation. The pretense is that all this occurs in a hothouse or a zoo, where one watches the flora or the curious beasts with amused and sympathetic detachment, making polite conversation all the while. But how intense the interest really is, how uncompromising the preciseness of detail, how persistent the drive toward universalizing ethical import; how irritated the poet is with soft-headedness of any kind! The ostrich "digesteth harde yron" and is therefore superior to all the absurdities of his appearance and, more important, to his ridiculous common mortality. Sometimes her famous "imaginary gardens with real toads in them"—Miss Moore's image for genuine poetic creations—are really not so far from [William] Blake's tiger-haunted forests.[7]

Rosenthal is not the only critic to point out Moore's battle against soft thinking; others have commented on her constant struggle for thought that is as direct as it is stimulating. Wallace Stevens says that she has "the faculty of digesting the 'harde yron' of appearance."[8] It is important to emphasize Stevens' use of the word "digesting," because Moore

Rees explains how Moore's concept of reality connects to questions that concern readers: who is and is not a poet, and how we can best evaluate a poet's creative work.

Topic sentences such as this one help readers anticipate what the writer will discuss in a paragraph—in this case, the importance of imagination to poets and its relationship to the factual and the sensed.

Rees circles back to the opening lines of the essay, where he presented different perspectives on reality.

Literary Analyses

accomplishes such a process through her imagination; she "digests" fact by using her imagination. Without such a function to act upon it, the fact itself would be of little or no importance to the individual. Imagination, then, has become the only criterion by which reality and actuality can be measured. •···

NOTES

1. Marianne Moore, "Poetry," *Collected Poems* (New York: Macmillan, 1951), p. 41. (All subsequent quotations from her poetry are from this work.)
2. Marianne Moore, "A Bold Virtuoso," *Predilections* (New York: Viking, 1955), p. 43.
3. Morton Zabel, "A Literalist of the Imagination," *Poetry*, 47 (March, 1936), 329–30.
4. R. P. Blackmur, "The Method of Marianne Moore," *Language As Gesture* (New York: Harcourt, Brace, 1952), p. 267.
5. Marianne Moore, "Paul Rosenfeld," *Nation*, 163 (Aug. 17, 1946), 192.
6. *Collected Poems*, "He 'Digesteth Harde Yron,'" p. 104.
7. M. L. Rosenthal, "Jubal, Jabal and Moore," *New Republic*, 126 (April 7, 1952), 21.
8. Wallace Stevens, "About One of Marianne Moore's Poems," *Quarterly Review of Literature*, 4 (1948), 149.

Rees continues this process of circling around to his introduction, as he uses this last sentence to present his final answer to the question he first suggested in that initial paragraph—what is the meaning of reality, and how do we assess and understand it?

Three Literary Works for Analysis

This section presents a short story, a poem, and a play on which you can practice and hone your skills in analytical reading and writing. Freewriting prompts will help you focus your readings of these texts and begin to identify the aspect of one text to which you'll respond in your essay. Your freewriting can also serve you well as you begin to compose the first draft of your essay.

Reading actively

Through this section, you'll construct your own reading of a text. Reading actively when you read a literary work is a first step toward making an argument about that work and its significance. There is no one specific way to make sense of any literary work; what's important is that you support your argument with evidence from the text. Moreover, you want to demonstrate to other readers, including your classmates, why your particular reading of the text is an important one for them to consider. That is, you want to convince readers that your interpretation helps them to understand the literary work in a new way.

To construct an interpretation that provides readers with significant insight, you first need to choose a feature of the literary work that genuinely interests you. Second, you formulate an interpretive question that you'll answer, with supporting evidence, throughout your essay. Actively reading the text—recording your reactions in the margins, highlighting passages that confuse you, noting sections that seem to be central to the events or the characters—will help you identify and begin to answer such a question.

Keeping a reading journal

To help you craft your interpretive question, consider keeping a reading journal in which you can freewrite in response to the following series of prompts. Reading these prompts *before* you read the literary text will help you focus your thinking as you read; you can draft responses to the prompts after you have read the text once or twice. Later, your journal freewrites will help you identify and clarify the interpretive question on which you will focus your analysis of the literary work.

> ### FREEWRITING PROMPTS FOR COMPOSING A LITERARY ANALYSIS

1. Freewrite for ten minutes in response to these questions about the characters in the literary work: Who do you think the most important character in the piece is? How does that character change or not change through the course of the piece? What is the significance of this change or lack of change? How do the other characters in the piece contribute to or prevent this change?
2. Freewrite for ten minutes on the importance of the setting in the literary work: Where does the piece take place? Do you notice anything significant about the setting that affects how you read the piece?
3. Freewrite for ten minutes about the point of view of the literary work: What is the point of view? What role does the narrator (or speaker) play? What does the narrator (or speaker) know and not know? How does the narrator's (or speaker's) knowledge about events and the ideas and attitudes of other characters shape how you read and understand the piece?
4. Freewrite for ten minutes about the plot of the literary work: What do you think is the single most important event or moment? Why do you think this moment is so important or crucial?
5. Freewrite for ten minutes about the theme, what the author is trying to say through the literary work: What does the piece make you think about? What does it make you see about the people or events?

A short story

Alice Walker was born in 1944 in Eaton, Georgia, the eighth child of sharecroppers Minnie Lou Grant and Willie Lee Walker. During Walker's teenage years, the Civil Rights Movement of the 1960s opened up opportunities for more African American children to attend college. Walker attended both Spelman College in Atlanta and Sarah Lawrence College near New York City, earning her undergraduate degree from the latter school. Two years later, in 1967, she published her first literary work, the short story "To Hell with Dying." In 1983, she became the first black woman to receive the Pulitzer Prize for fiction, for *The Color Purple*, her third novel.

Walker is credited with first using the term *womanist* to refer to a theoretical stance toward understanding, illuminating, and building on the lived experiences of African American women. Her literary works engage the dominant stereotypes and limiting conceptions about who African American women (particularly Southern black women) are and who they could be as well as provide spaces wherein these women have their own voices with which to articulate the significance of their lives. According to Barbara T. Christian, Walker's short story "Everyday Use" "is especially significant in that perhaps for the first time in contemporary United States literary history, a writer features a variety of *Southern* black women's perspectives."

> Everyday Use

Alice Walker

I will wait for her in the yard that Maggie and I made so clean and wavy yesterday afternoon. A yard like this is more comfortable than most people know. It is not just a yard. It is like an extended living room. When the hard clay is swept clean as a floor and the fine sand around the edges lined with tiny, irregular grooves, anyone can come and sit and look up into the elm tree and wait for the breezes that never come inside the house.

Maggie will be nervous until after her sister goes: she will stand hopelessly in corners, homely and ashamed of the burn scars down her arms and legs, eying her sister with a mixture of envy and awe. She thinks her sister has held life always in the palm of one hand, that "no" is a word the world never learned to say to her.

You've no doubt seen those TV shows where the child who has "made it" is confronted, as a surprise, by her own mother and father, tottering in weakly from backstage. (A pleasant surprise, of course: What would they do if parent and child came on the show only to curse out and insult each other?) On TV mother and child embrace and smile into each other's faces. Sometimes the mother and father weep, the child wraps them in her arms and leans across the table to tell how she would not have made it without their help. I have seen these programs.

Sometimes I dream a dream in which Dee and I are suddenly brought together on a TV program of this sort. Out of a dark and soft-seated limousine I am ushered into a bright room filled with many people. There I meet a smiling, gray, sporty man like Johnny Carson who shakes my hand and tells me what a fine girl I have. Then we are on the stage and Dee is embracing me with tears in her eyes. She pins on my dress a large orchid, even though she has told me once that she thinks orchids are tacky flowers.

In real life I am a large, big-boned woman with rough, man-working hands. In the winter I wear flannel nightgowns to bed and overalls during the day. I can kill and clean a hog as mercilessly as a man. My fat keeps me hot in zero weather. I can work outside all day, breaking ice to get water for washing; I can eat pork liver cooked over the open fire minutes after it

Alice Walker.

continued

comes steaming from the hog. One winter I knocked a bull calf straight in the brain between the eyes with a sledge hammer and had the meat hung up to chill before nightfall. But of course all this does not show on television. I am the way my daughter would want me to be: a hundred pounds lighter, my skin like an uncooked barley pancake. My hair glistens in the hot bright lights. Johnny Carson has much to do to keep up with my quick and witty tongue.

But that is a mistake. I know even before I wake up. Who ever knew a Johnson with a quick tongue? Who can even imagine me looking a strange white man in the eye? It seems to me I have talked to them always with one foot raised in flight, with my head turned in whichever way is farthest from them. Dee, though. She would always look anyone in the eye. Hesitation was no part of her nature.

"How do I look, Mama?" Maggie says, showing just enough of her thin body enveloped in pink skirt and red blouse for me to know she's there, almost hidden by the door.

"Come out into the yard," I say.

Have you ever seen a lame animal, perhaps a dog run over by some careless person rich enough to own a car, sidle up to someone who is ignorant enough to be kind to him? That is the way my Maggie walks. She has been like this, chin on chest, eyes on ground, feet in shuffle, ever since the fire that burned the other house to the ground.

Dee is lighter than Maggie, with nicer hair and a fuller figure. She's a woman now, though sometimes I forget. How long ago was it that the other house burned? Ten, twelve years? Sometimes I can still hear the flames and feel Maggie's arms sticking to me, her hair smoking and her dress falling off her in little black papery flakes. Her eyes seemed stretched open, blazed open by the flames reflected in them. And Dee. I see her standing off under the sweet gum tree she used to dig gum out of; a look of concentration on her face as she watched the last dingy gray board of the house fall in toward the red-hot brick chimney. Why don't you do a dance around the ashes? I'd wanted to ask her. She had hated the house that much.

I used to think she hated Maggie, too. But that was before we raised money, the church and me, to send her to Augusta to school. She used to read to us without pity; forcing words, lies, other folks' habits, whole lives upon us two, sitting trapped and ignorant underneath her voice. She washed us in a river of make-believe, burned us with a lot of knowledge we didn't necessarily need to know. Pressed us to her with the serious way she read, to shove us away at just the moment, like dimwits, we seemed about to understand.

Dee wanted nice things. A yellow organdy dress to wear to her graduation from high school; black pumps to match a green suit she'd made from an old suit somebody gave me. She was determined to stare down any disaster in her efforts. Her eyelids would not flicker for minutes at a time. Often I fought off the temptation to shake her. At sixteen she had a style of her own: and knew what style was.

I never had an education myself. After second grade the school was closed down. Don't ask me why: in 1927 colored asked fewer questions than they do now. Sometimes Maggie reads to me. She stumbles along good-naturedly but can't see well. She knows she is not bright. Like good looks and money, quickness passes her by. She will marry John Thomas (who has mossy teeth in an earnest face) and then I'll be free to sit here and I guess just sing church songs to myself. Although I never was a good singer. Never could carry a tune. I was always better at a man's job. I used to love to milk till I was hooked in the side in '49. Cows are soothing and slow and don't bother you, unless you try to milk them the wrong way.

I have deliberately turned my back on the house. It is three rooms, just like the one that burned, except the roof is tin; they don't make shingle roofs any more. There are no real windows, just some holes cut in the sides, like the portholes in a ship, but not round and not square, with rawhide holding the shutters up on the outside. This house is in a pasture, too, like the other one. No doubt when Dee sees it she will want to tear it down. She wrote me once that no matter where we "choose" to live, she will manage to come see us. But she will never bring her friends. Maggie and I thought about this and Maggie asked me, "Mama, when did Dee ever have any friends?"

She had a few. Furtive boys in pink shirts hanging about on washday after school. Nervous girls who never laughed. Impressed with her they worshiped the well-turned phrase, the cute shape, the scalding humor that erupted like bubbles in lye. She read to them.

When she was courting Jimmy T she didn't have much time to pay to us, but turned all her faultfinding power on him. He flew to marry a cheap city girl from a family of ignorant flashy people. She hardly had time to recompose herself.

When she comes I will meet—but there they are!

Maggie attempts to make a dash for the house, in her shuffling way, but I stay her with my hand. "Come back here," I say. And she stops and tries to dig a well in the sand with her toe.

It is hard to see them clearly through the strong sun. But even the first glimpse of leg out of the car tells me it is Dee. Her feet were always neat-looking, as if God himself had shaped them with a certain style. From the other side of the car comes a short, stocky man. Hair is all over his head a foot long and hanging from his chin like a kinky mule tail. I hear Maggie suck in her breath. "Uhnnnh," is what it sounds like. Like when you see the wriggling end of a snake just in front of your foot on the road. "Uhnnnh."

Dee next. A dress down to the ground, in this hot weather. A dress so loud it hurts my eyes. There are yellows and oranges enough to throw back the light of the sun. I feel my whole face warming from the heat waves it throws out. Earrings gold, too, and hanging down to her shoulders. Bracelets dangling and making noises when she moves her arm up to shake the folds of the dress out of her arm-pits. The dress is loose and flows, and as she walks closer, I like it. I hear Maggie go "Uhnnnh" again. It is her sister's hair. It stands straight up like the wool on a sheep. It is black as night and around the edges are two long pigtails that rope about like small lizards disappearing behind her ears.

"Wasuzo-Teano!" she says, coming on in that gliding way the dress makes her move. The short stocky fellow with the hair to his navel is all grinning and he fol-lows up with "Asalamalakim, my mother and sister!" He moves to hug Maggie but she falls back, right up against the back of my chair. I feel her trembling there and when I look up I see the perspiration falling off her chin.

continued

"Don't get up," says Dee. Since I am stout it takes something of a push. You can see me trying to move a second or two before I make it. She turns, showing white heels through her sandals, and goes back to the car. Out she peeks next with a Polaroid. She stoops down quickly and lines up picture after picture of me sitting there in front of the house with Maggie cowering behind me. She never takes a shot without making sure the house is included. When a cow comes nibbling around the edge of the yard she snaps it and me and Maggie and the house. Then she puts the Polaroid in the back seat of the car, and comes up and kisses me on the forehead.

Meanwhile Asalamalakim is going through motions with Maggie's hand. Maggie's hand is as limp as a fish, and probably as cold, despite the sweat, and she keeps trying to pull it back. It looks like Asalamalakim wants to shake hands but wants to do it fancy. Or maybe he don't know how people shake hands. Anyhow, he soon gives up on Maggie.

"Well," I say. "Dee."

"No, Mama," she says. "Not 'Dee,' Wangero Leewanika Kemanjo!"

"What happened to 'Dee'?" I wanted to know.

"She's dead," Wangero said. "I couldn't bear it any longer, being named after the people who oppress me."

"You know as well as me you was named after your aunt Dicie," I said. Dicie is my sister. She named Dee. We called her "Big Dee" after Dee was born.

"But who was she named after?" asked Wangero.

"I guess after Grandma Dee," I said.

"And who was she named after?" asked Wangero.

"Her mother," I said, and saw Wangero was getting tired. "That's about as far back as I can trace it," I said. Though, in fact, I probably could have carried it back beyond the Civil War through the branches.

"Well," said Asalamalakim, "there you are."

"Uhnnnh," I heard Maggie say.

"There I was not," I said, "before 'Dicie' cropped up in our family, so why should I try to trace it that far back?"

He just stood there grinning, looking down on me like somebody inspecting a Model A car. Every once in a while he and Wangero sent eye signals over my head.

"How do you pronounce this name?" I asked.

"You don't have to call me by it if you don't want to," said Wangero.

"Why shouldn't I?" I asked. "If that's what you want us to call you, we'll call you."

"I know it might sound awkward at first," said Wangero.

"I'll get used to it," I said. "Ream it out again."

Well, soon we got the name out of the way. Asalamalakim had a name twice as long and three times as hard. After I tripped over it two or three times he told me to just call him Hakim-a-barber. I wanted to ask him was he a barber, but I didn't really think he was, so I didn't ask.

"You must belong to those beef-cattle peoples down the road," I said. They said "Asalamalakim" when they met you, too, but they didn't shake hands. Always too busy: feeding the cattle, fixing the fences, putting up salt-lick shelters, throwing down hay. When the white folks poisoned some of the herd the men stayed up all night with rifles in their hands. I walked a mile and a half just to see the sight.

Hakim-a-barber said, "I accept some of their doctrines, but farming and raising cattle is not my style." (They didn't tell me, and I didn't ask, whether Wangero (Dee) had really gone and married him.)

We sat down to eat and right away he said he didn't eat collards and pork was unclean. Wangero, though, went on through the chitlins and corn bread, the greens and everything else. She talked a blue streak over the sweet potatoes. Everything delighted her. Even the fact that we still used the benches her daddy made for the table when we couldn't afford to buy chairs.

"Oh, Mama!" she cried. Then turned to Hakim-a-barber. "I never knew how lovely these benches are. You can feel the rump prints," she said, running her hands underneath her and along the bench. Then she gave a sigh and her hand closed over Grandma Dee's butter dish. "That's it!" she said. "I knew there was something I wanted to ask you if I could have." She jumped up from the table and went over in the corner where the churn stood, the milk in it clabber by now. She looked at the churn and looked at it.

"This churn top is what I need," she said. "Didn't Uncle Buddy whittle it out of a tree you all used to have?"

"Yes," I said.

"Uh huh," she said happily. "And I want the dasher, too."

"Uncle Buddy whittle that, too?" asked the barber.

Dee (Wangero) looked up at me.

"Aunt Dee's first husband whittled the dash," said Maggie so low you almost couldn't hear her. "His name was Henry, but they called him Stash."

"Maggie's brain is like an elephant's," Wangero said, laughing. "I can use the chute top as a centerpiece for the alcove table," she said, sliding a plate over the chute, "and I'll think of something artistic to do with the dasher."

When she finished wrapping the dasher the handle stuck out. I took it for a moment in my hands. You didn't even have to look close to see where hands pushing the dasher up and down to make butter had left a kind of sink in the wood. In fact, there were a lot of small sinks; you could see where thumbs and fingers had sunk into the wood. It was beautiful light yellow wood, from a tree that grew in the yard where Big Dee and Stash had lived.

After dinner Dee (Wangero) went to the trunk at the foot of my bed and started rifling through it. Maggie hung back in the kitchen over the dishpan. Out came Wangero with two quilts. They had been pieced by Grandma Dee and then Big Dee and me had hung them on the quilt frames on the front porch and quilted them. One was in the Lone Star pattern. The other was Walk Around the Mountain. In both of them were scraps of dresses Grandma Dee had worn fifty and more years ago. Bits and pieces of Grandpa Jattell's Paisley shirts. And one teeny faded blue piece, about the size of a penny

continued

matchbox, that was from Great Grandpa Ezra's uniform that he wore in the Civil War.

"Mama," Wangero said sweet as a bird. "Can I have these old quilts?"

I heard something fall in the kitchen, and a minute later the kitchen door slammed.

"Why don't you take one or two of the others?" I asked. "These old things was just done by me and Big Dee from some tops your grandma pieced before she died."

"No," said Wangero. "I don't want those. They are stitched around the borders by machine."

"That'll make them last better," I said.

"That's not the point," said Wangero. "These are all pieces of dresses Grandma used to wear. She did all this stitching by hand. Imagine!" She held the quilts securely in her arms, stroking them.

"Some of the pieces, like those lavender ones, come from old clothes her mother handed down to her," I said, moving up to touch the quilts. Dee (Wangero) moved back just enough so that I couldn't reach the quilts. They already belonged to her.

"Imagine!" she breathed again, clutching them closely to her bosom.

"The truth is," I said, "I promised to give them quilts to Maggie, for when she marries John Thomas."

She gasped like a bee had stung her.

"Maggie can't appreciate these quilts!" she said. "She'd probably be backward enough to put them to everyday use."

"I reckon she would," I said. "God knows I been saving 'em for long enough with nobody using 'em. I hope she will!" I didn't want to bring up how I had offered Dee (Wangero) a quilt when she went away to college. Then she had told they were old-fashioned, out of style.

"But they're priceless!" she was saying now, furiously; for she has a temper. "Maggie would put them on the bed and in five years they'd be in rags. Less than that!"

"She can always make some more," I said. "Maggie knows how to quilt."

Dee (Wangero) looked at me with hatred. "You just will not understand. The point is these quilts, these quilts!"

"Well," I said, stumped. "What would you do with them?"

"Hang them," she said. As if that was the only thing you could do with quilts.

Maggie by now was standing in the door. I could almost hear the sound her feet made as they scraped over each other.

"She can have them, Mama," she said, like somebody used to never winning anything, or having anything reserved for her. "I can 'member Grandma Dee without the quilts."

I looked at her hard. She had filled her bottom lip with checkerberry snuff and gave her face a kind of dopey, hangdog look. It was Grandma Dee and Big Dee who taught her how to quilt herself. She stood there with her scarred hands hidden in the folds of her skirt. She looked at her sister with something like fear but she wasn't mad at her. This was Maggie's portion. This was the way she knew God to work.

When I looked at her like that something hit me in the top of my head and ran down to the soles of my feet. Just like when I'm in church and the spirit of God touches me and I get happy and shout. I did something I never done before: hugged Maggie to me, then dragged her on into the room, snatched the quilts out of Miss Wangero's hands and dumped them into Maggie's lap. Maggie just sat there on my bed with her mouth open.

"Take one or two of the others," I said to Dee.

But she turned without a word and went out to Hakim-a-barber.

"You just don't understand," she said, as Maggie and I came out to the car.

"What don't I understand?" I wanted to know.

"Your heritage," she said, and then she turned to Maggie, kissed her, and said, "You ought to try to make something of yourself, too, Maggie. It's really a new day for us. But from the way you and Mama still live you'd never know it."

She put on some sunglasses that hid everything above the tip of her nose and chin.

Maggie smiled; maybe at the sunglasses. But a real smile, not scared. After we watched the car dust settle I asked Maggie to bring me a dip of snuff. And then the two of us sat there just enjoying, until it was time to go in the house and go to bed.

A poem

Joy Harjo was born in Tulsa, Oklahoma, in 1951 and is enrolled as a member of both the Creek and Muscogee Tribes. At the age of sixteen, she moved to the Southwest to attend the Institute of American Indian Arts in Santa Fe, New Mexico. Harjo eventually switched her major from the visual arts to poetry and moved to Albuquerque to attend the University of New Mexico, where she earned her BA in English. She went on to earn an MFA in creative writing from the University of Iowa. On the website she maintains (www.joyharjo.com), Harjo says that she "began writing poetry when the national Indian political climate demanded singers and speakers" and that she was quickly "taken by the intensity and beauty possible in the craft."

Harjo has published a number of books of poetry, one of which, *In Mad Love and War*, received an American Book Award from the Before Columbus Foundation in 1990. In the 1990s, Harjo also learned to play the saxophone and has combined her poetic and musical talents as the lead member of the

Joy Harjo.

Paul Abdoo/MPI/Getty Images

group Joy Harjo and Poetic Justice. The group has released two albums, *Letter from the End of the 20th Century* (1997) and *Native Joy for Real* (2005). In addition to her writing and performing, Harjo teaches as the Joseph M. Russo Professor of Creative Writing at the University of New Mexico. The following poem appears in the poetry collection *Sweeping Beauty: Contemporary Women Poets Do Housework.*

> Perhaps the World Ends Here

Joy Harjo

The world begins at a kitchen table. No matter what, we must eat to live.

The gifts of earth are brought and prepared, set on the table. So it has been since creation, and it will go on.

We chase chickens or dogs away from it. Babies teethe at the corners. They scrape their knees under it.

It is here that children are given instructions on what it means to be human. We make men at it, we make women.

At this table we gossip, recall enemies and the ghosts of lovers.

Our dreams drink coffee with us as they put their arms around our children. They laugh with us at our poor falling-down selves and as we put ourselves back together once again at the table.

The table has been a house in the rain, an umbrella in the sun.

Wars have begun and ended at this table. It is a place to hide in the shadow of terror. A place to celebrate the terrible victory.

We have given birth on this table, and have prepared our parents for burial here.

At this table we sing with joy, with sorrow. We pray of suffering and remorse. We give thanks.

Perhaps the world will end at the kitchen table, while we are laughing and crying, eating of the last sweet bite.

A play

According to the website for Kingston, Ontario's Fishbowl Theatre, Jane Martin "has been referred to as 'America's best known, unknown playwright.'" Although Martin has been nominated for the Pulitzer Prize and twice won the American Theatre Critics Association's New Play Award, she has never been photographed for publication or made public appearances. Indeed, many critics believe that "Jane Martin" is a pseudonym for a playwright who first garnered national attention for *Talking With . . .*, a collection of monologues produced by Actors' Theatre of Louisville for the 1981 Humana Festival of New American Plays.

Jon Jory, the former artistic director of Actors' Theatre, has accepted awards on Martin's behalf, and he has also served as Martin's spokesperson. Many critics believe that in fact, Jory *is* Jane Martin, since almost all of Martin's plays have premiered at the Actors' Theatre and have been directed by Jory. Jory has often refuted this, however, explaining that whoever writes the plays clearly feels that she would be unable to do so if her identity became public knowledge. Martin has written ten full-length plays, six one-act plays, and numerous short plays, of which the following, *Beauty*, is one.

> Beauty

Used by permission of Jon Jory.

Jane Martin

CHARACTERS
Carla
Bethany

An apartment. Minimalist set. A young woman, Carla, on the phone.

CARLA: In love with me? You're in love with me? Could you describe yourself again? Uh-huh. Uh-huh. And you spoke to me? (*A knock at the door.*) Listen, I always hate to interrupt a marriage proposal, but . . . could you possibly hold that thought? (*Puts phone down and goes to the door. Bethany, the same age as Carla and a friend, is there. She carries the sort of Mideastern lamp we know of from Aladdin.*)

BETHANY: Thank God you were home. I mean, you're not going to believe this!

CARLA: Somebody on the phone. (*Goes back to it.*)

BETHANY: I mean, I just had a beach urge, so I told them at work my uncle was dying. . .

CARLA: (*motions to Bethany for quiet*) And you were the one in the leather jacket with the tattoo? What was the tattoo? (*Carla again asks Bethany, who is gesturing wildly that she should hang up, to cool it.*) Look, a screaming eagle from shoulder to shoulder, maybe. There were a lot of people in the bar.

continued

Beauty *(continued)*

BETHANY: *(gesturing and mouthing)* I have to get back to work.

CARLA: *(on phone)* See, the thing is, I'm probably not going to marry someone I can't remember . . . particularly when I don't drink. Sorry. Sorry. Sorry. *(She hangs up.)* Madness.

BETHANY: So I ran out to the beach. . .

CARLA: This was some guy I never met who apparently offered me a beer . . .

BETHANY: . . . low tide and this . . . *(The lamp.)* . . . was just sitting there, lying there . . .

CARLA: . . . and he tracks me down . . .

BETHANY: . . . on the beach, and I lift this lid thing . . .

CARLA: . . . and seriously proposes marriage.

BETHANY: . . . and a genie comes out.

CARLA: I mean, that's twice in a . . . what?

BETHANY: A genie comes out of this thing.

CARLA: A genie?

BETHANY: I'm not kidding, the whole Disney kind of thing, swirling smoke, and then this twenty-foot-high, see-through guy in like an Arabian outfit.

CARLA: Very funny.

BETHANY: Yes, funny, but twenty feet high! I look up and down the beach, I'm alone. I don't have my pepper spray or my hand alarm. You know me, when I'm petrified I joke. I say his voice is too high for Robin Williams, and he says he's a castrati. Naturally. Who else would I meet?

CARLA: What's a castrati?

BETHANY: You know . . .

The appropriate gesture.

CARLA: Bethany, dear one, I have three modeling calls. I am meeting Ralph Lauren!

BETHANY: Okay, good. Ralph Lauren. Look, I am not kidding!

CARLA: You're not kidding what?!

BETHANY: There is a genie in this thingamajig.

CARLA: Uh-huh. I'll be back around eight.

BETHANY: And he offered me *wishes*!

CARLA: Is this some elaborate practical joke because it's my birthday?

BETHANY: No, happy birthday, but I'm like crazed because I'm on this deserted beach with a twenty-foot-high, see-through genie, so like sarcastically . . . you know how I need a new car . . . I said fine, gimme 25,000 dollars. . . .

CARLA: On the beach with the genie?

BETHANY: Yeah, right, exactly, and it rains down out of the sky.

CARLA: Oh sure.

BETHANY: (*pulls a wad out of her purse*) Count it, those are thousands. I lost one in the surf.

Carla sees the top bill. Looks at Bethany, who nods encouragement. Carla thumbs through them.

CARLA: These look real.

BETHANY: Yeah.

CARLA: And they rained down out of the sky?

BETHANY: Yeah.

CARLA: You've been really strange lately, are you dealing?

BETHANY: Dealing what, I've even given up chocolate.

CARLA: Let me see the genie.

BETHANY: Wait, wait.

CARLA: Bethany, I don't have time to screw around. Let me see the genie or let me go on my appointments.

BETHANY: Wait! So I pick up the money . . . see, there's sand on the money . . . and I'm like nuts so I say, you know, "Okay, look, ummm, big guy, my uncle is in the hospital" . . . because as you know when I said to the people at work my uncle was dying, I was on one level telling the truth although it had nothing to do with the beach, but he was in Intensive Care after the accident, and that's on my mind, so I say, okay, Genie, heal my uncle . . . which is like impossible given he was hit by two trucks, and the genie says, "Yes, Master" . . . like they're supposed to say, and he goes into this like kind of whirlwind, kicking up sand and stuff, and I'm like, "Oh my God!" and the air clears, and he bows, you know, and says, "It is done, Master," and I say, "Okay, whatever-you-are, I'm calling on my cell phone," and I get it out and I get this doctor who is like dumbstruck who says my uncle came to, walked out of Intensive Care and left the hospital! I'm not kidding, Carla.

CARLA: On your mother's grave?

BETHANY: On my mother's grave.

They look at each other.

CARLA: Let me see the genie.

BETHANY: No, no, look, that's the whole thing . . . I was just, like, reacting, you know, responding, and that's already two wishes . . . although I'm really pleased about my uncle, the $25,000 thing, I could have asked for $10 million, and there is only one wish left.

continued

CARLA: So ask for $10 million.

BETHANY: I don't think so. I don't think so. I mean, I gotta focus in here. Do you have a sparkling water?

CARLA: No. Bethany, I'm missing Ralph Lauren now. Very possibly my one chance to go from catalogue model to the very, very big time, so, if you are joking, stop joking.

BETHANY: Not joking. See, see, the thing is, I know what I want. In my guts. Yes. Underneath my entire bitch of a life is this unspoken, ferocious, all-consuming urge . . .

CARLA: *(trying to get her to move this along)* Ferocious, all-consuming urge . . .

BETHANY: I want to be like you.

CARLA: Me?

BETHANY: Yes.

CARLA: Half the time you don't even like me.

BETHANY: Jealous. The ogre of jealousy.

CARLA: You're the one with the $40,000 job straight out of school. You're the one who has published short stories. I'm the one hanging on by her fingernails in modeling. The one who has creeps calling her on the phone. The one who had to have a nose job.

BETHANY: I want to be beautiful.

CARLA: You are beautiful.

BETHANY: Carla, I'm not beautiful.

CARLA: You have charm. You have personality. You know perfectly well you're pretty.

BETHANY: "Pretty," see, that's it. Pretty is the minor leagues of beautiful. Pretty is what people discover about you after they know you. Beautiful is what knocks them out across the room. Pretty, you get called a couple of times a year; *beautiful* is twenty-four hours a day.

CARLA: Yeah? So?

BETHANY: So?! We're talking *beauty* here. Don't say "So?" Beauty is the real deal. You are the center of any moment of your life. People stare. Men flock. I've seen you get offered discounts on makeup for no reason. Parents treat beautiful children better. Studies show your income goes up. You can have sex anytime you want it. Men have to know me. That takes up to a year. I'm continually horny.

CARLA: Bethany, I don't even like sex. I can't have a conversation without men coming on to me. I have no privacy. I get hassled on the street. They start pressuring me from the beginning. Half the time, it never occurs to them to start with a conversation. Smart guys like you. You've had three long-term relationships, and you're only twenty-three. I haven't had one. The good guys, the smart guys are scared to death of me. I'm surrounded by male bimbos who think a preposition is when you go to school away from home. I have no woman friends except you. I don't even want to talk about this!

BETHANY: I knew you'd say something like this. See, you're "in the club" so you can say this. It's the way beauty functions as an elite. You're trying to keep it all for yourself.

CARLA: I'm trying to tell you it's no picnic.

BETHANY: But it's what everybody wants. It's the nasty secret at large in the world. It's the unspoken tidal desire in every room and on every street. It's the unspoken, the soundless whisper . . . millions upon millions of people longing hopelessly and forever to stop being whatever they are and be beautiful, but the difference between those ardent multitudes and me is that I have a goddamn genie and one more wish!

CARLA: Well, it's not what I want. This is me, Carla. I have never read a whole book. Page six, I can't remember page four. The last thing I read was *The Complete Idiot's Guide to WordPerfect.* I leave dinner parties right after the dessert because I'm out of conversation. You know the dumb blonde joke about the application where it says, "Sign here," she put Sagittarius? I've done that. Only beautiful guys approach me, and that's because they want to borrow my eye shadow. I barely exist outside a mirror! You don't want to be me.

BETHANY: None of you tell the truth. That's why you have no friends. We can all see you're just trying to make us feel better because we aren't in your league. This only proves to me it should be my third wish. Money can only buy things. Beauty makes you the center of the universe.

Bethany picks up the lamp.

CARLA: Don't do it. Bethany, don't wish it! I am telling you you'll regret it.

Bethany lifts the lid. There is a tremendous crash, and the lights go out. Then they flicker and come back up, revealing Bethany and Carla on the floor where they have been thrown by the explosion. We don't realize it at first, but they have exchanged places.

CARLA/BETHANY: Oh God.

BETHANY/CARLA: Oh God.

CARLA/BETHANY: Am I bleeding? Am I dying?

BETHANY/CARLA: I'm so dizzy. You're not bleeding.

CARLA/BETHANY: Neither are you.

BETHANY/CARLA: I feel so weird.

CARLA/BETHANY: Me too. I feel . . . (*Looking at her hands.*) Oh, my God, I'm wearing your jewelry. I'm wearing your nail polish.

continued

BETHANY/CARLA: I know I'm over here, but I can see myself over there.

CARLA/BETHANY: I'm wearing your dress. I have your legs!

BETHANY/CARLA: These aren't my shoes. I can't meet Ralph Lauren wearing these shoes!

CARLA/BETHANY: I wanted to be beautiful, but I didn't want to be you.

BETHANY/CARLA: Thanks a lot!!

CARLA/BETHANY: I've got to go. I want to pick someone out and get laid.

BETHANY/CARLA: You can't just walk out of here in my body!

CARLA/BETHANY: Wait a minute. Wait a minute. What's eleven eighteenths of 1,726?

BETHANY/CARLA: Why?

CARLA/BETHANY: I'm a public accountant. I want to know if you have my brain.

BETHANY/CARLA: One hundred thirty-two and a half.

CARLA/BETHANY: You have my brain.

BETHANY/CARLA: What shade of Rubinstein lipstick does Cindy Crawford wear with teal blue?

CARLA/BETHANY: Raging Storm.

BETHANY/CARLA: You have my brain. You poor bastard.

CARLA/BETHANY: I don't care. Don't you see?

BETHANY/CARLA: See what?

CARLA/BETHANY: We both have the one thing, the one and only thing everybody wants.

BETHANY/CARLA: What's that?

CARLA/BETHANY: It's better than beauty for me; it's better than brains for you.

BETHANY/CARLA: What? What?!

CARLA/BETHANY: Different problems.

Blackout.

■ GUIDE TO RESPONDING TO THE RHETORICAL SITUATION

Understanding the Rhetorical Situation

When you want to share your understanding of a literary work, consider composing a literary analysis. Whether you are writing or reading such an analysis, it has the following features:

- A literary analysis introduces interpretations of the literary work under investigation, often explaining what these perspectives might be missing.
- A literary analysis presents a specific question about the literary work that the writer believes needs to be answered.
- A literary analysis presents a clear argument, or thesis, about the literary work and explains how this thesis addresses some concern that other readers of this literary work have ignored or misrepresented.
- To provide evidence supporting its thesis, a literary analysis quotes specific passages from the text.
- A literary analysis explicates all quoted passages, directing readers' attention to particular aspects of the literary work that support the thesis.

The following sections will help you compose a literary analysis. To work with an online guide to the elements of the rhetorical situation, access your English CourseMate through cengagebrain.com.

Identifying an opportunity

To identify a rhetorical opportunity for your analysis, reread the journal free-writes you composed earlier. Reflect on those journal entries as you respond to these questions:

1. What features of the literary work interested you the most?
2. What features of the work seemed most problematic or most significant in terms of helping you to interpret it?
3. What features of the work do you disagree with your classmates about?
4. What were your initial reactions to the work when you read it for the first time, and how did those reactions change as you reflected on and wrote about its features?

Your responses to the preceding questions will likely allow you to pose an interpretive question on which you can base your essay. If you still need some help generating a question, think about important points where *change* occurs in the text. As novelist Raymond Carver has said, "In the best fiction, the central character, the hero or heroine, is also the 'moved' character, the one to whom something happens in the story that *makes a difference*. Something happens that changes the way that character looks at himself and hence the world."

So, in order to arrive at a question on which to focus your essay, respond to the following questions:

1. At what places within the text does some element—a character, the plot, the setting, the point of view—undergo a significant change?
2. What are the specific details of that change?
3. What might be the significance of the change in relation to the entire text?
4. What were your reactions to the change?
5. What might have been the writer's point in incorporating the change into the text?

Now, articulate a question about the work that readers could answer in different ways and will be genuinely interested in. Once you have articulated this question, spend several minutes freewriting an answer. Try to mention specific parts of the text that are informing your answer as you do this freewriting. Write about whatever ideas come into your head. Don't worry about punctuation, grammar, or organization. You want to allow your writing to move you toward identifying your opportunity and answering your interpretive question.

Locating an audience

The following questions can help you locate your rhetorical audience as well as identify the relationship it has to the question you have identified. Then, you'll be able to choose the best way to present and support your answer.

1. List the names of the persons or groups who are talking about the literary work you're analyzing or who have questions about its meaning or importance.
2. Next to the name of each potential audience, write reasons that audience might have for acknowledging your analysis of the literary work. In other words, what would persuade these people or groups to read the story, poem, or play and interpret it in a different way?
3. What responses could these audiences reasonably be persuaded to have to your essay and to the text you're analyzing?
4. With your audience's interests and capabilities in mind, look again at the question and initial answer you composed in the preceding section on identifying an opportunity. Decide how you can enable your audience to feel engaged by your question and invested in hearing how you interpret the text in ways that answer it. At this point, you may find it necessary to revise your question so that it speaks more directly to the concerns of your audience.

Identifying a fitting response

Identifying an interpretive question and getting others to recognize it as interesting or important is only the beginning of your efforts to transform your freewriting and planning into an analytical essay. You also need to identify an appropriate form in which to respond to this rhetorical situation. Your response should consider what you already know about your rhetorical opportunity and audience, such as the interpretations that audience has formed about the text. Your analysis should also be a fitting response in the sense that it addresses the context within which your audience is likely to consider it. For example, to analyze how Joy Harjo's "Perhaps the World Ends Here" demonstrates that everyday objects such as the kitchen table shape our personal interactions with others, you might consider writing an article for the "Arts & Entertainment" section of the local newspaper. To reinterpret the significance of the quilts in Alice Walker's "Everyday Use," you might want to create a newsletter that you could distribute at a local crafts store. Or, to explore how Jane Martin's *Beauty* speaks to the pressures of growing up in an image-obsessed culture, you might consider shaping your analysis into the form of a blog entry or a web page that could appear on a website devoted to activist efforts on the part of the world's young adults. The point here is that once you identify your opportunity, audience, and purpose, you need to consider what kind of text will best respond to the rhetorical situation.

Use the following two questions to help you narrow your purpose and shape your response:

1. Are you asking the audience to simply reread the literary work in a new light or to perform some particular action in response to this new way of interpreting the text?
2. What is the best way to contact this audience? That is, what kind of text is this audience most likely to respond to? (Chapter 13 can help you explore options for media and design.)

Writing a Literary Analysis: Working with Your Available Means

Shaping your literary analysis

You'll have done a good deal of thinking, writing, and planning by the time you begin to draft your literary analysis. As you start to draft it, your primary focus will be on establishing the significance of your interpretive question, providing sufficient evidence from the text to support your answer to this question, and explaining the larger implications of your answer for understanding the text.

Your introduction should explain which literary work you're going to analyze and why. Ralph Rees, for example, states that he will examine how Marianne Moore's poetry addresses the relationship between imagination and reality. The introduction also presents your interpretive question about the literary work as well as your initial attempt to persuade readers that this question is an interesting and important one to answer. At some point in the introduction, you need to pose this question explicitly for your readers. You can briefly summarize the different answers that other readers, including your classmates, have posed or might be likely to pose to this question. Rees, for example, reviews the three different perspectives that literary critics tend to have about reality.

Introduction
- ▶ Identifies the literary work being analyzed
- ▶ Presents an interpretive question and argues for its importance
- ▶ Summarizes other answers to the question
- ▶ Presents the thesis statement (writer's answer to the interpretive question)

Body
- ▶ Presents supporting reasons for writer's answer to the interpretive question, usually one reason per paragraph
- ▶ Strengthens writer's appeal to logos by building toward most interesting or persuasive reason
- ▶ Includes direct quotations from the literary work as evidence
- ▶ May directly address others' interpretations of the text

Conclusion
- ▶ Explains how this analysis helps deepen readers' understanding
- ▶ May point to related questions that could unlock additional meanings of the text

Keep in mind, too, that you might need to quickly summarize a main point or describe a main element of the text in order to help your readers understand the precise nature of the question that you're asking.

Finally, before you conclude your introduction, you should provide your readers with your thesis statement—in this case, a one-or two-sentence answer to the interpretive question you have posed. You can often present this answer in the form of a statement that begins "In this essay, I argue that . . . ." Some writers, like Rees, for example, prefer to phrase their thesis statement in a way that makes it sound as if the author of the work is arguing the particular point. In either case, the thesis statement advances a particular interpretation of the meaning of the text.

As you turn your attention to drafting the body of your literary analysis, focus on the main reasons that support your specific answer to the interpretive question. Use paragraph divisions to distinguish each supporting reason. Strengthen your appeal to logos by arranging these paragraphs in a pattern that moves readers progressively toward the most interesting or most persuasive of your supporting reasons.

The body paragraphs should provide readers with direct references to the literary work. These direct quotations are the primary means by which you provide evidence to support your reasons; consequently, the more compelling or appropriate the quoted passages are, the stronger your appeal to logos. Early in his analysis, Rees cites a long passage from the end of Moore's "Poetry." With this quotation, Rees introduces several key terms, *literal, imagination, real*, and *genuine*, that he will explore in more depth as he presents his interpretation of Moore's work. Rees wants readers to understand explicitly what meaning he takes away from this work.

Another way to support your thesis in the body paragraphs is to directly address other readers' interpretations of the text. Here you can strengthen your appeal to ethos by citing other literary critics who share your perspective. Rees does this several times in his analysis, as when he cites Morton Zabel's reference to Moore's definition of the poet as a "literalist of the imagination." Conversely, you can also work to support your thesis by conceding or refuting alternative interpretations.

After providing sufficient evidence to support your major reasons, conclude your literary analysis by situating it within a larger conversation about the work you're analyzing. In other words, explain to readers how your answer to your interpretive question helps deepen their understanding of the entire work. In his conclusion, Matthew Marusak (the writer of the sample paper on pages 383–387) explains how thinking carefully about what the narrator reveals makes us, as readers, "continually reevaluate our own perceptions of Alice Walker's story." You can also use the conclusion to point to other questions that, while related to the one you have answered in your analysis, remain unanswered and could help to unlock additional meanings of the text.

You should also consider whether visuals could strengthen your analysis. Consider sketching the scene for Jane Martin's *Beauty* if such a sketch would help readers to better understand a specific point you're making about how the two main characters interact. Photograph an object from your everyday life that has significance similar to that of the kitchen table in Joy Harjo's "Perhaps the World Ends Here." Or you might compile a slide presentation that incorporates digital photos and videos of Alice Walker speaking about "Everyday Use."

Revision and peer review

After you've drafted a strong version of your literary analysis, ask one of your classmates to read it. You'll want your classmate to respond to your work in a way that helps you revise it into the strongest analysis it can be, one that addresses your intended audience, helps you fulfill your purpose, and is delivered in the most appropriate means available to you.

Questions for a peer reviewer
1. To what rhetorical opportunity is the writer responding?
2. Where does the writer clearly state the interpretive question? How might he or she help the audience better understand—and care about—that question?
3. How does the writer establish ethos?
4. Who might comprise the writer's intended audience?
5. Identify the thesis statement, in which the writer clearly states his or her response to the interpretive question. If you cannot locate a thesis statement, what thesis statement might work for this analysis?
6. Identify the evidence (in the form of direct quotations and other references to the text) the writer provides in support of and against the claim. In what other ways does the writer strengthen the logos of the writing?
7. How does the writer establish pathos?
8. What did you learn from the conclusion that you didn't already know from reading the analysis? How did the writer give you a better understanding of the literary work overall?
9. What idea or passage in the analysis is handled most successfully and least successfully?
10. What are two questions you have for this writer?

Oral Literary Analysis

Slate's online Audio Book Club provides book reviews and discussions regularly. Among the archives is a podcast for *The Great Gatsby,* in which critics discuss what makes the novel endure, despite its flimsy plot. To access the podcast, find *Writing in Three Media* in your English Course-Mate, accessed through cengagebrain.com

The Granger Collection

Online Literary Analysis

J from Kent, Ohio, has posted more than 80 in-depth commentaries for his network of thirty-five friends on GoodReads.com. To view J's analysis of *The Historian,* by Elizabeth Kostova, find *Writing in Three Media* in your English Course-Mate, accessed through cengagebrain.com.

Courtesy of J. Keirn Swanson

Print Literary Analysis

In the following literary analysis, student Matthew Marusak articulates a clear objection to the way many readers have interpreted Alice Walker's story "Everyday Use."

Katrina Outland/Shutterstock.com

If Matthew had wanted to recommend summer reading, he could have submitted a literary review of the short story to the student newspaper. If he had wanted to join an online conversation about the story, he could have written comments on a blog devoted to Alice Walker's works. Knowing that his primary audience—his English instructor—would expect him to pose and respond to a specific question about the story and would be most receptive to an essay organized around a clear thesis statement, Matthew decided that the most appropriate genre was a print literary analysis.

Matthew Marusak

Professor Glenn

English 496

2 March 2011

Backward Enough: Alice Walker's Unreliable Narrator

Alice Walker's "Everyday Use" is a poignant short story about a dysfunctional family, whose members disagree over the meaning and importance of heritage—a disagreement stemming from the overarching tension already deeply seated among the family. Specifically, Walker presents an apparent contrast between heritage that is merely put on for show and that which is used on a daily basis. When the more sophisticated Dee returns home to visit her sister and mother, who live in the country, the characters inevitably grapple with one another in a clash of personalities, ideals, and belief systems. "Everyday Use" encompasses a wide range of human emotions and complex themes that we, as readers, have a responsibility to unravel throughout the course of the story. And while Walker's message about heritage is an undeniably important one, I see something more vital taking place concerning the nature of familial relationships. I will argue that we must effectively look beyond our initial interpretations of the text and focus instead on how the story brings us to those interpretations, a problem that lies entirely with the narrative voice.

Alice Walker crafts complex characters that truly encompass the themes of the story, yet this complexity relies heavily on the audience's own interpretation. If we read the story flat, it becomes impossible for the complexity and nuances of character to shine through. We must keep in mind that the only point of view expressed in "Everyday Use" is, in fact, the mother's. Therefore, I argue that the mother, as the speaking voice of the

> Matthew poses a specific question about this literary work: What does it reveal about familial relationships?

> Matthew moves easily from his observation that traditional interpretations must be re-evaluated to his argument (or thesis) that the mother's point of view used in the story disguises the fact that the mother is not a reliable narrator.

story, is not necessarily a reliable narrator, allowing us to see only what she sees in an entirely subjective manner. The narrator introduces herself and her daughters, immediately setting up the main theme (and conflict) in the story: familial relations. She explains: "Maggie will be nervous until after her sister [Dee] goes: she will stand hopelessly in corners, homely and ashamed of the burn scars down her arms and legs, eying her sister with a mixture of envy and awe" (23). But we never really know what Maggie is thinking. The only depiction we get of her is that, according to the mother, of a painfully reserved young woman left physically and emotionally scarred by tragedy; nothing more is learned about Maggie's past or her motivations except for what the mother tells us. "She thinks her sister has held life always in the palm of one hand," the mother continues, "that 'no' is a word the world never learned to say to her" (23). Her depiction of Maggie is certainly not a favorable one, and she seems to view her daughter with a mere observer's pity rather than a mother's empathy. The cause of Maggie's discomfort with her sister becomes clearer when we actually meet Dee. Yet even before Dee enters the scene, the mother gives us the sense that Dee is a force to be reckoned with.

The mother, too, seems to be in conflict with Dee, who, we are told, is embarrassed about her home and her family: "This house is in a pasture, too, like the other one. No doubt when Dee sees it she will want to tear it down. She wrote me once that no matter where we 'choose' to live, she will manage to come see us. But she will never bring her friends" (27). Yet herein lies another contradiction in the mother's narration: Dee does, in fact, bring her boyfriend home to meet her family. This is not the act of a woman as deeply ashamed of her family as we are meant to believe. Obviously, Dee wants her boyfriend to meet her family, or she would not have

Matthew focuses on specific features and passages of the text to support his thesis.

Matthew shows his readers that the narrator's evaluation of Maggie and Dee is biased.

Literary Analyses

made the effort. Not only is the mother's claim disproved, she never even acknowledges her own mistaken assumption. The mother paints an ugly and unfair portrait of Dee before she even arrives—a picture that only gets darker as the story progresses.

When Dee finally arrives with Hakim-a-barber, we meet a beautiful, poised, and sophisticated woman, yet the mother is quick to judge Dee's attire as "so loud it hurts my eyes" (28). (Perhaps worth mentioning here is that the film version of "Everyday Use" presents Dee as very chic and not nearly as garishly dressed as her mother would have us believe. This may have been a deliberate choice on the filmmaker's behalf to set up this contradiction between the mother's misguided opinion of Dee and how Dee is in reality.) Evidently, the mother does not and seemingly cannot understand Dee's personality, as Dee has undertaken a new way of life. Clearly, the tension when Dee arrives is the result of a clash of cultures, marked by Dee's embracing of all things trendy and metropolitan, having left behind a life of simplicity and stillness—in other words, everything her family has come to represent.

The mother views Dee as more or less going through the motions of being a good daughter but never fully understanding what that role truly entails. Then again, we only know as much as the mother tells us; in this context, getting into Dee's head is not likely in the least. In Dee's defense, leaving her family was tantamount to survival. She could never have thrived in such an environment, nor could she have been happy. And though we never get Dee's side of the story, this seems like a fairly reasonable conclusion to draw. Of course, the mother would never admit this. She is too stuck in her ironclad determination to resent her daughter, never once attempting to understand why Dee left, but only that she did.

Matthew's analysis of Dee's motivations helps him prove his point that the mother's point of view is not reliable.

Literary Analyses

When heritage comes into the picture, then, the tension within the family naturally grows even greater. When the mother calls her daughter "Dee," Dee is quick to correct her, saying that her name is "Wangero Leewanika Kemanjo," and that she could no longer bear "being named after the people who oppress me" (29). Even after her mother says she was named after her aunt, Wangero argues that the name "Dee" is a symbol of oppression, traceable back to slavery. Again, here we cannot fully understand Wangero's motives, yet our narrator in her tone is not hesitant to let us know that she thinks this name change is baloney. A skeptic might get the impression that Wangero seems less concerned about oppression than the novelty of having a recognizably and fashionably Afrocentric name. Yet if we take her character only at face value—only as the mother sees her—we, like the mother, end up making quick and harsh judgments that would be better reserved for a character we truly get to know.

The episode with the quilts addresses the theme of lived heritage versus heritage for show only. When Wangero suggests Maggie is "backward enough to put [the quilts] to everyday use" (33), we find Wangero seemingly arguing that heritage is only worth something when it is put on display. Her opinion of heritage is different from that of her mother and sister, but it's a valid opinion all the same, an idea that the mother never addresses. In these final scenes, Wangero comes across as selfish and ignorant upon first, even second, reading; but it bears reiterating that we only see her through the mother's eyes. Wangero seems far more in tune with her heritage than the mother would care to admit. And just because Wangero has a different way of expressing her affection for her heritage does not make her any less worthy of that heritage than the others.

"Everyday Use" demands meticulous reading of its audience, revealing themes that are universal but not always considered on a daily basis. My interpretation focuses on the narrative voice as an essential element in our understanding of a text. In this case, we are faced with an unreliable narrator and thus are forced to continually reevaluate our own perceptions of Alice Walker's story—an ambiguity that adds further richness to a text we can revisit over and over again.

> Matthew admits that his literary analysis differs from traditional ones of this work because he's focusing on the narrative voice.

> He ends his analysis by assuring readers that the work will reward those who revisit it.

Work Cited

Walker, Alice. "Everyday Use." *Everyday Use.* Ed. Barbara T. Christian. New

Brunswick: Rutgers UP, 1994. 23–35. Print.

Alternatives to the Literary Analysis

Fitting responses come in many forms, not just literary analyses. Your instructor might call upon you to consider one of the following opportunities for writing.

1. Tell the story of a literary work from the point of view of a minor character. Account for this character's different interpretation of events in the narrative.
2. Deliver an analysis of a literary work in which setting is paramount. First, describe the setting itself (the locale); then, demonstrate the ways in which the characters are constrained (limited) and empowered by the setting. Be sure to use descriptive details and examples as you make your case. If local color (details that relate to the specific setting and its inhabitants) contributes to the work's meaning, be sure to explain that contribution by pointing to the characters' behavior, speech, attitudes, actions, and inactions.

pages 67–68

pages 66–67

Everyday Use" demonstrates meticulous reading of its audience, revealing

themes that are universal but not always considered on a daily basis. My

interpretation focuses on the narrative voice as an essential element in our

understanding of a text. In this case we are faced with an unreliable narrator

and thus are forced to continually reevaluate our own perceptions of Alice

Walker's story—an ambiguity that adds further richness to a text we can

revisit over and over again.

Work Cited

Walker, Alice. "Everyday Use." Everyday Use. Ed. Barbara T. Christian. New

Brunswick, Rutgers UP 1994. 23–35. Print.

Alternatives to the Literary Analysis

Essay responses come in many forms, not just literary analyses. Your instructor
might call upon you to consider one of the following opportunities for writing:

1. Tell the story of a literary work from the point of view of a minor character. Account for this character's different interpretation of events in the narrative.

2. Deliver an analysis of a literary work in which setting is paramount. First, sketch the setting itself (the locale); then, demonstrate the ways in which the characters are constrained (limited) and empowered by the setting. Be sure to use descriptive details and examples as you make your case. If local color (details that relate to the specific setting and its imaginings) contributes to the work's meaning, be sure to explain that contribution by pointing to the characters' behavior, speech, attitudes, actions, and intentions.

3

Multimedia Compositions

Just as composing in traditional print media can be a challenge, so can composing with multimedia. In addition to requiring you to generate the most effective information and the most appropriate arrangement, multimedia composing asks you to consider new skills (using audio and visual technologies, for instance) as well as new audiences. You'll find yourself moving from writing for your instructor to writing for a much broader audience, many members of which you'll never meet. However, by paying attention to the elements of the rhetorical situation with which you are already familiar—opportunity, audience, purpose, fitting response, available means—you can compose and deliver effective multimedia pieces. Chapters 12 and 13 will help you approach multimedia compositions with rhetorical savvy.

12 Analyzing Multimedia

E-mail, websites, videos, and text messages may play such an integral part in your daily life that you barely notice them at all: they simply help you work, study, communicate, and entertain yourself. Much of the reading you do involves technology. Word processors, photo-editing and web page–editing software, smartphones, and video and audio recording equipment make it possible to create compositions that combine words, images, and sound. Many college students are already fluent in multimedia composition, able to create and upload images and videos to their blog posts, to make decisions about effective page layout, and even to use HTML coding to produce exactly the effects they want. Still, despite a familiarity with multimedia compositions, most students can benefit from learning how to critically analyze multimedia compositions. Such analysis is necessary when forming rhetorical responses to such compositions.

This chapter discusses critical analysis within a digital environment. Because the principles of multimedia analysis (identifying the purpose and audience for a composition, for instance) are the same as those for analyzing a text, the guidelines in this chapter should be easy to implement. The goal is for you not only to recognize the many options multimedia offer writers but also to understand how the elements of multimedia compositions work to produce their rhetorical effects.

> WRITE FOR FIVE

Write for five minutes in response to each of the following questions. Be prepared to share your answers with the rest of the class.

1. Describe your reading and writing practices, listing the technologies you use in each case. Keep in mind that pens and books are technologies in the sense that they are tools designed and created by humans with particular purposes in mind.
2. Which of your composing and reading experiences involve multimedia? What about your entertainment?
3. How is the reading you do on a website such as Facebook or Twitter, a blog, a news aggregator, or another online space different from other kinds of reading you do? List as many differences as you can.

Multimedia and the Rhetorical Situation

In the last few years, students have begun to use multimedia to address rhetorical opportunities in a number of inventive ways. "TXTmob," "coup de texte," "going mobile," "text brigades," "swarms"—these are some of the terms young people all over the world use for the ways political mobilizations are conducted, allowing group leaders to control, minute by minute, the appearance and movements of demonstrators. The demonstrators themselves—the TXT-mobbers and text brigaders—analyze the multimedia messages in order to read the situation, decide what to do, and stay synchronized.

A young woman whistles as she films the scene around her at a 2009 election rally in Tehran, Iran.

You might be familiar with the 2006 swarm of Filipino university students who organized and publicized a series of political rallies using text messages sent from cell phones. Similarly, after the 2009 Iranian presidential election, students in Tehran took to the streets in protest, relying on text messaging and the online social networking service Twitter to synchronize their swarm and to communicate with one another, the media, and the outside world. Twitter and texting were particularly important methods of communication during the Iran protests, because they provided alternatives to the traditional news media, which were heavily censored by the Iranian government.

Not all situations that call for multimedia responses or analysis involve wide-scale political movements, however. Some social situations also invite such responses and analysis. For instance, actress and activist Calpernia Addams uses YouTube videos to discuss transsexual issues that are often ignored by the mainstream media. She's posted a video entitled "Bad Questions to Ask a Transsexual" in order to achieve two goals: (1) to lampoon offensive questions people often ask her, and (2) to promote resources for transsexuals and education programs about transsexualism. Addams's video also provides links to websites such as Genderlife.com and to a response by one of her critics. A critical analysis of what Addams says (and what she leaves unspoken), how she chooses to deliver her message, who comprises her audience (and who does not), and the purpose of her message is the best means of assessing the overall success of her multimedia composition.

Multimedia compositions are frequently used to address organizational issues as well. Of course, the impact of these efforts depends on how successfully they are interpreted and analyzed. For instance, when student-run groups rely on multimedia for organizing and advertising their events, members of those groups realize that their achievement will be measured by attendance and interest. As you read about the student art show at Texas A&M in the following pages, you'll be analyzing how the students who organized it chose

Multimedia

A scene from one of Calpernia Addams's YouTube videos.

among different media in order to organize and promote their art exhibition as well as to shape their ultimate message for their various audiences. You will also be able to evaluate how well they accomplished their goals.

Using Multimedia to Address a Rhetorical Opportunity

For nearly twenty years now, students in visualization sciences classes at Texas A&M have held VizaGoGo, a visual art show that introduces multimedia student work to the student body and the larger college-town community. Spreading the word about and attracting an audience to the show constitute a rhetorical opportunity for VizaGoGo's student organizers each year. And each year, the organizers brainstorm different options for responding to that opportunity, options that require different media and have both advantages and disadvantages. For instance, when the organizers discussed whether to use a printed flyer or a website to advertise their event, they realized that printed flyers could display details about the event in visible spots around campus but would be competing for attention with any number of other flyers and visuals. A website, on the other hand, would allow organizers to take advantage of several types of media and reach a specific audience—but only that audience.

> ANALYZING THE RHETORICAL SITUATION

As you walk through any building on campus, look at the flyers covering a bulletin board. Which ones have you noticed before? Which ones do you notice now that you're actually stopping to look at the bulletin board? What

Courtesy of Texas A&M, Visualization Laboratory, www.viz.tamu.edu

This website for Texas A&M's VizaGoGo show reached a large and
diverse audience.

are the features of the most effective flyer on the bulletin board? Who is
the audience for the flyer? What is its purpose? What is the context of the
message? What is appealing or unappealing about that flyer? How will you
respond to it?

Using Multimedia to Address an Audience

Once a writer decides to respond to a rhetorical opportunity, he or she must
consider the audience, a rhetorical audience whose members can resolve or help
resolve the problem the writer has identified. The rhetorical opportunity for the
VizaGoGo organizers is figuring out how to attract an audience for the upcoming art show. They could use a blanket advertising campaign (such as the flyers) that might or might not attract interested audience members, or they could
target an audience already inclined to respond. Although a printed flyer on a
bulletin board in a café might reach hundreds of students, not all the students
who pass by will be interested in coming to the art show (assuming they notice
the flyer in the first place). At best, a few students might notice the quality of the
showcased artwork (if the flyer includes photos), that one of the artists is someone they know (if the artists are listed), or even that the art show provides a good
date destination and then decide to attend (if the exhibition dates and times are
prominently displayed). On the other hand, with a link to the VizaGoGo page
on the website of the Visualization Sciences Program, organizers could reach
other students taking courses in that program and encourage them to circulate
details about the show by pulling verbal, visual, or audio information from the

Visitors to the site can preview the artists' work in the Gallery.

site. The website could feature "teaser" clips of animations, image galleries of sketches and video stills, and even a history page documenting the development of the show. By giving individual artists and other interested students something to link to (via Twitter, Facebook, or an e-mail message), the website could involve more people in targeting a rhetorical audience for the show. In fact, once the organizers opened the website, it began to reach a wide audience, in part because program alumni who had moved on to careers at ILM, Dreamworks, Disney, and Microsoft shared the site with their coworkers. As the audience expanded, the rhetorical purpose of the website began to change as well.

> ANALYZING THE RHETORICAL SITUATION

Identify one multimedia composition (for instance, a website, podcast, or video) that you have recently been impressed by. Describe the various parts of the rhetorical situation to which the composer of that work is responding: What is the rhetorical opportunity? Who makes up the audience? What is the purpose? What is the context?

Using Multimedia with a Rhetorical Purpose

As you already know, purpose and audience cannot be separated. When the designers of the VizaGoGo website realized that their purpose had broadened, from simply publicizing the art show to interested parties to also promoting themselves to potential employers, they decided that they needed to address this more complicated (dual) rhetorical purpose. The expanded rhetorical purpose opened a new range of rhetorical choices for the organizers. As they considered their options, they generated a list of possibilities: they could expand the gallery section of the website to showcase more artists, include visual-audio biographies of the artists, feature online portfolios, describe the annual event as well as the current show, include a map and directions to the show, and even add a travel page that included information on accommodations for out-of-town attendees. After they narrowed down their options, they would need to concentrate on how they would arrange the material on the website.

> ANALYZING THE RHETORICAL SITUATION

Locate a multimedia message (delivered online, on television, or via another electronic medium) that affected you in some way: maybe it made you change an action, opinion, or attitude; maybe it entertained you or taught you something new. Identify the rhetorical purpose of and audience for that message, taking a few minutes to explain how purpose and audience work together in this message.

Using Multimedia as a Fitting Response

If you were one of the student organizers of the first VizaGoGo event, you and your fellow organizers might have weighed the ease of composing and circulating flyers against the time-consuming nature of composing with the more tantalizing multimedia. Or, together, you might have come to realize the advantage of adopting both approaches. After all, you can compose, print, and circulate flyers that include a link to your website, thereby reaping the benefits of both media. You have the flyer's broad distribution combined with the website's detailed, engaging, and easily transmitted content. The overlapping of print and digital media has already become common: business cards often have web and e-mail addresses printed on them, and a company's website may make printable coupons available.

The combination of website and flyers did prove successful for VizaGoGo organizers, who plastered the Texas A&M campus with printed flyers weeks before the show and put table tents (small flyers that can be propped up on a tabletop) in all of the student dining halls. The organizers also ran television and radio ads, which directed potential audience members to the website for more information about the show. In recent years, as its target audience and available means have grown, VizaGoGo has expanded its reach to social networking sites, with a Facebook profile that is integrated into the Visualization Sciences Program's website (viz.tamu.edu).

> ANALYZING THE RHETORICAL SITUATION

Multimedia presentation software such as PowerPoint allows speakers to create images and soundtracks to accompany their oral presentations. Evaluate the overall success of a multimedia presentation you've seen recently. In what ways was the presentation a fitting response to a rhetorical opportunity? List its strengths and its weaknesses. Be prepared to discuss your analysis with the rest of the class.

Using Multimedia as an Available Means

Like all other kinds of composing, multimedia composing requires that the writer assess the resources and the constraints of the available means of delivery. As you know well, multimedia compositions provide resources that traditional print documents do not. When the VizaGoGo organizers incorporated video on the show's website, for example, they were able to display teaser videos of student work as well as clips of the television ads for the event.

As you analyze multimedia, you should be aware of the types of media you might encounter (text, images, audio, and video), as well as the variety of digital composing environments used to produce those media. A digital composing environment is any software or online resource that allows writers to manipulate their compositions. The combination of the medium and the composing environment affords unique opportunities and limitations. For example, Microsoft Word, Twitter, and Adobe Photoshop offer different features for creating different types of compositions. Microsoft Word offers templates for managing long text-based documents, whereas Twitter won't let a writer type more than 140 characters. Photoshop focuses on the visual features of multimedia documents, allowing the editing of still images but offering very limited text-editing capabilities. In practice, however, these composing environments often overlap: a writer might compose text in Word and edit photos in Photoshop before combining these elements into a single blog post or web page. To analyze a multimedia composition, carefully consider the medium and composing environment.

> ANALYZING THE RHETORICAL SITUATION

You've been composing with multimedia ever since you stood in front of your class in elementary school, pointing to the poster you made to accompany your book report. And you've been analyzing multimedia ever since you sat back and listened to the book reports of your classmates, deciding which of the books you might like to read and which ones you never wanted to hear about again. Consider a multimedia composition by one of your current classmates. Determine the rhetorical opportunity, intended audience, purpose, context (constraints and resources), and overall effectiveness of the work. Refer back to the list of questions on pages 53–54 as you analyze the composition. Be prepared to share your analysis with the rest of the class.

Responding with Multimedia

The best composers, whether working with multimedia or not, take their rhetorical situation into consideration as they shape a message. This chapter focuses on the use of multimedia for responding to rhetorical situations. Each section discusses a different type of composing environment. Whether you're composing a website, a podcast, a video broadcast, or some other multimedia work, the rhetorical principles of invention and memory, arrangement, style, and delivery can inform your composing process.

A Rhetorical Approach to Websites, Wikis, and Blogs

When women and men all over the world realized that a greater awareness of symptoms and treatments could help prevent many deaths from breast cancer, activists generated ideas for how best to bring this issue to the public's awareness. As a result of their thinking, the pink ribbon movement was launched in 1991 to deliver the message about breast cancer via the now-familiar small pink ribbons. The Komen Foundation (a charitable foundation that supports breast cancer research and awareness) distributed pink ribbons to all the participants in its "Race for the Cure", celebrities wore pink ribbons at gala events, and many cars sported bumper stickers and magnets shaped like pink ribbons. The ribbons and the words that accompanied them were a form of multimedia, though a relatively low-tech form.

Wanting to spread breast cancer awareness globally, organizers chose to build a website to address that rhetorical opportunity in 1997. Pink Ribbon International organizers established the site PinkRibbon.org, which was "available for all people in the world connected to breast cancer." Not only did the website allow easy access to information about breast cancer, but it did so using multimedia such as images and educational videos. Of course, not all people have access to websites like PinkRibbon.org. In fact, many of the world's people have never used a computer, which is a constraint in this rhetorical situation. A resource, however, is the fact that healthcare providers in relatively undeveloped areas of the world sometimes have online access (or did when they were being trained and thus may have encountered the PinkRibbon.org site).

When organizations like Pink Ribbon International decide to use online multimedia, their web designers and content suppliers must choose from among

Pink Ribbon International's home page balances text and images to help its audience absorb information quickly.

a seemingly infinite assortment of images, texts, and layouts. Only by keeping their rhetorical situation—and the individual elements of that situation—in mind can website designers make the best decisions concerning these options. The PinkRibbon.org website balances text and images, using a layout that helps readers immediately identify the most important information. As a fundraising organization, Pink Ribbon International needs to solicit donations—a focus made prominent on its website. A visitor to the site is likely to notice immediately the large banner urging readers to "donate now." Keeping additional text in small, contained blocks is a rhetorical choice that makes it easy for the audience to scan and absorb large amounts of information quickly—an important feature, considering the organization's educational goals.

To organize multimedia elements like images and menus, web designers make use of some of the same fundamental principles of rhetoric that you use when writing an essay or drafting a speech: principles of invention and memory, arrangement, style, and delivery. As you compose, design, and format a website, you'll want to keep these basic principles in mind.

Invention and memory

Invention and memory are closely linked—they work together to provide you ideas and plans for any composition, including a website. Most broadly, *memory* refers to a storehouse of knowledge; the knowledge may be stored in a library, in an archive, on a bulletin board, or in your own memory. You draw from this storehouse when you use invention (or exploration) strategies such as listing, freewriting, and clustering (see Chapter 3). In digital environments, invention and memory can extend across space and time: you can share ideas with coauthors around the world and examine historical documents in online archives.

Arrangement

You should arrange the elements of a multimedia composition (including text and images) to create a *hierarchy* of information; that is, your arrangement should make obvious which information is most important and which is less so. For example, in this textbook, color-coded tabs, chapter titles, headings, and subheadings are used to organize the text visually. You've been taught to place your thesis in the introduction of an essay, and you'll use that technique in your multimedia compositions—placing the most important piece of information wherever your readers will be drawn to first. Because we read from left to right and from top to bottom, the top left corner of a page of type or a screen is often the first place we look. Thus, your decision about what to place in the top left corner of a web page has especially important rhetorical effects. PinkRibbon .org uses that space for a logo; as a result, the organization's promotional materials are always prominent on the website.

Ultimately, arrangement is connected with the rhetorical appeal to logos. As you know, logos is the logical appeal of your response to a rhetorical situation, and part of that appeal lies in the (literal) shape of the argument. A writer's attention (or inattention) to shape becomes especially evident on websites. Most websites use images to break up large blocks of text. The resulting shorter chunks of text, in conjunction with the images, help the audience focus on the important elements of the site. In addition, using headings to highlight major ideas can help an audience scan the content of a website more quickly as they scroll through it. (Remember that most people don't linger over a web page the way they might over a book page.)

Style

Style, the artful expression of ideas, is an important factor in any composition, but especially in a multimedia composition, which offers verbal, visual, and aural options for expression. Among a composition's visual elements, fonts in particular make an important (and immediate) rhetorical statement to a composition's audience. Many advertisements use clean, professional-looking fonts like Helvetica, while informal and light-hearted documents might use Comic Sans. *Serif* fonts such as Times New Roman (with those little foot-like tips, called *serifs*, on the ends of some letter strokes) make reading printed documents easier, but *sans serif* fonts such as Verdana (with no serifs on the ends of the strokes) have become the standard for websites. When deciding on fonts, consider your purpose. A good place to start is with these questions: What do I want this composition to do? What font best achieves that?

The colors you choose also have rhetorical effects on your audience. Specifically, colors are closely connected with appeals to pathos. You're probably already familiar with how colors influence thoughts and emotions in everyday life (red, blue, and yellow might conjure up a fond mental image of your elementary school classroom; just red and yellow might make you hungry for McDonald's fries). The same idea applies online: a color scheme featuring dark colors tends to look soberly professional, while a vibrant orange scheme might complement the mood of a humor blog. The PinkRibbon.org website uses a subtle gray as a secondary color to balance the thematic pink menu and highlights. Ultimately, just as you wouldn't write a scholarship application in lime green, you should choose color schemes for multimedia compositions based on your purpose and audience.

Delivery

Delivery is concerned with *how* something is said or presented—how a message is delivered. How you deliver a speech can be just as important as what you say. The same is true of a website. Not everyone will be able to stream videos or download podcasts. Some people might be browsing from a smartphone or a netbook; others might be using an older computer that lacks the memory capacity to deal with large video or audio downloads. In other words, accessibility is a rhetorical issue: the means of delivery influence what parts of your message an audience ultimately sees and hears. As a result, when you begin designing a multimedia composition such as a website, you should consider what information is accessible to which people in what ways. Just because some users can't access videos doesn't mean you should avoid them as a delivery method. After all, if your audience members are all digital movie aficionados, a video review would be completely appropriate. You should realize that your delivery choices determine not only who constitutes your audience but also how your audience experiences your composition.

WAIT A MINUTE . . .

How do blogs and wikis differ from websites? For one thing, they offer different levels of interactivity for the audience. Websites traditionally have offered few opportunities for the audience to contribute (though this is changing with the rise of social networking sites like Facebook and Web 2.0 sites like Amazon, which encourage reader reviews and contributions). Like websites, blogs are usually updated by one person (or a small group). However, most blogs also have a comment feature, allowing audience members to respond directly to blog posts, but not to edit them. Wikis have the highest level of interactivy, as they are created *by* site visitors *for* other site visitors. Thus, anyone can contribute to a wiki—developing text, adding images, and rewriting awkward sentences.

Wikis and blogs often address different rhetorical opportunities than websites do. Because of their interactivity, wikis are excellent tools for collaboration. For example, if you are working on a group project, you might set up a wiki where all the group members can contribute ideas and revise each other's work. Likewise, blogs often have a different purpose than websites do. Most blogs act as public journals, and journal writing has conventions that make it differ from the kind of concise, compressed writing you find on a website. You might use a blog to document your personal adventures in cooking, whereas a restaurant owner would probably choose a website to provide an appealing, unified image of his or her business. As you face the rhetorical decision of which genre to use (wiki, blog, or website), keep in mind that these often overlap—a website might have a blog component or a wiki might act like a collaborative journal.

If all of this technical talk seems intimidating, don't worry—websites can now be built and updated using Content Management Systems (CMSs) and design templates, tools that allow you to focus more on the rhetorical principles behind composing and less on the technical execution. A CMS lets users create and maintain websites through an Internet browser, meaning that little knowledge of HTML or the technical side of design is required. For example, the Composition Program's website (composition.la.psu.edu) at Penn State University is built and maintained using the open-source CMS Plone. In the screenshots in the Tricks of the Trade box, you can see that pages are edited using a WYSIWYG editor and constructed by Plone to fit the design template of the website. This is not to say that using a CMS puts all design elements out of your control: you still need to be comfortable with the rhetorical options for arranging images and formatting text, discussed earlier.

TRICKS OF THE TRADE

WYSIWYG Editors

WYSIWYG stands for "what you see is what you get," and WYSIWYG editors are a type of software that is commonly used with websites, blogs, and wikis. The advantage of WYSIWYG editors is familiarity—most have a toolbar for formatting text similar to the toolbar in Microsoft Word. This means you don't need an understanding of a mark-up language like HTML in order to create professional-looking content for a website. Because WYSIWYG interfaces make creating online documents so easy, hosts of many blogs and wikis have adopted them to increase user bases. The simple selling point of WYSIWYG is this: if you can send an e-mail, you can build a website, start a blog, or update a wiki.

continued

A page on the Penn State Composition Program's website being updated with a WYSIWYG editor. Notice that aside from the editing icons and text-boxes, this looks very much like the finished page shown below.

Courtesy of Pennsylvania State University

The finished page made public on the Composition Program's website.

Courtesy of Pennsylvania State University

A Rhetorical Approach to Podcasting

In your first-year writing class, you might be asked to produce a basic recording, such as a podcast. Such assignments offer an alternative to printed essays and give you practice with oral presentations. For example, you might be required to compose a critical review of your favorite band, to be delivered as a podcast. The podcast is a fitting medium for a music review, as it enhances the message itself. In addition, a podcast might appeal to the audience for such a review more than a print review would. If you have never done it, creating a podcast might seem technologically daunting—but it's not. In fact, composing a podcast is fairly easy, as you can use your personal computer and basic sound-editing software such as Apple's GarageBand or any of the audio editors available as free downloads, such as Audacity.

Invention and memory

You learned in the previous section that invention and memory work together to provide knowledge and generate new ideas when you are composing a website. Techniques such as freewriting and clustering can also help you prepare what you're going to say in a podcast. Like many writers, you may find that the act of imagining and planning a recording generates ideas that never

Multimedia

would have occurred to you if you had been composing a traditional print essay.

At this stage, particularly if podcasting is new to you, it might be helpful to listen to a few podcasts. As you do, try to think about what this medium makes possible and how you can best take advantage of this resource.

Arrangement

Compose and practice your script before you start. If you don't want to be tethered to a full script, write out a detailed outline of what you want to say (in order to avoid sounding nervous or rambling). Another good reason to practice is that written language often needs to be "translated" to spoken language. As you read aloud, you'll find that some passages flow smoothly but others are too complicated to allow good speaking or easy listening and need to be rewritten. You might need to break up long sentences, to enumerate your points, or to repeat key phrases. It also helps to mark in your script occasional pauses, so that your audience has time to process what you've said. Finally, by preparing and arranging your talk ahead of time and considering your audience and purpose, you can ensure that your word choice is suitable for the spoken medium. For example, instead of using a word like *disparage*, you might simply say "make fun of" or "put down."

Style

One advantage of an audio recording is that you can make stylistic changes after you've recorded it—that is, you can use sound-editing software to improve your composition. At the editing stage, you can also add effects. For example, if you are recording an album review, you might include background music from the album or brief samples of songs to illustrate the points you make in your review and thus build your ethos (that is, demonstrate that you know a good deal about the music). You can also make technical adjustments, such as lowering volume levels for individual tracks. Finally, with sound-editing software's visual interface, you can find and selectively edit out mistakes (much like correcting typos when using a word processor). Just as you practice before a live presentation and proofread your written essay before submitting it, you should always go back and make adjustments to an audio recording so that your finished composition sounds polished. As you know, a polished composition—whether written, spoken, or recorded—is important in establishing your ethos.

Delivery

Delivery has always been an important part of effective rhetoric. Once you've determined that you will use audio as the means of delivery, you need to be sure your listening audience can understand you. But the decision to speak clearly is a rhetorical choice; a good many underground or indie bands (such

TRICKS OF THE TRADE

Audio Technologies

The technologies used to make audio recordings can be as simple as a computer with a built-in microphone or as complicated as a full studio setup. You probably already have experience with audio recording as a medium of delivery. Think of all the times that you've planned out an important voice-mail message before recording it. You probably considered your audience and purpose before calling—you might have even practiced your delivery a few times. The point is that you're probably no stranger to audio recording as a rhetorical act.

Recording basic audio at home has become much easier in recent years, and recordings can even approach studio quality, as many personal computers have sound-editing software preinstalled. This software provides a visual representation of multiple recorded tracks that you have created or drawn from other sources; the tracks can be manipulated by cutting, pasting, rearranging, and recording over the segments of audio. You can adjust volume and equalization (treble and bass) levels using the slider bars or add sound effects with a single click of the mouse. Because of its visual interface, sound-editing software makes it easy for anyone to mix and layer multiple tracks into a professional audio composition.

as The White Stripes and T-Pain) purposefully distort their vocals. This voice distortion challenges the mainstream convention of recording clarity exhibited by artists like Justin Timberlake and Taylor Swift. In most cases, however, your audience will appreciate it if you speak clearly and slowly into the microphone to ensure that it picks up the sound of your voice properly. In addition to considering your voice quality, you'll also want to consider how fast you read. If you keep in mind that it should take about two and a half minutes to deliver a double-spaced page, you'll know how to pace yourself. And if you've followed the advice on arrangement and style, you will already have revised your composition so that your language is simple and clear enough to be understood by your listening audience.

A Rhetorical Approach to Broadcasting on YouTube

Video provides yet another available means for composing and delivering multimedia compositions. If you are going to review a movie, for example, you might decide to use the same medium as the piece you are reviewing: video. Like podcasting, composing a video gives you the chance to apply the rhetorical principles you're learning to a multimedia composition.

Invention and memory

Like a well-done audio recording, a well-composed video is based on the preparation that only invention and memory can supply. Thinking about videos you've enjoyed and replaying them online or on a television set may give you ideas about what you want to be sure to include visually and verbally in your video composition. Plenty of good information is stored in your own memory, as well as in your video library. These ideas can be the seeds of fresh visual, verbal, and musical concepts for your video composition. Invention and memory will work together to help you identify your message.

Arrangement

The material resulting from invention and memory must be given purposeful arrangement. Regardless of who performs in the video (you and/or others), you'll want to prepare a script, cue cards, or a flowchart so that you can closely track the arrangement of the video. Some videos are animated, some are *mashups* (a splicing together or layering of several existing clips), and still others are montages set to music or a narration (or both). You'll need to consider the resources and the constraints of your rhetorical situation as you choose among arrangement options. Your willingness to perform (or fear of performing) or your access to video equipment might be your richest resource or your strongest constraint. A variety of options will play a role in the arrangement of your composition, whether you add music, art, interviews, or performers—whatever visual or audio elements you choose to employ.

The ability to compose with video is itself a major resource, as video allows you to edit and polish your composition after the fact, just as you can with audio. With video-editing software you can rearrange your video composition frame by frame, as well as cut scenes and control audio. If, after finishing your composition, you decide that a different arrangement might appeal to your audience more, you can cut and paste segments into a different order, just as you might do with a word-processed essay. You might also cut parts of scenes that run too long. After all, as twentieth-century rhetorician Kenneth Burke put it, any composition is ultimately a selection, reflection, and deflection of reality.

Style

Once you have a draft of your video composition, you can enhance its style by adding soundtracks or special effects from your editing software's effects library. You'll want to keep in mind that every audio or visual enhancement has its own rhetorical as well as stylistic effect. Consider, for instance, James Cameron's *Titanic*, a pathos-drenched drama. Only a solemn, stately soundtrack could complement *Titanic*, whereas the lively musical score of *Mamma Mia!* brings the upbeat plot to life. As you consider various stylistic embellishments you might make to your video, keep in mind that even feature-length movies go through an intense editing process designed to produce a polished, stylistically appealing composition.

Delivery

Good delivery in a video follows many of the principles that apply to effective audio compositions—you should speak clearly into the microphone, pace yourself when delivering a monologue, and practice your performance ahead of time. However, you must also consider the visual dimensions of video, including what you and other performers wear and what material and visual elements you include in each scene. For instance, in the *Beyond the Trailer* segment in which she reviews *Shutter Island* (which is shown on the website Indy Mogul), Grace Randolph wears a sci-fi chic tee-shirt bearing a phrase referring to *Battlestar Galactica* and stands next to a giant digital movie poster while delivering her monologue. Even though Randolph is casually dressed, she has chosen her attire and props carefully: the combination of these visual elements immediately builds her ethos as a movie reviewer who focuses specifically on the sci-fi/indie genre. Her choices also display audience awareness, as the audience for the paranormal thriller *Shutter Island* would likely include sci-fi fans.

Delivery doesn't just apply to your performance on film, however. You also need to consider how you will distribute (or deliver) the video itself to your audience. YouTube and other sites that host streaming video have made distribution easier. However, because of the public nature of such sites, you may want to choose a different distribution method, such as e-mail, in order to more carefully control who is in your audience. Even something as mundane sounding as file format is a rhetorical issue: obscure video formats might limit who can view your composition, whereas more common formats (with the extension .avi or .mov) can be opened on most computers. These kinds

Grace Randolph hosts a review of Martin Scorsese's *Shutter Island* on YouTube.

Multimedia

of technical considerations can even affect your ethos. For example, the file extension .wma can be opened only on computers running Windows, so saving your video in this format aligns you with PC users and might hurt your ethos among Mac users. However, saving your composition as a .wma file might contribute to your ethos in an office environment, where PCs are more common than Macs.

Facebook and Twitter as Multimedia

In the past decade, social networking sites like Facebook and Twitter have become hugely popular. These sites allow you to construct an online profile, stay in touch with friends, and let people know what is happening in your life. Whenever you update your Facebook profile or post a photograph to Twitter, you are engaging in multimedia composing. After all, a Facebook profile is usually some combination of text, links, images, and video that you construct with a specific rhetorical purpose in mind. For example, if you wanted to persuade viewers of your profile that you were well read, you might post a long "Favorite Books" list, perhaps accompanied by a picture of your overburdened book shelves.

Although you probably don't think of the rhetorical principles of invention and memory, arrangement, style, and delivery each time you tweet or update your Facebook status, these principles are always at work. As you examine the following examples, one of a group's Facebook page and one of a Twitter stream, consider the ways the writers combined various media to form fitting responses.

The Brazos Gumbo Facebook page came about in response to a specific problem: the poetry community in the Brazos Valley of East Texas was loosely organized; poetry readings were advertised only by word of mouth, and the poets were unaware of other poets in the area. Identifying this problem as a rhetorical opportunity, a group of student poets realized that a Facebook page would allow poets whose work had been published in a local journal, *Brazos Gumbo*, to discuss their work, organize readings, and share news that was important to the community. The group eventually grew to encompass local poets and writers from a variety of backgrounds and a range of ages.

Some rhetorical advantages of using Facebook for such a project were the potential for wide distribution, the familiar and standardized interface, and the interactivity of the platform. Notice that the "Info" page for Brazos Gumbo has the same familiar layout as other group pages and profiles on Facebook—it provides a basic, easily accessible description and contact information for the group. This accessibility turned out to be important to the group as it tried to increase its visibility. However, another rhetorical purpose in forming the group was to build community among local poets. As a result, the group's formal discussion pages and informal wall began to develop as communication spaces.

For the poets of the Brazos Valley, a high-traffic online space like a Facebook page was ideal for building a network of local poets. But issues of audience can become complicated when you are working online with multimedia compositions, especially on sites like Facebook. The primary audience for your Facebook profile might be your friends, but unless you have adjusted your privacy

The Brazos Gumbo Facebook page provides an online space where local poets can discuss their work, plan upcoming events, and share photos of local poetry readings.

Multimedia

settings, anyone with an account could be part of the audience. Having such a large potential audience isn't necessarily a bad thing—as long as you are aware of it. After all, social networking sites can be effective tools for distributing compositions you think are important. Consider the university students in Iran who used Twitter to distribute information about protests to other Iranians and the outside world, discussed in Chapter 12. Or consider the VizaGoGo art show organizers, who linked their website to a Facebook profile as a way to reach beyond their small local audience and display their work to family members and potential employers. In both of these examples, the composers took full advantage of the interconnectedness and the potential for rapid distribution of information offered by social networking sites.

The rhetorical constraints of social networking sites have also spawned some unique and creative composing practices. Consider @cookbook, a Twitter stream by Maureen Evans, where all the recipes are condensed into 140-character tweets. As you can see in the screenshot, Evans had to develop her own cooking shorthand in order to adapt to her space constraint: writing "Cvr30m" instead of "Cover for 30 minutes" saves 14 valuable characters. Because this shorthand can be confusing, however, Evans also developed a glossary, using a wiki platform to define the shortened cooking terms she uses on Twitter. By

The Twitter stream @cookbook provides condensed, 140-character recipes.

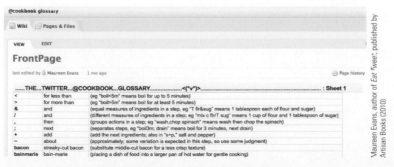

The companion glossary to @cookbook is a wiki.

connecting the two composing spaces (creating links to the wiki from @cookbook), Evans was able to work around one of the constraints of her rhetorical situation in a creative way.

One advantage of @cookbook's shortened recipes lies in the rhetorical principle of delivery: audience members can quickly and easily access these short recipes on small portable devices like smartphones. Such access may seem insignificant, but if you've ever been at the grocery store trying to remember the ingredients you need to make supper, you understand how important that access could be. Being able to access a recipe via a smartphone is also handy in the kitchen: you want to protect your laptop from boiling liquids and various other ingredients.

Challenges and Pleasures of Multimedia

The multimedia examples referred to throughout this chapter and Chapter 12 were composed by writers just like you, writers who came to realize the power and potential of multimedia. They approached their compositions—a Facebook page for poets, a revolutionary text message, and a website about a multimedia art show—with rhetorical savvy. As technology becomes an ever-present part of our lives, multimedia composing is becoming an important part of our rhetorical practices. Understanding how to meet the challenges posed by multimedia is key to participating in the emerging conversations of the twenty-first century.

A Guide to Research

Throughout this part of the book, you'll use your knowledge of the rhetorical situation to understand the research process. Chapter 14 will help you use the elements of the rhetorical situation to get started on your research projects. Chapters 15 and 16 describe the many different types of sources available to you and tell you where to find them. Chapter 17 provides strategies for managing the research process. Chapter 18 explains how to evaluate and use sources. Chapter 19 provides detailed guidelines on acknowledging sources and formatting research papers and presents a sample student paper.

Clues to Compulsive Collecting

SEPARATING USELESS JUNK FROM OBJECTS OF VALUE

AN INTRIGUING NEW STUDY MAY help researchers understand why some people are compelled to hoard useless objects. Steven W. Anderson, a neurologist, and his colleagues at the University of Iowa examined 63 people with brain damage from stroke, surgery or encephalitis. Before their brains were damaged, none had problems with hoarding, but afterward, nine began filling their houses with such things as old newspapers, broken appliances or boxes of junk mail, despite the intervention of family members.

WHY DO SOME PEOPLE COLLECT USELESS OBJECTS LIKE OLD NEWSPAPERS, BROKEN APPLIANCES AND JUNK MAIL?

© WR Publishing/Alamy.

These compulsive collectors had all suffered damage to the prefrontal cortex, a brain region involved in decision making, information processing and behavioral organization. The people whose collecting behavior remained normal also had brain damage, but it was instead distributed throughout the right and left hemispheres of the brain.

Anderson posits that the urge to collect derives from the need to store supplies such as food—a drive so basic it originates in the subcortical and limbic portions of the brain. Humans need the prefrontal cortex, he says, to determine what "supplies" are worth hoarding. His study was presented at the annual conference of the Society for Neuroscience.
—Richard A. Lovett

1. In "Clues to Compulsive Collecting," Richard Lovett describes research first presented by Steven Anderson and his colleagues at a neuroscience conference. After reading this article, write a paragraph or two in which you discuss the article in terms of Lovett's and the original researchers' rhetorical situations. How are they similar? How are they different?
2. In answering question 1, you likely noted significant differences in the rhetorical situations of the article writer and the original researchers, even though their subject matter was the same. In order to prepare for the research you may have to do for college classes, describe a rhetorical situation you might encounter in one of your classes. Explain how research would help you prepare a fitting response.

An Overview of Research

When people hear the word *research*, they often think of laboratory experiments, archaeological digs, or hours spent in the library or on the library's website. They overlook the ordinary research they do every day as they decide what to buy, how to fix something, how to perform a function on their computer, what books to read, or where to spend their vacation. Research is common to everyone's experience.

When people move to a new place, they must find information about schools, clinics, stores, and other locations of importance or interest. They must also find out about dentists, doctors, veterinarians, and accountants. They obtain the information they need by doing research—that is, by talking with other people, visiting websites, and reading brochures and other materials.

Many people do research at work. Business owners must keep abreast of new technology, marketing trends, and changes in the tax code. Doctors must have current information on diagnostic procedures and effective treatments, therapies, and pharmaceuticals. Some types of research that professionals do may be surprising. Librarians, for example, have to know about the latest print materials and information technology, but in order to prepare their operating budgets, they also have to know the costs of items and numbers of library users. The types of research people do in the workplace depend on their jobs, but most professionals consult other people they consider knowledgeable, read materials on specific topics, and visit useful websites.

Students, of course, conduct many types of research, starting in elementary school and continuing through college. Their research enables them to prepare lab reports, posters, term papers, multimedia presentations, and other types of assignments. Some of their research entails laboratory experimentation. Other research takes place in the field, as students conduct surveys, make observations, and attend performances. Much research focuses on written records such as articles and books, government documents, old letters, and personal journals.

Regardless of the form of the research or the context in which it takes place, all research is done in response to a *rhetorical opportunity*: a call or need for more information. Depending on the nature of the opportunity, you may or may not have to record the results of your research. Once you obtain the information on which store has the best prices for electronics, you simply go to that store. In contrast, research projects prepared in response to an assignment usually require writing—at all stages of the process. Researchers often freewrite to come up with ideas, create project designs and work plans, take notes, and eventually draft some kind of composition. It is hard to imagine a researcher in an academic setting without a pen, pencil, or keyboard.

For the results of research to be valuable, the process must be taken seriously. Researchers who chase down facts to attach to opinions they already have are doing only superficial research. These researchers are not interested in finding information that may cause them to question their beliefs or that may make their thinking more complicated. Genuine research, on the other hand, involves crafting a good research question and pursuing an answer to it, both of which require patience and care.

Rhetorical Opportunity and the Research Question

As you know from reading Chapter 3, the starting point for any writing project is determining your rhetorical opportunity—what has prompted you to write. For research assignments, that opportunity (or problem) also includes what has prompted you to look for more information. Once you are sure of your opportunity, you can craft a question to guide your research.

To make the most of your time, choose a specific question early in your research process. Having such a question helps you avoid collecting more sources than you can possibly use or finding sources that are only tangentially related. A student who chooses a general topic—say, the separation of church and state—will waste time if he or she neglects to narrow the topic into a question, such as one of the following: What did the framers of the Constitution have in mind when they discussed the separation of church and state? How should the separation of church and state be interpreted in law? Should the Ten Commandments be posted in government buildings? Should the phrase *under God* be removed from the Pledge of Allegiance?

Good questions often arise when you try to relate what you are studying in a course to your own experience. For instance, you may start wondering about the separation of church and state when, after reading about this topic in a history class, you notice the number of times politicians refer to God in their speeches, you remember reciting the phrase *under God* in the Pledge of Allegiance, or you read in the newspaper that a plaque inscribed with the Ten Commandments has been removed from the State House in Alabama. These observations may prompt you to look for more information on the topic. Each observation, however, may give rise to a different question. You will choose the question that interests you the most and that will best help you fulfill the assignment.

To generate research questions, you may find it helpful to return to Chapter 3, where you read about journalists' questions (Who? What? Where? When? Why? How?). Here are some more specific kinds of questions that commonly require research:

QUESTIONS ABOUT CAUSES

Why doesn't my college offer athletic scholarships?
What causes power outages in large areas of the country?

QUESTIONS ABOUT CONSEQUENCES

What are the consequences of taking antidepressants for a long period of time?
How would the atmosphere in a school change if a dress code were established?

QUESTIONS ABOUT PROCESSES

How can music lovers prevent corporations from controlling the development of music?
How does my hometown draw boundaries for school districts?

QUESTIONS ABOUT DEFINITIONS OR CATEGORIES

How do you know if you are addicted to something?
What kind of test is "the test of time"?

QUESTIONS ABOUT VALUES

Should the Makah tribe be allowed to hunt gray whales?
Would the construction of wind farms be detrimental to the environment?

TRICKS OF THE TRADE

If the assignment doesn't specify a topic and you are not sure what you want to write about, you may need some prompting. Consider these questions:

▶ Can you remember an experience that you did not understand fully or that made you feel uncertain? What was it that you didn't understand? What were you unsure of?

▶ What have you observed lately (on television, in the newspaper, on your way to school, or in the student union) that piqued your curiosity? What were you curious about?

▶ What local or national problem that you have recently heard or read about would you like to help solve?

▶ Is there anything you find unusual that you would like to explore? Lifestyles? Political views? Religious views?

As you consider which question will most appropriately guide your research, you may find it helpful to discuss your ideas with other people. Research and writing both require a great deal of time and effort, and you will find the tasks more pleasant—and maybe even easier—if you are sincerely interested in your question. Moreover, enthusiasm about your work will motivate you to do the best you can; indifference breeds mediocrity. By talking with other people, you may find out that the question you have chosen is a good one. Or, you may discover that you need to narrow the question or change it in some other way. You may even realize that the question you initially chose really does not interest you very much. To get a conversation about your ideas started, have someone you are familiar with ask you some of the following questions. You may also use these questions for a focused freewriting exercise in your research log (see Chapter 17 for more on research logs).

▶ Why is it important for you to answer the question? What is the answer's significance for you? How will answering the question help you? How is the question related to your rhetorical opportunity?

▶ Will the answer to your question require serious research? (A genuine research question does not have a simple or obvious answer.)

▶ What types of research might help you answer your question? (You may already have some ideas; see Chapter 15 for ideas about library and online research and Chapter 16 for suggestions on field research.) Will you be able to carry out these types of research in the amount of time you have been given?

TRICKS OF THE TRADE

by Cristian Nuñez, history and economics major

Don't be shy about reaching out to your professors for help. I've found that professors can help shape a fuzzy question or idea into a strong research question, saving time and agony. Take advantage of their office hours to do this.

Research and Audience

In Part 1, you learned that a fitting response satisfies your audience. In order to meet the expectations of your readers, you must know something about them. First, you must find out who your audience is. If you are writing in response to a course assignment, your instructor may define your audience for you (usually, it is the instructor and your classmates). However, sometimes your instructor may ask you to imagine a different audience so that you have experience writing for a wider range of people. For example, your instructor might ask you to write a letter to the editor of your local paper. In this case, your audience is much broader. It still comprises your instructor and classmates, but it also includes the editor of the newspaper as well as all the newspaper's readers.

As your writing career progresses, the number of audiences you write for will increase. You may be able to easily name your audience—college students, science teachers, mechanical engineers, pediatricians, or the general public—but to make sure that you satisfy any audience you choose to address, you need to go beyond labels. When you do research, you must take into account what types of sources your audience will expect you to use and which sources they will find engaging, convincing, or entertaining.

Keep in mind that when you write for an audience, you are joining an ongoing conversation. To enter that conversation, you need to pay attention to what's being said and who the participants are. You can begin by reading the sources the participants in the conversation use. By reading what they read, you'll learn what information is familiar to them and what information may need to be explained in detail.

The web page for the Pucker Gallery (below) and the brief article from *Bostonia,* Boston University's alumni magazine (on page 418) contain information about the artist Joseph Ablow. The audience for each is different, however. In the *Bostonia* article, the abbreviation CFA is not explained, because the intended audience, alumni of Boston University, will know that it refers to the College of Fine Arts. If you were writing an article for an alumni magazine, you too would be able to use abbreviations and acronyms familiar to those who attended that college or university. However, if your audience were broader, such abbreviations and acronyms would have to be explained the first time you used

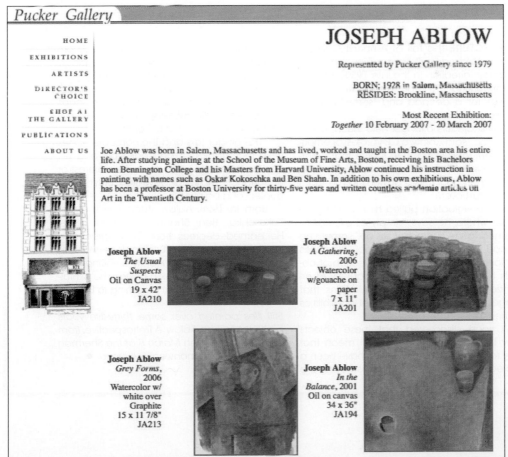

Pucker Gallery

HOME
EXHIBITIONS
ARTISTS
DIRECTOR'S CHOICE
SHOP AT THE GALLERY
PUBLICATIONS
ABOUT US

JOSEPH ABLOW

Represented by Pucker Gallery since 1979

BORN: 1928 in Salem, Massachusetts
RESIDES: Brookline, Massachusetts

Most Recent Exhibition:
Together 10 February 2007 - 20 March 2007

Joe Ablow was born in Salem, Massachusetts and has lived, worked and taught in the Boston area his entire life. After studying painting at the School of the Museum of Fine Arts, Boston, receiving his Bachelors from Bennington College and his Masters from Harvard University, Ablow continued his instruction in painting with names such as Oskar Kokoschka and Ben Shahn. In addition to his own exhibitions, Ablow has been a professor at Boston University for thirty-five years and written countless academic articles on Art in the Twentieth Century.

Joseph Ablow
The Usual Suspects
Oil on Canvas
19 x 42"
JA210

Joseph Ablow
A Gathering,
2006
Watercolor w/gouache on paper
7 x 11"
JA201

Joseph Ablow
Grey Forms,
2006
Watercolor w/ white over Graphite
15 x 11 7/8"
JA213

Joseph Ablow
In the Balance, 2001
Oil on canvas
34 x 36"
JA194

Ablow's Objets d'Art

Large Still Life Frieze, Joseph Ablow. Copyright © Joseph Ablow. Reprinted by permission of Pucker Gallery.

Large Still Life Frieze, oil on canvas, 32" x 66", 1986. Photograph by S. Petegorsky

IN A LECTURE this fall at Amherst College, Joseph Ablow described a major change in his artistic direction in the late 1950s. He had been working on large, classically inspired themes for a decade and "something did not feel right."

"My subjects no longer held much meaning for me," said Ablow, a CFA professor emeritus of art, "and I began to realize that painting and inventing from memory had left me visually parched. It was obvious to me that I had to start over."

The reevaluation pulled him back to the studio, where, he says, "simply as exercises, I returned to the subject of still life," something he had avoided since art school. "But it was not long before the motley collection of objects I had assembled began quietly to organize themselves into configurations that suggested unexpected pictorial possibilities to me.

"I soon discovered that these objects may be quiet, but that did not mean that they remained still. What was to have been a subject that suggested ways of studying the look of things within a manageable and concentrated situation became an increasingly involved world that could be surprisingly disquieting and provocative. I may have been the one responsible for arranging my cups and bowls on the tabletops, but that did not ensure that I was in control of them.

"The ginger jars and the compote dishes were real, particular, and palpable and yet had no inherent significance. Their interest or importance would be revealed only in the context of a painting."

Born in 1928, Ablow studied with Oskar Kokoschka, Ben Shahn, and Karl Zerbe. He earned degrees from Bennington and Harvard and taught at Boston University from 1963 until 1995. He is currently a visiting artist at Amherst College, which hosted the exhibition of his paintings that is coming to BU.

Still lifes painted over some thirty-five years highlight Joseph Ablow: A Retrospective, *from January 13 through March 5 at the Sherman Gallery, 775 Commonwealth Avenue.* ◆

Bostonia Magazine, Winter 2003–2004, page 16.

Research

them. The same criterion can be used to make decisions about content. If you were researching one of Joseph Ablow's still life paintings, you would find that sources on Ablow's work do not define what a still life painting is; the authors of these sources assume that their readers are familiar with the term. However, if you were writing for readers who knew next to nothing about painting, you would provide a definition for the term.

TRICKS OF THE TRADE

To determine which sources your audience will find authoritative, study any bibliographies that you encounter in your research. If a source is mentioned on several bibliographic lists, the source is likely considered authoritative.

Readers of an academic research paper expect the author to be knowledgeable. You can demonstrate your knowledge through the types of sources you use and the ways you handle them. Because you aren't likely to have established credibility as an expert on the topic you are researching, you'll usually have to depend on the credibility of the sources you use. Once you have done enough research to understand your audience, you'll be better able to select sources that will give you credibility. For example, to persuade your readers of the value of a vegetarian diet, you could choose among sources written by nutritionists, ethicists, religious leaders, and animal rights proponents. Your decision would be based on which kinds of sources your audience would find most credible.

Readers of an academic research paper also expect the author to be critical. They want to be assured that an author can tell whether the source information is accurate or deceptive, whether its logic is strong or weak, and whether its conclusions are justifiable. Your readers may accept your use of a questionable source as long as you show why it is problematic. You will learn ways of establishing your credibility and demonstrating your critical abilities in Chapter 18.

WAIT A MINUTE . . .

When you read sources critically, you are considering the rhetorical situation from the perspective of a reader. Since you're also thinking about how the sources might be used in your own writing, you're involved in a second rhetorical situation as a writer. Rarely will the rhetorical situation that led to the creation of the source you are consulting be the same as the rhetorical situation you confront in writing for a class. Of course, there may be overlap, particularly in audience, but the rhetorical opportunity and purpose of the two pieces of writing are likely to be different.

Research and Purpose

In Chapter 1, you saw how your rhetorical audience and your rhetorical purpose are interconnected. They cannot be separated. In general, your rhetorical purpose is to have an impact on your audience; more specifically, your aim may be to entertain them, to inform them, to explain something to them, or to influence them to do something. Research can help you achieve any of these purposes. For example, if you are writing a research paper on the roots of humor for a psychology class, your primary purpose is to inform. You may want to analyze a few jokes, in order to show how their construction can incite laughter, but you'll need research to support your claim. Your audience will be more inclined to believe you if you show them, say, experimental results indicating that people routinely find certain incidents funny.

Writers of research papers commonly define their rhetorical purposes in the following ways:

▶ *To inform an audience.* The researcher reports current thinking on a specific topic, including opposing views but not siding with any particular one.

Example: To inform the audience of current guidelines for developing a city park

▶ *To analyze and synthesize information and then offer tentative solutions to a problem.* The researcher analyzes and synthesizes information on a topic (for example, an argument, a text, an event, a technique, or a statistic), looking for points of agreement and disagreement and for gaps in coverage. Part of the research process consists of finding out what other researchers have already written about the subject. After presenting the analysis and synthesis, the researcher offers possible ways to address the problem.

Example: To analyze and synthesize various national health-care proposals

▶ *To persuade an audience or to issue an invitation to an audience.* The researcher states a position and backs it up with data, statistics, texts illustrating a point, or supporting arguments found through research. The researcher's purpose is to persuade or invite readers to take the same position.

Example: To persuade people to vote for a congressional candidate

Often, these purposes coexist in the same piece of writing. A researcher presenting results from an original experiment or study, for instance, must often achieve all of these purposes. In the introduction to a lab report, the researcher might describe previous work done in the area and identify a research niche—an area needing research. The researcher then explains how his or her current study will help fill the gap in existing research. The body of the text is informative, describing the materials used, explaining the procedures followed, and presenting the results. In the conclusion, the researcher may choose, given the results of the experiment or study, to persuade the audience to take some action (for example, give up smoking, eat fewer carbohydrates, or fund future research).

The sources you find through research can help you achieve your purpose. If your purpose is to inform, you can use the work of established scholars to enhance your credibility. If your purpose is to analyze and synthesize information, sources you find can provide not only data for you to work on but also a backdrop against which to highlight your own originality or your special research niche. If your purpose is to persuade, you can use sources to support your assertions and to counter the assertions of others.

Research and a Fitting Response

Like any other kind of writing you do, your research report needs to address the rhetorical situation. There are many different kinds of research, just as there are many different ways to present research findings. Shaping a fitting response means considering the following kinds of questions:

▶ *Is your researched response appropriate to the problem?* The focus, and thus the kind of research called for (library, Internet, naturalistic, laboratory, or some combination of these), depends on the nature of the problem. Engineers studying the question of how to prevent future natural disasters from causing the kind of damage wrought in New Orleans by Hurricane Katrina in 2005 would need to be sure their research focused on environmental and geographical conditions specific to that area. Research on the success of levees built along the Danube in Europe might not be applicable. The researchers would also likely need to combine many different kinds of research in order to determine the best method of prevention.

▶ *Is your researched response delivered in a medium that will reach its intended audience?* Writers presenting research findings want to be sure their work finds its way into the right hands. Engineers researching the issue of how best to rebuild the levees in New Orleans could certainly summarize their findings in a letter to the editor of the New Orleans *Times Picayune*. However, if they wanted approval from a government agency for future work, they would likely need to present the research in a document addressed directly to that agency, such as a written application for funding or a proposal in the form of a multimedia presentation.

▶ *Will your researched response successfully satisfy the intended audience?* Research papers in different academic disciplines have different types of content and formats. To help make sure their audience will be satisfied, researchers take care to notice the research methods used in the discipline and deliver writing that is presented and documented according to the accepted style of the discipline. (For information on different kinds of documentation styles, see Chapter 19.)

As always, a fitting response must also be considered in terms of the available means.

Research

Research: Constraints and Resources

In Chapter 1, you learned how the means available to you for responding are shaped by both the *constraints* (obstacles or limits) and the *resources* (positive influences) of the rhetorical situation. In reviewing the brief *Psychology Today* article that opened this chapter, you saw how one writer, Richard Lovett, worked with specific constraints and resources. You may have identified the primary elements of the rhetorical situation, noting constraints such as the need to deliver complex and specialized information from the field of neurology to readers of a popular magazine. To address this constraint, Lovett made allowances for his readers' perhaps limited knowledge of how the brain works by defining unfamiliar terms (*prefrontal cortex*, for example). You may also have noted some of the resources available to Lovett in writing for this kind of publication. The image that accompanies his text is a resource that allows readers to absorb the topic at a glance, while the pull-quote (the quotation in large type in the middle of the article) makes the scientists' research question explicit.

As a researcher in an academic setting, you are no doubt aware that many of your rhetorical situations share various constraints. For instance, an academic research assignment usually involves some kind of specifications from an instructor. Following are some common constraints for such writing assignments:

- ▶ *Expertise.* As a student, you rely to some degree on documenting what others have said in order to build credibility.
- ▶ *Geography.* Although the Internet gives researchers unprecedented access to materials not available locally, most students are still somewhat constrained by what's close at hand.
- ▶ *Time.* In most cases, your research will be subject to a time limit. Your readers—whether they are instructors, colleagues, or other decision makers—need to see your research before it goes out of date and before the deadline to make a decision (about what action to take or what grade to assign) has passed.

Constraints such as these can, however, suggest resources. What primary documents might you have access to in your geographical location? What unique opportunities do you have for reaching your audience that a recognized expert might not have? Can working within a particular time frame provide motivation?

Of course, each rhetorical situation is different. Every time you begin research, you'll face a new set of constraints and resources. To participate effectively in an ongoing conversation, you'll need to identify specific resources to help you manage your particular set of constraints.

Pop Cultures

REFRESCOS IN SPANISH, MASHROOB GHAZI in Arabic, kele in Chinese: the world has many words, and an unslakable thirst, for carbonated soft drinks. Since 1997 per capita consumption has nearly doubled in eastern Europe. In 2008 Coca-Cola tallied soda sales in some 200 countries. Even the global recession, says industry monitor Zenith International, has merely caused manufacturers to lean on promotional offers and try cheap social networking ads.

But some are sour on all this sweetness. U.S. obesity expert David Ludwig calls aggressive marketing in emerging nations—where people tend to eat more and move less as they prosper—"deeply irresponsible. That's the time of greatest risk for heart disease, diabetes, and obesity."

As that thinking catches on, places including New York and Romania are mulling levies on sugared drinks. Others argue that taxing a single product isn't the fix:

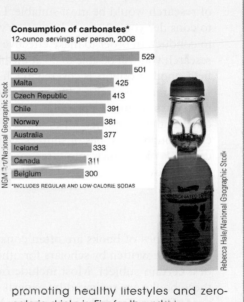

Consumption of carbonates*
12-ounce servings per person, 2008

U.S.	529
Mexico	501
Malta	425
Czech Republic	413
Chile	391
Norway	381
Australia	377
Iceland	333
Canada	311
Belgium	300

*INCLUDES REGULAR AND LOW-CALORIE SODAS

NGM Art/National Geographic Stock

Rebecca Hale/National Geographic Stock

promoting healthy lifestyles and zero-calorie drinks is Fizz for thought?

—Jeremy Berlin

1. Why do you think Jeremy Berlin (and the editors at *National Geographic*) decided to use a photograph and a list of statistics with the article "Pop Cultures"? What kind of research do you think he and his editors did to prepare this article and the accompanying graphics? In other words, what might they have read or observed, whom might they have questioned, and so on? If you wanted to check their facts, what would you do?

2. Think back to a research paper you wrote. What kind of research did you conduct for that project? Where did you go to find your sources? Given more time and more resources, what additional kinds of research might you have done?

Sources for Research

Although the library will probably play an important role in your research, it often will not be the only location in which you conduct research. During the research process, you might find yourself at home using the Internet, in your instructor's office getting suggestions for new sources, or even at the student union taking notes on what you observe about some aspect of student behavior. More than likely, the authors of the sources you gather did not confine themselves to one particular kind of research either—or do it all in one particular location. Responding to their own rhetorical situations, the authors of your sources specified a goal for their research, a group of readers who might be interested in their findings, and the type of document that would best express their thoughts. Based on their purpose, audience, and genre, the authors determined what kinds of research would be most suitable. Like the authors of your sources, you need to consider your rhetorical situation when determining which kinds of research to conduct. In order to make effective decisions, you need to know what kinds of research you will be able to do at the library and on the Internet. (Research in the field, another option, is covered in Chapter 16.)

Library research and Internet research continue to evolve, as librarians find new ways to make emerging technologies more accessible and scholars and other authors find new ways to use the Internet to deliver information. In general, though, the types of sources available through the library and the Internet can be broken down into three main categories: books, periodicals, and online and audiovisual sources.

Books

Three types of books are often consulted in the research process. **Scholarly books** are written by scholars for other scholars in order to advance knowledge of a certain subject. Most include original research. Before being published, these books are reviewed by experts in the field (in a process referred to as a peer review). **Trade books** may also be written by scholars, though they may be authored by journalists or freelance writers as well. But the audience and purpose of trade books differ from those of scholarly books. Rather than addressing other scholars, authors of trade books write to inform the general audience, often about research that has been done by others; thus, trade books are usually **secondary sources**—as opposed to **primary sources**, which contain original research. **Reference books** such as encyclopedias and dictionaries provide factual information. Reference books often contain short articles written and reviewed by experts in the field. The audience for these secondary sources includes both veteran scholars and those new to a field of study.

General encyclopedias and dictionaries such as the *Encyclopaedia Britannica* and the *American Heritage Dictionary* provide basic information on many topics. Specialized encyclopedias and dictionaries cover topics in greater depth. In addition to overviews of topics, they also include definitions of technical terminology, discussions of major issues, and bibliographies of related works.

Specialized encyclopedias and dictionaries exist for all major disciplines. Here is just a small sampling:

Art	*Grove Dictionary of Art, Encyclopedia of Visual Art*
Biology	*Concise Encyclopedia of Biology*
Chemistry	*Concise Macmillan Encyclopedia of Chemistry, Encyclopedia of Inorganic Chemistry*
Computers	*Encyclopedia of Computer Science and Technology*
Economics	*Fortune Encyclopedia of Economics*
Education	*Encyclopedia of Higher Education, Encyclopedia of Educational Research*
Environment	*Encyclopedia of the Environment*
History	*Dictionary of American History, New Cambridge Modern History*
Literature	*Encyclopedia of World Literature in the 20th Century*
Music	*New Grove Dictionary of Music and Musicians*
Philosophy	*Routledge Encyclopedia of Philosophy, Encyclopedia of Applied Ethics*
Psychology	*Encyclopedia of Psychology, Encyclopedia of Human Behavior*
Religion	*Encyclopedia of Religion*
Social sciences	*International Encyclopedia of the Social Sciences*
Women's studies	*Women's Studies Encyclopedia, Encyclopedia of Women and Gender*

You can find these kinds of sources by doing a title search of your library's online catalog. For other specialized encyclopedias, contact a reference librarian or consult *Kister's Best Encyclopedias*.

Periodicals

Periodicals include scholarly journals, magazines, and newspapers. Because these materials are published more frequently than books, the information they contain is more recent. Like scholarly books, **scholarly journals** contain original research (they are primary sources) and address a narrow, specialized audience. Many scholarly journals have the word *journal* in their names: examples are *Journal of Business Communication* and *Consulting Psychology Journal*. **Magazines** and **newspapers** are generally written by staff writers for the general public. These secondary sources carry a combination of news stories, which are intended to be objective, and essays, which reflect the opinions of editors or guest contributors. Both national newspapers (such as the *New York Times* and the *Washington Post*) and regional or local newspapers may have articles, letters, and editorials of interest to researchers.

Online and audiovisual sources

Books, journals, magazine articles, and newspaper articles can all be found online. But when you read documents on websites, created specifically for access by computer, you need to determine who is responsible for the site, why the site was established, and who the target audience is. To find answers to these questions, you can first check the domain name, which is at the end of the main part of the Internet address. This name will give you clues about the site. An Internet address with the domain name **.com** (for commerce) tells you that the website is associated with a profit-making business. The domain name **.edu** indicates that a site is connected to an educational institution. Websites maintained by the branches or agencies of a government have the domain name **.gov**. Nonprofit organizations such as Habitat for Humanity and National Public Radio have **.org** as their domain name.

You can also find out about the nature of a website by clicking on navigational buttons such as About Us or Vision. Here is an excerpt from a page entitled "About NPR" on the National Public Radio website:

What is NPR?

NPR is an internationally acclaimed producer and distributor of noncommercial news, talk, and entertainment programming. A privately supported, not-for-profit, membership organization, NPR serves more than 770 independently operated, noncommercial public radio stations. Each member station serves local listeners with a distinctive combination of national and local programming.

WAIT A MINUTE ...

Although it was once the case (and not so long ago!) that most sources accessed online were less reliable than those found in print, the difference is becoming less pronounced. Reputable scholarly (peer-reviewed) journals are found online, and personal web log entries (blogs) are being collected and published in books—even Twitter postings are being archived by the Library of Congress. It's generally still the case, however, that you'll locate the scholarly journals you need at your library or through your library's subscription service (such as LexisNexis). Likewise, standards for print publication are still higher than those for the Internet—after all, anyone can put up a website on any topic whatsoever, whereas most print materials have met a minimum set of standards.

The most common audiovisual sources are documentaries, lectures, and interviews. **Documentary films and television programs** are much like trade books and magazines. They are created for a popular audience, with the purpose of providing factual information, usually of a political, social, or historical nature. **Lectures** generally take place live at universities and in public auditoriums or are recorded as podcasts or for distribution through iTunes U or university websites. Lectures sponsored by a university are usually more technical or scholarly than those given in a public auditorium. Lecturers, who are usually experts in their field of study, deliver prepared speeches on a variety of topics. Sometimes lectures are like editorials in that the creator's perspective is presented in high profile. **Interviews** are a special type of conversation in which a reporter elicits responses from someone recognized for his or her status or accomplishments. Interviews, which are aired for a general audience, aim to provide information about the interviewee's achievements or about his or her views on a specific issue.

WAIT A MINUTE . . .

Images, such as photographs, drawings, and charts, also count as sources meant to be viewed. Although they aren't often accessed on their own in the same ways that books, periodicals, or documentaries are, they may constitute an important part of your research, whether or not your final project is meant to be multimedia. For example, you may use photographs to enhance written descriptions or maps and charts to support claims. Tips on locating still images will be provided later in this chapter.

Finding Sources in Print and Online

In the first part of this chapter, you learned about the different types of sources available to you. You'll find it easier to select your sources once you have a basic understanding of the genre, audience, and purpose of potential sources. For example, for an advanced course in your discipline, you'll want to consult primary sources, such as online or printed journal articles that present original research. However, if you have chosen a topic that is brand new to you, it may be more productive to consult secondary sources along with primary sources, as the primary sources may contain so much technical terminology that you might misunderstand the content. The rest of this chapter will help you find different types of sources in your library and online.

Finding books

The easiest way to find books on a particular topic is to consult your library's online catalog. Once you are logged on, navigate your way to the web page with search boxes similar to that shown on page 428. An author search or title search is useful when you already have a particular author or title in mind. When a research area is new to you, you can find many sources by doing either a keyword search

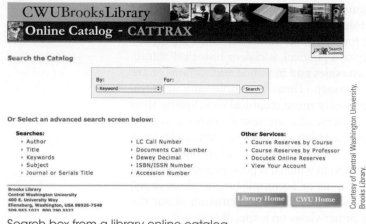

Search box from a library online catalog.

Courtesy of Central Washington University, Brooks Library.

or a subject search. For a keyword search, choose a word or phrase that you think is likely to be found in titles or notes in the catalog's records.

An advanced search page such as the one on page 429 allows the user to specify a language, a location in the library, a type of book (or a type of material other than a book), how the results should be organized, a publisher, and a date of publication. A keyword search page also provides some recommendations for entering words. By using a word or part of a word followed by asterisks, you can find all sources that have that word or word part, even when suffixes have been added. For example, if you entered *environment**, the search would return not only sources with *environment* in the title but also sources whose titles included *environments, environmental,* or *environmentalist.* This shortening technique is called **truncation.** You can enter multiple words by using an operator such as *and* or *or.* You can exclude words by using *and not.* When you enter multiple words, you can require that they be close to each other by using *near*; if you want to specify their proximity, you can use *within,* followed by a number indicating the greatest number of words that may separate them.

TRICKS OF THE TRADE

Searching Google Books (books.google.com) or using Amazon.com's "Look Inside!" feature can give you more information about books not available locally. Both sites allow you to search for keywords inside certain virtual texts. If the search locates the keywords, you can then preview the relevant pages of the text to determine if you want to purchase the book or order it from an interlibrary loan service. If the book is in the public domain, you may be able to access the entire text through Google Books.

Subject searches in most libraries are based on categories published by the Library of Congress. You may be able to find sources by entering words familiar to you. However, if your search does not yield any results, ask a reference librarian for a subject-heading guide or note the subject categories that accompany the search results for sources you have already found.

Once you locate a source, write down or print out its call number. The call number corresponds to a specific location in the library's shelving system, usually based on the classification system of the Library of Congress. Keys to the shelving system are usually posted on the walls of the library, but staff members will also be able to help you find sources.

In addition to using your library's online catalog, you can also access books online, downloading them as PDFs or in other formats for use on a handheld device such as a Kindle or an iPad. Over one million free books are listed on the University of Pennsylvania's Online Books Page (onlinebooks.library.upenn.edu).

Finding articles

Your library's online catalog lists the titles of periodicals (journals, magazines, and newspapers); however, it does not provide the titles of individual articles within these periodicals. Although many researchers head straight to an Internet search engine or web browser (Google, Bing, Yahoo!, Internet Explorer), type in the name of the desired article, and locate a copy, many others end up frustrated by such a broad search. You may find that the best strategy for finding reliable articles on your topic is to use an electronic database, available through your library portal. A database (such as ERIC, JSTOR, or PsycINFO) is similar to an online catalog in that it allows you to search for sources by author, title, subject, keyword, and other features. Because so much information is available, databases focus on specific subject areas.

You can access your library's databases from a computer in the library or, if you have a password, via an Internet link from a computer located elsewhere. Libraries subscribe to various vendors for these services, but the following are some of the most common databases:

OCLC FirstSearch or EBSCOhost: Contain articles and other types of records (for example, electronic books and DVDs) on a wide range of subjects.

Advanced keyword search page from a library online catalog.

ProQuest: Provides access to major newspapers such as the *New York Times* and the *Wall Street Journal* and to consumer and scholarly periodicals in areas including business, humanities, literature, and science.

LexisNexis: Includes articles on business, legal, and medical topics and on current events.

To find sources through a database, you can use some of the same strategies you use for navigating an online catalog. However, search pages often differ, so there is no substitute for hands-on experimentation. Your library may use a general database, such as OCLC FirstSearch or EBSCOhost. The first box on the EBSCOhost search page asks you to specify a subject area. Just underneath that box is a drop-down menu that lets you choose among several databases, including ERIC (Educational Resources Information Center), MLA (Modern Language Association), and PsycINFO (American Psychological Association's database of psychological literature). After you choose the particular database you would like to search, you can search by keyword, author, title, source, year, or a combination of these attributes. You click on the question-mark icon to the right of the search entry box to get directions for searching according to that attribute. In the Refine Search menu, you can click on a checkbox to limit a search to full texts only. In this case, your search will bring back only sources that include the complete text of an article, which can be downloaded and printed. Otherwise, the database search generally yields the source's bibliographic information and an **abstract**, which is a short summary of an article's content. To find the full text, you note the basic bibliographic information and then look up that book or periodical in the library's online catalog, as described earlier.

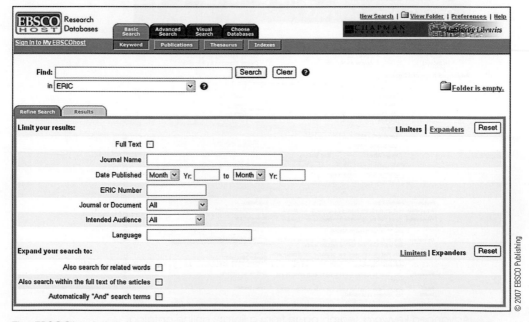

The EBSCOhost database allows you to search various smaller databases, such as ERIC.

TRICKS OF THE TRADE

Although most researchers use databases to find current articles, databases contain other types of information. LexisNexis, for example, provides the following kinds of reference material:

▶ Biographical information on politicians and other public figures

▶ Facts and statistics about countries and states

▶ Polls and surveys conducted by the Roper Center for Public Opinion Research

▶ Quotations on a range of topics

▶ A world almanac

Finally, some periodicals are available online. HighWire is a service that lists many scientific and medical journals that offer free articles or issues; you can find this list by going to highwire.stanford.edu/lists/freeart.dtl. The Global Development Network lists journals from a wide range of academic disciplines on its website (gdnet.org). Online articles are not always free, however. Be sure to check for subscription services that are available through your library's website before paying for an archived article on a newspaper's home page. You might save yourself a good deal of money!

Finding images

Internet and database searches yield all kinds of images for writers. You can search for images online by using a search engine such as Google Images. Also consider visiting the websites of specific libraries, museums, and government agencies, such as the Library of Congress, the Smithsonian Institution, and the U.S. Census Bureau; they often have databases of special collections.

Once you find an image that suits your purpose, download it from the website onto your desktop by right-clicking on the image and selecting Save Image As (or Save This Image As). To insert the image from your desktop into your paper, use the Insert command from your word processor's pull-down menu. (Some programs may allow you to drag the image into your text.) If you need to resize the image you have chosen, click on its corners and drag your mouse to enlarge it or reduce it. Hold down the Shift key while you are resizing the image to retain its original proportions.

The last step in using an image is to give credit to its creator and, if necessary, acquire permission to use it. If you are not publishing your paper in print or online, fair-use laws governing reproduction for educational purposes might allow you to use the image without permission. If you are uploading your paper to a website or publishing it in any other way, determine whether the image is copyrighted; if so, you'll have to contact its creator for permission to use it and then include a credit line underneath the image, after the caption.

Keep in mind that before you decide to include an image in your paper, you should be sure to identify your purpose for doing so. Avoid using images as mere decoration.

Finding government documents

You can find government documents by using library databases such as Lexis-Nexis Academic. In addition, the following websites are helpful:

FedWorld Information Network	fedworld.gov
Government Printing Office	gpoaccess.gov
U.S. Courts	uscourts.gov

Finding resources in special collections

Most academic libraries have special collections that you might also find useful, such as art collections, including drawings and paintings; audio and video collections, including records, audiotapes, CDs, videotapes, and DVDs; and computer resources, usually consisting of programs that combine text, audio, and video. You can find these resources by navigating through your library's website or by asking a reference librarian for help.

Additional advice for finding sources online

To find text, image, video, and audio sources relevant to your project, your first instinct might be to look online. Although searching the Internet is a popular research technique, it is not always the most appropriate technique. Search engines cover only the portion of the Internet that allows free access. Many books available at your school's library or periodicals available through the library's database materials cannot be found using a search engine because library and database services are available only to paid subscribers (students fall into this category). If you do decide to use the Internet, remember that no one search engine covers all of it, and surprisingly little overlap occurs when different search engines are used to find information on the same topic. Thus, using more than one search engine is a good idea. The following are commonly used search engines:

Ask.com	ask.com
Bing	bing.com
Google	google.com
Yahoo!	yahoo.com

When using a search engine for research, you'll probably want to check the Help links to learn about advanced search options. Using these options will allow you to weed out results that are not of interest to you. Advanced searches are performed in much the same way with search engines as they are with online catalogs and databases. You can specify words or phrases, how close words should be to each other, which words should be excluded, and whether the search should return longer versions of truncated words.

Metasearch engines are also available. *Meta* means "transcending" or "more comprehensive." Metasearch engines check numerous search engines, including those listed on the facing page. Try these for starters:

Dogpile   dogpile.com

Mamma   mamma.com

MetaCrawler   metacrawler.com

WebCrawler   webcrawler.com

Finally, be aware that sometimes when you click on a link, you end up at a totally different website. You can keep track of your location by looking at the Internet address, or URL, at the top of your screen. URLs generally include the following information: server name, domain name, directory and perhaps subdirectory, file name, and file type.

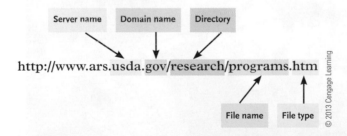

Be sure to check the server and domain names whenever you are unsure of your location. (See Chapter 18 for help in evaluating websites.)

USING RESEARCH IN YOUR WRITING

Using the same keywords, perform a database search and then an Internet search. For each type of search, print the first screen of results you get. Compare the two printouts, explaining how the results of the two searches differ.

Field Research

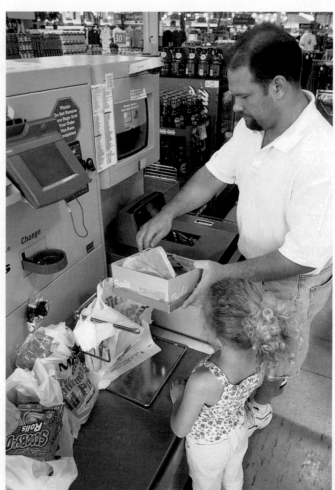

AP Photo/David Kohl

1. Even if your local supermarket doesn't have a machine that allows customers to check out their groceries by themselves, like the self-checkout machine above, you're no doubt familiar with various technologies designed to make our hectic lives a little easier by making routine tasks more efficient. Take a moment to list several such newer technologies that you've encountered recently.

Research

2. Choose one item on your list and consider its effect(s): What or whom does it replace? How is it changing human behavior? To take this activity further, go to a place where the technology is in use. Observe the scene for twenty minutes or so, noting effects of the technology on human behavior. Do your observations differ from your assumptions? If so, what is unexpected or surprising?

Basic Principles of Fieldwork

By now, you are familiar with the rhetorical situation and how it supports reading, writing, speaking—and research. In this chapter, you'll apply your knowledge of the rhetorical situation to develop an understanding of a local situation, an understanding that usually cannot be easily reached through traditional library, online, or laboratory research. Although these methods are effective, they cannot address all research questions.

Some research questions can be answered only by **fieldwork**, research carried out in the field, rather than in a library, laboratory, or some other controlled environment. Fieldwork usually takes place in a real-world, or naturalistic, environment. Following are some research questions calling for the collection of data in a naturalistic environment:

What nights of the week are busiest at the student union?
How popular is the foreign film series shown on campus, in terms of both attendance
   and satisfaction? How do the responses of students, faculty, and staff differ?
What do hair stylists do at work?
What is the effect of self-checkout machines in local grocery stores?
How do mothers and adult daughters communicate?
How has the day-to-day nature of nurses' work changed during the last 40 years?
How useful is the library's help desk? Who uses it? How often? When? Why?

All of these questions call for careful observation in the field (even though the field is actually the library in the case of the final question) and some means of data collection.

Observation in a real-world environment

A **naturalistic study** is based on observation in a real-world environment. The researcher observes and records some human behavior or phenomenon in its natural setting. Whether the goal is to establish the learning patterns of museum visitors, the daily driving habits of commuters, or the benefits of home schooling, the researcher conducting a naturalistic study observes, employing any or all of the following research methods:

▶ Watching the behavior or phenomenon and recording what he or she sees

▶ Using audiovisual equipment, such as digital recorders or video cameras

▶ Listening in on conversations or comments and taking notes

- ▶ Distributing questionnaires or administering pretests and posttests about a situation, phenomenon, or behavior
- ▶ Conducting interviews with individuals or focus groups

Whichever of these methods is employed, the researcher himself or herself is the most significant instrument for the collection and analysis of data.

Testing assumptions

Researchers often undertake a naturalistic study because they want to investigate an **assumption,** an idea taken for granted or accepted as true without proof. Whether expressed as a problem ("English majors dominate class discussion"), a question ("How much do hair stylists think as they do their job?"), or a belief ("The student union is always busy"), the assumption may be the researcher's alone or be commonly held. By collecting and analyzing data, the researcher compares the assumption with possible conclusions. The researcher tests the assumption with two goals in mind: (1) to interfere as little as possible with the subject or phenomenon under observation and (2) to minimize systematically the ways in which mere participation in the study influences patterns and outcomes. In other words, the fact that the researcher is observing, listening, or conducting interviews should not affect the behavior or beliefs of the participants. The researcher's goals overlap with the researcher's ethics.

Triangulation

To minimize inaccuracies and distortions, a researcher usually sets up a three-way process for gathering information, referred to as **triangulation**. When the process depends on using different sets of information from a variety of sources, it is called **data triangulation**. For instance, to triangulate responses to the question of how useful the library's help desk is, you might gather opinions from several different groups of people, looking for commonalities in their responses. When two or more researchers work together in order to compare their observations and findings, the approach is known as **investigator triangulation**. And, finally, **methodological triangulation** involves using multiple methods (observation, questionnaires, and so on) to study a single problem, person, or phenomenon.

Basic principles at work: Deborah Tannen's naturalistic study

After publishing a book about adult family relationships, *I Only Say This Because I Love You,* Deborah Tannen discovered that her readers were most interested in the chapter on communication between mothers and adult daughters. With that knowledge, she launched the naturalistic study that became the book *You're Wearing That?* Tannen's preresearch assumption was that mothers and their adult daughters have a uniquely intense relationship; she felt sure this was true, given her own relationship with her mother. Tannen observed, re-

Research

corded, and then transcribed many conversations; she also conducted interviews (or what she refers to as "focused conversations"), asked people she knew for examples from their own lives, and drew on her own ongoing communication with her mother. This process of observing, talking, asking questions, recording, and listening to the opinions of others was an example of methodological triangulation.

Deborah Tannen, author of *You're Wearing That?*

As Tannen observed and recorded, she also began to analyze what she was witnessing, an analysis based on her expertise in sociolinguistics (and on her status as an adult daughter). Toward the end of her research process, she compared her preresearch assumption (that the mother–adult daughter relationship is uniquely intense) with the emerging conclusion that mother–adult daughter communication "continues to evoke powerful emotions long after it has ceased."

Like all experienced researchers, Tannen knows that naturalistic studies may be generalizable—but only to a point. Naturalistic studies are like the rhetorical situation itself: time-bound and context-bound, with all the entities of the study (observer or recorder, analysis, and subject or behavior under observation) shaping one another simultaneously.

Methods for Fieldwork

Observing, taking notes, and asking questions are the three activities at the heart of a naturalistic study, as you have probably gathered from reading about Deborah Tannen's research and trying your hand at a brief study of your own. In his study of the intellectual processes necessary for conducting ordinary kinds of work, Mike Rose describes these three elements at work together:

> When at a job site or in a classroom, I observed people at work, writing notes on their activity and, when permissible, taking photographs of the task at hand. Once I got a sense of the rhythms of the work—its moments of less intense focus and its pauses—I would begin asking questions about what people were doing and why, trying to gain an understanding of their behavior and the thinking that directed it. As they got more familiar with me and I with them and their work, I was able to ask increasingly specific questions, probing the reasons for using one implement rather than another, for a particular positioning of the body, for the benefits of this procedure over that one. I wondered aloud how they knew what to do, given the materials and constraints of the present task, what they had in mind to do next, how they knew something was wrong. . . . Over time, the exchanges became more conversational, and frequently people on their own began explaining what they were doing and what their thinking was for doing it, a kind of modified think-aloud procedure, long used in studies of problem solving. —**Mike Rose,** *The Mind at Work* (New York: Viking/Penguin, 2004)

Notice how Rose talks about the material conditions of his observation: he watches, takes notes, sometimes takes photographs, and asks increasingly sophisticated questions as he begins to understand the procedures more and more. Each activity occurs in coordination with the others, but we'll look at them one at a time.

Using observation

Observation—watching closely what is happening and trying to figure out why—plays a central role in naturalistic studies of all kinds. After all, a naturalistic study depends most heavily on the researcher himself or herself, which is its advantage. The researcher is right there on the scene, conducting the research, with direct access to the person or phenomenon.

By the time Rose was ready to write up his observation, he was able to describe the results of his naturalistic study with style, grace, and a good deal of detail. In the following passage, he writes about the thinking that goes into the hair styling that Vanessa does.

Excerpt from

The Mind at Work

Mike Rose

Already readers can see how much information Rose has gleaned by talking with Vanessa as he observes her.

Vanessa works in a trendy salon but also cuts hair in her apartment—for a few friends and friends of friends. Her client Lynn sits in a small barber's chair by the window, the place where you'd imagine a breakfast table, a mirror leaning against the wall in front of her. On the floor by the mirror there is a small bowl for Vanessa's dog and a vase with three yellow flowers. Vanessa stands behind Lynn, asking her questions about her hair, chitchatting a little. She keeps her eyes on Lynn's hair as she moves her fingers through it, lifting up, then pulling down one section, then another, then gesturing with her hands around the hair, indicating shape and movement. "How did you like the last haircut?" she asks. How did it handle? Was it easy to manage? What's bugging you now? Does it feel heavy up front? Lynn answers these questions, describing what she wants, relying on adjectives that have more to do with feeling than shape. She wants the cut "freshened," wants it "sassy." •

Rose includes details that could be retained only with careful note taking or tape recording.

Rose has taken the time to learn the vocabulary of the people he's observing.

A pair of scissors, a comb, and a round hand mirror sit on the stove, to Vanessa's side. She reaches for the scissors and begins. She starts at the crown and moves around Lynn's head, picking a strand of hair, pulling it down gently along Lynn's face, eyeballing it, then elevating it, cutting into it, "point cutting," she calls it, not a "blunt" cut, her scissors angling into the hair, layering it, "giving it a softer look."

Vanessa likes to cut dry hair—at least hair like Lynn's, baby fine, short—because she "can see what it's doing immediately . . . where it's heavy, where it needs to be cut into." •("You can comb hair and cut it," she explains, "only to have it move into a different shape than the one you just cut.") When she does cut hair wet, because a particular style demands it, she "can't wait to dry it and then go in and do *my* work. . . . The initial shape might be there, but the whole interior can change. Eighty percent of the haircut is after you dry it."

This information could have been obtained only by asking interview questions, not by observation.

You can almost hear Rose asking the questions that elicited these specific answers.

As Vanessa continues, cutting, comparing one length of hair to another, her gaze circling her client's head, she tells me more about her work. Though she can do "technical, precise" cuts, like a graduated bob (a bob tapered at the nape of the neck), she most likes to cut "freehand," as she is doing now, a more "flowing" cut, and flowing process. "I don't like authority," she laughs, "so I love cutting this way." Even with that graduated bob, she adds, after it's dry, she'll "go in and add my own touch, a signature."

Research

Vanessa certainly has an idea of how a haircut should look, an idea based on the characteristics of the hair she's cutting and the client's desires, discerned from those opening questions, and, if the client's a regular, from their history together. And she is methodical. But she does not plan her cut in advance to the degree that some stylists do; cognitive psychologists would characterize her planning style as incremental or opportunistic. As the cut progresses, she observes what the hair is doing, how it's falling and moving, and reacts to that. "I do a lot of visual when I cut." And, in fact, about two-thirds of the way through Lynn's haircut, Vanessa exclaims, "Oh, this is starting to look really cute!" Moments like this are pivotal to Vanessa, aesthetically and motivationally. It excites her, is the art of it all, to use her skill in a way that is responsive to, interactive with, the medium of hair, watching the cut emerge, shaping it incrementally, guided by her aesthetic sense and enabled by her repertoire of techniques. Lynn is pleased with the outcome. It *is* a "sassy" cut. "Vanessa understands hair like mine."

> Rose invokes his library research, which underpins the assumption he is exploring with his study.

> Notice how Rose is weaving in his results, conclusions, and inferences.

> Readers do not know whether Vanessa actually told Rose these things; he seems to be making inferences based on his naturalistic study.

> ANALYZING THE RHETORICAL SITUATION

With a classmate or two, reread Rose's description of Vanessa's work and then answer the following questions:

1. What assumption, problem, or question is Rose exploring?
2. Why is observation a necessary component of his research?
3. Whom is Rose observing? Why?
4. What behaviors or actions is Rose observing? Why?
5. Where is he conducting his observations? Why?
6. How does he use observation to advance his exploration of the assumption?
7. Why does Rose need to use more than observation to conduct his study?

Be prepared to share your answers with the rest of the class.

USING OBSERVATION IN YOUR WRITING

Now apply the questions in the preceding Analyzing the Rhetorical Situation to a naturalistic study that you would like to conduct. Provide written answers and be prepared to share them with the class.

Taking notes

The second part of the naturalistic research process is **note taking**, writing down what you observe or hear. You can tell by reading Mike Rose's account of his observations that he took copious notes as he watched Vanessa work. Otherwise, he would not have been able to compose such a realistic and compelling narrative about his observations. An important feature of note taking, however,

Research

Lisa F. Young/Shutterstock.com

is rhetorical listening, a concept Krista Ratcliffe refers to in her book *Rhetorical Listening: Identification, Gender, Whiteness.* "Rhetorical listening is a stance of openness that a person may choose to assume in relation to any person, text, or culture. Because we all have a tendency to allow our expectations and experiences to influence how we process what we encounter, the openness that we adopt when listening rhetorically keeps us aware of difference and newness." Rhetorical listening also helps researchers translate what they observe and hear into spoken and written language (questions and research drafts). If we listen with the intent to understand (rather than waiting for a spot to insert our own voice), we'll have an easier time writing and speaking about unfamiliar topics from a standpoint of authentic knowledge and goodwill. Thus, careful observing, listening, and note taking all support the researcher's perceptions—and improve the results.

Researchers like Rose take notes during observations for two reasons: to record very specific detail and to record their own reactions to what they observe. Without notes, few people can remember all the details of what they have observed. While observing, researchers can experience a range of reactions: they might find what they've observed to be in line with what they expected, or they might find it comforting, puzzling, or even infuriating or distressing. By jotting down their reactions as they occur, researchers can minimize the degree to which their preconceptions influence those reactions. Some naturalistic researchers simply (or not so simply) take notes about what they observe, trying to jot down snatches of conversation and specialized terms or insider phrases that they will need to ask about later. They might also record specific actions or sequences of movements.

Whether you keep your notes in a notebook, on separate note cards or pieces of paper, or on your laptop, you can choose among various ways of recording what you observe and your responses. You might write notes that combine narration, description, and evaluation. In the following passage, student Bethanie Orban uses a combination of narration, description, and evaluation to focus on the question "Who talks the most, and what are the different ways of communicating?"

Cody, Andrea, and Tom are friends who eat lunch together. Andrea comes to the table first, followed by Tom. Both wait for Cody to join them before they start to eat. Cody comes to the table humming. As soon as he sits down, he immediately begins talking about his history exam. "I don't know where the professor got the questions!" Cody says. Andrea assures Cody he did fine, trying to comfort him. Tom makes a joke that Cody probably didn't study. Cody begins gesturing with his hands that he did study a lot. Tom laughs and holds up his hand. He tells Cody it was a joke. Cody begins to eat his soup and Tom takes a drink of his milk. Andrea begins telling them about her weekend in New

(continued)

Research

York with her friend. She describes the Broadway show she saw. Andrea keeps describing how great it was. Cody begins a story about going to a movie over the weekend. Tom says he saw the movie a while back. Cody thinks it was the best movie he ever saw. "It was awesome." Cody looks around at the other tables to see if anyone is listening to what he's saying, which makes him look like he likes to be the center of attention. Andrea excuses herself to go get a cookie. She asks if anyone else wants anything, but both Tom and Cody say they are full.

You might begin by describing what you observe and then go back later to add your evaluation of what you saw, as Bethanie did in the following passage from her double-entry notebook. A **double-entry notebook** is a journal that has two distinct parts: observational details and personal response to those details. The double-entry notebook thus allows researchers to keep their observations separate from their responses (including biases and preferences) toward what they observe. In addition, it encourages researchers to push their observations further, with responses to and questions about what they see or think they see. Some researchers draw a heavy line down the middle of each page of the notebook, putting "Observations" at the top of the left-hand side of the page and "Response" at the top of the right-hand side. Others lay the notebook flat and use the right-hand page for recording their observations and the left-hand page for responding to those observations. If you're using a computer, you can format your entries the way Bethanie did:

OBSERVATIONS	RESPONSE
Andrea, Cody, and Tom meet up for lunch. Andrea thinks they need to find a table first before they get food. Cody thinks it would be nice to sit by the window, so they put their stuff down. Andrea is the first back to the table and waits for everyone else before eating. Cody tells the other two about his exam. He doesn't think he did well. Andrea thinks he probably did fine, but Tom makes a joke about it. Eventually Andrea begins talking about her weekend in New York. Cody tells about the movie he saw. When he's done, Andrea goes to get a cookie. Tom and Cody continue to talk about their weekends. The dining commons smells like fried food and cookies. Everyone thinks the food tastes good. The tables feel a little sticky. There is the constant noise of students talking. Andrea returns with her cookie while Tom and Cody continue their conversation about the weekend.	I felt that Cody seems to talk the most. However, my response could be based on my own opinions about Cody. Cody is shorter and has glasses—and he really likes to be the center of attention, possibly because he wants to make up for something (his height, maybe?). He tends to be loud and look around at other tables to see if anyone else heard. Andrea waits her turn to speak, but gets really passionate when she talks about Broadway. I feel like maybe she feels out of place with two guys, but wants to engage others in conversation. Tom seems the most laid back and likes to joke around. He has really curly hair so he doesn't mind teasing, perhaps to take it off himself. I believe many of my observations were colored by my own take on each student: Cody wanting attention, Andrea feeling uncomfortable, and Tom's use of humor.

Like all human beings, Bethanie brings her personal experience and disposition to every research situation. Bethanie labels one student's excitement about Broadway "passionate" while she characterizes another's loud speaking as evidence that he "likes to be the center of attention." She suspects that a third student uses jokes to relieve social pressure. Chances are many observers would agree with Bethanie, but few would come to the same conclusion that she does about the very same scene. The double-entry format Bethanie chose to use helped her separate her observations from her responses and judgments.

Our biases and preferences sometimes prevent us from seeing what is going on right in front of our eyes. Besides bringing our personal preferences to what we observe, we also bring our personal understanding— or lack thereof. Our level of expertise with procedures, history, and terminology can enhance our understanding or prevent us from understanding what we are seeing. For these reasons, most of us need to train ourselves to become better observers of our surroundings, better at seeing and hearing, more attuned to all of our senses. As award-winning writer Diane Ackerman reminds us in *A Natural History of the Senses,* "There is no way in which to understand the world without first detecting it through the radar-net of our senses."

Researchers conducting naturalistic studies have to push themselves to see more clearly, and questioning often helps. The best researchers ask many questions before, during, and after their observations. Successful researchers also rely on other means to triangulate what they think they are seeing and hearing: interviews, questionnaires, tape recordings, or the work of another researcher.

Asking questions

The third part of the naturalistic research process consists of asking questions. Researchers may ask their questions all at once or over an extended period of time during their observations and afterward. They may ask questions face to face, over the phone, online, or in a distributed questionnaire. We'll first consider face-to-face interviews and then explore methods for preparing and distributing questionnaires. Understanding how to prepare for and conduct interviews will advance your ability to carry on conversations all through your research study and beyond. This understanding will also help you think through the design of a questionnaire, if you decide to compose one.

Interviews An interview conducted as part of a naturalistic study can be formal, based on a set of predetermined questions, or more casual, almost like a conversation. But the friendly nature of good conversational interviews belies the serious planning that goes into them. After all, asking questions (interviewing) is an important component of data collection, often just as valuable as observing and taking notes.

Whatever method you decide to use for your interview, you must obtain permission to conduct the interview, schedule the interview, and obtain permission to tape record or take notes during the interview. After the interview (or series of conversations) is complete, you'll want to send a thank-you note to the person and include a complimentary copy of your study.

Perhaps the most important element of interviewing is choosing **interview subjects**, the specific people who can provide useful information for your naturalistic study. In other words, whom do you want to interview and why? Your interview subjects might be key participants in the phenomenon you are studying, or they might be experts on the subject you are studying. Whatever rationale you use for choosing interview subjects, the most important criterion should be that each person can provide you with information you need to proceed with your research.

All successful questioning involves **background research**—in other words, doing your homework before you begin asking questions. Many television programs, from shows on MTV and BET to *The Today Show* and *The Colbert Report*, feature interviews. When you watch an interview (especially one in the guise of a casual conversation), you can see how well or badly the interviewer prepared. The burden is on the researcher or interviewer to know enough about the person or phenomenon to ask intelligent questions, just as Mike Rose did when studying the hairstylist. Good interview questions will help guide your research.

Your **interview questions** should serve your research in two ways. First, they should put your subjects at ease so that they willingly talk, amplify their answers, and provide rich examples. Second, your interview questions should progress purposefully from one subject to another. Successful researchers write out a series of questions to which they want answers, arranging them so that one question leads logically to the next. In addition, your interview questions should indicate that you have done your homework about the interviewee and the process or phenomenon you are studying—and that you have been paying close attention during your observations. They should also demonstrate that you appreciate the time and information the interviewee is giving you.

Interview questions that can be answered with yes or no will not yield much information unless they are followed with a related question. For example, if you follow a question like "Do you like your job?" with a journalist's question ("Why?" "When?" or "How?"), you give your interviewee a chance to elaborate. Effective interviews usually contain a blend of open, or broad, questions and focused, or narrow, questions. Here are a few examples:

OPEN QUESTIONS

What do you think about _____?
What are your views on _____?
Why do you believe _____?

FOCUSED QUESTIONS

How long have you worked as a _____?
When did you start _____?
What does _____ mean?
Why did you _____?

Whatever kind of interview you conduct—face to face, telephone, e-mail, or online—you should not rely on your memory alone, no matter how good it is. You need to take notes or record the conversation in order to keep track of the questions you pose and the responses you receive. Many researchers use a tape recorder during face-to-face interviews so that they can focus their attention on the interviewee, establishing the personal rapport that invigorates any interview. During telephone interviews, you may want to use the speakerphone function so that you can tape the interview or take notes. Because taking notes and transcribing recordings are both time-consuming (and sometimes tedious) tasks, some researchers conduct e-mail or online interviews. These electronic techniques have the advantage of providing a written record of your questions and the answers. They also allow you a convenient way to "meet" the person. Perhaps the biggest disadvantage of electronic interviews is the burden they place on the interviewee, who has to take the time and energy to think through and then compose cogent answers. Talking is often much easier for the interviewee.

After the interview, you need to read through your notes and listen to any recordings. Many researchers find this to be the best point in the process for transcribing recordings. As you read your materials, consider a number of questions:

- ▶ What information surprised you? Why?
- ▶ How does that reaction affect your study?
- ▶ What do you now understand better than you did? What was said that illuminated your understanding?
- ▶ What specific passages best forward the purpose of your research? How does that information help answer or address your research assumption?
- ▶ What exactly would you like to know more about?

When you have answered these questions, you'll know what else needs to be done. You may find that you need to make further observations, go to the library, or conduct more interviews.

After you have read through your notes and listened to any recordings, you can begin writing up results, based on what you have observed, listened to,

Research

asked about, and perhaps researched in other ways. Writing up results launches the analysis that will shape your final report.

Gillian Petrie, interview of Jan Frese

The following selections are written transcripts of an interview conducted by Gillian Petrie, a student who decided to interview a long-time nurse, Jan Frese, about the changes she had seen in the profession during her thirty-eight years on the job. Gillian's first question is open-ended and aimed at making her interviewee comfortable.

> GILLIAN: Would you like to tell me, How did you get into nursing in the first place, Jan?
>
> JAN: I was a little late getting into nursing, because I was married and I had four children and . . . things were not going well at home and I was going to get a divorce. Well now, how am I going to take care of my children? So, . . . a friend of mine told me about this LPN [Licensed Practical Nurse] school and, um, it was only a year, it only took a year to be a licensed practical nurse, and I thought that—that sounds like a good idea. So, I went to the school and, um, graduated from there, and was an LPN for, um, 10 years, and most of that time I worked in a nursing home.
>
> But at the nursing home, um, there wasn't a—there was like one RN [Registered Nurse], and I worked night shift and there were no RNs and I ended up doing pretty much everything the RNs did but still getting the LPN pay. And I thought, This isn't a good idea! I'm going to do RN work, even though it was a nursing home, which isn't as complicated as a hospital, of course. I, um, thought I'll go back to school and be an RN; and I had every intention of going back to work at the nursing home. Go to school, be an RN, go back to the nursing home [laughs], do pretty much what I was doing before, but at least I'll get paid for it!

As the interview progresses, Gillian steers her subject to the topic of changes that she has seen over the years in patients' perception of nurses. Gillian now mixes prepared questions with follow-up prompts that encourage her subject to expand on her responses.

> JAN: When I worked, um, as an LPN, in fact, we had to wear white dresses, white socks, white shoes, *and* a *cap*. You *absolutely had* to wear a cap. And, um, people respected you. They—they knew you were a nurse. They knew you were a nurse and they res—respected what you did. They could tell the difference between,
>
> *(continued)*

er, um, a nurse's aide [laughs], because you dressed differently and you looked quite respectable. Neat. Uh huh, very neat, hair up [laughs] 'cos I learnt that when I went to school: you keep your hair up, you keep your fingernails short [laughs]. And we didn't wear much makeup either. And, er, people just seemed to respect you then. They'd say, Well, this is a nurse, she *knows* what she's doing.

GILLIAN: As opposed to . . . ?

JAN: As opposed to now. Well, working in Intensive Care I wear scrubs, which looks like pajamas. You can wear, well—I hate to tell you what I wear on my feet! I've gotten lax in my old age [laughs]. Sloppy old shoes . . . .

GILLIAN: So you think the change in dress has, um—we've sacrificed a little . . .

JAN: I think it has *something* to do with it.

GILLIAN: . . . professional authority?

JAN: When I go into a patient's room, *they* don't know *who* I am. I could be the housekeeper, 'cos they have to wear scrubs too. I could be the housekeeper; I could be dietary, bringing them their tray. They don't know *what* I am and I just, um, . . . I *long* for the old days when I really *looked* like a nurse [laughs]! Because now I—I—I look like somebody who just got out of bed [laughs]!

Toward the end of the interview, Gillian asks if Jan sees any differences in how well people take care of themselves. This question leads into a discussion of nurses' roles as educators. Notice that in the following passage and else-where, Gillian summarizes or rephrases what her subject has said to demon-strate that she is listening rhetorically ("So you feel that *now* it is a continuous process . . .").

GILLIAN: An important part of the RN, um, *job* is supposed to be *educating* people. . . .

JAN: Well, I did that, when I was first graduated from RN and went to telemetry. Darn, I was pretty good at it too, I'm tellin' you! I never—I saw a lot of open heart surgeries and that helped, because when I was a—a student that's what I loved to do. So I had a flip chart that had all the information on it, and I really liked doing that. I really liked, um, . . . and the *people*—they—they *looked* at me with *respect*. Like, *Wow! She* knows what she's *talking* about. Although I'd never taken care of a open heart patient *after* surgery, until I went to these, um, ICU classes. But I could *tell* them about what to *expect,* and it was—I—I thought I was pretty good at it. I *liked* it. Was a good job.

GILLIAN: Do you find it more difficult to educate people now?

JAN: Um, well, I don't do *that* anymore because I don't work on telemetry. But you just *automatically educate* people as you go. You don't sit down with the *flip*

(continued)

chart like I used to, and educate the whole *family* sittin' there in *front* of yer. You just, um, . . . *talk* to 'em when they come out of—of surgery, you just *tell* 'em what's gonna happen. You know, "You've got this breathing tube and when you're a little more awake and your blood gases are good and the tube will come out and then you'll be able to talk. You can't talk now because of the tube." And you just *talk* to 'em. You know, but it isn't like sittin' down, givin' a lesson. But you *teach* all the *time*.

GILLIAN: Mm huh. So you feel that *now* it is a continuous process . . .

JAN: It *is*!

GILLIAN: . . . rather than a sit down, formalized . . .

JAN: Well, that's, you know—it *was* kinda fun [laughs], sitting down and—and being "the teacher." But now it's just like a continuous process; you're right.

You can listen to the full interview, which Gillian recorded, at your English CourseMate, accessed through cengagebrain.com.

Questionnaires Whereas an interview elicits information from one person whose name you know, questionnaires provide information from a number of anonymous people. To be effective, questionnaires need to be short and focused. If they are too long, people may not be willing to take the time to fill them out. If they are not focused on your research, you'll find it difficult to integrate the results into your paper.

The questions on questionnaires take a variety of forms:

▶ Questions that require a simple yes-or-no answer

Do you commute to work in a car? (Circle one.)
  Yes No

▶ Multiple-choice questions

How many people do you commute with? (Circle one.)
  0 1 2 3 4

▶ Questions with answers on a checklist

How long does it take you to commute to work? (Check one.)
  ___ 0–30 minutes   ___ 30–60 minutes
  ___ 60–90 minutes   ___ 90–120 minutes

▶ Questions with a ranking scale

If the car you drive or ride in is not working, which of the following types of transportation do you rely on? (Rank the choices from 1 for most frequently used to 4 for least frequently used.)
  ___ bus ___ shuttle van ___ subway ___ taxi

▶ Open questions

What feature of commuting do you find most irritating?

The types of questions you decide to use will depend on the purpose of your project. The first four types of questions are the easiest for respondents to answer and the least complicated for you to process. Open questions should be asked only when other types of questions cannot elicit the information you want.

Be sure to begin your questionnaire with an introduction stating what the purpose of the questionnaire is, how the results will be used, and how long it will take to complete the questionnaire. In the introduction, you should also assure participants that their answers will be kept confidential. To protect participants' privacy, colleges and universities have committees set up to review questionnaires. These committees are often referred to as **institutional review boards (IRBs)**. Before you distribute your questionnaire, check with the institutional review board on your campus to make certain you are following its guidelines.

Administering a questionnaire can sometimes be problematic. Many questionnaires sent through the mail are never returned. If you do decide to mail out your questionnaire, provide a self-addressed envelope and directions for returning the questionnaire. It is always a good idea to send out twice as many questionnaires as you think you need, because the response rate for such mailings is generally low. If you are on campus, questionnaires can sometimes be distributed in dormitories or in classes, but such a procedure must be approved by campus officials.

Once your questionnaires have been completed and returned, tally the results for all but the open questions on a single unused questionnaire. To assess responses to the open questions, first read through them all. You might find that you can create categories for the responses. Answers to the open question "What feature of commuting do you find most irritating?" might fall into such categories as "length of time," "amount of traffic," and "bad weather conditions." By first creating categories, you'll be able to tally the answers to the open questions.

To put the results of a questionnaire to work in your research, ask yourself questions similar to the ones you reflect on after an interview:

- ▶ What information surprised you? Why?
- ▶ How does that reaction affect your study?
- ▶ What do you now understand better than you did? Which particular results illuminated your understanding?
- ▶ What exactly would you like to know more about?

These reflective questions will guide you in determining what else needs to be done, such as to make further observations, go to the library, or conduct interviews. The questions will also help with your analysis. Analysis is part of a naturalistic study from the beginning, when you conceive an assumption you want to explore. But analysis becomes particularly important as you bring together all three parts of your methodology (observing, note taking, and asking questions) and begin the final step of writing up your research.

Organizing a Field Research Report

Like other kinds of research papers, a report on a naturalistic study is arranged into distinct sections. Many effective writers use headings to differentiate among the sections of a long piece of writing. Besides making reading easier, headings make writing easier. You can end one section and start another one, rather than spending time on building transitions between sections.

▶ The **introduction** presents the assumption under investigation, expressed as a problem, a question, or a belief. You might also use the introduction to explain the significance of your assumption.

▶ A **literature review** can be part of the introduction or can form a separate section. In the literature review, you demonstrate that you have conducted some library or online research about the assumption under examination. In fact, your assumption might even have grown out of that prior work.

▶ A **methodology** section explains the process you used to study the assumption you set out in your introduction. In the case of a naturalistic study, you explain how you gathered information. Whatever method of triangulation you used is also explained in this section.

▶ In the **results** section, you report your findings. Your findings might be a solution to a problem, an explanation or answer to a question, or an evaluation of an assumption. In this section, you might include graphs, photographs, or other kinds of visuals that help support your verbal explanation of your results.

▶ A **discussion** section provides a place to interpret your findings, compare them with what others have discovered or believe, and relate them to the assumption with which you started.

▶ Finally, a **conclusion** closes a field research report. One way to shape a conclusion is to break it into three subsections: (1) the clear-cut, obvious conclusions you can draw from your study; (2) the inferences you can draw, given your current knowledge of the subject under study; and (3) the implications of your research in terms of further research or practical application.

Many field research reports also merit a references or a works-cited list (see Chapter 19).

Mon	Tue	Wed	Thu	Fri	Tasks ☒
28	Mar 1 ☐ Research Journal: freewrite (C	2	3 ☐ Library homepage: database	4 10 Prof. Adams: office hours 8:30 Work 4p Work	**Media and Politics** ⊟ **Tuesday, Mar 1, 2011** ☐ Research Journal: › freewrite (Ch 17 questions)
7 ☐ Find Jon Stewart interview? 4:30p Meet JK in lab	8 BIO: lab report rewrite DUE	9	10 8:30 Work	11 4p Work	⊟ **Thursday, Mar 3, 2011** ☐ Library homepage: database search ⊟ **Monday, Mar 7, 2011** ☐ Find Jon Stewart interview?
14	15 8:30 Work	16	17 8:30 Work	18 4p Work	⊟ **Tuesday, Mar 29, 2011** ☐ Works Cited! [see notes and Zotero] ⊟ **No due date** ☐ Visit Prof. Adams during office hours to talk about research question
21	22 8:30 Work	23 6:30p BIO review session, Markle	24 8:30 Work 6:30p Take draft to writing center	25 revise Jon Stewart paper ▸ 4p Work	
28 revise Jon Stewart paper	29	30	31	Apr 1 Media/Politics Project DUE	

1. How do you organize your research process? What tools (electronic or manual) do you use?
2. What features and tasks on this Google Calendar page seem to relate to the ways you work?

Now that you've considered what kinds of sources might be useful to you and where to find them, you need a plan for proceeding with the research process. Without a clear plan and a method of tracking your progress, it's easy to lose track of your ideas and goals. Not even experienced researchers attempt to remember which sources they've consulted, how those sources fit into their research, and what their next steps will be. To keep their research moving ahead, researchers take advantage of tools such as research logs and use ordered methods similar to the ones described in this chapter.

Keeping a Research Log

Research logs come in different forms, but whatever their form—electronic or printed, detailed or brief—they help researchers stay focused. The items included on a log depend on the particular kind of research. For instance, a sociologist's log of field observations might include spaces for recording descriptions of the location, the time, and even the weather conditions—in addition to comments about observed events and notes about what steps should be taken next. (See Chapter 16 for more on field observations.) An architect working on a proposal for renovating an old courthouse might use a log to document her findings on the history of the building, noting locations and details of the photographs, sketches, and correspondence she comes across. A psychology student beginning a research project by using the database PsycINFO may save himself time in the long run by recording keyword combinations he uses in his searches, circling the keywords he wants to plug into similar databases. (See pages 427–428 for help in choosing keywords.)

Researchers make decisions about what to include in their logs by anticipating what kind of information will be most important in helping them answer their research question and document their results. Generally, entries in a research log relate to one of the following activities:

▶ Establishing the rhetorical opportunity, purpose, and research question
▶ Identifying the sources
▶ Taking notes
▶ Responding to notes
▶ Establishing the audience

Your research log may also be where you keep track of progress on the following activities, which are important to the writing process:

▶ Preparing a working bibliography
▶ Annotating a bibliography
▶ Crafting a working thesis
▶ Dealing with areas of tension in the research

Depending on your assignment, you may want to include entries related to all of these types of activities or just a few of them. We'll discuss each kind of entry in this chapter.

Establishing the purpose and identifying the research question

In the introductory entry in your research log, identify your research question and your reasons for choosing it. You might include some preliminary, tentative answers to your question if you have any, given what you already know. Your introductory entry should also establish your overall research purpose. What is your purpose in presenting your research to others: to inform, to analyze, or to persuade? Rereading this initial entry every so often may help you stay focused. Here is the first entry in a research log kept by student Hannah Lewis for a paper for a class called Media and Politics.

MY PURPOSE AND RESEARCH QUESTION

I've been thinking I'd like to learn more about a show I really enjoy, *The Daily Show with Jon Stewart*. I've heard people criticize my generation for getting most of our news from this show, instead of watching CNN or the nightly news on a local station like my parents do. I think I learn a lot from Jon Stewart's show, but it's important to me to know how reliable the information he delivers is—just because I'm young doesn't mean I don't care about current events and I want to be sure I'm paying attention to the right sources.

I think my main purpose will be to inform other *Daily Show* viewers about its reliability and usefulness. Depending on what I find out, maybe I will also be trying to persuade my audience to take some kind of action or to look differently at the show. I might start by asking *How reliable is the* Daily Show *as a news source—and how can we know?*

Identifying the sources

Before you start to take notes from any source, jot down important identifying features of the source, in case you need to return to it or cite it. If you expect to have only a few sources, you may want to include complete bibliographic information with your notes. If you will be consulting a number of sources, create an entry in your working bibliography (see pages 455–456) and then include with your content notes only basic information, such as the author's name and the page number.

Taking notes

Most of your entries, whether in an electronic or paper research log or other note-taking system, will consist of detailed notes about the research you have done. Often these notes will be based on your reading, but they may also cover observations, interviews, and other types of research. As you take notes, you may choose to quote, paraphrase, or summarize your sources. These ways of recording research findings are discussed in more detail in Chapter 18.

As you write, keep in mind the purpose of your notes. Ask yourself how you might use each source in your paper; how you intend to use a source generally determines the nature of the notes you take. You might use a source to provide context for your readers or deeper understanding for yourself. If you were researching a problem, for instance, you would look for information on what's already been done to try to address the problem. You might refer to sources that explain why previous attempts failed—or why they succeeded to some degree but not completely. A pithy quotation from an expert may encourage your readers to consider your proposed solution. If you find a quotation or a statistic that you might want to use in your introduction, write it down word for word, and then double-check to make sure that you have recorded it and identified the source accurately.

TRICKS OF THE TRADE

Instead of keeping a research log, some researchers use the time-tested method of writing information on note cards. Most of these researchers use four-by-six-inch cards, recording one note per card. If a note is particularly long, they staple a second card to it. Keeping separate cards allows a researcher to test different arrangements of information during the drafting stage. If you decide to use note cards, be sure to indicate the source of each note at the bottom of the card so that you will have the information you need to cite or document the source in your paper. See pages 455–456 for a list of source information to write down.

Responding to notes

With your notes, you'll want to include your responses to what you have recorded from the sources. You may wish to comment on what you agree or disagree with, what you question, why you find some item of information particularly interesting, and what connections you draw between one source and another. Like your notes, your responses should be purposeful. When you find a source with which you agree or disagree, you'll probably copy down or paraphrase excerpts you wish to emphasize or dispute; if you do not also note *why* you agree or disagree, however, you may not be able to reconstruct your initial response later when you are composing your essay. If you take the time to carefully record your responses to sources, you will be able to make a smooth transition from taking notes to composing your essay.

Especially when you are recording source notes and your responses to those notes in the same place, it's crucial to have a system for making clear which ideas come from the source and which are your own. Even professional authors have damaged their research—and their credibility—by assuming that they would remember which ideas came from their sources and which were their responses to those sources. Guard against this danger by writing your responses in a different color ink or using a different font, enclosing your responses in brackets, or using some other technique to make the distinction. You might want to use a double-entry notebook, as described in Chapter 16.

Here is another excerpt from Hannah Lewis's research log. It contains bibliographic information about a magazine article she is considering using as a source, her summary of the article, and her response to it.

A research log helps you keep track of your investigation. It also serves as a testing ground for information and thoughts you may include in your paper. For example, in the preceding entry from her log, Hannah identified satire as an important concept for her paper, and this concept does appear in her final draft (pages 501–511). When you are writing in your log, then, remember that composing your entries carefully may save you time when you write your paper. Notice that Hannah wrote down an idea for further research. Like most students, Hannah has many obligations besides writing this research paper, so she makes a note about follow-up research she intends to do.

Establishing the audience

A research log is a good place to jot notes about your audience so that you can keep your readers in mind as you compose. Let's say you're interested in finding out about the possibilities of commuting by bicycle in your town. If you are aware that your audience knows nothing about bike commuting, you may want to provide an explanation (or process analysis) of how bike commuters get to and from work safely and comfortably. You might even include a photograph of the kind of bike made for commuting—one with fenders to keep work clothes clean and panniers to hold cargo. However, if you are writing

AP Photo/Bizuayeh Tesfaye

Commuting to work by bike is uncommon in some communities, so an audience for a paper on this topic may need explanation or description.

Research

for an audience that has already been introduced to this type of transportation, a detailed description is unnecessary.

USING A RESEARCH LOG IN YOUR WRITING

1. In your research log, write two or three paragraphs in which you introduce your research question and articulate your purpose. Be sure to discuss why you are asking the question in the first place, what the benefits of answering the question will be, and what types of research are likely to be helpful.

2. After you've written notes about a source in your log, take a moment to write out a response, making sure to clearly distinguish your response from the notes you took. Here are some questions to ask yourself as you respond: What do I agree and disagree with? What do I not understand fully? What do I want to know more about? How does what this source says relate to (agree or disagree with) what other sources have said? What purpose might this source serve in my paper? What other research should I do?

3. In your research log, create an entry that describes your prospective readers and explains what you need to keep in mind to ensure that you are addressing them. In addition, make a list of the types of sources that you think this audience will find credible and explain why.

Preparing a Working Bibliography

Whenever you plan to consult a number of sources in a research project, dedicate a section of your research log to your working bibliography. A **working bibliography** is a preliminary record of the sources you find as you conduct your research. The working bibliography serves as a draft for your final list of references or works cited.

The following sample templates indicate what bibliographic information you should record for books, articles, and websites. Even though your citation may not require each piece of information, it will all be useful, should you need to relocate a source. To save yourself work later as you prepare the bibliography for your paper, you may find it worthwhile to take a few moments to look at how bibliographic information is conventionally recorded in your field. If you have been asked to follow the conventions of the Modern Language Association (MLA) or the American Psychological Association (APA), see Chapter 19.

BOOKS

Author(s) and/or Editor(s): _____

Title: _____

Publisher: _____

Place of Publication: _____

Date of Publication: _____

Page Numbers of Particular Interest: _____

For online books, also provide as much of the following information as possible:

Title of the Website: _____

Editor of the Site: _____

Version Number: _____

Date of Electronic Publication: _____

Name of Sponsoring Institution or Organization: _____

Date of Access: _____

URL for Book: _____

ARTICLES

Author(s): _____

Title of Article: _____

Title of Journal or Magazine: _____

Volume and Issue Numbers: _____

Date of Publication: _____

Page Numbers of Entire Article: _____

Page Numbers of Particular Interest: _____

For articles from a database, also provide as much of the following information as possible:

Name of Database: _____

Name of Service: _____

Name of Library: _____

Location (City and State) of Library: _____

Date of Access: _____

URL for the Service's Home Page: _____

WEBSITES

Name of Site: _____

Name of Sponsoring Entity: _____

Author(s) or Editor(s) (if any): _____

URL: _____

Date of Publication: _____

Date of Last Update: _____

Date of Access: _____

USING A WORKING BIBLIOGRAPHY IN YOUR WRITING

Find three sources related to your research question and list them in your working bibliography with all relevant information.

Annotating a Bibliography

An **annotated bibliography** is a list of works cited, or sometimes works consulted, that includes descriptive or critical commentary with each entry. By preparing an annotated bibliography, you show that you have understood your sources and have thought about how to incorporate them into your paper. Some instructors require students to include annotated bibliographies with their papers. However, even if an annotated bibliography is not required, you might want to create one if you are working on a research project that will take several weeks to complete, as this type of list can help you keep track of sources. To prepare entries that will help you solidify your knowledge of sources and your plans for using them, follow these guidelines:

▶ Begin each entry with bibliographic information. Follow the guidelines on pages 483–500 for MLA documentation style or those on pages 515–525 for APA documentation style if your instructor requires you to use one of these styles.

▶ Below the bibliographic information, write two or three sentences that summarize the source.

▶ After summarizing the source, write two or three sentences explaining the usefulness of the source for your specific research project.

Here is an example of an entry that Hannah Lewis might have included in an annotated bibliography:

Research

Young, Donnagal G., and Russell M. Tisinger. "Dispelling Late-Night Myths: News Consumption among Late-Night Comedy Viewers and the Predictors of Exposure to Various Late-Night Shows." *Harvard International Journal of Press/Politics* 11 (2006): 113–34. *Sage.* Web. 28 Dec. 2009.

Young and Tisinger consulted studies by the Pew Research Center and the Annenberg School for Communication to determine whether it is true that young people get all of their news from *The Daily Show.* They also wanted to consider whether or not it is safe to assume that the late-night audience is a homogenous group or whether those watching, say, David Letterman's show have characteristics different from those watching *The Daily Show.* They found that Stewart's audience regularly receives information from both traditional network news programs and his show. Stewart's audience also tends to be more politically informed than regular viewers of other programs.

This source will be useful because it relies on numerical data collected about *The Daily Show*'s audience. I've already found some sources that analyze the effects of the show, but this is the only one that tries to make sense of the various studies. The fact that viewers of the show tend to consult other news sources frequently is something I hadn't considered. If I use this source in my paper, it could make people wonder where Bill O'Reilly gets the idea that the audience is made up of "stoned slackers."

USING AN ANNOTATED BIBLIOGRAPHY IN YOUR WRITING

If you have already constructed a working bibliography, add annotations for the sources you think will be most useful. Be sure to include both a summary of the source and an explanation of how the source will be useful to you.

Planning a Research Paper

Strategies for planning a research paper are not that different from the general strategies you learned in Chapter 3: listing, keeping a journal, freewriting, questioning, clustering, and outlining. If you have been keeping a research log, you have already used many of these methods. When writing the first draft of your paper, you may want to use some of these methods to generate or organize ideas.

Crafting a working thesis

The most important step to take as you begin to prepare your first draft is to write your thesis. If you started the research process with a question, now is the time to answer that question. A **working thesis** is a tentative answer to a research question. By forming such a thesis, you can test a possible framework

Research

for your fitting response. For example, Hannah Lewis started with the question "How reliable is *The Daily Show* as a news source?" She transformed her question into this thesis: "*The Daily Show* offers critical viewers a chance to understand important news through its satirical delivery." As she read more sources and continued to write about them in her research log, she began to become more interested in the function *The Daily Show* serves—in how it differs from mainstream news sources in ways other than the use of humor.

Keep in mind that once you have written a working thesis, you may find that you need to adjust it, as Hannah eventually did. You can test your thesis as you try to support it in the body of your paper. Do not be concerned if you change your mind; writers often do. Writing a thesis is just a starting point in the drafting process.

Dealing with areas of tension in the research findings

As you sifted through all your information in an attempt to find an answer to your research question, you probably encountered information that was at odds with other information. Perhaps two authors disagreed, perhaps one study contradicted another, or perhaps your own experience provided evidence counter to another author's thesis. You may also have found flaws in the reasoning or gaps in the evidence. Look closely at these areas of tension, because they can provide a rhetorical opportunity and a purpose for your writing. You may even find ways to introduce them into your thesis. Kendra Fry's experience provides an illustration.

Kendra had been studying how mathematics is taught in elementary schools and observing students in a fifth-grade classroom. Her research question was "What are the most effective methods for teaching mathematics to students in elementary school?" Both in the articles Kendra read and in the classes she observed, she found a great deal of emphasis placed on writing. Students were often asked to write down explanations for their answers to math problems. The initial working thesis she drafted was "Although language arts and mathematics are often kept separate in coursework, writing may be key to teaching mathematics in elementary school." When observing students, though, Kendra found that some students who were able to solve math equations easily still had difficulty explaining the process. She thought this difficulty made a few of them dislike their math lessons. As Kendra started to draft her paper, she changed her thesis to take into account the tension between the type of mathematics teaching that was prescribed and the effect on learning that she was witnessing: "Although students in elementary schools are encouraged to explain their mathematical reasoning, this practice may have an adverse effect on some students' motivation to study math." In the process of trying to answer a broader question, Kendra found an opportunity and a purpose for a research paper she was really interested in writing.

Like Kendra, you can find a genuine research agenda when you pay attention to what doesn't fit neatly into an early outline you have or into your initial plans for what you will say.

Research

Reading, Evaluating, and Responding to Sources

The following is an excerpt from an interview conducted by Sharifa Rhodes-Pitts with Debra Dickerson, author of *The End of Blackness: Returning the Souls of Black Folks to Their Rightful Owners* (New York: Pantheon, 2004).

RHODES-PITTS: You've spoken about how *The End of Blackness* grew out of your frustration with the way racial politics get played out in what you call "black liberal" sectors. Can you elaborate a bit on what you mean?

DICKERSON: Part of what brought about the book in the first place was a lifetime spent having to bite my tongue because of the way black liberals wage the battle on race. It doesn't need to be a battle. It ought to be a dialogue—it ought to be a family discussion. Instead you're either with them or you're against them. If you don't think exactly like them you're the enemy or you're insane.

I think that comes from a couple of things. The moral urgency that there once was—when people were being lynched or were sitting in the back of the bus or being defrauded of their citizenship—is no more. But even though it's 2004 and we don't confront the same problems, people go at it as if it's still 1950 and nothing has changed. A lot of people read about what Fannie Lou Hamer and Martin Luther King went through and slip into an us-against-the-world kind of mode and pretend that things are more dire than they are. There's a temptation to want to feel like you're waging a crusade and the forces of evil are arrayed against you. But I think there's a real sloppiness of thought there.

1. In one paragraph, summarize the interview excerpt as objectively as you can.
2. Look over your paragraph and reflect in writing on the following questions: (a) What strategies did you use to put the source's ideas into your own words? (b) How did you indicate the source of any direct quotes you included? (c) How did you respond to the ideas expressed in the interview? (d) How did you credit and cite the source? If you were expanding your written response, which parts of your summary paragraph would you include? How would you alter those parts, if at all?

Reading with Your Audience and Purpose in Mind

Keeping purposeful notes as you read sources can save you from needless scrambling the night before your paper is due. In Chapter 17, you learned that your notes will be more useful to you in the later stages of the writing process if you keep your purpose and audience in mind as you write them. In the first part of this chapter, you'll learn to summarize, paraphrase, and quote from sources. Each of these techniques for recording information can help you achieve your purpose and satisfy your audience. In the second part of this chapter, you'll learn strategies for evaluating and responding to your sources.

Summarizing

Researchers regularly use summaries in their writing to indicate that they have done their homework—that is, that they are familiar with other work done on a topic. In summarizing their sources, researchers restate the information they have read as concisely and objectively as they can, thereby demonstrating their understanding of it and establishing their credibility. Researchers may have additional reasons for using summaries. For instance, they may use the information to support their own view, to deepen an explanation, or to contest other information they have found. In academic research papers, summaries appear most frequently as introductory material.

Using function statements

Depending on your purpose, you may decide to summarize an entire source or just part of it. Summarizing an entire source can help you understand it. To compose such a summary, you may find it useful to first write a **function statement** for each paragraph. A function statement goes beyond restating the content of the paragraph; it captures the intention of the author. For example, an author may introduce a topic, provide background information, present alternative views, refute other writers' positions, or draw conclusions based on evidence provided.

The words you use to indicate who the author is and what he or she is doing are called **attributive tags** because they attribute information to a source. Attributive tags help you assign credit where credit is due. Most tags consist of the author's name and a verb. These verbs are often used in attributive tags:

acknowledge	criticize	insist
advise	declare	list
agree	deny	maintain
analyze	describe	note
argue	disagree	object
assert	discuss	offer
believe	emphasize	oppose
claim	endorse	reject
compare	explain	report
concede	find	state
conclude	illustrate	suggest
consider	imply	think

Other attributive tags are phrases, such as *according to the researcher, from the author's perspective,* and *in the author's mind.*

Jacob Thomas used function statements to develop a summary of the following article. Jacob chose the article as a possible source for a research paper addressing the question "How do the media use language to deceive the public?" His function statements follow the article.

> Doubts about Doublespeak

William Lutz

During the past year, we learned that we can shop at a "unique retail biosphere" instead of a farmers' market, where we can buy items made of "synthetic glass" instead of plastic, or purchase a "high-velocity, multipurpose air circulator," or electric fan. A "wastewater conveyance facility" may "exceed the odor threshold" from time to time due to the presence of "regulated human nutrients," but that is not to be confused with a sewage plant that stinks up the neighborhood with sewage sludge. Nor should we confuse a "resource development park" with a dump. Thus does doublespeak continue to spread.

Doublespeak is language which pretends to communicate but doesn't. It is language which makes the bad seem good, the negative seem positive, the unpleasant seem attractive, or at least tolerable. It is language which avoids, shifts or denies responsibility; language which is at variance with its real or purported meaning. It is language which conceals or prevents thought.

Doublespeak is all around us. We are asked to check our packages at the desk "for our convenience" when it's not for our convenience at all but for someone else's convenience. We see advertisements for "preowned," "experienced" or "previously distinguished" cars, not used cars, and for "genuine imitation leather," "virgin vinyl" or "real counterfeit diamonds." Television offers not reruns but "encore telecasts." There are no slums or ghettos, just the "inner city" or "substandard housing" where the "disadvantaged" or "economically nonaffluent" live and where there might be a problem with "substance abuse." Nonprofit organizations don't make a profit, they have "negative deficits" or experience "revenue excesses." With doublespeak it's not dying but "terminal living" or "negative patient care outcome."

There are four kinds of doublespeak. The first kind is the euphemism, a word or phrase designed to avoid a harsh or distasteful reality. Used to mislead or deceive, the euphemism becomes doublespeak. In 1984 the U.S. State Department's annual reports on the status of human rights around the world ceased using the word "killing." Instead the State Department used the phrase "unlawful or arbitrary deprivation of life," thus avoiding the embarrassing situation of government-sanctioned killing in countries supported by the United States.

A second kind of doublespeak is jargon, the specialized language of a trade, profession or similar group, such as doctors, lawyers, plumbers or car mechanics. Legitimately used, jargon allows members of a group to communicate with each other clearly, efficiently and quickly. Lawyers and tax accountants speak to each other of an "involuntary conversion" of property, a legal term that means the loss or destruction of property through theft, accident or condemnation. But when lawyers or tax accountants use unfamiliar terms to speak to others, then the jargon becomes doublespeak.

In 1978 a commercial 727 crashed on takeoff, killing three passengers, injuring 21 others and destroying the airplane. The insured value of the airplane was greater than its book value, so the airline made a profit of $1.7 million, creating two problems: the airline didn't want to talk about one of its airplanes crashing, yet it had to account for that $1.7 million profit in its annual report to its stockholders. The airline solved both problems by inserting a footnote in its annual report which explained that the $1.7 million was due to "the involuntary conversion of a 727."

A third kind of doublespeak is gobbledygook or bureaucratese. Such doublespeak is simply a matter of overwhelming the audience with words—the more the better. Alan Greenspan, a polished practitioner of bureaucratese, once testified before a Senate committee that "it is a tricky problem to find the particular calibration in timing that would be appropriate to stem the acceleration in risk premiums created by falling incomes without prematurely aborting the decline in the inflation-generated risk premiums."

The fourth kind of doublespeak is inflated language, which is designed to make the ordinary seem extraordinary, to make everyday things seem impressive, to give an air of importance to people or situations, to make the simple seem complex. Thus do car mechanics become "automotive internists," elevator operators become "members of the vertical transportation corps," grocery store checkout clerks become "career associate scanning professionals," and smelling something becomes "organoleptic analysis."

Doublespeak is not the product of careless language or sloppy thinking. Quite the opposite. Doublespeak is language carefully designed and constructed to appear to communicate when in fact it doesn't. It is language designed not to lead but mislead. Thus, it's not a tax increase but "revenue enhancement" or "tax-base broadening." So how can you complain about higher taxes? Those aren't useless, billion dollar pork barrel projects; they're really "congressional projects of national significance," so don't complain about wasteful government spending. That isn't the Mafia in Atlantic City; those are just "members of a career-offender cartel," so don't worry about the influence of organized crime in the city.

New doublespeak is created every day. The Environmental Protection Agency once called acid rain "poorly buffered precipitation," then dropped that term in favor of "atmospheric deposition of anthropogenically-derived acidic substances," but recently decided that acid rain should be called "wet deposition." The Pentagon, which has in the past given us such classic doublespeak as "hexiform rotatable surface compression unit" for steel nut, just published a pamphlet warning soldiers that exposure to nerve gas will lead to "immediate permanent incapacitation." That's almost as good as the Pentagon's official term "servicing the target," meaning to kill the enemy. Meanwhile, the Department of Energy

continued

wants to establish a "monitored retrievable storage site," a place once known as a dump for spent nuclear fuel.

Bad economic times give rise to lots of new doublespeak designed to avoid some very unpleasant economic realities. As the "contained depression" continues, so does the corporate policy of making up even more new terms to avoid the simple, and easily understandable, term "layoff." So it is that corporations "reposition," "restructure," "reshape" or "realign" the company and "reduce duplication" through "release of resources" that involves a "permanent downsizing" or a "payroll adjustment" that results in a number of employees being "involuntarily terminated."

Other countries regularly contribute to doublespeak. In Japan, where baldness is called "hair disadvantaged," the economy is undergoing a "severe adjustment process," while in Canada there is an "involuntary downward development" of the work force. For some government agencies in Canada, wastepaper baskets have become "user friendly, space effective, flexible, deskside sortation units." Politicians in Canada may engage in "reality augmentation," but they never lie. As part of their new freedom, the people of Moscow can visit "intimacy salons," or sex shops as they're known in other countries. When dealing with the bureaucracy in Russia, people know that they should show officials "normal gratitude," or give them a bribe.

The worst doublespeak is the doublespeak of death. It is the language, wrote George Orwell in 1945, that is "largely the defense of the indefensible designed to make lies sound truthful and murder respectable, and to give an appearance of solidity to pure wind." In the doublespeak of death, Orwell continued, "defenseless villages are bombarded from the air, the inhabitants driven out into the countryside, the cattle machine-gunned, the huts set on fire with incendiary bullets. This is called pacification. Millions of peasants are robbed of their farms and sent trudging along the roads with no more than they can carry. This is called transfer of population or rectification of frontiers." Today, in a country once called Yugoslavia, this is called "ethnic cleansing."

It's easy to laugh off doublespeak. After all, we all know what's going on, so what's the harm? But we don't always know what's going on, and when that happens, doublespeak accomplishes its ends. It alters our perception of reality. It deprives us of the tools we need to develop, advance and preserve our society, our culture, our civilization. It breeds suspicion, cynicism, distrust and, ultimately, hostility. It delivers us into the hands of those who do not have our interests at heart. As Samuel Johnson noted in 18th century England, even the devils in hell do not lie to one another, since the society of hell could not subsist without the truth, any more than any other society.

Research

SAMPLE FUNCTION STATEMENTS

Paragraph 1: Lutz begins his article on doublespeak by providing some examples: a "unique retail biosphere" is really a farmers' market; "synthetic glass" is really plastic.

Paragraph 2: Lutz defines *doublespeak* as devious language–"language which pretends to communicate but doesn't" (22).

Paragraph 3: Lutz describes the wide use of doublespeak. It is used in all media.

Paragraph 4: Lutz defines the first of four types of doublespeak—euphemism, which is a word or phrase that sugarcoats a harsher meaning. He provides an example from the U.S. State Department.

Paragraph 5: Lutz identifies jargon as the second type of doublespeak. It is the specialized language used by trades or professions such as car mechanics or doctors. But Lutz believes the use of jargon is legitimate when it enables efficient communication among group members. Jargon is considered doublespeak when in-group members use it to communicate with nonmembers who cannot understand it.

Paragraph 6: Lutz shows how an airline's annual report includes devious use of jargon to camouflage a disaster.

Paragraph 7: According to Lutz, the third type of doublespeak has two alternative labels: *gobbledygook* or *bureaucratese*. The distinguishing feature of this type of doublespeak is the large number of words used.

Paragraph 8: Lutz states that the final type of doublespeak is inflated language.

Paragraph 9: Lutz is careful to note that doublespeak is not the product of carelessness or "sloppy thinking" (23) but rather an attempt to deceive.

Paragraph 10: Lutz emphasizes that instances of doublespeak are created on a daily basis and provides examples.

Paragraph 11: Lutz attributes increases in the use of doublespeak to a bad economy. Doublespeak serves to gloss over the hardships people experience.

Paragraph 12: Lutz notes that doublespeak is also used in other countries.

Paragraph 13: Lutz singles out the doublespeak surrounding the topic of death as the worst type of doublespeak.

Paragraph 14: Lutz concludes his article by establishing the harmfulness of doublespeak, which can leave us without "the tools we need to develop, advance and preserve our society, our culture, our civilization" (24).

Clustering and ordering information in a summary

After you have written a function statement for each paragraph of an essay, you may find that statements cluster together. For example, the statements Jacob Thomas wrote for paragraphs 4 through 8 of William Lutz's article all deal with the different categories of doublespeak. If an essay includes subheadings, you can use them to understand how the original author grouped ideas. By finding clusters of ideas, you take a major step toward condensing information. Instead of using a sentence or two to summarize each paragraph, you can use a sentence or two to summarize three paragraphs. For example, Jacob might have condensed his function statements for paragraphs 4 through 8 into one sentence: "Lutz claims that euphemism, jargon, gobbledygook (or bureaucratese), and inflated language are four types of doublespeak."

Summaries often present the main points in the same order as in the original source, usually with the thesis statement of the original source first, followed by supporting information. Even if the thesis statement appears at the end of the original source, you should still state it at the beginning of your summary. If there is no explicit thesis statement in the original source, you should state at the beginning of your summary the thesis (or main idea) that you have inferred from reading that source. Including a thesis statement, which captures the essence of the original source, in the first or second sentence of a summary provides a reference point for other information reported in the summary. The introductory sentences of a summary should also include the source author's name and the title of the source.

After you finish your summary, ask yourself the following questions to ensure that it is effective:

- ▶ Have I included the author's name and the title of the source?
- ▶ Have I mentioned the thesis (or main idea) of the original source?
- ▶ Have I used attributive tags to show that I am referring to someone else's ideas?
- ▶ Have I remained objective, not evaluating or judging the material I am summarizing?
- ▶ Have I remained faithful to the source by accurately representing the material?

Direct quotations can be used in summaries, but they should be used sparingly. Guidelines for quotations are discussed in more detail on pages 470–472. All quotations and references to source material require accurate citation and documentation. In-text citation and documentation formats are presented in Chapter 19.

Sample student summary

Jacob Thomas followed the MLA citation and documentation guidelines when writing the following summary. Notice that Jacob chose to include only those details he found most important. The notes he took on paragraphs 3, 6, 9, 11, and 13 were not included.

Jacob Thomas

Professor Brown

English 101, Section 13

22 January 2011

Summary of "Doubts about Doublespeak"

In "Doubts about Doublespeak," William Lutz describes the deviousness of

doublespeak, which he defines as "language which pretends to communicate

but doesn't" (22). It is language meant to deceive. "Unique retail biosphere"

for *farmers' market* and "revenue enhancement" for *taxes* are just a few of

the examples Lutz provides. Such use of deceptive language is widespread.

According to Lutz, it can be found around the world and is created anew on

a daily basis. Lutz defines four types of doublespeak. Euphemisms are words

or phrases that sugarcoat harsher meanings. The U.S. State Department's

use of "unlawful or arbitrary deprivation of life" for *killing* is an example (22).

Jargon is the second type of doublespeak Lutz discusses. It is the specialized

language used by trades or professions such as car mechanics or doctors.

Although Lutz believes the use of jargon is legitimate when it enables efficient

communication among group members, he considers it doublespeak when

in-group members use it to communicate with nonmembers who cannot

understand it. Lutz distinguishes the third type of doublespeak, gobbledygook

(or bureaucratese), by the large number of words used, which, he says, serve

to overwhelm those in an audience. The final type of doublespeak, according

to Lutz, is inflated language, which is the use of overelaborate terms to describe

something quite ordinary. Lutz concludes his article by establishing the

harmfulness of doublespeak. He believes that doublespeak can alter how we

perceive the world and thus leave us without "the tools we need to develop,

advance and preserve our society, our culture, our civilization" (24).

Work Cited

Lutz, William. "Doubts about Doublespeak." *State Government News* July 1993: 22–24. Print.

Partial summaries

Jacob Thomas summarized an entire article. Depending on his purpose and the expectations of his audience, he might have chosen to write a partial summary instead. Partial summaries of varying size are frequently found in research papers. A one-sentence summary may be appropriate when a researcher wants to focus on a specific piece of information. If Jacob had been interested in noting what various writers have said about abuses of language, he could have represented William Lutz's ideas as follows:

> In "Doubts about Doublespeak," William Lutz describes abuses of language and explains why they are harmful.

Partial summaries of the same source may vary depending on the researcher's purpose. The following partial summary of Lutz's article focuses on its reference to George Orwell's work, rather than on the uses of doublespeak.

> **SAMPLE PARTIAL SUMMARY**
>
> Authors frequently cite the work of George Orwell when discussing the abuses of language. In "Doubts about Doublespeak," William Lutz describes different types of doublespeak—language used to deceive—and explains why they are harmful. He quotes a passage from Orwell's "Politics and the English Language" in order to emphasize his own belief that the doublespeak surrounding the topic of death is the worst form of language abuse: "defenseless villages are bombarded from the air, the inhabitants driven out into the countryside, the cattle machine-gunned, the huts set on fire with incendiary bullets. This is called pacification. Millions of peasants are robbed of their farms and sent trudging along the roads with no more than they can carry. This is called transfer of population or rectification of frontiers" (qtd. in Lutz 24).

Paraphrasing

A **paraphrase** is like a summary in that it is a restatement of someone else's ideas, but a paraphrase differs from a summary in coverage. A summary condenses information to a greater extent than a paraphrase does. When you paraphrase, you translate the original source into your own words; thus, your paraphrase will be approximately the same length as the original. Researchers usually paraphrase material when they want to clarify it or integrate its content smoothly into their own work.

A paraphrase, then, should be written in your own words and should cite the original author. A restatement of an author's ideas that maintains the original sentence structure but substitutes a few synonyms is not an adequate paraphrase. In fact, such a restatement is plagiarism—even when the author's name is cited. Your paraphrase should contain different words and a new word order; however, the content of the original source should not be altered. In short, a paraphrase must be accurate. Any intentional misrepresentation of another person's work is unethical.

Below are some examples of problematic and successful paraphrases. The source citations in the examples are formatted according to MLA guidelines.

SOURCE

Wardhaugh, Ronald. *How Conversation Works*. Oxford: Blackwell, 1985.
    Print.

ORIGINAL

Conversation, like daily living, requires you to exhibit a considerable trust in
    others.

PROBLEMATIC PARAPHRASE

Conversation, like everyday life, requires you to show your trust in others
(Wardhaugh 5).

SUCCESSFUL PARAPHRASE

Ronald Wardhaugh compares conversation to everyday life because it requires
people to trust one another (5).

ORIGINAL

Without routine ways of doing things and in the absence of norms of behaviour, life would be too difficult, too uncertain for most of us. The routines, patterns, rituals, stereotypes even of everyday existence provide us with many of the means for coping with that existence, for reducing uncertainty and anxiety, and for providing us with the appearance of stability and continuity in the outside world. They let us get on with the actual business of living. However, many are beneath our conscious awareness; what, therefore, is of particular interest is bringing to awareness just those aspects of our lives that make living endurable (and even enjoyable) just because they are so commonly taken for granted.

PROBLEMATIC PARAPHRASE

Without habitual ways of acting and without behavioral norms, life would be too uncertain for us and thus too difficult. Our routines and rituals of everyday life provide us with many of the ways for coping with our lives, for decreasing the amount of uncertainty and anxiety we feel, and for giving us a sense of stability and continuity. They let us live our lives. But many are beneath our awareness, so what is of interest is bringing to consciousness just those parts of our lives that make life livable (and even fun) just because we generally take them for granted (Wardhaugh 21-22).

SUCCESSFUL PARAPHRASE

Ronald Wardhaugh believes that without routines and other types of conventional behavior we would find life hard because it would be too unstable and unpredictable. Our habitual ways of going about our everyday lives enable us to cope with the lack of certainty we would experience otherwise. Many of our daily routines and rituals, however, are not in our conscious awareness. Wardhaugh maintains that becoming aware of the ways we make life seem certain and continuous can be quite interesting (21-22).

Notice how the attributive tags in the successful paraphrases help the writer vary sentence structure.

Quoting Sources in Your Paper

Whenever you find a quotation that you would like to use in your paper, you should think about your reasons for including it. Quotations should be used only sparingly; therefore, make sure that when you quote a source, you do so because the language in the quotation is striking and not easily paraphrased. A pithy quotation in just the right place can help you emphasize a point you have mentioned or, alternatively, set up a point of view you wish to refute. If you overuse quotations, though, readers may decide that laziness prevented you from making sufficient effort to express your own thoughts.

TRICKS OF THE TRADE

by Keith Evans, history major

After completing a developed draft of my paper, I identify all the direct quotes I have used and critically analyze their effectiveness. I try to remember that a paraphrase will work *better* than a quote if all the quote's information is useful but couched in difficult or inexpressive language, and a summary will be preferable if the quote is taking too long to arrive at its crucial point. Only if the exact wording of the quote is what makes it so valuable should it be kept.

Using attributive tags

The direct quotations in your paper should be exact replicas of the originals. This means replicating not only the words but also punctuation and capitalization. Full sentences require quotation marks and usually commas to set them off from attributive tags. Such a tag can be placed at the beginning, middle, or end of your own sentence.

ATTRIBUTIVE TAG AT THE BEGINNING OF A SENTENCE

André Aciman reminisces, "Life begins somewhere with the scent of lavender" (1).

ATTRIBUTIVE TAG IN THE MIDDLE OF A SENTENCE

"Life," according to André Aciman, "begins somewhere with the scent of lavender" (1).

ATTRIBUTIVE TAG AT THE END OF A SENTENCE

"Life begins somewhere with the scent of lavender," writes André Aciman (1).

Including question marks or exclamation points

If you choose to quote a sentence that ends with a question mark or an exclamation point, the punctuation should be maintained, no comma is necessary.

"Why are New Yorkers always bumping into Charlie Ravioli and grabbing lunch, instead of sitting down with him and exchanging intimacies, as friends should, as people do in Paris and Rome?" asks Adam Gopnik (106).

"Incompatibility is unacceptable in mathematics! It must be resolved!" claims William Byers (29).

Quoting memorable words or phrases

You may want to quote just a memorable word or phrase. Only the word or phrase you are quoting appears within quotation marks.

Part of what Ken Wilber calls "boomeritis" is attributable to excessive emotional preoccupation with the self (27).

Modifying quotations with square brackets or ellipsis points

In order to make a quotation fit your sentence, you may need to modify the capitalization of a word. To indicate such a modification, use square brackets:

> Pollan believes that "[t]hough animals are still very much 'things' in the eyes of American law, change is in the air" (191).

You can also use square brackets to insert words needed for clarification:

> Ben Metcalf reports, "She [Sacajawea] seems to have dug up a good deal of the topsoil along the route in an effort to find edible roots with which to impress Lewis and Clark . . ." (164).

For partial quotations, as in the example above, use ellipsis points to indicate that some of the original sentence was omitted.

Using block quotations

If you want to quote an extremely long sentence or more than one sentence, you may need to use a block quotation. MLA guidelines call for a block quotation to be set off by being indented one inch from the left margin. You should use a block quotation only if the quoted material would take up more than four lines if formatted as part of the regular text of your paper. No quotation marks are used around a block quotation.

> Francis Spufford describes his experience reading *The Hobbit* as a young child:
>
> > By the time I reached *The Hobbit*'s last page, though, writing had softened, and lost the outlines of the printed alphabet, and become a transparent liquid, first viscous and sluggish, like a jelly of meaning, then ever thinner and more mobile, flowing faster and faster, until it reached me at the speed of thinking and I could not entirely distinguish the suggestions it was making from my own thoughts. (279)

APA guidelines call for using a block format when quoting forty or more words. The page number for the in-text citation follows *p.* for "page." More information about in-text citations can be found in Chapter 19.

Evaluating and Responding to Your Sources

To incorporate sources effectively, you should not only summarize, paraphrase, or quote them and document them but also respond to them. Your research log is a good place to record your initial responses (see Chapter 17). You can then craft more complete responses to your sources during the process of writing your paper.

TRICKS OF THE TRADE

by Alyse Murphy Leininger, English major

After reading eight or nine articles, I tend to forget where I read each quote or idea, so I always use several methods to annotate my sources as I'm researching. I like using different colored Post-it notes, highlighting, underlining, and taking notes in the margins. I also put the especially important quotes that I know I want to use on a separate document on the computer so I can just search through the document instead of having to read all the articles again to find what I'm looking for.

Your response to a source will be based on your evaluation of it. Readers of academic research papers expect the authors to be critical. They want to know whether facts are accurate or erroneous, whether logic is apt or weak, whether plans are comprehensive or ill-conceived, and whether conclusions are valid or invalid. Thus, researchers evaluate their sources to ensure that their readers' concerns are being addressed; however, they also critique sources to set up their own research niche. They try to show that previous research is lacking in some way in order to establish a rhetorical opportunity for their study.

Questions that can help you evaluate your sources fall into five categories: currency, coverage, reliability, reasoning, and author stance. In the following sections, you'll learn more about these categories and read brief sample notes that illustrate them.

Currency

Depending on the nature of your research, the currency of sources or of the data they present may be important to consider. Using up-to-date sources is crucial when you are writing about events that have taken place recently or issues that have arisen recently. However, if you are doing historical research, you may want to use primary sources from the period you are focusing on.

QUESTIONS ABOUT CURRENCY

▶ Do your sources and the data presented in them need to be up to date? If so, are they?

▶ If you are doing historical research, are your sources from the relevant period?

▶ Since you began your project, have events occurred that you should take into account? Do you need to find new sources?

SAMPLE NOTES ABOUT A SOURCE'S CURRENCY

According to the author, only 50 percent of all public schools have Web pages (23); however, this statistic is taken from a report published in 1997. A more recent count would likely yield a much higher percentage.

Coverage

Coverage refers to the comprehensiveness of research. The more comprehensive a study is, the more convincing are its findings. Similarly, the more examples a writer provides, the more compelling are the writer's conclusions. Claims that are based on only one instance are likely to be criticized for being merely anecdotal.

QUESTIONS ABOUT COVERAGE

▶ How many examples is the claim based on?

▶ Is this number of examples convincing or are more examples needed?

▶ Are the conclusions based on a sufficient amount of data?

SAMPLE NOTES ABOUT A SOURCE'S COVERAGE

Johnson concludes that middle-school students are expected to complete an inordinate amount of homework given their age, but he bases his conclusion on research conducted in only three schools (90). To be more convincing, Johnson would need to conduct research in more schools, preferably located in different parts of the country.

Reliability

Research, especially research based on experiments or surveys, must be reliable. Experimental results are reliable if they can be replicated in other studies—that is, if other researchers who perform the same experiment or survey get the same results. Any claims based on results supported by only one experiment are extremely tentative.

Reliability also refers to the accuracy of data reported as factual. Researchers are expected to report their findings honestly, not distorting them to support their own beliefs and not claiming ideas of others as their own. Researchers must resist the temptation to exclude information that might weaken their conclusions.

Sometimes, evaluating the publisher can provide a gauge of the reliability of the material. As a rule, reliable source material is published by reputable companies, institutions, and organizations. If you are using a book, check to see whether it was published by a university press or a commercial press. Books published by university presses are normally reviewed by experts before publication to ensure the accuracy of facts. Books published by commercial presses may or may not have received the same scrutiny, so you will have to depend on the reputation of the author and/or postpublication reviews to determine reliability. If you are using an article, remember that articles published in journals, like books published by academic presses, have been reviewed in draft form by two or three experts. Journal articles also include extensive bibliographies so that readers can examine the sources used in the research. Magazine articles, in contrast, seldom undergo expert review and rarely include documentation of sources.

If you decide to use an online source, be sure to consider the nature of its sponsor. Is it a college or university (identified by the suffix *.edu*), a government agency (*.gov*), a nonprofit organization (*.org*), a network site (*.net*), or a commercial business (*.com*)? There is no easy way to ascertain the reliability of online sources. If you are unsure about an online source, try to find out as much as you can about it. First click on links that tell you about the mission of the site sponsor and then perform an online search of the sponsor's name to see what other researchers have written about the company, institution, or organization. (See Chapter 15 for more on finding and evaluating online sources.)

QUESTIONS ABOUT RELIABILITY

▶ Could the experiment or survey that yielded these data be replicated?

▶ Are the facts reported indeed facts?

▶ Is the coverage balanced and the information relevant?

▶ Are the sources used acknowledged properly?

▶ Are there any disputes regarding the data? If so, are these disputes discussed sufficiently?

▶ Was the material published by a reputable company, institution, or organization?

SAMPLE NOTES ABOUT A SOURCE'S RELIABILITY

The author blames business for practically all of our nation's woes without providing details to bolster her argument. It is not clear how business has the impact on health care and education that she says it does.

Soundness of reasoning

When writing is logical, the reasoning is sound. Lapses in logic may be the result of using evidence that does not directly support a claim, appealing primarily (or exclusively) to the reader's emotions, or encouraging belief in false authority. Faulty logic is often due to the presence of rhetorical fallacies. These fallacies occur often enough that each one has its own name. Some of the most common rhetorical fallacies are listed below; after each is a question for you to ask yourself as you consider an author's reasoning. (See Chapter 7 for a more detailed discussion of rhetorical fallacies, with examples of each of the following.)

▶ *Ad hominem* (Latin for "toward the man himself"). Has the author criticized or attacked the author of another source based solely on his or her character, not taking into account the reasoning or evidence provided in the source?

▶ *Appeal to tradition.* Does the author support or encourage some action merely by referring to what has traditionally been done?

▶ *Bandwagon.* Does the author claim that an action is appropriate because many other people do it?

▶ *False authority.* When reporting the opinions of experts in one field, does the author incorrectly assume that they have expertise in other fields?

▶ *False cause* (sometimes referred to as *post hoc, ergo propter hoc,* a Latin phrase that translates as "after this, so because of this"). When reporting two events, does the author incorrectly believe (or suggest) that the first event caused the second event?

▶ *False dilemma* (also called the *either/or fallacy*). Does the author provide only two options when more than two exist?

▶ *Hasty generalization.* Are the author's conclusions based on too little evidence?

▶ *Oversimplification.* Does the author provide unreasonably simple solutions?

▶ *Slippery slope.* Does the author predict an unreasonable sequence of events?

Stance of the author

All authors have beliefs and values that influence their work. As you read a work as part of your research, it is your job to decide whether the author is expressing strong views because of deep commitment or because of a desire to deceive. As long as authors represent information truthfully and respectfully, they are acting ethically. If they twist facts or otherwise intentionally misrepresent ideas, they are being dishonest.

QUESTIONS ABOUT THE STANCE OF THE AUTHOR

▶ Has the author adequately conveyed information, or has the author over-simplified information or ignored relevant information?

▶ Has the author been faithful to source material, or has the author distorted information and quoted out of context?

▶ Has the author adequately supported claims, or has the author used un-supported generalizations?

SAMPLE NOTES ABOUT AN AUTHOR'S STANCE

The author believes that artificial environments are detrimental to the natural environment because they draw people away from the outdoors. In his mind, one must spend time outside in order to be an environmentalist (78). The author, though, owns a rafting service and thus is promoting his own business, which occurs in a natural environment. He fails to account for the many benefits of artificial environments, such as providing exercise opportunities to people who do not live near natural areas.

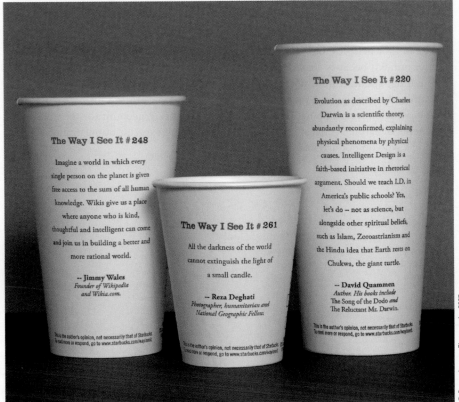

The Way I See It # 248

Imagine a world in which every single person on the planet is given free access to the sum of all human knowledge. Wikis give us a place where anyone who is kind, thoughtful and intelligent can come and join us in building a better and more rational world.

-- **Jimmy Wales**
Founder of Wikipedia and Wikia.com.

The Way I See It # 261

All the darkness of the world cannot extinguish the light of a small candle.

-- **Reza Deghati**
Photographer, humanitarian and National Geographic Fellow.

The Way I See It # 220

Evolution as described by Charles Darwin is a scientific theory, abundantly reconfirmed, explaining physical phenomena by physical causes. Intelligent Design is a faith-based initiative in rhetorical argument. Should we teach I.D. in America's public schools? Yes, let's do — not as science, but alongside other spiritual beliefs, such as Islam, Zoroastrianism and the Hindu idea that Earth rests on Chukwa, the giant turtle.

-- **David Quammen**
Author. His books include The Song of the Dodo *and* The Reluctant Mr. Darwin.

© Steven Lunetta Photography, 2007

1. The coffee cups pictured here may have been familiar to you, but you may not have thought of them as demonstrating the use of sources. How does Starbucks credit the sources of the quotations? What information is given? What does that information tell you? What information about the sources is left out?

2. Even if you haven't seen quotations on coffee cups, you've likely seen them elsewhere; they appear on everything from teabags to tee shirts, bumper stickers to baseball caps. If you wanted to place a quotation on something you own, what item and what quotation would you choose? What source information, if any, would you provide to accompany it?

Why Acknowledge Sources?

Just as you decide whether authors of sources are credible, your readers will decide whether your work is trustworthy. One of the most important ways to demonstrate credibility as an author is to acknowledge the sources from which you have drawn. Writers who do not provide adequate acknowledgment are accused of **plagiarism**, the unethical and illegal use of others' words and ideas. By acknowledging your sources, you also give your readers the information they need to find those sources in case they would like to consult them on their own. Such acknowledgment should occur in the body of your paper (in-text citations) and in the bibliography at the end of your paper (documentation). The Modern Language Association (MLA) and the American Psychological Association (APA) provide guidelines for both formatting papers and acknowledging sources. These guidelines are summarized in the following sections.

Which Sources to Cite

If the information you use is considered common knowledge, you do not have to include an in-text citation. Common knowledge is information that most educated people know and many reference books report. For example, you would not have to include an in-text citation if you mentioned that New Orleans was devastated by Hurricane Katrina. However, if you quoted or paraphrased what various politicians said about relief efforts following Katrina, you would need to include such citations.

You should include citations for all facts that are not common knowledge, statistics (whether from a text, table, graph, or chart), visuals, research findings, and quotations and paraphrases of statements made by other people. Be sure that when you acknowledge sources you include the following:

▶ The name(s) of the author(s) or, if unknown, the title of the text
▶ Page number(s)
▶ A bibliographic entry that corresponds to the in-text citation
▶ Quotation marks around material quoted exactly

Common Citation Errors

To avoid being accused of plagiarism, be on the lookout for the following errors:

▶ No author (or title) mentioned
▶ No page numbers listed
▶ No quotation marks used
▶ Paraphrase worded too similarly to the source
▶ Inaccurate paraphrase
▶ Images used with no indication of the source
▶ No bibliographic entry corresponding to the in-text citation

MLA Guidelines for In-Text Citations

If you are following the style recommended by the Modern Language Association, you will acknowledge your sources within the text of your paper by referring just to authors and page numbers. If the author's name is unknown, you use the title of the source in the in-text citation. By providing in-text citations and a works-cited list at the end of your paper, you offer your readers the opportunity to consult the sources you used.

You will likely consult a variety of sources for any research paper. The following examples are representative of the types of in-text citations you might use.

DIRECTORY OF IN-TEXT CITATIONS ACCORDING TO MLA GUIDELINES

1. Work by one to three authors 480
2. Work by four or more authors 481
3. Work by an unknown author 481
4. An entire work 481
5. A multivolume work 481
6. Two or more works by the same author(s) 481
7. Two or more works by different authors with the same last name 481
8. Work by a corporate or government author 482
9. Indirect source 482
10. Work in an anthology 482
11. Poem 482
12. Drama 482
13. Bible 482
14. Two or more works in one parenthetical citation 482
15. Material from the Internet 483

---

1.   Work by one to three authors

Although the state of New York publishes a booklet of driving rules, **Katha Pollit** has found no books on "the art of driving" (**217**).

No books exist on "the art of driving" (**Pollit 217**).

Other researchers, such as **Steven Reiss and James Wiltz**, rely on tools like surveys to explain why we watch reality television (**734-36**).

Survey results can help us understand why we watch reality television (**Reiss and Wiltz 734-36**).

Citizens passed the bond issue in 2004, even though they originally voted it down in 2001 (**Jacobs, Manzow, and Holst 120**).

The authors' last names can be placed in the text or within parentheses with the page number. The parenthetical citation should appear as close as possible to the information documented—usually at the end of the sentence or after any quotation marks. When citing a range of page numbers of three digits, do not repeat the hundreds' digit for the higher number: 201-97.

2. Work by four or more authors

When citing parenthetically a source by more than three authors, you can either include all the authors' last names or provide just the first author's last name followed by the abbreviation *et al.* (Latin for "and others"): (Stafford, Suzuki, Li, and Brown 67) or (Stafford et al. 67). The abbreviation *et al.* should not be underlined or italicized in citations.

3. Work by an unknown author

The Tehuelche people left their handprints on the walls of a cave, now called Cave of the Hands (**"Hands of Time"** 124).

If the author is unknown, use the title of the work in place of the author's name. If the title is long, shorten it, beginning with the first word used in the corresponding works-cited entry ("Wandering" for "Wandering with Cameras in the Himalaya"). If you use the title in the text, however, you do not have to place it in the parenthetical reference.

4. An entire work

Using literary examples, **Alain de Botton** explores the reasons people decide to travel.

Notice that no page numbers are necessary when an entire work is cited.

5. A multivolume work

President Truman asked that all soldiers be treated equally (**Merrill 11: 741**).

The volume number and page number(s) are separated by a colon.

6. Two or more works by the same author(s)

Kress refers to the kinds of interpretive skills required of children who play video games to argue that we should recognize multiple forms of reading, not just those already encouraged in our school systems (*Literacy* 174).

Marianne Celce-Murcia and Diane Larsen-Freeman claim that grammar involves three dimensions (*Grammar Book* 4).

To distinguish one work from another, include a title. If the title is long (such as *Literacy in the New Media Age*), shorten it, beginning with the first word used in the corresponding works-cited entry.

7. Two or more works by different authors with the same last name

If the military were to use solely conventional weapons, the draft would likely be reinstated (**E. Scarry** 241).

To distinguish one author from another, use their initials. If the initials are the same, spell out their first names.

8. Work by a corporate or government author

Strawbale constructions are now popular across the nation (**Natl. Ecobuilders Group 2**).

Provide the name of the corporate or government author and a page reference. You may use common abbreviations for terms in the name—for example, *Assn.* for "Association" and *Natl.* for "National."

9. Indirect source

According to **Sir George Dasent**, a reader "must be satisfied with the soup that is set before him, and not desire to see the bones of the ox out of which it has been boiled" (**qtd. in Shippey 289**).

Use the abbreviation *qtd.* to indicate that you found the quotation in another source.

10. Work in an anthology

"Good cooking," claims **Jane Kramer**, "is much easier to master than good writing" (**153**).

Either in the text or within parentheses with the page number, use the name of the author of the particular section (chapter, essay, or article) you are citing, not the editor of the entire book, unless they are the same.

11. Poem

The final sentence in **Philip Levine's** "Homecoming" is framed by conditional clauses: "If we're quiet / . . . if the place had a spirit" (**38-43**).

Instead of page numbers, provide line numbers, preceded by *line(s)* for the first citation; use numbers only for subsequent citations.

12. Drama

After some hesitation, the messenger tells Macbeth what he saw: "As I did stand my watch upon the hill / I looked toward Birnam and anon methought / The wood began to move" (**5.5.35-37**).

Instead of page numbers, indicate act, scene, and line numbers.

13. Bible

The image of seeds covering the sidewalk reminded her of the parable in which a seed falls on stony ground (**Matt. 13.18-23**).

Identify the book of the Bible (using the conventional abbreviation) and, instead of page numbers, provide chapter and verse(s).

14. Two or more works in one parenthetical citation

Usage issues are discussed in both academic and popular periodicals (**Bex and Watts 5; Lippi-Green 53**).

Use a semicolon to separate citations.

15. Material from the Internet

Alston describes three types of rubrics that teachers can use to evaluate student writing (**pars. 2-15**).

McGowan finds one possible cause of tensions between science and religion in "our cultural terror of curiosity."

If an online publication numbers pages, paragraphs, or screens, provide those numbers in the citation. Precede paragraph numbers with *par.* or *pars.* and screen numbers with *screen* or *screens*. If the source does not number pages, paragraphs, or screens, refer to the entire work in your text by citing the author.

MLA Guidelines for Documenting Works Cited

To provide readers with the information they need to find all the sources you have used in your paper, you must prepare a bibliography. According to MLA guidelines, your bibliography should be entitled *Works Cited* (not in italics). It should contain an entry for every source you cite in your text, and, conversely, every bibliographic entry you list should have a corresponding in-text citation. (If you want to include entries for works that you consulted but did not cite in your paper, the bibliography should be entitled *Works Consulted.*)

The guidelines in the *MLA Handbook for Writers of Research Papers,* 7th edition, require that titles of books, magazines, Web sites, and other sources be italicized. MLA format also requires identification of the medium of publication at the end of each entry—for example, *Print, Web, CD-ROM, LP, Television,* or *Radio,* none of which are italicized. Alphabetize the entries in your works-cited list according to the author's (or the first author's) last name. When the author is unknown, alphabetize according to title. Use the first major word of the title; in other words, ignore any initial article (*a, an,* or *the*). If a source was written by four or more authors, you have two options: either list all the authors' names or provide just the first author's name followed by the abbreviation *et al.* (not italicized). Many people prefer to list all the authors so that their contributions are recognized equally.

Double-space the entire works-cited list. The first line of each entry begins flush with the left margin, and subsequent lines are indented one-half inch. If you have used more than one work by the same author (or team of authors), alphabetize the entries according to title. For the first entry, provide the author's name; for any subsequent entries, substitute three hyphens (---).

Rodriguez, Richard. *Brown: The Last Discovery of America.* New York: Viking, 2002. Print.

---. *Hunger of Memory: The Education of Richard Rodriguez.* New York: Bantam, 1982. Print.

If two or more entries have the same first author, alphabetize the entries according to the second author's last name.

Bailey, Guy, and Natalie Maynor. "The Divergence Controversy." *American Speech* 64.1 (1989): 12-39. Print.

Bailey, Guy, and Jan Tillery. "Southern American English." *American Language Review* 4.4 (2000): 27-29. Print.

For more details on various types of sources, use the following directory to find relevant sections. For an example of a works-cited list, see page 510. If you would like to use a checklist to help ensure that you have followed MLA guidelines, see page 500.

Books

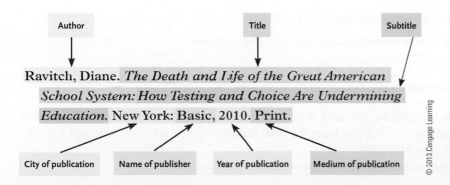

Author

Title

Subtitle

Ravitch, Diane. *The Death and Life of the Great American School System: How Testing and Choice Are Undermining Education.* New York: Basic, 2010. Print.

City of publication

Name of publisher

Year of publication

Medium of publication

© 2013 Cengage Learning

Research

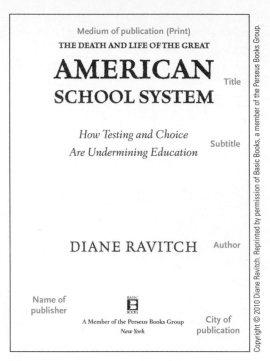

Medium of publication (Print)

THE DEATH AND LIFE OF THE GREAT

AMERICAN Title
SCHOOL SYSTEM

How Testing and Choice Subtitle
Are Undermining Education

DIANE RAVITCH Author

Name of
publisher

BASIC
B BOOKS

A Member of the Perseus Books Group City of
New York publication

Copyright © 2010 Diane Ravitch. Reprinted by permission of Basic Books, a member of the Perseus Books Group.

Copyright © 2010 by Diane Ravitch Year of
Published by Basic Books, publication
A Member of the Perseus Books Group

All rights reserved. Printed in the United States of America. No part of this book may
be reproduced in any manner whatsoever without written permission except in the
case of brief quotations embodied in critical articles and reviews. For information,
address Basic Books, 387 Park Avenue South, New York, NY 10016-8810.

Books published by Basic Books are available at special discounts for bulk purchases
in the United States by corporations, institutions, and other organizations. For more
information, please contact the Special Markets Department at the Perseus Books
Group, 2300 Chestnut Street, Suite 200, Philadelphia, PA 19103, or call
(800) 810-4145, ext. 5000, or e-mail special.markets@perseusbooks.com.

Designed by Pauline Brown

Library of Congress Cataloging-in-Publication Data

Ravitch, Diane.
The death and life of the great American school system : how testing and choice are
undermining education / Diane Ravitch.
    p. cm.
Includes bibliographical references and index.
ISBN 978-0-465-01491-0 (alk. paper)
1. Public schools—United States. 2. Educational accountability—United States.
3. Educational tests and measurements—United States. 4. School choice—United
States. I. Title.
LA217.2.R38 2009
379.1—dc22

2009050406

10 9 8

Copyright © 2010 Diane Ravitch. Reprinted by permission of Basic Books, a member of the Perseus Books Group.

Title page of *The Death and Life of the
Great American School System.*

Copyright page of *The Death and Life of
the Great American School System.*

Most of the information you need for a works-cited entry can be found on a
book's title page. If you cannot find the date of publication on the title page,
turn to the copyright page. Works-cited entries for books generally include three
units of information: author, title, and publication data.

Author The author's last name is given first. Use a comma to separate the last
name from the first, and place a period at the end of this unit of information.
When two or more authors are listed, only the first author's name is inverted. For
a work by more than three authors, either list all the authors' names or provide just
the first author's name followed by the abbreviation *et al.* (not italicized).

Atherton, Lewis.

Blyth, Carl, Sigrid Becktenwald, and Jenny Wang.

Rand, George, Peter Mathis, Sali Hudson, and Victor Singler.

OR

Rand, George, et al.

Title Include the title and, if there is one, the subtitle of the book. Use a colon
to separate the subtitle from the title. *Italicize* every part of the title and subtitle,
including any colon.

Visual Explanations: Images and Quantities, Evidence and Narrative.

Research

Publication data For the third unit of information, list the city of publication, the publisher's name, the copyright date, and the medium of publication you consulted (in this case, *Print*). Place a colon between the city of publication and the publisher's name, a comma between the publisher's name and the copyright date, a period between the date and the medium of publication, and a period at the end of this unit of information. When more than one city appears on the title page, use only the first one listed. You can usually shorten a publisher's name by using the principal name (*Random* for Random House or *Knopf* for Alfred A. Knopf) or by using the abbreviation *UP* for University Press (*Yale UP* for Yale University Press).

1. Book by one author

You, Xiaoye. *Writing in the Devil's Tongue: A History of English Composition in China.*
 Carbondale: Southern Illinois UP, 2009. Print.

2. Book by two or three authors

Gies, Joseph, and Frances Gies. *Life in a Medieval City.* New York: Harper, 1981. Print.

List the authors' names in the order in which they appear on the title page, not in alphabetical order. Include full names for all of the authors, even if they have the same last name. Invert the name of only the first author.

3. Book by four or more authors

Belenky, Mary, Blythe Clincy, Nancy Goldberger, and Jill Tarule. *Women's Ways of Knowing:*
 The Development of Self, Voice, and Mind. New York: Basic, 1986. Print.

Belenky, Mary, et al. *Women's Ways of Knowing: The Development of Self, Voice, and Mind.* New York:
 Basic, 1986. Print.

Provide the names of all the authors in the order in which they appear on the title page, with the first author's name inverted, or list only the first author's name, followed by a comma and *et al.*

4. Book by a corporate author

American Heart Association. *The New American Heart Association Cookbook.* 6th ed. New York:
 Potter, 2001. Print.

Omit any article (*a, an,* or *the*) that begins the name of a corporate author, and alphabetize the entry in the works-cited list according to the first major word of the corporate author's name.

5. Book by an anonymous author

Primary Colors: A Novel of Politics. New York: Warner, 1996. Print.

Alphabetize the entry according to the first major word in the title of the work.

6. Book with an author and an editor

Dickens, Charles. *Pickwick Papers*. Ed. Malcolm Andrews. Boston: Tuttle, 1997. Print.

Begin the entry with the author's name. Place the editor's name after the title of the book, preceded by *Ed.* for "edited by."

7. Book with an editor instead of an author

Baxter, Leslie A., and Dawn O. Braithwaite, eds. *Engaging Theories in Interpersonal Communication: Multiple Perspectives*. Los Angeles: SAGE, 2008. Print.

Begin the entry with the name(s) of the editor(s), using the abbreviation *ed.* for "editor" or *eds.* for "editors."

8. Second or subsequent edition

Cameron, Rondo, and Larry Neal. *A Concise Economic History of the World: From Paleolithic Times to the Present*. 4th ed. New York: Oxford UP, 2003. Print.

After the title, place the number of the edition in its ordinal form, followed by *ed.* for "edition." Note that the letters *th* following the number appear in regular type, not as a superscript.

9. Introduction, preface, foreword, or afterword to a book

Peri, Yoram. Afterword. *The Rabin Memoirs*. By Yitzhak Rabin. Berkeley: U of California P, 1996. 422-32. Print.

Begin the entry with the name of the author of the introduction, preface, foreword, or afterword, followed by the name of the part being cited (e.g., *Afterword*). If the part being cited has a title, include the title in quotation marks between the author's name and the name of the part being cited. Provide the name of the author of the book, preceded by *By,* after the title of the book. Provide the page number(s) of the part being cited after the publication information and complete the entry with the medium of publication.

10. Anthology

Ramazani, Jahan, Robert O'Clair, and Richard Ellman, eds. *The Norton Anthology of Modern and Contemporary Poetry*. 3rd ed. New York: Norton, 2003. Print.

The entry begins with the anthology's editor(s), with the first (or only) editor's name inverted. Use the abbreviation *ed.* for "editor" or *eds.* for "editors."

11. Single work from an anthology

Muños, Gabriel Trujillo. "Once Upon a Time on the Border." *How I Learned English*. Ed. Tom Miller. Washington, DC: Natl. Geographic Soc., 2007. 141-48. Print.

Begin the entry with the name of the author of the work you are citing, not the name of the anthology's editor. The title of the work appears in quotation marks between the author's name and the title of the anthology. The editor's name is preceded by *Ed.* for "Edited by." (Note that because *Ed.* does not stand for "Editor," it is not changed to *Eds.* when a work has multiple editors, as you do when listing editors before the title.) After the publication information, include the numbers of the pages on which the work appears and conclude with the medium of publication.

12. Two or more works from the same anthology

Miller, Tom, ed. *How I Learned English.* Washington, DC: National Geographic, 2007. Print.

Montero, Mayra. "How I Learned English . . . or Did I?" Miller 221-25.

Padilla, Ignacio. "El Dobbing and My English." Miller 237-41.

When citing more than one work from the same anthology, include an entry for the entire anthology as well as entries for the individual works. In entries for individual works, list the names of the author(s) and the editor(s) and the title of the work, but not the title of the anthology. Then specify the page or range of pages on which the work appears. Note that only the first, complete entry ends with the medium of publication.

13. Book with a title within the title

Koon, Helene Wickham. *Twentieth Century Interpretations of* Death of a Salesman:
    A Collection of Critical Essays. Englewood Cliffs: Prentice, 1983. Print.

When an italicized title includes the title of another work that would normally be italicized, do not italicize the embedded title. If the embedded title normally requires quotation marks, it should be italicized as well as enclosed in quotation marks.

14. Translated book

Rilke, Rainer Maria. *Duino Elegies.* Trans. David Young. New York: Norton, 1978. Print.

The translator's name appears after the book title, preceded by *Trans.* However, if the material cited in your paper refers primarily to the translator's comments rather than to the translated text, the entry should appear as follows:

Young, David, trans. *Duino Elegies.* By Rainer Maria Rilke. New York: Norton, 1978. Print.

15. Republished book

Alcott, Louisa May. *Work: A Story of Experience.* 1873. Harmondsworth, Eng.: Penguin, 1995. Print.

Provide the publication date of the original work after the title.

16. Multivolume work

Banks, Lynne Reid. *The Indian in the Cupboard.* Vol. 3. New York: Morrow, 1994. Print.

Feynman, Richard Phillips, Robert B. Leighton, and Matthew L. Sands. *The Feynman Lectures on Physics.* 3 vols. Boston: Addison, 1989. Print.

Provide only the specific volume number (e.g., *Vol. 3*) after the title if you cite material from one volume. Provide the total number of volumes if you cite material from more than one volume.

17. Book in a series

Restle, David, and Dietmar Zaefferer, eds. *Sounds and Systems*. Berlin: de Gruyter, 2002. Print.
> Trends in Linguistics 141.

After the medium of publication at the end of the entry, provide the name of the series and the series number, separated by a period.

Articles

ARTICLE IN A JOURNAL

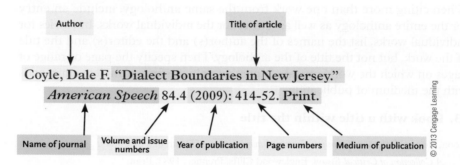

You can generally find the name of the journal, the volume and issue numbers, and the year of publication on the cover of the journal. Sometimes this information is also included in the journal's page headers or footers. To find the title of the article, the author's name, and the page numbers, you'll need to locate the article within the journal.

ARTICLE IN A MAGAZINE

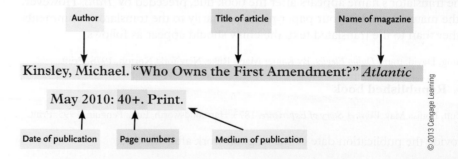

To find the name of the magazine and the date of publication (ignore volume and issue numbers), look on the cover of the magazine. Sometimes this information is also included in the magazine's page headers or footers. To find the title of the article, the author's name, and the page numbers, you'll have to look at the article itself. If the article is not printed on consecutive pages, as often happens in magazines, give the number of the first page, followed by a plus sign.

Works-cited entries for articles generally include three units of information: author, title of article, and publication data.

Author List the author, last name first. Use a comma to separate the last name from the first, and place a period at the end of this unit of information. If there is more than one author, see the information given for book entries on pages 485–487.

Title of article Include the title and, if there is one, the subtitle of the article. Use a colon to separate the subtitle from the title. Place the entire title within quotation marks, including the period that marks the end of the unit of information.

"Sounding Cajun: The Rhetorical Use of Dialect in Speech and Writing."

Publication data The publication data that you provide depends on the type of periodical in which the article appeared. However, for all entries, include the title of the periodical (italicized), the date of publication, the page numbers of the article, and the medium of publication. When citing a range of three-digit page numbers, do not repeat the hundreds' digit (for example, write 154-59). If you are using a journal, include the volume and issue numbers as well. Next, provide the date of publication. For journals, put the year of publication within parentheses. For magazines, give the day, month (all months except May, June, and July are abbreviated to three letters), and year. No punctuation sepa-

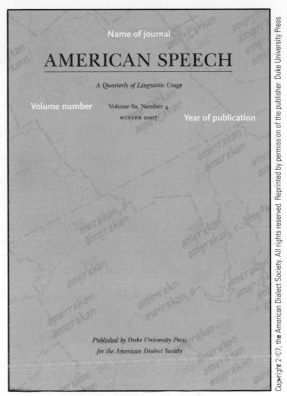

Cover of an academic journal.

rates the title and the date of publication. After the date of publication, place a colon and then the page numbers for the article. Conclude with the medium of publication. Note that the current MLA guidelines no longer make a distinction between journals that are numbered continuously (for example, Vol. 1 ends on page 208, and Vol. 2 starts on page 209) and those numbered separately (that is, each volume starts on page 1). No matter how the journal is paginated, all entries must contain volume and issue numbers. One exception is journals with issue numbers only; simply cite the issue number alone as though it were a volume number.

18. Article in a journal

Burt, Susan Meredith. "Solicitudes in American English." *International Journal of Applied Linguistics* 13.1 (2003): 78-95. Print.

Place the title of the article in quotation marks between the author's name and the name of the journal. Provide the volume and issue numbers separated by a period, the year of publication (in parentheses and followed by a colon), the range of pages on which the article appears, and the medium of publication.

19. Article in a monthly magazine

Moran, Thomas E. "Just for Kicks Soccer Program." *Exceptional Parent* Feb. 2004: 36-37. Print.

Provide the publication month and year after the title of the magazine. Abbreviate the names of all months except May, June, and July.

20. Article in a weekly magazine or newspaper

Gonzalez, Jennifer. "Community-College Professor, Visiting Yale, Explores the Ethics of Treating
 Animals." *Chronicle of Higher Education* 23 Apr. 2010: A4. Print.

Provide the day, month, and year of publication after the title of the publication.

21. Article in a daily newspaper

Lewin, Tamara. "Teenage Insults, Scrawled on Web, Not on Walls." *New York Times*
 6 May 2010: A1+. Print.

Provide the day, month, and year of publication. If the article does not appear
on consecutive pages, add a plus sign after the first page number.

22. Unsigned article

"Beware the Herd." *Newsweek* 8 Mar. 2004: 61. Print.

Alphabetize the entry according to the first major word in the title, ignoring any
article (*a, an,* or *the*).

23. Editorial in a newspaper or magazine

Marcus, Ruth. "In Arizona, Election Reform's Surprising Consequences." Editorial. *Washington
 Post* 5 May 2010: A21. Print.

Place the word *Editorial,* followed by a period, between the title of the editorial
and the name of the newspaper or magazine.

24. Book or film review

Morgenstern, Joe. "See Spot Sing and Dance: Dog Cartoon 'Teacher's Pet' Has Enough Bite
 for Adults." Rev. of *Teacher's Pet*, dir. Timothy Björklund. *Wall Street Journal* 16 Jan. 2004:
 W1+. Print.

Place the reviewer's name first, followed by the title of the review (if any) in quotation
marks. Next, provide the title of the work reviewed, preceded by *Rev. of* for "Review
of," and then mention the name of the author, translator, editor, or director of the
original work. The word *by* precedes an author's name, *trans.* precedes a translator's
name, *ed.* precedes an editor's name, and *dir.* precedes a director's name.

Other print sources

25. Letter to the editor

Willens, Peggy A. Letter. *New York Times* 5 May 2010: A30. Print.

Following the author's name, insert *Letter.* Then provide the name of the periodical, the date of publication, the page number, and the medium of publication.

26. Encyclopedia entry

"Heckelphone." *The Encyclopedia Americana.* 2001. Print.

Begin with the title of the entry, unless an author's name is provided. Provide the edition number (if any) and the year of publication after the title of the encyclopedia. Conclude with the medium of publication. Other publication information is unnecessary for familiar reference books.

27. Dictionary entry

"Foolscap." Def. 3. *Merriam-Webster's Collegiate Dictionary.* 11th ed. 2003. Print.

A dictionary entry is documented similarly to an encyclopedia entry. If the definition is one of several listed for the word, provide the definition number or letter, preceded by *Def.* for "Definition."

28. Government publication

United States. Executive Office of the President and Council of Economic Advisors. *Economic Report of the President.* Washington: GPO, 2010. Print.

If no author is provided, list the name of the government (e.g., *United States, Montana,* or *New York City*), followed by the name of the agency issuing the publication.

29. Pamphlet or bulletin

Ten Ways to Be a Better Dad. Gaithersburg: Natl. Fatherhood Inst., 2000. Print.

An entry for a pamphlet is similar to one for a book. List the author's name first, if an author is identified.

30. Dissertation

Eves, Rosalyn Collings. "Mapping Rhetorical Frontiers: Women's Spatial Rhetorics in the Nineteenth-Century American West." Diss. Penn State U, 2008. Print.

If the dissertation has been published, proceed as for a book, but add *Diss.* for "Dissertation" after the title, followed by the name of the institution that issued the degree and the year the degree was granted. If the dissertation has not been published, enclose the title of the dissertation in quotation marks rather than italicizing it.

Live performances and recordings

31. Play performance

Roulette. By Paul Weitz. Dir. Tripp Cullmann. John Houseman Theater, New York. 9 Feb. 2004. Performance.

Begin with the title of the play (italicized), followed by the names of key contributors such as author, director, performers, and/or translator. The location of the performance (the theater and the city), the date of the performance, and the word *Performance* complete the entry.

32. Lecture or presentation

Joseph, Peniel. "The 1960's, Black History, and the Role of the NC A&T Four." Gibbs Lecture. General Classroom Building, North Carolina A&T State University, Greensboro. 5 Apr. 2010. Lecture.

Ryken, Leland. Class lecture. English 216. Breyer 103, Wheaton College, Wheaton. 4 Feb. 2010. Lecture.

Provide the name of the speaker, the title of the lecture (if any) in quotation marks, the sponsoring organization (if applicable), the location and date of the lecture or presentation, and the form of delivery. If the lecture or presentation is untitled, provide a description after the name of the speaker.

33. Interview

Blauwkamp, Joan. Telephone interview. 14 Mar. 2010.

Kotapish, Dawn. Personal interview. 3 Jan. 2009.

Provide the name of the interviewee, a description of the type of interview conducted (e.g., *Telephone interview* or *Personal interview*), and the date on which the interview occurred.

34. Film

Bus Stop. Dir. Joshua Logan. Twentieth Century Fox, 1956. Film.

Monroe, Marilyn, perf. *Bus Stop*. Screenplay by George Axelrod. Dir. Joshua Logan. Twentieth Century Fox, 1956. Film.

Give the title of the film, the name of the director (preceded by *Dir.* for "Directed by"), the distributor, the year of release, and the medium consulted. To highlight the contribution of a particular individual, start with the individual's name, followed by an indication of the nature of the contribution, abbreviated if possible. For example, *perf.* means "performer."

35. Radio or television program

"Blue Blood and Beans." Narr. Garrison Keillor. *A Prairie Home Companion*. Natl. Public Radio. KJZZ, Phoenix. 21 Feb. 2004. Radio.

Simon, Scott, narr. *Affluenza*. Prod. John de Graaf and Vivia Boe. PBS. KCTS, Seattle. 2 July 1998. Television.

Provide the title of the segment (in quotation marks), the title of the program (italicized), the name of the network, the call letters and city of the broadcasting station, the date of the broadcast, and the medium of reception. Information such as the name of an author, performer, director, or narrator may appear after the title of the segment. When referring especially to the contribution of a specific individual, however, place the individual's name and an abbreviated identification of the contribution before the title.

36. Sound recording or compact disc

The White Stripes. *Under Great White Northern Lights*. Warner Bros., 2010. CD.

Begin with the name of the performer, composer, or conductor, depending on which you prefer to emphasize. Then provide the title of the recording, the manufacturer's name, the date of the recording, and the medium (in this case, *CD*). Other types of media include *LP, Audiocassette,* and *DVD*. When referring to an individual song, provide its name in quotation marks after the name of the performer, composer, or conductor. Note that the above entry should be alphabetized as though it begins with *w*, not *t*.

Images

37. Work of art

Vermeer, Johannes. *Woman Holding a Balance*. 1664. Oil on canvas. Natl. Gallery of Art, Washington.

Begin with the artist's name and the title of the work (italicized). Then provide the date the work was created (if not available, use the abbreviation *n.d.* for "no date") and the medium of composition. End your citation with the location where the artwork is housed (that is, the name of the museum or institution that owns the piece) and the city in which it is located.

38. Photograph

Lange, Dorothea. *Migrant Mother*. 1936. Photograph. Prints and Photographs Div., Lib. of Cong., Washington.

Provide the photographer's name, the title of the work (italicized), the medium of composition, and the name and location of the institution that houses the work. If the photograph has no title, briefly describe its subject.

39. Cartoon or comic strip

Cheney, Tom. "Back Page by Tom Cheney." Cartoon. *New Yorker* 12 Jan. 2004: 88. Print.

The description *Cartoon* appears before the title of the publication.

40. Advertisement

McCormick Pure Vanilla Extract. Advertisement. *Cooking Light* Mar. 2004: 177. Print.

Identify the item being advertised, and then include the description *Advertisement* before the usual publication information.

41. Map or chart

Scottsdale and Vicinity. Map. Chicago: Rand, 2000. Print.

Treat the map or chart as you would an anonymous book, including the description *Map* or *Chart* before the usual publication information.

Online sources and databases

Current MLA guidelines do not require you to include an Internet address (URL) if your readers can easily locate the online source by searching for the author's name and the title of the work. For cases in which your readers cannot easily locate a source, provide the complete URL (between angle brackets) following the date of access and a period. The closing angle bracket should also be followed by a period.

JOURNAL ARTICLE FROM A LIBRARY SUBSCRIPTION SERVICE

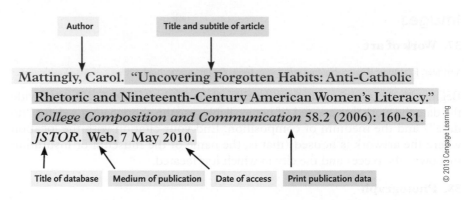

You can usually find much of the information you will need for your works-cited entry at the beginning of the article. Works-cited entries for online periodicals generally include six units of information: author, title (and subtitle, if any) of the article, print publication data, electronic publication data, medium of publication, and date of access (URL if needed).

Author The author's name is given, last name first. Use a comma to separate the last name from the first, and place a period at the end of this unit of information. If there is more than one author, see the information given for book entries on pages 485–487.

Title of article Include the title and, if there is one, the subtitle of the article. Use a colon to separate the subtitle from the title. Place the entire title within quotation marks, including the period that marks the end of the unit of information.

Print publication data The publication data that you provide depends on the type of periodical in which the article appeared. For detailed information, see the discussion of publication data for periodicals on page 491.

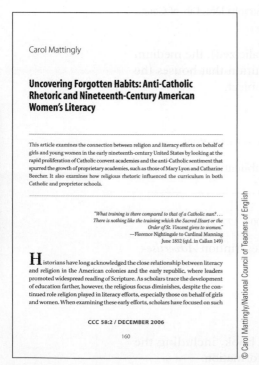

First page of article in an online journal.

Electronic publication data If possible, include the name of the database in which the periodical can be found.

Medium of publication The medium of publication identifies the medium consulted, in this case, Web.

Date of access (with URL if needed) The date of access is the date on which you consulted a source. It can be found on any printout of the material you used. For cases in which your readers cannot easily locate a source, place the URL—the Internet address at which the source is located—between angle brackets (< >). Be sure to include the access-mode identifier (*http*, *ftp*, or *telnet*) and all punctuation. If the address must continue onto a second line, break it after a slash. If the URL is excessively long or complicated (more than one full line), provide just the search page you used to find the article. If there is no search page, use the site's home page.

Electronic sources vary significantly; thus, as you prepare your works-cited list, you'll need to follow the models shown here closely. On occasion, you may not be able to find all the information mentioned. In such cases, provide as much of the information as you can. When no publication date is available, use the abbreviation *n.d.* for "no date." When no publisher or sponsor is available, use *N.p.* for "No publisher."

42. Online book

Austen, Jane. *Emma.* London: Murray, 1815. *Gutenberg.net.* 1994. Web. 20 Nov. 2009.

Begin with the information you always provide for an entry for a book (author, title, and publication information, if available). Then provide as much of the following electronic publication information as possible: title of the Internet site (italicized), version number (if provided), date of electronic publication, and name of any sponsoring organization. Conclude with the medium of publication and the date of access.

43. Article in an online journal

Ballard, Karen. "Patient Safety: A Shared Responsibility." *NursingWorld* 8.3 (2003). Web. 15 Jan. 2010.

Begin with the information you provide for an entry for an article in a print journal, and conclude with the medium of publication and the date of access.

44. Article in an online magazine

Cloud, John. "The Gurus of YouTube." *Time.* Time, 16 Dec. 2006. Web. 18 Dec. 2009.

Begin with the information you provide for an entry for an article in a print magazine, adding the name of any sponsor. Conclude with the medium of publication and the date of access.

45. Article in an online newspaper

Connelly, Joel. "Lessons from the Gulf Oil Spill." *Seattle Post-Intelligencer.* Hearst Seattle Media, 3 May 2010. Web. 7 May 2010.

Research

Begin with the information you provide for an entry for an article in a print newspaper, adding the name of any sponsor before the date. Conclude with the medium of publication and the date of access.

46. Review in an online newspaper

Safire, William. "Not Peace, but a Sword." Rev. of *The Passion of the Christ*, dir. Mel Gibson. *New York Times*. New York Times, 1 Mar. 2004. Web. 6 Sept. 2009.

Begin with the information you provide for an entry for a review in a print newspaper, adding the name of any sponsor before the date. Conclude with the medium of publication and the date of access.

47. Article from a library subscription service

Fenn, Donna. "Can the Boss Make the Grade?" *Inc.* May 1996: n. pag. *ABI/INFORM*. Web. 11 Mar. 2010.

After providing the usual information for the article, include the italicized name of the database, the medium consulted, and the date of access. If a complete range of pages is not known for the original publication, use *n. pag.*

48. Online work of art

Picasso, Pablo. *Guitar*. 1912. Museum of Mod. Art, New York. Web. 17 Feb. 2010.

Begin with the information you always provide in an entry for a work of art and conclude with the medium of publication and the date of access. Note that the medium of composition is omitted.

49. Online government publication

United States. Dept. of Health and Human Services. *2008 Physical Activity Guidelines for Americans*. 22 Sept. 2008. Web. 13 Apr. 2010.

Begin with the information you provide for an entry for a print government publication and conclude with the publication medium and the date of access.

50. Web site

OMB Watch. OMB Watch, 2010. Web. 19 Apr. 2010.

Provide the title of the site (italicized), the version number (if provided), the name of any sponsoring organization, and the date of publication or latest update. Conclude with the medium of publication and the date of access.

51. Section of a Web site

"Creating a 21st Century Environmental Right-to-Know Agenda." *OMB Watch*. OMB Watch, 2010. Web. 20 Apr. 2010.

Provide the information you include in an entry for an entire Web site (see item 50), but place the title of the section you are citing in quotation marks before the title of the Web site. If the section has an author, list his or her name (inverted) first.

52. Course home page

Owens, Kalyn. General Chemistry. Course home page. Jan.-Mar. 2010. Chemistry Dept., Central
    Washington U. Web. 18 Feb. 2010.

List the instructor's name (inverted), the course title, the description *Course home page*, the course dates, the name of the department offering the course, and the name of the institution. Conclude with the medium consulted and the date of access.

53. Podcast

DiMeo, Nate. "The Sisters Fox." *The Memory Palace*. 12 Mar. 2010. Web. 14 Apr. 2010.

Provide the information you include in an entry for a section of a Web site (see item 51). List the producer's name first, if available.

54. Online video clip

First+Main Media. *Built to Last*. 7 May 2009. *YouTube*. Web. 8 May 2010.

Provide the name of the production company, the title of the video clip, the date it appeared online, the online venue, the medium of delivery, and the access date.

55. E-mail message

Kivett, George. "Hydrogen Fuel Cell Technology." Message to Theodore Ellis. 28 Jan. 2010. E-mail.

Give the name of the author of the message, the title (taken from the subject line of the message and enclosed in quotation marks), a description of the communication (including the recipient's name), the date the message was sent, and the medium of transmission.

56. Posting to a discussion group or forum

Everett, Rebecca. "Searching for a Perfect Life 'In That House'." Online posting. 5 May 2010.
    Talk of the Nation. Web. 8 May 2010.

Provide the name of the author (inverted) and the title of the posting (in quotation marks), followed by the description *Online posting*. Include the date the material was posted, the name of the forum, the medium consulted, and the date of your access.

57. Synchronous communication

Bruckman, Amy. 8th Birthday Symposium. "Educational MOOs: State of the Art." 17 Jan. 2001.
    MediaMOO. Web. 10 Mar. 2005.

Provide the name of the writer (inverted) and a description of the discussion. Indicate any discussion title in quotation marks. The name of the forum appears between the date of the communication and the medium. The entry concludes with your date of access.

58. CD-ROM

Ultimate Human Body. Camberwell, Austral.: DK, 2002. CD-ROM.

Provide all the information you include for a print book. Add a description of the medium, followed by a period, after the publication information.

CHECKING OVER A WORKS-CITED LIST

✓ Is the title, *Works Cited* (not italicized), centered one inch from the top of the page? Is the first letter of each word capitalized?

✓ Is the entire list double-spaced?

✓ Are initial lines of entries flush with the left margin and subsequent lines indented one-half inch?

✓ Is there a works-cited entry for each in-text citation? Is there an in-text citation for each works-cited entry?

✓ Are the entries alphabetized according to the first author's last name? If the author of an entry is unknown, is the entry alphabetized according to title (ignoring any initial *a, an,* or *the*)?

✓ If the list contains two or more entries by the same author, are the entries alphabetized according to title? After the author's full name is used for the first entry, are three hyphens substituted for the name in subsequent entries?

✓ Are book and periodical titles italicized? Are names of databases italicized?

✓ Are quotation marks used to indicate article titles?

✓ Are URLs (when needed) enclosed in angle brackets?

Sample MLA Research Paper

The MLA recommends omitting a title page (unless your instructor requires one) and instead providing the identification on the first page of the paper. One inch from the top, on the left-hand side of the page, list your name, the name of the instructor, the name of the course, and the date—all double-spaced. Below these lines, center the title of the paper, which is in plain type (no italics, underlining, or boldface). On the right-hand side of each page, one-half inch from the top, use your last name and the page number as a header. Double-space the text throughout the paper, and use one-inch margins on the sides and bottom. Indent every paragraph (including the first one) one-half inch.

The running head includes the author's last name and the page number.

Hannah Lewis

Professor Adams

Media and Politics, English 305

The heading and the rest of the paper are double-spaced.

1 March 2010

The Daily Show with Jon Stewart: Contextualizing, Criticizing, and Mobilizing

The title of the paper is centered.

> *Crossfire* or *Hardball?* Which is funnier? Which is more soul-crushing,
>
> do you mean? Both are equally dispiriting.... The whole idea
>
> that political discourse has degenerated into shows that have to
>
> be entitled *Crossfire* and *Hardball* ... is mind-boggling. *Crossfire*,
>
> especially, is completely an apropos name. It's what innocent
>
> bystanders are caught in when gangs are fighting. (Stewart, *Now*)

A block quotation is indented one inch (or ten spaces) on the left. The right-hand margin remains the same as in the rest of the paper.

In a 2003 PBS interview with Bill Moyers, Jon Stewart of *The Daily Show*

evaluated so-called news programs, criticizing them for presenting polar

views as the only and final views: "It's the left and it's the right, and well, we've

had that discussion and that's done" (Stewart, *Now*).

"*Now*" in the parenthetical citation refers to the name of the show on which the interview of Stewart was broadcast.

The partisan politics that Stewart describes is not limited to *Hardball*

and *Crossfire.* News networks and talk radio programs as well as politicians

continue to enact political discourse and democratic deliberation as nothing

but the crossfire of partisan views. In the 2003 interview with Moyers, Stewart

argues that "even cartoon characters have more than left and right. They

have up and down." For this reason, Stewart uses *The Daily Show* as a political

cartoon that provides a richer context to the partisan narratives constituting

contemporary political discourse (see Fig. 1). *The Daily Show* also employs

satire and irony to model—for viewers and news agencies alike—what a

critical approach to such partisan debates looks and sounds like.

Each paragraph begins with an indent of one-half inch (or five spaces).

According to its Web site, *The Daily Show with Jon Stewart* "takes a

Research

AP Photo/Jason DeCrow

Fig. 1. *The Daily Show with Jon Stewart* criticizes the current state of the media through parody, using irony and exaggerated imitation as critical tools.

reality-based look at news, trends, pop culture, current events, politics, sports and entertainment with an alternative point of view" (thedailyshow.com).

As parody, the show mimics other news programs, highlighting the absurdity of the practices they employ while distinguishing its point of view from that of the partisan narratives. For example, *The Daily Show* features mock reports from "senior correspondents," who mimic the biased opinions that so many other network journalists perpetuate. *The Daily Show* also offers a rundown of the day's news, delivered as a series of jokes that dissect the media and political absurdities and contradictions within a fuller context. For instance, Stewart might juxtapose a recent clip of a senator's "I've *always* been against the war in Iraq" speech with an earlier clip of the senator rallying support for that war. At the conclusion of each show, Stewart interviews a

This parenthetical citation refers to a source that has no author or page numbers.

Research

public figure who has recently written or spoken about a serious political or social issue. Stewart and his guest carry on a brief, but serious discussion of this issue.

Outside of his show, Stewart frequently speaks on political issues and the work he and his team try to accomplish. During his interviews with Moyers, Stewart twice refused any categorization of *The Daily Show* while acknowledging the importance of the work it does. In the 2003 interview, Stewart denied that he is either a social critic or a media critic, calling himself "a comedian who has the pleasure of writing jokes about things that I actually care about" (Stewart, *Now*). Stewart's resistance to these titles is consistent with the show's characterization of itself as "alternative"—it is able to be properly critical only because of its separation from the roles that exist in mainstream media and scholarship (thedailyshow.com).

Resisting labels gives Stewart the flexibility to speak up and reach out, especially to the people who share his frustration with the current state of political discourse. In the 2007 interview with Moyers, Stewart declined the label of journalist, even when Moyers asserted, "Young people that work with me now think they're getting better journalism from you than they do from the Sunday morning [programs]." Stewart replied, "I can assure you, they're not getting any journalism from us.... if anything, I do believe we function as a sort of editorial cartoon. We are a digestive process" (*Bill Moyers Journal*). So while Stewart resists the title of journalist, he does admit that *The Daily Show* functions in a useful way, as a "sort of editorial cartoon" that allows the audience to put the other news sources into a larger context.

Research

In the 2007 Moyers interview, Stewart characterized as problematic partisan politics and current political discourse because they both undervalue context. *The Daily Show* itself strives to provide that context, as it did when Stewart revealed that Fox News anchor Sean Hannity's narration of scenes from an allegedly well-attended anti–health-care reform rally were actually clips from Glenn Beck's much more well-attended 9/12 rally (*The Daily Show*, Nov. 10, 2009). In the drive to uphold its narrative that the majority of Americans are anti–health-care reform and politically conservative, Fox News, according to Stewart, intentionally used one set of images to represent something else. As far as Stewart is concerned, this is but one example of Fox News deliberately obscuring context in order to protect its narrative.

This parenthetical citation provides the airdate of an episode of Stewart's show.

The Daily Show not only discredits "debate" shows that obscure the context of their positions, it also places within a context issues that other networks do not. To that end, Stewart criticized Fox News for indicting other networks as elitist while celebrating the ignorance of its own reporters in a ploy to identify with the viewing audience. For instance, Fox News reporter Gretchen Carlson regularly claims to have to look up in a dictionary words such as "ignoramus," "double-dip recession," and "czar" in order to deliver her report to her viewers (*The Daily Show*, Dec. 8, 2009). *The Daily Show*, though, outed her performance as purposefully devious, given that she has a degree from Stanford University.

Stewart also criticizes the lengths to which some networks go for material gain. When MSNBC's *The Morning Joe* began, Stewart provided the context that MSNBC would not: he showed a cascade of clips from the show to demonstrate the shameless product placement of Starbucks coffee. When the show's hosts repeatedly extolled the great taste of Starbucks coffee and

Research

then interviewed Starbucks's CEO, Stewart asserted that the CEO should have been asked about layoffs and cutbacks, not about the coffee's merit (*The Daily Show*, June 3, 2009).

Of course, the format of *The Daily Show* itself also critically engages the content of other news shows and the opinions of their "experts." Typically, each show includes the outrageous opinion of a "senior correspondent." When "senior British correspondent" Jon Oliver expressed outrage that the tea party movement cites health-care legislation as taxation without representation, he claimed to be insulted that the tyranny of the sixteenth-century British empire was seen as comparable to health-care legislation. His ironic report highlights the extent to which other networks air ridiculous content and use the term "expert" loosely (*The Daily Show*, Apr. 16, 2009).

Because *The Daily Show* criticizes contemporary political discourse, it is, in turn, itself criticized. For example, Stewart has been accused of being entertaining and thus pressing "hard" news networks to become more entertaining (Tucker). He has also been accused of deceiving his audiences into thinking of his show as "real news," thereby getting them to rely on it for facts rather than watching other networks (Cosgrove-Mather). But data from the Pew Research Center for the People and the Press provide evidence that *The Daily Show*'s criticism of other networks' content is justified, since coverage by those networks compares poorly to *The Daily Show*'s news coverage.

As Table 1 shows, the Pew Research Center's Project for Excellence in Journalism (PEJ) found that both *The Daily Show* and the mainstream media covered US foreign affairs and elections/politics most frequently. And even though *The Daily Show* is comedic, it covered "hard news" topics almost as frequently as the mainstream media. The show's coverage emphasized

Research

Table 1

Top Ten Topics on *The Daily Show* vs. Mainstream News Media[a]

The Daily Show	Mainstream Media
1. US Foreign affairs	1. US Foreign affairs
2. Elections/Politics	2. Elections/Politics
3. Government	3. Foreign/Non-US
4. Lifestyle	4. Crime
5. Press/Media	5. Government
6. Foreign/Non-US	6. Disasters
7. Celebrities	7. Health/Medicine
8. Race/Gender/Gay	8. Lifestyle
9. Crime	9. Business
10. Science/Technology	10. Economy

Source: Pew Research Center's Project for Excellence in Journalism. *Journalism, Satire or Just Laughs? "The Daily Show with Jon Stewart" Examined. Journalism.org.* Pew Research Center, 8 May 2008. Web. 8 Jan. 2009. <http://www.journalism.org/node/10959>.

The source of the information in the table is identified.

a. The information and language in this table are taken directly from PEJ.

lifestyle topics and stories about celebrities more than the mainstream media did, but deemphasized crime.

The Daily Show, though extremely critical, is not negative merely for the sake of being negative. Its criticism productively exposes the way political discourse could be and offers hope to those who have become jaded by the partisanship of political discourse. Since *The Daily Show* criticizes the status quo of political discourse, it is inevitably labeled cynical by those who misunderstand its positive critical function. Even some of those who defend Jon Stewart, including W. Lance Bennett, a professor of political science at the University of Washington, find him cynical but consider his cynicism a natural reaction to a political climate in which the media have already adopted an attitude of cynicism and can no longer be taken very seriously (Bennett 278).

However, Stewart's attitude cannot rightly be labeled cynical—he expresses optimism at the tenacity of Americans and their ability to overcome any adversity, even the partisan politics that pervade discourse. In a 2009 interview with Lou Dobbs, Stewart said,

> I don't think we're a fragile country. I think that we're incredibly
> tenacious. The whole fabric of this country was born of people who
> came ... to a place they wanted to be to do whatever they had to
> do ... and that ethos still lives within this country and the idea that
> [policy issues] will destroy us is trumped-up fear that's being used
> as a wedge to flatter people into voting [a certain way] and it is
> absolutely not a part of our national character. (*The Daily Show*, Nov.
> 18, 2009)

The writer attributes the following quotation to Stewart.

For Stewart, then, Americans have the potential to overcome the dogmatic partisanship and all of the other obstacles to democracy that present themselves.

Not only does Stewart talk optimistically about American potential but he mobilizes his audience. Despite Bill O'Reilly's concern that *The Daily Show's* audience is made up of "stoned slackers who love Obama" (O'Reilly), who can be easily motivated by Stewart's comedy to make bad decisions

Research

about politics, the Pew Research Center found otherwise. In a 2004 study, Pew found that twenty-one percent of eighteen- to twenty-nine-year-olds cited *The Daily Show* as one of their sources for 2004 election information (Young and Tisinger 114). And when political scientists Donnagal Young and Russell Tisinger analyzed Pew and Annenberg School for Communication data, they determined that Stewart's viewers are more knowledgeable than their peers about current events and more regular followers of politics, as they regularly receive information from both traditional network news programs and *The Daily Show*. These findings suggest that viewers who are more knowledgeable about politics and current events are perhaps more likely to enjoy *The Daily Show* and, conversely, that people who regularly watch *The Daily Show* will tune in to other news programs as a result of Stewart's influence (Young and Tisinger 129-30).

The writer cites a journal article that has two authors and includes a page number.

Katarina Whalen and Abigail Vladeck of *Yale Daily News* speak for many of the intelligent and informed young people who are attracted to and mobilized by *The Daily Show*: "Though no one could deny that all news reporting is somehow biased, there is still not a spectrum of critical analyses represented in the mainstream media. That is why, for many of us, *The Daily Show with Jon Stewart* has taken the place of the traditional news media" (Whalen). Terrance Macmullan, contributor to Jason Holt's book *The Daily Show and Philosophy*, points out another way in which Stewart affects his well-informed audience—encouraging them to carry the torch of critical analysis. Macmullan calls Stewart "the new public intellectual," who "fosters critical thinking principles across an enormous audience and defends democratic principles from erosion by partisan punditry and the government's apparent disregard for genuine debate" (57). After *The Daily Show*'s criticism of Fox

Research

News's use of misleading anti–health-care reform footage, for instance, *Mlive* blogger Troy Reimick started watching the news more closely. Citing *The Daily Show*'s catch and Hannity's subsequent apology to Stewart, Reimick pointed to another so-called mix-up: Fox's use of McCain-Palin campaign footage of huge crowds when covering Palin's *Going Rogue* book tour in 2009 (*mlive.com*). Jason Linkins, a blogger for the *Huffington Post*, followed Stewart's lead, further criticizing a program that succumbs to corporate sponsorship. Bloggers like Reimink and Linkins are learning from *The Daily Show*'s methods, taking note of the problems that the show points out and using the same tools that the show uses to hold the media responsible for their content.

Stewart is obviously influencing mainstream news agencies as well, as Hannity's on-air apology to him for the footage "mix-up" demonstrates. In fact, Lauren Feldman of the University of Pennsylvania thinks that Stewart's approach to the news is catching and that other journalists will soon be looking to him to correct their partisan practices. She compares *The Daily Show* to a "critical incident" to which the media must respond and which they must use to reexamine their practices (Feldman 411). Geoffrey Baym of the University of North Carolina at Greensboro agrees. He calls *The Daily Show* "a rethinking of discursive styles and standards that may be opening spaces for significant innovation" (262). In addition, several contributors to Holt's *The Daily Show and Philosophy* compare Stewart's work to that of Socrates because of the impact both men have on those they criticize, as well as on their audiences.

Jon Stewart clearly mobilizes people to use the criticism and the context he provides to correct problems in today's partisan political discourse. He does so effectively, drawing viewers, catching the attention of the reporters and networks he criticizes, and rallying online writers and bloggers. If *The*

Daily Show really functions to hold the media accountable, it is not surprising that O'Reilly and others in the field hesitate to take the show seriously. If they acknowledged its influence, then they would be forced to acknowledge, as Feldman predicts and as many of *The Daily Show*'s viewers insist, that they practice flawed journalism. In fact, an increasing number of viewers are questioning *and* talking about *and* writing about the practices that Stewart criticizes. *The Daily Show* clearly challenges its viewers to take on civic responsibilities and engage in dialogue with those in power, a powerful tool for the correction of political discourse. If the show's influence continues to grow, citizens and consumers of news will certainly be able to press for changes in the current partisan practices of news networks.

The works-cited list begins on a new page, with the heading centered

Works Cited

Every entry on the list begins flush with the left margin and has subsequent lines indented one-half inch (a hanging indent). Entries are listed in alphabetical order.

Baym, Geoffrey. "*The Daily Show*: Discursive Integration and the Reinvention of Political Journalism." *Political Communication* 22.3 (2005): 259-76. *Informaworld*. Web. 28 Dec. 2009.

Bennett, Lance W. "Relief in Hard Times: A Defense of Jon Stewart's Comedy in an Age of Cynicism." *Critical Studies in Media Communication* 24.3 (2007): 278-83. *Informaworld*. Web. 28 Dec. 2009.

This entry documents an article from a professional journal.

Cosgrove-Mather, Bootie. "Young Get News From Comedy Central." *CBS News.com*. CBS News, 1 Mar. 2004. Web. 28 Dec. 2009.

This entry is for a source taken from the Internet.

Crossfire. CNN. Atlanta, 15 Oct. 2004. Television.

The Daily Show with Jon Stewart. Comedy Central. New York, 16 Apr. 2009. Television.

---. Comedy Central. New York, 3 June 2009. Television.

---. Comedy Central. New York, 10 Nov. 2009. Television.

---. Comedy Central. New York, 18 Nov. 2009. Television.

---. Comedy Central. New York, 8 Dec. 2009. Television.

---. Comedy Partners. 1995. Web. 15 Dec. 2009.

Feldman, Lauren. "The News about Comedy: Young Audiences, *The Daily Show,* and the Evolving Notions of Journalism." *Journalism* 8.4 (2007): 406-27. *Sage.* Web. 28 Dec. 2009.

Macmullan, Terrance. "Jon Stewart and the New Public Intellectual." *The Daily Show and Philosophy.* Ed. Jason Holt. Malden, MA: Blackwell, 2007. 57-68. Print.

Linkins, Jason. "*Daily Show* Offers 'Correction' to *Morning Joe* for Making 'Sarcastic' Product Placement." *Huffington Post.com.* Huffington Post, 9 June 2009. Web. 8 Jan. 2010.

Reimink, Troy. "Fox News Uses Misleading Footage in Coverage of Palin Book Tour?" *mlive.com,* Michigan Live LLC, 19 Nov. 2009. Web. 8 Jan. 2010.

Stewart, Jon. Interview by Bill O'Reilly. *The O'Reilly Factor.* Fox News. 4 Feb. 2010. Television.

---. Interview by Bill Moyers. *Bill Moyers Journal.* PBS. 27 Apr. 2007. Web. 8 Jan. 2010. <http://video.pbs.org/video/1162731332/program/1113570149#>.

---. Interview by Bill Moyers. *Now.* PBS. 11 July 2003. Web. 8 Jan. 2010 <http://www.pbs.org/moyers/journal/archives/jonstewartnow.html>.

Tucker, Ken. "You Can't Be Serious!" *New York Magazine* 1 Nov. 2004: 63. Print.

Whalen, Katrina, and Abigail Vladeck. "2004 Class Day Speaker Needs Irony, Wit." *Yale Daily News.* 12 Jan. 2004. Web. 8 Jan. 2010.

Young, Donnagal G., and Russell M. Tisinger. "Dispelling Late-Night Myths: News Consumption among Late-Night Comedy Viewers and the Predictors of Exposure to Various Late-Night Shows." *Harvard International Journal of Press Politics* 11 (2006): 113-34. *Sage.* Web. 28 Dec. 2009.

APA Guidelines for In-Text Citations

If you are following the style recommended by the American Psychological Association, your in-text citations will refer to the author(s) of the text you consulted and the year of its publication. In addition, you must specify the page number(s) for any quotations you include; the abbreviation *p.* (for "page") or *pp.* (for "pages") should precede the number(s). For electronic sources that do not include page numbers, specify the paragraph number and precede it with the abbreviation *para.* or the symbol ¶. When no author's name is listed, provide a shortened version of the title of the source. If your readers want to find more information about your source, they will look for the author's name or the title of the material in the bibliography at the end of your paper.

You will likely consult a variety of sources for your research paper. The following examples are representative of the types of in-text citations you might use.

DIRECTORY OF IN-TEXT CITATIONS ACCORDING TO APA GUIDELINES

---

1. Work by one or two authors

Wachal (**2002**) discusses dictionary labels for words considered taboo.

Dictionary labels for taboo words include *offensive* and *derogatory* (**Wachal, 2002**).

Lance and Pulliam (**2002**) believe that an introductory linguistics text should have "persuasive power" (**p. 223**).

On learning of dialect bias, some students expressed outrage, often making "a 180-degree turnaround" from their original attitudes toward a standard language (**Lance & Pulliam, 2002, p. 223**).

Authors' names may be placed either in the text, followed by the date of publication in parentheses, or in parentheses along with the date. When you mention an author in the text, place the date of publication directly after the author's name. If you include a quotation, provide the page number(s) at the end of the quotation, after the quotation marks but before the period. When citing a work by two authors, use the word *and* between their names; when citing two authors in parentheses, use an ampersand (&) between their names. Always use a comma to separate the last author's name from the date.

2. Work by three, four, or five authors

First Mention

Johnstone, Bhasin, and Wittkofski (2002) describe the speech of Pittsburgh, Pennsylvania, as *Pittsburghese*.

The speech of Pittsburgh, Pennsylvania, is called *Pittsburghese* (**Johnstone, Bhasin, & Wittkofski, 2002**).

Subsequent Mention

Johnstone et al. (2002) cite *gumband* and *nebby* as words used in *Pittsburghese*.

The words *gumband* and *nebby* are used by speakers of *Pittsburghese* (**Johnstone et al., 2002**).

When first citing a source by three, four, or five authors, list all the authors' last names. In subsequent parenthetical citations, use just the first author's last name along with the abbreviation *et al.* (Latin for "and others"). The abbreviation *et al.* should not be italicized in citations.

3. Work by six or more authors

Taylor et al. (2001) have stressed the importance of prohibiting the dumping of plastic garbage into the oceans.

In both the first and subsequent mentions of the source, use only the first author's last name and the abbreviation *et al.*

4. Work by an unknown author

A recent survey indicated increased willingness of college students to vote in national elections (**"Ending Apathy," 2004**).

The documents leaked to the press could damage the governor's reputation (**Anonymous, 2010**).

When no author is mentioned, use a shortened version of the title instead. If the word *Anonymous* is used in the source to designate the author, use that word in place of the author's name.

5. Two or more works by the same author

Smith (2001, 2003, 2005) has consistently argued in support of language immersion.

Bayard (1995a, 1995b) discusses the acquisition of English in New Zealand.

In most cases, the year of publication will distinguish the works. However, if the works were published in the same year, distinguish them with lowercase letters, assigned based on the order of the titles in the bibliography.

6. Two or more works by different authors with the same last name

J. P. Hill and Giles (2001) and **G. S. Hill and Kellner** (2002) confirmed these findings.

When two or more authors have the same last name, always include first initials with that last name.

7. Work by a group

Style refers to publishing guidelines that encourage the clear and coherent presentation of written text (**American Psychological Association [APA], 2009**).

Spell out the name of the group when you first mention it. If the group has a widely recognizable abbreviation, place that abbreviation in square brackets after the first mention. You can then use the abbreviation in subsequent citations: (APA, 2009).

8. Work by a government author

Taxpayers encounter significant problems with two different taxes: the sole proprietor tax and the alternative minimum tax (**Internal Revenue Service [IRS], 2010**).

Spell out the name of the government entity when you first mention it. If the entity has a widely recognizable abbreviation, place that abbreviation in square brackets after the first mention. You can then use the abbreviation in subsequent citations: (IRS, 2010).

9. Indirect source

According to Ronald Butters, the word *go* is frequently used by speakers born after 1955 to introduce a quotation (**as cited in Cukor-Avila, 2002**).

Use *as cited in* to indicate that you found the information in another source.

10. Two or more works in one parenthetical citation

A speaker may use the word *like* to focus the listener's attention (**Eriksson, 1995; Ferrar & Bell, 1995**).

When you include two or more works within the same parentheses, order them alphabetically. Arrange two or more works by the same author by year of publication, mentioning the author's name only once: (Kamil, 2002, 2004).

11. Personal communication

Revisions will be made to the agreement this month (**K. M. Liebenow, personal communication, February 11, 2010**).

Letters, e-mail messages, and interviews are all considered personal communications, which you should cite in the text of a paper. Because personal communications do not represent recoverable data, you should not include entries for them in the references list.

APA Guidelines for Documenting References

To provide readers with the information they need to find all the sources you have used in your paper, you must prepare a bibliography. According to APA guidelines, your bibliography should be titled *References* (not italicized). It should contain all the information your readers need to retrieve the sources if they wish to consult them on their own. Except for personal communications, each source you cite in your text should appear in the references list.

Alphabetize your references according to the author's (or the first author's) last name. If the author is unknown, alphabetize according to title (ignoring any initial article—*a, an,* or *the*). When you have more than one source by the same author(s), order them according to the year of publication, with the earliest first.

Frazer, B. (2000).

Frazer, B. (2004).

If two or more works by the same author(s) have the same year of publication, the entries are ordered alphabetically according to the works' titles, and lowercase letters are added to the date to distinguish the entries.

Fairclough, N. (1992a). The appropriacy of "appropriateness."

Fairclough, N. (1992b). *Critical language awareness.*

Fairclough, N. (1992c). *Discourse and social change.*

When an author you have cited is also the first of two or more authors of another entry, list the source with a single author first.

Allen, J. P. (1982).

Allen, J. P., & Turner, E. J. (1988).

When two or more entries have the same first author, alphabetize the list according to the names of subsequent authors.

Fallows, M. R., & Andrews, R. J. (1999).

Fallows, M. R., & Laver, J. T. (2002).

Double-space all of your entries, leaving the first line flush with the left margin and indenting subsequent lines one-half inch. (Your word processor may refer to the indented line as a *hanging indent.*)

For more details on various types of sources, use the following directory to find relevant sections. For an example of a references list, see pages 531–532. If you would like to use a checklist to help ensure that you have followed APA guidelines, see page 526.

DIRECTORY OF REFERENCES ENTRIES ACCORDING TO APA GUIDELINES

Books

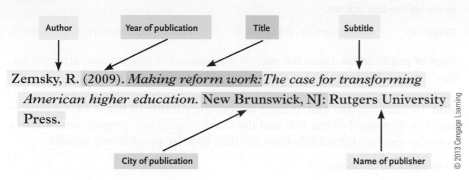

You can find most of the information you need to write a reference entry on a book's title page. If you cannot find the date of publication on the title page, turn to the copyright page. Reference entries for books generally include four units of information: author, year of publication, title, and publication data.

Author The author's last name appears first, followed by the first and (if given) second initial. Use a comma to separate the last name from the initials, and place a period at the end of this unit of information. If there is more than one author, invert all the authors' names, following the pattern described for a single

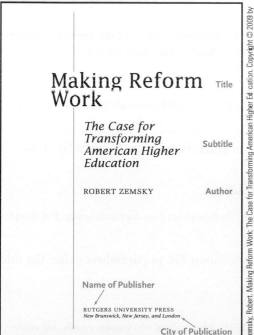

Title page of *Making Reform Work*.

Copyright page of *Making Reform Work*.

author. Separate the names with commas, adding an ampersand (&) before the name of the last author.

Hooker, R.   Montgomery, M., & Morgan, E.   McCrum, D., Kurath, H., & Middleton, S.

Year of publication Place the year of publication in parentheses after the author's name. Mark the end of this unit of information with a period.

Title Include the title and, if there is one, the subtitle of the book. Capitalize *only* the first word of the title and the subtitle, plus any proper nouns. Use a colon to separate the subtitle from the title. Italicize the title and subtitle.

Social cognition: Key readings.

Publication data For the fourth unit of information, start with the city of publication, followed by the common two-letter state abbreviation. Place a colon between the state abbreviation and the publisher's name. Use a shortened version of the publisher's name if possible. Although the word *Press* or *Books* should be retained, *Publishers, Company* (or *Co.*), or *Incorporated* (or *Inc.*) is omitted.

1. Book by one author

Gladwell, M. (2008). *Outliers: The story of success.* New York, NY: Little, Brown.

2. Book by two or more authors

Alberts, B., Lewis, J., & Johnson, A. (2002). *Molecular biology of the cell.* Philadelphia, PA:
    Taylor & Francis.

If there are more than seven authors, provide the names of the first six authors, inverted, followed by an ellipsis and the name of the final author.

3. Book with editor(s)

Good, T. L., & Warshauer, L. B. (Eds.). (2002). *In our own voice: Graduate students teach writing.*
    Needham Heights, MA: Allyn & Bacon.

Include the abbreviation *Ed.* or *Eds.* in parentheses after the name(s) of the editor(s).

4. Book with an author and an editor

Lewis, C. S. (2003). *A year with C. S. Lewis: Daily readings from his classic works* (P. S. Klein,
    Ed.). Grand Rapids, MI: Zondervan.

Place the editor's name and the abbreviation *Ed.* in parentheses after the title of the book.

5. Book by a corporate author

Modern Language Association of America. (1978). *International bibliography of books and articles*
    on the modern languages and literatures, 1976. New York, NY: Author.

Alphabetize by the first major word in the corporate author's name. List the publisher as *Author* when the author and the publisher are the same.

6. Book by an anonymous author

Primary colors: A novel of politics. (1996). New York, NY: Warner.

List the title of the book in place of an author. Alphabetize the entry by the first major word of the title.

7. Second or subsequent edition

Cember, H. (1996). *Introduction to health physics* (3rd ed.). New York, NY: McGraw-Hill.

Maples, W. (2002). *Opportunities in aerospace careers* (Rev. ed.). New York, NY: McGraw-Hill.

Provide the edition number in parentheses after the title of the book. If the revision is not numbered, place *Rev. ed.* for "Revised edition" in parentheses after the title.

8. Translated book

De Beauvoir, S. (1987). *The woman destroyed* (P. O'Brien, Trans.). New York, NY: Pantheon. (Original work published 1969)

Insert the name(s) of the translator(s) in parentheses after the title, and conclude with the original publication date. Note the absence of a period at the end of the entry. In the text, provide both publication dates as follows: (De Beauvoir, 1969/1987).

9. Republished book

Freire, P. (1982). *Pedagogy of the oppressed* (2nd ed.). London, England: Penguin. (Original work published 1972)

Conclude the entry with the original publication date. Note the absence of a period at the end of the entry. In the text provide both dates: (Freire, 1972/1982).

10. Multivolume work

Doyle, A. C. (2003). *The complete Sherlock Holmes* (Vols. 1–2). New York, NY: Barnes & Noble.

Maugham, S. W. (1977–1978). *Collected short stories* (Vols. 1–4). New York, NY: Penguin.

Include the number of volumes after the title of the work. If the volumes were published over a period of time, provide the date range after the author's name.

11. Government report

Executive Office of the President. (2003). *Economic report of the President, 2003* (GPO Publication No. 040-000-0760-1). Washington, DC: Government Printing Office.

Provide the publication number in parentheses after the name of the report. If the report is available from the Government Printing Office (GPO), that entity is the publisher. If the report is not available from the GPO, use *Author* as the publisher.

12. Selection from an edited book

Muños, G. T. (2007). Once upon a time on the border. In T. Miller (Ed.), *How I learned English* (pp. 141–148). Washington, DC: National Geographic Society.

The title of the selection is not italicized. The editor's name appears before the title of the book. Provide the page or range of pages on which the selection appears.

13. Selection from a reference book

Layering. (2003). In W. Lidwell, K. Holden, & J. Butler (Eds.), *Universal principles of design* (pp. 122–123). Gloucester, MA: Rockport.

Provide the page number or range of pages after the title of the book. If the selection has an author, give that author's name first.

Bruce, F. F. (1991). Hermeneutics. In *New Bible dictionary* (p. 476). Wheaton, IL: Tyndale.

Articles in print

ARTICLE IN A JOURNAL

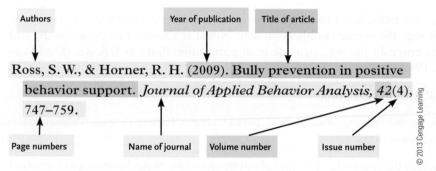

You can generally find the name of the journal, the volume and issue numbers, and the year of publication on the cover of the journal. Sometimes this information is also included in the journal's page headers or footers. To find the title of the article, the author's name, and the page numbers, you'll have to locate the article within the journal.

ARTICLE IN A MAGAZINE

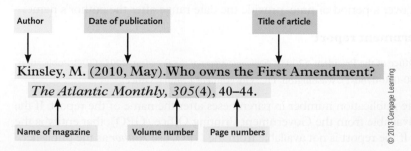

To find the name of the magazine, the volume and issue numbers, and the date of publication, look on the cover of the magazine. Sometimes this information is also included in the magazine's page headers or footers. For the title of the article, the author's name, and the page numbers, look at the article itself. Reference entries for articles generally include four units of information: author, date of publication, title of article, and publication data.

Author The author's last name appears first, followed by the first and (if given) the second initial. Use a comma to separate the last name from the initial(s), and place a period at the end of this unit of information. For articles with more than one author, see the information given for book entries on pages 517–518.

Date of publication For journals, place just the year of publication in parentheses after the author's name. For magazines, also specify the month and the day (if given). Mark the end of this unit of information with a period.

Title of article Include the title and, if there is one, the subtitle of the article. Capitalize *only* the first word of the title and the subtitle, plus any proper nouns. Use a colon to separate the subtitle from the title. Place a period at the end of this unit of information.

Cover of an academic journal showing the year of publication, volume and issue numbers (vertically, on left side), and title of the journal.

Publication data The publication data that you provide depends on the type of periodical in which the article appeared. However, for all entries, include the title of the periodical (italicized), the volume number (also italicized), and the page numbers of the article. If you are using a magazine or a journal that paginates each issue separately, include the issue number as well. Place the issue number (not italicized) in parentheses following the volume number. After the issue number, place a comma and then the article's page numbers.

14. Article in a journal with continuous pagination

McCarthy, M., & Carter, R. (2001). Size isn't everything: Spoken English, corpus, and the classroom. *TESOL Quarterly, 35,* 337–340.

Provide the volume number in italics after the title of the journal. Conclude with the page number or page range.

15. Article in a journal with each issue paginated separately

Smiles, T. (2008). Connecting literacy and learning through collaborative action research. *Voices from the Middle, 15*(4), 32–39.

16. Article with three to seven authors

Biber, D., Conrad, S., & Reppen, R. (1996). Corpus-based investigations of language use. *Annual Review of Applied Linguistics, 16,* 115–136.

If there are seven or fewer authors, list all of the authors' names.

17. Article with more than seven authors

Stone, G. W., Ellis, S. G., Cox, D. A., Hermiller, J., O'Shaughnessy, C., Mann, J. T., . . . Russell, M. E. (2004). A polymer-based, paclitaxel-eluting stent in patients with coronary artery disease. *The New England Journal of Medicine, 350,* 221–231.

Provide the names of the first six authors, inverted, followed by an ellipsis and the name of the final author.

18. Article in a monthly or weekly magazine

Gross, D. (2010, May 3). The days the Earth stood still. *Newsweek,* 46–48.

Warne, K. (2004, March). Harp seals. *National Geographic, 205,* 50–67.

Provide the month and year of publication for monthly magazines or the day, month, and year for weekly magazines. Names of months are not abbreviated. Include the volume number (italicized), if any, issue number (not italicized), and the page number or page range (not italicized) after the name of the magazine.

19. Anonymous article

Ohio police hunt for highway sniper suspect. (2004, March 16). *The New York Times,* p. A4.

Begin the entry with the title of the article, followed by the date of publication.

20. Article in a newspaper

Lewin, T. (2010, May 6). Teenage insults, scrawled on Web, not on walls. *The New York Times,* pp. A1, A18.

Use *p.* or *pp.* before the page number(s) of newspaper articles. If the article appears on discontinuous pages, provide all of the page numbers, separated by commas: pp. A8, A10–11, A13.

21. Letter to the editor

Richard, J. (2004, March 8). Diabetic children: Every day a challenge [Letter to the editor]. *The Wall Street Journal,* p. A17.

Include the description *Letter to the editor* in square brackets after the title of the letter.

22. Editorial in a newspaper

Marcus, R. (2010, May 5). In Arizona, election reform's surprising consequences. [Editorial]. *The Washington Post,* p. A21.

Include the description *Editorial* in square brackets after the title.

23. Book review

Kakutani, M. (2004, February 13). All aflutter, existentially [Review of the book *Dot in the universe*]. *The New York Times,* p. E31.

In square brackets after the title of the review, indicate that the work cited is a review, provide a description of the medium of the work (e.g., book, film, or play), and include the title of the work.

Sources produced for access by computer

JOURNAL ARTICLE FROM A DATABASE

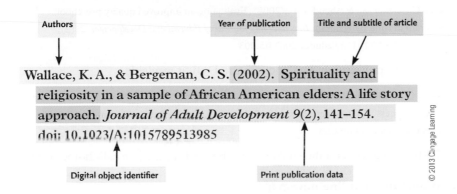

You can usually find much of the information you will need for your reference entry on the first page of the article. Each entry generally includes five units of information: author, year of publication, title and subtitle of the article, print publication data, and digital object identifier (DOI).

Author The author's last name appears first, followed by the first and (if given) the second initial. Use a comma to separate the last name from the initials, and place a period at the end of this unit of information. For articles with more than one author, see the information given for book entries on pages 517–518.

Date of publication For journals, place just the year of publication in parentheses after the author's name. Mark the end of this unit of information with a period.

Title of article Include the title and, if there is one, the subtitle of the article. Capitalize only the first word of the title and subtitle, plus any proper nouns. Use a colon to separate the subtitle from the main title. Place a period at the end of this unit of information.

Print publication data The publication data that you provide depends on the type of periodical in which the article appeared. See the information on publication data for periodicals on page 521.

Digital object identifier Rather than provide a URL for the database or article, include the digital object identifier (DOI), if available. A DOI is assigned to many scholarly articles found online and has the great advantage of being stable. You will usually find the DOI on the first page of the article, near the copyright notice. In cases in which a DOI is unavailable, provide the URL for the source's home page after the words *Retrieved from (*not italicized).

Electronic sources vary significantly; therefore, as you prepare your list of references, follow the models below closely. On occasion, you may not be able to find all the information presented in a particular model. In such cases, provide as much of the information as you can.

24. Article from a database or from a journal published only online

Moore, A. C., Akhter, S., & Aboud, F. E. (2008). Evaluating an improved quality preschool program in rural Bangladesh. *International Journal of Educational Development, 28*(2), 118–131. doi:10.1016/j.ijedudev.2007.05.003

After the print publication data, include the DOI, if available.

Andersson, G., Carlbring, P., & Cuijpers, P. (2009). Internet interventions: Moving from efficacy to effectiveness. *E-Journal of Applied Psychology, 5*(2), 18–24. Retrieved from http://ojs.lib .swin.edu.au/index.php/ejap

If no DOI is assigned, end the citation with the URL of the journal's home page.

25. Article in an online newspaper

Connelly, J. (2010, May 3). Lessons from the Gulf oil spill. *Seattle Post-Intelligencer.* Retrieved from http://www.seattlepi.com

Provide the full date of the article after the author's name. Conclude with the URL of the newspaper's home page.

26. Message posted to a newsgroup, forum, or discussion group

Skrecky, D. (2004, February 27). Free radical theory of aging falsified [Newsgroup message]. Retrieved from news://ageing/bionet.molbio.ageing

Bradstreet, J. (2010, May 6). The over diagnosis of ADHD and why. [Electronic mailing list message]. Retrieved from http://groups.google.com/group/natural-health/browse_thread /thread/690cbd531a1ea39e

If the author's name is unavailable, the author's screen name may be used. A brief description of the source (such as *Online forum comment*) should be provided in square brackets after the subject line of the message.

27. Document from a website

Robinson, J. (2010). *Grass-fed basics.* Retrieved from http://www.eatwild.com/basics.html

Slow Food USA. (2010). *Slow food on campus.* Retrieved from http://www.slowfoodusa.org/index .php/programs/details/slow_food_on_campus

If no author is given, use the name of the organization hosting the website as the author of the document. Provide the date, the name of the document, and the URL for the specific page where the document can be found.

28. E-mail message

Personal communications such as e-mail messages, letters, telephone conversations, and personal interviews do not appear in the references list, but should be cited in the text as follows: (S. L. Johnson, personal communication, September 3, 2009).

29. Podcast

DiMeo, N. (Producer). (2010, March 12). The sisters Fox. *The memory palace*. [Audio podcast].
    Retrieved from http://thememorypalace.us

Other sources

30. Motion picture

Jurow, M. (Producer), & Edwards, B. (Writer/Director). (1963). *The pink panther* [Motion
    picture]. United States: United Artists.

Begin with the name of the producer or the director, or both. Include the description *Motion picture* in square brackets after the title of the film. Conclude with the country of origin and the name of the movie studio.

31. Television program

Godeanu, R. (Producer). (2004, March 17). *In search of ancient Ireland* [Television broadcast].
    Alexandria, VA: Public Broadcasting Service.

Begin with the name of the producer. Italicize the title of the program, and follow the title with the description *Television broadcast* in square brackets.

32. Music recording

 Porter, C. (1936). Easy to love [Recorded by H. Connick, Jr.]. On *Come by me* [CD]. New York,
    NY: Columbia. (1999)

White, J. (2003). Seven nation army [Recorded by The White Stripes]. On *Under great white
    northern lights* [CD]. Burbank, CA: Warner Bros. Records. (2010)

Start with the name of the songwriter and the date the song was written. If someone other than the songwriter recorded the song, add *Recorded by* and the singer's name in square brackets after the song title. Indicate the medium of the recording in square brackets after the album title. Conclude the entry with the year the song was recorded, in parentheses, if that date is not the same as the date the song was written.

33. Interview

Brock, A. C. (2006). Rediscovering the history of psychology: Interview with Kurt Danziger.
    History of Psychology, 9(1), 1–16.

For a published interview, follow the format for an entry for an article. If you conducted the interview yourself, cite the name of the person you interviewed in the body of your paper and include in parentheses the words *personal communication,* followed by a comma and the interview date. Do not include an entry for a personal interview in the list of references.

CHECKING OVER A REFERENCES LIST

✓ Is the title, *References* (not italicized), centered one inch from the top of the page? Is the first letter capitalized?

✓ Is the entire list double-spaced?

✓ Are initial lines flush with the left margin and subsequent lines indented one-half inch?

✓ Is there an entry in the references list for each in-text citation (except for personal communications)? Is there an in-text citation for each entry in the references list?

✓ Are the entries alphabetized according to the first author's last name? If the author of an entry is unknown, is the entry alphabetized according to title (ignoring any initial *a, an,* or *the*)?

✓ If the list contains two or more entries by the same author, are the entries arranged according to year of publication (earliest one first)?

✓ Are book and periodical titles italicized?

✓ Is capitalization used for only the first words of book and article titles and subtitles and any proper nouns they contain?

Sample APA Research Paper

The APA provides the following general guidelines for formatting a research paper. The title page is page 1 of your paper. In the upper left-hand corner, place a shortened version of your title (no more than fifty characters), all in capital letters; on page 1 only, precede the header with the words *Running head* and a colon. In the upper right-hand corner, put the page number. This manuscript page header should appear on every page, one-half inch from the top of the page and one inch from the left and right edges. Center the full title in the upper half of the title page, using both uppercase and lowercase letters. Below it, put your name and affiliation (double-spaced)—unless your instructor asks you to include such information as the date and the course name and number instead of your affiliation.

If your instructor requires one, include an abstract—a short summary of your research—as the second page of your paper. The abstract should be no longer than 250 words. The word *Abstract* (not italicized) should be centered at the top of the page.

The first page of text is usually page 3 of the paper (following the title page and the abstract). The full title of the paper should be centered one inch from the top of the page. Double-space between the title and the first line of text. Use a one-inch margin on all sides of your paper (left, right, top, and bottom). Do not justify the text; that is, leave the right margin uneven. Indent paragraphs and block quotations one-half inch. Double-space your entire paper, including block quotations.

Running head: PERCEPTIONS OF PEERS' DRINKING 1

The page header has a running head (no more than 50 characters) on the left and page number on the right. The label *Running head:* appears only on page 1.

Perceptions of Peers' Drinking Behavior

The title is typed in uppercase and lowercase letters and is centered.

Catherine L. Davis

Central Washington University

An instructor may require such information as the date and the course name and number instead of an affiliation.

PERCEPTIONS OF PEERS' DRINKING 2

Abstract

This study is an examination of how students' perceptions of their peers' drinking behavior are related to alcohol consumption and alcohol-related problems on campus. Four hundred nine randomly selected college students were interviewed using a modified version of the Core Survey (Presley, Meilman, & Lyeria, 1995) to assess alcohol consumption and its related problems.

The abstract appears on a separate page, with the heading centered on the page width. The abstract should not exceed 250 words.

Research

Perceptions of Peers' Drinking Behavior

Studies typically report the dangers associated with college students' use of alcohol (Beck et al., 2008). Nonetheless, drinking is still highly prevalent on American campuses. Johnston, O'Malley, and Bachman (1998) found that 87% of the college students surveyed reported drinking during their lifetime. Most of the students are 21 or 22 years old and report frequent episodes of heavy drinking (i.e., binge drinking).

Heavy episodic drinking is particularly problematic. Johnston et al. (1998) found that 41% of college students engage in heavy episodic drinking, which they defined as having at least five or more drinks in a row at least once in the 2 weeks prior to being surveyed. Heavy episodic drinking is related to impaired academic performance, interpersonal problems, unsafe sexual activity, and sexual assault and other criminal violations (Moore, Smith, & Catford, 1994). The magnitude of such problems has led Neighbors, Lee, Lewis, Fossos, and Larimer (2007) to conclude that binge drinking is a widespread problem among college students.

Massad and Rauhe (1997) report that college students engage in heavy episodic drinking in response to social pressure or physical discomfort. Almost half of college students in a survey stated their reason for drinking was to get drunk (Jessor, Costa, Krueger, & Turbin, 2006). Recent research suggests that students' misperceptions of their peers' drinking behavior contribute to increased alcohol consumption (Perkins, 2002).

College students commonly perceive their social peers as drinking more often and in greater quantities than they actually do (Neighbors et al., 2007). When these students see their peers as heavy drinkers, they are more likely to engage in heavy drinking (Neighbors et al., 2007; Perkins &

The full title of the paper is centered on the page width.

When a work with six or more authors is cited, et al. is used in the citation.

This is a subsequent mention of a work by three authors.

When authors are named in the text, the year of publication is placed in parentheses after the names.

This is a subsequent mention of a work by five authors.

Wechsler, 1996). The goal of this study was to determine whether students' perceptions of their peers' use of alcohol are related to alcohol consumption and alcohol-related problems on campus.

> Two or more sources in the same parenthetical citation are separated by semicolons and listed alphabetically.

Method

Participants

For the purposes of this study, a randomly selected sample ($N = 409$) of undergraduate students from a university in the Pacific Northwest was drawn. The mean age of participants, 55.8% of whom were female, was 24 years; 54.5% of participants were White, 19% were Hispanic, 14.8% were Asian/Pacific Islander, 5% were African American, 0.5% were American Indian, and 6.3% indicated "Other" as their ethnicity.

Instrument

The study used a modified version of the short form of the Core Survey (Presley, Meilman, & Lyeria, 1995). The Core Survey measures alcohol and other drug (AOD) use as well as related problems experienced by college students. For the purposes of this study, the Core was modified from a self-administered format to an interview format.

Procedure

Interviews were conducted by telephone. Each interview took an average of 16 minutes to complete. The refusal rate for this survey was 12%, and those refusing to participate were replaced randomly.

Alcohol use was defined as the number of days (during the past 30 days) that respondents drank alcohol. *Heavy episodic drinking* was defined as five or more drinks in a single sitting, with a drink consisting of one beer, one glass of wine, one shot of hard liquor, or one mixed drink (Presley et al., 1995). Respondents indicated the number of occasions in the past 2 weeks that they engaged in heavy episodic drinking. *Alcohol-related problems* were defined as the number of times in the past 30 days respondents experienced any of 20 specific incidents.

To determine alcohol-related problems, the interviewer asked students how many times they (a) had a hangover, (b) damaged property, (c) got into a physical fight, (d) got into a verbal fight, (e) got nauseous or vomited, (f) drove a vehicle while under the influence, (g) were criticized by someone they knew, (h) had memory loss, or (i) did something they later regretted. To determine their perceptions of their peers' drinking, students were asked to respond on a 7-point ordinal scale that ranged from 0 = never to 6 = almost daily.

[The data analysis and statistical report of results have been omitted.]

Discussion

The relationship found here concerning the normative perception of alcohol use is somewhat consistent with past research (Baer & Carney, 1993; Perkins, 2002) that suggested drinking norms are related to alcohol use. Readers should note, however, that respondents' perceptions of the drinking norm were consistent with the actual norm for 30-day use. This indicates that students are fairly accurate in assessing their peers' drinking frequencies. Unfortunately, the current study did not include a perception question for heavy episodic drinking, making it unclear whether respondents accurately perceive their peers' drinking quantity. Conceptually, misperceptions of drinking quantity might be better predictors of heavy episodic drinking. That is, students might falsely believe that their peers drink heavily when they drink. Such a misperception would be compounded by the fact that most students accurately estimate frequency of their peers' drinking. The combination of an accurate perception of frequency coupled with an inaccurate perception of quantity might result in an overall perception of most students being heavy, frequent drinkers. As expected, this study also revealed a positive and moderately strong pathway from alcohol use, both heavy episodic drinking and 30-day drinking, to alcohol-related problems.

This study represents an effort to add to the literature concerning college students' alcohol consumption and its related problems. The results of the study suggest that students' perceptions of their peers' drinking habits are important predictors of drinking or drinking-related problems. Future studies along similar lines might help prevention specialists better design media campaigns related to drinking norms and high-risk behaviors.

References

Baer, J. S., & Carnoy, M. M. (1993). Biases in the perceptions of the consequences of alcohol use among college students. *Journal of Studies on Alcohol, 54,* 54–60.

Beck, K. H., Arria, A. M., Caldeira, K. M., Vincent, K. B., O'Grady, K. E., & Wish, E. D. (2008). Social context of drinking and alcohol problems among college students. *American Journal of Health Behavior, 32*(4), 420–430.

Jessor, R., Costa, F. M., Krueger, P. M., & Turbin, M. S. (2006). A developmental study of heavy episodic drinking among college students: The role of psychosocial and behavioral protective and risk factors. *Journal of Studies on Alcohol, 67,* 86–94.

References begin on a new page. The heading is centered on the page width.

The entries are alphabetized according to the first author's last name. If two or more entries have the same first author, the second author's last name determines the order of the entries.

All entries have a hanging indent of one-half inch and are double-spaced.

Research

Johnston, L. D., O'Malley, P. M., & Bachman, J. G. (1998). *National survey results on drug use from the Monitoring the Future Study. 1975–1997: Vol. 11* (NIH Publication No. 98-4346). Washington, DC: U.S. Government Printing Office.

Massad, S. J., & Rauhe, B. J. (1997). Alcohol consumption patterns in college students: A comparison by various socioeconomic indicators. *Journal for the International Council of Health, Physical Education, Recreation, Sport, and Dance, 23*(4), 60–64.

Moore, L., Smith, C., & Catford, J. (1994). Binge drinking: Prevalence, patterns and policy. *Health Education Research, 9,* 497–505. doi:10.1093/her /9.4.497

Neighbors, C., Lee, C. M., Lewis, M. A., Fossos, N., & Larimer, M. E. (2007). Are social norms the best predictor of outcomes among heavy-drinking college students? *Journal of Studies on Alcohol and Drugs, 68,* 556–565.

Perkins, H. W. (2002). Social norms and the prevention of alcohol misuse in collegiate contexts. *Journal of American Studies on Alcohol, 14,* 164–172.

Perkins, H. W., & Wechsler, H. (1996). Variation in perceived college drinking norms and its impact on alcohol abuse: A nationwide study. *Journal of Drug Issues, 26,* 961–974.

Presley, C. A., Meilman, P. W., & Lyeria, R. (1995). Development of the Core Alcohol and Drug Survey: Initial findings and future directions. *Journal of American College Health, 42,* 248–255.

When available for an article accessed through a database, a DOI is included in the entry.

Entries with a single author come before entries with that author and one or more coauthors.

Research

A Rhetorical Guide to Grammar and Sentence Style

5

When you think of the word *grammar*, you probably also think of the word *rules*—lawlike statements that you can't ignore if you want to stay out of trouble. But *rule* has another meaning: "a description of what is true in most cases." You might think of grammar rules as statements about how language is commonly used. However, language, as you know, is used differently by different people and in different situations. You can probably list a number of people whose language, perhaps in just small ways, differs from your own. You also adjust what you say or write to suit more formal and less formal occasions. Like all writers and speakers, you have a wide variety of options for language use, and your choices depend on your rhetorical situation. (Linguists refer to this variety that language users employ as *register*.) When you express your thoughts, you have any number of words and word arrangements at your disposal.

In the following chapters, you will learn to identify rhetorical options at the word and sentence levels. Understanding your options will help you craft a fitting response to any rhetorical situation.

20 Word Classes and Rhetorical Effects

When you look up a word in the dictionary, you will usually find it followed by one of these labels: *adj., adv., conj., det., interj., n., prep., pron.,* or *v.* (or *vb.*) These are the abbreviations for the traditional word classes, or parts of speech: adjectives, adverbs, conjunctions, determiners, interjections, nouns, prepositions, pronouns, and verbs. The definition of a word depends on which of these labels applies to the word. For example, when labeled as a noun, the word *turn* has several meanings, one of which is "curve":

> We were surprised by the <u>turn</u> in the road.

When *turn* is labeled as a verb, one of its possible meanings is "to change color":

> The leaves have <u>turned</u>.

By learning the word classes, not only will you be able to use a dictionary effectively, you will also better understand the feedback your teacher, supervisor, or peers give you and provide fellow writers with more specific recommendations. Someone reading your work, for example, may suggest that you use more action verbs. And you may note, as you read another's work, that it would be improved by balancing abstract nouns such as *nutrition* with concrete nouns such as *spinach*.

Nouns

Most nouns are labels for people, places, things, events, or ideas. A **common noun** refers to a member of a class or category: *student, university, document, protest, education.* In contrast, a **proper noun** is a specific name: *Jean Fadiman, Western Washington University,* the *Constitution,* the *Boston Tea Party.* Proper nouns are capitalized.

A common noun that has both singular and plural forms is called a **count noun**: *book, books.* A **noncount noun** has only one form because it refers to something that is not normally counted: *democracy, architecture.* A **collective noun** refers to a group of people or things: *clergy, committee, herd, bunch.*

Decide whether each noun is common or proper. If it is common, decide whether it is a count, noncount, or collective noun.

1. the Sun Belt
2. university
3. team
4. senator
5. Senator John Glenn

Thinking rhetorically about nouns

The best time to think about whether you've chosen appropriate nouns and other words is usually during the revision process. If you worry too much about word choices during planning or drafting, you may not be able to generate all the ideas you need for a comprehensive response. So write a rough draft first. Then, when you feel that your ideas are in place, look at your nouns and decide whether they are abstract or concrete. An **abstract noun** like *entertainment* refers to a concept. A **concrete noun** refers to someone or something perceivable by the senses: *guitar, vocalist.*

Choose nouns that express precisely what you want your readers to sense or to understand. Some rhetorical situations call for the use of abstract terms. For example, you may be asked to write an art history paper using words like *impressionism* and *cubism.* Nonetheless, many writers forget to include the tangible details conveyed through concrete terms, which would, for example, enable readers to see in their minds the colors and brushstrokes of Claude Monet, Pablo Picasso, or any of a number of other painters.

> EXERCISE 20.2

Fill in the topic sentence with your favorite type of music (an abstract noun), Then write several supporting sentences that include concrete nouns.

If I could listen to only one type of music, it would be _____ _____.

Determiners

A **determiner** narrows the reference of a common noun. Either of the determiners *a* and *the* can combine with *building,* but the scope of their reference differs. *A building* refers to one nonspecific member of a category consisting of buildings; *the building* refers to a specific building. The determiners *this* and *that* also affect the reference to a noun. *This* indicates physical or mental proximity: *this book, this idea. That* indicates physical or psychological distance: *that book, that idea.* The following are the five main types of determiners:

▶ Articles: *a, an, the*
▶ Demonstrative determiners: *this, that, these, those*

Grammar and Style

- Possessive determiners: *my, your, his, her, its, our, their* (sometimes called *possessive pronouns*)
- Quantifiers: *some, many, both, few, little*
- Numerals: *one, two, fourteen, three hundred,* and so on

> EXERCISE 20.3

Underline each determiner in the following paragraph and identify its type.

> The rivalry between the Boston Red Sox and the New York Yankees is legendary. These two teams have faced each other in many dramatic playoff games. According to tradition, the rivalry began in 1918, when a financially strapped Red Sox owner sold his star player, Babe Ruth, to the Yankees. Up until 2004, the Yankees had won every decisive match the two teams had played. In 2004, what Red Sox fans call "the curse of the Bambino" was broken.

Thinking rhetorically about determiners

Sometimes sentences in a rough draft are only loosely related. You can make the connection between two sentences tighter by using a combination of determiner plus noun. Articles, demonstrative determiners, or possessive determiners can combine with nouns to refer to information in the previous sentence, creating coherence.

My chemistry professor invented a new material. The/This/His invention was patented in 2003.

The researchers published an article on avalanche control in a well-known journal. The/This/Their report described several new methods for controlling avalanches in recreational areas.

> EXERCISE 20.4

For each sentence, provide a determiner plus noun combination that could begin a subsequent sentence.

1. The journalist investigated the politician's fund-raising record.
2. My friend explained string theory to me.
3. Alan Lee illustrated Tolkien's trilogy.

Verbs

Verbs refer to actions, sensations, events, or states of being. **Action verbs** are verbs that convey activity or change, such as *eat, happen, write,* and *study.* **Linking verbs** can be divided into two types. The linking verbs *be, seem,* and *become* refer to states of being. The linking verbs *look, taste, smell, feel,* and *sound,* also called **sensory verbs**, refer to perceptions.

Sometimes the verb in a sentence is just one word, such as the action verb *attend* in this sentence:

We <u>attended</u> the caucus.

However, at other times, a main verb may be accompanied by one or more **auxiliary verbs**, such as the following:

Be (am, is, are, was, were, been):	aux main verb The students <u>are registering</u> for classes today.
Have (has, had):	aux main verb My friend <u>has studied</u> in Japan.
Do (does, did):	aux main verb They <u>do</u> not <u>support</u> the proposal.
Modal verbs (can, may, should, will, and others):	aux main verb We <u>should finish</u> by five o'clock.

Some words can be a main verb or an auxiliary verb. In fact, sometimes the same word is used twice in a sentence—once as a main verb and once as an auxiliary.

Jamie <u>did</u> not help prepare lunch, but he <u>did</u> the dishes.

> EXERCISE 20.5

Underline the verbs, including auxiliary verbs, in the following sentences.

1. The chair of the committee explained the proposal.
2. Everyone was talking at the same time.
3. No one could understand the logic of the proposal.
4. A similar proposal had been introduced a week ago.
5. The motion did not pass.

Thinking rhetorically about verbs

Decide which of the following sentences evokes a clearer image.

The team captain <u>was</u> happy. In fact, she <u>was</u> absolutely ecstatic.

Grinning broadly, the team captain <u>shot</u> both her arms into the air.

Although *be* in its many forms is the most frequently used verb, it is often avoided by writers whose rhetorical situation calls for vibrant imagery and stylistic variety. Instead, these writers favor strong action verbs.

Revise the following sentences so that the verbs help to evoke vivid images. You'll likely need to include sensory details.

1. We were tired.
2. My friend was surprised.
3. The road was extremely treacherous.

Phrasal Verbs

A **phrasal verb** has two parts: a verb and an adverbial particle (see page 544), such as *down, in,* or *up.* The two parts of a phrasal verb work together to create meaning. When not forming the phrasal verb, the two parts have their own distinct meanings. For instance, the two individual words *run* and *up* might make you think of an action and a direction: *running up a hill* or *running up the road.* When the two words work together in the phrasal verb *run up,* though, the meaning changes. If someone runs up a bill or a debt, that person is buying items on credit that he or she will have to pay for later.

Occasionally, the meaning of a phrasal verb can be derived from the meanings of its parts, especially when the particle *up* or *down* adds a sense of completion, as in *eat up* or *gobble down.* If you are unsure of the meaning of a phrasal verb, you can look for its verb in a comprehensive dictionary. Phrasal verbs are usually listed at the end of a verb's entry.

There are two types of phrasal verbs: separable and inseparable. As their name suggests, **separable phrasal verbs** can be separated. Notice how the parts of a separable phrasal verb can be separated by a pronoun or a short noun phrase (see page 544) but not by a long noun phrase:

I turned <u>it</u> in.

I turned <u>the test</u> in early.

I turned in <u>my paper on the harmful effects of secondhand smoke</u>.

The verb and the adverbial particle of an **inseparable phrasal verb** must always occur together:

into
I ran ^ some friends into yesterday.

> EXERCISE 20.7

Only one sentence in each of the following pairs contains a phrasal verb. Decide which sentence it is and explain how you know.

1. They looked up the road.
   They looked up the word.
2. I put the book on the shelf.
   I put the costume on.
3. He carried out the plan.
   He carried the specimens out the door.

Thinking rhetorically about phrasal verbs

As you know, informal language is appropriate for some rhetorical situations, but not for all. Because many phrasal verbs are considered conversational, you should find one-word synonyms for those that may sound too informal to your audience.

> *understood*
>
> They ∧ caught on to the idea immediately.

> ### EXERCISE 20.8

Replace the phrasal verbs with more formal one-word verbs.

1. You and your lab partner left out one step.
2. The stock prices went down rapidly.
3. The firefighters put out the wildfire.
4. The assistants put away the new shipment of paper.
5. The news editor blew up the old photograph.
6. Her explanation mixed me up even more.
7. The sponge did not take up much water.
8. The builders threw up that house in a month.
9. She turned down the job offer.
10. The young actress tried out for the play.

Adjectives

Adjectives modify nouns. *Modify* means to "qualify or limit the meaning of." If you use the noun *car* but want to limit the many different cars that may come to mind for your readers, you can add a modifier such as *black, rusty,* or *used.* **Attributive adjectives** usually precede, but occasionally follow, nouns or pronouns, as in *something special.* **Predicative adjectives** follow linking verbs such as *be, seem,* and *look* (when its meaning is "seem or appear"):

My schedule is <u>full</u>.   She seems <u>nervous</u>.   His face looks <u>familiar</u>.

> ### EXERCISE 20.9

Use both attributive and predicative adjectives to modify the following nouns.

1. building
2. book
3. song
4. idea
5. dinner

Thinking rhetorically about adjectives

You have already learned that using concrete nouns and action verbs can make your writing vivid. Not all rhetorical situations call for such writing, but if yours does, you should also choose precise adjectives that help you convey sensation or intensity. So instead of describing a movie you did not like with the overused adjective *bad* or *boring,* you could call it *tedious* or *predictable.* When you sense that you might be using a lackluster adjective, search for an alternative in a thesaurus. If you come across unfamiliar words, be sure to look them up in a dictionary so that you do not misuse them.

> EXERCISE 20.10

Find a movie review in a newspaper or online. Identify the adjectives used to describe the film and its actors, and note whether they are as precise as they can be.

Adverbs

Like adjectives, **adverbs** are modifiers. Instead of modifying nouns, however, they modify verbs, adjectives, and other adverbs. As modifiers of verbs, they provide information about time, manner, place, and frequency.

Time:	The festival begins <u>today</u>.
Manner:	She stated her position <u>forcefully</u>.
Place:	We will meet you <u>there</u> after lunch.
Frequency:	They <u>usually</u> close at five.

Depending on which words in a sentence you want to stress, you can move an adverb modifying a verb to other positions within the sentence:

<u>Today</u> the festival begins.

She <u>forcefully</u> stated her position.

Adverbs that modify adjectives or other adverbs intensify or otherwise qualify the meanings of these words.

Adverb modifying adjective:	The child was <u>mysteriously</u> clever.
Adverb modifying another adverb:	He ran <u>astonishingly</u> fast.

Thinking rhetorically about adverbs

Adverbs of manner can enliven your prose in a number of ways. Adding such an adverb can help you create a sharp portrayal of an action.

After he entered the end zone, the fullback <u>delicately</u> set the ball down beneath the goalposts.

When you are writing dialogue, you can use an adverb of manner to depict how somebody is speaking.

"You're late," he whispered <u>vehemently</u>.

Adverbs of manner modify not only action verbs but adjectives as well. Adverbs can add detail to a description:

He was curiously intelligent.

Adverb-adjective combinations are common in book, movie, and theater reviews. Here are a few from *The New Yorker: blazingly apt, fastidiously elegant, enchantingly quaint, fascinatingly indecipherable, cautiously hopeful, mesmerizingly persuasive.*

> ## > EXERCISE 20.11

Write a short paragraph in which you describe a movie or someone performing a task. Include at least three adverbs.

Pronouns

As its name suggests, a **pronoun** is similar to a noun. Like nouns, pronouns refer to people, places, things, events, or ideas. However, without context, determining which person, place, thing, event, or idea is the referent for a pronoun is impossible. If you read just the sentence *They are visiting campus today,* you would not know who the visitors were. In contrast, if that sentence were preceded by *Ten students from Japan arrived yesterday,* you would know immediately that *they* refers to the ten students from Japan. Pronouns fall into several categories: personal, demonstrative, interrogative, reflexive or intensive, and indefinite.

Personal pronouns

To understand the usage of personal pronouns, you must first learn about person, number, and case. The **person** of a pronoun distinguishes between the writer (first person), the reader (second person), and the person or thing discussed (third person). The **number** of a pronoun indicates whether there is just one or more than one referent. That is, pronouns can be either singular or plural. **Case** refers to the form a pronoun takes depending on its function in the sentence. Pronouns can be subjects, objects, or possessives. (You will learn more about subjects and objects in Chapter 21.) When they function as subjects, personal pronouns are in the subjective case; when they function as objects, they are in the objective case; and when they are possessives, they are in the possessive case.

	Subjective		Objective		Possessive	
Number	*Singular*	*Plural*	*Singular*	*Plural*	*Singular*	*Plural*
Person						
First person	I	we	me	us	mine	ours
Second person	you	you	you	you	yours	yours
Third person	he, she, it	they	him, her, it	them	his, hers, its	theirs

Grammar and Style

Demonstrative pronouns

The **demonstrative pronouns** are *this, that, these,* and *those.*

> <u>That</u> was the year when more people voted than ever before.

Demonstrative pronouns indicate physical or psychological proximity in either space or time.

Interrogative pronouns

Interrogative pronouns are question words that appear in the same positions in sentences as nouns do. *What* and *which* can be subjects or objects. *Who* is used as a subject, while its counterpart, *whom,* is used as an object. *Whose* is a possessive interrogative pronoun.

Subjective interrogative pronoun:	<u>Who</u> won the award?
Objective interrogative pronoun:	<u>Whom</u> did you consult?
Possessive interrogative pronoun:	<u>Whose</u> is it?

Who, which, whom, and *whose* can also be found in relative clauses, which are discussed on pages 567–569.

Reflexive or intensive pronouns

Myself, yourself, himself, herself, itself, ourselves, yourselves, and *themselves* are used as either **reflexive pronouns** or **intensive pronouns.** Both types of pronouns are objects and must be accompanied by subjects. Reflexive pronouns are used when the performer and recipient of an action are the same. Intensive pronouns are used to provide emphasis.

Reflexive pronoun:	<u>He</u> was always talking to <u>himself</u>.
Intensive pronoun:	I, <u>myself</u>, delivered the letter.

Indefinite pronouns

Indefinite pronouns do not have specific referents. Here are some of the most common indefinite pronouns:

everybody	everything	everyone
somebody	something	someone
nobody	nothing	none
one	each	any
few	some	many

Circle each pronoun in the paragraph below. Then, indicate what kind of pronoun each is (personal, demonstrative, interrogative, reflexive, intensive, or indefinite).

> I ran across a dim photograph of him the other day, going through some old things. He's been dead about forty years. His name was Rex (my two brothers and I named him when we were in our early teens) and he was a bull terrier. "An American bull terrier," we used to say, proudly; none of your English bulls. He had one brindle eye that sometimes made him look like a clown and sometimes reminded you of a politician with derby hat and cigar. The rest of him was white except for a brindle saddle that always seemed to be slipping off and a brindle stocking on a hind leg.
>
> —**James Thurber,** "A Snapshot of Rex"

Thinking rhetorically about pronouns

Because pronouns must have context to make their referents clear, be sure that you provide your readers with enough information to understand who or what each pronoun represents. Vague uses of *it, they, this,* and *that* can make your writing hard to follow. Notice the difficulty of identifying what *this* is in the following sentence:

> The study found that students succeed when they have clear directions, consistent and focused feedback, and access to help. This has led to the development of a tutoring center at our university.

This could refer to the study, the information provided by the study, or perhaps just to the finding that students need access to help. If you find that you have used a vague pronoun, add enough text to make the referent easily identifiable:

> The finding that successful students have access to help has led to the development of a tutoring center at our university.

> EXERCISE 20.13

Underline vague uses of pronouns in the following sentences. Then revise the sentences so that the pronouns have clear referents.

1. Has anyone proposed removing the tax on textbooks, or is this unlikely?
2. The young and innovative research team used unconventional procedures to produce provocative results. They will be described in today's newspaper.
3. When employees suggested that management might be guilty of some wrongdoing, it attracted the attention of journalists.

Prepositions and Adverbial Particles

Prepositions combine with pronouns, nouns, or noun phrases (see page 550) to form prepositional phrases: _at us, toward midnight, in an argument._ A prepositional phrase functions as either an adjective or an adverb.

My parents immediately noticed the stain <u>on the carpet</u>. [modifying _the stain_]

She put the check <u>on the table</u>. [modifying _put_]

Prepositions usually consist of only one word. Prepositions containing more than one word are called **phrasal prepositions.**

COMMON PREPOSITIONS

about	beneath	in	regarding
above	beside	inside	round
across	between	into	since
after	beyond	like	through
against	by	near	to
among	concerning	of	toward
around	despite	off	under
as	down	on	unlike
at	during	out	until
before	except	outside	up
behind	for	over	upon
below	from	past	with

PHRASAL PREPOSITIONS

according to	by way of	in spite of
along with	due to	instead of
apart from	except for	on account of
as for	in addition to	out of
as regards	in case of	with reference to
as to	in front of	in/with regard to
because of	in lieu of	with respect to
by means of	in place of	

An **adverbial particle** may look like a preposition, but its function is different. Whereas a preposition combines with a noun or noun substitute, an adverbial particle combines with a verb. The resulting verb plus particle unit is a **phrasal verb** (see page 538). The adverbial particle may sometimes be separated from the verb by pronouns or short noun phrases:

I <u>turned</u> my paper <u>in</u> yesterday.   I <u>blew</u> it <u>out</u>.

COMMON ADVERBIAL PARTICLES

about	back	on
across	down	out
ahead	forward	over
along	in	through
apart	off	

> EXERCISE 20.14

Identify the prepositions and adverbial particles in the following paragraph.

> As a Columbia College freshman, in 1960, I took the Humanities (Great Books) course with a gruff, crewcut philosophy instructor named Robert G. Olson, who was genially contemptuous of us and the institution. He used to stub his cigarettes out on the floor and mumble a wish that one day the place would burn down. I liked his irreverent, sardonic manner—even when he dressed me down for stealing others' ideas—and at last it dawned on me, after he chose me as the best student in his section (an honor that came with a $20 certificate at the university bookstore) that he liked me.
>
> —**Philip Lopate,** in *For the Love of Books* by Ronald B. Shwartz

Thinking rhetorically about prepositions and adverbial particles

Prepositions and adverbial particles are often found in idioms. An **idiom** is a word combination that has a meaning independent of the meanings of its individual words. For example, when we *come across* some money, we find it by chance. When we *come into* some money, we inherit it. Knowing the typical meanings of *come, across,* and *into* does not lead you to these definitions. There is no simple explanation as to why we use *across* with *come* in one idiom and *into* in the other.

Using idioms accurately will help ensure that you are expressing your thoughts clearly. Because many idioms are not included in conventional dictionaries, it is important to study how writers use them and to consult a specialized reference book such as *The BBI Dictionary of Word Combinations*.

> EXERCISE 20.15

Use each of the following idioms correctly in a sentence.

1. give back, give in, give out, give up
2. show regard for, in regard to, to regard someone as, to regard someone with
3. to chance upon, to leave something to chance, by chance, on the off chance

Conjunctions

The English word *conjunction* has its roots in the Greek word *sundesmos,* which means "binding together." And that is exactly what a conjunction does. A **coordinating conjunction** joins words or groups of words of the same grammatical category; for example, it links noun to noun, verb phrase to verb phrase, or independent clause to independent clause (see page 566).

> Gabon <u>and</u> Cameroon share a border. [connecting proper nouns]

> They were successful entrepreneurs, <u>but</u> they never boasted of their achievements. [connecting independent clauses]

There are seven coordinating conjunctions: *for, and, nor, but, or, yet, so.* Combining the first letters of these words gives *fanboys.* This made-up word can help you remember the coordinating conjunctions.

A **correlative conjunction** is a two-part conjunction. The four most common correlative conjunctions are *both . . . and, either . . . or, neither . . . nor,* and *not only . . . but also.* Like coordinating conjunctions, correlative conjunctions link words or groups of words of the same category.

> She has a degree <u>not only</u> in medicine <u>but also</u> in law. [connecting prepositional phrases]

Subordinating conjunctions introduce dependent clauses—clauses that must be linked to a main clause, or independent clause.

COMMON SUBORDINATING CONJUNCTIONS

after	in case	though
although	in that	till
as if	inasmuch as	unless
as though	insofar as	until
because	lest	when, whenever
before	now that	where, wherever
even if	once	whether
even though	since	while
how	so that	why
if	than	

> EXERCISE 20.16

The paragraph below is from Stacy Simkanin's first draft of the essay that is featured in Chapter 3. Identify the underlined words as coordinating or subordinating conjunctions. Be prepared to explain your answers.

> <u>But</u> at the same time <u>that</u> technology brings these advantages, it also inhibits learning <u>and</u> writing. I know <u>that when</u> I'm conducting online research I may be missing out on information <u>or</u> lowering the quality of information

because I'm limiting my searching to electronic sources. Nowadays, students don't really have to learn to use the library, where often more information can be found than what appears in an online search. I fear that students are placing convenience over quality. I know I do sometimes. The information online isn't always reliable, either. Students don't often take the time to investigate sources.

Thinking rhetorically about conjunctions

Your use of conjunctions conveys how you think ideas are related, so you must choose conjunctions carefully. Determining whether ideas are being compared, contrasted, or just presented sequentially is the first step in choosing an appropriate conjunction. Conjunctions convey a variety of meanings—addition, comparison, contrast, and purpose, to mention just a few. Some conjunctions are more specific than others, however. The conjunction *and,* for instance, can often be replaced by a more exact conjunction.

> so
>
> My grandparents moved away when I was little, ∧ and I seldom saw them.

Be sure that the meaning of the conjunction you use is not ambiguous. In the following sentence, *since* could mean either "after" or "because of":

> Since he arrived, we decided to leave.

The subordinating conjunction *after* or *because* would clarify the meaning in this sentence.

> EXERCISE 20.17

Revise the following sentences so that the connections are more precise.

1. As we were discussing my performance, the coach mentioned my slow times in the freestyle.
2. The clock struck one, and we were not finished.
3. Since she was elected to office, the deficit has decreased.

Expletives

The word *expletive* has its origin in a Latin word meaning "to fill out." The expletives *there* and *it* take the subject position in sentences either because there is no clear subject, as in *It's raining,* or because the information usually placed in the subject position has been moved to a position after the verb, as in *There's a fly in my soup.* Note that the expletive *there* is different from the adverb *there,* and the expletive *it* is different from the personal pronoun *it:*

> I live over there. [adverb]
>
> There is a full moon tonight. [expletive]
>
> We liked the apartment, but it was too expensive. [pronoun]
>
> It was surprising to see so many people at the rally. [expletive]

Thinking rhetorically about expletives

The expletives *it* and *there* allow information to be presented later in a sentence and thus stressed.

> A storm will be moving in tonight.

> There will be a storm moving in tonight.

When *there* opens the sentence, *storm* receives more emphasis than when it is in the subject position. Similarly, the placement of *it* at the beginning of the second sentence in the following pair allows the underlined information to be emphasized:

> That <u>we survived the ordeal</u> was amazing.

> It is amazing that <u>we survived the ordeal</u>.

> ### > EXERCISE 20.18
>
> Revise the following sentences so that the information in the subject position comes later in each sentence. Identify which words are stressed in the original and which are stressed in your revision.
>
> 1. A pod of orcas is hunting in Puget Sound.
> 2. That we have actually finished the project is hard to believe.
> 3. A quartet is singing in the alleyway.
> 4. A crowd is waiting outside the courthouse.
> 5. That no one noticed the problem earlier was odd.

Interjections

Some types of writing call for expressions of emotion. Such expressions are called **interjections**, which usually appear at the beginning of a sentence but may also occur in the middle or at the end of a sentence.

> <u>Phew</u>! That test burned up my synapses.

> My brothers, <u>alas</u>, were left to fend for themselves.

Thinking rhetorically about interjections

Most likely you will use interjections only in writing that is meant to mimic speech, as in this excerpt:

> Rosemary unlatches their tool kit, a tackle box. From it, Peter extracts a pair of jeweler's spectacles, a plastic mask with bulging lenses, which make him look like Robinson Crusoe from Mars. "<u>Okay</u>, Famous Bird," Peter says. "<u>Ow</u>! Famous Bird has decided to bite the hand that feeds him." He grasps the finch with one hand and its head sticks out observantly from his fist. The bird is about the size of a sparrow, and jet-black, with a black beak and shiny dark eyes.
>
> —Jonathan Weiner, *The Beak of the Finch*

Write a short paragraph in which you use one or two of the following interjections, or choose your own.

oh	yow	phew
hey	sheesh	wow
yay	hooray	ouch
well	no way	no

Sentence Structure and Rhetorical Effects

In Chapter 20, you studied the smaller parts of sentences—word classes such as nouns, pronouns, verbs, and so on. In this chapter, you'll see how these parts combine to form phrases and sentences and how they can be manipulated to help you achieve rhetorical effect. Studying elements of sentence structure will help you write clear, concise, and complete sentences.

Phrases

If you were asked to define *phrase*, the first definition to pop into your head might be "a group of words." Though this definition is accurate, its vagueness becomes apparent when you try to apply it. Try locating all the groups of words in the following sentence:

> Just as we painstakingly fit photos into albums or, in the new age, organize them into computer folders and make digital copies for safekeeping, so I hang on to the impression of a stainless-steel wristwatch that once applied a familiar force of weight to my left wrist. —**Marshall Jon Fisher**, "Memoria ex Machina"

Is *applied a familiar* a phrase? Is *weight to my left* a phrase? Clearly, these are groups of words, but the words in them are not related in a way that seems as natural to us as the groupings *a familiar force* and *my left wrist*.

Groupings occur at various levels in English. At the level of the word, a group consists of a root word and its prefix and/or suffix: <u>reexamining</u>. At the level of the phrase, most groups form around a **head word**. For example, *force* is the head word of *a familiar force,* and *wrist* is the head word of *my left wrist.* Types of phrases are named for their head words: in noun phrases, the head word is a noun; in verb phrases, the head word is a verb; and so on.

Noun phrases

A **noun phrase** is a group of words with a noun as the head word. The other words in the group modify the head word. In *the new age,* the determiner *the* indicates a specific referent, and the adjective *new* provides information to distinguish the age being referred to from other ages. See if you can pick out the head words in these noun phrases: *computer folders, a stainless-steel wristwatch, digital copies.* If you chose *folders, wristwatch,* and *copies,* you are right.

Complete the following sentence with noun phrases. Identify the head word in each.

_____ bumped and lurched along _____, _____ flying left and right, _____ brushing _____.

Thinking rhetorically about noun phrases

When you studied word classes, you learned the importance of being precise. A corollary of being precise is being concise. To write concisely, though, does not mean using only short sentences; rather, it means that you make each word count. During the editing stages of writing, look for words that can be deleted. Here are some likely candidates that you may find in noun phrases:

Nouns that are close in meaning:	The significance ~~and importance~~ of this new law was not immediately apparent.
Adjectives that are close in meaning:	She was given an award for her new ~~and innovative~~ design.
Unnecessary determiners:	Each ~~and every~~ student in the program received a progress report.
Unnecessary adjective:	You will receive a ~~complimentary~~ gift.

> EXERCISE 21.2

Delete any unnecessary words in the noun phrases of the following sentences.

1. Our future plans include a vacation in the Rockies.
2. The staff responded to each and every letter.
3. The children all have their own individual idiosyncrasies.
4. Listen for the full and complete report on the six o'clock news.
5. In a letter to her best friend, she expressed all her hopes and desires.

Prepositional phrases

A **prepositional phrase** is a combination of a preposition and a noun phrase. Such a phrase normally modifies another element in a sentence, providing information about time, location, direction, cause, accompaniment, and so on.

They moved <u>to a small town</u> <u>near Boise</u>. [*To a small town* modifies *moved*, providing information about direction. *Near Boise* modifies *town*, providing information about location.]

Because prepositions are generally followed by noun phrases, they do not usually appear at the ends of sentences. In fact, you may have heard the rule "Never end a sentence with a preposition." However, most style manuals, including *The Chicago Manual of Style* (probably the most widely used style guide), consider this rule outmoded, especially regarding prepositional phrases found in adjectival clauses (see page 567). Notice how much more natural this sentence sounds with a final preposition:

> Those are the principles <u>on</u> which we relied.

> Those are the principles we relied <u>on</u>.

Thinking rhetorically about prepositional phrases

When you are writing descriptive passages, you can use prepositional phrases beginning with *like* or *as* to make comparisons.

> He had always been so strange and had lived, <u>like a prophet</u>, in such unimaginably close communion with the Lord that his long silences which were punctuated by moans and hallelujahs and snatches of old songs while he sat at the living-room window never seemed odd to us. —**James Baldwin**, "Notes of a Native Son"

> Fog, melancholy <u>as a rain-soaked dog</u>, drifts through the highlands, beading my hair with moisture. On the path ahead a vermilion flycatcher, burning scarlet against the muted greens of the cloud forest, bursts up in flight. He flies to a space just over my head and flutters there furiously, an acrobatic stall, a tiny wild commotion that hounds me down the muddy trail, until I pass beyond the small arena of his life.
>
> —**Barry Lopez**, "Wide-Eyed in Galápagos"

These prepositional phrases are called **similes**. By including a simile, you can add details to a sentence or paragraph that needs further development.

> EXERCISE 21.3

Add similes to the following sentences.

1. Fireworks drifted down from the black heavens.
2. His diagram confused us all.
3. The crowd surged from the subway doors.

Verb phrases and tenses

Like a noun phrase, a **verb phrase** has a head word, which, in this type of phrase, is the main verb. Although a sentence may contain just a main verb, it also often includes **auxiliary verbs**, sometimes called **helping verbs**. In the following sentences, *work* is the main verb; *is, has, does,* and *might* are auxiliary verbs.

> She <u>works</u> for IBM.

> She <u>is working</u> this Saturday.

> She <u>has worked</u> there since 1995.

> <u>Does</u> she <u>work</u> near her home?

> She <u>might work</u> late tonight.

Notice that the main verb *work* has four different forms:

> work, works, working, worked

All **regular verbs** have four forms: (1) a base form, which is the form you find in the dictionary (*play, carry*); (2) an *-s* form, which consists of the base form and the suffix *-s* or, in some cases, *-es* (*plays, carries*); (3) an *-ing* form, also called the *present participle*, which is a combination of the base form and the suffix *-ing* (*playing, carrying*); and (4) an *-ed* form, which consists of the base form and the suffix *-ed* (*played, carried*). The *-ed* form has two alternative labels. When used without any auxiliary verb, it is called the *past form*:

> They *played* soccer together.

When used with an auxiliary verb, it is called the *past participle*:

> She *has carried* a heavy load.

VERB FORMS OF REGULAR VERBS

Base Form	-s *Form* (Present Tense, Third Person, Singular)	-ing *Form* (Present Participle)	-ed *Form* (Past Form or Past Participle)
talk	talks	talking	talked
match	matches	matching	matched
reply	replies	replying	replied
shop	shops	shopping	shopped

Irregular verbs have as few as three forms (*put, puts, putting*) up to as many as eight forms (*be, am, is, are, was, were, being, been*). The base form, the *-s* form, and the *-ing* form of an irregular verb (*drive, drives, driving*) are often similar to those forms of a regular verb. However, the past form (*drove*) and the past participle (*driven*) are not the regular *-ed* form. Some irregular verbs even have two acceptable past forms (*dived, dove*) or past participles (*beat, beaten*). For irregular verbs with only three forms, the base form, the past form, and the past participle are all the same (*let*). If you are unsure about verb forms, consult the following chart or a dictionary.

VERB FORMS OF IRREGULAR VERBS

Base Form	-s *Form* (Present Tense, Third Person, Singular)	-ing *Form* (Present Participle)	Past Form	Past Participle
beat	beats	beating	beat	beaten, beat
begin	begins	beginning	began	begun
forget	forgets	forgetting	forgot	forgotten
give	gives	giving	gave	given
lay	lays	laying	laid	laid
lie	lies	lying	lay	lain
put	puts	putting	put	put
rise	rises	rising	rose	risen
set	sets	setting	set	set

VERB FORMS OF IRREGULAR VERBS *(continued)*

Base Form	-s *Form* (Present Tense, Third Person, Singular)	-ing *Form* (Present Participle)	Past Form	Past Participle
steal	steals	stealing	stole	stolen
swim	swims	swimming	swam	swum
write	writes	writing	wrote	written

There are four types of auxiliary verbs: (1) *do, does, did;* (2) modal auxiliary verbs; (3) *will, be, have;* and (4) auxiliary verbs used in the passive voice (see page 562).

The auxiliary verb *do* is used to form yes/no questions, negations, and emphatic sentences.

<u>Do</u> you <u>like</u> your classes?

He <u>does</u> not <u>spend</u> much money.

I <u>did</u> return his phone call.

A **modal auxiliary verb**, the second type, adds information about such conditions as possibility and obligation to the main verb.

COMMON MEANINGS OF MODAL AUXILIARY VERBS

Meaning	Modal Auxiliary	Main Verb	Example
ability	can	solve	He *can* solve the problem.
advice	should	wear	You *should* wear sunscreen.
certainty	will	finish	They *will* finish before the deadline.
obligation	must	pay	She *must* pay the fine by Friday.
permission	may	use	They *may* use our equipment.
possibility	might	go	I *might* go to China this summer.

The auxiliary verbs *will, be,* and *have* are used to indicate verb tense and verb aspect. To fully understand how these auxiliary verbs work in verb phrases, you'll need to recognize the difference between tense and aspect.

English has three tenses: present, past, and future. Verbs are marked for aspect as well as for tense. **Aspect** provides information about the completion of an action, event, or state and about the relation of one verb to other verbs in a time sequence. The sentences *The wind blows in the spring* and *The wind is blowing hard* both use the present tense, but they differ in aspect. *Blows,* in the first sentence, refers to a habitual action; *is blowing,* in the second sentence, refers to an incomplete action. To indicate the difference in aspect, *blows* is labeled as the **simple present** and *is blowing* is labeled as the **present progressive**. There are four aspect labels: simple, progressive, perfect, and perfect progressive.

Sometimes two different aspects are used in one sentence to show a sequence of actions:

I had been talking on the telephone when the storm hit.

The past perfect progressive *had been talking* indicates that the action was ongoing and occurred prior to the action indicated by the simple past *hit*.

The following chart provides labels for and examples of verb tense–aspect combinations.

TENSE–ASPECT COMBINATIONS AND THEIR USES

	Tense		
Aspect	*Present*	*Past*	*Future*
Simple	Simple present **study, studies** Use to refer to current states, habitual actions, and general truths: *Judith studies every night she's not working.*	Simple past **studied** Use to refer to completed past events or actions: *We studied together last night.*	Simple future **will study** Use to refer to future states or actions: *I will study for my French exam over the weekend.*
Progressive	Present progressive **am, is, are studying** Use to refer to activities in progress or situations considered temporary: *Carlos is studying until he has to leave for class.*	Past progressive **was, were studying** Use to signal a repeated or ongoing action or event in the past: *Reese and Krissi were studying architecture while in Italy.*	Future progressive **will be studying** Use to refer to actions that will be ongoing in the future: *You will be studying while I am at the gym.*
Perfect	Present perfect **has, have studied** Use to refer to a situation originating in the past but continuing into the present or to a past action or state with current relevance: *I have studied Japanese for five years now.*	Past perfect **had studied** Use to indicate that a completed action occurred prior to another action in the past: *Marie thought that she had studied long enough.*	Future perfect **will have studied** Use to refer to a future action that will be completed by a specified time: *By the time I have to leave for work, I will have studied my biology notes.*

	Tense		
Aspect	*Present*	*Past*	*Future*
Perfect progressive	*Present perfect progressive*	*Past perfect progressive*	*Future perfect progressive*
	has been, have been studying	**had been studying**	**will have been studying**
	Use to show that an action or state originating in the past is ongoing or incomplete: *Ryan has been studying for less than ten minutes.*	Use to show that an ongoing past action occurred prior to another completed action: *Lori had been studying so hard that she overslept the next morning.*	Use to refer to an ongoing action that will continue for a specific amount of time: *In 30 minutes, we will have been studying for five straight hours.*

> EXERCISE 21.4

Identify the tense and aspect of the verb phrases in the following sentences; explain why they have been used, inventing context as necessary.

1. He will deliver your package tomorrow.
2. She has taught kindergarten for twenty years.
3. The team has been practicing since October.
4. I have read that book already.
5. My neighbor usually goes to the park on Sundays.
6. It had snowed two feet that day.
7. Earlier that afternoon, they had been playing chess.
8. They are experts in their field.
9. He is planning a party.
10. By the end of 2015, we will have visited all the states.
11. My friend and I are working in a national park this summer.
12. We paid for our own tickets.
13. Everyone will be celebrating this weekend.
14. In ten minutes, I will have been dancing for twenty-four hours.
15. My son was laughing through the entire movie.

Thinking rhetorically about verb tense

A fiction writer may use the present tense to tell a story because it makes the events seem immediate.

We <u>drive</u> past Half Moon Bay and Pacifica and Seaside, the condos on the left and the surfers on the right, the ocean exploding pink. We <u>pass</u> through cheering eucalyptus and waving pines, cars <u>reflect</u> wildly as they <u>come</u> at us, they <u>seem</u> to come right for us, and I <u>look</u> through their windshields for the faces of those coming at us, for a sign, for their understanding, for their trust, and I <u>find</u> their trust and they <u>go</u> by. Our car <u>thrums</u> loudly and I <u>turn</u> up the radio because I <u>can</u>. I <u>drum</u> the steering wheel with open palms, then fists, because I <u>can</u>. Toph <u>looks</u> at me. I <u>nod</u> gravely.

—**Dave Eggers**, *A Heartbreaking Work of Staggering Genius*

> EXERCISE 21.5

To get a sense of the difference between the uses of the present and past tenses, change all of the underlined verbs in the excerpt by Dave Eggers to the past tense.

Verbal phrases

Verbal phrases are phrases with verb forms that are not marked for tense: the present participle (*asking*), the past participle (*asked*), and the infinitive (*to ask*). Depending on which form is used and what its role is in the sentence, a verbal phrase may be a gerund phrase, a participial phrase, or an infinitive phrase.

A **gerund phrase** has the present participle (*-ing* form) at its core. Even though a gerund is a verb form, it plays the role of a noun. Notice how the gerund phrase in the following sentences can be replaced by a pronoun—just as a noun phrase can:

It
~~Wrapping presents~~ is easy for some people.

A **participial phrase** is formed with either the present participle (the *-ing* form) or the past participle (the *-ed* form for regular verbs or a special form for irregular verbs). (Consult the chart on pages 553–554 for some irregular past participles.) A participial phrase differs from a gerund phrase in that it takes the role of a modifier, not a noun phrase.

Hoping to graduate in May, the students worked diligently on their final projects.

A participial phrase often begins a sentence, but it can appear in the middle or at the end of a sentence.

Encouraged by job prospects, the students worked diligently to graduate.

The students, hoping to graduate in May, worked diligently on their final projects.

The students worked diligently on their final projects, hoping to graduate in May.

An **infinitive phrase** comprises the infinitive marker *to* and the base form of a verb. An infinitive phrase takes the role of either a noun phrase or a modifier.

He continued to play the trumpet after he graduated from high school.

To solve the traffic problem, the city manager has proposed a subway system.

Notice that the infinitive phrase in the first sentence cannot be moved because it is taking the role of a noun phrase; the infinitive phrase in the second sentence could be moved to the middle or end of the sentence because it is a nonessential modifier, simply providing additional information.

> The city manager, <u>to solve the traffic problem</u>, has proposed a subway system.

> The city manager has proposed a subway system <u>to solve the traffic problem</u>.

> EXERCISE 21.6

Identify the verbal phrases in the following paragraph.

> I see four kinds of pressure working on college students today: economic pressure, parental pressure, peer pressure, and self-induced pressure. It is easy to look around for villains—to blame the colleges for charging too much money, the professors for assigning too much work, the parents for pushing their children too far, the students for driving themselves too hard. But there are no villains, only victims.
>
> —**William Zinsser,** "College Pressures"

Thinking rhetorically about verbal phrases

By using verbal phrases, you can make your writing both concise and varied. If some sentences sound monotonous or choppy, try combining them with a verbal phrase.

Choppy: The ecstatic fans crowded the city streets. They were celebrating their team's first state championship.

Revised: <u>Crowding the city streets</u>, the ecstatic fans celebrated their team's first state championship.

OR

<u>Celebrating their team's first state championship</u>, the ecstatic fans crowded the city streets.

Using a verbal phrase also allows you to focus on action, rather than on the agents of action.

> They bundle products together, which often results in higher consumer costs.

> <u>Bundling products together</u> often results in higher consumer costs.

It is the bundling that is the focus, not the bundlers.

> EXERCISE 21.7

Combine the following pairs of sentences, using a participial phrase for the first pair, a gerund phrase for the second, and an infinitive phrase for the third.

1. He wrote frantically throughout the night.
He completed his portfolio by class time.

2. Some drivers try to beat red lights.
This behavior often causes accidents.

3. You could argue about this point.
But such argument is useless in the end.

Subjects and Predicates

Every complete sentence has a subject and a predicate. The **subject** has a noun or noun substitute at its core; the **predicate** has a verb at its core. If only the core words are used, a sentence consists of two words: *Everyone laughed.* Most sentences, though, include modifiers: *Everyone in the audience laughed uproariously.* Even with modifiers, this sentence still has just two parts. *Everyone in the audience* is the subject, and *laughed uproariously* is the predicate.

The subject of a sentence generally corresponds to the topic of the sentence, and the predicate provides a comment about the topic. Most native speakers of English can easily separate the subject and the predicate. Try to do so with the following sentences:

Many people in the United States study karate.

Japanese forms of karate focus on simple movement.

If you separated the first sentence between *States* and *study* and the second between *karate* and *focus,* you have a head start in understanding sentence composition.

> ## EXERCISE 21.8

Identify the subjects and the predicates in the following proverbs.

1. Practice makes perfect.
2. A rolling stone gathers no moss.
3. A stitch in time saves nine.

Thinking rhetorically about subjects and predicates

If you would like to add some variety to your sentence patterns, try moving the predicate to the front of a sentence.

A small dog with large brown eyes <u>was peering through the window.</u>

<u>Peering through the window was</u> a small dog with large brown eyes.

Sentences in which a verb phrase includes the present participle (-*ing* form) are good candidates for this type of inversion. When you move the -*ing* form of the verb to the beginning of the sentence and place the subject at the end of the sentence, you not only vary the sentence structure but also create some suspense. The reader must wait to find out who or what was peering through the window—that is, who or what is the agent of the action.

> ## EXERCISE 21.9

Rewrite each sentence so that the predicate occurs before the subject.

1. A group of protestors were standing by the door.
2. Two of my friends were vying for first place.
3. A distant cloud of smoke was attracting everyone's attention.

Sentence Patterns

Sentence patterns are determined by the type of verb found in the predicate—a linking verb or an action verb (see pages 536–537). There are six common patterns. The first pattern includes a linking verb, such as *be, seem,* or *look,* followed by a **subject complement**, usually a noun phrase or an adjectival phrase (a phrase in which the head word is an adjective).

1. SUBJECT + LINKING VERB + SUBJECT COMPLEMENT

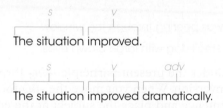

s   v   sc: noun phrase
I was the chair of the committee.

s   v   sc: adjectival phrase
Some people are allergic to cat hair.

Related to this pattern is another in which the linking verb is followed by an adverbial phrase, usually signaling time or place.

2. SUBJECT + LINKING VERB + ADVERBIAL PHRASE

s   v   adv: prepositional phrase (place)
They are in the library.

The remaining patterns all have action verbs as their predicate cores. Action verbs can be divided into two types: transitive and intransitive. These labels come from the stem *trans,* meaning "over or across." The action of a **transitive verb** carries over to an object—most frequently a noun phrase. The action of an **intransitive verb** does not carry over; the verb occurs by itself or with an adverb or adverb substitute.

3. SUBJECT + INTRANSITIVE VERB

s   v
The situation improved.

s   v   adv
The situation improved dramatically.

In contrast, a transitive verb is followed by at least one noun phrase (or sometimes just a noun or pronoun) called the **direct object**. The direct object generally receives the action of the verb.

4. SUBJECT + TRANSITIVE VERB + DIRECT OBJECT

s   v   do
He wrote detective stories.

In some sentences, the direct object is followed by a noun phrase or adjectival phrase that identifies or describes it. This type of phrase is called an **object**

complement. Object complements help complete the meaning of such verbs as *consider, call,* and *elect.*

5. SUBJECT + TRANSITIVE VERB + DIRECT OBJECT + OBJECT COMPLEMENT

$$\begin{array}{cccc} s & v & do & \text{oc: noun phrase} \end{array}$$

They considered her the best candidate.

$$\begin{array}{cccc} s & v & do & \text{oc: adjectival phrase} \end{array}$$

The judges called my project somewhat unconventional.

In addition to a direct object, an **indirect object** may follow a transitive verb. Like a direct object, an indirect object may be a noun, a pronoun, or a noun phrase. It is most commonly used to indicate the recipient of the direct object and thus follows verbs such as *buy, give,* and *send.*

6. SUBJECT + TRANSITIVE VERB + INDIRECT OBJECT + DIRECT OBJECT

$$\begin{array}{cccc} s & v & io & do \end{array}$$

My father sent me a care package.

> ### EXERCISE 21.10

Identify the pattern of each of the following sentences.

1. The volcano erupted.
2. The electrician clipped the wires.
3. Your license expires tomorrow.
4. His followers considered him a guru.
5. His argument seems persuasive.
6. They are in Indonesia right now.
7. She is a member of the marketing team.
8. The judge declared him the winner.
9. The photographer showed me her recent work.
10. I found the lecture provocative.

Thinking rhetorically about sentence patterns

If you want to emphasize a contrast or intensify a feeling, use a sentence with a transitive verb and a direct object and place the direct object at the start of the sentence.

They loved the queen. They despised the king.

They loved the queen. The king they despised.

I acquired English in the crib. I learned Japanese on the street.

I acquired English in the crib. Japanese I learned on the street.

Read the preceding example sentences aloud and put a mark by the words receiving major stress. In a sentence with conventional word order (subject-verb-object), the main stress usually occurs near the end of the sentence. When you move the object to the front of the sentence, you also move the stress forward.

> EXERCISE 21.11

Move the direct object to the beginning of the second sentence of each pair to make it more emphatic. Note the differences in sentence stress.

1. Leah considers her medical studies her priority. She calls her rock band a hobby.
2. He learned to play the clarinet when he was eight. He mastered the saxophone later on.
3. They renovated the state house. They condemned the old hotel.

Passive Voice

The voice of a sentence is either active or passive. (Do not confuse these labels with aggression or submission. They simply designate the way the subject is related to the verb.) In a sentence written in the active voice, the focus is on a subject (an agent) that usually initiates an action. Conversely, in a sentence written in the passive voice, the focus is on a subject that receives or undergoes the action of the verb.

Active voice: Robert Goddard launched the first liquid-fuel rocket in 1926.

Passive voice: The first liquid-fuel rocket was launched by Robert Goddard in 1926.

Notice that the verbs in these two example sentences differ. In the passive voice, the verb phrase consists of a form of the auxiliary verb *be* and the past participle of the main verb. Depending on the tense and aspect, the auxiliary verbs *have* (or *has* or *had*), *will,* and/or a second form of *be* are also necessary parts of the verb phrase.

ASPECT AND TENSE WITH PASSIVE VOICE

Aspect	Tense		
	Present	*Past*	*Future*
Simple	Simple present **am, is, are asked**	Simple past **was, were asked**	Simple future **will be asked**
Progressive	Present progressive **am, is, are being asked**	Past progressive **was, were being asked**	Future progressive **uncommon**
Perfect	Present perfect **has, have been asked**	Past perfect **had been asked**	Future perfect **will have been asked**

In a sentence written in the passive voice, an agent may appear as the object of the preposition *by.* If a passive sentence does not have an agent, it is called a **short passive.**

Full passive: The East Building of the National Gallery was designed by I. M. Pei.

Short passive: The East Building of the National Gallery was completed in 1978.

> EXERCISE 21.12

Identify each sentence as active or passive.

1. Alexander Graham Bell invented the telephone.
2. Radium and polonium were discovered by Marie Curie.
3. More than a thousand devices, including the phonograph, were patented by Thomas Edison.

Thinking rhetorically about the passive voice

Although the passive voice is often used in academic writing, it is not the best choice for all writing. The following tips will help you determine when to use the passive voice and when to avoid using it.

USING THE PASSIVE VOICE

▶ Use the passive voice to provide cohesion. The noun near the end of one sentence and the noun at the beginning of the next sentence will be closely linked.

She wrote most of her **stories** between 1936 and 1954. Her first **story** was published when she was just sixteen.

▶ Use the passive voice to focus on someone or something receiving or undergoing the action of the verb.

As early as 1000 BCE, a writing system had been devised by the Phoenicians. Its twenty-two consonants were written horizontally, from right to left.

▶ Use a short passive when the identity of the agent is unknown, unimportant, or obvious from the larger context.

John F. Kennedy was elected president in 1962.

▶ Use a short passive when it is tactful to leave the agent unmentioned.

Some members of the staff were excluded.

▶ Use a full passive when the agent is new information that should be emphasized.

They were surrounded by people cheering and throwing confetti.

AVOIDING THE PASSIVE VOICE

▶ Avoid the passive voice if your goal is to be concise. A sentence in the passive voice will be longer than its active counterpart.

The new route <u>was discovered</u> by Lewis and Clark.

Lewis and Clark <u>discovered</u> the new route.

▶ Avoid using a short passive if your readers should know who is responsible for an action.

The documents <u>were not released</u> until May.

The corporation <u>did not release</u> the documents until May.

▶ Avoid shifting to the passive voice if it would cause a distracting change in focus.

The travel agent printed the itinerary, which <u>was then sent</u> to the client.

The travel agent printed the itinerary and sent it to the client.

OR

The travel agent printed the itinerary; her assistant sent it to the client.

> EXERCISE 21.13

Find the active and passive sentences in the passage below. In each instance, explain why the writer chose to use active or passive voice.

Korean was once written with Chinese characters, which had been introduced in the first centuries AD. However, Korean suffixes could not be easily represented by Chinese writing. Various devices were tried to alleviate this problem but inadequacies persisted. Finally, King Sejong (1419–1452) commissioned an alphabetic script, called *hangul*, consisting of eleven vowels and seventeen consonants that, after some modifications over the centuries, became the standard Korean writing system. An especially interesting feature of hangul is that symbols are grouped together into syllable-sized clusters rather than being arranged in a completely linear fashion.

—William O'Grady, Michael Dobrovolsky, and Mark Aronoff,
Contemporary Linguistics

Sentence Types

Think of all the ways you use sentences every day. You probably ask questions, give directions, make suggestions, report news, give compliments, tell jokes—to mention just a few. To accomplish your purposes when writing, you'll use four common sentence types: declarative, imperative, interrogative, and exclamatory.

Declarative sentences

A **declarative sentence**, the most common type, is often used to report facts, express opinions, or share information. Declarative sentences follow the sentence patterns presented on pages 560–561.

> We camped out at Crater Lake.

Imperative sentences

An **imperative sentence** differs from a declarative sentence in that its subject is rarely stated. In fact, the subject of such a sentence is often referred to as the *understood you*. You use imperative sentences when you are giving directions.

> Turn left at the corner of Elm and Fairview.

Interrogative sentences

An **interrogative sentence** is a question. **Yes/no questions** are those that can be answered with *yes, no,* or a word indicating possibility such as *maybe* or *perhaps*. In contrast, **wh- questions** are used to elicit specific information. They begin with *wh-* words: *what, who, whom, where, when, why,* and *how*. Interrogative sentences are punctuated with question marks.

> *Yes/no question:*   Can we improve the design?
>
> *Wh- question:*   Why did the expedition succeed?

Exclamatory sentences

Any of the types of sentences just described can be written as an **exclamatory sentence** by placing an exclamation point at the end. This punctuation mark indicates emphasis, either positive or negative.

> They won all three games!
>
> Report accidents immediately!
>
> How could they have believed such a lie!

> ### > EXERCISE 21.14
>
> Identify the type of each sentence.
>
> 1. Who is going to the concert?
> 2. Go early to get good seats.
> 3. The concert was six hours long.
> 4. What an amazing night that was!

Thinking rhetorically about sentence types

One type of interrogative sentence, the rhetorical question, is not a true question because an answer is not expected. Instead, like a declarative sentence, a rhetorical question is used to state an opinion. However, a comparison between declarative sentences and rhetorical questions reveals a surprising difference. A positive question often corresponds to a negative assertion, and vice versa.

Should we allow our rights to be taken away?

We shouldn't allow our rights to be taken away.

Isn't it time to make a difference?

It's time to make a difference.

Because they are more emphatic than declarative sentences, rhetorical questions are used to focus the reader's attention on major points.

> EXERCISE 21.15

Find the rhetorical question in the following excerpt. State the author's claim.

I also take a dim, or perhaps a buffaloed, view of electronic slang. Perhaps I should view it as a linguistic milestone, as historic as the evolution of Cockney rhyming slang in the 1840s. But will the future generations who reopen our hard drives be stirred by the eloquence of the e-acronyms recommended by a Web site on "netiquette"?

—Anne Fadiman, "Mail"

Clauses

If you have not studied grammar before, you may not have realized that you have already studied clauses in this book. You have learned the essential parts of a sentence and the different types of sentences. A sentence, basically, is a clause—an **independent clause**. Sentences can include other clauses as well. Specifically, **dependent clauses** can be embedded within sentences. The following independent clause consists of a subject, transitive verb, and a direct object:

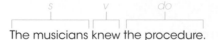

The musicians knew the procedure.

Notice how this sentence becomes more precise with the addition of embedded dependent clauses:

adjectival clause

The musicians, who had played the same song hundreds of times, knew

noun clause   *adverbial clause*

that they were supposed to begin playing when Joe turned his head to the right.

The adjectival clause provides information about the musicians, the noun clause elaborates on the procedure, and the adverbial clause adds information about time.

Relative (adjectival) clauses

A **relative clause**, also called an **adjectival clause**, modifies a pronoun, a noun, or a noun phrase. Like an adjective, then, it provides descriptive or qualifying information that helps the reader identify or recognize a referent. Compare *the architect* and *the architect who designs schools*. The latter noun phrase is more precise because it has a modifying clause.

A relative clause ordinarily begins with one of these relative pronouns: *who, whom, which,* or *that.* To provide a link to the independent clause, the relative pronoun corresponds to a word or words in the independent clause, called the **antecedent**.

antecedent relative pronoun

The students talked to a reporter who had just returned from overseas.

Notice that the dependent clause can become an independent clause if you replace the relative pronoun with its antecedent:

A reporter had just returned from overseas.

Who versus whom Although a relative pronoun always begins a dependent clause, it is not always the subject.

s

Who as subject: They will hire someone who is trustworthy.

do

Whom as direct object: They will hire someone whom they can trust.

You can determine whether to use *who* or *whom* by rewriting the dependent clause as an independent clause using *someone* in place of the relative pronoun.

who [subject]

Someone is trustworthy.

whom [direct object]

They can trust someone.

By noting the relationship of the relative pronoun to the verb, you will be able to identify whether it is subject or direct object. (See the Glossary of Usage for more on *who* versus *whom.*)

Essential (restrictive) versus nonessential (nonrestrictive) relative clauses Knowing the difference between an essential clause and a nonessential clause will help you decide how to punctuate sentences containing such clauses. A clause that a reader needs in order to correctly identify the referent is an **essential clause**.

antecedent   essential relative clause

The person who presented the award was last year's winner.

A **nonessential clause** is *not* needed for correct identification of the referent and thus is set off by commas. A nonessential clause often follows a proper noun (a specific name).

antecedent   nonessential relative clause

Andrea Bowen, who presented the award, was last year's winner.

That* versus *which According to the traditional rule, *that* is used in essential relative clauses, and *which* is used in nonessential relative clauses.

I need a job that pays well.

I took a job, which pays well enough.

However, some professional writers do not follow both parts of this rule. Although they will not use *that* in nonessential relative clauses, they will use *which* in essential relative clauses.

According to Trask, *pragmatics* is "the branch of linguistics which studies how utterances communicate meaning in context."

> EXERCISE 21.16

Punctuate the following sentences as needed. Be prepared to state whether a sentence has an essential or a nonessential relative clause.

1. Hippocrates who is credited with writing many books on the medical aspects of animal science lived in the fourth and fifth centuries BCE.
2. Zoology which is the study of animals has its origin in the works of Aristotle.
3. There are four areas of study that form the cornerstones of biology: taxonomy, anatomy, physiology, and genetics.
4. What is the name of the scientist whose contributions shaped the cornerstones of biology?
5. Binomial nomenclature which was introduced by Linnaeus assigns a two-word Latin name to each species.

> EXERCISE 21.17

Complete each sentence with *who* or *whom*.

1. Charles Darwin, _____ was born on February 12, 1809, was the son of a physician.
2. A professor _____ was also a good friend recommended him for a position on a scientific expedition.
3. Emma Wedgewood, _____ Darwin married in 1839, was the scientist's cousin.

Thinking rhetorically about relative clauses

If some of your sentences sound monotonous or choppy, try to combine them by using a relative clause.

> *Dub* is a car magazine. It appeals to drivers with a hip-hop attitude.

> *Dub* is a car magazine that appeals to drivers with a hip-hop attitude.

> A Hovercraft can go where many vehicles cannot. It is practically amphibious.

> A Hovercraft, which can go where many vehicles cannot, is practically amphibious.

> EXERCISE 21.18

Combine the following pairs of sentences, using relative clauses.

1. Charles Darwin showed no early academic promise.
   He was interested in natural history as a boy.
2. Evolution was also studied by earlier thinkers.
   Evolution was first called "descent with modification" by Darwin.
3. Earthworms are not guided by instinct alone.
   Darwin studied earthworms for forty years.

Adverbial clauses

An **adverbial clause** provides information about time, manner, place, condition, concession, or reason. The type of information contained in such a clause is signaled by the word that begins it—a subordinating conjunction (see page 546).

Time:	You must pay a fee <u>when you register</u>.
Manner:	It looked <u>as though it were written a long time ago</u>.
Place:	<u>Wherever you find balsam root</u>, you will find lupine.
Condition:	I will be surprised <u>if my proposal is accepted</u>.
Concession:	<u>Although they were far away</u>, I could still hear their voices.
Reason:	My friends, <u>because they arrived late</u>, were asked to sit in the back row.

Another function of the adverbial clause is to add meaning to an adjective or an adjectival phrase.

After an adjective:	She was pleased <u>that so many people attended the seminar</u>.

An adverbial clause may also be used in a comparison.

Comparison:	The schools in this district received more funding <u>than the schools in the adjacent district did</u>.

Adverbial clauses appear at various places in sentences—at the beginning, middle, or end. Notice that when an adverbial clause begins or interrupts a sentence, it is separated from the rest of the sentence by a comma or commas.

An adverbial clause that appears at the end of a sentence is not set off by a comma unless it is nonessential.

> She must have been in her office, because the lights were on.

> ### EXERCISE 21.19

Identify the adverbial clause in each sentence.

   1. I went for a walk because the weather was nice.
   2. I was glad that the weather was nice.
   3. The weather was nicer than it usually is.
   4. The wind blew less gustily than it usually does.
   5. I walked until I could walk no further.
   6. I had walked further than I had intended to.

Thinking rhetorically about adverbial clauses

To make your writing concise, you can condense adverbial clauses beginning with *while, when,* or *though.* You can often omit the subject and auxiliary verb *be* as long as the subject of the dependent clause is the same as the subject of the independent clause.

> While we were rafting, we saw a rare owl.

> While rafting, we saw a rare owl.

If the subjects of the dependent and independent clauses are not the same, the independent clause may have to be revised to ensure clarity and coherence.

>   *I thought of*
> While reading the statistics, ~~a few questions occurred to me.~~

> ### EXERCISE 21.20

Write three sentences with condensed adverbial clauses. Use a different subordinating conjunction (*while, when,* or *though*) in each sentence.

Noun clauses

As its name suggests, a **noun clause** is similar to a noun or a noun phrase. Although a noun clause differs from a noun or a noun phrase because it contains a verb, it too can be a subject, a direct object, or a subject complement. To test whether a clause is a noun clause, try replacing it with a pronoun. If such a substitution is possible, then the clause is a noun clause.

>   *It [subject]*
> Whether we win or lose is not important.

>   *this [direct object]*
> The pollsters asked many students whether they would vote this year.

>   *this [subject complement]*
> The question is whether we have sufficient funding.

Noun clauses usually begin with *if, that,* or a *wh-* word such as *what* or *why.* You can omit *that* from the beginning of a noun clause as long as the sentence retains its meaning.

> The author said <u>he traveled to India to do research for his book</u>.

Be sure to retain the introductory *that* when you have more than one noun clause in a sentence.

> The author said <u>that</u> he traveled to India to do research for his book but <u>that</u> the story was not autobiographical.

> EXERCISE 21.21

Identify the noun clauses in these sentences.

1. Some researchers believe that tests can verify the existence of intelligence.
2. Some parents ask if the tests are reliable.
3. Researchers must explain how the scores are calculated.

Thinking rhetorically about noun clauses

You may sometimes use an adjective to express your attitude toward a piece of information expressed in a noun clause.

> *noun clause*   *adj*
> That she will run for office again is doubtful.

When the noun clause is extremely long or when you want to emphasize it, you can start your sentence with the expletive *it* and place the noun clause after the adjective.

> *exp*   *adj*   *noun clause*
> It is doubtful that she will run for office again.

If you read these two example sentences aloud, you'll be able to hear the difference in stress. The following adjectives frequently occur with the expletive *it* and a noun clause: *possible, clear, amazing, funny, nice, odd, sad, understandable, crucial, essential, important, necessary.*

> EXERCISE 21.22

Rewrite each sentence, using the expletive *it,* an adjective, and a noun clause.

1. The defendant was not guilty.
2. Many citizens volunteered to help the flood victims.
3. The nighttime temperatures have dropped dramatically.

Sentence Classification

Sentences are often classified according to the number and type of clauses they contain.

Simple sentences

A **simple sentence** has one independent clause.

> They solved the problem easily.

Even when a prepositional phrase or a verbal phrase is added, the sentence is still considered simple.

> Having studied hard the night before, they solved the problem easily.

Compound sentences

A **compound sentence** consists of at least two independent clauses, joined by a coordinating conjunction or a semicolon.

> Books were expensive, but magazines were affordable.

> Books were expensive; magazines were affordable.

Complex sentences

A **complex sentence** includes at least one independent clause and at least one dependent clause. Noun clauses, adjectival clauses, and adverbial clauses are dependent clauses.

> *dependent clause*
>
> Everyone shook hands after the game was over.

> *dependent clause*
>
> Whoever designed that building was a genius.

Compound-complex sentences

A **compound-complex sentence** has the features of a compound sentence (at least two independent clauses) and a complex sentence (at least one dependent clause).

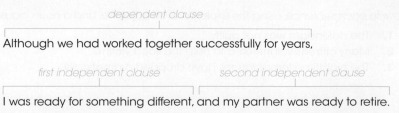

> *dependent clause*
>
> Although we had worked together successfully for years,
>
> *first independent clause*   *second independent clause*
>
> I was ready for something different, and my partner was ready to retire.

Identify each sentence as simple, compound, complex, or compound-complex.

1. Designed by Frank Gehry, the Walt Disney Concert Hall is unusual yet appealing.
2. The Disney Concert Hall is the home of the Los Angeles Philharmonic.
3. Not only is the concert hall an awe-inspiring piece of architecture, it is also the perfect place to hear music.
4. Because the hall's acoustical design is excellent, many musicians hope to play there.
5. Although audiences for concert music are not as large as they used to be, the novelty of this concert hall may bring old concert-goers back, and it may lure new concert-goers in.

Thinking rhetorically about sentence structure

If you find that one of your paragraphs consists of simple sentences only, try combining some of your ideas into compound, complex, or compound-complex sentences. Here is an example of a paragraph that could use some help:

> I rode the school bus every day. I didn't like to, though. The bus smelled bad. And it was always packed. The worst part was the bumpy ride. Riding the bus was like riding in a worn-out sneaker.

Once you try combining some of your ideas, you might find that you need to add information as well.

> As a kid, I rode the school bus every day, but I didn't like to. I hated the smell, the crowd, and the ride itself. Every seat was filled with a kid, and many of the kids took their shoes off for the long ride home down a road so bumpy you couldn't even read a comic book. Riding that bus was like riding inside a worn-out sneaker.

> EXERCISE 21.24

Vary the sentence structure in the following paragraph. Add details as needed.

> We arrived at the afternoon jazz concert late. We couldn't find any seats. It was hot, so we stood in the shade. We finally found seats under an umbrella. The shade didn't help, though. We could feel our brains melting. The music was cool, but we sure weren't.

22

Editing for Clarity and Style

Jack Finney began his book *Invasion of the Body Snatchers* with this sentence:

> I warn you that what you're about to read is full of loose ends and unanswered questions.

But he could have written other sentences to express a similar idea:

> Warning: what you are about to read is full of loose ends and unanswered questions.

> I warn you that you are about to read something that has many loose ends and questions that have not been answered yet.

> What you are about to read, I warn you, is full of unanswered questions and loose ends.

Can you add other versions to this list? We do not know whether Finney tried any of these or similar sentences before he settled on his first line, but we do know that the sentence he chose has lured many readers into his dystopian fantasy.

Ultimately, the decisions a writer makes form what is commonly referred to as *style*. You might be wondering, though, what style has to do with grammar. *Grammar* refers to the structure of words and sentences. When you add an *s* to a noun to make it plural or when you put the article *the* before a noun, you are dealing with grammatical structure. *Style* refers to the way ideas are expressed in sentences. Although style depends on grammar, grammar and style are so closely related that they could be called two different sides of the language coin.

Because of the numerous grammatical (and stylistic) options available to writers, characterizing effective writing is difficult. A sentence considered succinct in one circumstance might be considered overly simplistic in another. A long passage may seem wordy under some conditions but comprehensive under others. Nonetheless, readers and writers do agree on some ways of speaking about style. The following stylistic features may or may not be relevant, depending on the rhetorical situation.

Descriptors Used to Discuss Style

1. *Precise.* Sentences are precise when they include fitting and very specific words and word combinations. Precision is important in rhetorical situations calling for exactness. If you were writing an instruction manual, you would be expected to state exactly what is supposed to be done, when,

and how. However, there are rhetorical situations in which you may have to be vague. For example, if you are writing a news report of a recent crime but do not know who is responsible for the action, you may have to use a sentence that does not specify the person responsible:

Several of the campaign signs were defaced.

2. *Conventional.* Sentences are conventional when they conform to the expectations of a particular writing community. For most of your academic assignments, you will be expected to use Standardized English, the language most often used in governmental, educational, and professional settings. But on occasion—say, if you are writing dialogue for a play, essay, or story—you might use a regional variation or a home dialect instead.

3. *Complete and consistent.* A piece of writing is complete and consistent when the writer has omitted none of the words often dropped in speech and has maintained the same tone and style throughout, even when varying the sentence structure. A piece that is not consistent seems to have been written by more than one person. Writing that is incomplete has words left out, often in a way that is conversational:

We discussed a couple [of] issues at the meeting.

It is hard to think of a rhetorical situation that would not call for complete, consistent prose, but imagine that you are writing a narrative essay, short story, or poem in which you want to capture a variety of voices in dialogue. In this case, to be effective, you would not employ one consistent style.

4. *Concise.* Concise prose has been weeded—that is, all redundant or otherwise useless words have been thrown out. If you are writing a science report, your readers will expect you to report your findings as succinctly as possible:

The results of the current study suggest that students' perceptions of their peers' drinking habits are important predictors of drinking or drinking-related problems.
—**Catherine Davis,** "Perceptions of Peers' Drinking Behavior"

If you are describing an unusual event or experience, however, your readers will appreciate sentences that are long and luxurious, such as this one:

One night about eleven o'clock in Las Vegas I watched a bride in an orange minidress and masses of flame-colored hair stumble from a Strip chapel on the arm of her bridegroom, who looked the part of the expendable nephew in movies like *Miami Syndicate.* —**Joan Didion,** "Marrying Absurd"

5. *Coherent.* Coherent writing has adjacent sentences that are clearly connected to each other. Words such as pronouns and synonyms often provide strong links that make the progression from one idea to the next easy for readers to follow. In a letter to the editor, for example, a writer might use restatement to link a sentence to the one that came before:

Members of the community planning board failed to consider affordable living alternatives for tenants of the old apartment building before approving the high-cost condominiums. This unfortunate oversight has put an additional burden on social services that were already strained.

The great majority of the writing you do in college should be coherent, but the degree of coherence may vary. A student in a creative writing class may choose to write a poem that reflects the senseless nature of an experience; that poem would not have to be coherent according to the standards applicable to a business report.

6. *Varied.* Variation is the spice of paragraph structure. In order to write appealing paragraphs, a writer uses both short sentences and longer ones. When sentences vary in length, they usually also vary in rhythm and emphasis. The optimal degree of variation can change from one writing situation to another. Whereas a reader of a friendly letter will quickly become bored with a lack of variety, someone reading a lab report isn't likely to notice such a lack.

7. *Parallel.* Parallelism refers to the expression of related ideas in similar structures. For example, if you want to say that you enjoy three activities, you could write

I like skiing, golfing, and swimming.

Notice that each of the activities ends in *-ing*. These parallel words express the meaning clearly and rhythmically. But there may be a situation in which you break from the expectation in order to emphasize a point. To describe a friend, you could start with two adjectives and then switch to a noun phrase:

My friend Alison is pretty, kind, and <u>the smartest mathematician at this school.</u>

As you already know, the *common* stylistic features listed here may not apply to *uncommon* rhetorical situations. For instance, poets, short story writers, and novelists often use language in unusual ways to create an atmosphere that is out of the ordinary—that may make readers slow down, weigh each word, and see connections between words they might not otherwise notice. But even when writers are playing *with* the rules, instead of *by* the rules, they benefit by knowing the difference between what is commonly expected and what may not be.

The revision process requires you to move back and forth between large-scale revision (often called **global revision**) and small-scale revision (often called **sentence-level revision**)—between making sure that you have provided enough information for your readers to understand your message and ensuring that the information is presented in a way that is easy for them to read. Many students believe that all they need to do is check for spelling and punctuation before submitting their first draft to their instructor. However, if you read your own writing carefully, especially if you let your writing "cool off" for a while, you will probably discover that you need to rethink some of your original ideas, connections, and examples. One revision can quickly lead to another. Your rewrite of a sentence, for example, might reveal the need to add more information or to rethink some of your ideas entirely. Novelist Robert Boswell describes such a possibility:

If the first sentence of a story is the classic cliché "It was a dark and stormy night," then the writer will likely begin revising by trying to rescue the idea from the expression. Perhaps, he will first try to eradicate "was," as it is the most generic of verbs.

"Dark, the stormy night blew." If he has the good sense to recognize the comedy of this sentence, he will revise again. "The air was filled with lightning." Again he sees "was" and wishes to get rid of it. Finally, he writes, "Lightning struck the fencepost." This sentence is not only much better than the original, he now has a charred fencepost in the story, and that image may well become important to the reader's understanding of the events. It may even alter the events in future drafts of the story.

—**Robert Boswell**, *The Place of Grammar in Writing Instruction*

Boswell's hypothetical writer starts the revision process by trying to eliminate the verb *was*. This change eventually leads him to a completely different opening line. In the following pages, you will learn form-based revision, but do not be surprised if your revisions of form lead to revisions of meaning—to your own "charred fencepost."

Precision

Accurate words

Accurate words convey precise meanings. Although you may use words such as *thing* and *nice* in a rough draft, you'll want to choose words with denotations and connotations that help you accurately portray your ideas. **Denotations** refer to dictionary definitions; **connotations** refer to associated meanings. A good dictionary includes entries that help you understand how one word is related to words with similar meanings, explaining connotations as well as denotations. For example, the following entry from *Heinle's Newbury House Dictionary* could help you choose the best word for describing an event that was extremely loud. Listed first are the definitions, followed by some synonyms.

> **loud** /laud/ *adj.* **-er, -est 1** having an intense sound, noisy: *The sound of city traffic is loud.* **2** unpleasantly bright in color: *He wears bright reds and other loud colors. n.* **loudness.**

> **loud 1** deafening, earsplitting | shrill, strident *frml.* **2** flashy, gurlish, gaudy.

Also be sure to consider your choice of verb when revising for accuracy: writers too often depend on a form of the verb *to be* (*am, is, are, was, were*). As Boswell points out in the excerpt above, *was* is "the most generic of verbs." (See page 582 for help with revising *to be* verbs.)

Fresh expressions

As you explain a concept, you may want to use an image to make your point. Fresh images can help your readers "see" what you mean, what you're talking about. For instance, Susan Gubar wanted to explain how her mind was working as she listened to various arguments:

> While others, judging by their ardent notetaking, found enlightenment, or, at least, points for debate, I precariously moved along a spider web of speculation.

—**Susan Gubar**, *Rooms of Our Own*

Grammar and Style

Spider web of speculation is a fresh phrase that expresses the jumbled mental state the author experienced.

You'll often find that what were once fresh expressions or examples of vivid language have become so common that they've lost their impact: *white as snow, sick as a dog,* and *strong as an ox* are just a few examples of the cobwebbed expressions called **clichés.** If you find yourself resorting to clichés in your writing, or if a peer reviewer identifies a phrase as a cliché, you will want to revise your prose in one of the following ways: you can use language that does not call forth an image or make a comparison, try to invent a new expression, or tweak the original expression to make it fresh.

Cliché: *at the drop of a hat*

Literal synonym: *immediately*

New expression: *at the click of the Send button*

Original expression with a slight change:

> We know by now that whenever politics and art collide, art loses—at least, in these United States, where anything cultural can become politicized *at the drop of a grievance.* —Peter Schjeldahl, "Those Nasty Brits"

Clear metaphors

When you use language that evokes images, make sure that the images are clearly related. **Mixed metaphors** include parts of two or more unrelated metaphors. The following sentence has the image of a spiral and the image of drowning, but is it possible to drown in a downward spiral?

> *sliding down*
> Despite this ~~downward~~ spiral that we seem to be ∧~~drowning in~~, there is hope.

Changing one of the images makes them better related.

Clear definitions

When you use a specialized term, one specific to your topic, ask yourself whether your audience will know its definition. When writing her essay on technology and learning that appears in Chapter 3, Stacy Simkanin had to ask herself if her audience needed a definition of terms such as *interlibrary loan.* Since her audience (her instructor) was in the field of college education, Stacy knew that *interlibrary loan* wouldn't need a definition, but that she should provide a description of her school's ANGEL site so that her instructor would understand which features of this online course management system students actually use.

If there is any chance that readers could confuse a term's intended meaning with another of its meanings (for example, the word *reservoir* has both a general and a technical meaning) or that readers may be unfamiliar with the term, provide a definition to help them choose the meaning you have in mind.

A definition can be a formal definition, a dictionary definition, a synonym, a stipulative definition, or a negative definition (see pages 64–66). A **formal definition** places the term in a class and then differentiates it from other members of the class.

> A *reservoir* [term] is an artificial body of water [class] that is retained by a dam [differentiation].

A definition from a general or specialized dictionary may also be used.

> *Reservoir* can refer to an "underground accumulation of petroleum or natural gas" ("Reservoir," def. 3).

If you choose to quote from a dictionary, be sure to cite the number of the definition you used and include an entry for it in your bibliography (see page 493). Another way to define a word is to use a synonymous word or phrase set off by commas or dashes (see pages 615 and 618).

> They searched for a reservoir, a rock formation that retains natural gas underground, in an uninhabited area.

When you use a definition, especially a formal definition, be sure that your subject and predicate (see page 559) fit together grammatically. The term being defined should be followed by a noun or a noun phrase, not an adverbial clause. In particular, avoid using any construction that includes *is when* or *is where*.

> *the designing of systems*
> Resource development is when systems are designed for using natural resources.

> *the contest between* *vying*
> Exploitative competition is where two or more organisms vie for a limited resource such as food.

Clear pronoun use

When you use pronouns, you may know whom or what the pronoun refers to, but if your reference is not clear to your readers, they will be confused. As you revise your writing, be on the lookout for any pronoun that does not have a clear **antecedent** (the word, phrase, or clause that makes the pronoun's reference clear).

> Many wildfires ignite when someone leaves a fire unattended or fails to ensure that it is extinguished. <u>This</u> has led to a stricter burn ban.

The antecedent for *this* is unclear. Is the cause for the new burn ban the unattended fire, the unextinguished fire, or something related to both? One way to clear up the murkiness of such a sentence is to add a noun.

> <u>This carelessness</u> has led to stricter burn bans.

The pronouns *this, that, it,* and *which* often lack clear antecedents. Take a second look when you come across one of these pronouns in your writing to be sure the antecedent is clear.

> *These changes*
> The team has a new coach and a new stadium. That will certainly improve team morale.

The researcher used innovative procedures to produce provocative

. These innovations

results, which will be reported in the next edition of *Science Journal*.

When you use pronouns such as *we, you,* and *they* to refer to people, be sure that the referents are clear and consistent. In written texts, *we* and *us* always refer to the writer or writers; however, other people may also be included: readers of the text, associates, or the general public.

> We [coauthors] advocate the development of writing-intensive courses.

> Let us [writer and readers] look at another example.

> As a profession, we [writer and others in the profession] need to address some difficult issues.

> Let us endeavor so to live that when we [general public] come to die even the undertaker will be sorry. —**Mark Twain**, *The Tragedy of Pudd'nhead Wilson and the Comedy of Those Extraordinary Twins*

Most writers avoid using the word *we* for self-reference because readers will want to know just who that word includes. Rather than using what has long been called the "royal" *we* (used by royalty to include God), writers should refer to themselves as *I*. Despite the acceptability of using *I* in writing, though, many teachers and professions continue to frown on the usage. You should ask your instructor or supervisor before using *I* in your writing.

If you decide to address readers directly, you'll undoubtedly use the pronoun *you* (as in this sentence). In this case, you'll want to be sure to clarify whether *you* refers to just one person or to people in general. Be sure to check with your teacher as to whether using *you* is acceptable. If you are told to avoid using the indefinite *you,* recast your sentences. For example, use *one* instead of *you.*

> Even in huge, anonymous cities, you find community spirit.

> Even in huge, anonymous cities, one finds community spirit.

However, owing to the formality of *one,* it might not always be the best choice. Changing the word order is another possibility.

> Community spirit can even be found in huge, anonymous cities.

If you are unsatisfied with either of these strategies, use different words.

> Community spirit arises even in huge, anonymous cities.

The pronoun *they* is used to refer to an outside group. When you revise, make sure that the outside group is specific.

the reporter from Cairo

On the news, they said the situation had improved.

If you are unsure of who comprises the outside group, try using a short passive sentence (see page 563).

> They revised the original forecast.

> The original forecast was revised.

Revise the following paragraph for precision. Be sure words are accurate, expressions are fresh, imagery is consistent, definitions are aptly worded, and pronouns have clear antecedents.

[1]Roller-skating is when you use shoes fitted with small wheels for movement that is smooth as silk on rinks and paved surfaces. [2]Although they introduced roller skates in the eighteenth century, the design that made them all the rage was created in 1863. [3]The four-wheel skate originally had wooden and later metal wheels. [4]In the twentieth century, these wheels were replaced by polyurethane plastic wheels that could grab various surfaces better. [5]Another innovation that greatly affected the sport was the development of in-line skates, where there is a single row of wheels in place of the standard four-wheel configuration. [6]In-line skating rolled to a quick take-off in popularity. [7]In-line skaters now speed down most parkways, sidewalks, and even some store aisles.

Conciseness

Making every word count

After writing your first draft, review it to make sure that your sentences are not empty or repetitive. If you draft quickly or are worried about making the length requirement for your assignment, you may be writing rambling sentences that obscure your message rather than clarify it.

As you revise, check to be sure that you are not using three or four words when one or two will suffice. Sometimes you can just delete extra words; other times you may be able to think of a more concise alternative. (See also pages 551 and 570.)

WORDS THAT CAN BE DELETED

square ~~in shape~~
large ~~in size~~
orange ~~in color~~
at 8:00 p.m. ~~in the evening~~
~~basic~~ fundamentals
sweet-~~tasting~~ dessert
medium-~~size~~ onions
poor ~~and impoverished~~ country
~~really and truly~~ funny
return ~~back~~
connect ~~up~~
secondly, he ~~also~~

REPLACEMENTS FOR WORDY EXPRESSIONS

at this moment (*or* point) in time	now, today
due to the fact that	because
in view of the fact that	because

REPLACEMENTS FOR WORDY EXPRESSIONS (*continued*)

for the purpose of	for
it is clear (*or* obvious) that	clearly (obviously)
there is no question that	unquestionably, certainly
without a doubt	undoubtedly
beyond the shadow of a doubt	certainly, surely
it is my opinion that	I think (believe)
in this day and age	today
in the final analysis	finally

With some adjustment, the frequently overused constructions *there are* and *it is* (called *expletives*) can be deleted.

> *Nobody*
> ^There was nobody home.

> *The   was dark*
> It was dark in the ^house^.

Eliminating wordiness from clauses

Nonessential (nonrestrictive) adjectival clauses can often be made less wordy. Sometimes just the relative pronoun (*who, which,* or *that*) can be dropped. Other times both the relative pronoun and a form of *be* (*am, is, are, was, were*) can be deleted.

> The research that he did on endangered species was published last year.

> The Endangered Species Act, which was passed in 1973, protects the habitat of endangered plants and animals.

When deleting a relative pronoun and a verb, you may have to make other changes to your sentence as well.

> *infected us with laughter.*
> His boisterous guffaw, ^which was infectious, made us all laugh.

Using elliptical constructions

The term *ellipsis* comes from the Greek word meaning "to leave out." You might recognize ellipsis points (. . .), which tell you that words have been omitted (see pages 619–620). Similarly, **elliptical constructions** leave out words readily understood from the context. By occasionally using elliptical constructions, you make your writing concise. In the following sentence, *was* has been omitted from the last two clauses:

> In their successful collaboration, Louise was the courageous innovator, Jerome the methodical critic, and Scott the relentless editor.

Commas may be used also to indicate omissions.

> The winner in 2005 was Jacqui; in 2006, Ben; and in 2007, Alison.

> EXERCISE 22.2

Revise the following paragraph so that it is more concise.

¹Louis Leakey was born in the country of Kenya in 1903 but earned a doctorate in the country of England. ²When people hear his name in this day and age, they think of the search for the beginnings and origins of humankind. ³But in the 1920s he caused surprise, disapproval, and dismay when he insisted that humans evolved on the continent of Africa, which was a contradiction of the common belief at the time that they originated in Asia or Europe. ⁴He proved his hypothesis by returning back to Africa and finding in 1960 *Homo habilis,* which was considered the earliest known human ancestor at that time. ⁵Louis was not the only Leakey curious about and interested in archaeology. ⁶Other Leakeys interested in digging have made important and significant discoveries. ⁷His wife, Mary, found fossil footprints that were 3.5 million years old. ⁸His son, Richard, found the most complete early-human skeleton. ⁹His daughter-in-law, Meave, found important new fossils. ¹⁰His granddaughter Louise currently runs expeditions in Kenya.

Conventions

Usage

Usage refers to the types of words appropriate for a particular rhetorical situation, especially the types of words your audience expects within a specific context. Sometimes it's perfectly acceptable and expected to use slang, regionalisms, or conversational (or colloquial) words. A truck driver who hears "What's your twenty?" on the CB radio knows the other driver is asking for a location. In Philadelphia, many cheesesteak aficionados order a "Whiz without" if they have a hankering for a cheesesteak with Cheez Whiz and without onions. Among friends, you might gripe that you have "tons" of research to do. Other times your rhetorical situation calls for technical language and Standardized English. However, be aware that the concept of *standard* is often accompanied by the assumption that grammatical structures or words not considered standard are incorrect and therefore inferior, even though they may be used frequently by a specific group of people. For example, if you are from the northeastern part of the United States, you might know the word *youse* as a conversational term meaning "all of you," but that usage is not favored in all parts of the country.

Instead of judging words as "correct" or "incorrect," you'll find it more productive to think of them as conventional or unconventional in relation to a specific language community. Many of the words listed in the Glossary of Usage are those that cause difficulties in rhetorical situations calling for conventional language used in academic writing.

Idioms

Idioms are fixed expressions whose meaning cannot be entirely determined by knowing the meanings of their parts—examples are *bear in mind, cut to the chase, in a nutshell,* and *a pushover.* Idioms can be particularly difficult to make sense of when

English is not your native language—or when you're an outsider to any language community, since every one of these has its own idiomatic expressions. Even small variations of familiar idioms can be distracting or confusing to your audience.

> *low*
> She tried to keep a ~~small~~ profile.

> *a vested*
> They had ~~an invested~~ interest in the project.

As you edit your writing, keep an eye out for idioms you think might not be worded correctly. Then check a general dictionary or a dictionary of idioms to make sure that your usage is appropriate.

Spelling

When drafting, you may be writing so fast or concentrating so deeply that you do not pay attention to spelling. Proofreading for spelling mistakes is essential—though only after you have a solid draft. As a starting point, use a spell checker to catch your errors. However, keep in mind that the spell checker will not detect misspellings of specialized vocabulary and foreign words, keyboarding errors (*as* for *is*), or misuses of words that sound alike (*here* for *hear*). The spell checker also cannot detect words that are spelled correctly but used incorrectly.

> *by*
> We must abide ~~with~~ his decision.

A spell checker will also overlook a single word that should be spelled as two words or two words that should be spelled as a single word.

> *may be*
> The researchers ~~maybe~~ able to answer that question.

> *Someday maybe*
> ~~Some day may be~~ these conditions will no longer pose a problem.

TRICKS OF THE TRADE

The following strategies can help you check your spelling effectively.

▶ Create a special file for words you frequently misspell. Then use the Find command to locate possible misspellings in your draft.

▶ Add new technical or foreign words to your spell checker's dictionary by clicking on the Add button. The spell checker will then be able to check for these words.

▶ Reject the offer from the spell checker to correct all instances of a particular error. You are better off examining each instance yourself.

▶ Check suggested alternative spellings in a dictionary if you doubt their accuracy.

▶ After using the spell checker, be sure to proofread your draft yourself.

In addition to spell checking, learning a few basic spelling rules will help you find mistakes during the proofreading process. Spelling errors often occur when suffixes, but not prefixes, are added to base words. When a prefix is added to a base word (or root), no letters are added or dropped.

dissatisfy   misspell   unnecessary   immaterial

When you add a suffix, however, the spelling is often affected.

mercy, merciful   subscribe, subscription   BUT electric, electricity

The spellings of words with suffixes are not totally irregular, though. Note the following patterns.

BASE WORD ENDING IN *E*

▶ When adding a suffix that begins with a vowel to a word that ends in *e*, drop the *e*.

behave, behaving   love, lovable   combine, combination

A few exceptions to this rule have to be memorized: *dyeing* (changing a color), *canoeing*, and *snowshoeing.*

▶ The letters *c* and *g* each have two different sounds. To signal the *s* sound of *ce* or the *j* sound of *ge*, keep the final *e* before *-able* or *-ous*.

outrageous   changeable   noticeable

▶ If the suffix begins with a consonant sound, the final *e* is retained.

polite, politeness   sincere, sincerely   hope, hopeful

This rule also has some exceptions: *argument, judgment, awful, ninth, truly,* and *wholly.*

DOUBLING CONSONANTS BEFORE SUFFIXES BEGINNING WITH VOWELS (*-ED, -ING, -ANCE, -ENCE*)

▶ If a consonant is preceded by a vowel in either a one-syllable word or a two-syllable word with a stressed second syllable, double the final consonant.

VC   VCC   VCC   VC   VCC   VCC
stop, sto**pped**, sto**pping**   omit, omi**tted**, omi**tting**

▶ If there are two vowels before the consonant, the consonant is not doubled.

VVC   VVC   VVC   VVC   VVC   VVC
group, group**ed**, group**ing**   review, review**ed**, review**ing**

▶ If the second syllable is not stressed, the consonant is not doubled.

edit, edit**ed**, edit**ing**   cover, cover**ed**, cover**ing**

CHANGING *Y* TO *I* BEFORE SUFFIXES

▶ Change the *y* following a consonant to *i* before adding a suffix (except *-ing*).

rely, rel**ies,** rel**ied,** rel**iance**   certify, certif**ies,** certif**ied,** certif**ication**
BUT rel**ying**   BUT certif**ying**

▶ If *y* is preceded by a vowel, retain the *y.*

stay, stay**s,** stay**ed**   convey, convey**s,** convey**ed,** convey**ance**

▶ Some verb forms are irregular and thus can cause difficulties: *says, said; pays, paid.* For a list of irregular verbs, see pages 553–554.

ADDING *-LY*

▶ When adding *-ly* to a word ending in *l,* retain both *l*'s.

normal, normal**ly**   real, real**ly**   usual, usual**ly**

PLURALS

▶ For most nouns ending in *s, z, ch, sh,* or *x,* add *-es.*

pass, pass**es**   beach, beach**es**

▶ For nouns ending in a consonant and *y,* add *-es* after changing the *y* to *i.*

army, arm**ies**   company, compan**ies**   twenty, twent**ies**

▶ For some nouns ending in a consonant and *o,* add *-es.*

hero, hero**es**   potato, potato**es**

For others, *-s* will suffice.

video, video**s**   memo, memo**s**

Sometimes either an *-s* or *-es* suffix is correct.

tornado**s,** tornado**es**   volcano**s,** volcano**es**

▶ For nouns ending in *f* or *fe,* change the ending to *ve* before adding *-s* if the sound of the plural changes from *f* to *v.*

sel**f,** sel**ves**   li**fe,** li**ves**   BUT belie**f,** belie**fs**

▶ Certain nouns have irregular plural forms.

woman, wom**en**   child, child**ren**   foot, f**eet**   tooth, t**eeth**

▶ For the plural of most proper nouns, add *-s:* the Lees; the Kennedys. Add *-es* when the plural ending is pronounced as a separate syllable: the Rodriguez**es,** the Jones**es.**

▶ Some words borrowed from Greek or Latin form their plurals as in the original language: *alumnus, alumni; alumna, alumnae; analysis, analyses.* (For *criteria, data,* and *media,* see the Glossary of Usage.)

One other rule that may improve your proofreading is often taught as a rhyme. This rule can help you remember which words include *ie* and which include *ei*.

> Put *i* before *e*
> Except after *c*
> Or when sounded like *a*
> As in *neighbor* and *weigh*.

Words with *i* before *e:* bel**ie**ve, br**ie**f, f**ie**ld
Words with *e* before *i,* after *c*: c**ei**ling, perc**ei**ve, rec**ei**pt
Words with *ei* sounding like *a* in *cake:* fr**ei**ght, th**ei**r, h**ei**r

Exceptions to this rule include *caffeine, either, neither, species, foreign, leisure,* and *weird.*

Inclusive language

When you respond to a rhetorical situation, you are asking an audience to read or listen to what you have to say. Using respectful, inclusive language is essential to this endeavor. Otherwise, your readers or listeners may not bother to consider your ideas. It is important not to assume that all of your readers are part of the majority in terms of religion, race, ethnicity, sexual preference, or physical ability. A letter to the editor of a local newspaper proposing that a busy city park be made off limits to all cars may be disrespectful if it does not take into account park users who must use handicapped parking to access the park.

Language used to identify groups of people in terms of their religion, race, education, politics, or other characteristic presents a distinctive challenge. In fact, try to avoid categorizing a person or persons unless such a reference is absolutely necessary for your discussion. Most people feel that their individuality transcends their membership in any one group. If you must mention others as belonging to a group, the best way to show them respect is to use the name they themselves have chosen (whether that's *American Indians, Native Americans, Indigenous People, First Americans,* or *Indians; Latino/Latina* or *Chicano/Chicana;* or some other name). Although there are countless groups, only a few frequently found in print are discussed in the following sections.

Referring to gender Sentences that needlessly single out a person as being male or female can be revised fairly easily.

▶ Make a pronoun or determiner and its antecedent plural.

    Reporters   *they describe*
    A reporter should be sure that ~~he describes~~ events accurately.

Some authors choose to use *they* or *she* as an alternative to the generic *he*. However, sentences such as *A reporter should be sure that they describe events accurately* and *A reporter should be sure that she describes events accurately* are not considered standard.

▶ Rephrase to avoid using a pronoun.

    A reporter should be sure to describe events accurately.

▶ Use a noun phrase instead of a pronoun.

that person
If someone questions the procedures, ~~he~~ should consult the supervisor.

▶ Use both *he* and *she*.

or she
If an individual questions the procedures, he should consult the supervisor.

This option should be avoided when possible because of its awkwardness.

▶ Use an article instead of a possessive determiner.

a
Every employee has ~~his own~~ locker.

▶ Drop the possessive determiner.

A student should submit ~~his~~ papers on time.

▶ Choose gender-neutral terms.

working people
Labor unions benefit ~~the working man~~.

Other gender-neutral terms include the following:

~~anchorman, anchorwoman~~	anchor, news anchor
~~businessman~~	business executive, businessperson
~~chairman, chairwoman~~	chair, chairperson
~~clergyman~~	member of the clergy
~~congressman~~	member of Congress, representative, senator
~~man, mankind~~	human, human beings, humanity, humankind
~~repairman~~	technician, repair technician
~~salesman~~	salesperson, sales representative, salesclerk
~~workman~~	worker

Referring to race and ethnicity Determining which terms a particular group prefers can be difficult because preferences sometimes vary within a group and change over time. One conventional way to refer to Americans of a specific descent is to include an adjective before the term *American: African American, Asian American, European American, Latin American, Mexican American, Native American.* These words are widely used, especially by people who are not members of a given group. However, members of a particular group may identify themselves in more than one way. In addition to *African American* and *European American, black* and *white* have long been used. People of Spanish-speaking descent may prefer *Chicano/Chicana, Hispanic, Latino/Latina, Puerto Rican, Mexican,* or another term. Descendants of peoples who were indigenous to North America before European settlers arrived may prefer a specific name such as *Diné* or *Haida,* though some also accept *American Indian.* An up-to-date dictionary that includes notes on usage can help you choose appropriate terms.

Referring to age Although some people object to the term *senior citizen*, a better alternative has not yet been suggested. When used respectfully, the term refers to a person who has reached the age of retirement (but may not have decided to retire) and is eligible for certain privileges granted by society. However, if you know your audience would object to this word, find out what term is preferred.

Referring to disability or illness A current recommendation for referring to disabilities and illnesses is "to put the person first"; in this way, it is believed, the focus will be on the individual rather than on the limitation. Thus, *persons with disabilities* is preferred over *disabled persons*. When you are writing, you can find out whether such person-first expressions are preferred by noting whether they are used in the articles and books (or by the people) you consult. Be aware, though, that some writers and readers find this type of expression unnatural sounding, and others think that it does not serve its purpose because the last word in a phrase can carry the greater weight, especially at the end of a sentence.

Referring to sexual orientation Terms for sexual orientation such as *gay*, *lesbian*, and *bisexual* are used most often as adjectives rather than as nouns. In fact, using a noun to refer to specific people may be considered offensive. Noting professions or participation is thought to be more respectful: two gay lawyers, three lesbian participants. But again, note sexual orientation only when it is relevant to the discourse.

Referring to geographical areas Certain geographical terms need to be used with special care. Though most frequently used to refer to people from the United States, the term *American* may also refer to people from Canada, Mexico, and Central or South America. If your audience may be offended by this term, use *people from the United States* or *U.S. citizens* instead.

The term *Arab* refers to people of Arabic-speaking descent. Use this term only when you cannot use more specific terms, such as *Iraqi* or *Saudi Arabian*, and only when you are sure that a country's people speak Arabic and not another language. Iranians, for example, are not Arabs because they speak Farsi.

It is often helpful to distinguish between the terms *British* and *English*. *British* is the preferred term for referring to people from the island of Great Britain or from the United Kingdom. *English* refers to people from England (a part of the United Kingdom).

Negation

You may be unaware of the number of ways negation is used. Negative words can be formed by the addition of prefixes: *patient, impatient; logical, illogical*. Phrases, too, can be negated: *time, no time; to be, not to be*. Sentences are most frequently negated by the word *not: We do not have sufficient funding*. In some dialects of English, multiple negation signals emphasis: *They don't understand nothing*. However, when the rhetorical situation calls for the use of Standardized

English, refrain from using this type of negation. Although a word with a negative prefix or a negated infinitive phrase may be used in a negative sentence (*He is <u>not</u> impatient* or *It would <u>not</u> be right <u>not</u> to intervene*), other types of multiple negation should be revised.

I don't have _^*any* ~~no~~ time.   OR   I don't have ~~no~~ time.

The words *barely, hardly,* and *scarcely* carry with them the sense of negative conditions, so they should not be used with *not* or *nothing.*

He couldn't hardly see.   OR   He couldn't ~~hardly~~ see.

She could hear hardly _^*anything* ~~nothing~~.

> EXERCISE 22.3

Revise the following sentences so that they follow the conventions of Standardized English.

[1]According to Cheryl Dolven, a registered deitician, a kid in the United States will consume 1,500 peanut butter sandwiches before he leaves high school in the dust. [2]Although some parents think that peanut butter is unhealthy for their children because it contains alot of fat, Dolven explains that this popular sandwich spread consists in protien, folate, niacin, and other important vitamins and minerals. [3]She does not say that peanut butter does not have no fat; she admits that there is fat but it is good fat (the unsaturated stuff). [4]Dolven recommends picking up natural peanut butter because other types of peanut butter contain sugar and partialy hydrogenated fats.

Completeness and Consistency

Talking versus writing

Conversation differs from academic writing in the number of shortcuts we use. We might say to someone, "You ready? Time to go." This snippet of conversation becomes "Are you ready? It's time to go" when the two utterances are written as full sentences. Because you might be using your conversational voice when you write your first draft, be sure to revise so that all words are included, especially the small ones that are easily overlooked.

Missing article:	Starting _^*a* new job does not have to be stressful.
Missing preposition:	He mentioned a couple _^*of* reasons for the success.
Missing pronoun:	The clear directions made _^*it* easy for us to understand the process.
Missing verb:	She _^*has* spoken to the director about a raise.

It is also a good idea to look at the parts of a sentence where *and* is used.

Missing preposition: He was interested ^*in*^ and thus focused on cellular biology.

Missing verb: We have never ^*ignored*^ and will never ignore our responsibilities.

Complete and consistent comparisons

A comparison has two parts: something is compared to something else. As you edit your writing, make sure your audience knows what is being compared. A comparison can frequently be completed by adding a phrase or clause to the sentence.

Printers today are quite different ^*from those built in the early 1990s*^ .

His first novel was better ^*than the one just published*^ .

If you include both parts of a comparison in the same sentence, be sure the comparison is logical.

Her test scores are higher than ^*those of*^ the other students.

In the original sentence, *scores* were being compared to *students*. You could also rewrite the sentence as follows:

Her test scores are higher than the other students'.

Because *test scores* have already been mentioned, it is clear that *students'* (with an apostrophe) is short for *students' test scores.*

Verb tense consistency

Verbs in English are described according to both tense and aspect (see pages 554–556). Consistency in the use of tense, though not necessarily in the use of aspect, ensures that your sentences link together logically. In the following paragraph, notice that the tense remains in the past, but the aspect varies among simple, perfect, and progressive.

In the summer of 1983, I *had* just *finished* [*past perfect*] my third year of architecture school and *had* [*simple past*] to find a six-month internship. I *had grown* up and *gone* [*past perfect (compound verb phrase)*] through my entire education in the Midwest, but I *had been* [*past perfect*] to New York City once on a class field trip and I *thought* [*simple past*] it *seemed* [*simple past*] like a pretty good place to live. So, armed with *simple past*

little more than an inflated ego and my school portfolio, I <u>was</u> off to Manhattan,

past progressive

oblivious to the bad economy and the fact that the city <u>was overflowing</u> with young architects. —**Paul K. Humiston,** "Small World"

If you do need to shift to another tense, you can use time markers such as these to indicate a different time period:

now, then, today, yesterday
in two years, during the 1920s
after you finish, before we left

The verb tense shifts back and forth between present and past in the following comparison of different time periods—today, when Edward O. Wilson is studying ants in the woods around Walden Pond, and the nineteenth century, when Thoreau lived there. The time markers used to cue readers are blue.

     simple present   *simple past*

These woods <u>are</u> not wild; indeed, they <u>were</u> not wild in Thoreau's day. Today, the

                         simple present

beach and trails of Walden Pond State Reservation <u>draw</u> about 500,000 visitors a

    simple present   *simple present*

year. Few of them <u>hunt</u> ants, however. Underfoot and under the leaf litter there <u>is</u>

    simple past   *simple past*

a world as wild as it <u>was</u> before human beings <u>came</u> to this part of North America.
—**James Gorman,** "Finding a Wild, Fearsome World Beneath Every Fallen Leaf"

A shift in time is sometimes indicated implicitly—that is, without an explicit time marker. A writer may change tenses without including time markers for any of several reasons: (1) to explain or support a general statement with information about the past, (2) to compare and contrast two different time periods, or (3) to comment on a topic. Why do you think the author of the following paragraph used different tenses?

Thomas Jefferson, author of the Declaration of Independence, <u>is</u> considered one of our country's most brilliant citizens. His achievements <u>were</u> many, as <u>were</u> his interests. Some historians <u>describe</u> his work as a naturalist, scientist, and inventor; others <u>focus</u> on his accomplishments as an educator and politician. Yet Jefferson <u>is</u> best known as a spokesman for democracy.

Except for the two uses of *were* in the second sentence, all verb phrases are in the present tense. The author uses the past tense in the second sentence to provide evidence from the past that supports the thesis sentence.

Consistency of pronoun usage through agreement

If you were writing about a woman named Martha, you would use the pronouns *she* and *her* to refer to that person, not *it, he, they,* or *him.* This principle of pronoun usage is called **pronoun-antecedent agreement**.

Pronouns must reflect the number, the person, and sometimes the gender of the nouns they refer to.

third person, singular, feminine   *third person, singular, feminine*

Martha went to Argentina to visit her grandparents.

When indefinite pronouns, instead of nouns, are antecedents for personal pronouns, confusion often ensues. Although we often say or write a sentence such as *Everyone has the right to their own opinion,* this usage is not acceptable in most academic writing. *Everyone* and *they* agree in number; that is, they both indicate more than one person. However, they do not agree grammatically. The indefinite pronouns *everybody, everyone, somebody, someone, anybody,* and *anyone* are grammatically singular. Note that the verb following these words is in the same form as the verb following the singular pronoun *he* or *she.*

Everybody/Everyone is welcome.

Somebody/Someone is coming.

Anybody/Anyone is welcome.

He is here.

She is here.

The pronouns *they* and *them,* as well as the determiner *their,* however, are plural.

They are here.

The problem with the sentence *Everyone has the right to their own opinion* is that *everyone* is grammatically singular but *their* is grammatically plural. You could revise this sentence in a number of ways. You could replace *their* with singular determiners: *Everyone has the right to his or her own opinion.* This option should rarely be used because the phrasing *his or her* is cumbersome. However, using just one pronoun (*Everyone has the right to his opinion*) is also frowned on because of sexist overtones (see pages 587–588). Another possible revision of the sentence is to use a noun instead of an indefinite pronoun: *All citizens have the right to their own opinions.* You could also use an article instead of a possessive determiner: *Everyone has the right to an opinion.*

> EXERCISE 22.4

Revise the following paragraph so that it is complete and consistent.

¹When I am so hungry that my stomach starts barking orders, I skip over to the closest Chinese restaurant and order dim sum. ²*Dim sum* referred to variety of small sweet and savory dishes such as fried dumplings or pastries filled with pork, shrimp, or vegetables. ³Everyone I know says they like *dim sum,* but I'm sure I snack on dim sum more than them. ⁴For me, these little dishes really "dot the heart," which is what *dim sum* literally meant. ⁵As an English idiom, it means "hit the spot."

Coherence

Placement of old and new information

Good writers forge strong links between their sentences. One way they do this is by presenting old, or given, information at the beginning of a sentence, saving the new information for the end of the sentence. The given information is familiar and expected; the new information is unknown or unanticipated until the sentence has been read. Think of it this way: if you are at an awards ceremony, you expect the announcer to say, "The winner is Carlos Rico," not "Carlos Rico is the winner." *The winner* is old information (you are at an awards ceremony and so you assume a winner will be chosen); the name of the winner is the new, highly anticipated information.

By ordering information in this way, you create a chain: old new old new old new. What was new becomes old. After declaring the winner at the awards ceremony, the announcer may continue by describing the person's accomplishments: "Mr. Rico has starred in five Broadway plays in just eight years." Notice that in this sentence the winner's name is now old information placed at the beginning of the sentence, with the new information following it. Although there are other ways to ensure text coherence, if you want to provide this type of linking, alter the order of some of your sentences so that new and old information are tightly connected.

> *On top of one of the snow banks sat three teenagers.*

The snow plow left ample evidence of its work. ^~~Three teenagers sat on top of one of the snow banks.~~

> *Her first poem was published when she was only sixteen.*

She wrote most of her poems between 1936 and 1954. ^~~She was only sixteen when her first poem was published.~~

Linking through words

Words with associated meanings By choosing specific nouns, determiners, and pronouns, you can tightly connect one sentence to the next. Here is a brief overview of strategies for making your writing coherent through word choice:

▶ Use nouns with related meanings.

We found most of the <u>directions</u> easy to follow, especially those in the first three chapters. Several of us, though, had difficulty understanding the <u>instructions</u> in Chapter 4.

▶ Use determiners to indicate old information.

The students had to write a paper comparing American and Japanese management styles. <u>The assignment</u> was due Thursday.

▶ Use pronouns to refer to old information.

Susan started playing the piano at the age of six. <u>She</u> was eighteen when she began strumming the guitar.

Repetition of words and phrases Repeating words or phrases will provide coherence in a paragraph, especially when your focus is a specific item or concept. In the following paragraph, the author focuses on taboos and thus, of course, repeats this word.

> **Taboos** come in all sizes. Big **taboos**: when I was a kid in the Italian neighborhoods of Brooklyn, to insult someone's mother meant a brutal fight—the kind of fight no one interferes with until one of the combatants goes down and stays down. Little **taboos**: until the sixties, it was an insult to use someone's first name without asking or being offered permission. Personal **taboos**: Cyrano de Bergerac would not tolerate the mention of his enormous nose. **Taboos** peculiar to one city: in Brooklyn (again), when the Dodgers were still at Ebbets Field, if you rooted for the Yankees you kept it to yourself unless you wanted a brawl. **Taboos**, big or small, are always about having to respect somebody's (often irrational) boundary—or else.
>
> —**Michael Ventura,** "Taboo: Don't Even Think About It!"

Be careful, though, not to overdo repetition. Repetition in the following sentences is ineffective because the word being repeated is not significant:

Some shoppers ^*spend endless time browsing without buying anything.* ~~shop around but do not buy anything. They have time to shop, so they spend it looking through all the shops in the mall.~~

> EXERCISE 22.5

Discuss the repetition in the following paragraph.

> [1]The cowboy icon has two basic incarnations: the cowboy hero and the cowboy villain. [2]Cowboy heroes often appear in roles such as sheriff, leader of a cattle drive, or what I'll call a "wandering hero," such as the Lone Ranger, who appears much like a frontier Superman wherever and whenever help is needed. [3]Writers and producers most commonly place cowboy heroes in conflict either with "Indians" or with the cowboy villain. [4]In contrast to the other classic bad guys of the Western genre, cowboy villains pose a special challenge because they are essentially the alter ego of the cowboy hero; the cowboy villain shares the hero's skill with a gun, his horse-riding maneuvers, and his knowledge of the land. [5]What distinguishes the two, of course, is character: the cowboy hero is essentially good, while the cowboy villain is essentially evil.
>
> —**Jody M. Roy,** "The Case of the Cowboy"

Parallelism—linking through structure

Parallelism refers to the repetition of a grammatical structure. Like repeated words and phrases, this type of repetition makes your writing more cohesive, but it is also considered aesthetically pleasing, just like the repeated patterns in waves, leaves, or textiles. In the following excerpt from John F. Kennedy's inauguration speech, you will find examples of parallel words, phrases, and clauses. Note that some of these elements are embedded within others.

> We dare not forget today that we are the heirs of that first revolution. Let the word go forth from this <u>time</u> and <u>place</u>, to <u>friend</u> and <u>foe</u> alike, that the torch has been passed to a new generation of Americans, <u>born in this century</u>, <u>tempered by war</u>, <u>disciplined</u>

by a hard and bitter peace, <u>proud of our ancient heritage,</u> and <u>unwilling to witness or</u> <u>permit the slow undoing of these human rights</u> to which this nation has always been committed, and <u>to which we are committed today at home</u> and <u>around the world.</u>

You can use correlative conjunctions to link parallel elements, and in doing so, emphasize the connection between them.

He won gold medals in the 100-meter dash and the 400-meter relay.

He won gold medals in <u>both</u> the 100-meter dash <u>and</u> the 400-meter relay.

As you revise, make sure that elements joined by *both . . . and, either . . . or, neither . . . nor,* and *not only . . . but also* are parallel in structure.

They will ~~either~~ meet with the supervisor _∧ *either* today or tomorrow.

They not only give money to charities but they also do ~~they~~ charitable work.

Effective nominalizations

Look at the following pairs of words:

discuss/discussion	*occur/occurrence*	*apply/application*
describe/description	*depend/dependence*	*recommend/recommendation*
allude/allusion	*prescribe/prescription*	*present/presentation*

The first word in each pair is a verb; the second word, derived from the verb, is a noun. You can use this feature of English, called **nominalizing,** to link sentences together (the root of *nominalize* means "noun" or "name"). After using the verb in the first sentence, you can use the noun in the second. The noun becomes the old information that is linked to the new information of the previous sentence. Here is an example:

The grammar of the written language <u>differs</u> profoundly from that of the spoken language. This <u>difference</u> is attributable to the constant innovations of spoken language.

Most verbs take endings when they are nominalized, but some do not—for example, *request, address,* and *excerpt.*

Adjectives can also be nominalized (*sad/sadness, scarce/scarcity*). Note, though, that nominalizations, whether derived from verbs or adjectives, are abstractions. A sentence with too many nominalizations seems static, because verbs showing movement have crystallized and forms of *be* have replaced them as the main verbs. A sentence with too many nominalizations may also frustrate readers because it demands that they mentally record a number of nominalized actions or states. In the following sentence, the reader has to determine how four nominalized actions are related.

The firm is now engaged in an <u>assessment</u> of its <u>procedures</u> for the <u>development</u> of new <u>products.</u>

To revise a sentence like this one, locate the most important action and recast the sentence with this action as the main verb. The revised sentence is more concise—and quite likely clearer to your readers.

The firm is now <u>assessing</u> its procedures for <u>developing</u> new products.

You may also decide that some actions or ideas are less important and thus can be discarded. For the preceding example sentence, the action of engaging was not important enough to be included.

Subject-verb agreement

A subject (see page 559) and a verb are linked and thus need to match in person and number. This is called *subject-verb agreement*. Notice in the chart below how the verb *be* changes according to whether the subject is singular or plural and whether the subject refers to the person(s) writing, the person(s) addressed, or the person(s) or item(s) discussed.

	Number	
Person	*Singular*	*Plural*
First	I *am*	Joe and I *are*
Second	You *are*	All of you *are*
Third	Joe *is*	The papers *are*

Because subjects can be more than one word long (*assignment* versus *tough assignment* versus *tough assignment due tomorrow*), choosing the correct verb can sometimes be a challenge. The following chart gives examples of various types of subjects and an explanation of the agreement principle that applies in each case.

Examples	Explanation
The ideal workshop **has** good ventilation. [singular subject, singular verb] Safe workshops **have** good ventilation. [plural subject, plural verb]	A verb agrees in person and number with the noun that is the head of the subject. The head noun is the noun that will affect the form the verb takes. It is underlined twice in the examples.
Workshops without good ventilation **are** dangerous. [plural head noun, plural verb]	A verb agrees in person and number with the noun that is the head of the subject, regardless of an intervening phrase (here, *without good ventilation*).
Garages and basements **are** sometimes used as workshops. [compound subject, plural verb]	A compound subject—two nouns usually connected by *and*—takes a plural verb.
The designer and owner **is** responsible for employee safety. [In this case, *designer* and *owner* refer to a single person.]	If a compound subject refers to one person, the verb is singular.

(continued)

Examples	Explanation
Neither smoke alarms nor <u>a fire extinguisher</u> **was** installed properly. [The noun closer to the verb is singular.] Neither a fire extinguisher nor <u>smoke alarms</u> **were** installed properly. [The noun closer to verb is plural.]	In formal English, when subjects are joined by *or, either . . . or,* or *neither . . . nor,* the verb agrees in person and number with the closer noun. If a sentence with both a singular and a plural noun seems awkward, reword it so that the plural noun is closer to the verb.
There **is** <u>a workbench</u> at the center of any good shop. [singular subject, singular verb] There **are** <u>shelves</u> for small tools. [plural subject, plural verb] There **are** <u>a first aid kit and a list of emergency numbers</u> by the door. [compound subject, plural verb]	The verb following the expletive *there* agrees in person and number with the noun phrase or coordinated noun phrases that follow it. The expletive *there* is sometimes called the dummy subject; the actual subject then follows the verb.
The whole <u>family</u> **uses** the shop. [Here the family is unified: It uses the shop.]	A collective noun refers to a group of people, animals, or objects as a single unit. When the unity of the group is the focus, a collective noun takes a singular verb. The pronoun *it* can substitute for the noun.
The <u>family</u> **disagree** on the use of the shop. [The individual family members are involved: They disagree on the use of the shop.]	When the individuality of the members is the focus, a collective noun takes a plural verb.

Placing modifiers

Modifiers (words or word groups that describe, limit, or qualify) enliven writing with details, but if they are not placed correctly, they can disrupt coherence. As you revise, be sure that you place your modifiers as close as you can to the words they modify.

Limiting modifiers **Limiting modifiers** such as *almost, even, hardly, just,* and *only* are clearest when they are placed right before the words they modify. Altering the placement of any of these modifiers can alter meaning.

The committee can <u>only</u> nominate two members for the position.

[The committee cannot appoint or elect the members.]

The committee can nominate <u>only</u> two members for the position.

[The committee cannot nominate more than two members.]

<u>Only</u> the committee can nominate two members for the position.

[No person or group other than the committee can nominate members.]

Squinting modifiers A **squinting modifier** is confusing because it is not clear whether it is modifying what is before it or what comes after it. To avoid such lack of clarity, reposition the modifier or provide appropriate punctuation.

Even though Erikson lists some advantages <u>overall</u> his vision of a successful business is faulty.

Reposition: Even though Erikson lists some <u>overall</u> advantages, his vision of a successful business is faulty.

Punctuate: Even though Erikson lists some advantages, <u>overall</u> his vision of a successful business is faulty.

Dangling modifiers **Dangling modifiers** are words, phrases, or elliptical clauses without an appropriate noun to modify. The dangling modifier may contain a verb form that has no clear agent, or it may consist of adjectives with no noun to modify. You can revise such sentences in one of the following ways:

▶ Provide a noun or pronoun.

I didn't know the difference between
Flubbing chemistry, ∧*silicon* and *silicone* were the same to me.

[According to the original sentence, *silicon* and *silicone* flubbed chemistry.]

▶ Move the modifier.

candy-colored and versatile
Candy-colored and versatile, I use my ∧silicone spatulas every day.

[According to the original sentence, the writer is candy-colored and versatile.]

▶ Reword the modifier.

Feeding my addiction to kitchen gadgets,
∧A kitchen-gadget junkie, silicone baking pans thrill me.

[In the original sentence, an illogical connection is made between "a kitchen-gadget junkie" and "silicone baking pans."]

Connecting words, phrases, or clauses

Using conjunctions or conjunctive adverbs **Coordinating conjunctions** join words, phrases, or even clauses. Coordinating conjunctions do more than link, however; they specify a type of link.

▶ *For* signals cause.

They won the court case, <u>for</u> their argument was strong and their evidence unassailable.

► *And* signals addition.

They made strong claims <u>and</u> supported them with convincing evidence.

► *Nor* signals negative alternatives.

They didn't have a strong argument, <u>nor</u> did they have convincing evidence.

► *But* signals contrast.

They made strong claims, <u>but</u> they were unable to support them with convincing evidence.

► *Or* signals positive alternatives.

They will win the case <u>or</u> appeal it.

► *Yet* signals contrast.

They made strong claims, <u>yet</u> they were unable to support them with convincing evidence.

► *So* signals consequence.

Their evidence was unassailable, <u>so</u> they won the case.

Writers sometimes use more than one coordinating conjunction to slow down the rhythm of a sentence: *The lecture was long and far-reaching and tedious.* In this sentence, each adjective receives emphasis. Note also that the sentence stretches out just as the lecture it refers to does. (The rhetorical term for this stretching strategy is **polysyndeton**.) In contrast, writers may also choose to omit an expected coordinating conjunction in order to take advantage of the resulting change in rhythm. In *His response was quick, pointed, painful,* three adjectives end the sentence in three strong beats. This type of sentence rhythm can produce the sense that a longer list could have been presented: *They served the usual—soup, salad, sandwiches, pasta.* (The strategy of omitting coordinating conjunctions is called **asyndeton**.)

Conjunctive adverbs form links between sentences. Like coordinating conjunctions, these adverbs provide *meaningful* links. Writers use them to indicate their logic—for example, to show how two sentences contrast or how one sentence builds on another. Here are some of the more common types of logical links:

► Contrast: *however, conversely*

Many patients fear that generic drugs are not safe. <u>However</u>, the Food and Drug Administration has reported that these drugs pose no risks for patients.

► Result: *thus, therefore, consequently, then*

The patents for several drugs will expire this year. <u>Therefore</u>, patients will be able to buy cheaper generic versions of these drugs.

► Concession: *nevertheless, nonetheless, still*

A recent study reported differing results for generic and brand-name drugs. <u>Nonetheless</u>, no adverse effects were reported.

► Enumeration: *first, second, next*

<u>First</u>, consult a physician.

- Addition: *furthermore, moreover, also*

  The FDA requires the generic drug to contain the same active ingredient as the brand-name drug. The agency <u>also</u> expects manufacturers of generic drugs to perform laboratory tests.

- Comparison: *similarly, likewise*

  Research studies of the brand-name drug reported no adverse side effects. <u>Similarly</u>, studies of the generic drug listed no serious health issues associated with taking the drug.

When a conjunctive adverb comes at the beginning of a clause, you can indicate the separation between the two independent clauses in two ways: (1) use a semicolon, or (2) use a period and begin a new sentence.

> Many patients fear that generic drugs are not safe; <u>however</u>, the Food and Drug Administration has reported that generic medicines pose no risks for patients.

> Many patients fear that generic drugs are not safe. <u>However</u>, the Food and Drug Administration has reported that generic medicines pose no risks for patients.

Although conjunctive adverbs usually appear at the beginning of a sentence or clause, some, such as *however* and *nevertheless,* can appear in the middle or at the end. In either case, use a comma or commas to set off the adverb.

> <u>However</u>, the generic drug did not sell well.

> The generic drug, <u>however</u>, did not sell well.

> The generic drug did not sell well, <u>however</u>.

Using prepositional phrases Prepositional phrases (see pages 551–552) are often used as transitions between sentences or paragraphs. They signal various logical relationships.

- Time and sequence: *at first, in addition*

  <u>At first</u>, musicals were labeled *musical comedies.*

- Contrast: *in contrast, on the one hand/on the other hand*

  For musicals, you need actors who can sing. <u>In contrast</u>, for operettas, you need singers who can act.

- Example: *for example, for instance*

  There are several differences between operettas and musicals. <u>For example</u>, operettas often include aristocratic characters, while musicals involve more ordinary people.

- Emphasis: *in fact, above all*

  Because of the seriousness of its plot, *Porgy and Bess* should not be placed in the same category as *My Fair Lady*. <u>In fact</u>, it should be labeled an *opera* rather than a *musical.*

- Restatement: *in other words, in sum*

  <u>In sum</u>, what matters is the audience's appreciation of the piece.

Using participial phrases Participial phrases (see page 557) express a variety of meanings that can affect the coherence of your writing.

▶ Cause:

<u>Noting our confusion</u>, the lecturer provided additional examples.

▶ Purpose:

He came to the lecture <u>looking for a debate</u>.

▶ Result:

She concluded by presenting several provocative perspectives—<u>effectively opening the door for further discussion</u>.

Using subordinating conjunctions with dependent clauses Like the other connectors presented in this chapter, subordinating conjunctions signal several different types of connections, including the following:

▶ Cause: *because, since, as*

The election results were unknown <u>because</u> the polls were still open.

▶ Time: *after, before, since, while, until*

<u>After</u> the polls closed, the votes were quickly counted.

▶ Concession: *although, even though, though, while*

<u>Although</u> the polls were still open, news programs predicted the winner.

▶ Condition: *if, unless*

<u>If</u> the polls are still open, there is no winner.

Three subordinating conjunctions sometimes cause problems because they can be used in two different ways. *While* can refer to both time and concession, so *While we had disagreements, we never threw bottles* could mean either that bottles were not thrown during disagreements or that bottles were not thrown even though there were disagreements. *Since* and *as* are also potentially ambiguous; they both can refer to time or cause. When you edit your sentences, make sure that the meanings of these words are clear.

> EXERCISE 22.6

Choose an essay in this book and identify ten different ways the author makes the work coherent.

Variety and Emphasis

Sentence length

Both short and long sentences have their uses. Short sentences sound direct and emphatic, so they can highlight your feelings and impressions. Long sentences allow you to develop your ideas fully. However, if you use too many short sentences, no one sentence will stand out. Instead, your writing will sound choppy. Similarly, if you overuse long sentences, you send a signal to your readers that you have not thought through your ideas enough to present them succinctly. Your sentences will seem rambling.

Using a variety of sentence lengths, Louise Rafkin recounts a sixth-grade memory in all its horror.

> In sixth grade I was shown a filmstrip on hygiene. My teacher, good-hearted but simple, screened this gem of an educational tool directly before lunch. It was a "follow the fly" documentary. We witnessed the fly in its full furry glory, magnified to horror-film proportions. We followed it to a raw-sewage treatment plant, and watched it set down and gulp a huge dollop of crud through its hydraulic pump of a mouth, the surface of the sewage swamp roiling about its hairy legs. Then the little monster up and flew right over to a nearby playground and landed on an unsuspecting kid's baloney sandwich. There, it threw up.
>
> —Louise Rafkin, *Other People's Dirt*

You can see the varying lengths more clearly in this list of the sentences from her paragraph:

1. In sixth grade I was shown a filmstrip on hygiene.
2. My teacher, good-hearted but simple, screened this gem of an educational tool directly before lunch.
3. It was a "follow the fly" documentary.
4. We witnessed the fly in its full furry glory, magnified to horror-film proportions.
5. We followed it to a raw-sewage treatment plant, and watched it set down and gulp a huge dollop of crud through its hydraulic pump of a mouth, the surface of the sewage swamp roiling about its hairy legs.
6. Then the little monster up and flew right over to a nearby playground and landed on an unsuspecting kid's baloney sandwich.
7. There, it threw up.

Notice how Rafkin's longer sentences carry evocative details, while her shorter ones highlight a significant event or action.

Unusual sentence patterns

A sentence usually consists of a subject followed by a predicate. However, other sentence patterns are available (see pages 560–562). When used judiciously, the unusual sentence patterns in the following chart can add variety and emphasis to your writing. Sensing a change in the expected order of words, readers will shift their attention to the stressed word that is out of place.

Pattern	Original Sentence	Revised Sentence
Begin the sentence with the complement.	He expected <u>an insult</u>. He could not accept <u>a compliment</u>.	<u>An insult</u>, he expected. <u>A compliment</u>, he could not accept.
Begin the sentence with the verb or part of the verb.	Then the brass band <u>came</u>, marching to a military cadence.	Then <u>came</u> the brass band, marching to a military cadence.
Begin the sentence with a negative word.	She did <u>not</u> understand the consequences of her action until she lost her job.	<u>Not</u> until she lost her job did she understand the consequences of her action.
Begin the sentence with an expression of location or direction.	Stacks of old magazines were <u>inside the garage</u>.	<u>Inside the garage</u> were stacks of old magazines.

Combining sentences

If you find during the revision stage that your sentences lack variety, try joining two or three short sentences into one longer one. The following chart presents several sentence-combining strategies.

Strategy	Original Sentences	Combined Sentences
Join sentences or parts of sentences with a coordinating conjunction.	My parents live in Maryland. My brother lives in Iowa. I live in Arizona.	My parents live in Maryland, my brother lives in Iowa, **and** I live in Arizona.
	The Bradleys have <u>contributed money</u>. They have also <u>volunteered to work</u>.	The Bradleys <u>have contributed money</u> **and** <u>volunteered to work</u>.
Join sentences with a semicolon.	Johnson won the gold medal. His best friend won the silver medal.	Johnson won the gold medal**;** his best friend won the silver medal.
Reduce the information in one sentence to a prepositional phrase.	<u>They worried about their mounting debt and their tense relationship.</u> As a result, they consulted a financial advisor.	**Because of** <u>their mounting debt and tense relationship</u>, they consulted a financial advisor.

Strategy	Original Sentences	Combined Sentences
Reduce the information in one sentence to a verbal phrase.	<u>I walked into the kitchen</u>. I saw something on the counter that was not supposed to be there.	**Walking** <u>into the kitchen</u>, I saw something on the counter that was not supposed to be there.
Reduce the information in one sentence to an appositive.	David is the head of the department. He will be leading the discussion.	David, <u>the head of the department</u>, will be leading the discussion.
Place the information in one sentence in a dependent clause.	The guide recommended staying away from the cave. The couple entered anyway.	**Although** <u>the guide recommended staying away from the cave</u>, the couple entered anyway.

If you end up with too many long sentences in an essay, you can separate some into two sentences.

Visitors to Olympic National Park, located on Washington's Olympic Peninsula,

often want to see a glacier,~~especially~~ Blue Glacier, which cascades down
      ^*Many glimpse*

Mount Olympus, but only those willing to carry a heavy pack and walk

seventeen miles can get a close-up view.

Questions, exclamations, and imperative sentences

If your rhetorical situation allows you to take on a conversational voice—one in which you are able to ask questions, emphasize impressions, or give instructions—you can use interrogative, exclamatory, and imperative sentences.

Interrogative sentences Some questions introduce a new topic. These questions are answered within the text.

> <u>So, how does a coach motivate?</u> Well, any number of ways. Coaches, in many ways, are like child psychologists, dealing with a variety of maturity and intelligence levels. The truth is, no one method works for every player. Some players need to be kicked in the butt. Some need to be stroked and coddled. Each method could backfire if used on the wrong player. —**Joe Theismann**, *The Complete Idiot's Guide to Football*

Other questions used by writers are **rhetorical questions**—questions that are used as statements rather than as sincere questions (see pages 565–566).

Exclamatory sentences To express emotional responses, some writers use exclamatory sentences.

> But at other moments, the classroom is so lifeless or painful or confused—and I so powerless to do anything about it—that my claim to be a teacher seems a transparent sham. Then the enemy is everywhere: in those students from some alien planet, in the subject I thought I knew, and in the personal pathology that keeps me earning my living this way. <u>What a fool I was to imagine that I had mastered this occult art—harder to divine than tea leaves and impossible for mortals to do even passably well!</u>
>
> —**Parker Palmer**, *The Courage to Teach*

Beware of overusing exclamation points. Your readers might decide you are being cute or melodramatic. If you are emphasizing something humorous, you don't need to signal it with your punctuation. In fact, understatement can enhance the humor of a scene.

Imperative sentences If you want to direct your readers to do something, consider using an imperative sentence.

> Now I stare and stare at people shamelessly. <u>Stare</u>. It's the way to educate your eye.
>
> —**Walker Evans**, *Unclassified*

> EXERCISE 22.7

Choose an essay in this book and find ten different ways the author has added variety to the work.

Punctuation, Mechanics, and Rhetorical Effects

23

Take a few minutes to thumb through this book, looking at just the punctuation marks. Stop to compare the different uses of punctuation in the excerpts from various authors. More than likely, you'll notice some personal preferences in punctuation. Now consider this description of a large Christian nightclub:

> Enter her three-level, 18,000-square-foot club—a new space inaugurated in October—and you won't find any overtly religious symbols. In the lounge below, patrons can shoot pool and order pizzas and smoothies from the bar (the closest you'll get to a stimulant is Red Bull). Upstairs, they can experience acts with a state-of-the-art sound and light system. The price tag for all the renovations: $3 million, raised through donations and loans guaranteed by the club's founder, the Living Word Christian Center. —**Arian Camp-Flores**, "Get Your Praise On"

First, notice the variety of punctuation marks: commas, hyphens, dashes, periods, apostrophes, parentheses, and a colon. The writer's choice of punctuation marks becomes part of her message, as they are meant to serve as beacons to help readers navigate her prose. Some help us understand where one idea starts and ends. Without seeing a period after the first sentence and a capital letter at the beginning of the next, a reader could experience a few moments of confusion while trying to figure out whether religious symbols are not present in the entire club or whether they are just not visible in the lounge. Other punctuation marks help us understand which parts of the paragraph the author deems most important and which parts she considers significant but only tangentially related to her main idea. By enclosing a clause in parentheses, Camp-Flores is signaling that the remark should be understood as an aside—the equivalent of saying, "Just in case you're interested in stimulants, Red Bull is the only one available."

Now let's look at another description—an excerpt from an article in *Scientific American.*

> To understand the birth process from the mother's point of view, imagine you are about to give birth. The baby is most likely upside down, facing your side, when its head enters the birth canal. Midway through the canal, however, it must turn to face your back, and the back of its head is pressed against your pubic bones. At that time, its shoulders are oriented side to side. When the baby exits your body, it is still facing backward, but it will turn its head slightly to the side. This rotation helps to turn the baby's shoulders so that they can also fit between your pubic bones and tailbone.
> —**Karen R. Rosenberg and Wenda R. Trevathan**, "The Evolution of Human Birth"

In this paragraph, you can quickly pick out commas, periods, and apostrophes—conventional punctuation found in almost any piece of nonfiction writing. However, there are no dashes, colons, or parentheses. The punctuation style in this paragraph differs from that in the paragraph by Camp-Flores because the authors' rhetorical situation differs. Rosenberg and Trevathan's primary purpose is to describe the human birthing process as concisely and as straightforwardly as possible. Their readers expect to be informed, and the authors meet this expectation by using a limited number of punctuation marks so that the information is easy to read. In contrast, Camp-Flores's purpose is to be entertaining and conversational as well as informative; thus, she uses punctuation as the owner of a nightclub uses stage lights, directing bright lights toward some parts of the stage but providing subdued lighting elsewhere.

In this chapter, you will learn the punctuation options that are available to you for crafting a fitting response to each particular rhetorical situation. The Guide to Punctuation provides detailed information about each punctuation mark. This section is followed by a discussion of punctuation trouble spots and the Guide to Mechanics, which provides style guidelines for writing in an academic setting. **Mechanics** refers to the use of abbreviations, acronyms, initialisms, capital letters, italics, and numbers.

Guide to Punctuation

As you have seen by examining some of the excerpts in this book, writers punctuate purposefully—to indicate boundaries, to control sentence rhythm, and to modify or clarify meaning. The following guide, arranged alphabetically, provides details on uses of the individual punctuation marks.

The punctuation conventions listed here are based on those provided in *The Chicago Manual of Style* (CMS), sixteenth edition. The great majority of these conventions are also included in *The MLA Handbook for Writers of Research Papers* (MLA) and in the *Publication Manual of the American Psychological Association* (APA). When MLA or APA conventions differ from those of the CMS, those alternatives are also listed.

' Apostrophe

To mark omissions An apostrophe is used to mark an omission in a contraction, number, or word mimicking speech.

we will → we'll   class of 2008 → class of '08   you all → y'all

Contractions are not appropriate for all rhetorical situations. In formal contexts, your audience may expect you to use full words and numbers.

To form the possessive case of singular and plural nouns An apostrophe is commonly used to indicate possession, ownership, or origin.

Sandra's dog   Sandra's car   Sandra's idea

It can also signal other types of relationships.

Relationship between people:	Sandra's friend
Traits or features of humans, plants, and animals:	Sandra's tenacity, the cat's yowl, the plant's stem
Features of objects:	the fabric's sheen, the room's lighting
Features of abstract nouns:	greed's hold
Identification of buildings:	St. John's Cathedral
Identification of illnesses:	Huntington's disease
Identification of holidays:	Valentine's Day, Presidents' Day
Type of certification:	bachelor's degree, driver's license
Measurement:	a month's vacation, ten dollars' worth of gas

An apostrophe and the letter *s* indicate the possessive case of singular nouns, indefinite pronouns, abbreviations, and acronyms.

the director's office   Dr. Seuss's stories   everyone's hope

the UN's announcement   NAFTA's history

A noun may end with the letter *s* in both its singular and plural forms. In such a case, only an apostrophe is added.

politics' attraction   physics' contribution

WAIT A MINUTE . . .

The words *its* and *it's* are often confused. *Its* is a possessive pronoun; *it's* is a contraction for "it is." The words *whose* and *who's* are also frequently confused. *Whose* is a pronoun; *who's* is a contraction for "who is."

Possessive Pronoun	**Contraction**
Its roof is sleep.	It's a steep roof.
Whose is it?	Who's in charge?

Only an apostrophe is added to indicate the possessive case of a plural noun ending in the letter *s*.

the students' petition   the Lopezes' company

However, both an apostrophe and the letter *s* are needed to indicate the possessive case of an irregular plural not ending in *s*.

children's activities   men's health   women's programs

> ## WAIT A MINUTE . . .
>
> It is easy to confuse the *s* ending that makes a noun plural and the *s* ending used to indicate the possessive case. Use an apostrophe only to indicate possession, ownership, origin, and the other relationships listed on page 609.
>
> *planets*
> The planets' were visible without the use of a telescope.
>
> [COMPARE: The planets' orbits vary in shape.]
>
> *Joneses*
> The Joneses' donated $500.
>
> [COMPARE: The Joneses' donation was unsolicited.]

To show joint ownership or collaboration An apostrophe and the letter *s* are added to the second noun to indicate shared ownership or collaboration on a project.

> David Ayo and Jill Michelucci's studio
>
> the director and the producer's decision

To show separate ownership or individual contributions An apostrophe and the letter *s* are added to each noun to indicate that ownership is separate or that contributions have been made independently.

> David Ayo's and Jill Michelucci's apartments
>
> the director's and the producer's ideas

For possessive forms of compound nouns An apostrophe and the letter *s* are added to the last word of a compound noun to make it possessive.

> sister-in-law's job, the attorney general's report [singular]
>
> sisters-in-law's jobs, the attorneys general's reports [plural]

The awkwardness of making plural compounds possessive can be eliminated by using a prepositional phrase beginning with *of* instead of an apostrophe and *s*.

> the jobs of my sisters-in-law, the reports of the attorneys general

Before gerunds A noun used before a gerund should be in the possessive case.

> Jeff's <u>objecting</u> caused many members to feel uncomfortable.
>
> We were awakened by the neighbors' <u>shouting</u>.

WAIT A MINUTE . . .

If a noun precedes a participle, no apostrophe is needed.

I remember my aunt <u>telling</u> me stories about my parents.

A good way to tell the difference between a gerund and a participle is to ask whether the emphasis is on an action or on a person. In a phrase or clause containing a gerund, the emphasis is on the action (in *Jeff's objecting*, the emphasis is on the objecting). In a phrase or clause containing a participle, the emphasis is on the person (in *my aunt telling me*, the emphasis is on the aunt).

[ ] Brackets

In quotations Brackets indicate that a clarification or explanation has been added to a quotation. In other words, the brackets indicate that the enclosed text was not written by the original author of the quoted passage.

Three years after the death of Joseph Stalin, President Dwight D. Eisenhower asked, "Is it [the Soviet Union] prepared to allow other nations, including those of Eastern Europe, the free choice of their own forms of government?"

Within parentheses Brackets, instead of another set of parentheses, are used inside a parenthetical remark.

(According to Stewart, the Battle of Little Bighorn [Custer's last stand] was a poorly planned attack.)

: Colon

To introduce a list In academic writing, a colon is used after a complete independent clause to introduce a list.

Musicians producing the neo-soul sound have been inspired by artists from the seventies: James Brown, Isaac Hayes, Curtis Mayfield, and Stevie Wonder, to mention a few.

For formal writing assignments, lists not preceded by a full independent clause must be revised, either by removing the colon or by using *as follows* or *the following* to fill out the clause.

The books that most influenced Mario Puzo, author of *The Godfather,*
included ‸ *the following* : *The Brothers Karamazov, The House by the Medlar Tree, Madame Bovary,* and *Vanity Fair.*

In less formal contexts (as in an article in a popular magazine or newspaper), a full introductory clause may not be needed. Arian Camp-Flores (writing for the magazine *Newsweek*) does not use one in her description of a Christian nightclub.

> The price tag for all the renovations: $3 million, raised through donations and loans guaranteed by the club's founder, the Living Word Christian Center.

In academic writing, a complete independent clause precedes a colon, but a word or a phrase can follow it.

> She had only one word on her mind: success.

To direct attention to an explanation, an example, or a summary A colon is used between two independent clauses when the second clause expands, exemplifies, or summarizes the idea expressed in the first. Unless the second clause is a direct question or is the first of two or more sentences, the first letter of the second clause is not capitalized.

> After weeks of conflict, the couple reached an impasse: Could they possibly stay together, or should they split up?

> After several reports of elephants being overworked and then attacking humans, government officials took action: they sent the fatigued animals to a wildlife sanctuary for a short vacation.

According to APA guidelines, the first letter of the second clause should always be capitalized. In MLA style, the first letter is capitalized only if the second clause is a rule or principle.

> The trainer wrote the first rule on the board: Never promise what you cannot deliver, and always deliver what you promise.

To introduce a quotation A quotation is often introduced by an introductory independent clause followed by a colon.

> In "High-Tech Bibliophilia," Paul Goldberger praises the newest building in downtown Seattle: "The complex polygonal form of the Seattle library, which is sheathed almost entirely in glass set in a diamond-shaped grid, has a dazzling energy; it's the most alluring architectural object to arrive in this city's downtown since the Space Needle."

After a salutation in a formal letter A colon is used in formal letters after the salutation.

> To Whom It May Concern:

> Dear Dr. Elmore:

, Comma

One of the most important punctuation marks to learn to use effectively is the comma. It can be difficult to decide whether to use a comma because this mark has so many functions. But commas are essential: they give sentences clarity and rhythm. See if you agree as you read the following passage—first with the commas removed and then in the original form.

Without Commas

Eighty years ago when I was about thirteen my elder brother Edwin was about eighteen and in his freshman year at Columbia College commuting from our home in Brooklyn. He was taking a survey course in English literature. He decided because I was interested in books to give me the same course at home that he was taking in college. So every day when he came home he would sit down with me and tell me what the assignment was for the next day. I had to read everything he read and take all the tests he took. I also had to write the papers he had to write. So what I got was a thorough survey course in English literature based on a textbook which I remember as being titled *Century Readings in English Literature*. I'm not sure that was the exact title but I think so because it was published by the Century Company. The editors however I do remember: Cunliffe Pyre and Young.

With Commas (Original)

Eighty years ago, when I was about thirteen, my elder brother, Edwin, was about eighteen and in his freshman year at Columbia College, commuting from our home in Brooklyn. He was taking a survey course in English literature. He decided, because I was interested in books, to give me the same course at home that he was taking in college. So every day, when he came home, he would sit down with me and tell me what the assignment was for the next day. I had to read everything he read and take all the tests he took. I also had to write the papers he had to write. So what I got was a thorough survey course in English literature based on a textbook which I remember as being titled *Century Readings in English Literature*. I'm not sure that was the exact title but I think so, because it was published by the Century Company. The editors, however, I do remember: Cunliffe, Pyre, and Young.

—**Clifton Fadiman,** in *For the Love of Books* by Ronald B. Shwartz

Knowing a few basic functions of commas will help you use them to clarify the meaning and enhance the rhythm of your sentences.

WAIT A MINUTE . . .

Some novice writers believe that they should place a comma wherever they would pause if they were speaking. The result of holding such a notion is the overuse or misplacement of commas. As you can hear when you read a sentence aloud, a comma indicates more than mere hesitation; it also affects intonation and stress and causes lengthening of certain words.

Two or more elements

To separate items in a series A comma separates words, phrases, and clauses in a series. A comma has not always been considered necessary before a conjunction (*and* or *or*) in a series; however, its use is now strongly recommended to ensure clarity.

Grammar and Style

Words:	Diplomats from England, France, and Spain met on Tuesday.
Phrases:	He worked before school, after school, and on weekends.
Clauses:	We should support this candidate because she supports higher funding for education, because she has a plan for improving health care, and because her economic policies are sound.

If a pair of words combined with *and* are considered a single item, a comma should not separate them.

> The children's menu included hamburgers, hot dogs, and <u>macaroni and cheese</u>.

To separate coordinate adjectives Two or more adjectives that modify the same noun are called **coordinate adjectives**. To test whether adjectives are coordinate, either interchange them or put *and* between them. If the meaning does not change, the adjectives are coordinate and so should be separated by a comma or commas.

> The company honored their dedicated, energetic interns.
>
> [COMPARE: energetic, dedicated interns OR dedicated and energetic interns]

The adjectives in the following sentence are not separated by a comma. Notice that they cannot be interchanged or joined by *and*.

> The old wooden bridge was featured in a documentary.
>
> [NOT the wooden old bridge OR the old and wooden bridge]

To separate independent clauses A comma is generally used between two independent clauses in a compound sentence when they are linked by a coordinating conjunction. The comma appears before the conjunction.

Two clauses:	The ultraviolet rays used in tanning beds differ from those produced by the sun, but they are still dangerous.

If there are more than two clauses, each clause is followed by a comma.

Four clauses:	Responding to a flood of adrenaline, your heart pounds faster, your breathing quickens, your muscles contract, and your eyes dilate.

If the clauses are short and closely related in meaning, the comma is not always necessary.

> I collect pottery and my sister collects jewelry.

Introductory elements

After introductory words and phrases A comma usually follows a word or phrase that precedes the subject of a sentence. It indicates that the typical sentence structure has been altered.

> Rapidly, I calculated the total cost.
>
> In contrast, a counterculture defines itself by opposing the dominant culture.

> Backed by a bass and a keyboard, the guitarist played a familiar song.

A comma is not required after a single word or short prepositional phrase as long as there is no chance of misreading.

> On Monday we will discuss the new design.

After introductory attributive tags A comma follows an attributive tag, a short phrase that signals the source of a remark or quoted information. Although these tags may appear in the middle or at the end of a sentence, they often appear at the beginning in order to introduce the material.

> She replied, "Yeah, right."

> As Bill would say, "Where there's no hope, there's no hurry."

> According to Azar Nafisi, "What we search for in fiction is not so much reality but the epiphany of truth."

A comma is not used with indirect questions.

> He asked me when I would be able to finish the report.

After introductory dependent clauses A comma follows an introductory dependent clause.

> Even though traffic was heavy, we arrived on time.

Parenthetical elements

To set off parenthetical expressions A comma is used to set off a **parenthetical expression**—words, phrases, or clauses that make a transition in thought or add emotive details. When the parenthetical expression is placed in the middle of the sentence, two commas are used (before and after it) to indicate that it is a transition, an interruption, an interjection, an aside, or an additional but unnecessary detail.

> We all laughed, in nervous titters, as we introduced ourselves.

When the parenthetical expression is placed at the end of the sentence, just one comma is used to set off the element from the rest of the sentence.

> He did not mention his destination, however.

To set off nonessential verbal phrases Commas are used to set off nonessential verbal phrases. The term *nonessential* means that these phrases are not necessary for their referents to be specifically identified. These verbal phrases begin with either a present participle (*laughing, walking*) or a past participle (*offered, written*).

> Fans waited in line at the box office, hoping to get tickets to the evening concert.

> *nonessential*

> The annual Ellensburg Rodeo, held on Labor Day weekend, attracts many tourists.

When the information in the verbal phrase is essential for the referent to be identified, commas are not used.

> The rodeo planned for Labor Day weekend will attract many tourists.

To set off nonessential appositives A **nonessential appositive** is a word or phrase that provides extra information about an adjacent noun or pronoun. Because this type of appositive is not necessary for the identification of a referent, it is set off from the rest of the sentence—by two commas when it occurs in the middle of a sentence or by a single comma when it appears at the end of a sentence.

> Suzanne Dittmer, president of the company, announced the opening of a new factory in Greenville.

> Delegates met in Hanoi, the capital of Vietnam.

To set off nonessential dependent clauses A nonessential dependent clause may be an adverbial clause, an adjectival clause, or a noun clause. These clauses add extra details rather than providing essential information for completing the meaning of a sentence, so they are set off by commas.

Adverbial clauses that begin with *although, even though,* or *while* are usually set off by commas because they provide nonessential, contrasting information.

> Sea Biscuit, although the odds were against him, won the race by a nose.

Adverbial clauses indicating time, cause, or purpose are usually not set off by commas.

> She studied in Tokyo for a year so that she could improve her Japanese.

A nonessential adjectival clause begins with a relative pronoun, most commonly *who* or *which*. The information conveyed in the clause adds details about a referent that has already been identified.

> Many families enjoy hiking on the Scout Trail, which is located at the end of Bay Road.

> Joel Cavanaugh, who reported the accident, was on his way home from work.

Adjectival clauses that are necessary for the identification of the referent are not set off by commas.

> The person who reported the accident was on his way home from work.

A nonessential noun clause adds information about or renames a preceding noun.

> His suggestion, that the application deadline be extended, resulted in a larger pool of candidates.

The exact content of the suggestion referred to here would have been mentioned earlier in the passage. The nonessential noun clause, then, is a repetition of that old information and is thus set off by commas. If the sentence were introducing the suggestion for the first time, no commas would be used.

> His suggestion that the application deadline be extended resulted in a larger pool of candidates.

If you read both versions of this sentence aloud, you should be able to hear a difference in rhythm.

To set off contrasting information Commas set off contrasting information. The phrase that is set off often contains the word *not*.

> The business owners, not the employees, were responsible for the accident.

With attributive tags Commas separate the words in a quotation or dialogue from an attributive tag (see page 461).

> "Being a hippie," explains DiFilippo, "means approaching life's obstacles in a way that promotes freedom, peace, love, and respect for our earth and all of humankind."
>
> No one was injured, according to the sheriff's report.

Special uses

To indicate the omission of words When two or more adjacent parts of a sentence have similar structures (that is, they are parallel in form), a comma can be used in the element(s) after the first to indicate the omission of a word or words. The missing words should be easily retrievable from the context.

> June brought two severe storms; July, three; and August, four.

If there is no chance of misreading, no commas are needed to indicate omitted words.

> I played the piano, my sister the trumpet, and my brother the saxophone.

With the more, the less, and other comparatives When comparative forms (e.g., *the more* or *the less*) are followed by clauses, a comma is used to separate the clauses.

> The more we study this topic, the more complicated it becomes.
>
> The less time I spend worrying about baseball, the better I feel.

To set off state or year A comma is used to set off the name of a state when it follows the name of a city. It is also used to set off the year in a complete date.

> My parents moved to Athens, Vermont, on January 1, 1954.

A comma is not used between a month or specific day (without numerical date) and year.

> My parents moved there in January 1954.
>
> My parents moved to their new home on New Year's Day 1954.

Unnecessary or misplaced commas

Separating a subject and its verb or a verb and its object Although speakers often pause after the subject or before the object of a sentence, such a pause should not be indicated by a comma.

In this climate, rain at frequent intervals, produces mosquitoes.
[no separation between subject (*rain*) and verb (*produces*)]

Following a coordinating conjunction Avoid using a comma after a coordinating conjunction (*and, but, for, nor, or, so,* or *yet*).

We worked very hard on her campaign for state representative, but, the incumbent was too strong in the northern part of the district.

Separating elements in a compound predicate Avoid using a comma between two elements of a compound predicate.

She picked up her baby, and ran out the door.

Occasionally, a comma is used in a compound predicate to provide emphasis. Use this option sparingly, however, or it will lose its effectiveness.

I looked around the room at all the boxes of junk, and despaired.

Setting off words, phrases, and clauses that are clearly essential In the following sentences, the elements in boldface are clearly essential and so should not be set off by commas. (See also pages 615–616.)

Kelly was born, **in Chicago in 1987.**

Everyone, **who has a mortgage,** is required to have fire insurance.

— Dash

After an introductory list A dash follows an introductory list of nouns. No spaces are used before or after the dash.

Frodo, Sam, Pippin, and Merry—these were the hobbits who left the Shire together.

Notice that a pronoun follows the dash; it refers to the list of nouns.

To set off comments Dashes are used to set off comments that interrupt or conclude a sentence.

My story—it is a long one, so bear with me—begins in 1959.

They had never been in trouble before—as far as we knew.

To indicate faltering speech A dash is used to indicate that a speaker is struggling to find the right word.

May I—would you—is it possible for us to disagree and still be friends?

To set off nonessential appositives A nonessential appositive can be set off by dashes instead of commas. However, the dash, because it suggests a longer pause, emphasizes the content of the appositive.

Sylvia—an avid videogame player—also likes to read books.

He never tired of watching his favorite movie—*The Matrix.*

WAIT A MINUTE . . .

Which punctuation is better to use with a nonessential appositive—commas, dashes, or a colon? Any of these marks can be used. As a guide, though, consider the comma as neutral, the dash as semiformal and emphatic, and the colon as formal.

He always had the same lunch, a turkey sandwich.

He always had the same lunch—a turkey sandwich.

He always had the same lunch: a turkey sandwich.

. . . Ellipsis points

To indicate omitted words in a quotation Ellipsis points—three periods separated from each other and adjacent words by spaces—indicate the omission of words from quoted sentences. An omission may occur within a quoted sentence or at the end of a quoted sentence. The examples of the use of ellipsis points that follow are based on this excerpt.

> Within months of their 1st birthday, most kids start attaching names to things. And whether they're learning Swahili or Swedish, they go about it in much the same way. Instead of proceeding by trial and error—unsure whether "doggie" refers to a part of a dog, to one dog in particular, or to anything with four legs—children start with a set of innate biases. They assume that labels refer to wholes instead of parts (the creature, not the tail) and to classes instead of items (all dogs, not one dog). They also figure that one name is for any class of object (if it's a dog, it's not a cow). These assumptions are not always valid—there's only one Lassie, after all, and any dog qualifies as a mammal—but they enable kids to catalog new words with breathtaking efficiency. A typical child is socking away a dozen words a day by 18 months, and may command 2,000 of them by the age of 2.
>
> —**Geoffrey Cowley,** "For the Love of Language"

Within a quoted sentence

According to Geoffrey Cowley, "Instead of proceeding by trial and error . . . children start with a set of innate biases."

End of a quoted sentence Ellipsis points that replace words at the end of a sentence must be followed by an end punctuation mark (a period, a question mark, or an exclamation point).

According to Geoffrey Cowley, "A typical child is socking away a dozen words a day by 18 months . . . ."

Beginning of a quoted sentence No ellipsis points are needed to indicate an omission at the beginning of a sentence.

> According to Geoffrey Cowley, children learn "a dozen words a day by 18 months, and may command 2,000 of them by the age of 2."

Omission of a sentence or more For an omission of a sentence or more, the ellipsis points should follow the end punctuation of the preceding sentence.

> Geoffrey Cowley explains how young children learn language:
>
> > Within months of their 1st birthday, most kids start attaching names to things. . . . They assume that labels refer to wholes instead of parts (the creature, not the tail) and to classes instead of items (all dogs, not one dog). They also figure that one name is for any class of object (if it's a dog, it's not a cow). These assumptions are not always valid—there's only one Lassie, after all, and any dog qualifies as a mammal—but they enable kids to catalog new words with breathtaking efficiency. A typical child is socking away a dozen words a day by 18 months, and may command 2,000 of them by the age of 2.

To indicate pauses or hesitation in speech Ellipsis points are used to indicate interrupted speech.

> I talked to her once . . . twice . . . maybe three times.

! Exclamation Point

To indicate strong feeling Because an exclamation point signals an emphatic comment, it should be used sparingly. Academic writing rarely calls for an exclamation point.

> What an incredible day!

- Hyphen

To form compound words A hyphen is used in some compound words.

> father-in-law   nurse-practitioner   president-elect

A hyphen is used in a compound number.

> sixty-three   seventy-eight   forty-two

A hyphen is also used with certain prefixes and suffixes.

self-confidence	self-reliance
ex-mayor	ex-president
cross-cultural	cross-reference
e-greeting	e-commerce
toll-free	debt-free

A hyphen in a compound adjective indicates that words in the compound should be considered as a single unit.

fifteenth-century church   fourth-floor apartment

six-year-old child   two-hour delay

down-and-dirty campaign   tit-for-tat response

Notice that when these modifiers do not come before a noun, they are not hyphenated.

The church was built in the fifteenth century.

The child is six years old.

A dictionary is a helpful source when trying to decide which compound words include hyphens. A compound consisting of an adverb that ends in -*ly* and an adjective never has a hyphen.

The rarely used church was finally abandoned.

In fractions A hyphen is used between the numerator and the denominator when a fraction is written as words.

two-thirds   eight-tenths

( ) Parentheses

To enclose numbers or letters in a list Parentheses enclose numbers or letters used in lists within paragraphs.

Use insect repellent carefully: (1) apply repellent just to clothing and shoes if possible, (2) wash off repellent applied to the skin when you go indoors, and (3) avoid putting repellent on your hands.

To enclose source information Parentheses enclose dates, authors' names, page numbers, and other types of source information.

Around this time, the first Penn State student donned a "furry lion outfit" for athletic events (Bezilla 30).

To enclose explanatory or supplementary material Parentheses enclose words, phrases, or sentences that explain or supplement the information in the main text.

Paragraphs can be organized chronologically (along a time line) or emphatically (starting or ending with the most important point).

If a complete sentence enclosed in parentheses appears within a sentence, the first letter is not capitalized, nor is end punctuation included within the parentheses.

Nosebleeds are common throughout childhood (see page 23 for common causes). You can usually stop a nose from bleeding by squeezing the soft part of the nose against the center wall. However, if the bleeding does not stop after you have applied pressure for twenty minutes, you should call your pediatrician.

If a complete sentence enclosed in parentheses is separate from other sentences, the first letter of the sentence is capitalized, and end punctuation is used.

Nosebleeds are common throughout childhood. (See page 23 for common causes.) You can usually stop a nose from bleeding by squeezing the soft part of the nose against the center wall. However, if the bleeding does not stop after you have applied pressure for twenty minutes, you should call your pediatrician.

. Period

To mark the end of a sentence A period signals the end of a sentence.

Both teachers and students attended the forum.

Be prepared to explain your answers.

Be careful not to use a period at the end of a phrase or clause. Although occasional sentence fragments may be effective, their use is generally discouraged in academic contexts. (See pages 627–628 and 630 for more information on sentence fragments.)

After initials and some abbreviations A period, followed by a space, is used after each initial in a person's name.

A. A. Milne   B. B. King

Some abbreviations commonly include periods, regardless of which style manual you refer to.

Mr.   Mrs.   Ms.   Dr.

et al.   e.g.   i.e.   etc.   a.m.   p.m.

Other types of abbreviations, such as those created by the U.S. Postal Service for the names of states, do not include periods (see page 632). MLA and CMS now recommend omitting periods from abbreviations such as *MA, PhD,* and *MD.*

? Question mark

At the end of a direct question A question mark is used at the end of a direct question—that is, one that is not embedded in a statement.

Who will present the report?

A question that is embedded within a statement does not require a question mark.

Everyone wondered when the war would end.

In quotations A question mark is placed within quotation marks unless it does not belong with the quoted material.

> He asked simply, "Why are we here?"

When the question mark is not part of the quoted material, it is placed outside the quotation marks.

> Do you agree with James Surowiecki's claim that "collective intelligence relies on a certain degree of innocence"**?**

" " Quotation marks

For direct quotations Double quotation marks appear before and after a direct quotation—the exact words from a source.

> I remember my teacher saying, "Be good to your sentences, and they will be good to you."

> According to the research reported by Natalie Angier, "There is a reason children are perpetually yearning for the flour-dusted, mythical figure called grandma or granny or oma or abuelita."

See pages 471–472 for information on capitalizing within direct quotations.

For titles of short works Quotation marks are used around titles of short works, such as essays, short stories, articles, short poems, songs, and episodes in a television series. Short works usually appear within larger works—a poem in a collection of poems, an article in a magazine.

> In "It's Easy Being Green," Bill McKibben argues that politicians should be encouraging the car industry to develop and produce more hybrid electric cars.

> "Outlaws" is just one of several episodes of *Lost* that rely on flashback techniques. [Note that the name of the program is italicized or underlined.]

For special uses of words or phrases Quotation marks around a word or phrase signal that the word is being used in an unusual way—ironically or informally, for example. Quotation marks used for such a purpose are often called **scare quotes.**

> His "health kick" consisted of eating cereal instead of doughnuts for breakfast.

Notice the change in intonation of words or phrases placed between quotation marks. Overuse of scare quotes distracts readers because it results in constant and abrupt changes in intonation and because it suggests that the writer has not put enough effort into finding more suitable words or phrases.

WAIT A MINUTE . . .

You may be wondering about single quotation marks. CMS, MLA, and APA recommend not using single quotation marks around words or phrases used in special ways. However, you should use single quotation marks when a word or phrase in a passage you are quoting was placed between double quotation marks by the original author.

According to the author, some work "the 'optimizers' do is reasonable."

; Semicolon

To connect independent clauses A semicolon is used to link two independent clauses that are not already connected by a coordinating conjunction (*and, but, or, yet, so, nor,* or *for*).

Sweet basil is essential in many Mediterranean foods; Thai basil is equally important in many Asian and East Indian recipes.

With transitional words and phrases A semicolon is often accompanied by a transitional word or phrase to establish a specific type of connection between ideas. For example, *however* and *on the contrary* signal contrast, and *thus* and *as a result* signal consequence.

Rap music was once considered a fad; however, it has now lasted over twenty years.

I just found out that funding is not forthcoming; as a result, we will have to postpone the project.

The following are common transitional words and phrases:

however	therefore	thus	then
instead	also	besides	as a result
at any rate	for example	for instance	in addition
in fact	in other words	on the contrary	

When these words and phrases are placed within a clause, a semicolon is not used. They are set off by two commas instead.

Voter registration, however, has been above normal.

WAIT A MINUTE . . .

Most transitional words and phrases are followed by a comma. However, the comma may be omitted after a transitional word such as *thus* or *then* when no pause is desired and no risk of misreading exists.

Turn right at the corner; then go straight for six miles.

To separate items in a series that contain commas A semicolon separates items in a series that also contain commas.

> The student teacher focused on the bottom half of the food pyramid, including the vegetable group; the fruit group; and the bread, cereal, rice, and pasta group.

/ Slash

To signal alternatives A slash between two words indicates that either is acceptable.

> Sometimes oppositions such as good/evil and right/wrong are hard to distinguish.

Slashes are rarely used in formal writing, especially when the word *or* would suffice.

> The form must be signed by the patient or a guardian.

To indicate line breaks in quoted poetry A slash with a space on either side is used to indicate line breaks in poetry quoted within a sentence.

> A secret message is introduced in the first lines of Tess Gallagher's "Under Stars": "The sleep of this night deepens / because I have walked coatless from the house / carrying the white envelope."

> EXERCISE 23.1

The following excerpt consists of just one sentence. Circle, or highlight, all punctuation marks in the sentence and explain their functions.

> If you sit on the periphery of a group of men telling jokes and you listen for a while and laugh appropriately and don't thrust yourself into the group but wait an appropriate length of time until there is a lull and then offer your joke and if it's a joke that is new to them and if you tell it well and don't flounder around in the setup, the crucial part of the joke, but tell it cleanly and simply with no missteps and not too much topspin, remembering this is Minnesota and we like it dry, no wheezing and chortling, and then you get to the elaboration where you can embroider a little and draw it out, if they're in the mood, and you do this gracefully, not overselling the joke, read your audience and just when they're ready for it you feed them the fat part, and then the punch line, and not laugh at the joke yourself until they do—then you'll be welcome here. **—Garrison Keillor,** *A Prairie Home Companion Pretty Good Joke Book*

Circle, or highlight, all punctuation marks in the following passage and explain their functions.

> The founding fathers of modern environmentalism, Henry David Thoreau and John Muir, promised "that in wildness is the preservation of the world." The presumption was that the wilderness was out there, somewhere, in the western heart of America, awaiting discovery, and that it would be the antidote for the poisons of industrial society. But of course the healing wilderness was as much the product of culture's craving and culture's framing as any other imagined garden. Take the first and most famous American Eden: Yosemite. Though the parking is almost as big as the park and there are bears rooting among the McDonald's cartons, we still imagine Yosemite the way Albert Bierstadt painted it or Carleton Watkins and Ansel Adams photographed it: with no trace of human presence. But of course the very act of identifying (not to mention photographing) the place presupposes our presence, and along with us all the heavy cultural backpacks that we lug with us on the trail.

—**Simon Schama,** *Landscape and Memory*

> ## EXERCISE 23.3

Find two passages that consist of no more than 250 words each and were written in response to widely different rhetorical situations. Circle, or highlight, every punctuation mark; then count the number of times each punctuation mark is used in each passage. Discuss your findings in terms of the rhetorical situation within which each author was writing.

> ## EXERCISE 23.4

Find two passages that consist of no more than 250 words each and were written in response to similar rhetorical situations. Circle, or highlight, every punctuation mark; then count the number of times each punctuation mark is used in each passage. Discuss how your findings help you understand the punctuation choices made by each writer.

> ## EXERCISE 23.5

In an essay you have written recently, circle and number all of the punctuation marks. Identify the punctuation conventions covered in this chapter that you followed.

> ## EXERCISE 23.6

Insert an appropriate punctuation mark in each blank. Explain the function of each punctuation mark that you add.

> In 2002 Dr. Richard Wiseman__ a professor at the University of Hertfordshire__ in collaboration with the British Association for the Advancement of Science__ released the first findings of LaughLab__ a worldwide experiment into the psychology of humor__ The

project consisted of two parts_ _1_ the collection of jokes and _2_ the collection of joke reviews_ Based on over forty thousand jokes submitted and nearly two million ratings_ the following joke written by Geoff Anandappa_ from Blackpool in Great Britain_ was rated number two_

Sherlock Holmes and Dr. Watson go on a camping trip_ After a good dinner and a bottle of wine_ they retire for the night and go to sleep_

Some hours later_ Holmes wakes up and nudges his faithful friend_ _Watson_ Look up at the sky and tell me what you see_ _

I see millions and millions of stars Holmes_ _ replies Watson_

And what do you deduce from that _

Watson ponders for a minute_

Well astronomically_ it tells me that there are millions of galaxies and potentially billions of planets_ Astrologically_ I observe that Saturn is in Leo_ Horologically_ I deduce that the time is approximately a quarter past three_ Meteorologically_ I suspect that we will have a beautiful day tomorrow_ Theologically_ I can see that God is all_powerful and that we are a small and insignificant part of the universe_ What does it tell you_ Holmes_ _

Holmes is silent for a moment_ _Watson_ you idiot_ _ he says_ _ Someone has stolen our tent_ _

To find the joke rated number one_ visit Laughlab.co.uk_

Punctuation Trouble Spots

For most of the rhetorical situations you'll respond to, you'll be expected to use complete, accurately punctuated sentences. Incorrect punctuation of sentences often results in one of these common errors: a sentence fragment, a comma splice, or a fused sentence. When you edit your writing, check to make sure you have not made these typical mistakes. You may be able to help yourself notice these errors by reading your work aloud or having someone else read it aloud to you. Other helpful hints for finding trouble spots and making effective revisions are described in the following subsections.

Sentence fragments

A **sentence fragment** is only a piece of a sentence. It is missing either a complete subject or a complete predicate, or both. Phrases are often mispunctuated as complete sentences.

Prepositional phrase:	They live in northeastern Iowa. ~~Near~~ the Mississippi River. *(, near)*
Verbal phrase:	The fullback scored the final points. ~~Twisting~~ past and leaping over would-be tacklers to reach the goal line. *(, twisting)*
Appositive phrase:	The discussion bounced between two topics. ~~How~~ to increase the amount of oil available and how to avoid damaging the environment. *(; how)*

Mispunctuated dependent clauses are also sentence fragments.

Adverbial clause: New buildings were continually constructed. ~~While~~ old buildings sat empty. *[, while]*

Adjectival clause: The library changed its lending policy in January. ~~Which~~ resulted in much confusion at the end of the term. *[, which]*

Sentence fragments can be revised by either joining the fragment to an adjacent sentence, as above, or making it a complete sentence. When you recast a sentence fragment as a full sentence, you elevate the importance of the information it conveys.

> The library changed its lending policy in January. This change resulted in much confusion at the end of the term.

In most academic rhetorical situations, sentence fragments are not appropriate. However, when a rhetorical situation calls for an intimate or playful tone, sentence fragments can be used judiciously to emphasize ideas, add surprise, or improve the rhythm of a paragraph.

> My pity for Mrs. Cullinan preceded me the next morning like the Cheshire cat's smile. Those girls, who could have been her daughters, were beautiful. They didn't have to straighten their hair. Even when they were caught in the rain, their braids still hung down straight like tamed snakes. Their mouths were pouty little cupid's bows. Mrs. Cullinan didn't know what she missed. Or maybe she did. *Poor Mrs. Cullinan.*
>
> —**Maya Angelou,** "Finishing School"

See page 630 for help in determining whether you have written a sentence fragment.

Comma splices

A **comma splice**, or **comma fault**, is the incorrect use of a comma between two independent clauses. This problem can be corrected either by including a coordinating conjunction (usually *and* or *but*) or by using a stronger mark of punctuation, such as a period or a semicolon.

> Color filters can reduce the atmospheric haze in a photograph, they can also increase it. *[, but]*

> Many millennia ago, human groups started evolving into complex societies, most of these groups settled in villages. *[;]*

Comma splices often occur in the following situations:

▶ The second independent clause begins with a transition word or phrase, such as *however* or *for example*.

> All nurses care for patients, however their responsibilities and working conditions vary according to the shift they work. *[; ,]*

- The second independent clause provides an explanation or an example.

  I became obsessive about programming, *.My* my desire to be at the computer blocked out all other concerns.

- The second independent clause presents an alternative, usually negative.

  A written argument is an opportunity to explore various perspectives and

  reach an informed position, *.It* it is not just a quarrel.

- The second independent clause begins with a pronoun whose antecedent is in the first clause.

  Earth's atmosphere lets light in, *but* ∧ it also keeps dangerous levels of ultraviolet light out.

Although they sometimes appear in pieces of fiction, comma splices are not used in most academic contexts. See page 630 for help in determining whether you have written a comma splice.

Fused sentences

A **fused sentence**, also called a **run-on sentence**, is actually two sentences (independent clauses) joined together without adequate punctuation. This type of problem can be corrected by adding appropriate punctuation and any necessary connecting words.

They spent a great deal of time socializing their puppy ∧ *First.* they held "people-

puppy parties" and ∧ *later* "puppy-puppy parties."

Fused sentences occur in the same situations that comma splices do.

- The second independent clause begins with a transition word or phrase, such as *however* or *for example*.

  Some historians claim that Andrew Carnegie was a benevolent

  philanthropist ∧ however ∧ others consider him a pitiless taskmaster.

- The second independent clause provides an explanation or an example.

  Myopia is a condition of the eye that results in blurry vision ∧ *Light* light rays entering the eye come together in front of the retina.

- The second independent clause presents an alternative.

  The vote was not just an instance of majority rule ∧ *.It* it was an act of tyranny.

▶ The second independent clause begins with a pronoun whose antecedent is in the first clause.

They
Some people expect others to solve their problems ∧ they ignore their own responsibility to come up with a solution.

The following box can help you determine whether you have written a fused sentence.

WAIT A MINUTE . . .

If you suspect that you have written a sentence fragment, comma splice, or fused sentence but you are not sure, try placing the words in the following test-sentence frame.

They do not understand the idea that _____.

Sentence Fragment

A complete sentence will make sense when embedded in the test-sentence frame because it is an independent clause.

Test sentence fails: They do not understand the idea that <u>near the Mississippi River</u> (The underlined phrase is a sentence fragment.)

Test sentence succeeds: They do not understand the idea that <u>the town is located in northeastern Iowa, near the Mississippi River.</u> (This independent clause fits into the test-sentence frame and therefore could be written as a sentence.)

Comma Splice

A comma splice will not make sense when embedded in the test-sentence frame because the second independent clause will sound tacked on.

Test sentence fails: They do not understand the idea that <u>Earth's atmosphere lets light in, it also keeps dangerous levels of ultraviolet light out.</u> (The underlined test sentence is a comma splice. The second clause sounds tacked on.)

Test sentence succeeds: They do not understand the idea that <u>Earth's atmosphere lets light in but also keeps dangerous levels of ultraviolet light out.</u> (The test sentence fits into the frame and therefore could be written as a sentence.)

Fused Sentence

A fused sentence will not make sense when embedded in the test-sentence frame because it will sound muddled. The boundary between the two independent clauses will be indistinct.

Test sentence fails:	They do not understand the idea that <u>myopia is a condition of the eye that results in blurry vision light rays entering the eye come together in front of the retina.</u> (The underlined test sentence is a fused sentence. It is difficult to determine the boundary between the two independent clauses.)
Test sentence succeeds:	They do not understand the idea that <u>myopia makes vision blurry because light rays entering the eye come together in front of the retina.</u> (The test sentence fits into the frame and therefore could be written as its own sentence.)

> EXERCISE 23.7

Identify sentence fragments in an essay in this book (or in one assigned by your instructor) and explain their rhetorical effects.

> EXERCISE 23.8

Find two or three advertisements that include sentence fragments and explain their rhetorical effects.

> EXERCISE 23.9

Look for comma splices in the following excerpt from a novel. Why do you think writers of fiction sometimes use comma splices, while writers of academic prose generally do not?

[1]When she didn't show up for several days on end to play the organ, it was known that Ms. DeWitt was suffering from nerves again. [2]Incrementally, tortuously, unnecessarily, she was unblessed by tiny fragments of memory. [3]Berndt materialized, cruelly, touch by touch, until he was all there but not there. [4]A word and a look, a moment they had spent together, had apparently entered the heart of Agnes to be kept sealed and safe until, for no particular reason, she was to be tormented by an elusive recovery. [5]She shut herself away. [6]Some people grieve by holding fast to the love of others, some by rejecting all companionship. [7]Some grieve with tears and some with dry howls. [8]Some grieve like water, some burn. [9]Some are fuel for the fire of sorrow and some are stone. [10]Agnes was pure slate, dark and impenetrable.

> **—Louise Erdrich,** *The Last Report on the Miracles at Little No Horse*

> EXERCISE 23.10

Revise all fragments, comma splices, and fused sentences in the following paragraph. Change the wording, if necessary.

[1]Traditionally an instrument used to accompany a vocalist. [2]The guitar has a humble origin. [3]Once plugged in, though, it gained center stage.

[4]Along with the person playing it. [5]Any fan of jazz, blues, or rock can state an all-time favorite guitar player when I asked my office mates which guitar players they revered, they mentioned Charlie Christian, B. B. King, and Jimi Hendrix. [6]Without even pausing to consider my question. [7]The need for amplified guitars arose during the 1920s and 1930s when the public was listening and dancing to big-band jazz, the guitar had to match the sounds of the other, louder instruments and voices. [8]Coincidentally, a new style of guitar and guitar playing gained popularity the Hawaiian guitar, a flat guitar with six to eight strings, was played while resting in the player's lap. [9]As early as 1923, experiments were being conducted in an attempt to amplify the sound of the Hawaiian guitar however it was not until 1932 that the first electric guitar was created. [10]Built by Harry Watson and sold by the company Ro-Pat-In, the new Hawaiian-style electric guitar was nicknamed the frying pan. [11]More than seventy years have passed since the guitar was electrified. [12]And began to electrify audiences. [13]It has evolved tremendously since its conception. [14]Even influencing the kinds of music it is used to produce.

Guide to Mechanics

The conventions listed here are based on those presented in *The Chicago Manual of Style* (CMS), sixteenth edition. MLA or APA conventions that differ from those of CMS are mentioned.

Abbreviations, acronyms, and initialisms

Standard abbreviations An **abbreviation** is the shortened form of a word or phrase. Some abbreviations are acceptable in both formal and informal writing:

Mr.   Mrs.   Ms.   Dr.   Jr.   Sr.   a.m.   p.m.

Correspondence abbreviations Words such as *Street, Road,* and *Corporation* are written out when they appear in sentences, but they are usually abbreviated when used in addresses on envelopes.

Sentence: Ben & Jerry's Foundation is located on Community Drive in South Burlington, Vermont.

Address: Ben & Jerry's Foundation

30 Community Dr.

S. Burlington, VT 05403

When addressing correspondence within the United States, use the abbreviations designated by the U.S. Postal Service for the names of the states. (No period follows these abbreviations.)

Documentation abbreviations *The Chicago Manual of Style,* the *MLA Handbook for Writers of Research Papers,* and the *Publication Manual of the American Psychological Association* all mention specific abbreviations to use in citations and bibliographies. These abbreviations include the following:

anon.	anonymous
c., ca.	circa, about (for example, c. 1840)
ch., chs.	chapter, chapters
fig.	figure
illus.	illustrated by, illustrator, illustration
intl.	international
ms., mss.	manuscript, manuscripts
natl.	national
n.d.	no date
n.p.	no page number, no publisher
p., pp.	page, pages
trans.	translation, translated by
vol., vols.	volume, volumes
Jan.	January
Feb.	February
Mar.	March
Apr.	April
Aug.	August
Sept.	September
Oct.	October
Nov.	November
Dec.	December

LATIN ABBREVIATIONS

cf.	compare
e.g.	for example
et al.	and others
etc.	and so forth, and others of the same kind
i.e.	that is
v., vs.	versus

Abbreviations of people's names When first and middle names are abbreviated as initials, they should be followed by a space.

E. B. White   J. R. R. Tolkien   H. G. Wells

Acronyms An **acronym** is a shortened form of a name pronounced as a word. It is formed from the first letters or successive parts of words in a multiword name. Each letter is a capital, and no periods are required.

AIDS	acquired immunodeficiency syndrome
NASA	National Aeronautics and Space Administration
NATO	North Atlantic Treaty Organization
OSHA	Occupational Safety and Health Administration
SWAT	special weapons and tactics

Grammar and Style

The words an acronym stands for should be spelled out the first time the entity is mentioned; the acronym should follow in parentheses. This convention ensures that readers unfamiliar with the acronym will understand the reference.

> The Federal Emergency Management Administration (FEMA) issued revised evacuation guidelines for coastal cities.

Initialisms An **initialism** is similar to an acronym in that each letter is a capital. However, unlike the letters constituting acronyms, the letters of initialisms are pronounced individually.

CIA	Central Intelligence Agency
FBI	Federal Bureau of Investigation
UN	United Nations
SUV	sport-utility vehicle

The first time an initialism is used, the words it stands for should be spelled out.

Capitalization

Proper nouns All proper nouns are capitalized.

Buildings, bridges, monuments	Empire State Building, Golden Gate Bridge, World War II Memorial
Course titles	History of the Civil War [BUT history, the general subject]
Days, months, holidays	Monday, May, Memorial Day [NOT the names of the seasons: fall, winter, spring, summer]
Ethnic groups and languages	Latinos/Latinas, Spanish, Chinese
Geographical names	North America, Canada, Minnesota, Boston, Interstate 90, the Southwest, Lake Michigan, the Mississippi River, Central Park [NOT a direction, as in south of the park]
Historical documents, events, movements, and periods	Declaration of Independence, Allentown Fair, Renaissance, Stone Age
Military terms	Eighth Air Force, United States Army, Gulf War, Battle of the Bulge, Silver Star [NOT general military terms: the air force, the army, the war, the battle]
Names of people	Rosa Vargas, Dr. Lee, Alexander the Great
Organizations, agencies, companies, institutions	National Endowment for the Arts, Internal Revenue Service, Ford Motor Company, Yakima Valley Community College [BUT a university in New York]

Religious terms	Buddha, God, Allah, Yahweh, Buddhism, Christianity, Islam, Judaism, Buddhist, Christian, Muslim, Jew, Sutras, Bible, Koran, Talmud [NOT adjectives, such as biblical, talmudic]
Trade names	Nike, Oscar Mayer, Chevrolet

Earth, sun, and moon Except in technical contexts, the words *earth, sun,* and *moon* are not capitalized.

> The earth, the sun, and the moon appear in many myths.

> The Sun contains more than 99.8 percent of the total mass of the Solar System.

Words derived from names and trade names Adjectives and verbs that are derived from names of people or places are capitalized.

> Whitmanesque   Americanize

Trade names are capitalized unless such a name has become the term for a general class of objects or ideas, such as *zipper* (which was originally a trademark).

Words used as names or proper nouns When words are used as names or parts of names, they are capitalized.

> Mom   Uncle Tom   Senator Wellston   Professor Brown

WAIT A MINUTE . . .

Sometimes words such as *mom* and *dad* are capitalized, and sometimes they are not. The key to knowing when to use an uppercase letter and when to use a lowercase letter is understanding the difference between proper nouns and common nouns. Proper nouns can be replaced by a person's actual name.

> Every Saturday, Mom [Catherine] took me to the park.

Such a substitution cannot be made if the word is a common noun.

> Every Saturday, my mom [NOT my Catherine] took me to the park.

Titles of literary and artistic works All major words in titles and subtitles of literary and artistic works mentioned within a text are capitalized. Minor words, unless they are the first or last word in the title, are not. Minor words include articles (*a*, *an*, and *the*), coordinating conjunctions (see pages 599–600), prepositions (see pages 544–545), and the infinitive marker *to*.

> *Reading* Lolita *in Tehran*
>
> *The Return of the King*
>
> "Once More to the Lake"

APA style for capitalizing titles of works differs. According to APA style, any word of four or more letters should be capitalized.

All words in a hyphenated compound are capitalized unless they are minor words such as prepositions and conjunctions.

> "The Texas-Mexico Border"
>
> "Touch-and-Go Decisions"

WAIT A MINUTE . . .

You'll sometimes notice that the title of a source has only the first word capitalized. Titles found in databases are often listed this way.

> A meeting of minds

Nonetheless, if you use such a source in your paper, you should capitalize all major words.

> The authors of "A Meeting of Minds" discussed cross-cultural similarities.

First words of sentences The first word of every sentence, and of every complete quoted sentence, is capitalized.

> Based on his experience as a cub reporter, James Alexander Thom asserts, "Human suffering has become a spectator sport."

Italics

The use of italics lets readers know that a word or a group of words is being used in a special way. CMS, APA, and MLA allow the use of italics. However, in handwritten or typewritten documents, underlining can be used instead of italics. On the Internet, underlining often indicates a hyperlink. In e-mail messages that cannot include italicized words, an underscore should be placed before and after words normally italicized.

> _The Novel of the Future_ was published in 1968.

For emphasis Italics indicate that a word is being given extra stress.

> She *is* our only hope.

Italics can also emphasize emotional content.

>   We have to act *now*.

Italicized words should be used sparingly; otherwise, they will lose their impact.

Foreign words Italics indicate foreign words.

>   I respect and serve my parents, prepare food for the family, eat rice and stew, *Iyan* and *Eba* with *egusi* stew. —**Omotayo Banjo,** "Under My Skin"

Latin words used to identify genus and species are also italicized. The genus name is capitalized.

>   *Stenella frontalis* (Atlantic spotted dolphin)
>
>   *Raphus cucullatus* (dodo)

Legal cases The names of legal cases are italicized.

>   *Roe v. Wade*   *Brown v. Board of Education*   *Miranda v. Arizona*

The shortened name of a well-known legal case is also italicized.

>   The *Miranda* decision gave criminal suspects the right to remain silent and the right to legal advice.

Names of transporting vehicles The names of ships, submarines, aircraft, spacecraft, and satellites are italicized.

>   *Titanic*   USS *Hawkbill*   *Spirit of St. Louis*   *Atlantis*

However, the names of trains and the trade names of aircraft are not italicized.

>   Orient Express   Boeing 747   Concorde

Titles Works published or produced as a whole rather than as a part of a larger work are italicized. Thus, the name of a newspaper is italicized, but the title of an editorial is not. The titles of the following types of works are italicized.

Book	*Cold Mountain*
Magazine	*Wired*
Newspaper	*Wall Street Journal*
Play or film	*Monster*
Television or radio program	*American Idol*
Music recording	*Kind of Blue*
Work of art	*The Thinker*
Long poem	*Paradise Lost*
Pamphlet	*Saving Energy*
Comic strip	*Doonesbury*

When one title is embedded in another title, the embedded title is not italicized.

The main character in *The Making of* Kind of Blue is a young bass player.

Words, letters, or numbers referred to as such A word, letter, or number is italicized when it represents the word, letter, or number itself.

The *k* in words such as *knight* and *knock* was pronounced in Old English.

Who decided that the number *911* should be used for emergencies?

Numbers

For general purposes, numbers from one through one hundred are spelled out.

forty-five points   sixty-two pages

If the words *thousand, million,* or *billion* follow whole numbers from one through one hundred, the numbers should still be spelled out. For any other number, a numeral is used unless the number begins a sentence.

They earned 145 extra points.

According to APA style, words should be used only for numbers below ten.

Addresses The numbers in addresses do not need to be spelled out.

For years, they lived at 25 East 45th Street.

Dates and times of day Numbers are used to indicate dates and times of day.

The meeting is scheduled for 9:00 a.m. on June 7, 2014.

Except for specific years, dates and times may be spelled out.

3 p.m.   OR   three o'clock in the afternoon

the first of March   OR   March 1

the sixties   OR   the 1960s

Decimals and percentages Decimals and percentages are expressed in numbers.

a 3.0 grade point average   80 percent

Identification numbers Numbers are used for identification of specific people and places.

Henry IV   Interstate 90   Room 415

Large fractional numbers Large fractional numbers can be expressed numerically.

3.5 billion years   2.3 million inhabitants

Monetary amounts When monetary amounts are frequently mentioned, they can be written as numbers. However, if they are mentioned only rarely, they should be spelled out.

$6,000   OR   six thousand dollars

Page numbers and divisions in books and plays Numerals are used for page numbers and for book or play divisions.

page 82   chapter 16   act 1, scene 2   OR   Act II, Scene I

> EXERCISE 23.11

Underline or highlight seven different uses of capital letters, italics, abbreviations, acronyms, or numbers in an essay in this book (or in one assigned by your instructor). Explain their functions.

> EXERCISE 23.12

Describe the functions of capitalization and italics in an essay in this book (or in one assigned by your instructor). Are any of these uses unconventional? If so, are they still effective?

> EXERCISE 23.13

Edit the following paragraph so that it follows the conventions for academic writing.

[1]On october first, nineteen fifty-eight, congress and president eisenhower created the national aeronautics and space administration (nasa). [2]The creation of nasa was related to national defense. [3]After world war two, political tensions and rivalry divided the united states and the soviet union. [4]Although no full-scale battles occurred, the friction was so intense that this period was called the cold war. [5]space exploration became a major arena for competition. [6]When the soviets launched sputnik one, americans feared that they were at a technological disadvantage and immediately directed more effort and funding to space exploration. [7]Nasa began its operation with 8,000 employees and an annual budget of $100,000,000. [8]Within months of its conception, nasa conducted space missions. [9]By the time it was 20 years old, apollo eleven had been launched, and a human being had actually walked on the moon.

> EXERCISE 23.14

In an essay you have written recently, circle and number all capital letters, abbreviations, acronyms, initialisms, numbers, and italicized words. Identify the mechanics conventions covered in this chapter that you followed.

As the introduction to Chapter 22, **Editing for Clarity and Style**, explains, Standardized English is the stylistic option you'll most often choose when working in an academic context. This glossary presents many of those standardized usages and spellings, as well as usages and spellings considered to be conversational (or informal) and even unconventional (or nonstandardized). Using the information in this glossary, you'll be able to make informed decisions about the words you use.

The following labels will help you choose appropriate words for your rhetorical situation.

Conventional Words or phrases listed in dictionaries without special usage labels; generally considered appropriate in academic and professional writing.

Conversational Words or phrases that dictionaries label *informal, slang,* or *colloquial;* although often used in informal speech and writing, not generally appropriate for formal writing assignments.

Unconventional Words or phrases not generally considered appropriate in academic or professional writing and often labeled *nonstandard* in dictionaries; best avoided in formal contexts.

a half a, a half an Unconventional; instead use *half a, half an,* or *a half:* He commutes **a half an** hour to work.

a lot of A conversational expression for *many, much,* or *a great deal of:* A lot of **Many** people attended the concert. *A lot* is spelled as two words.

a while, awhile *A while* means "a period of time" and most frequently follows the preposition *after, for,* or *in:* They stopped for **a while**. *Awhile* means "a short time." It is not used after a preposition: We rested **awhile**.

accept, except *Accept* is a verb meaning "to receive": He will **accept** the offer. *Except* can be a verb meaning "to exclude": Her criminal record will **except** her from consideration for this job. However, *except* is more commonly used as a preposition meaning "other than": No one knew **except** us. Other forms: *acceptable, acceptance; exception.*

adapt, adopt *Adapt* means "to adjust or change": He will **adapt** to the new climate. *Adopt* means "to take as one's own": The board of directors will **adopt** a new policy. Other forms: *adaptable, adaptation; adoption.*

adverse, averse *Adverse* means "unfavorable": The storm had **adverse** effects on the county's economy. Usually followed by *to, averse* means "reluctant" or "opposed": They are not **averse** to negotiating a compromise. Other forms: *adversity; aversion.*

advice, advise *Advice* is a noun: They asked an expert for **advice**. *Advise* is a verb: He should be able to **advise** us.

affect, effect *Affect* is a verb that means either "to influence" or "to touch the emotions": The threatened strike did not **affect** the company's decision to keep the factory open. The news **affected** us deeply. Psychologists use *affect* as a noun (with the stress on the first syllable) meaning "emotional expression": She noted the patient's lack of **affect**. As a noun, *effect* means "a result": Maren discussed the **effects** of secondhand smoke. When used as a verb, *effect* means "to bring about": They hoped to **effect** real political change. Other forms: *affective; effective.*

agree on, agree to, agree with *Agree on* means "to be in accord with others about something": We **agreed on** the arrangements. *Agree to* means "to accept something" or "to consent to do something": They **agreed to** our terms. They **agreed to** discuss the matter. *Agree with* means "to share an opinion with someone" or "to approve of something": Everyone **agreed with** the chair of the committee. No one **agreed with** my position.

all ready, already *All ready* means "completely prepared": The documents are **all ready** for the meeting. *Already* means "by or before a specified time": We have **already** submitted our final report.

all right Two of the most common meanings of *all right* are "permissible" and "safe." They asked whether it was **all right** to arrive a few minutes late. Everyone in the accident was **all right**. The spelling *alright* is not a generally accepted alternative for *all right,* although it is frequently used in popular writing.

all together, altogether *All together* means "as a group": We sang **all together**. *Altogether* means "wholly, thoroughly": This song is **altogether** too difficult to play.

allude, elude *Allude* means "to refer to indirectly": She **alluded** to the poetry of Elizabeth Bishop. *Elude* means "to evade" or "to escape from": For months, the solution **eluded** the researchers.

allusion, illusion *Allusion* means "a casual or indirect reference": Her **allusion** was to Elizabeth Bishop's poetry. *Illusion* means "a false idea or an unreal image": The magician's trick was based on **illusion**.

among, between According to traditional usage, *among* is used when three or more individuals or entities are discussed: He must choose **among** several good job offers. *Between* is used when referring to only two entities: We studied the differences **between** the two proposals. Current dictionaries also mention the use of *between* to refer to more than two entities when the relationships between these entities are considered distinct: Connections **between** the four coastal communities were restored.

amoral, immoral *Amoral* means "not caring about right or wrong": The prosecutor in the case accused the defendant of **amoral** acts of random violence. *Immoral* means "not moral": Students discussed whether abortion should be considered **immoral**. Other forms: *amorality; immorality.*

amount of, number of Use *amount of* before nouns that cannot be counted: The **amount of** rain that fell last year was insufficient. Use *number of* with nouns that can be counted: The **number of** students attending college has increased. *A number of* means "many" and thus takes a plural verb: **A number of** opportunities **are** listed. *The number of* takes a singular verb: **The number of** opportunities available to students **is** rising.

angry at, angry with *Angry* is commonly followed by either *at* or *with,* although according to traditional usage, *with* should be used when the cause of the anger is a person: She was **angry at** the school for denying her admission. He was **angry with** me because I corrected him in public.

anxious, eager *Anxious,* related to *anxiety,* means "worried" or "nervous": They are **anxious** about the test results. *Eager* means "keenly interested" or "desirous": We were **eager** to find a compromise. Current dictionaries report that *anxious* is often used as a synonym for *eager,* but such usage is still considered conversational.

anymore, any more *Anymore* means "any longer" or "now" and most frequently occurs in questions or negative sentences: We do not carry that product **anymore**. Its use in positive sentences is considered conversational; *now* is generally used instead: All they do ~~anymore~~ now is fight. *Any more* means "additional": Do you need **any more** help?

anyone, any one *Anyone* means "anybody": I did not see **anyone** familiar. *Any one* means "one from a group": **Any one** of them will suffice.

anyplace, everyplace, someplace As synonyms for *anywhere, everywhere,* and *somewhere,* these words are considered informal.

as, like According to traditional usage, *as,* not *like,* should begin a clause: Her son talked **~~like~~ as** she did. When used as a preposition, *like* can introduce a phrase: He looks **like** his father. That scarf feels **like** silk.

as regards See **regard, regarding, regards.**

assure, ensure, insure *Assure* means "to state with confidence": He **assured** us that the neighborhood was safe. *Ensure* and *insure* can often be interchanged to mean "to make certain," but only *insure* means "to protect against loss": The researcher **ensured** [OR **insured**] the accuracy of the test results. Homeowners **insure** their houses and furnishings.

averse See **adverse, averse.**

awhile See **a while, awhile.**

bad Unconventional as an adverb; use *badly* instead: Some fans behaved **~~bad~~ badly** during the game. However, as an adjective, *bad* can be used after sensory verbs (*feel, look, sound, smell,* and *taste*): I felt **bad** that I could not attend her recital.

being as, being that Unconventional; use *because* instead: **~~Being as~~ Because** it was Sunday, many of the stores were closed.

better, had better *Better* is conversational. Use *had better* instead: They **~~better~~ had better** buy their tickets tomorrow.

between See **among, between.**

breath, breathe *Breath* is a noun: I was out of **breath**. *Breathe* is a verb: It was hard to **breathe**.

bunch Conversational to refer to a group: A **~~bunch~~ group** of students gathered in front of the student union.

busted Unconventional. Use *broken* instead: The printer was ~~busted~~ broken, so none of us had our papers ready on time.

can, may According to traditional definitions, *can* refers to ability, and *may* refers to permission: He **can** read music. You **may** not read the newspaper during class. According to current dictionaries, *can* and *may* are sometimes used interchangeably to denote permission, though *may* is generally preferred in formal contexts.

can't hardly, can't scarcely Both are examples of a double negative, used in some regions of the United States but unconventional. Use *can hardly* or *can scarcely* instead: I ~~can't~~ hardly believe it happened.

capital, capitol, Capitol A *capital* is a governing city; it also means "funds": The **capital** of California is Sacramento. They invested a large amount of **capital** in the organization. As an adjective, *capital* means "chief" or "principal": This year's election is of **capital** importance. It may also refer to the death penalty: In some countries, espionage is a **capital** offence. A *capitol* is a statehouse; the *Capitol* is the U.S. congressional building in Washington, DC.

censor, censure, sensor As a verb, *censor* means "to remove or suppress material that is deemed objectionable or classified": In some countries, the government **censors** the news. As a noun, *censor* refers to a person authorized to remove material considered objectionable or classified: The **censor** cleared the report. The verb *censure* means "to blame or criticize": The committee **censured** her. The noun *censure* is an expression of disapproval or blame: She received a **censure** from the committee. A *sensor* is a device that responds to a stimulus: The motion **sensor** detected an approaching car.

center on, center around *Center around* is conversational. Use *center on* or *revolve around* for formal occasions. The critic's comments **centered** ~~around~~ on health care.

cite, sight, site *Cite* means "to mention": She could easily **cite** several examples of altruism. *Sight,* as a verb, means "to see": The crew **sighted** land. As a noun, *sight* refers to the ability to see or to a view: Her **sight** worsened as she aged. We had never seen such a **sight!** *Site,* as a verb, means "to situate": They **sited** their new house near the river. As a noun, *site* means "a location": The **site** for the new library was approved. Other forms: *citation, citing; sighting.*

climactic, climatic *Climactic* refers to a high point (a climax): The film's **climactic** scene riveted the viewers to their seats. *Climatic* refers to the climate: Global warming is creating **climatic** changes.

coarse, course *Coarse* means "rough" or "ill-mannered": Several people objected to his **coarse** language. A *course* is "a route" or "a plan of study": Because of the bad weather, we had to alter our **course**. She must take a **course** in anatomy. *Course* is used in the expression *of course.*

compare to, compare with *Compare to* means "to consider as similar": The film critic **compared** the actor **to** Humphrey Bogart. *Compare with* means "to examine to discover similarities or differences": He **compared** early morning traffic patterns **with** late afternoon ones.

complement, compliment *Complement* means "to balance" or "to complete": Their voices **complement** each other. *Compliment* means "to express praise": After the reading, several people **complimented** the author. Other forms: *complementary* (they have **complementary** personalities); *complimentary* (her remarks were **complimentary**). *Complimentary* may also mean "provided free of charge": I received two **complimentary** books.

compose, comprise *Compose* means "to form by putting together": The panel is **composed** of several experts. *Comprise* means "to consist of": The course package **comprises** a textbook, a workbook, and a CD-ROM.

conscience, conscientious, conscious, consciousness *Conscience* means "a sense of right and wrong": His questionable actions weighed on his **conscience**. *Conscientious* means "careful": She appreciated her **conscientious** research assistant. A *conscientious objector* is a person who refuses to join the military for moral reasons. *Conscious* means "awake": For a few minutes, I wasn't **conscious**. I lost **consciousness** for a few minutes. *Conscious* may also mean "aware": I was **conscious** of the risks involved in starting a new business.

consequently, subsequently *Consequently* means "as a result": They exceeded their budget and **consequently** had little to spend during the holidays. *Subsequently* means "then" or "later": He was arrested and **subsequently** convicted of fraud.

continual, continuous *Continual* means "recurring": **Continual** work stoppages delayed progress. *Continuous* means "uninterrupted": The high-pitched **continuous** noise distracted everyone. Other forms: *continually; continuously.*

convince, persuade *Convince* means "to make someone believe something": She **convinced** us that she was the best candidate for the office. *Persuade* means "to motivate someone to act": They **persuaded** me to write a letter to the editor. According to current dictionaries, many speakers and writers now use *convince* as a synonym for *persuade*.

could of See **of**.

council, counsel A *council* is a committee that advises or makes decisions: The library **council** proposed a special program for children. A *counsel* is a legal adviser: The **counsel** said he would appeal the case. *Counsel* also means "advice": They sought her out for her wise **counsel**. As a verb, *counsel* means "to give advice": The adviser **counsels** people considering career changes.

course See **coarse, course**.

criteria, criterion A *criterion* is "a standard": The most important **criterion** for judging the competition was originality. *Criteria* is the plural form of *criterion*: To pass, the students had to satisfy three **criteria** for the assignment.

data, datum *Datum* means "fact"; *data,* the plural form, is used more often: The **data were** difficult to interpret. Some current dictionaries note that *data* is frequently used as a mass entity (like the word *furniture*), appearing with a singular verb.

desert, dessert *Desert,* with the stress on the first syllable, is a noun meaning "a barren land": Cacti grow in the **deserts** of Arizona. As a verb, with the second syllable stressed, *desert* means "to leave": Because of his behavior, his research partners **deserted** him. *Dessert* means "something sweet eaten at the end of a meal": I ordered chocolate ice cream for **dessert**.

device, devise *Device* means "mechanism": The **device** indicates whether a runner has made a false start. *Devise* means "to create": They **devised** a new way of packaging juice.

differ from, differ with *Differ from* means "to be different": His management style **differs from** mine. *Differ with* means "to disagree": We **differed with** each other on just one point.

different from, different than *Different from* is normally used before a noun, a pronoun, a noun phrase, or a noun clause: His technique is **different from** yours. The results were **different from** what we had predicted. *Different than* is used to introduce an adverbial clause, with *than* serving as the conjunction: The style is **different than** it was ten years ago.

discreet, discrete, discretion *Discreet* means "tactful": Because most people are sensitive to this issue, you must be **discreet**. Related to *discreet, discretion*

means "caution or self-restraint": Concerned about their privacy, the donors appreciated the fundraiser's **discretion**. *Discrete* means "distinct": The course was presented as three **discrete** units.

disinterested, uninterested *Disinterested* means "neutral": Scientists are expected to be **disinterested**. *Uninterested* means "lacking interest": Knowing nothing about the sport, I was **uninterested** in the score.

distinct, distinctive *Distinct* means "well-defined" or "easily perceived": We noticed a **distinct** change in the weather. *Distinctive* means "characteristic": The **distinctive** odor of chlorine met us in the entryway to the pool.

dyeing, dying *Dyeing,* from *dye,* means "coloring something, usually by soaking it": They are **dyeing** the wool today. *Dying,* from *die,* means "losing life" or "fading": We finished our hike just as the light was **dying**.

eager See **anxious, eager**.

effect See **affect, effect**.

elicit, illicit *Elicit* means "to draw out": Her joke **elicited** an unexpected response from the audience. *Illicit* means "illegal": The police searched for **illicit** drugs.

elude See **allude, elude**.

emigrate from, immigrate to *Emigrate* means "to move from one's own country": His ancestors **emigrated from** Norway. *Immigrate* means "to move to a different country": They **immigrated to** Australia. Other forms: *emigrant; immigrant*.

eminent, imminent *Eminent* means "well-known and respected": An **eminent** scientist from the University of Montana received the award. *Imminent* means "about to happen": As conditions worsened, a strike was **imminent**.

ensure See **assure, ensure, insure**.

especially, specially *Especially* means "remarkably": The summer was **especially** warm. *Especially* also means "particularly": Tourists flock to the island, **especially** during the spring and summer months. *Specially* means "for a particular purpose": The seeds were **specially** selected for this climate.

etc. Abbreviation of *et cetera,* meaning "and others of the same kind" or "and so forth." In academic writing, it is generally used only within parentheses. Avoid using *and etc.*: A noise forecast is based on several factors (time of day noise occurs, frequency of noise, duration of noise, **and etc.**).

everyday, every day *Everyday* means "routine": They took advantage of **everyday** opportunities. *Every day* means "each day": He practiced **every day**.

everyplace See **anyplace, everyplace, someplace.**

except See **accept, except.**

explicit, implicit *Explicit* means "expressed directly": The **explicit** statement of her expectations left little room for misinterpretation. *Implicit* means "expressed indirectly": Our **implicit** agreement was to remain silent.

farther, further *Farther* usually refers to geographic distance: They drove **farther** than they had planned. *Further* indicates additional effort or time: Tomorrow they will discuss the issue **further**.

fewer, less *Fewer* is used before nouns referring to people or objects that can be counted: **fewer** students, **fewer** printers. *Less* is used before noncount or abstract nouns: **less** water, **less** interest. *Less than* may be used with measurements of distance or time: **less than** ten miles, **less than** two years.

first, firstly, second, secondly Although *first* and *second* are generally preferred, current dictionaries state that *firstly* and *secondly* are well-established forms.

foreword, forward A *foreword* is a preface or introduction to a book: In the **foreword**, the author discussed his reasons for writing the book. *Forward* means "in a frontward direction": The crowd lunged **forward**.

former, latter *Former* refers to the first and *latter* refers to the second of two people or items mentioned in the previous sentence: Employees could choose between a state pension plan or a private pension plan. The majority chose the **former**, but a few believed the **latter** would provide them with more retirement income.

further See **farther, further.**

good, well Use *well* instead of *good* to modify a verb. You played ~~good~~ well today. *Good* and *well* can be used interchangeably to mean "in good health": I did not feel **well** [OR **good**] when I woke up.

had better See **better, had better.**

hanged, hung *Hanged* means "executed by hanging": They were **hanged** at dusk. *Hung* means "suspended" or "draped": She **hung** a family photo in her office.

herself, himself, myself, yourself Unconventional when not used as reflexive or intensive pronouns. Jean and ~~myself~~ I prepared the presentation. I **myself** led the discussion.

hopefully Conversational for "I hope": ~~Hopefully,~~ I hope the weather will improve.

hung See **hanged, hung.**

i.e. Abbreviation of *id est*, meaning "that is." In academic writing, it is generally used only within parentheses and is followed by a comma: Everyone donated the same amount (**i.e.,** fifty dollars). Outside of parentheses, use *that is* rather than *i.e.:* The office will be closed for the autumn holidays, **that is**, Labor Day, Columbus Day, Veterans' Day, and Thanksgiving.

illicit See **elicit, illicit.**

illusion See **allusion, illusion.**

immigrate to See **emigrate from, immigrate to.**

imminent See **eminent, imminent.**

immoral See **amoral, immoral.**

impact Considered unconventional in academic writing when used as a verb to mean "to affect": The hurricane will ~~impact~~ affect coastal residents. However, according to current dictionaries, this usage is common in business writing.

implicit See **explicit, implicit.**

imply, infer *Imply* means "to suggest indirectly": I did not mean to **imply** that you were at fault. *Infer* means "to conclude or deduce": Given his participation at the meeting, I **inferred** that he would support the proposal.

in regards to Unconventional. See **regard, regarding, regards.**

ingenious, ingenuous *Ingenious* means "creative": This **ingenious** plan will satisfy everyone. *Ingenuous* means "innocent or naive": No one knew for sure whether she was truly **ingenuous** or just shrewd.

inside of, outside of Delete *of* when unnecessary: They met **outside** ~~of~~ the fortress.

insure See **assure, ensure, insure.**

irregardless A double negative (*ir-* means "not" and *-less* means "not having") that is used in some regions of the United States for *regardless* but is unconventional.

its, it's *Its* indicates possession: The Republican Party concludes **its** convention today. *It's* is a contraction of *it is*: **It's** difficult to predict the outcome. Confusion over *its* and *it's* is responsible for many usage errors.

kind, sort, type Use *this* or *that* to refer to one *kind, sort,* or *type;* avoid using the word *a:* **This kind** [OR **sort** OR **type**] of **a** leader is most effective. Use *these* or *those* to refer to more than one: **These kinds** [OR **sorts** OR **types**] of leaders are most effective.

kind of, sort of Conversational to mean "somewhat": The rock-climbing course was ~~kind of~~ somewhat difficult.

later, latter *Later* means "afterward": The concert ended **later** than we had expected. *Latter* refers to the second of two people or items mentioned in the previous sentence. See also **former, latter**.

lay, lie *Lay* (*laid, laying*) means "to put" or "to place": I will **lay** the book on your desk. *Lie* (*lay, lain, lying*) means "to rest" or "to recline": She **lay** perfectly still, trying to hear what they were saying. *Lay* takes an object (to **lay** something), but *lie* does not. The present tense of *lay* and the past tense of *lie* (which is *lay*) are often confused because they are spelled the same way.

lead, led The noun *lead* is a kind of metal: The gas had **lead** added to it. The verb *lead* means "to show the way" or "to go in front": The director will **lead** the campaign. The past tense of the verb *lead* is *led*: He **led** a discussion on the origins of abstract art.

less, less than See **fewer, less**.

liable *Liable* generally means "likely" but with a negative connotation: If they do not wear the appropriate gear, they are **liable** to harm themselves. Because of her experience, she is ~~liable~~ likely to win easily.

lie See **lay, lie**.

like See **as, like**.

literally Used in conversation for emphasis. In academic writing, *literally* indicates that an expression is not being used figuratively: My friend **literally** took the cake—at least the few pieces that were left after the party.

lose, loose *Lose* means "to misplace" or "to fail to succeed": She hates to **lose** an argument. *Loose* means "unfastened" or "movable": One of the boards had come **loose**.

lots, lots of Conversational for *many* or *much*: ~~Lots of~~ Many fans traveled to see the championship game. You will have ~~lots~~ much to do this year. See also **a lot of**.

may See **can, may**.

may of, might of See **of**.

maybe, may be *Maybe* means "possibly": **Maybe** we will have better luck next year. *May* and *be* are both verbs: I **may be** late.

media, medium *Media,* the plural form of *medium,* should be followed by a plural verb. The **media** ~~is~~ are covering the event. However, current dictionaries note the frequent use of *media* as a collective noun taking a singular verb.

morale, moral *Morale* means "confidence" or "spirits": **Morale** was always high. *Moral* means "ethical": She confronted a **moral** dilemma. *Moral* may also mean "the lesson of a story": The **moral** of the story is live and let live.

myself See **herself, himself, myself, yourself**.

number of See **amount of, number of**.

of Often mistakenly used for the unstressed auxiliary verb *have:* They must ~~of~~ have [OR could have, might have, may have, should have, would have] left early.

OK, O.K., okay All three spellings are acceptable, but usage of any of the forms is considered conversational: The teacher gave her ~~O.K.~~ permission to the students. Did the manager ~~okay~~ agree to the expense?

outside of See **inside of, outside of**.

passed, past *Passed* is the past tense of the verb *pass:* I **passed** city hall on my way to work. *Past* means "beyond": The band marched **past** the bleachers.

persecute, prosecute *Persecute* means "to harass" or "to oppress": The group had been **persecuted** because of its religious beliefs. *Prosecute* means "to take legal action against": They decided not to **prosecute** because of insufficient evidence. Other forms: *persecution; prosecution*.

perspective, prospective *Perspective* means "point of view": Our **perspectives** on the issue differ. *Prospective* means "potential": **Prospective** graduate students must take an entrance exam.

persuade See **convince, persuade**.

plus *Plus* joins nouns or noun phrases to make a sentence seem like an equation: Supreme talent **plus** rigorous training **makes** this runner hard to beat. Note that a singular form of the verb is required. Avoid using *plus* to join clauses: She takes classes Monday through Friday, ~~plus~~ and she works on weekends.

precede, proceed To *precede* is to "go before": A determiner **precedes** a noun. To *proceed* is to "go on": After a layover in Chicago, we will **proceed** to New York. Other forms: *precedence, precedent; procedure, proceedings*.

prejudice, prejudiced *Prejudice* can be a noun or a verb: Because of his **prejudice**, he was unable to make a fair decision. Be aware of your own bias so that you do not **prejudice** others. *Prejudiced* is an adjective: The authorities were racially **prejudiced**.

principal, principle *Principal* is a noun meaning "head" or an adjective meaning "main": The **principal** met the students at the door. The state's **principal** crop is wheat. *Principle* is a noun meaning "standard or belief": The doctrine was derived from three moral **principles**.

proceed See **precede, proceed.**

prosecute See **persecute, prosecute.**

prospective See **perspective, prospective.**

quotation, quote In academic writing, use *quotation,* rather than *quote,* to refer to a copied sentence or passage: Her introduction included a ~~quote~~ quotation from *Rebecca. Quote* expresses an action: My friend likes to **quote** lines from recent movies.

raise, rise *Raise (raised, raising)* means "to cause to increase or move upward": The Federal Reserve Board **raised** interest rates. *Rise (rose, risen, rising)* means "to get up" or "to increase": Prices **rose** sharply. *Raise* takes an object (to **raise** something); *rise* does not.

regard, regarding, regards These words are used appropriately in the expressions *with regard to, as regards, in regard to,* and *regarding:* I am writing **with regard to** [OR **as regards** OR **in regard to** OR **regarding**] your purchasing my computer. (*As regarding, in regards to,* and *with regards to* are unconventional.)

respectfully, respectively *Respectfully* means "considerately": The scholars **respectfully** disagreed with each other. *Respectively* means "in that order". The diplomat introduced her to the representative, the senator, and the governor, **respectively**.

rise See **raise, rise.**

second, secondly See **first, firstly, second, secondly.**

sensor See **censor, censure, sensor.**

sensual, sensuous *Sensual* refers to physical pleasure, especially sexual pleasure or indulgence of an appetite: The band's lead singer was renowned for his **sensual** movements. *Sensuous* refers to aesthetic pleasure, for example, in response to art: She found the **sensuous** colors of the painting very soothing. Other forms: *sensuality; sensuousness.*

set, sit *Set* means "to place" or "to establish": We **set** the date for the meeting: May 4. *Sit* means "to take a seat": The judges of the competition **sat** on the left side of the stage. *Set* takes an object (to **set** something), but *sit* does not.

should of See **of.**

sight See **cite, sight, site.**

sit See **set, sit.**

site See **cite, sight, site.**

so *So* emphasizes another word that is followed by a *that* clause: We arrived **so** late **that** we could not find a place to stay. Avoid using *so* without a *that* clause; find a more precise modifier instead: She was **so** ~~spectacularly~~ successful.

someplace See **anyplace, everyplace, someplace.**

sometime, sometimes, some time *Sometime* means "at an unspecified time": We will move **sometime** in June. *Sometimes* means "every so often": **Sometimes** the weather changes abruptly. *Some time* means "a short period": After **some time** had passed, they were able to reach a compromise.

sort See **kind, sort, type.**

sort of See **kind of, sort of.**

specially See **especially, specially.**

stationary, stationery *Stationary* means "at a standstill": The planes on the runway were **stationary** for two hours. *Stationery* means "writing paper and envelopes": He objected to the new logo on the **stationery**.

subsequently See **consequently, subsequently.**

than, then *Than* links both parts of a comparison: The game lasted longer **than** we had expected. *Then* means "after that": Read the contract closely; **then** sign it.

that, which *Which* introduces nonessential (nonrestrictive) clauses and is preceded by a comma: The world's tiniest fish, **which** is *Hippocampus denise,* was found in Indonesia. *That* generally introduces essential (restrictive) clauses: He wants to develop a bar code **that** can be used to identify animals. *Which* can be used in an essential clause introduced by a preposition: The legal battle **in which** we find ourselves seems endless.

that, who In essential (restrictive) clauses, *who* is generally used to refer to people: They did not know the protestors **who** [OR **that**] organized the rally.

their, there, they're *Their* is a possessive form: **Their** donation was made anonymously. *There* refers to location: We worked **there** together. *There* can also be used as an expletive: **There** are some unanswered questions. *They're* is a contraction of *they are:* **They're** performing on Wednesday.

theirself, theirselves Unconventional for *themselves.* They discussed the topic among ~~theirselves~~ themselves.

then See **than, then.**

there See **their, there, they're.**

they're See **their, there, they're.**

thru Use *through* in academic writing: He lived **thru** ~~through~~ two world wars.

to, too, two *To* is a preposition, usually signaling a direction: They sent the petition **to** everyone in the neighborhood. *To* is also an infinitive marker: They planned **to** finish their work by Friday. *Too* means "also": She goes to school and works **too.** *Too* also means "excessively": We have made **too** many commitments. *Two* is a number: She moved here **two** months ago.

toward, towards *Toward* is preferred in American English.

type See **kind, sort, type.**

uninterested See **disinterested, uninterested.**

unique *Unique* means "one of a kind" and thus is not preceded by a word such as *most* or *very:* San Francisco is **very** ~~unique~~. However, according to current dictionaries, *unique* is frequently used to mean "extraordinary."

weather, whether *Weather* refers to the condition of the atmosphere: The **weather** report is usually accurate. *Whether* introduces alternatives: He must decide **whether** to sell now or wait for the market to improve.

well See **good, well.**

whether See **weather, whether.**

which See **that, which.**

who, whom *Who* is the subject or subject complement of a clause: Leon Bates, ~~whom~~ **who** I believe has great potential, will soon be competing in international events. (*Who* is the subject of *who has great potential.*) *Whom* is used as an object: Anna Holmes, ~~who~~ **whom** I met at a convention three years ago, has agreed to speak to our study group. (*Whom* is the object of *I met.*) According to current dictionaries, *who* is frequently used in the object position when it does not follow a preposition. See also **that, who.**

whose, who's *Whose* is a possessive form: The procedure was developed by a researcher **whose** mother will benefit from the innovation. *Who's* is the contraction of *who is:* **Who's** responsible for writing the report?

with regards to Unconventional. See **regard, regarding, regards.**

would of See **of.**

your, you're *Your* is a possessive form: **Your** review was chosen for publication. *You're* is the contraction of *you are:* **You're** almost finished.

yourself See **herself, himself, myself, yourself.**

Essay Exams and the Rhetorical Situation

You will not always have the luxury of planning, drafting, revising, getting feedback on, and editing a piece of writing over a stretch of days or weeks. Frequently, your college instructor or your employer will ask you to produce an essay or a report during a class period or within a day or two. No matter when a deadline falls, most writers feel some pressure. But when they are asked to write quickly or on demand, that pressure intensifies. This section will help you write well when faced with the constraints of time and place that come with essay examinations.

Using exam answers to address rhetorical opportunities

You can begin preparing for an essay exam by thinking of answers as responses to specific rhetorical opportunities. In an exam, the opportunities have been provided for you by your instructor, although you may not know immediately just how you'll proceed. A good way to begin is to skim through the questions, if the exam has more than one, to be sure you understand them. If you don't, ask your instructor for clarification.

Once you can clearly identify the opportunity posed by each question, figure out how much time to allot to answering each one. If you are faced with two questions that are worth the same number of points, give half the time to one and half to the other. When certain questions are weighted more heavily than others, however, you need to divide your time accordingly. However you allocate your time, allow ten minutes for final revising and proofreading.

Stick to your time allotment for each question. If you do not finish, leave room to complete it later and move on to the next question. Partial answers to *all* questions usually gain you more points than complete answers to only *some* questions. Besides, you can use the ten minutes you saved to put the finishing touches on any incomplete answers, even if you have to draw arrows to the margins or to the back of the page, or if you have to supply rough notes. Your instructor will probably appreciate the extra effort.

Using exam answers to address an audience and fulfill a purpose

Unlike most rhetorical situations, an essay exam usually has an audience that is easy to identify: your instructor. The questions on an exam offer big clues about what that audience wants to see in your responses and what kind of purpose you should have in writing; be sure to read all instructions and questions carefully. Invest a few minutes in studying each question, putting that question in your own words, and then jotting down a few notes in the margin next to it. If you have been given a choice of questions to answer, choose those that best suit your knowledge yet do not overlap.

Most questions contain specific instructions about how, as well as what, to answer. Be alert for words such as *compare, define,* and *argue,* which identify the writing task and provide specific cues for organizing your response. Other words, such as *discuss* and *explain,* are less specific, so try to determine exactly what it is your instructor wants you to do. When these more general directions appear, be tuned in to such accompanying words as *similar* or *different* (which signal, respectively, comparison or contrast), *identify* (which signals definition or description), and *why* (which signals the need to identify causes). You will also want to be clear as to whether you are being asked to call up course-related information from memory or to respond with your own ideas. Words such as *think, defend,* and *opinion* signal that you are to frame a thesis and support it.

Most essay exam questions begin with or contain one of the words in the following list and end with a reference to the information you are to discuss. Understanding these terms and framing your answer in response to them will help you focus on what is being asked.

TERMS USED IN ESSAY QUESTIONS

Compare	Examine the points of similarity (compare) or difference (contrast) between two ideas or things.
Define	State the class to which the item to be defined belongs, and clarify what distinguishes it from the others of that class.
Describe	Use details in a clearly defined order to give the reader a clear mental picture of the item you are being asked to describe.
Discuss	Examine, analyze, evaluate, or state pros and cons. This word gives you wide latitude in addressing the topic and thus makes your task more difficult than do some of the others in this set, since you must choose your own focus. It is also the one that appears most frequently on exam questions.
Evaluate	Appraise the advantages and disadvantages of the idea or thing specified.
Explain	Clarify and interpret, reconcile differences, or state causes.
Illustrate	Offer concrete examples or, if possible, create figures, charts, or tables that provide information about the item.

| Summarize | State the main points in a condensed form; omit details and curtail examples. |
| Trace | Narrate a sequence of events that show progress toward a goal or comprise a process. |

Using exam answers as a fitting response

Preparing a fitting response to the rhetorical opportunity is another consideration (along with satisfying a specific audience) as you compose essay exam answers. You'll need to decide how to present your ideas and organize your responses in a way that fits the problem, can be delivered in a medium that will reach your audience, and successfully satisfies that audience.

Even under time constraints, you should be able to draft a rough outline or jot down a few phrases for an informal list. Identify your thesis; then list the most important points you plan to cover. You might decide to rearrange ideas later, but the first step is to get some down on paper. Before you begin to write the answer, quickly review the list, deleting any irrelevant or unimportant points and adding any better ones that come to you (keeping in mind how much time you have allotted to the specific question). Number the points in a logical sequence determined by chronology (reporting events in the order in which they occurred), by causation (showing how one thing led to another), or by order of importance (going from the most important point to the least important). Although arranging points in order of increasing importance is often effective, it can be risky in an exam situation because you might run out of time and not get to your most important point.

On the following page is a thesis statement and a list of supporting points that biology major Trish Parsons quickly composed and edited during the first few minutes of an essay exam. Trish was responding to the following question:

> Discuss whether the term *junk DNA* is an appropriate name for the nucleic DNA that does not code for proteins.

Sometimes, the language of the question will tell you how you should organize your answer. Consider this example:

> Discuss how the two-party political system of the United States influenced the outcome of the Bush-Gore presidential election.

At first glance, this exam question might seem to state the topic without indicating how to organize a discussion of it. *To influence,* however, is to be responsible for certain consequences. In this case, the two-party political system is a cause, and you are being asked to identify its effects. Once you have recognized this, you might decide to discuss different effects in different paragraphs.

Here is another example:

> Consider Picasso's treatment of the human body early and late in his career. How did his concept of bodily form persist throughout his career? How did it change?

THESIS: The term "junk" applied to DNA with no apparent purpose is a misnomer; there are many possible purposes, both past and present, for the allegedly "junk" DNA.

1a.

1b. Though junk DNA sequences do not code for specific proteins, they may play an important role in DNA regulation. ⟶ go to point #5

2. Microbiology technology has had many amazing advances since the discovery of DNA. Indeed, DNA itself was not immediately recognized as the "plan for life." Further technological advances that are sure to come may find a definite purpose for "junk" DNA.

3. Junk DNA may have coded for proteins in our evolutionary past and a mechanism for disposing of it never has ∧evolved. (yet to evolve)

4. During DNA replication, the possibilities for mistakes are endless. The junk (filler) DNA decreases the chances of the more important, protein-coding DNA being mutated during this process.

5. Junk DNA may yet play an important role in the new field of eugenics, where it has been found that certain traits are heritable, but not directly coded for (possible relation to DNA regulation role in point #1)

1a Many terms have been applied in genetics that end up creating confusion because scientists come to conclusions too quickly—e.g., dominant and recessive alleles are too simplistic. b/c genetics is a relatively new field we have only recently begun to understand.
BEGIN WITH THIS ONE

The reference to two different points in the artist's career, along with the words *persist* and *change,* indicates that your task is to compare and contrast. You could organize your response to this question by discussing Picasso's concept of the bodily form when his paintings were realistic and when they were cubist—preferably covering the same points in the same order in each part of the response. Or you could begin by establishing similarities and then move on to discuss differences. There is almost always more than one way to organize a thoughtful response. Devoting at least a few minutes to organizing your answer can help you better demonstrate what you know.

Once you have identified and organized your main points, try to make them stand out from the rest of the answer to the exam question. For instance, you can make a main point be the first sentence of each paragraph. Or you can use transitional words such as *first, second,* and *third.* You might even create headings to separate your points. By the time you have outlined your essay exam answer, you should know which points you want to highlight, even if the points change slightly as you begin writing. Use your conclusion to summarize your main points. If you tend to make points that differ from those you had in mind when you started, try leaving space for an introduction at the beginning of the answer and then writing it after you have written the rest. Or simply draw a line pointing into the margin (or to the other side of the paper), and write the introduction there.

Using exam answers as an available means

Finally, the success of your answers on an essay exam depends on your strategic employment of the available means. In most cases, the physical means available to you for delivering the required information are fairly limited and mostly predetermined. But what are the resources and constraints of your rhetorical situation?

As you already know, one major constraint is time. However, a time limit can also be seen as a resource to help keep you on track, focused clearly on the particular question you're trying to answer. It's critical while completing an essay exam to stick to the question at hand. Always answer each question as precisely and directly as you can, perhaps using some of the instructor's language in your thesis statement. If your thesis statement implies an organizational plan, follow that plan as closely as possible. If you move away from your original thesis because better ideas occur to you as you write, simply go back and revise your thesis statement. If you find yourself drifting into irrelevant material, stop and draw a line through it.

If you face a vague or truly confusing question, construct a clear question and then answer it. Rewriting the instructor's question can seem like a risky thing to do, especially if you have never done it before. But figuring out a reasonable question that is related to what the instructor has written is actually a responsible move if you can answer the question you have posed.

Since you'll have reserved time to reread your answers after you've drafted the last one, use this time as a resource to help you improve what you've already written. You can make whatever deletions and corrections you think are necessary. If time allows, ask yourself if there is anything you have left out that you can still manage to include (even if you have to write in the margins or on the back of the page). Most instructors will not mind if you draw a caret (∧), marking the exact place in the text where you want an addition or correction to be placed. Making corrections will allow you to focus on improving what you have already written, whereas recopying your answer just to make it look neat is an inefficient use of time (and you may have recopied only half your essay when the time is up). Finally, check spelling, punctuation, and sentence structure.

Oral Presentations and the Rhetorical Situation

In nearly every course you'll take, your grade will be based in part on participation, a term that is defined according to the subject, the course level, and the instructor. But regardless of the range of expectations this term implies, it nearly always includes oral presentations to the class. You might be expected to contribute to ongoing class discussions or a group project, as a way to demonstrate that you've done your homework and can engage productively with the subject matter and your classmates. Or you might be required to lead a class discussion, teach a lesson, or present research results.

Whether you're someone who feels confident participating in class discussions and who speaks regularly and knowledgeably in class or one of many people who cite public speaking as their greatest fear (even greater than the fear of dying), you can learn some ways to make oral presentations easier on you and better for your audience. Like preparing for an essay examination, preparing for an oral presentation means just that: preparing!

Using oral presentations to address rhetorical opportunities

You can begin preparing by considering your oral presentation as a response to a specific rhetorical opportunity. For instance, you may have identified a problem that you can address by way of research, a public controversy that you want to investigate, or a personal problem that you want to resolve. If, however, the rhetorical opportunity has been provided for you by your instructor, you may not know immediately just how to proceed. In either situation (you've identified your own opportunity or an opportunity has been provided for you), you'll need to begin to gather information right away. As soon as you have your assignment and due date, start keeping a computer or paper file of your ideas and information. That way, as the term moves forward, you'll continually bank ideas and materials. Even if you don't know for sure what you'll end up speaking about (you may have in mind a general subject but not a more specific topic), your accumulation of ideas and materials will help you when it's time to begin addressing the specific opportunity.

Using oral presentations to address an audience

As you consider the opportunity to be addressed, you'll also need to consider your audience. First, you need to consider to whom you'll be speaking: Will you be speaking to your entire class, a smaller group, or several sections of the same course? Or will you be able to seek out the specific audience you most want to reach with your information? As you begin to envision an audience for your presentation, you'll need to consider the level of expertise of that audience so that you can shape your material and your oral presentation accordingly. In order to do so, you'll want to consider the following questions: How much (if anything) does your intended audience know about your subject? What opinions do members of the audience hold, if any? What role will you take in delivering your information? Will you deliver the information as an expert, a novice, a careful observer or researcher, or a peer? And, of course, you'll need to consider how you're going be evaluated. Finally, you'll need to consider the audience's role in evaluating your presentation. Will the audience evaluate or help evaluate your presentation, or will your instructor be the only one making an evaluation?

Using oral presentations with a rhetorical purpose

You know by now that it's impossible to separate purpose from audience. After all, your purpose is dependent on your audience. Do you want to gather, arrange, and deliver your information (assertions and detailed support) in order to help those in your audience make a decision, change their attitude or behavior, enrich their understanding, or give them pleasure? Your in-class oral presentations will usually be informative, but you'll occasionally be required to provide information that is argumentative or entertaining.

Using oral presentations as a fitting response

Offering a fitting response to the rhetorical opportunity is another consideration in planning your oral presentation. You need to decide whether the information you've gathered and organized fits the problem, can be delivered in a medium that will reach your audience, and successfully satisfies that audience. You must make decisions about whether to deliver your information in spoken words only or with spoken words and visuals, making sure that the words you use sound as though they should be spoken. To that end, read aloud slowly what you've written, making changes in sentence structure and word choices as you go along, so that the final presentation moves along smoothly and sounds natural. Another benefit of reading aloud is that you'll hear assertions that need support. You may find yourself simplifying your sentence structure (by breaking long, complex sentences into two or more simpler sentences) and following each of your assertions with explicit examples. You might add the type of sensory details that are elemental to narration, description, and definition. You might emphasize transitional words and phrases, so that your audience can hear the movement of your words: "first," "second," and so on. If audience members expect to hear three reasons or five main parts, then they will listen for those reasons or parts and be able to follow your words more easily—and with better comprehension. Finally, you can decide whether your presentation might benefit from visuals or audio clips: items that you bring in to show (sometimes referred to as realia), a handout, a flip chart, a transparency, a poster, a film clip, a podcast or an audio stream, or a PowerPoint, Prezi, or other type of digital presentation. (For help using video or podcast technology in a presentation, see Chapter 13.)

None of these items will automatically improve your presentation, but all of them hold the potential for bringing your points to life. Nothing can be more persuasive than a series of powerful visuals or audio clips that complement (or complete) a speaker's argument. Nothing can be more aggravating than a series of bulleted points that a speaker reads to the audience while the audience is reading it from a display. Thus, as you consider the use of visuals and audio, keep in mind that they should complement your words—not mirror them. Some of the most effective digital presentations are cascades of visuals that accompany—and enhance—a speaker's words.

Using oral presentations as an available means

Finally, the success of an oral presentation depends on your strategic employment of the available means. What are the physical means available to you for delivering the information you want to deliver? Where will you be presenting your information? And what are the resources and constraints of your rhetorical situation?

An oral presentation by definition requires the use of spoken words—your own spoken words. Therefore, you need to practice by reading and/or reciting your information aloud several times. You want to be sure that you are presenting your information loudly, clearly, and slowly enough for all of the audience members to hear you. If you've ever left a presentation thinking "I don't listen as quickly as that speaker speaks," you know why practicing the delivery of your words is important: if you're going to all the trouble of putting together an oral presentation, you want your audience to be able to follow it. Another reason for practicing aloud is to ensure that your presentation comes in at a little less than the maximum time your instructor has allotted you. If you need to trim your presentation, consider which parts could be delivered through another means, such as a handout that lists additional resources or a URL for a website that supports your presentation. You'll also want to practice using your audio clips or visuals to make sure that all of your equipment (even something as simple as a flip chart) actually works.

Be sure to consider the resources and constraints of the physical location in which your presentation is to be delivered. If you're speaking in front of a classroom, you'll reach all of your classmates if you speak clearly and take time to look up from your notes as often as possible. If you're speaking in a lecture hall, however, you may find yourself dependent on a microphone, and you may want to practice with it beforehand. A lecture hall offers a few other challenges as well, not the least of which is the need to ensure that audience members who are hearing impaired or visually impaired can follow your presentation. You may want to make printed handouts available so that hearing-impaired individuals can follow along more easily. And you'll want to concentrate on facing your audience so that they can see your facial expressions and even read your lips, all the better to "hear" your words.

Again, you'll want to practice presenting your words aloud to make sure that your voice is clear enough, that your ideas move forward logically (with lots of transitional flags), and that your visuals or audio clips work to bring alive your words. You cannot overpractice or overprepare an oral presentation.

For many speakers, the problem isn't researching a topic, writing a text, or translating it into an oral presentation. The problem is getting up in front of a group and delivering the results of their hard work. The best prevention for overcoming this problem is practice, practice, practice—and preparation. The better you know your information, the more familiar your words are as you speak them, the more familiar you are with your speaking space and with any electronic equipment you're using, the easier time you'll have with oral presentations.

Portfolios and the Rhetorical Situation

Many instructors have undoubtedly asked you to keep a portfolio of your work—whether your work consists of drawings, blueprints, or writing.

WAIT A MINUTE . . .

What if your oral presentation is part of an ongoing class discussion—a situation in which, for instance, you need to contribute your ideas about a reading assignment? In such a rhetorical situation, you won't be able to practice delivering your presentation ahead of time. You can, however, do several things to take advantage of your available means and deliver a fitting response:

▶ It may sound obvious, but be sure to keep up with your assigned reading and take notes as you read so that you're familiar with the main subject under discussion. Responding to the text by "talking back" to the author in the margins of your book is one way of preparing for in-class discussions.

▶ Listen to what your classmates have said so that you can frame your ideas in terms of that larger conversation, making clear the relevance of your point. Listening carefully can also help you avoid repeating a point that has already been made.

▶ Jot down a couple of key words so that you remember what you want to say when it comes time for you to speak.

▶ Don't hesitate to offer a response that is inconclusive or that raises more questions than it answers: class discussions are a time to clarify your understanding of the subject, not just demonstrate what you already know.

Student writers are asked to keep portfolios that include both works in progress and final projects so that their instructors can review the writing and rewriting that has been done over the course of a term. Rather than grade each formal paper individually, an instructor can look at a student's performance and progress in a variety of writing situations. A portfolio reveals the strengths and weaknesses of a student writer, the kinds of risks the student is willing to take, and the progress the student has made. Perhaps most important, portfolios give students the opportunity to declare what they see and value in their own writing.

Using portfolios to address a rhetorical opportunity

If your instructor requires an end-of-term portfolio, then the rhetorical opportunity for your portfolio is his or her evaluation. The basis of evaluation might be your ability to accomplish a sequence of challenging and complex writing tasks; to use writing as a means for in-depth learning; to write for different audiences, with different purposes, and with different kinds of responses; or to assess your own progress and to set your own goals as a writer. Your job, then, is to put together a portfolio that addresses the opportunity of evaluation.

Using portfolios to address an audience

The audience for a portfolio is most often someone who will judge it, whether that person is you (as you decide what to include or take out of the portfolio) or your instructor. Of course, you're always an audience for your portfolio, for you are the one who writes the cover letter that introduces and reflects on the work included. Your instructor is the primary audience, however, in terms of evaluation, so you'll want to be sure to include the materials that your instructor has required and will most value.

Using portfolios with a rhetorical purpose

The purpose of your portfolio becomes clear as you select the materials you want to include (unless, of course, your instructor asks you to include every word you've written all term). Your purpose is to demonstrate how well your writing and critical thinking have progressed, how much you've learned about meeting the demands of any rhetorical situation, and what goals you have already achieved and plan to achieve. In your portfolio, you are making an argument about your development as a writer and using your writing as support for that argument (for strategies for writing arguments, see Chapters 2 and 3). Thus, you'll want to decide not only what materials to include in your portfolio but also how to organize those materials.

Using portfolios as a fitting response

Many instructors ask for writing samples that best represent you as a writer. If all the samples must come from the course taught by that instructor, then your selection task is simplified. You include what the instructor has asked for and concentrate on your cover letter, describing the contents of the portfolio, commenting on the strengths and weaknesses of each piece of your writing, and explaining why you believe you've earned a specific grade in the course.

However, if your instructor wants you to choose the contents of the portfolio, you'll need to decide whether all your samples will come from the course or you should include materials from outside the course. (In either case, check with your instructor to make sure that your decision about what to include is acceptable.) If your writing portfolio is to represent you as a writer, you'll want to include both academic and nonacademic pieces: a course essay that argues a point, a personal essay that reveals your self-insight, a group or collaborative project and your evaluation of how the group worked, a successful writing assignment from another academic course, a sample of professional writing (perhaps your résumé or a job application letter), and a piece of writing that you simply like. Again, you'll want to reflect on the writing samples in your cover letter, showing your instructor that you understand your progress and have set reasonable goals for yourself throughout the term and for the future. Together, then, the contents of the portfolio, the arrangement of those contents, and the cover letter make a fitting response to the rhetorical opportunity at the same time as they satisfy your audience.

Using portfolios as an available means

Finally, the success of your portfolio ultimately depends on your means of delivery. Whether you deliver your portfolio on paper or electronically, you'll want to take advantage of the features that can be used to present your work more effectively. To that end, you'll want to include a title page and a table of contents, allowing your reader to decide which materials he or she will read. Your cover letter should include an explanation of your choices as well as an evaluation of each of those choices. It should also describe your perceived progress, your achievements, and your goals. If your writing includes a good deal of online and multimedia work (web pages, multimedia presentations, PDF files, and the like), you might be better off delivering your portfolio electronically so that it can feature visuals, graphics, and audios. Some students create a link to their writing portfolio from their home page or print the URL on their résumé.

Like all important writing you do, you'll want your portfolio to reflect you at your best. So be sure to organize it effectively, proofread and edit it carefully, and showcase your most persuasive and engaging writing in your cover letter.

TEXT

pp. 11–13: Judy Brady, "Why I Want a Wife," *Ms.* magazine, inaugural issue, 1971. Used by permission of the author.

pp. 22–24: From *Life as We Know It* by Michael Bérubé, copyright © 1996 by Michael Bérubé. Used by permission of Pantheon Books, a division of Random House, Inc., and by The Doe Coover Literary Agency.

p. 26: Christopher Cokinos, from *Hope Is the Thing with Feathers: A Personal Chronicle of Vanished Birds* (New York: Grand Central Publishing, 2001).

pp. 32–33: Statement of George A. Hacker, "Support 21" Coalition Press Conference on Minimum Drinking Age Law. Used by permission of Center for Science in the Public Interest.

p. 35: Academic Senate of San Francisco State University, "Resolution Regarding the Rodney King Verdict," http://sfsu .edu/~senate/documents/resolutions/RS92-107.pdf

pp. 37–38: Barbara Smith, from *The Truth That Never Hurts*, pp. 102–105 (New Brunswick, NJ: Rutgers University Press, 1998).

p. 45: Sojourner Truth, from speech given at 1851 Women's Rights Convention in Akron, Ohio.

p. 49: "Susan Orlean Delivers 2001 Johnston Lecture," *Flash: Newsletter of the School of Journalism and Communication*, vol. 16, no. 3 (2001), http://flash.uoregon.edu/S01/orlean.html

pp. 49–51: "The American Man, Age Ten," from *The Bullfighter Checks Her Makeup* by Susan Orlean, copyright © 2001 by Susan Orlean. Used by permission of Random House, Inc. For online information about other Random House, Inc. books and authors, see the Internet Web Site at http://www.randomhouse.com.

p. 56: Joyce Carol Oates, "To Invigorate Literary Mind, Start Moving Literary Feet," in *Writers on Writing: Collected Essays from The New York Times* (New York: Times Books/Holt, 2001), 165–71.

p. 57: Susan Sontag, in *Writers on Writing: Collected Essays from The New York Times* (New York: Times Books/Holt, 2001), 223–9.

pp. 59, 60, 61, 63, 78–79, 82, 83–88: Anastasia Simkanin.

p. 65: Britannica definition of "primates," http://www.britannica .com/eb/article-9105977/primate

p. 65: Primate Conservation, Inc., http://www.primate.org/about.htm

p. 65: ChimpanZoo: Research, Education and Enrichment 2003, www.chimpanzoo.org/history%20of%20primates.html

p. 66: W. E. Le Gros Clark, *The Antecedents of Man*, 3rd ed. (Chicago: Quadrangle Books, 1971).

p. 67: William Styron, *Darkness Visible* (New York: Random House, 1990), p. 52.

pp. 67–68: Burciaga, José Antonio, "I Remember Masa" from *Weedee Peepo*. Published by Pan American University Press, Edinburgh, TX (1988).

pp. 72–73: From Michael McGarrity, *Everyone Dies* (New York: Dutton-Penguin, 2003), pp. 169–71.

p. 76: http://www.fns.usda.gov/cnd/Breakfast/expansion /10reasons-breakfast_flyer.pdf

p. 90: Taryn Plumb, *Boston Globe*, May 4, 2006.

p. 90: Jonathan Kibera, from "Fond Memories of a Congenital Glutton," http://www.epinions.com/educ-review-229A-80FFD6-388E720C-bd3, January 5, 2000.

p. 93: http://chocolateandzucchini.com/archives.2003/10 /happinessarecipe

pp. 93–94: Ruth Reichl, "The Queen of Mold," from *Tender at the Bone*, by Ruth Reichl. Random House, Inc. and Random House, UK.

p. 94: Eric Schlosser, *Fast Food Nation* (Boston: Houghton Mifflin, 2001).

pp. 96–97: © 2007 National Public Radio, Inc. NPR® news report titled "Ruth Reichl: Favorite Food Memoirs" by NPR's Steve Inskeep was originally broadcast on NPR's *Morning Edition*® on June 28, 2007, and is used with the permission of NPR. Any unauthorized duplication is strictly prohibited.

pp. 98–99: Julie Powell, from "The Julie/Julia Project," July 8, 2003, http://blogs.salon.com/0001399/2003/07/08.html

p. 101: Margaret Mead, from "The Wider Food Situation," *Food Habits Research: Problems of the 1960s,* National Research Council's Committee for the Study of Food Habits Update.

p. 103: Margaret Mead, from "The Changing Significance of Food," *American Scientist* 58 (March/April 1970): 176–81.

pp. 105–106: Used with permission of *The Atlantic Monthly,* from "Good-bye Cryovac," Corby Kummer, volume 294, no. 3, Copyright 2004 The Atlantic Monthly Group, as first published in *The Atlantic Monthly.* Distributed by Tribune Media Services, permission conveyed through Copyright Clearance Center, Inc.

pp. 108–112: Pooja Makhijani, "School Lunch," from *Women Who Eat,* Copyright © 2003 Leslie Miller. Reprinted by permission of Seal Press, a member of the Perseus Books Group.

pp. 120–123: Courtesy of Anna Seitz Hickey.

p. 125: Reprinted by arrangement with The Heirs to the Estate of Martin Luther King Jr., c/o Writers House as agent for the proprietor New York, NY. Copyright 1963 Dr. Martin Luther King Jr; copyright renewed 1991 Coretta Scott King.

pp. 128, 140–141: "Uncovering Steve Jobs' Presentation Secrets," by Carmine Gallo. *Business Week,* October 6, 2009. Used with permission of Bloomberg Businessweek.com Permissions Copyright © 2010. All rights reserved.

pp. 130–132: "What Would Obama Say?" by Ashley Parker. From the *New York Times,* January 20, 2008 © 2008 The New York Times. All rights reserved. Used by permission and protected by the Copyright Laws of the United States. The printing, copying, redistribution, or retransmission of this Content without express written permission is prohibited.

pp. 133–135: Transcript of Senator Barack Obama's address to supporters after the Iowa caucuses, as provided by *Congressional Quarterly* via The Associated Press.

pp. 135–136: From *What I Saw at the Revolution,* by Peggy Noonan, copyright © 1989 by Peggy Noonan. Used by permission of Random House, Inc. Reprinted by permission of International Creative Management, Inc. Copyright © 1989 by Peggy Noonan.

pp. 138–139: "Confessions of a TED Addict," by Virginia Heffernan. From the *New York Times,* January 25, 2009 © 2009. The New York Times. All rights reserved. Used by permission and protected by the Copyright Laws of the United States. The printing, copying, redistribution, or retransmission of this Content without express written permission is prohibited.

pp. 143–145: "Successes Speak Well for Debate Coach" written by Marisa Lagos, published October 6, 2004. Copyright © 2004, *Los Angeles Times.* Reprinted with permission.

pp. 152–157: Courtesy of Matthew Glasgow.

p. 160: www.beloit.edu/mindset

p. 164: Eric Hoover, "The Millennial Muddle: How Stereotyping Students Became a Thriving Industry and a Bundle of Contradictions," *The Chronicle of Higher Education,* October 11, 2009, http:// chronicle.com/article/The-Millennial-Muddle-How/48772/

pp. 164–168: Pew Research Center, Pew Social & Demographic Trends, "Millennials: Confident. Connected. Open to Change." Executive Summary, February 24, 2010, www.pewsocialtrends .org/2010/02/24/millennials-confident-connected-open-to-change/

pp. 169–170: Derek Thompson, "What's Really the Matter with 20-Somethings," *The Atlantic,* August 23, 2010, http://www .theatlantic.com/business/archive/2010/08/what's-really-the-matter-with-20-somethings/61938

pp. 171–174: Mano Singham, "More Than 'Millennials': Colleges Must Look Beyond Generational Stereotypes," *The Chronicle of Higher Education,* October 11, 2009, http://chronicle.com/article /More-Than-Millennials-/48751/

pp. 175–176: David Fallarme, "A Look at How Gen Y Communicates," *The Marketing Student*, June 16, 2008, http://www.themarketingstudent.com/2008/06/16/a-look-at-how-gen-y-communicates/

pp. 177–178: Mark Bauerlein, "Why Gen-Y Johnny Can't Read Non-Verbal Cues." Reprinted from the *Wall Street Journal* © 2009. Dow Jones & Company. All rights reserved.

pp. 178–179: Laurie Fendrich, "Bad Student Writing? Not So Fast," *The Chronicle of Higher Education*, August 28, 2009, http://chronicle.com/blogs/brainstorm/bad-student-writing-not-so-fast/7853

pp. 181–184: Christine Rosen, "The Myth of Multitasking," *The New Atlantis*, Number 20, Spring 2008, pp. 105–110.

pp. 191–193: "The Last of the Music Videos" by Jenn Mayer, the *Columbia Daily Spectator*.

pp. 195, 196: Copyright 2007 The Atlantic Monthly Group, as first published in *The Atlantic Monthly*. Distributed by Tribune Media Services.

p. 198: Zitkala-Sa, "Impressions of an Indian Childhood," *The Atlantic Monthly*, vol. 85, no. 507 (January 1900), pp. 37–47.

p. 199: From "Not Neither" by Sandra Maria Esteves, quoted in Juan Flores, *From Bamboo to Hip-Hip: Puerto Rican Culture and Latino Identity* (New York: Columbia University Press, 2000), p. 56.

p. 201: Lines from "Nuestro Himno" ("Our Anthem"), produced by British music producer Adam Kidron by Adam Kidron. Urban Box Office/Beyond Oblivion. Used by permission.

p. 201: "Sen. Alexander to Introduce Senate Resolution on Singing National Anthem in English." Press release of U.S. Senator Lamar Alexander. 28 Apr. 2006. 19 May 2006.

pp. 204–206: Constitutional Values and Contemporary Policy, sponsored by the Washington Institute for Values in Public Policy. Used by permission of The Regional Oral History Office, Berkeley, CA.

p. 206: U.S. Senate, Bill 992, http://www.govtrack.us/congress/billtext.xpd?bill=s111-992.

p. 206: Quote from EPIC on English Plus from "The English Plus Alternative," in James Crawford (ed.), *Language Loyalties: A Source Book on the Official English Controversy* (Chicago: University of Chicago Press, 1992), pp. 151–53.

p. 207: Geoffrey Nunberg, "The Official English Movement: Reimagining America." From *Language Loyalties: A Source Book on the Official English Controversy*, edited by James Crawford (Chicago: University of Chicago Press, 1992), pp. 479–494.

pp. 208–209: Hyon B. Shin, with Rosalind Bruno, from *Language Use and English-Speaking Ability: Census 2000 Brief*. Washington, DC: U.S. Dept. of Commerce, 2003.

pp. 210–212: "Los Olvidados: On the Making of Invisible People" by Juan F. Perea, 70, *N.Y.U. Law Review*, 965 (1995).

p. 213: "Hunger of Memory" by Richard Rodriguez, from *Hunger of Memory: The Education of Richard Rodriguez* (New York: Bantam Books, 1982) pp. 19–20.

pp. 215–217: Gabriela Kuntz, "My Spanish Standoff," From *Newsweek*, May 4, 1998. © 1998 The Newsweek/Daily Beast Company LLC. All rights reserved. Used by permission and protected by the Copyright Laws of the United States. The printing, copying, redistribution, or retransmission of the Material without express written permission is prohibited.

p. 223: Generation Rescue/13636 Ventura Blvd. #259 / Sherman Oaks, CA 91423.

pp. 228–233: Courtesy of the author.

pp. 239–241: "The Future of College May Be Virtual" by Gregory M. Lamb. Reproduced with permission from the October 15, 2009 issue of *The Christian Science Monitor* (www.CSMonitor.com). © 2009 The Christian Science Monitor.

pp. 242–247: "How Web-Savvy Edupunks Are Transforming American Higher Education" by Anya Kamenetz © *Fast Company*, September 1, 2009. Used with permission of Fast Company Copyright © 2011. All rights reserved.

pp. 248–251: Mark David Milliron, "Online Education vs. Traditional Learning: Time to End the Family Feud," *The Chronicle of Higher Education*, October 31, 2010, http://chronicle.com/article/Online-vs.-Traditional/125115

pp. 252–255: "Will Higher Education Be the Next Bubble to Burst?" by Joseph Marr Cronin and Howard E. Horton. *The Chronicle of Higher Education*, May 22, 2009.

pp. 255–257: "Maybe Experience Really Can Be the Best Teacher" by George D. Kuh. *The Chronicle of Higher Education*, November 21, 2010.

p. 258: http://www.centerforcollegeaffordability.org/25-ways/use-lower-cost-alternatives/encourage-community-colleges. Center for College Affordability and Productivity

pp. 260–262: Reprinted from the *Wall Street Journal* © 2010, Dow Jones & Company. All rights reserved. Reprinted by permission of Alain de Botton and Aragi Inc.

pp. 269–273: "OpenCourseWare and the Future of Education" by Ryan T. Normandin. *The Tech Online Edition*. Volume 129, Issue 59, Tuesday, December 8, 2009.

p. 279: Charles A. Hill, *Intertexts: Reading Pedagogy in College Writing Classrooms* (Mahwah, NJ: Lawrence Erlbaum, 2003), p. 123.

p. 281: Jane Dark, "Reloaded Questions: Hacking the 'Matrix' Master Code," *The Village Voice*, May 14–20, 2003.

p. 281: Joshua Clover, "The Matrix," *British Film Institute Modern Classics Series* (London: BFI Publishing, 2004), p. 15.

pp. 282–284: "An Apocalypse of Kinetic Joy," written by Kenneth Turan, published March 31, 1999. Copyright, 1999, *Los Angeles Times*. Reprinted with permission.

pp. 284–285: Used with permission of *San Francisco Chronicle*, from "Lost in the Matrix" by Bob Graham, March 31, 1999. Copyright 1999; permission conveyed through Copyright Clearance Center, Inc.

pp. 287–290: "Paper, Plastic, or Canvas?" by Dmitri Siegel. Originally published on *Design Observer*. Used by permission, Winterhouse, Falls Village, CT. January 20, 2009.

p. 291: "Classics of Everyday Design No 12" by Jonathan Glancey. 13 March 2007. Copyright Guardian News & Media Ltd. 2007.

pp. 293–294: Mike D'Angelo, "Unreally, Really Cool: Stop-Motion Movies May Be Old School, but They Still Eat Other Animation for Breakfast," *Esquire*, October 2005, pp. 72–73. Use by permission of the author.

pp. 301–304: Courtesy of Alexis Walker.

p. 309: Jeffrey T. Grabill, "Community Computing and Citizen Productivity," *Computers and Composition*, vol. 20 (2003), p. 144.

pp. 310–311: From interview with Marshall McLuhan by Eric Norden, in Marshall McLuhan, Eric McLuhan, and Frank Zingrone, *Essential McLuhan* (New York: Basic Books, 1996), p. 236.

p. 311: From interview with Marshall McLuhan on *Explorations*, video, http://archives.cbc.ca/IDC-1-74-342-1818/people/mcluhan/clip2

pp. 311–312: McLuhan, Marshall, *Understanding Media: the Extensions of Man*, Critical Edition, Gordon, W. Terrence, ed. Corte Madera, CA: Ginko Press, 2003.

pp. 313–315: "A Brief Interview with Michael Wesch" by John Battelle. Found at http://battellemedia.com/archives/003386.php (John Battelle's Searchblog).

pp. 317–318: © 2010 Time Inc. All rights reserved. Reprinted from *Time* Magazine and published with permission of Time Inc. Reproduction in any manner in any language in whole or in part without written permission is prohibited. *Time* is registered trademark of Time Inc. Used Under License.

pp. 319–320: Used with permission of MSNBC.COM, from "Twitterverse Draws More Black Followers into Its Orbit" by Michael E. Ross, May 7, 2010. Copyright 2010; permission conveyed through Copyright Clearance Center, Inc.

pp. 322–324: From *Newsweek* February 27, 1995 © 1995 The Newsweek/Daily Beast Company LLC. All rights reserved. Used by permission and protected by the Copyright Laws of the United States. The printing, copying, redistribution, or retransmission of the Material without express written permission is prohibited.

pp. 332–335: Courtesy of Anna Seitz Hickey.

p. 338: Jonathan Franzen, quote from interview with Terry Gross, *Fresh Air*, WHYY, Philadelphia, October 15, 2001.

p. 338: Sonny Mehta, quoted in Edward Wyatt, "Oprah's Book Club Reopening to Writers Who'll Sit and Chat," *New York Times*, September 23, 2006, p. A2.

p. 340: Maya Angelou, quoted in "Literary Legend Lends Name and Creates Original Poetry for New Hallmark Product Line; 'The Maya Angelou Collection from Hallmark' Will Feature

Inspirational Greeting Cards and Specialty Products," *PR Newswire*, November 14, 2000. Hallmark Cards, Inc. http://www.prnewswire.com

p. 341: Harold Bloom, "The Man in the Back Row Has a Question VI," *Paris Review*, vol. 42, no. 154 (Spring 2000): p. 379.

p. 342: Matt Morden.

pp. 345–348: Mortimer Adler, "How to Mark a Book," in *The Sundance Writer*, 3rd ed. (Boston: Thomson/Wadsworth). Originally published in *Saturday Review of Literature* in 1940.

pp. 348–350: Copyright © 1998 Sherman Alexie. All rights reserved. Used by permission of Nancy Stauffer Associates.

pp. 351–352: Marianne Gingher, "The Most Double-D-Daring Book I Read." From *Remarkable Reads: 34 Writers and Their Adventures in Reading* (New York: W.W. Norton & Co., 2004), pp. 95–104. Used by permission of the author.

p. 352: Elaine Oswald and Robert L. Gale, "On Marianne Moore's Life and Career," *Modern American Poetry 2000.* The Department of English, University of Illinois at Urbana-Champaign, July 10, 2007. http://www.english.uiuc.edu/maps/poets/m_r/moore/life.htm

p. 353: Reprinted with the permission of Scribner, a Division of Simon & Schuster, Inc., from *The Collected Poems of Marianne Moore* by Marianne Moore. Copyright © 1935 by Marianne Moore, renewed 1963 by Marianne Moore and T. S. Eliot. All rights reserved. Electronic reproduction with permission of the Estate of Marianne C. Moore. David M. Moore, Esq., Administrator. All rights reserved.

p. 357: Quote from Hisaye Yamamoto, "Las Vegas Charley," in *Seventeen Syllables* (New Brunswick, NJ: Rutgers University Press, 1994).

p. 357: Quote from Alice Walker, *To Hell with Dying* (San Diego, CA: Harcourt, 1988).

pp. 358–361: Ralph Rees, "The Reality of Imagination in the Poetry of Marianne Moore." Originally published in *Twentieth Century Literature*, vol. 30, nos. 2–3 (Summer–Autumn 1984): pp. 231–41.

p. 363: Barbara T. Christian, *Everyday Use by Alice Walker* (New Brunswick, NJ: Rutgers University Press, 1994), introduction, p. 9.

pp. 363–369: "Everyday Use" from *In Love & Trouble: Stories of Black Women*, copyright © 1973 by Alice Walker, reproduced by permission of Houghton Mifflin Harcourt Publishing Company. Reprinted by permission of The Wendy Weil Agency, Inc. First published by Harcourt © 1973 by Alice Walker.

p. 369: Joy Harjo, quoted at http://www.joyharjo.org

p. 370: "Perhaps the World Ends Here," from *The Woman Who Fell from the Sky* by Joy Harjo. Copyright © 1994 by Joy Harjo. Used by permission of W.W. Norton & Company, Inc. Copyright © 1994 by Joy Harjo. Reprinted with the permission of the author c/o The Permissions Company, Inc., www.permissionscompany.com.

p. 371: Quote from Fishbowl Theatre's website, http://fishbowltheatre.ca/jane_martin.html

pp. 371–376: Used by permission of Jon Jory.

p. 377: Raymond Carver quoted in William L. Stull, "Raymond Carver," http://whitman.edu/english/carver/biography.html. Originally published in *Dictionary of Literary Biography*.

pp. 383–387: Courtesy of Matthew Marusak.

p. 412: REPRINTED WITH PERMISSION FROM PSYCHOLOGY TODAY MAGAZINE (Mar./Apr. 2004), p. 29. Copyright © 2004 Sussex Publishers, LLC.

p. 416: Tricks of the Trade courtesy of Christian Nuñez.

p. 418: *Bostonia* Magazine, Winter 2003-2004, page 16.

p. 405: Kenneth Burke, *A Grammar of Motives* (Berkeley: University of California Press, 1969), p. 59.

p. 423: Chart credit: NGM Art/National Geographic Stock. Text credit: Jeremy Berlin/National Geographic Stock.

p. 426: Tricks of the Trade courtesy of Alyse Murphy Leininger.

p. 426: "What is NPR?" from www.npr.org/about/

p. 433: Tricks of the Trade courtesy of Christian Nuñez.

p. 437: Deborah Tannen, *You're Wearing That? Understanding Mothers and Daughters in Conversation* (New York: Random House, 2006) pp. 5–6.

pp. 437, 438–439: Mike Rose, from *The Mind at Work* (New York) Viking/Penguin, 2004.

p. 440: Krista Ratcliff, *Rhetorical Listening: Identification, Gender, Whiteness* (Carbondale: Illinois University Press, 2005), p. xiii.

p. 440–441: Courtesy of Bethanie Orban.

p. 442: Diane Ackerman, *A Natural History of the Senses* (New York: Vintage, 1991).

pp. 445–447: Courtesy of Gillian Petrie.

pp. 452, 454, 458: Courtesy of Hannah Lewis.

p. 457: Tricks of the Trade courtesy of Keith Evans.

p. 459: Courtesy of Kendra Fry.

p. 460: From interview with Debra Dickerson, author of *The End of Blackness: Returning the Souls of Black Folks to Their Rightful Owners*, in Sharifa Rhodes-Pitts, "Getting Over Race," *The Atlantic*, vol. 293, no. 1 (February 27, 2004).

pp. 462–464: William Lutz, "Doubts about Doublespeak." From *State Government News* (July 1993).

pp. 465, 467–468: Courtesy of Jacob Thomas.

p. 469: Ronald Wardhaugh, *How Conversation Works* (Oxford: Blackwell, 1985).

p. 470: Tricks of the Trade courtesy of Keith Evans.

p. 472: Francis Spufford, *The Child That Books Built: A Life in Reading* (New York: Picador, 2003).

p. 473: Tricks of the Trade courtesy of Alyse Murphy Leininger.

pp. 501–511: Hannah L. Lewis.

pp. 527–532, 575: Courtesy of Catherine L. Davis.

p. 543: James Thurber, from "A Snapshot of Rex," in *The Dog Department: James Thurber on Hounds, Scotties, and Talking Poodles* (New York: HarperCollins, 2001), p. 90.

p. 545: Philip Lopate, in *For the Love of Books* (New York: Putnam, 1992), edited by Ronald B. Shwartz.

pp. 546–547: Courtesy of Anastasia Simkanin.

p. 548: Jonathan Weiner, *The Beak of the Finch: A Story of Evolution in Our Time* (New York: Vintage Books, 1995).

p. 550: Marshall Jon Fisher, "Memoria ex Machina," in *The Best American Essays 2003*, eds. Anne Fadiman and Robert Atwan (Boston: Mariner Books, 2003), p. 64.

p. 552: James Baldwin, "Notes of a Native Son," in *Collected Essays*, ed. Toni Morrison (New York: Library of America, 1998).

p. 552: Barry Lopez, "Wide-Eyed in Galapagos," http://dir.salon.com/story/travel/feature/1998/06/25/pass, March 4, 2008.

pp. 556–557: Dave Eggers, *A Heartbreaking Work of Staggering Genius* (New York: Simon & Schuster, 2000), p. 48.

p. 558: William Zinsser, "College Pressures," *Blair and Ketchum's Country Journal* (April 1970).

p. 564: William O'Grady, Michael Dobrovolsky, and Mark Aronoff, eds., *Contemporary Linguistics: An Introduction*, 3rd ed. (New York: St. Martin's, 1997).

p. 566: Anne Fadiman, "Mail," in *At Large and At Small: Familiar Essays* (New York: Farrar, Straus, & Giroux, 2007).

p. 574: Jack Finney, *Invasion of the Body Snatchers* (New York: Prion Books, 1997), p. 1.

p. 575: Joan Didion, from "Marrying Absurd," in *Slouching Towards Bethlehem* (New York: Farrar, Straus, & Giroux, 1990).

pp. 576–577: Robert Boswell, in *The Place of Grammar in Writing Instruction: Past, Present, Future* (Portsmouth, NH: Boynton/Cook, 1995), edited by Susan Hunter and Ray Wallace.

p. 577: "Loud," *Heinle's Newbury House Dictionary of American English*, 4th ed. (Boston: Thomson/Heinle, 2004), p. 557.

p. 577: Susan Gubar, *Rooms of Our Own* (Champaign: University of Illinois Press, 2006).

p. 578: Peter Schjeldahl, "Those Nasty Brits," *The New Yorker*, October 11, 1999, p. 104.

p. 580: Mark Twain, *The Tragedy of Pudd'nhead Wilson and the Comedy of Those Extraordinary Twins* (New York: Oxford University Press, 1894/1996).

pp. 591–592: Paul K. Humiston, "Small World," in *I Thought My Father Was God* by Paul Auster (New York: Henry Holt, 2001), p. 183.

p. 592: James Gorman, "Finding a Wild, Fearsome World Beneath Every Fallen Leaf," in *The Best American Science and Nature Writing 2003*, ed. Richard Dawkins (Boston: Houghton Mifflin, 2003), p. 67.

p. 595: Michael Ventura, "Taboo: Don't Even Think About It," *Psychology Today* (January/February, 1998).

p. 595: Jody M. Roy, "The Case of the Cowboy," in *Love to Hate: America's Obsession with Hatred and Violence* (New York: Columbia University Press, 2002).

pp. 595–596: John F. Kennedy, inaugural address, Washington, DC, January 1961.

p. 603: Louise Rafkin, *Other People's Dirt: A Housecleaner's Curious Adventures* (Chapel Hill, NC: Algonquin Books, 1998), p. 34.

p. 605: Joe Theismann, *The Complete Idiot's Guide to Football* (Royersford, PA: Alpha, 2001).

p. 606: Parker Palmer, *The Courage to Teach: Exploring the Inner Landscape of a Teacher's Life* (San Francisco: Jossey-Bass, 2007).

p. 606: Walker Evans, *Unclassified* (Zurich: Scalo Publishers, 2000).

pp. 607, 611–612: Arian Camp-Flores, from "Get Your Praise On," *Newsweek*, April 19, 2004, p. 57.

pp. 607–608: Karen R. Rosenberg and Wenda R. Trevathan, "The Evolution of Human Birth," *Scientific American Special Edition: A New Look at Human Evolution*, August 25, 2003, p. 82.

p. 612: Paul Goldberger, "High-Tech Bibliophilia," *The New Yorker* (May 24, 2004).

p. 613: Clifton Fadiman, in *For the Love of Books* (New York: Putnam, 1992), edited by Ronald B. Shwartz, p. 85.

pp. 619–620: Geoffrey Cowley, "For the Love of Language," *Newsweek* (Fall/Winter, 2000), pp. 12–15.

p. 625: Garrison Keillor, ed., *A Prairie Home Companion Pretty Good Joke Book* (St. Paul, MN: High Bridge, 2000), p. 8.

p. 626: Simon Schama, *Landscape and Memory* (New York: Alfred A. Knopf, 1995), p. 7.

p. 628: Maya Angelou, "Finishing School," in *Heritage: African American Readings for Writers*, 2nd ed., by Joyce M. Jarrett, Doreatha D. Mbalia, and Margaret G. Lee (Upper Saddle River, NJ: Prentice Hall, 2002).

p. 631: Louise Erdrich, *The Last Report on the Miracles at Little No Horse* (New York: HarperCollins, 2001), p. 34.

p. 637: From a paper written by Omatayo Banjo during an internship with Professor Cheryl Glenn, 2007.

PHOTOS AND ILLUSTRATIONS

p. 338: Cover from *How I Found the Strong: A Novel of the Civil War* by Margaret McMullan. © 2004 by Margaret McMullan. Reprinted by permission of Houghton Mifflin Company. All rights reserved. Poster provided courtesy of Evansville Vanderburgh Public Library. Photography by Matt Wegner.

p. 340: "Out Beyond Ideas of Wrongdoing and Rightdoing" by Jelaluddin Rumi, translated by Coleman Barks and John Moyne from *The Essential Rumi*. Copyright © 1995 by Coleman Barks. Used by permission of Poetry in Motion, Metropolitan Transit Authority and Barnes & Noble.

p. 352: © Gordon Converse/© 1955 *The Christian Science Monitor* (http://www.csmonitor.com). All rights reserved.

p. 382: The Granger Collection, NYC GREAT GATSBY COVER, 1925. Cover of the first edition, 1925, of *The Great Gatsby* by F. Scott Fitzgerald.

English
as official U.S. language, 200, 201, 203–209
Standardized, 195, 196, 202
English Plus Information Clearinghouse (EPIC), 206
Erdrich, Louise, 631
ERIC (Educational Resources Information Center), 429, 430
essay exams, 649–653
essential clause, 567–568
Esteves, Sandra Marià, 199
ethnicity, referring to, 588
ethos
and audio recording, 403
in critical analysis, 328, 329
in evaluation, 297
in investigative report, 188
in literary analysis, 380
in memoir, 115, 116, 119
in position argument, 221
in proposal, 265
as rhetorical appeal, 44, 45, 76
and video presentation, 406, 407
"Ethos of American Sign Language, The" (Williams), 228–233
evaluations, 276
alternatives to, 304
characteristics of, 295
contextual, 298–299
as fitting response, 293
shaping, 297–299
Evans, Keith, 457, 470
Evans, Maureen, 409–410
Evans, Walker, 606
"Everyday Use" (Walker), 363–369, 379, 382–387
Everyone Dies (McGarrity), 72–73
evidence, 45–46, 221, 265, 298, 299, 380, 381

"Evolution of Human Birth, The" (Rosenberg and Trevathan), 607
examples. *See* exemplification
exclamation points, 471, 565, 606, 620
exclamatory sentences, 565, 606
exemplification, 46, 64, 66–67, 149, 180, 188, 221, 328
exigence, 6, 9
expletive(s), 547–548, 571, 598
exploration, 58–61, 399
exposition, 356
extended definition, 65
Eye, The, 190

Facebook, 14, 15, 129, 278, 317–318, 395
as multimedia, 407–410
facts, 187, 188, 221
Fadiman, Anne, 566
Fadiman, Clifton, 613
Faimon, Peg, 268
Fairey, Shepard, 129, 130
Fallarme, David, 175–176
falling action, 356
false analogy (rhetorical fallacy), 223
false authority (rhetorical fallacy), 223–224, 476
false cause (rhetorical fallacy), 224, 476
false dilemma (rhetorical fallacy), 224, 476
Family Violence Prevention Fund, 14
Fast Food Nation (Schlosser), 94, 124
Favorite Poem Project, 342, 343
Favreau, Jon, 130–132
feasibility, of proposal, 265
Federal Bilingual Education Act of 1968, 199
Fendrich, Laurie, 178–179
fiction, 355

field research (fieldwork). *See also* naturalistic study
basic principles of, 435–437
methods for, 437–445
figurative language, 357
file format, 406–407
film
APA style for, in references list, 525
MLA style for, in works-cited list, 494
Final Cut Express, 407
"Finding a Wild, Fearsome World Beneath Every Fallen Leaf" (Gorman), 592
"Finishing School" (Angelou), 628
Finney, Jack, 574
Fishburne, Laurence, 281
Fisher, Marshall Jon, 550
fitting response, 2, 6, 389
critical analysis as, 321–322
development methods for, 64–77
drafting, 77–79
editing and proofreading, 82
essay exam as, 651–652
evaluation as, 293
exploration and, 58–61
identifying, 27–32, 33–34, 115, 148, 187, 219–220, 264–265, 296–297, 327–328, 378–379
investigative report as, 180–181
literary analysis as, 354–355
memoir as, 107–108
multimedia as, 395
oral presentation as, 655
organization of, 62–64
political commentary as, 37–38
portfolio as, 658–659
position argument as, 215
profile as, 143
proposal as, 260

persuasion, 4–5, 75, 129–130
available means of, 39–46
petition, 31
Petrie, Gillian, 445–447
Pew Research Center, 162, 164–168, 190
photograph, MLA style for, in works-cited list, 495
phrasal verb, 538–539
phrase(s), 550–558
noun, 550–551
prepositional, 551–552
verbal, 557–558
Pillsbury, Barbara, 329
Pink Ribbon International, 397–398
PinkRibbon.org, 397–398, 399, 400
Pinsky, Robert, 342
Pitbull, 201
Place of Grammar in Writing Instruction, The (Boswell), 576–577
plagiarism, 469, 479
Plath, Sylvia, 352
Platt, Glenn, 268
play, MLA style for, in works-cited list, 493
plot, 73, 355, 356, 358
podcast(s)
APA style for, in references list, 525
MLA style for, in works-cited list, 499
rhetorical approach to, 402–404
poem, MLA style for in-text citation of, 482
poetry (genre), 355, 357, 625
"Poetry" (Moore), 353, 380
Poetry in Motion, 339–340
Poetry Slam Face Off, 341
point of view, 74, 356, 358
points of comparison, 68
political commentary, as fitting response, 37–38
polysyndeton, 600

Ponce, Carlos, 201
"Pop Cultures" (Berlin), 423
portfolios, 657–659
position argument, 196. *See also* argument
alternatives to, 234
characteristics of, 218
as fitting response, 215
shaping, 220–222
possessive
pronoun as, 541, 542
use of apostrophe to indicate, 608–610
Powell, Julie, 98–99
Prairie Home Companion Pretty Good Joke Book, The (Keillor), 625
"Praise Song for the Day" (Alexander), 340
precision, 574–575, 577–581
predicate(s), 559, 618
predicative adjective, 539
prefix, 620
preposition(s), 544–545, 636
prepositional phrase, 551–552, 601, 604, 627
present participle, 553, 557
primary sources, 424, 425, 427
process analysis, 43, 46, 71–73
profile, 126
alternatives to, 158
characteristics of, 146
as fitting response, 143
shaping, 148–150
pronoun(s), 542–543
clear use of, 579–580
indefinite, 593
relative, 567
pronoun-antecedent agreement, 592–593
proper noun, 534
proposals, 236
acceptability and feasibility of, 265
alternatives to, 273–274
characteristics of, 263

as fitting response, 260
shaping, 265–266
proposition, 199, 227
ProQuest, 430
protagonist, 355
PsycINFO, 429, 430
public speaking, 127–128, 653–654
APA style for, in references list, 518, 521, 523
MLA style for, in works-cited list, 487, 491, 496–497
Publication Manual of the American Psychological Association, 608, 633
publisher, reliability of, 475
punctuation, 607–608. *See also names of specific punctuation marks*
problems with, 627–631
purpose. *See* rhetorical purpose

"Queen of Mold, The" (Reichl), 93–94
Quest for Truth: Scientific Progress and Religious Beliefs (Singham), 171
question marks, 471, 622–623
questioning, 61
in naturalistic research, 442–445
questionnaires, 447–448
questions
in interviews, 443
indirect, 615
open vs. focused, 443, 448
in questionnaires, 447
rhetorical, 565–566
wh- questions, 565
yes/no, 565
quotation marks, 623–624
quotations, 466, 470–472
block, 472
punctuation with, 611, 612, 617, 619–620, 623
as support for logos, 187–188, 221, 298, 329, 380

rhetorical situation, 5, 7, 89
  analyzing, 5–8
  elements of, 2
  essay exam and, 649
  language conventions and, 583–590
  oral presentation and, 653–654
  portfolio and, 657
Rhodes-Pitts, Sharifa, 460
rhyme, 357
rhythm, 357
Robinson, Ken, 268
Rodriguez, Richard, 212–213, 215
Rooms of Our Own (Gubar), 577
Rose, Mike, 437, 438–439, 440
Rosen, Christine, 160, 181–184
Rosenberg, Karen, R., 607, 608
Ross, Michael, 319–320
Roy, Jody M., 595
Rumi, Jelaluddin, 340
run-on sentence, 629–631

Samth, Ruwanga, 129
Savage, Dan, 313
scare quotes, 623
Schama, Simon, 626
Schjeldahl, Peter, 578
Schlosser, Eric, 94, 124
scholarly books, 424
scholarly journals, 425, 426
"School Days of an Indian Girl, The" (Zitkala-Ša), 198
"School Lunch" (Makhijani), 107–112
School of Life, 260
search engines, 432–433
secondary sources, 424, 425, 427
Seitz, Anna, 119–123, 331–335
semicolon, 604, 624–625
sensibility details, 67
sensory details, 67, 116, 298
sensory verb, 536
sentence fragment, 627–628, 630

sentence(s)
  classification of, 572–573
  combining, 604–605
  exclamatory, 565, 606
  fragment, 627–628, 630
  fused (run-on), 629–631
  imperative, 565, 606
  interrogative, 565, 605
  length of, 602–603
  patterns of, 560–562, 603–604
  types of, 564–566
sentence-level revision, 576
separable phrasal verb, 538
series, separation of words in, 613–614, 625
setting, 73, 355, 356, 358
sexual orientation, referring to, 589
Shalit, Gene, 280
Shin, Hyon B., 208–209
short passive, 563
Shutter Island, 406
Sia, Beau, 341
Siegel, Dmitri, 287–290
Silent Generation, 161, 162
simile, 357, 552
Simkanin, Stacy, 58, 59–61, 62, 63, 64, 78–79, 82–88, 546–547, 578
simple present tense, 554
simple sentence, 572
since, 602
Singham, Mano, 171–174
slang, 583
slash, 625
Slate Audio Book Club, 382
slippery slope (rhetorical fallacy), 225, 476
"Small World" (Humiston), 591–592
Smith, Barbara, 37–38
"Snapshot of Rex, A" (Thurber), 543
so, 600
social networking. *See* Facebook; Twitter
Song, Cindy, 15–16

Sontag, Susan, 57
sound recording
  APA style for, in references list, 525
  MLA style for, in works-cited list, 495
sources, in research, 424–427
  acknowledging, 478–479, 621
  coverage of, 474
  currency of, 473–474
  evaluating and responding to, 473–477
  identifying, 452
  online, 475
  quoting, 470–472
  reliability of, 474–475
Southwest Minnesota State University, 300
speaker, 356
special collections, for research, 432
spell checker, 584
spelling, conventions of, 584–587
square brackets, 472
squinting modifier, 599
Standardized English, 46, 195, 196, 202, 575, 583, 589–590
Stanford University, 278, 279
"Star Wars Kid," 331
"Statement by George A. Hacker on Minimum Drinking Age Law," 32–33
statistics, 188, 329
Stengel, Richard, 317–318
stipulative definition, 66
style, 574. *See also* APA; CMS; mechanics; MLA
  conventions of, 46
  descriptors for, 574–577
  of multimedia compositions, 399–400, 408
  in podcasting, 403
  as rhetorical principle, 397, 398
  in YouTube broadcasts, 405